THE JEWS
IN MEDIEVAL GERMANY

A Study of
Their Legal and Social Status

THE JEWS
IN
MEDIEVAL GERMANY

A Study of
Their Legal and Social Status

By

GUIDO KISCH

THE UNIVERSITY OF CHICAGO PRESS
CHICAGO · ILLINOIS

THE UNIVERSITY OF CHICAGO PRESS, CHICAGO 37
Cambridge University Press, London, N.W. 1, England
W. J. Gage & Co., Limited, Toronto 2B, Canada

To the Memory of My Parents

ALEXANDER KISCH

and

CHARLOTTE KISCH

in Admiration and Gratitude

PREFACE

AMONG the infinite number of events and developments, causes and effects, which together are Jewish history, law is but one aspect. Even though in this book stress has been laid on the basic importance of law, the interaction of other factors has not been overlooked. It has not been intended to emphasize the mere content of government regulations affecting Jews (Jewry-law) or their specific effects, which, for the most part, are evident from the primary sources used. The purpose of the study is rather to interpret and evaluate Jewry-law against the background of the history of law and legal institutions generally. Jewry-law, which belongs both to the realm of legal history and to the realm of Jewish history, must be studied from the point of view of the jurist, as well as from that of the historian and the sociologist. True, the ultimate aim must be achieved by a comparative method. Only the comparison of the various Jewry-laws in different countries and in different periods will permit a just and accurate scholarly appreciation of the numerous problems involved. But the study of individual countries and individual periods, based on every available primary source, is an indispensable preliminary for the final evaluation.

The literature of legal history is not rich in comprehensive monographs on Jewry-law. The well-known works by Otto Stobbe and by Johannes E. Scherer are still important for central Europe in the Middle Ages. Their presentations, based mainly on laws and deeds, will be supplemented by the treatment of medieval judicature and legal theory in the present work. Needless to say, it owes much to many valuable monographs in the fields of political, legal, economic, and social history. The author has, of course, used extensively his own preliminary studies, which have been published over a period of more than three decades and particularly during the last thirteen years. None of them, however, has been completely embodied in the present work, and none is entirely superseded. There is only one excep-

vii

tion: Parts I and II of this book represent a new and considerably enlarged version of essays published previously in a different form. The source material on which this study is based—regulations from lawbooks and texts of court decisions, taken mainly from medieval manuscripts—was published in a separate volume (see Bibliography, p. 567).

Much work still remains to be done. The complexity of subjects such as the Jewry-law of the town laws or canon Jewry-law during the Middle Ages—not to speak of the problems posed by the legal and social status of the Jews in later periods—almost surpasses the capacity of any single scholar. Still, they must be studied, in order not only to illuminate the past but also to understand the present in a historical perspective. Modern research cannot be satisfied with the present state of knowledge or with mere generalizations derived from it. The mosaic composed of court decisions in individual cases involving juridical technicalities, which is presented in Part III, seems perhaps to need specific justification. Scholars will readily recognize that only laborious and detailed work of this nature can offer a solid basis for the evaluation of general aspects and theories which is contained in Part IV.

During the long years of preparatory research, the author has been generously aided by many institutions of learning, by libraries, and interested friends. Their support has made possible the completion and publication of this work. He is greatly indebted to all of them. The American Academy for Jewish Research, by its kind invitation and several fellowships awarded during the initial years of research, has given stimulus and important aid to this undertaking. Mr. Paul Baerwald, Honorary Chairman of the Joint Distribution Committee, by his fine understanding of the author's scholarly endeavors, has been a constant source of encouragement; it was he who secured a substantial grant toward the publication of this volume. Professor Richard P. McKeon, of the University of Chicago, who read part of the work in manuscript, was kind enough to recommend it to the University of Chicago Press for publication. Dr. Joshua Trachtenberg of Easton, Pennsylvania, and Professor Judah Goldin of the State University of Iowa assisted in the stylistic revision of an earlier version. My wife, Hilde Kisch, took care of many technicalities, patiently and skilfully preparing the typescript from the often difficult manuscript. To all of them I wish to express my deep-felt gratitude.

This work was written in the midst of the greatest war ever experienced by man and of the greatest distress ever suffered by the Jewish people. In such epochs of history the individual's fate recedes before the destiny of mankind. Yet the collectivity must, in the final analysis, serve the "pursuit of happiness" of its individual members. Thus, in concluding this work, the author fervently repeats the wishes and hopes for the growth of right and justice that went out from Stobbe's and Scherer's earlier books. *Per aspera ad astra!*

GUIDO KISCH

NEW YORK CITY
February 2, 1948

IT IS hardly necessary for me to justify the fact that I have dealt only with the Jews in Germany, and only during the Middle Ages. This is not meant to imply that the position of the Jews has been essentially different in other countries or in subsequent centuries. The opposite is true. Even at the beginning of modern times the status of the Jews remained what it had been at the end of the Middle Ages. In spite of all the advances of the modern age, in spite of our political evolution and of a legislation which has advanced along the roads of humaneness and freedom, medieval conceptions, until late in the eighteenth century, have predominated, not only in life, but even in legislation wherever national hatred, religious zeal, and envy found the old conditions more to their liking. Even though the latest legislation, in many places, has pronounced the complete emancipation of the Jews, much is lacking still for its full realization. And if the State did not protect the Jew against gross injustice, Jewry today would still be exposed to persecution and abuse by the mob.—OTTO STOBBE, Preface to *Die Juden in Deutschland während des Mittelalters*.

BRESLAU
April 10, 1866

I HAVE written the present peaceful work from a historical perspective, in the service of mankind and of truth, disregarding the strife and confusion of the present. I offer it to the public with the wish that the advancing civilization of the twentieth century, on whose threshold we stand, may see the sun of pure and noble love rising over a humanity which has been cleansed of religious, national, social, and economic prejudices. May the time come at last when "man will be man's brother in spite of everything and everything." May God will it so.—J. E. SCHERER, Preface to *Die Rechtsverhältnisse der Juden in den deutsch-österreichischen Ländern*.

PRAGUE
January 1901

CONTENTS

PART I. MEDIEVAL JEWRY-LAW, ITS SOURCES AND SCOPE

xi

PART IV. GENERAL ASPECTS OF MEDIEVAL JEWRY-LAW

PART I

Medieval Jewry-Law, Its Sources and Scope

CHAPTER ONE

Jewry-Law and Its Investigation

I. The Jews in Medieval Germany[1]

IT IS well known that Jewish settlements on German soil can be traced back to very early times. Roman colonial policy, the general history of German settlement, and the spread of Christian propaganda all speak for the assumption that Jews made their home on German soil at a very early date. In a decree issued by Emperor Constantine in 321, Jews are explicitly mentioned as Roman citizens in Cologne. In all probability, Mayence and Treves likewise saw Jewish settlers in Roman days. The same may be assumed of other places along the Rhine and the Meuse, as well as for the territory along the Danube, for example, Augsburg, Regensburg, and the region of Vienna.

After the stormy period of the barbarian invasions, documentary evidence of Jewish settlements within the territory of the later German Empire does not reappear until the time of Charlemagne. The Jews of the medieval German communities came to the realm, for the most part, as immigrants. Their migration followed the great commercial highways and the gradual development of civilization in the territory. The important trade routes, which stretched along the Rhine and the Moselle, led along the Danube to eastern Europe and extended along the Main and across the Saale territory to the Elbe and the Slavic countries. Along these routes there also traveled Jewish merchants, many of whom settled permanently in those regions. Thus, in the main, the Jewish settlements in central Europe spread out gradually from west to east and from the south northward.[2]

With the rise of the German cities in the tenth and eleventh centuries, many Jews began to settle in urban centers. For obvious reasons statistical data are not available. In part the urban

3

Jewish settlements were due to efforts made by the founders of the cities to attract Jews, who were granted favors like those mentioned in the well-known charter of Bishop Rüdiger for Speyer in 1084.[3] A large network of Jewish communities rose quickly to commercial importance and cultural renown.[4] The Jewish persecutions in the period of the Crusades could interrupt or retard, but not put an end to, this course of development.[5] Nor was the Jewish spirit broken by the ordeal through which it passed in this period. In the middle of the fourteenth century, however, when the plague of the "Black Death" broke over Europe, decimating the population and raising the fury against the Jews to its peak, most of the flourishing Jewish settlements were destroyed.[6] There was hardly a German city that did not witness persecution either by expulsion or by burning of its Jews. But, despite the frightful bitterness against the alleged enemies of Christ and poisoners of the wells which is reflected in the catastrophic events of 1348–50, the Jews were soon received again into the German cities.[7] Their numbers, to be sure, were not considerable, and their distribution over the empire remained unequal. Nevertheless, once more Jewish life was revived in German lands, albeit on a restricted scale.

Hardly a century and a half later, economic and political conditions were such that the Jews were no longer regarded as indispensable. Toward the end of the fifteenth century and in the beginning of the sixteenth, expulsions brought the Jewish communities in most of the large German cities to a tragic end.[8]

II. "JEWRY-LAW"[9]

Law, as everyone knows, is a main pillar of social life in all times. A comprehensive inquiry into the legal status of medieval Jewry in Germany thus needs no specific justification.

This inquiry takes its point of departure from the established fact that the medieval Jewish pioneers entered German territory as traveling merchants. From their ranks, through permanent settlement, came the "founding fathers" of the medieval Jewish communities. In those early days the commercial situation conditioned by such factors as geography and trade communication prevailed without difference for all merchants, Jewish and non-

Jewish. This resulted in an identical legal treatment of all, with very slight modifications in favor of Jewish merchants. Those modifications of rights were caused by their difference in religion.[10] The difference, however, was not regarded as a discrimination sufficient to exclude them from permanent settlement in central Europe. In contrast to Jews, for example, heathen and Saracens were denied the right of settling in some Christian countries of Europe.[11] The admittance of Jews as permanent settlers, at times upon invitation, is thus itself conclusive evidence that they were not considered "unassimilable aliens," to use a modern sociological term.

Despite the tremendous growth of commerce and the increase of foreign trade from the twelfth century onward, in Germany territorial law did not produce a body of rules by which the status of aliens in general or foreign merchants in particular was regulated in a clear or complete form. As in the early, so in the later, Middle Ages, this regulation was effected by the general and local conditions in a given territory. Therefore, in the sources of territorial law there is only very rare mention of Jewish merchants. Only the rise of a municipal law, specifically favoring commerce and trade, resulted in an attempt to solve the burning legal problems of the local, as well as the foreign and inter-territorial, trade and its representatives, the different types of merchants. In accordance with the well-planned political economy of the medieval cities, this was done in a great body of legal regulations usually designated by the term *Gästerecht*, that is, "alien law."[12] The rules of *Gästerecht*, comprising many exemptions and privileges as compared with the prevailing common law, included Jews only in so far as the general definition of *Gast*, or "alien," applied to them, that is, if they were "foreign" Jews, living abroad or not having a permanent home in the city or territory in question. In other words, like other city dwellers, Jews with a permanent domicile were regarded as *Gäste* and designated as such only outside their home town. There can be no doubt that Jews as such and in general were not considered aliens according to medieval German law.

Another fact, however, is as certain as this conclusion drawn from relevant source material which will be presented and discussed in detail later:[13] the legal status of medieval Jewry shows some specific traits. In fact, it must be characterized as a legal status *sui generis*. Two historical factors closely co-operated to bring about the peculiar situation of the Jews in medieval law: their traditional adherence to Judaism and their integration into the medieval state.

The Bible and the Talmud have always accompanied the Jews in their wanderings through the world. Biblical law was always dominant in Jewish life, and the teachings of the Talmud played a great role in shaping Jewish intellect and character. Jewish spiritual leaders have at all times endeavored to take account of the changing political and social conditions under which Jewish life in the Diaspora had to be carried on. Traditional Jewish law had thus to be reinterpreted, adjusted, and supplemented to meet the needs of everyday life. Besides being studied and interpreted, Jewish law was further developed through ordinances, or *Takka-not*, issued from time to time by rabbinical authorities, individually or collectively. Rules were established for the internal administration of Jewish communities within the limits of their autonomy. Jewish law remained alive in the rabbinical court, or *Beth Din*, which was authoritative for legal disputes between Jewish litigants. It was even recognized by the state to some extent. An immense store of rabbinical decisions and legal opinions, *Sheelot u-Teshubot*, gives evidence of the extent of Jewish jurisdiction and administration of justice.

Jewish law is deeply rooted in religion and based on religious institutions. But Judaism recognizes no cleavage between religious-"ecclesiastical" and moral-secular law. On the contrary, the laws of ethics are regarded as part of the Jewish system of law. Moral life was religious life. Jewish law thus remained the guiding rule of Jewish life in the Diaspora; it was, indeed, essential for Jewish survival. The problem of the relation of Jews to their Christian environment was therefore a permanent concern of medieval Jewish jurisprudence.

This relationship definitely determined the Jews' position in the medieval state and society. In spite of the fact that they were not regarded as "unassimilable" and despite their permanent settlement under the protection of the law of the land, the complete "assimilation" of Jews into medieval society and their full integration into the medieval state was never accomplished. Their unshakable devotion to their religion put medieval Jewry in a separate category, for this religion was, of course, different from, and, according to the medieval conception, opposed to, the dominant faith. On the other hand, the Jews did not enjoy the faintest shadow of political independence and had ceased to be regarded as a separate nation ever since the dissolution of the Jewish state. Wherever in the world they had settled and found admission, their places of residence and spheres of activity were assigned to them by those powers to whose control they were, willy-nilly, subjected. In other words, the political and legal status of the Jewish community in the Diaspora was always determined by forces and influences foreign to the Jews and, as a rule, beyond their control.

The special rules of law determining the status of the Jews within the structure of the medieval state are comprised in the term "Jewry-law," formed after and equivalent to the expression *Judenrecht*, a compound found—characteristically—in the German language only. It is obvious that both these terms, unlike designations such as "Roman law" or "English law," meaning the law of the Romans or the English, do not refer to the Jews as the law-creating factor. Jewry-law is, on the contrary, of non-Jewish origin, the product of legislation, administration of justice, and legal theory in Christian states dealing with the legal status of the Jews. As a rule, they are treated as passive objects of legislation and law enforcement.

In its strictest sense the term "Jewry-law" includes laws enacted for the Jews collectively as a separate social group, by means of which laws their legal status in general was determined. This specific meaning of the word thus carries with it a discriminative connotation.

In research the term "Jewry-law" is to be strictly differentiated from, and not to be confused with, the designation "Jewish law."[14] The latter, comprising the legal material of a religious character based on the Bible, the Talmud, and later rabbinical ordinances and decisions, regulated the internal life of the Jewish community. In the constant flow and re-enactment of their religious laws the Jews remained, even in the Middle Ages, active agents, a law-creating factor, a role denied them for obvious reasons with regard to Jewry-law. Through its independence in formulating the rules of Jewry-law, the medieval state was in a position to extend or deny recognition to Jewish law and thus in some measure to exert influence, positive as well as negative, on its application and further development.

However, the power to secure and to create for the individual the subjective rights to which the general legal order gives him a claim—a power inherent in Roman and modern law—was lacking in the law of the Middle Ages. For this reason those who wrote down the law were very seldom concerned with objective law and never with a complete and systematic codification of objective law, but rather with determining the subjective rights of individual persons. In other words, the predominant form of recorded law was the privilege.[15] The special law for the Jews followed the same pattern; it appears specifically in the typical form of a charter or "privilege" (*privilegium*).[16] All the more was this legal form to be employed if rights or prerogatives deviating from the common or regular order of law had to be conferred upon Jews because of their difference in religion. Emperors, kings, and princes thus granted privileges, first, to individual Jews, then to individual Jewish groups, and, finally, to all Jews in a definite territory, for example, the empire.[17] Only gradually was the legal position of all Jews made the subject of general legislation for smaller or larger territories. The further unfolding of Jewry-law and its adaptation to the special conditions of Jewish life, on the one hand, and to their legal relations with their environment, on the other, took place in the medieval cities. They were the natural foci of commerce and trade in general and also became the centers of Jewish settlement and economic activity. However, despite the creation of direct relationships of Jews to municipal authorities or territorial rulers as such or as town lords, the emperor continued to consider them as his immediate subjects and to exercise his rule over them. This resulted in a complication of the Jewry-law regulations; for municipal Jewry legislation, despite its refinement and inclusiveness, could not completely replace the Jewry privileges of the emperor or territorial ruler. The complexity of the medieval legal status of the Jews and, consequently, of medieval Jewry-law is due to their living as Jews among the Christian population within the closed municipal area and to their continued legal dependence on the emperor and the town lord. The political and financial interests of these powers, often antagonistic to one another and overlapping those of the municipal government, increased that complexity all the more.

The political constellation and the peculiarity of the law-making factors involved indicate also the form and nature of the rules which constitute the composite and complex body of "medieval Jewry-law." The status of the Jews was, as a rule, not regulated by any general act of imperial legislation for the entire territory of Germany. Just as in medieval German law generally, so in German Jewry-law, uniformity was lacking. German Jewry-law was of a disintegrated character like German law itself. Imperial law (*Reichsrecht*), territorial law (*Landrecht*), and town law (*Stadtrecht*) contain regulations of Jewry-law.[18] They were the products of and appeared in the forms of law, statute, and custom. In all the privileges and statutes, first the political status of the Jews was determined, their relationship to state and government, their obligations to pay taxes and render services. But they also included regulations concerning the Jews' standing in civil law, their protection under criminal law, their rights and duties in legal procedure, and their subjection to the ordinances of administrative law. Provisions were also made for the application of Jewish law and the measure of recognition that it should be accorded. All these legal regulations were not dictated by a definite political attitude toward the Jews. Instead, the controlling factors were the will and interest of those in power, the time, place, and special circumstances. Curtailment and abrogation of granted rights or privileges depended also on these ever changing elements.

Privileges, laws, statutes, and customary law as sources of Jewry-law in medieval Germany are supplemented by records of legal transactions and recorded decisions of law cases in courts of law or arbitration. The judgments in legal disputes between Jewish and Christian litigants, especially, shed light on the functioning of the courts and on the actual application of the general rules, as well as specific regulations, in relation to Jews.

In this voluminous body of "applied" Jewry-law the available source material is not yet exhausted, however. From the beginnings of a legal science, medieval jurisprudence also concerned itself with the status of the Jews. The medieval "lawyers" sought to reveal and discuss the principles of, and motives for, the special legal treatment of Jews. This "theoretical" Jewry-law, slowly developing from the summit of the medieval period onward, acquired increasing scope and importance in the period of the adoption of Roman and canon law in the late Middle Ages.[19]

Secular Jewry-law in all its branches, as described hitherto, found a counterpart in canon Jewry-law. The church, too, even earlier than the medieval state, saw fit not only to define its attitude toward Judaism and Jewry dogmatically but also to determine the relationship of its institutions and adherents to the Jews in all spheres of potential contact in everyday life. Founded in Christian theology and supported by a powerful system of law enforcement, the ecclesiastical regulations concerning Jews were recognized in their validity throughout the Christian world. They affected the Jewish status directly, of course, and also bore heavily on the secular Jewry legislation, which could not escape this impact. There was even a mutual supplementary jurisdiction of secular and ecclesiastical courts to enforce rules concerning Jews and their relationships to Christians. "If one fails, the other shall act."[20]

The status in law assigned to the Jew by the world around him by Jewry-law exerted a determining influence on his entire intellectual, economic, social, and cultural life and development. This non-Jewish element in the history of the Jews, therefore, deserves the serious attention of both historian and sociologist. All the more so since it was, at the same time, a segment of the national law of those peoples among whom the Jews had to live.

III. LEGAL HISTORY OF THE JEWS[21]

At the present time, when the social conditions of Germany, and especially her legal status and system, have undergone so many important changes, with many of equal importance still in prospect, when everything is in the making and in process of transition, it seems more than ever necessary to turn one's eyes to the past and become familiar with the spirit of the former situation. Whether much or little of the old be adopted in the new institutions—without a profound knowledge of that which was and of the manner and method by which it came to be what it was—it will always be impossible properly to understand its spirit and its relation to that which will endure.

One might suppose that these words were coined for and spoken in our time, about ten to fifteen years ago, or even as recently as the immediate present. They are quoted, however, from the Preface to the voluminous work, *Deutsche Staats- und Rechtsgeschichte*, which—published in 1808—is almost forgotten today. Yet it ushered in a new era in the study of history and law, first in Germany and later all over Europe.[22] It laid the foundation for the science of German legal history. Its author, Karl Friedrich Eichhorn (1781–1854), is representative of the epoch of the awakening historical sense and modern historical research in the field of German law. He is the peer of his internationally better-known contemporary, Friedrich Carl von Savigny (1779–1861), head of the "historical school of law."[23] His book was the starting-point for a large number of learned investigations and has long served as a stimulus for research in the history of national laws.

Almost one hundred and forty years have elapsed, yet Eichhorn's words have retained full value and have even grown in significance for a large and important section of German legal history—that of German Jewry. This is a very large field of research—in fact, an independent science with many branches, embracing a period of about fifteen hundred years. It is rooted in history as well as in law and presents an unexpected wealth of source material and research problems, historical, juridical, and sociological. Up to the present it has almost completely escaped scholarly investigation, historical survey, juridical analysis, and sociological elucidation. Today, perhaps less than ever, should it be necessary to point out the importance and need of such researches. They should not be regarded merely as an object of learned play or a scholarly hobby, nor are they a negligible matter of historical speculation of interest to lawyers alone. Basic problems of the legal status of European Jewry in its historical development are involved here. Their solution can help considerably in providing a solid foundation for a history of the Jews to be written with detached objectivity and in accordance with the requirements of modern scholarship.

Eichhorn, in his works on the history of German law, had already given careful attention to the legal status of the Jews and to individual regulations of medieval Jewry-law.[24] Fifteen years were to pass after the publication of Eichhorn's *Staats- und Rechtsgeschichte* before the problem of a legal history of the Jews in the Diaspora caught the attention of a Jewish scholar. He was Eduard Gans (1798–1839), well known as a learned Hegelian, fervent antagonist of Savigny, and professor of law at the University of Berlin.[25] In 1823 Gans published a profound essay, "The Legislation Concerning Jews in Rome, According to the Sources of Roman Law."[26] To him, the laws of the various peoples in various countries represented an expression of the stage of civilization which these peoples had reached in their historical development. Thus he thought of legal history as a part of universal history. This idea, generally recognized and accepted only two generations later, was also basic for his essay on Roman Jewry-law. Although his study remained a literary torso, as it were, it is nevertheless noteworthy, because Gans, in the introduction to his essay, was the first to recognize the essential basis for, as well as the main difficulty in, a historical investigation of European Jewry-law. "A collection of all laws and regulations concerning the Jews, issued in Europe," seemed to him the most important preliminary task. The main difficulty lay, according to Gans, "in the circumstance that the general laws of individual countries and the general collections of laws are to serve as source material to a much lesser degree than individual town laws of Germany as well as of the other European countries, for in no section of public legislation do particularisms and differences prevail more than in that to be used here." The project as outlined by Gans is naturally of tremendous dimensions and therefore could not be accomplished except for that fragmentary study on Roman Jewry-law.

After this unsuccessful attempt, almost half a century elapsed before Otto Stobbe, celebrated historian of medieval German law, founded and firmly established a science worthy to bear the name of "legal history of the Jews."[27] His monumental and classical work, *Die Juden in Deutschland während des Mittelalters in politischer, sozialer und rechtlicher Beziehung*, was published some eighty years ago, in April, 1866.[28] For more than ten years Stobbe had carefully mustered the vast store of all German law sources, from the *Leges barbarorum* to the contemporary territorial legislation; and on this material he based his two-volume history of the sources of German law.[29] It was certainly no accident that Stobbe's investigations in the medieval law sources and their numerous individual regulations led him to study carefully the political, social, and legal status of the Jews—a group which played an important role in medieval economic life, although it was numerically small and never fully integrated into Christian society. The observation that this group remained a plaything among the nations, subject to every variety of law and violence, induced that unprejudiced Christian scholar to write a legal and social history of the Jews in the territories of the former Holy Roman Empire. For the legal history of the Jews of Germany, Stobbe's comprehensive work is easily as significant as Eichhorn's work for the general field. The fifth edition of Eichhorn's *Staats- und Rechtsgeschichte*, published in 1843-44, has remained the last. It was superseded by other leading works in the second half of the nineteenth century, when legal history attained full development in central Europe. Not so the book by Stobbe. Research in the legal history of the Jews did not keep pace with the progress of its mother-science. The reason for this lag must be sought in the favorable development of the political and legal status of central European Jewry during the second half of the nineteenth and the first third of the twentieth centuries. As a rule, neither in Germany nor in other countries, was further attention paid to the problems offered by the legal and social past of European Jewry. The few exceptions worthy of note (the works of men like Johannes Scherer, Georg Caro, Werner Sombart, or Jean Juster) could not change the general trend in the investigation of the legal history of the Jews. This applies particularly to the medieval period. Stobbe's work, therefore, offering a comprehensive survey for central Europe and particularly

Germany, has maintained its place to this very day.[30] Its scholarly value has endured and proved to be of permanent character. Jewish and non-Jewish historians, as well as apologists and anti-Semites, draw their "material" from this inexhaustible source. A Catholic legal historian stated in 1928: "In general, Stobbe offers the best survey and information of the pertinent facts, although with a judgment very favorable to the Jews."[31] A leading Jewish historian wrote in 1937: "Even today Stobbe's book offers guidance and support for the Jewish historian, because it was only little surpassed by research, and the problem of Jewry-law was hardly touched by the science of legal history."[32] Even a National Socialist pseudo-scholar and propagandist had to confess in 1935: "Efforts like those of Stobbe resulted in a good picture of the legal status of the Jews in medieval Germany, but they have remained isolated. . . ."[33]

Stobbe's book remains a classic in spite of the fact that some of its details call for re-examination, clarification, and supplementation. Of course, today a legal history of the Jews must be written in a different way; and, in order to replace Stobbe's collection of sketchy studies by comprehensive and systematic presentations, considerable research in the legal history of the Jews will be required. But the scholarly goal as established and pursued by Stobbe is still valid.

Unfortunately, no matter how desirable and necessary such a new comprehensive work on the medieval legal history of the Jews may be, it still cannot be produced. The task is too great, the subject too vast, the preliminary studies available are inadequate, the powers of one man are insufficient. Thus the first endeavor must limit and direct itself to a much more restricted scope. Only special problems or individual groups of problems can be selected for investigation. In this way alone can single stones be supplied, with the hope that in the future they may be used for the larger structure of a comprehensive legal history of the Jews.

Such is the aim of the present study. Others may follow. It seems appropriate, therefore, not only to define the subject and to give a detailed account of the sources of these researches but also briefly to describe the specific methods to be employed and to discuss some general problems of historical methodology in this field.

IV. RESEARCH IN MEDIEVAL LEGAL HISTORY OF THE JEWS

As was previously stated, the legal history of the Jews in Germany is simultaneously a part of German legal history and of the history of the Jews in Germany. The life of German Jewry ran its course on German territory, within the state, and therefore according to the law, of the German people. The fact that the connection between the special field of Jewish historical research and German legal history is given first place here is thus due to a particular reason. Jewry-law, imposed on the Jewish community from outside, not even leaving untouched the practice of Jewish law, was the determining factor in the legal, economic, social, and, to some extent, cultural life of the Jews.

The fact that the legal history of the Jews represents merely a section of general legal history has fundamental importance for its investigation. The inquiry into the problems in this restricted field is dependent not only on the source material specifically referring to Jews but also on general sources available. The method to be applied is determined thereby. Sources and methods of German legal history, in general, are of decisive importance for the investigation of the legal history of the Jews in Germany.[34] Jewish sources, namely, sources of Jewish origin, as far as such are available, must, of course, also be drawn upon. Rabbinical ordinances, decisions, or legal opinions in lawsuits (*responsa*) and other rabbinical writings, as well as Jewish community statutes and regulations, offer welcome supplementary material to complete the picture.[35]

A legal history of the Jews must obviously be based on the entire rich and varied source material available for the Middle Ages. The policy of state and church in regard to Jews and Jewry-law, the product of this policy, were then as important politically and economically as the Jewish question and legislation affecting Jews are considered to be in our time. The task now facing the scholar cannot be accomplished through a mere collection of the sources of medieval Jewry-law, a description of their contents, and perhaps, on the basis of these, a construction of an ideal picture of the legal situation of the time. Such a picture may well mirror the Jewry-law regulations contained in princely charters or town laws; but will it also bring to light the legal thinking and reasoning with reference to Jewry-law, the legal principles involved, and the actual enforcement of the laws in those days? This is the question which automatically forces itself into the foreground. To delve into these problems, it is necessary to probe the source material more deeply and with a more refined method. In other words, it is no longer satisfactory to collect, survey, or compare in a descriptive manner the statements found in legal sources, so that, in the end, a structure of imaginary legal history may be erected. What is required is insight into the inner interrelationships, general as well as specific. The forces and factors working within the legal organisms must be uncovered, and the dynamics of their functioning must be revealed. The spiritual foundation of the pertinent legal institutions must be searched for. Such is the task of modern legal history in general.[36] It is likewise the task of research in the legal history of the Jews.

In this field, too, the available "historical-legal" material must be penetratingly examined and analyzed by means of the refined methods of legal science with a historical orientation. This is self-evident and should be considered as a matter of course. Yet it is not superfluous to point this out and emphasize especially the need for legal-historical methods. Since the legal history of the Jews is, at the same time, a part of the general history of civilization and of Jewish history, the legal historian still finds his field of research contested,[37] as can be seen at once from the literature produced in Europe. Even here it was so, although the prerogatives of legal-historical research were already well established by a tradition of one and a half centuries. All the more is it so in America, where legal history has not yet been generally recognized as a separate field of historical studies (as, for instance, the history of art or medicine has been) and research in legal history is only in its incipient stages.[38] Yet thoroughgoing training in the specific materials and methods of legal history is indispensable for a profound insight into the legal ideas and principles, as well as into their historical developments and connections. Only a positive "legal-historical" training can teach the manner of juridical thinking and analysis and give the knowledge of juristic expression, all so essential for an exact description and full appreciation of institutions and developments in the history of law. The historian, theologian, and philologist usually lack this training, as does also the lawyer, who, without specializing in the field, has merely gone through the ordinary law-school curriculum. Moreover, a historian who attacks or treats problems of legal history, even if he produces essays or books on themes in this field, does not thereby become a legal historian. For researches of this special type a specific and specialized training is indispensable if works of full scientific value are to be produced. It is by no means accidental that the authors of the few generally recognized standard works on the legal history of the Jews—Stobbe, Scherer, and Juster—all were jurists and specifically legal historians. "The legal historian," explained Stobbe in the Preface to his work on the Jews, "has a richer material at his command than one who searches the sources merely for the history of the Jews; for interesting information is found in places where one would hardly search for material, and the general study of historical and legal sources yields a rich harvest also for that theme. Moreover," he continues, "many a regulation concerning the Jews appears to a legal historian in a different light and he is in a position to put it into organic connection with the general legal life. . . ."[39]

To realize the proposed purpose as well as possible, it is necessary, in addition, to exercise a fine sense of discrimination in the appreciation and evaluation of the several types of sources in accordance with points of view of legal history. The charters or privileges granted the Jews by the rulers and the legal enactments of the Empire, territories, and cities will therefore not suffice to afford a true picture of the actual legal status of the Jews in the Middle Ages; for in many instances it is not known whether these laws were carried into effect or, if so, to what extent. Even outside the sphere of law concerned with Jews, examples are not lacking in medieval legal history of regulations which remained empty laws, on paper only.[40] Therefore, the largest possible number of legal facts or *Rechtstatsachen* should be taken into account, this is, those sources which demonstrate the actual validity and specific application of the various Jewry-law regulations. One must think, above all, of records of legal transactions, of judgments in legal disputes, and of decisions of courts of law or arbitration. These alone offer clear evidence of the actual legal treatment of the Jews. They alone reveal the true attitude of the Christian to the Jew in the legal sphere. They alone can disclose, furthermore, whether and to what extent the "dark" Middle Ages permitted the Jew to enjoy the rights accorded him. They alone, finally, can indicate in what spirit those lofty ideals of right and justice, stated and extolled everywhere in medieval literature, were translated into reality.

But even all this will not result in a complete and well-rounded picture. Ever since a science of law has developed, it has concerned itself also with the legal status of the Jews. The basic ideas in their legal treatment which it has sought to discover and to discuss or prove theoretically must serve to round out the legal-historical picture. It will therefore be well worth a separate investigation to find out whether and how far legal doctrine exerted any influence upon legislation and the administration of justice with reference to Jews.

The formulation of the last-mentioned problem clearly proves that the discriminating evaluation of the various types of source material must not lead to a breaking of historical connections. From the point of view of methodology, however, it seems desirable to start by investigating the several bodies of source material separately, in order, for instance, to uncover the attitude of legal doctrine and judicial practice toward Jews. But it will have to remain the ultimate goal of the legal-historical inquiry finally to bring into a synthesis all the forces that determined the attitude of medieval law toward Jews and thus shaped their legal status.

In the pursuit of this aim, it will further be desirable to pay attention to the Christian population in general, as well as to some individual groups of medieval society whose legal position may be comparable to that of the Jews.[41] By including their legal history in the picture it may be possible to obtain valuable points

of comparison for the historical foundations and legal development and for the nature of, and the course followed by, medieval
Jewry-law. Such a comparison may lead to a discriminating evaluation of the legal status of the Jews. Not only will the comparison make evident whether and how, if at all, the Jewish legal
status differed from that of non-Jews, but it will also establish in
which respects Jews were equal to, or in a better or worse position than, other special groups. Such a comparative inquiry will
open up important vistas sociologically, as well as juridically
and historically.

In our day every scientific investigation into the field of the
medieval legal history of the Jews should be conducted in accordance with the ideas and principles outlined. Otherwise the
requirements of modern research will never be met or present-day
standards of scholarship reached. These, too, are the points of
view which have motivated the attitude toward the problems
set forth and determined the course of the following investigation. It will be confined to the study of medieval lawbooks and
court decisions as sources of German Jewry-law. Each of these
two groups of sources will first be subjected to a separate inquiry.
At times the inquiry will have to be extended to the textual development of individual laws, formulas, or even single passages;
for this may well be of basic importance not only for interpretation but also for an understanding of the entire historical development or the significance of the legal institution involved.[42]
Then the following questions are to serve as a starting-point for
the researches: What do the lawbooks and court decisions relate
about the legal treatment of the Jews? How was their legal position regulated in the law or ruled upon by the courts? Did the
general medieval conception of the Jew find expression in some
way? What was the mental attitude and actual behavior of medieval man toward Jews in the sphere of legal life? What were
specifically the attitude and behavior of the authors of the lawbooks, of the adversaries of Jews in lawsuits, and of the men who
rendered the decisions and handed down the law to the litigants?

Even the fullest reply to these questions, however, will shed
only partial, if any, light on the religious and social history of
the Jews within their own community, dominated by the rule of

Jewish law. This is quite obvious. The legal history of the Jews is intended to supplement, not to supplant, Jewish history or Jewish legal history. No one would suggest making that specialized field the main or central task for the Jewish historian.[43] Needless to say, knowledge of Jewish history is essential for the historian of Jewry-law. Likewise, knowledge of the history of Jewry-law is indispensable for research in Jewish history. In medieval times, Jewish law had hardly any direct influence on the shaping of the rules of Jewry-law, at least in central Europe.[44] The latter, on the other hand, determined the conditions under which Jewish life was allowed to be governed by Jewish law.[45] Thus principles of Jewry-law may well have found their way into Jewish law, owing particularly to the latter's well-known principle, *dina de-malkuta dina* ("law of the kingdom [country] is law").[46] Jewry-law made important and lasting inroads even into the process of development of Jewish life and thought as conditioned and effected by internal Jewish forces; it affected Jewish character, Jewish religious tradition, and Jewish historical values. It gave a particular tinge to the Jewish conception of *Galut* or Diaspora in the Middle Ages, and in the age of Enlightenment it became a causative factor in the emergence of the Jewish "emancipation" ideology.[47]

Thus the significance of Jewry-law and its historical investigation should not be underestimated. It should be granted its due place in the research in, and presentation of, Jewish history. At present, this postulate is being more and more recognized also among Jewish scholars.[48] The fact that it had won full recognition for long among anti-Semitic propagandists is perhaps the best and most convincing, though most sorrowful, confirmation of the thesis set forth.

V. An Inquiry into the Methodology and Philosophy of History[49]

At the beginning of a series of investigations into the history of medieval Jewry-law, a general inquiry into the methods of research to be applied seems appropriate.

The starting-point is again the fact that the legal history of the Jews belongs to the field of German legal history, on the one hand, and to that of Jewish history, on the other. Two problems of historical methodology are involved. One is the scientific approach as expressed in a definite formulation of the historical inquiry. The other is the manner of scientific investigation as expressed in the methods of examination and evaluation of the historical sources. Both problems are inseparable. Unsatisfactory as it is to present one's point of view in brief only, nevertheless it seems that a discussion on fundamentals should not be omitted altogether.

Two factors compel a clear stand. One rests on grounds of Jewish history; the other lies in the field of general legal history.

To begin with, Jewish historical research, the new *Wissenschaft des Judentums*, or "science of Judaism," was founded in Germany in the early part of the nineteenth century and came as an aftermath of the first discussions on the problem of Jewish emancipation.[50] "The Jews must again prove themselves as vigorous collaborators in the common work of mankind; they must raise themselves and the basic ideas of Judaism to the level of science, for this is the level of European life." The "father" of the science of Judaism, Leopold Zunz, put an essay containing this postulate at the head of his new journal, which was intended to be the mouthpiece of a circle of Jewish youth who believed in the preservation and revival of Judaism on the basis of scholarship.[51] In fact, from about 1830 on, Jewish historians displayed an intensive activity in various fields and produced valuable works of scholarship on the basis of a thorough historical-philological training. But their historical outlook was dimmed by the ghetto experiences, which were perceived in their full tragedy only after the ghetto gates had been thrown open. Instead of objective research, a new period of increasing exaltation of Jewish martyrdom began. Jewish history was viewed as "a sheer succession of miseries and persecutions," a conception which goes far back in Jewish history and historiography. Its foremost representatives in the nineteenth century were the great Jewish historians, Leopold Zunz and Heinrich Graetz. Their point of view impressed itself on generations of historians, Jewish and non-Jewish. Salo Baron, more recently, denounced the one-sidedness and partiality of this "lachrymose conception of

Jewish history," from which Jewish historiography has not been able to free itself even to this day.[52]

· This conception also entered the field of the legal history of the Jews, even in works by non-Jewish scholars. Some reflections of this attitude can be found in Stobbe's book. Upon its publication, however, that conception was criticized by Konrad Maurer, a renowned German scholar and outstanding investigator of northern Germanic law. In his review of Stobbe's work he pointed out that "reference to blind fanaticism, on the one hand, and suffering martyrdom, on the other," could not satisfactorily explain or justify medieval Jewry-law. To oppose that attitude he ventured an interpretation of his own, emphasizing "the tragic conflict between the national-religious conception of Judaism and the German political system of federation likewise founded on a national-religious basis."[53] But in spite of this new theory, Maurer himself did not escape the lachrymose conception of Jewish history, since he made the corporate structure of the political and legal organization in medieval Germany responsible for "the most unjust oppressions of Jews under the cover of law." This phrase was written in 1867. At that time, of course, no trace of modern racial doctrines can be found. Yet Maurer's thoughts moved distinctly in a direction which is on the same plane as modern racism, although the conclusions were different at the time.

In fact, it would be a worth-while, though difficult, research problem to find out whether conceptions like Maurer's prepared the way for the National Socialist ideologies. However this may be, the latter produced a new and very peculiar approach to Jewish history, as early as 1933. If "eternal self-pity" was characteristic of the lachrymose conception in Jewish historiography, now a boundless hatred of the Jews was to become the keynote for the new approach to Jewish history. The National Socialist system of values was raised to the position of a criterion in historical research. This system was to be introduced into a new historical domain, called *Judentumskunde*, to determine the selection of material and the manner of its evaluation, to found a new "scholarly" attitude, and to establish new laws of scholarship. This was to be "political science" (*politische Wissenschaft*) in its

special application to the Jewish problem and its historical
analysis.[54] In opposition to the "misconceived objectivity"
(*falsch verstandene Objektivität*) of the pre-Nazi era, the demand
was made for a *gegenwartsnahe Fragestellung*, that is to say, a formulation of the research problems in present-day ideology. The
formulation of the question—the conception and investigation of
historical sources—was to be viewed from the standpoint of current politics, with which the results, of course, had to be in harmony.[55] Thus a pseudo-science was created to serve the political
aim of exterminating the Jews. This was preceded by a world-
wide propaganda of Jew-baiting, well camouflaged under the
veil of scholarship. The dangers of this pseudo-science—the most
vicious and deleterious kind of propaganda—are not completely
removed with the downfall of the Third Reich; for its products—
books, essays, and articles, not confined merely to German-language publications—will continue to be used in research, and it
will often be very difficult to apply discriminating judgment.[56]
It should also not be overlooked that the tendency characterized
here does not appear always and everywhere as openly as it was
allowed to be in Hitler's Germany.

All told, it does not seem superfluous to point out and to emphasize the method of a truly scholarly approach to Jewish history and the legal history of the Jews in particular. The application of this method alone will insure the historian of whatever
religious or political affiliation against the pitfalls of lachrymose, as well as of pseudo-scientific, conceptions. The method
alluded to is that which has for long been generally recognized
as genuine in the field of historical research. The past cannot be
measured exclusively by the standard of values of a totally different present. Historical events must be understood and interpreted from the standpoint of their own time and from the laws
inherent in them. Only such a historical attitude rests on secure
ground. It was by no means unknown among German historians
prior to 1933 and was, indeed, slowly and steadily developed by
them in the course of the nineteenth century.[57] The scientific
clarification and solution of all the problems involved obviously
meets with extraordinary difficulties.[58] A thoroughgoing analysis would have to aim at and result in no less than an elaborate

philosophy of Jewish history, nonexistent at present.[59] However, it is neither possible nor necessary to present an extensive discourse on this theme in this connection.

Instead, a few references to some fine historical and psychological observations by some old-time German scholars of international reputation may perhaps prove useful. To be sure, Gustav Schmoller (1838–1917), the well-known German historian of economics, did not take into consideration in his researches such one-sided approaches as those exposed on the preceding pages. To him, however, even the mere difference in personality and the approach of different scholars to the same problem, though prompted by an identical endeavor for truth and impartiality, seemed to entail pitfalls for historical research. He discussed this in a preliminary study to his work on medieval German cities, at the time a much disputed problem of medieval constitutional, legal, and economic history.[60] As a kind of introduction to his inquiry into and presentation of the facts, he briefly characterized each of those scholars who had had a leading part in the discussion; for this was his reasoning:

Practically everyone who deals with the subject formulates the question differently and gives a different answer. These differences cannot reside in the sources, which are the same for everyone, but must inhere in the varieties of talent and temperament, in the diversity of educational training and life-experience. Has anyone ever heard of a variety of readers getting the same impression from the same book? Each one reads with a different object in view; each one gets a different impression; each overlooks a different thing and retains something else. In the same way different scholars, utilizing the same source-material, obtain dissimilar impressions and arrive at different conclusions, even if their training in method has resulted in the elimination of the sources of many a mistake. That is why one frequently finds that, of different scholars in the same field, each grasps but part of the truth.

How much more must this conclusion be justified when the very approach to the sources is colored by a definite preconception, intentional or subconscious. True, even such an approach may bring forth parts of the truth. No one can deny the great accomplishments of German-Jewish historiography, particularly during the nineteenth century, despite the lachrymose conception. But these results need correction. Therefore, emphasis should also be placed on another conclusion reached by Schmoller: "Only from the totality of the answers can the full truth be apprehended."[61] This is meant to be applied not only to the different individualities of scholars but also to the different types of historical approach, such as the political, legal, economic, social, or religious. "Historical science," Johan Huizinga, the Dutch historian, once said, "is a process of civilization, a world-function, a Father's house of many mansions."[62] Finally, in this connection a related idea of a noted church historian should not be forgotten: "The historical method alone is conservative, for it assures a sense of awe—not for tradition, but in the face of the facts—and puts an end to arbitrariness which would transform lead into gold and gold into lead."[63]

Approaching historical problems with an epistemological attitude of this kind, one is bound to arrive at a self-evident conclusion: Despite all transformations continuously affecting the historical picture, a view of history is necessary which earnestly strives to free itself from self-reflection as well as from current notions. To be sure, human efforts can never succeed in attaining the ideal of scientific objectivity. But, "if complete objectivity is denied us, then the will to objectivity must be all the stronger, the striving after it the more indefatigable. True history demands awe and humility, and more than anything else, honesty and the purest love of truth."[64]

After this discussion of questions of the general philosophy of history, thought must be given to some questions of methodology, purely legal-historical in their nature. This seems to be in place here for two reasons: first, for the benefit of those not acquainted with the aims and methods of legal-historical research; second, for the sake of the legal history of the Jews which, being a young and little-cultivated field of study, has to develop its own method from that of its mother-science.

During the one hundred and twenty-five years after Eichhorn laid the foundations for the science of the history of German law, the legal-historical methods have been successfully improved and thoroughly refined. With these methods, during the second half of the nineteenth century, scholars of world renown, such as

Heinrich Brunner and Otto Gierke, have led the science of German legal history to the pinnacle of success. Their scholarship also exerted considerable influence on the development of the science of, and research in, legal history all over Europe and in America.[65] How these men conceived the aim and method of research is reflected in every one of their works. In the Introduction to the second volume of his standard work, *Das deutsche Genossenschaftsrecht*, Otto Gierke developed clearly and fundamentally his thoughts on the subject of the "task" of legal history. He explained in detail the difficulties encountered by scholarship in legal history as a result of the imperfections of method, the incongruity of human thinking, and the inconsistency prevailing in the world in general.[66] One must read Gierke's significant conclusions completely and in his own words in order to get some idea of the earnestness and sense of responsibility with which such men as he approached the problems and of the way in which they sought to master them.[67] It might be well to offer just one illustration, contained in the following few sentences, upon which particular emphasis was placed and should be placed even today.

Finally, the understanding of a mental process whose existence belongs to the past is made difficult for us by subjective causes; for, since we think not with the thoughts of others but with our own, therefore, as soon as we make the thinking of others the object of our thought, we are always in danger of insinuating our own thoughts into that of the others. Therein lies the mistake of many legal historians. In their striving to give as definite a picture as possible of the past, they substitute for the flux characteristic of the evolution of the state and law in Germany's past the sharply formulated categories of modern juridical dogma. A picture of this sort, presented in bold outline as a finished work of art, all too easily lures the jurist who is accustomed to think in methodical and systematic terms and leads him to the false conclusion that such a conception is the only true "juristic" one. What is forgotten, however, is the fact that legal history is, first of all, history, a discipline dealing with the process of the evolution of law. Legal history dare not defer to our own ways of thinking by giving up the difficult task of coming as close as possible to the actual manner of development, in favor of a more attractive delineation of a number of static situations. It all depends solely on the ability to operate with the ideas of an age, the thought-processes of which were different from ours, in order to understand that age. Hence, as soon as the genesis and nature of old legal concepts are involved, we must try to put aside, so to speak, our own more finished concepts. The most we dare do is subsequently to subject the old concepts to a comparison with the new and extract the germ of the latter from the former. It is true that we shall hardly be able, even in this way, to revive within ourselves the positive content of a vanished consciousness, but at least we shall obtain a fair reflection of it.[68]

Essentially the same thought was expressed later by Claudius von Schwerin when he described the proper scholarly manner of approaching and evaluating sources of legal history and made the following statements:

The task is to enter into the spirit of the time and place represented by the source, to adjust one's own thinking to that of the source. . . . If the aim of interpretation is to establish what the originator of the source wanted to express or expressed unconsciously, then the interpreter, on his part, must be warned most emphatically against the very common mistake of reading into the source what it never meant to express. This danger is extraordinarily great, since it reposes within the very nature of the investigator and can be avoided only by constant and conscious watchfulness. . . . Every use of a source implies a question put to the source. The user of it wants the source to unlock its secret. Therein already resides the temptation to extract an answer from the source where one is not easily obtainable. . . . The danger becomes particularly great when the general wish for elucidation turns into a wish for elucidation in a special sense. An interpretation which starts out with a preconceived result can hardly escape this danger. Therefore, a cautious user of sources should ask only what the source says and never whether it says this or that. No rules exist by which reading into a source, or, as it has also been called, "hyperhermeneutics," can be avoided. This is a case where only a determined will can act as a check against the desire to force out of the source that which it cannot give.[69]

These words are in themselves a clear indication of the anxiety lest the danger of hyperhermeneutics become an actuality. The fear was not unfounded. Modern legal thinking, based as it is upon a system of specific concepts, has grown up in an atmosphere of predominant occupation with codes of legislation, while legal-historical training was pushed even further into the background. In the end, legal-historical scholarship in Germany was also brought under such influence. The concepts, the constructions, and the methodology of modern law were, to a large extent, utilized without discrimination for research in problems of legal history. An impartial observer, Gotthelf Bergsträsser, the investigator of the history of Islamic law, noted this tendency many years ago. He foresaw clearly whither such a mistaken attitude toward the aims of legal history was bound to lead.[70] But his warning has gone unheeded by the younger generation of German legal historians.[71] And yet, every age and every community has a conception of law peculiarly its own. It is this conception which we must let speak. Therefore, we must also apply the utmost caution in comparing developments or institutions belonging to different periods.

Before the doctrines of national socialism infected and perverted all science in Germany, the danger described was also felt among German legal historians. A program for the reformation of research in legal history was launched, with a plea for a "historical view" in Gierke's sense, to be assisted by "the inner power of truth." It reached its climax in the postulate: "Back to Gierke." "Gierke was an apostle of the new era, the acknowledged leader of our youngest generation; his works should be read better and consulted more frequently by his disciples. Thus they would avoid wrong ways and escape many an error."[72]

Whoever enters the realm of research in the legal history of the Jews should unconditionally adopt this watchword as a guiding principle. It was also the way which had successfully been followed by Otto Stobbe, the incorruptible seeker of truth and first scholar representative of research in the legal history of the Jews. Put into one sentence, that watchword means: with a full sense of responsibility toward scholarship and with indefatigable striving after objective judgment, to penetrate into the sources both as historian and as jurist.

CHAPTER TWO

Sources and Literature

I. MEDIEVAL GERMAN LAWBOOKS

A. THE LITERATURE OF THE LAWBOOKS[1]

IN THE mind of medieval man, law and legal matters played a far more important role than they do in our thinking today. In the Middle Ages legal doctrine and legal practice constituted an important function and an organic part of the cultural activity of the people. Lawbooks and judicial decisions therefore mirror, better than almost any other source, medieval law and life. Their real nature and evolution emerge from these sources in clear and unmistakable design. These types of sources are valuable for legal history because of their specifically juridical content. On the other hand, their social and cultural foundations make them particularly fit to serve the purposes of a legal-historical investigation with a broad scope as described in chapter i.

When, therefore, these sources offer information about the legal status and treatment of Jews, it is well to pay careful attention to what they say and to attribute particular importance to their statements. They supplement our knowledge of the legal past at many points where other sources leave us in the dark. In fact, they, and the judicial decisions in particular, reveal how the German of the Middle Ages, in his thoughts and feelings, saw himself in relation to the Jew and how he brought his legal attitude and action into agreement with the leading ideas of his time. All this lends an unusual significance and value to the two different bodies of source material, each of a special type and complete in itself, namely, the medieval lawbooks and the court decisions. They are, indeed, indispensable for an investigation of

the legal history of the Jews. This is true even if the historical
information which they disclose proves to have some gaps; for,
even then, these sources afford material of great factual value, by
means of which a check might be kept, at least to a certain extent, on the several laws and regulations concerned with Jews
which have until now served as the principal or only sources of
our knowledge.

The German "lawbooks" (*Rechtsbücher*) or "mirrors of the
law" (*Spiegel des Rechts*) first appeared in the thirteenth century.
The term *Rechtsbuch*, as well as *Spiegel*, is used in legal sources
as early as the second half of the thirteenth century.[2] Accordingly, the period between 1200 and 1500 is designated in the history of German law as the "age of the lawbooks" (*die Rechts-
bücherzeit*), whereby importance and value attached to these law
sources are clearly brought out.

By the term "lawbooks" we designate private records or di-
gests of customary law, compiled by expert lawmen and intended
to give a comprehensive account of the whole body of legal material in specific spheres of law within a certain territory and
covering a certain subject matter. They do not represent products
of the legislative activity of the Holy Roman Empire, its territories, cities, or rural districts. The lawbooks are, rather, the
literary work of individual men who were experienced in the
legal field; they are private compilations of customary law; i.e.,
they are the earliest "scholarly" treatises on German law. Some
of them came into being at a time when Roman law was not yet
known in most parts of Germany and when it had won no influence of any moment anywhere. Not only are they national in
origin; the older ones among them are purely German in content, without any traces of Roman law. Furthermore, these
works possess a national character in still another respect: they
were composed in the German language. They are thus the first
German records of German law, as well as the earliest monuments of German prose. In the beginning none of these private
works possessed the authority of codified law. But in practice
some of them were looked upon and employed as codes of law.
Hence they contributed greatly to the further development of
law. Their value as sources of legal history is evident and
acknowledged.

Research in the medieval German lawbooks (once furthered by scholars in the field of legal history, such as Carl Gustav Homeyer, Karl von Amira, and Ferdinand Frensdorff) had a gratifying and promising revival in Germany after the conclusion of the first World War. The numerous and, in part, extremely complicated problems which they presented were attacked anew from the most diverse angles. The common goal of all these endeavors was to pave the way for definitive editions of the most outstanding among these medieval legal monuments, in accordance with the standards of modern scientific research.[3] For obvious reasons, such editions are of as great an importance for research in the legal history of the Jews as they are for all other branches of legal history. Although only little progress was made after 1933, this type of source material is a suitable and sufficient basis for the study of the history of Jewry-law. True, reference to the manuscripts will prove necessary, and sometimes their unavailability will cause some difficulties or leave certain problems open. Nevertheless, it is safe to assume that hardly any decisive change in the basic lines of the legal-historical picture is to be expected from future critical research in these sources. The present investigation is built only on completely solid ground.

B. THE LAWBOOKS AS A SOURCE OF JEWRY-LAW

In the medieval conception "law" comprised, in general, customary law. It was written down for the sole purpose of preventing it from falling into oblivion and of thus insuring its permanent validity. Furthermore, customary law, as it was, was identified with the law as it ought to be.[4]

Law regarding Jews, as fixed in a medieval lawbook, must be viewed under the same aspect. Moreover, such law, reduced to writing and intended for permanent use, is indicative of a more or less finished state of development of the rules that it contains. These rules disclose the Jewish status in several special spheres, such as in territorial or municipal law. The omission of Jewry-law regulations from a certain lawbook may indicate the absence of Jews from a certain territory. The fact that such provisions are missing in all books of feudal law offers evidence that Jews played no role in this domain, which was of fundamental importance in the stratification of medieval society. Although not explicitly mentioned among the groups excluded from the feudal system in the *Sachsenspiegel*'s *Lehnrecht* (2, 1), Jews were excluded in fact, since they were not of knightly descent (*von ritteris art*). On the other hand, the participation of Jews in almost all other branches of legal life is attested by a voluminous body of pertinent Jewry-law regulations in the various lawbooks.

The lawbooks also bear witness to the fact that the legal status of the Jews, its juridical conception, and historical foundation were of concern to medieval experts in law. The problem of chamber serfdom discussed in some of the lawbooks is perhaps the best example of this. The legal treatment of the Jews, different as it was in point of time and place, is clearly mirrored in the lawbooks. Some of them adopted or imitated the elaborate rules of canon law concerning Jews, as was the case in southern Germany, whereas in others no trace of ecclesiastical influence can be found. Various reasons may account for this divergence. The reception of canon-law rules in books of secular law effected, to some degree, a unification of the principles of Jewry-law extending over large territories. If a lawbook was disseminated over wide areas and enjoyed recognition in many lands, the same result was brought about even if canon law did not come into play, as in the case of the *Sachsenspiegel*. In other lawbooks, again, there can be observed a patent deviation from that uniformity which was to become almost a rule. The personal standpoint— political, religious, or juridical—of the author determined, of course, his attitude toward, and presentation of, the problems of Jewry-law. In this respect each lawbook has its own distinct character, which gives it its particular significance. Every lawbook must thus be studied and analyzed individually.

For an investigation and evaluation of the Jewry-law in the German lawbooks, two circumstances are to be taken into consideration: the importance of each individual lawbook in legal history and the fulness and quality of its regulations on Jewry-law.

The center of the presentation must be occupied by those lawbooks which are of greatest value for legal history in general. They are the books which stood out for their juristic significance and, for this reason, were widely used and held in greatest esteem by lawyers and laymen. These lawbooks obviously exercised great and sometimes lasting influence on the life of medieval man. In this group must be reckoned, above all, the *Sachsenspiegel*, the *Schwabenspiegel*, the *Sächsisches Weichbild*, and the *Meissener Rechtsbuch*.

But legal-historical research depends also on the fulness and importance of the regulations on the subject of Jewry-law which each lawbook contains. It is fortunate that both circumstances overlap or are interwoven in the source material at hand. The only exception is the *Sächsisches Weichbild*, which, in its earlier versions, did not concern itself with the Jews. The *Schwabenspiegel* and the *Meissener Rechtsbuch* treat the legal conditions of Jewry in great detail. The regulations of the *Sachsenspiegel* dealing with Jews and their status in law are not numerous, to be sure; but they are of a fundamental character and clear enough to bring to life the basic principles which governed medieval German Jewry-law. In fact, they were of utmost importance for its further development. As an essential part of the *Sachsenspiegel*, they were put into practice in a very large territory, and they also served as a model for the formulation of the Jewry-law in other lawbooks. Therefore, first place must be assigned to the Jewry-law of the *Sachsenspiegel*. Naturally, other lawbooks of a comparatively more restricted circulation (comprising territorial law or town law) must also receive due consideration.[5]

The lawbooks on which the present investigation is chiefly based are treated individually below. Each of them is briefly analyzed in accordance with the present state of secure knowledge of legal source history. Obviously, their origin had a bearing upon the formulation of their Jewry-law, and their dissemination was important for its influence on the legal life in various countries. Therefore, a summary of their history will prove useful for understanding their content. For every lawbook the exact places in which the regulations regarding Jews are to be found are indicated. The historical origin of these regulations is traced, in so far as source history permits us to do so and in so far as valid results can be derived from the sources involved. Finally, the spirit of each individual lawbook, manifest in the specific formulation of the Jewry-law regulations, is briefly characterized. Thereby an attempt is made to offer a basic orientation toward each source used for the present study.

In the course of the inquiry the regulations of Jewry-law are given in faithful translation, accompanied by precise citation of the original.[6]

C. INDIVIDUAL LAWBOOKS AND THEIR JEWRY-LAW REGULATIONS[7]

1. *Sachsenspiegel* OR *Sächsisches Landrecht*[8]

Among the great German lawbooks—indeed, among all European lawbooks of the thirteenth century—the *Sachsenspiegel*, or "Saxon Mirror," merits a special place. In fact, it must be considered as one of the most important of all medieval lawbooks. It is not only the oldest among them, but in originality and depth it is an outstanding legal monument. With it the literary treatment of German law in the Middle Ages begins and culminates.

The *Sachsenspiegel*—a statement or digest of Saxon, especially Eastphalian, law—was composed probably between 1221 and 1224, by Eike von Repgow of Anhalt, a lay judge of knightly rank (born about 1180, died after 1233). It was the author's intention to present the law handed down from the forefathers, to exhibit to the free Saxons their law as in a mirror. The German version of his lawbook, written in Low German but possibly avoiding dialectical expressions, replaced a Latin original which has been lost. The *Sachsenspiegel* is divided into two parts: *Landrecht* and *Lehnrecht*, "territorial law" and "feudal law." The former contains the principal features of what is now called "public" or "constitutional" law, of criminal and civil law as well as of the law of procedure. The other part is confined to feudal law.

Eike von Repgow had a comprehensive knowledge of the positive law as displayed in his *Spiegel*. The juridical reasoning with which he expounded all legal phenomena and arranged them under categories was, in his day, a great achievement. He produced a trustworthy account of contemporary law, complementing his extensive familiarity with it by painstaking investigation; his results he brought into harmony with the ethical sense with which he was imbued. His lawbook is purely German in character. Roman law was known to him only from hearsay, so that hardly a trace of it is found in his work. Since he considered God the beginning of all things, it followed as a matter of course that the law also had a relation to this fountain-head of all being, that all law must be in harmony with the Word of God. Thus the Bible served as a source for the *Sachsenspiegel*.

Eike was an expert in his native East Saxon law. He cherished especially the law handed down by the forefathers.[9] Up to his time one could gain knowledge of it only through oral tradition and court proceedings. Henceforward, the *Sachsenspiegel* was to guide all those in need of the law, all who wished to know which laws were valid in the country. Eike's aim was to set down this law, as it had been transmitted from of old, in unadulterated form.[10] He desired to present the legal regulations which he considered valid and whose validity he sought to reinforce. In this light the *Sachsenspiegel* is seen to be a profoundly reasoned codification rather than a legal textbook.[11] Eike's presentation is reliable, although, with his unique combination of conservative attitude and progressive creative power, he occasionally views the obsolescent and the nascent as equally present and actual. In a conflict of opposing opinions he knows how to take a purposeful and independent stand. He is always more jurist than politician. The only reproach from which he is not free is that of the subjectivity of genius. His work must not be used uncritically. Critically employed, the *Sachsenspiegel* represents a historical source of inestimable importance.

The *Sachsenspiegel* achieved great popularity. Fully two hundred complete manuscripts of its *Landrecht* and not quite one hundred and fifty of its *Lehnrecht* have been preserved—surely, the most impressive proof of the wide dissemination and influence of this lawbook. As early as the thirteenth century two other important German lawbooks were composed in southern Germany on the basis of Eike's work, the *Deutschenspiegel* and the *Schwabenspiegel*. With the drift of the German colonists eastward, *Sachsenspiegel* law penetrated beyond the German-language border, deep into Slavic territory.[12] The lawbook was rendered into various German dialects and was translated into Latin, Dutch, and

Polish. Although it did not take into particular account the special law of the cities, town law of the north and east also frequently accepted the legal ideas of the *Sachsenspiegel* as a model. These ideas became, for instance, of decisive importance for the development of the town law of Magdeburg. Thus it was again *Sachsenspiegel* law which gained authority in numerous towns under Magdeburg law in East Saxony and in the territories of German colonization. For the development of German law in the Middle Ages, the "Saxon Mirror" has an importance attained by no other code of law.

Besides the practical influence which the *Sachsenspiegel* exercised as valid law, there is its scientific significance: It was the first literary work on German law; it became a model for numerous lawbooks; and with it German jurisprudence, indeed, begins.

Soon after 1325 Johann von Buch, judge at the court of the Elector of Brandenburg, wrote a commentary (*Glosse*) on the *Landrecht*. This *Gloss* utilized the Roman and canon law for the interpretation of the *Sachsenspiegel*, with the objective of demonstrating extensive agreement between the German and the Romanic laws. It was later (before 1386) revised by Nicholas Wurm of Neuruppin, a pupil of Johannes de Lignano and a prolific juridical author. Other commentaries followed. Among them, the so-called "Stendal Gloss" (before 1434)—independent of Buch—commented on the German, as well as on the Latin, text.[13]

As early as the thirteenth century some texts of the *Sachsenspiegel* were illustrated throughout with pen drawings, so as to give a clear idea of the legal contents by means of pictures. They elucidate and comment, they supplement and often particularize, legal institutions and legal regulations on which the lawbook itself is silent. Apart from their importance for the study of law, the pictures are representative of almost every phase of medieval Saxon life. All the picture manuscripts that are preserved originate from one archetype, which presumably came into existence in Meissen in 1290, but unfortunately is lost. Of those preserved, the Heidelberg manuscript of about 1300–1315 is the oldest, the Dresden picture manuscript of the middle of the fourteenth century the richest in content and form.

The *Sachsenspiegel* is the first German lawbook which purposefully and systematically deals with Jewry-law in a series of articles, namely, *Landrecht*, II, 66, 1; III, 2; and III, 7, 1–4. Its author clearly saw the practical importance of Jewry-law. It is possible and even probable that this awareness came to him during his activity as *Schöffe* ("juror"). It may well have been that there were Jews living in Eike's own judiciary district. We have only scanty information concerning the presence of Jews and their living conditions in medieval Eastphalia, especially in the districts of Anhalt and northern Thuringia.[14] Margrave Otto the Rich of Meissen (1156–90) probably employed a Jewish master of the mint, for bracteates with Hebrew lettering have been preserved from the period of his reign.[15] Between 1160 and 1200 there originated a Thuringian legal document frequently mentioned, the Jewry Oath of Erfurt. It is an official parchment designed in the manner of a charter and provided with the pendent great seal of the city of Erfurt. Evidently, it was used by the city authorities when Jews had to be sworn.[16] In the first quarter of the thirteenth century the Jewish community in this central German city must certainly have been not inconsiderable.[17] There is evidence that a number of small and middle-sized, as well as some larger, Jewish communities existed scattered throughout the region of Saxony-Thuringia,[18] and that a substantial number of learned rabbis taught and worked there.[19] The imperial lawbook of Mühlhausen, the *Mühlhäuser Reichsrechtsbuch*, possibly even older than the *Sachsenspiegel*, composed at Mühlhausen in Thuringia about 1200 or not much later and thence transmitted to other Thuringian towns, mentions Jews as pawnbrokers in a manner which implies that they had been settled there for some time.[20]

In addition to this documentary evidence for the presence of Jews in medieval Saxony and Thuringia, the most important testimony is the fact that Eike himself in his *Sachsenspiegel* included Jews and Jewry-law. The way this is done shows clearly that in the first quarter of the thirteenth century Jews subject to Eastphalian law were already of considerable economic importance. This again warrants the inference of long-time settlement and rather extensive business activity in those districts.[21] It is obviously for this group of Jews and their legal relations to non-Jews that the Jewry-law clauses of the *Sachsenspiegel* were formulated; and to this group these clauses were applicable. That such regulations found a place at all in this Saxon lawbook is also the best proof of their practical importance and of the author's interest in the subject.

Eike was undoubtedly interested in, and occupied with, the problem of the legal status of the Jews, their peculiar position in various relations to the law, and the theoretical analysis and justification of their special legal treatment. In the *Sachsenspiegel* he deals with the questions of Jewry-law without bias, with calm sobriety, philosophic acumen, and a keen sense of justice. This attitude is also revealed in his stand toward the massacre of Jews during the First Crusade as he expressed it in the *Saxon World Chronicle*, his other important work. Here we read words of rebuke for the persecution of the Jews by the crusaders under Peter of Amiens, words which may perhaps be indicative of sympathy for these innocent victims of rabid passion.[22]

2. *Schwabenspiegel*[23]

The southern German counterpart of the *Sachsenspiegel* is the *Kaiserliches Land- und Lehnrecht* or *Kaiserrecht* ("Imperial Territorial and Feudal Law"), which, from the seventeenth century on, has come to be known as *Schwabenspiegel*. It is largely based on the *Sachsenspiegel* but adds new material and transforms much of what it took over. Yet, compared with its model, the *Schwabenspiegel* must be considered as a lawbook of second rank. It lacks the originality and independence of thought characteristic of the *Sachsenspiegel* and its author. Nevertheless, this lawbook is to be given a place by the side of its Saxon predecessor not for its content but because of the influence which its ideas exerted on the development of law, particularly in southern Germany.

The *Schwabenspiegel* was compiled in Augsburg, Bavaria, probably in the years 1274–75. The author was an ecclesiastic of markedly papal orientation, equipped with some knowledge of law and history. He seems to have been connected with the Franciscan monastery at Augsburg. Roman law was apparently not foreign to him. Ecclesiastical sources, in particular, were at his command, and he employed them freely. He sought to bring the legal doctrines into harmony with the prevailing canon-law views and accordingly gave first place in his presentation to pope and church. This comes clearly to light at the very opening of the lawbook, in the curialistic version of the doctrine of the two swords. In his thoroughly ecclesiastical Weltanschauung, the compiler of the *Schwabenspiegel* is the direct opposite of the author of the *Sachsenspiegel;* for Eike von Repgow regarded the spiritual and the secular powers as equals and avoided taking sides explicitly, although he made no secret of his sympathy for the imperial standpoint. The Franciscan friar did not succeed in welding into a well-rounded unity the materials obtained from diverse sources. On the whole, his lawbook, again in contrast to the *Sachsenspiegel*, must be characterized as a diffuse, uncritical compilation by a man not profoundly versed in legal theory and philosophy.

The *Schwabenspiegel*, too, soon gained great authority and popularity. It was esteemed as highly and disseminated as widely in the south as was the *Sachsenspiegel* in the north and east.[24] It even penetrated northern Germany, Bohemia, Moravia, and also reached Burgundy. Indeed, the number of the manuscripts preserved of the *Schwabenspiegel*, amounting to about three hundred and fifty, by far exceeds that of its Saxon model. It was rendered into Latin, French, and Czech. In the thirteenth and fourteenth centuries other lawbooks were composed on the basis of the *Schwabenspiegel*, among them the *Freisinger Rechtsbuch*. Its model had far-reaching and authoritative influence in those regions which had not been conquered by the *Sachsenspiegel*.

The Jewry-law of the *Schwabenspiegel* is more comprehensive and detailed than that of its predecessor. It was originally intended for the Jewish communities in southern Germany and their legal relations with their Christian neighbors.[25] It contains numerous regulations unknown to the *Sachsenspiegel*. The accompanying table offers a survey of all regulations pertaining to Jewry-law which are found in the *Schwabenspiegel*. The individual articles appear in parallel columns arranged according to the three independent editions of the lawbook, representing several manuscripts. In a fourth column, for the sake of comparison, those articles of the *Sachsenspiegel* are listed which served as a basis for the *Schwabenspiegel*.

Lassberg (L)	Wackernagel (W)	Gengler (G)	Ssp. Ldr.
81	66	66	
86	71	71, 2	
87	72	72, 1	
	102	101, 3	
125	106	105, 2	
192	165	165, 7	
248	205	205, 1–2	II, 66, 1
255	210	210	III, 2
260	214	214, 1–5	III, 7, 1–3
261	214	214, 6–7	III, 7, 3(2), 4
262	214	214, 8–13	
263	215	215	
322	268	272	

The Jewry-law of the *Schwabenspiegel*, like its contents in general, is diffuse and uncritical. The very fact that the author drew not only on canon-law sources but also on medieval literature, such as the sermons of Berthold of Regensburg (*ca.* 1220–72) and the writings of the latter's teacher, David of Augsburg (*ca.* 1210/20–1272), both of the Franciscan order, is indicative of his attitude toward the Jews.[26] He is strongly influenced by anti-Jewish sentiment and lets himself be guided by the anti-Jewish regulations of the canon law, almost all of which were incorporated in the *Schwabenspiegel*, whereas the *Sachsenspiegel* was still free from such influence. The *Schwabenspiegel* stands out as an example of how and to what extent canon Jewry-law was integrated into the system of secular law. Eike von Repgow's original systematization of secular Jewry-law appears here considerably enlarged, revised, and supplemented on the basis of canon Jewry-law, for the first time introduced into a medieval German lawbook (L 262, 322; G 214, 8–13; 272). In one place (L 262; G 214, 12) there is even an explicit reference to the sixth section of the fifth book of Gregory IX's collection of decretals (*Liber Extra*, chap. 5, *de judaeis*, 5, 6). According to the *Schwabenspiegel* (L 262; G 214, 13) a mutually supplementary jurisdiction of secular and ecclesiastical courts is to enforce the rules concerning the Jews and their relationships to Christians. Its author's legal doctrines concerning the status of the Jews also betray theological and canon-law conceptions. *Servitus Judeorum* and "chamber serfdom," both unknown to Eike von Repgow, are taken for granted in concept and validity in the *Schwabenspiegel*.[27]

All told, there is no doubt that the author's attitude must be defined as decidedly anti-Jewish.[28] In his work no trace is found of Éike von Repgow's sense of justice, fairness, and objectivity in the attitude toward Jews and in the treatment of Jewry-law.

The *Sachsenspiegel* and the *Schwabenspiegel* were imitated in a series of lawbooks of a similar kind. The objective of the latter, however, was not to describe the law of a particular territory, such as Eastphalia, or a definite stratum of society within it, as in the case of feudal law. Rather, they aimed at a much broader scope: they intended to comprise the common territorial law in general. But the limited outlook of the several authors kept them—quite naturally—within narrow confines. Thus, despite their intentions, their works took on a local coloring. They were also somewhat confused by Roman and canon-law influences. It is mere book-learning and lack of criticism in the choice of their sources which distinguish these compilers from their great Saxon predecessor, both in aim and in performance.[29]

The formulation of the Jewry-law regulations in later lawbooks mirrors the same attitude in general. Nevertheless, the need for a law applicable in daily practice must have played some role in their setting forth the definite rules which should govern the life of the Jews and their relations to non-Jews. These rules, in turn, were dependent on the presence and the importance of Jews within the territory for which the individual lawbook was to define a system of laws. Hence the lawbooks, to which we have to turn now, must be considered under these different, specific aspects.

3. *Meissener Rechtsbuch*[30]

Among the lawbooks which were derived from or influenced by the *Sachsenspiegel*, the *Meissener Rechtsbuch* deserves first mention because of the considerable volume and the detailed character of its Jewry-law regulations. The Meissen lawbook, also known as *Vermehrter Sachsenspiegel* ("Enlarged *Sachsenspiegel*") or *Rechtsbuch nach Distinctionen*, was composed more than one hundred years later than the *Sachsenspiegel*, between 1357 and 1387.[31] It originated in a country town of the March of Meissen (today a part of Saxony) and rests to a large extent on the *Sachsenspiegel*, the municipal law of Goslar, an unknown source of Magdeburg law, and the lawbook of Zwickau of 1348. The aim of its author was to describe the common municipal law of Saxony ("in sächsischer Art").

The *Meissener Rechtsbuch* contains a large mass of the most detailed legal regulations and must be considered as one of the most interesting lawbooks because of its presentation, side by side, of municipal law and territorial law based on the *Sachsenspiegel*. The seventy-six manuscripts which have come down to us, bear witness to the great importance that it had attained among lawyers and in court practice. From Meissen as a center of its realm of application, its recognition and validity spread to Thuringia, to parts of Silesia, and, in particular, to Bohemia and Moravia. Its wide dissemination in the territory which is today Czechoslovakia, is attested to by no less than twenty-four manuscripts still preserved in that country, among them sixteen in Czech translation.

Despite all this esteem accorded to the Meissen lawbook in wide circles of lawyers and in legal practice within a large territory, the "Supreme Court" of medieval Germany, the *Oberhof* of Magdeburg, refused to grant it official recognition on grounds which were officially pointed out as follows:

Know ye with regard to the book *Distinctiones* that we think nothing of it; for it has not been confirmed by either the pope or the emperor. It has made its appearance but recently, nor is it known how it was composed. Also, it contains several articles contrary to our old laws which have been written down and confirmed.[32]

In spite of this nonrecognition by the most outstanding judicial body, the *Meissener Rechtsbuch* was introduced and even regarded as valid law in most of the cities subject to the law of Magdeburg.

It is a long-established historical fact that Jews in considerable numbers lived in the territory in which the *Meissener Rechtsbuch* attained influence on legal life.[33] It is little wonder, therefore, that its Jewry-law regulations are numerous in volume and comprehensive in character. They take up the entire seventeenth chapter of the third book, comprising forty-eight *distinctiones* ("paragraphs"). In addition, legal rules concerning Jews are found in the following articles: III, 1, 3; III, 11, 4–5; III, 14, 4; IV, 42, 22; IV, 46, 12; V, 5, 3; VI, 2, 2; VI, 2, 6. The compiler not only drew them from older lawbooks, such as the *Sachsenspiegel*,[34] but also utilized various princely charters granted to Jews, such as those issued by Margrave Henry the Illustrious of Meissen in 1265; by King Ottokar of Bohemia in 1268; by Duke Bolco I of Schweidnitz, Silesia, in 1295; and by King Casimir the Great of Poland in 1343.[35] The numerous borrowings from older law sources notwithstanding, the legal material in the Meissen lawbook is worked up in an original and interesting manner.

The inquiry into its source history is only in its incipient stage. The text, origin, and content of each individual *distinctio* must still be studied on the basis of all manuscripts available, and the mutual relationship of the latter is still to be established. This applies in particular to the regulations of Jewry-law. Such researches, however, would reach far beyond the limits of the present study. They must obviously be left to the scholars who are preparing a modern edition of this lawbook. Moreover, only on the basis of such an edition will it be possible to study the influence of the Jewry-law in the Meissen lawbook on the law practice concerning Jews in Bohemia and Moravia and, specifically, on that of the superior court of Brünn.[36]

Among all the medieval German lawbooks, the *Meissener Rechtsbuch* assumes the most favorable attitude toward the Jews.[37] In fact, here they are treated basically on the same level as Christians. One example may illustrate this. The oath of office prescribed for the judges' executive officers, explicitly includes a clause providing that "in all matters they would lawfully treat the poor as the rich, foreigners as all people, Jews as Christians" (III, 1, 3). Several provisions are intended to afford Jews particular legal protection and are motivated by special regard for their religious feelings or institutions. No Christian debtor, it was stated, could force his Jewish creditor to return pledges "on his holiday" (III, 17, 28). The sanctity of synagogues and Jewish cemeteries was under the special protection of criminal law (III, 17, 36 and 37). Jews were to be given assistance by their Christian neighbors in cases of legal emergency (III, 17, 45). But, obviously, another conclusion must also be drawn from regulations of this sort: at the time of the composition of the lawbook anti-Jewish sentiment was to be found in Meissen. Even the tale of ritual murder did not remain unknown to the author, for provisions for cases of blood accusation are included (III, 17, 41 and 43). True, regulations unfavorable to Jews are not missing from the lawbook. Yet, all in all, they are moderate and mild. Sometimes even in such provisions consideration for the Jews found expression. In one article, for example, the obligation is imposed on the Jews to retreat when meeting a procession bearing the Host (III, 17, 34), an obligation which, by the way, cannot be traced back to any analogous rule in ecclesiastic law. After having it included in his lawbook, the author considered it appropriate to add the following clause: "But no one should inflict any injury upon the Jews."

To sum up, the Jewry-law of the *Meissener Rechtsbuch* is inspired by a sense of justice and is permeated by an understanding for the peculiar situation in which the Jews were placed.

Each of the three lawbooks thus far mentioned represents, in its regulations of Jewry-law, a specific type all its own. The differences inhere in the originality of their conception and in the significance of their actual influence on the medieval practice of law. In both these respects the Jewry-law of the other lawbooks which are to be taken into consideration here falls far short of that of their respective models.

Nonetheless, for the sake of scholarly inquiry into the history of Jewry-law, it does not seem appropriate to eliminate the later lawbooks from the present investigation, even if they show a complete lack of originality. Research should establish which of the Jewry-law regulations found in the earlier lawbooks were taken over by the later ones, which were excluded, and what transformations and developments the accepted legal regulations underwent.

4. *Deutschenspiegel*[38]

The *Deutschenspiegel* which aims at a presentation of common German law, shows relations to both the *Schwabenspiegel* and the *Sachsenspiegel*. Whether it is the connecting link between them or rests upon both is a problem for which medieval source history has not yet found a definite solution. Accordingly, the date at which the *Deutschenspiegel* was probably composed would fall shortly before or shortly after the composition of the *Schwaben-spiegel*. Both seem to have originated in the same place, namely, Augsburg, southern Germany, and the author of the *Deutschen-spiegel* must also be sought in the circle of the Augsburg Franciscan friars. He employed for his work customary law and municipal statutes of Augsburg, but also used sources of Roman and canon law. Only one manuscript of the *Deutschenspiegel* has survived.

This lawbook does not seem to have enjoyed any importance worth mentioning in legal practice, nor is there any proof that it had actual validity anywhere. From the point of view of legal history it cannot be overlooked, however, because of its close relation to the two most important and widely disseminated German lawbooks.

The Jewry-law of the *Deutschenspiegel* shows no originality whatever. Its regulations are completely dependent upon those of the *Sachsenspiegel* and the *Schwabenspiegel*, for the most part agreeing with them. The variations in wording are, as a rule, inconsiderable and of little importance for the juridical interpretation of the regulations.

Article 73, 3, stating that no forfeited pledge should be pawned with Jews without the owner's consent, does not seem to have its source in chapter 59 of the Bavarian Land Peace Law of the year 1256, as has been suggested in the most recent edition of the *Deutschenspiegel;*[39] for in the regulation of 1256 an entirely different rule is set forth: "No Christian shall take usury nor pawn goods usuriously except with Jews."[40] This general principle has no logical connection at all with the specific rule laid down in the *Deutschenspiegel* and, correspondingly, in the *Schwabenspiegel* (L 81; W 66; G 66).

The dependence of the *Deutschenspiegel*'s Jewry-law regulations on those of the *Sachsenspiegel* and their relationship to those contained in the *Schwabenspiegel* are evident from the accompanying synoptical survey.

Dsp.*	Ssp.	Schwsp.
FE 73, 3		L 81; W 66; G 66
FE 77, 2		L 86; W 71; G 71
FE 78, 1		L 87; W 72; G 72, 1
F 187	II, 66, 1	L 248; W 205; G 205
FE 198	III, 2	L 255; W 210; G 210
FE 207	III, 7, 1	Cf. L 260; W 214; G 214, 1
F 208	III, 7, 2, 3	L 260; W 214; G 214, 4–5
F 209	III, 7, 4	Cf. L 261; W 214; G 214, 7

* The symbol "F" refers to Ficker's, "E" to Eckhardt and Hübner's, editions.

5. *Weichbild-Vulgata*[41]

Among the private records of municipal law, the *Sächsisches Weichbild* was the most influential. It consists of two parts connected externally only: the *Weichbildrecht*, which originated in Magdeburg or Halle between 1241 and 1269, probably between 1257 and 1261, and the *Magdeburger Schöffenrecht*, which may be dated between 1261 and 1295, possibly about 1270. While these two lawbooks were already combined in their early versions, supplementary regulations, partly taken from the *Sachsenspiegel* and partly formed independently, gradually were added and helped to produce a comprehensive new lawbook, known as *Weichbild-Vulgata*. This lawbook became widespread, was provided with a Gloss, and was translated into Latin, Polish, and Czech. Unfortunately, we are still completely in the dark about the historical details of this development as mirrored in the various manuscripts preserved.

Originally, the *Sächsisches Weichbild* contained no regulations bearing on Jewry-law. These are found, however, in that body of supplementary regulations in the *Weichbild-Vulgata* which, "in formulation if not in content seem to be for the most part independent."[42] Yet, until now, research has not succeeded in discovering their sources.

The most comprehensive form of these Jewry-law regulations, comprising rules on court jurisdiction and legal procedure and including a formula of the judicial oath to be taken by Jews, is found in articles 116 and 117 of the Berlin manuscript, dated 1369 (Homeyer, Rbb., No. 41), which served as the basis for the first edition by A. von Daniels. The Jewry oath is noteworthy for its formulation. It is placed at the end of the lawbook, and its integration in it is evident from its inclusion in the numeration of articles. The texts which served the editions of Ludovici and von Daniels and von Gruben are not so complete. The same applies to the unpublished version in the manuscript of the Preussische Staatsbibliothek in Berlin, Germ. fol. 391, dated 1382 (Homeyer, Rbb., No. 50), fol. 18v. The Heidelberg manuscript, Codex Palatinus 461, dated 1504 (Homeyer, Rbb., No. 533), published in von Thüngen's edition, shows noteworthy peculiarities. Here, article 116 is, in part, formulated differently. The most important variant is in article 352, 2 (116, 4): *uberczeugen selbsybennde*, instead of *overtugen selve dridde [ader selbandern] he mit eme cristen und mit eme juden*. The Jewry oath is more detailed than in either of the two last-mentioned editions and is not placed at the end of the book as it is in these editions. But the chief difference between the Heidelberg text of the *Weichbild-Vulgata* and all others is that it alone took over from *Sachsenspiegel Landrecht* its Jewry-law regulations (III, 2 and 7).

Of the other *Weichbild* manuscripts here under consideration, only one contains a mere reference to the *Sachsenspiegel*'s Jewry-law (III, 7). It is the so-called "Berlin-Steinbeck manuscript" of the Preussische Staatsbibliothek in Berlin, Germ. fol. 631, dating from the fourteenth century (Homeyer, Rbb., No. 63). The text of its Jewry-law comes closest to that found in the Berlin manuscript of 1382 and seems to be related to the Heidelberg manuscript. In the Berlin-Steinbeck manuscript, between article 112, 3 (116, 5) and the formula of the Jewry oath, there is an important insertion which has remained unnoticed hitherto. It reads: "The law concerning Jews is treated in the *Landrecht* which is called the *Sachsenspiegel*, in the third book in the seventh article; therefore, I do not intend to write about it here."[43] This passage seems to offer a historical clue for an explanation of the fuller wording found in later manuscripts. In all probability it was this very reference to the Jewry-law in *Sachsenspiegel Land-*

recht, contained in the same codex though in a different context, which led to the inclusion of the full wording of the *Sachsenspiegel*'s Jewry-law regulations in later manuscripts of the *Weichbild-Vulgata*, for instance that of Heidelberg, dated 1504.

In the original, common version of the *Gloss* on the *Weichbild-Vulgata*, which was composed in the fourteenth century in Magdeburg,[44] Jewry-law is also discussed in detail and with reference to Roman and to canon law.[45]

The accompanying table affords a view of the textual content of the *Weichbild-Vulgata* in the matter of Jewry-law.

MS Berlin 1369 Homeyer, No. 41. Ed. Daniels	Ed. Ludovici	Ed. Daniels and Gruben	MS Berlin 14th cent. Homeyer, No. 63. Unpublished	MS Berlin 1382 Homeyer, No. 50. Unpublished	MS Heidelberg 1504 Homeyer, No. 533. Ed. Thüngen	Sachsenspiegel Landrecht
116, 1	135, 1	134, 1	111, 1	18, 1*	351, 1	
116, 2	135, 2	134, 2	111, 2	18, 2	351, 2	
116, 3	136, 1	135, 1	112, 1	18, 3	352, 1	
116, 4	136, 2	135, 2	112, 2	18, 4	352, 2	
116, 5	136, 3	135, 3	112, 3	18, 5	352, 3	
117, 1 I			Insertion†			
117, 1 II‡	136, 4	136	Oath 1 II§	18, 1 II	181, pr.-3	
117, 2		‖	2	18, 2	181, 4	
					175	III, 2
					176	III, 7, 2
					177	III, 7, 3
					178	III, 7, 1
					179	III, 7, 4 (1)
					180	III, 7, 4 (2)

* MS Germ., fol. 391, of the Preussische Staatsbibliothek (Homeyer, Rbb., No. 50), has no numeration of articles or paragraphs. For this reason the paragraph numeration of von Daniels' edition is retained in this survey. The number "18" refers to leaf 18v of the manuscript.

† Reference to Ssp., III, 7.

‡ Formula of Jewry oath.

§ The oath formula is preceded by the special addition which follows :"Tu salt wissen, ab ein jude dem andern entghen solde mit sinem eyde, so sol der steber da sin und sol im dy vinger legen uffe Moyses buch, und der jude sol voran alsus sprechin." At the end there follows: "Amen sprechin dy andern juden alle." Cf. also Emil Steffenhagen, "Die Entwicklung der Landrechtsglosse des Sachsenspiegels, I," *Sitzungsberichte der kaiserlichen Akademie der Wissenschaften in Wien, phil.-hist. Klasse*, XCVIII (1881), 80; Thea Bernstein, *Die Geschichte der deutschen Judeneide im Mittelalter* (see below, pp. 73 f.), pp. 60 f.; Guido Kisch, "Studien zur Geschichte des Judeneides im Mittelalter," *Hebrew Union College Annual*, XIV (1939), 437 f.

‖ The paragraph missing here is found, however, in the Latin translation, in von Daniels and von Gruben, p. 176, as well as in the *Gloss* on the *Weichbild* to art. 135 (von Daniels and von Gruben, p. 438). Cf. G. Kisch, "The Yellow Badge in History," *Historia Judaica*, IV (1942), 138, n. 15.

6. SPECIAL LAWBOOKS BASED ON THE *Sachsenspiegel*[46]

There is a number of lawbooks of a more local character which were directly derived from, or based to a greater or lesser extent on, the *Sachsenspiegel*, while several other sources were used in them as well. It is quite obvious that the *Sachsenspiegel*'s regulations of Jewry-law often served as a model for these lawbooks, or even were taken over literally, if a need for the inclusion of such rules was felt at all. Through them the *Sachsenspiegel*'s original Jewry-law gained a still wider area of validity and ever broadening influence. The latter can well be studied on the basis of these—so to speak—special versions of the *Sachsenspiegel*.

The following lawbooks bear mention here.[47]

The *Breslauer Landrecht*, also known as *Schlesisches Landrecht*, is a collection of customary law, composed in 1356 for the principality of Breslau by a collegium of six city councilmen of the city of Breslau. As to Jewry-law, it adopted from the *Sachsenspiegel Landrecht* articles II, 66, 1 in its article 237; III, 2 in its article 245; III, 7 in its article 251.[48]

The *Berliner Stadtbuch* of 1397, based on the *Sachsenspiegel* and its *Gloss*, on the *Richtsteig Landrechts*, on the *Sächsisches Weichbildrecht*, and on local customary law, contains detailed regulations of Jewry-law. It belongs to this group of lawbooks but will be discussed separately, in section 9 below.

The *Neumarkter Rechtsbuch*, a local adaptation of the Silesian form of the *Sachsenspiegel*, with additions (*Extravaganten*), composed probably in the first half of the fourteenth century, contained all the Jewry-law regulations found in the *Sachsenspiegel*. Chapter 398 represents *Sachsenspiegel*, II, 66; chapter 411 corresponded to *Sachsenspiegel*, III, 2; chapters 423–25 were identical with *Sachsenspiegel*, III, 7. In chapter 606 a Jewry-oath formula was added. But the text of only the first passage has been preserved in full. The section treating of Jewry-law shows no deviation from the *Sachsenspiegel*. As a result of textual losses in the only manuscript extant, none of the other articles concerning Jews has come down to us, being known only through a register appended to the manuscript.[49]

The *Niederländischer Sachsenspiegel* took over the Jewry-law regulations of the *Sachsenspiegel* without change.[50]

The *Holländischer Sachsenspiegel*, an independent lawbook (date of origin unknown), based on Dutch manuscripts of the *Sachsenspiegel*, shows a different attitude toward Jewry-law. In article 16, "Van papen ende joden recht," and article 65, "Van joden recht," the Jewry-law regulations from *Sachsenspiegel*, III, 2 and 7 are found again. But they are in a singular connection with the pertinent comments of the *Gloss*, supplemented by additions taken from the *Gloss* to *Sachsenspiegel*, III, 53, 2 and III, 70, 1, and by some independent statements.[51]

The *Görlitzer Rechtsbuch*, transmitted in one manuscript only, dates from the beginning of the fourteenth century.[52] Among its excerpts from the *Landrecht* of the *Sachsenspiegel*, only article III, 2 is indirectly referred to in chapter 32, 4; but mention of the Jews is omitted. Nor are they referred to anywhere else in the lawbook. This is all the more surprising, since this lawbook shows a distinct relationship to the Magdeburg-Görlitz law instruction of 1304,[53] which contains the *Sachsenspiegel*'s Jewry-law regulations (art. 118 = Ssp., III, 7, 1–3[1]) within a section (arts. 81–121) borrowed from the *Sachsenspiegel*.[54]

The *Livländischer Spiegel*, composed between 1322 and 1337 on the basis of the *Sachsenspiegel* and of Livonian law sources, also omitted the regulations concerning Jews.[55] Here this fact is less surprising, for such laws would have been superfluous in Livonia, where, at the time, Jews were denied the right of residence.[56]

7. Freisinger Rechtsbuch[57]

Aside from those mentioned, there are several lawbooks which offer more detailed and coherent regulations of Jewry-law, whereas in others the subject is treated merely in a more or less fragmentary manner. For the most part, however, the Jewry-law is derived or adapted from older lawbooks.

The *Freisinger Stadtrechtsbuch*, by Ruprecht of Freising, the *Fürsprech* (spokesman and legal adviser), compiled in 1328, leans heavily on the *Schwabenspiegel*. The dissemination of that lawbook was considerable, although its sphere of influence was more limited than that of its Swabian model. Nevertheless, it won an important place in legal practice and, in particular, exerted influence on the law of Bavarian cities. In the fifteenth century the

Freisinger Stadtrechtsbuch was combined with a *Landrechtsbuch* by the same author, which was also based on the *Schwabenspiegel*, thus forming a book of municipal, as well as territorial, law.

The *Stadt- und Landrechtsbuch* of Ruprecht of Freising reproduces in its Jewry-law the respective regulations of the *Schwabenspiegel*, at times in a somewhat changed or amplified form.[58] Only one article (Knapp 263, Claussen 264, Westenrieder 87, missing in Maurer) seems to be either independent or taken from an unidentified source.

One article is worth mentioning, although it treats only of Christians (Maurer, II, 75[29], Knapp 212, Claussen 213; cf. Schwsp., L 160; W 141; G 140). "Christian usurers," the author points out, "are commonly called 'baptized Jews' [*getaufte Juden*]."[59]

The accompanying table shows a survey of the Jewry-law regulations of the Freising lawbook and their relationship to those contained in the *Schwabenspiegel*.

Freisinger Rechtsbuch			Schwabenspiegel
Ed. Maurer	Ed. Knapp	Ed. Claussen	
I, 163			L 248; W 205; G 205
168			L 255; W 210; G 210
172	121, 122, I	122, 123, I	L 261; W 214; G 214, 1, 2, 7
173	122, II	123, II	L 262; W 214; G 214, 8–12
	122, III	123, III	L 262; W 214; G 214, 13
174	218	219	L 263; W 215; G 215
204	123	124	L 322; W 268; G 272
Cf. II, 211[11]	38	41	L 260; W 214; G 214, 4
	39	42	L 260; W 214; G 214, 5
Cf. II, 102[6]	263	264	

8. *Glogauer Rechtsbuch*[60]

The *Glogauer Rechtsbuch* of 1386, although a daughter-lawbook of the so-called *Systematisches Schöffenrecht*, is to be mentioned in this connection; for its regulations on the legal treatment of Jews are dependent mostly on those found in the *Sachsenspiegel* and the *Weichbild-Vulgata*. They are variously remolded, supplemented, or amplified. The Jewry oath in article 485 is in conformity with that of the *Breslauer Landrecht* of 1356.

The relationship between the regulations on Jewry-law in the

Glogau lawbook and those in its sources is given in the following tabulation:

Glogauer Rechtsbuch Ed. Wasserschleben	Sachsenspiegel Landrecht	Weichbild-Vulgata Ed. Daniels	Other Sources
475			Magdeburg jury-court decision in Codex Bregensis (*ca.* 1339), Böhme, VI, 113, 3*
476			Cf. Breslau-Glogau Law Instruction of 1302, 5†
477	Cf. III, 7, 4		
478		116, 1	
479		116, 2	
480			Cf. *Breslauer Landrecht* of 1356, 365‡
481		116, 4, 5	
482		Cf. 116, 3	
483	III, 7, 2		
484	{ III, 2 { III, 7, 3		
485			*Breslauer Landrecht* of 1356, 365§

* [Johannes Ehrenfried Böhme], *Diplomatische Beyträge zur Untersuchung der schlesischen Rechte und Geschichte*, VI (Berlin, 1775), 113.

† G. A. Tzschoppe and G. A. Stenzel, *Urkundensammlung zur Geschichte des Ursprungs der Städte und der Einführung und Verbreitung deutscher Kolonisten und Rechte in Schlesien und der Oberlausitz* (Hamburg, 1832), p. 445 and n. 2.

‡ Ernst Theodor Gaupp, *Das Schlesische Landrecht* (Leipzig, 1828), p. 199.

§ See preceding note. This Jewry-oath formula is also found in MS J 7 of the fifteenth century in the Stadtarchiv of Breslau (fol. 241 v). It was published in G. Kisch, "Studien zur Geschichte des Judeneides im Mittelalter," *Hebrew Union College Annual*, XIV (1939), 438, n. 18b, where—by a printer's mistake—the number mark of the manuscript was given as "J 5," instead of J 7.

9. Berliner Stadtbuch[61]

Like the *Glogauer Rechtsbuch*, the *Berliner Stadtbuch* of 1397, whose main sources have already been enumerated,[62] drew its Jewry-law regulations primarily from the *Sachsenspiegel* and the *Weichbild-Vulgata*. The inverted order of the passages adopted from article 116 of the *Weichbild-Vulgata* (116, 4, 5, 3) and the Jewry oath following them, arranged in the same way as in the *Glogauer Rechtsbuch*, indicate that both lawbooks must have used the same type of text. Buch's *Gloss* on *Sachsenspiegel Landrecht* was also employed by the compiler.[63]

The author of the *Berliner Stadtbuch* shows an attitude favorable to Jews. He tried in particular to soften the anti-Jewish attitude of the citizenry of Berlin, which apparently did not escape his attention. In an introductory paragraph to the section on Jewry-law he offered four reasons why Jews should be permitted to dwell among Christians, in spite of their being "opponents of all Christendom."[64]

The accompanying table offers a comparison of the various laws.

Berliner Stadtbuch		Sachsenspiegel Landrecht	Weichbild-Vulgata Ed. Daniels 1853
Ed. Fidicin (Page and Paragraph)	Ed. Clauswitz		
149, 3 Prooemium	III, 14		
149, 4–150, 1	III, 15, 1–2	III, 7, 1–3	
150, 2	III, 15, 3	III, 7, 4	
150, 3	III, 15, 4–5		
150, 4	III, 16, 1	III, 2	
150, 5–151, 1	III, 16, 2	II, 66, 1	
151, 2	III, 16, 3	II, 66, 2	
151, 3	III, 17		⎰116, 4 ⎱116, 5 116, 3
152, 1 Vom Wucher	III, 18, 1–2	Cf. Gl., I, 54, 2	
152, 2–153, 1 Eid	III, 19, 1–3	Cf. Gl., III, 7, 1 *i. f.*	117, 1
	III, 19, 4		
153, 2	III, 19, 5		
153, 3	III, 19, 6		117, 2

10. *Zwickauer Stadtrechtsbuch*[65]

The influence of the *Sachsenspiegel* and the *Weichbildrecht* can also be observed in the *Zwickauer Stadtrechtsbuch* of about 1348, which, in turn, was used as a source by the *Meissener Rechtsbuch*. Only the published parts of this lawbook have been investigated by the writer, for the only manuscript in existence was not available to him. In the published parts, one single passage is found mentioning Jews (I, 15, 3). It is reminiscent of a passage in the *Sachsenspiegel Landrecht* (I, 61, 4) and of one in the *Gloss* to its article I, 60. But the exclusion of Jews from the office of *vorsprecher* ("spokesman") stated in the Zwickau lawbook was originally not found in the *Sachsenspiegel*. Only the *Gloss* and two late *Sachsenspiegel* manuscripts contain that anti-Jewish clause, though in different wording. But none of these manuscripts can possibly have served as a source for the Zwickau lawbook.[66] Its exclusion of Jews from spokesmanship is very rigid. It is reminiscent of a similar clause in *Richtsteig Landrechts* (II, 4).[67] The question must remain open whether this widely used lawbook on legal procedure, composed by Johann von Buch between 1325 and 1333, might have served as a source for the Zwickau lawbook.

11. *Neun Bücher Magdeburger Rechts*[68]

This work, also known as *Poelmannsche Distinctionen*, was compiled between 1400 and 1402 by Walter Ekhardi of Bunzlau, *Stadtschreiber*, or "town clerk," of the city of Thorn. He drew on various lawbooks, including the *Sachsenspiegel* with *Gloss*, the *Weichbild*, and the *Meissener Rechtsbuch*: "us der *Sachsinspigel* mit der glosen und us vil andern buchern des rechten." This lawbook was revised and published in 1574 by the notary Albert Poelmann of Königsberg. It includes a large part of the Jewry-law regulations of the *Meissener Rechtsbuch*.

12. *Prager Rechtsbuch*[69]

The lawbook of Prague is probably not a "lawbook" in the technical meaning of the term but a compilation of legal material for the royal towns in Bohemia.

Dating from the fourteenth century, it includes in its article 206 the Jewry-law regulations from *Sachsenspiegel*, III, 7, 2 and 3.

13. *Salzwedeler Stadtrechtsbuch*[70]

This "lawbook," probably of the early fifteenth century or possibly of the late fourteenth, represents merely a compilation of the contents of two charters for Salzwedel of 1273 and 1278 and of excerpts from the *Sachsenspiegel Landrecht*.

While the latter's articles III, 2 and III, 7, 1 were taken over in the paragraphs 77 and 83, 1, with some less significant changes, article III, 7, 2 was completely reversed in paragraph 83, 2. By completely denying justice to Jews, the author here expressed his religiopolitical attitude toward Jews and Judaism: ". . . the Jew must suffer in silence what the law appoints, for he has no claim on Christendom, and is God's persecutor, and a murderer of

Christendom." Such a penetration of religiopolitical sentiment into the realm of legal literature occurs rarely indeed, even in the Middle Ages.[71]

14. *Blume von Magdeburg*[72]

At the end of the fourteenth century, possibly in 1386–87, Nicholas Wurm composed the *Blume von Magdeburg*, with the *Richtsteig Landrechts* as its model. Some of its regulations were drawn from the *Sachsenspiegel* and the *Weichbild*.

This lawbook contains but few paragraphs on Jewry-law in its *Particula* II, namely, 2, 45 and 150–51. The latter passage is taken, with some changes, from *Sachsenspiegel*, III, 7, 4(1).

15. *Mühlhäuser Reichsrechtsbuch*[73]

The imperial lawbook of Mühlhausen, the *Mühlhäuser Reichsrechtsbuch*, to be attributed to about 1200 or to the first third of the thirteenth century because of its archaic language, was composed in Thuringia and thence transmitted to other towns, such as Nordhausen and Eschwege.

It contains no general regulation of Jewry-law or even single rules for Jews. But in article 45, 8, Jews are mentioned as pawnbrokers in a manner which implies that they had been settled in Thuringia for some time. The same article declares lawful the peculiar legal transaction of *Schadennehmen*, in which Jews functioned as lenders.[74] It is surprising, therefore, that no elaborate rules of Jewry-law were included in this lawbook. This fact could well be quoted to support the hypothesis that the Mühlhausen lawbook is older than the *Sachsenspiegel*, and hence perhaps the oldest German lawbook. If the author had been familiar with the *Sachsenspiegel*, he certainly would have availed himself of its provisions concerning Jews.

16. *Wiener Stadtrechtsbuch*[75]

The *Wiener Stadtrechtsbuch*, dating from the second half of the fourteenth century, is based on local customary law and on municipal statutes, but it also incorporated a considerable excerpt from later versions of the *Schwabenspiegel*.

Yet just in the regulations concerned with Jews—articles 10, 79, 135, and 145—the author kept his lawbook free of foreign, that is to say, non-Viennese, influences. The *Schwabenspiegel*'s Jewry-law was not employed by him. The explanation for this lies in the fact that the charter of Emperor Frederick II for the Jews of Vienna, issued in 1238, contained very elaborate Jewry-law. In fact, the author of the Vienna lawbook explicitly refers to it in article 145 as "der juden hantvest."[76] The regulations on Jews which he found fit to include in his lawbook concerned local customary law only or supplemented the privilege of 1238.

These regulations stand out for only one reason. The expression of Jew-hatred in some of the articles is very intense, one may even say passionate, in character. In article 79 it comes to the fore in an unfriendly remark addressed to the Jews "of whom there are only few as compared with us Christians." In article 145, moreover, hatred reveals itself in the compiler's exclamation that "the accursed Jews have much better rights with regard to Christians than the Christians have with regard to Jews." Even the Christian editor of this lawbook was impressed by such utterances of intense hatred of Jews ("äusserst lebhaften Judenhasses"). Another Catholic scholar designated the Jewry-law of the southern German lawbooks as "hard, degrading, indeed directly spiteful."[77]

17. *Frankenspiegel*[78]

The *Frankenspiegel* or *Kleines Kaiserrecht* originated in a *Reichsstadt* of Frankish Hesse at the time of Louis the Bavarian, probably between 1328 and 1338. It was based on local sources and influenced by the *Schwabenspiegel*.

Originally, Jewry-law regulations were completely lacking in this lawbook, of which a considerable number of manuscripts has been preserved. In a certain group of them, however, at the end of the text (IV, 24) only a Jewry-oath formula was inserted. It is drawn from the *Schwabenspiegel*.[79] It was obviously needed for court proceedings.

18. JOHANNES PURGOLDT's *Rechtsbuch*[80]

Johannes Purgoldt, mentioned in 1490 as town clerk of Eisenach, Thuringia, completed—probably about 1503-4—a lawbook that has come to be known under his name. It was based on a work compiled about one hundred and ten years earlier by the Thuringian chronicler, Johann Rothe, from several law sources, such as the Meissen lawbook, the *Sachsenspiegel* with *Gloss*, the *Schwabenspiegel*, and from local customs of Eisenach. The significance of Johannes Purgoldt's revision of this work (of his original version only the name *Eisenacher Kettenbuch* has come down to us) lies in the fact that he presents simultaneously *Landrecht* (defined as "the common law of Saxony, Meissen, Thuringia, and Hesse"), the municipal law of these countries (called *Weichbildrecht* by Purgoldt), and the town law of Eisenach. Purgoldt belonged to that group of medieval *Stadt-schreiber* whose training in Roman and canon law paved the way for the "reception of Roman law" in German court practice.[81] There can be no doubt that harmonizing the autochthonous with the foreign laws was the main goal that the author had set for himself. In order to accomplish this better, he drew also on the Bible and Greek and Roman classics and often referred to some "masters" of the canon law, whose doctrines patently had a considerable influence upon his legal thought.

This general attitude of the author found specific expression in his treatment of the laws which governed the status of the Jews and their economic activities in the midst of the general community. The pertinent rules are contained in Book VII, articles 97–99, 102, and in Book VIII, articles 30, 31, 52, 59–106, of Purgoldt's lawbook. Their main body is derived from, or based on, the Meissen lawbook. The other sources mentioned were also drawn on. But the method of compilation, arrangement as well as presentation, is original. The relationship of the individual articles in Purgoldt's *Rechtsbuch* to those in the Meissen lawbook appears in the tabulation shown on the next page.

After its publication in 1860 in a then modern edition, Purgoldt's lawbook almost entirely eluded scholarly investigation. The same is true especially of its Jewry-law. Yet its particular form is not only noteworthy in itself but sheds light also on the author's individuality. To characterize Purgoldt's attitude toward the Jews as mirrored in his compilation is, however, a difficult task, much more so than in the case of the authors of the *Sachsenspiegel*, *Schwabenspiegel*, and *Meissener Rechtsbuch*.

Doubtless the author shows interest in the legal, economic,

and social status of the Jews. In Book VIII, article 85, he offers a summary of his knowledge on this subject:

By custom and law the Jews' status differs in one country from that in another country, also the laws concerning them differ in one city from those in another city. In some cities and countries they own hereditary possessions, fields, vineyards, meadows, and woods; there they have privileges and laws accordingly. In some countries such as Italy, where Rome is situated, they must busy themselves with handicrafts and are compelled to wear special garments different from those of Christians. In some countries no more than two or three of them are tolerated in one city. But in German lands, they indulge in idleness and usury.

Purgoldts Rb.	Meissener Rb.	Purgoldts Rb.	Meissener Rb.
VII, 97	III, 11, 4 (1)	VIII, 77	III, 17, 15
98	III, 11, 4 (2)	78	III, 17, 17
99	III, 11, 5	79	III, 17, 9
102	III, 14, 4	80	III, 17, 8
VIII, 31	Cf. III, 17, 1	81	III, 17, 23
59	Cf. Berlin St B. III, 14	82	III, 17, 11
62	III, 17, 27	83	III, 17, 12
63	III, 17, 23	84	Cf. III, 17, 4 (2)
64	Cf. III, 17, 20	86	III, 17, 3 (1)
65	Cf. III, 17, 25	87	III, 17, 3 (2)
68	III, 17, 48	88	III, 17, 4
70	Cf. III, 17, 20	89	Cf. III, 17, 17
71	III, 17, 18	91	Cf. III, 17, 5
72	III, 17, 19	92	Cf. III, 17, 5
73	Cf. III, 17, 21	93	III, 17, 5, 6
74	III, 17, 26	95	Cf. Ssp., III, 7, 1
75	III, 17, 13	96	Cf. III, 17, 42
76	III, 17, 16		

In Book VIII, article 61, Purgoldt explains why it is the privilege of Jews to engage in usury: "To engage in usury is more fitting for Jews than for other people. For Saint Jerome, the teacher, writes that no people is greedier and more unchaste than the Jews. This is the cause for their indulging in idleness. Thereby greediness grows in the males and unchastity in the females."

It would be a mistake, however, to attribute to Purgoldt a special preoccupation with, or animosity against, Jews on the basis of these utterances.[82] Only in the preceding chapter of his lawbook (VIII, 60) he stated, referring to the canon law: "One should not impose on the Jews too heavy and unseemly a lot, one should tolerate them among Christians, but not extend this treatment to heathen, according to ecclesiastical law." In another chapter of his lawbook (VIII, 31) he visualizes the situation of Jews realistically, describes vividly their exclusion from ownership of real property and from handicrafts, guilds, and trading companies, and the hostile attitude of their Christian neighbors. Finally, he arrives at this conclusion: "Therefore, they must engage in usury, and this is their excuse. But Christian usurers have no such excuse, since they do it out of greed and because of their abandon and malice."[83]

This almost apologetic explanation does not seem consistent at all, in view of the quite different characterization and motivating idea offered by Purgoldt in VIII, 61 of his lawbook.

A similar discrepancy with reference to enforced baptism reveals itself in VIII, 96. True, Purgoldt does not take over from the Meissen lawbook the provision against kidnapping of Jewish children (III, 17, 42), which placed such acts under death penalty. But he states as a rule (VIII, 96): "Their children shall not be taken away from Jews, according to law, nor be made Christians without consent of their parents." Nevertheless, Purgoldt quotes "Meister Wilhelmus" as saying that "the princes may well take away from Jews their children lawfully without their consent and have them baptized, and thereby earn heavenly reward . . . if this be done solely for the children's salvation and happiness."

The author's dependence on theological doctrine and canon-law theory is clearly discernible. In the one case it is St. Jerome, in the other "Meister Wilhelmus" on whom he leans. Moreover, at the end of his section on Jewry-law, he embodied in his lawbook (VIII, 97–106) the entire canon of ecclesiastical restrictions and prohibitions of social intercourse between Jews and Christians.

In view of all this, no definite attitude toward Jews and Judaism can be found in Johannes Purgoldt's lawbook. It is the product of an uncritical compilation. As a rule, the differing regulations are marked by the author as taken from *Landrecht*, municipal, or ecclesiastical law: "Dit ist der stat recht und lantrecht," or "Dit ist geistlich recht." This clearly indicates that the different rules from several sources were merely put to-

gether in a superficial manner. By this method the author obviously could not succeed in welding them into a unity.

Johannes Purgoldt and his *Rechtsbuch* thus serve as a striking
example for the statement made previously, and confirm it fully:
that mere book-learning and lack of criticism in the choice of
their sources are what distinguish such compilers, both in aim
and work, from their Saxon predecessor, Eike von Repgow.

19. *Abecedaria* AND *Remissoria*[84]

Finally mention must be made of two types of medieval juristic
compilations which are derived from the lawbooks analyzed on
the preceding pages, but which considerably differ from them in
character.

The *Abecedaria* set themselves the task of making superfluous
the use of all the lawbooks registered therein by presenting their
total legal content in alphabetical form. One of the most important of these works is the *Schlüssel des [Sächsischen] Landrechts*. It
is a comprehensive remolding of the legal material contained
in the *Sachsenspiegel Landrecht*, including its *Gloss*, and in the
Schwabenspiegel. In part this was done through the utilization and
reformulation, in an independent manner, of the sources named.
The work was completed in 1432. It has remained in manuscript
form, but copies of it became widespread. The Jewry-law of the
lawbooks was worked up in similar fashion in the *Schlüssel des
Landrechts* as has been done in the *Remissoria*.[85]

The *Remissoria* are alphabetically, and sometimes even systematically, arranged registers of the main rules and principles of
law, drawn usually from several lawbooks. The designation
Remissorium indicates the aim of the book, namely, to serve as a
means to which one who is seeking legal information can turn
(*se remittit*). As a rule, the *Remissoria* were not intended to replace
the lawbooks, the contents of which were difficult to survey.
Their purpose was rather to facilitate the use of the lawbooks,
just as it was the case with the *Vocabularia*.[86] For this reason the
Remissoria are considerably briefer and afford, under the rubric
Jude ("Jew"), a complete survey of the regulations of Jewry-
law contained in the lawbooks which had been excerpted. The
custom of compiling *Remissoria* originated as early as the middle

of the fourteenth century, but flourished particularly in the second half of the fifteenth century and in the sixteenth. It is therefore not accidental that the sources of Roman and canon law were also employed for this type of lawbooks.

It is self-evident that such alphabetical registers and systematic excerpts from the most popular lawbooks contributed much to the further spread and practical application of Jewry-law. By collecting under the rubric *Jude* all the material on that subject in the legal sources, these registers offer for the first time a systematic survey of Jewry-law in the Middle Ages, as developed and described in the lawbooks.

In the course of the sixteenth century, some of the *Abecedaria* and *Remissoria* were printed in connection with, or as appendixes to, the lawbooks from which they offered excerpts. Many such books, however, compiled by industrious town clerks, jurists, or lay members of municipal tribunals for use in local courts, remained unpublished, in the form of voluminous manuscripts.

The municipal archives of Breslau are particularly rich in such manuscripts. Two of them, J 15 (Homeyer, Rbb., No. 210) and J 3 (Homeyer, Rbb., No. 204) contain a collection called *Regulae juris "Ad decus,"* compiled possibly by Nicholas Wurm at the end of the fourteenth century, but both written in the fifteenth century. The Jewry-law regulations are here arranged alphabetically as well as systematically. They are drawn from the *Sachsenspiegel* and are accompanied by the pertinent references to the *Corpus juris canonici* and the *Corpus juris civilis*.

Particularly widespread was the *Remissorium* of Dietrich (Theoderich) von Bocksdorf, of the middle of the fifteenth century (1449), of which an early copy (of 1468) is found in the Breslau MS J 16 (Homeyer, Rbb., No. 211). In its Jewry-law the *Sachsenspiegel* with *Gloss* and the *Weichbildrecht* were utilized.

More comprehensive and peculiar is the section on Jewry-law of another *Remissorium* which was compiled, between 1484 and 1493, by Caspar Popplaw of Breslau and is preserved in the Breslau MS J 8 (Homeyer, Rbb., No. 207). Caspar Popplaw (d. 1499), who also collected a comprehensive compilation of jury-court decisions, chiefly of the Magdeburg *Oberhof*, was a lay member of the municipal court of Breslau, with no training in Roman law. He drew from the *Sachsenspiegel* and *Weichbildrecht* and from the *Glosses* to both these lawbooks and, in addition, from the municipal law of Breslau.[87]

From 1482 on, a *Remissorium* was appended to the editions of the *Sächsisches Weichbild und Lehnrecht*. There the Jewry-law is registered under an independent arrangement.[88]

II. MAGDEBURG JURY-COURT DECISIONS

A. MAGDEBURG LAW AND THE *Oberhof* OF MAGDEBURG[89]

Very few cities in medieval Germany developed a town law of their own as an *Urrecht*, representing an original and independent system of law. In the twelfth and thirteenth centuries most of the then rising towns obtained their constitution and statutory laws by way of *Bewidmung*, that is, by transmission of an older system of town law which had originally grown up in one of Germany's ancient cities. These, through the act of conferring their law and constitution upon younger municipal foundations, became "mother"-towns of these "daughter"-towns. The latter derived their "daughter"-law from the "mother"-law of their models. It was therefore only in the natural course of legal development that, in difficult or doubtful law cases, court authorities or litigating parties applied for legal advice or instruction in law to the jurors or the court of their mother-city, on whose laws their own statutes were founded. Such "recourse to the superior court," or *Zug an den Oberhof*, developed in the early centuries of medieval city life and soon became a widespread, common, and regular legal practice all over Germany.

As early as the twelfth century, Magdeburg town law, *Magdeburger Recht*, was the legal system predominant in central Germany. The law of this old city, whose origin reaches back to the tenth century, owed its popularity and rapid expansion to its progressive and commerce-favoring character. In the era of the spontaneous rise and systematic founding of towns, franchises and privileges according to Magdeburg law were striven after by most of the new municipal settlements in the east. "Magdeburg law" then won its universal importance for the dissemination of law and civilization. It was first adopted by Halle, Stendal, and

Leipzig. It conquered almost all large cities in the March of Brandenburg and in the Lausitz. In the course of the thirteenth century it came to Silesia, Pomerania, and the domain of the Teutonic Order. Subsequently, it spread over Bohemia, Moravia, Hungary, over the whole Polish realm, Lithuania, Galicia, Volhynia, Podolia; and in the beginning of the sixteenth century it became the dominant system of law even in numerous cities of Russia.

This tremendous expansion of Magdeburg law east, north, and south of the province of its origin effected a very lively legal intercourse of the younger settlements with their common mother-city. Recourse to the *Schöffenstuhl*, or superior court of Magdeburg, was by no means obligatory or in any way prescribed in the customary charters which endowed individual towns with Magdeburg law. It was rather the great respect for the mother-city's model institutions of law and the almost unbounded esteem accorded to the Magdeburg jury-court decisions for their juridical value which raised this *Oberhof* of Saxon provincial law and jurisdiction to the level of a supreme tribunal of European authority. At the height of its fame it was often consulted by more than four hundred local courts and provincial *Oberhöfe*. Such secondary superior courts which, in the course of time, became to a certain extent competitors of the *Schöffenstuhl* of Magdeburg and, after its decline, its successors, rose in Halle, Leipzig, Dresden, Naumburg, Leitmeritz, Breslau, Görlitz, Lemberg, Cracow, Thorn, Culm, and other capitals of diverse provinces. All of them maintained, expounded, and at times developed more fully the original principles of Magdeburg law.

B. MAGDEBURG JURY-COURT DECISIONS AS A SOURCE OF JEWRY-LAW[90]

After this—though only very sketchy—description of the historical development and legal significance of Magdeburg law and the *Oberhof* of Magdeburg, there is no need to stress the particular importance and priceless value for legal-historical research of the decisions which emanated from that medieval "supreme court" or its younger offspring. They comprised instructions in law of a general character called *Weistümer*, or decisions in individual lawsuits, *Schöffensprüche*. Both groups have long been recognized as mines of information on the legal and social past in general.

Their paramount importance as sources for the legal history of medieval German Jewry, however, has hitherto hardly been noticed. The range of Magdeburg jurisdiction extended over numerous cities and provinces inhabited by Jews, and Jews therefore took a place, even if only a modest one, as subjects of Magdeburg jury-court activity. This fact alone puts Magdeburg decisions, from the point of view of Jewish history, on a level shared only by the *Sheelot u-Teshubot*, the rabbinic decisions of individual cases according to Jewish law, which are universally recognized as source material of the first rank.

It is well known that Jews were among the first settlers of Magdeburg and, together with non-Jewish traders, formed the early free community established there on the bank of the Elbe.[91] Members of the Magdeburg courts thus had at an early date an opportunity to come into contact with Jews and Jewish affairs of secular character. From their general acquaintance with the *Sachsenspiegel* and other lawbooks, on which many of their *Weistümer* and decisions were based, the conclusion may be drawn that the Jewry-law of the Saxon lawbook did not escape the attention of the Magdeburg jurors. Indeed, it was to a great extent incorporated in the law-instruction which they transmitted to the city of Görlitz, in 1304.[92] Moreover, there are many references to its basic principles in the regulations of Magdeburg law. It is a matter of fact that lawsuits of Jews against non-Jewish litigants and vice versa were brought before the *Schöppen* of Magdeburg and decided by their *Oberhof*.

This meant much more than merely an application of the principles of the *Sachsenspiegel* Jewry-law in cases involving Jewish litigants. It involved, indeed, an authentic and authoritative interpretation of these principles and their logical expansion and unfolding, with the ultimate tendency toward developing a unified Magdeburg Jewry-law. This evolution is to be regarded as a reflection of the general trend in the development of Magdeburg law: to remodel and adjust with a unifying tendency the principles of territorial law to the requirements of municipal law. In the case under consideration such legal practice exercised its influence upon a special sphere of law, the medieval Jewry-law. The Jewry regulations in the *Sachsenspiegel* were peculiarly suited for adoption and logical development by the Magdeburg town law: in contradistinction to law matter of territorial or feudal character, the *Sachsenspiegel* Jewry-law itself refers to municipal conditions, medieval Jews being predominantly city dwellers. The unifying tendency in the evolution of a specific Magdeburg Jewry-law was twofold. First, the jurors, as a rule, would be inclined to adhere to their established practice. Second, the decisions handed down from Magdeburg were not only respected by the provincial courts but regarded as precedents for future cases of the same or a similar nature, so to be decided even by subsequent generations of jurors.[93]

But it is not the tendency toward unification alone which, in the medieval German realm, makes the Magdeburg Jewry-law stand out from the unparalleled provincial and local diversity of laws, including the laws for the Jews. Even more remarkable may be considered the high standard of ethics in law as generally applied by the *Schöppen* of Magdeburg in their judicial practice, with respect to Jews no less than to non-Jews.

Thus, the "fact" value to the historian of the Magdeburg jury-court decisions, which exhibit the actual application of the rules of law to human life and relations, is only too evident. But it is not surprising that so important and promising a source of legal history as the Magdeburg jury-court decisions has not yet been systematically explored, collected, and expounded for the history of medieval Jewry. True, the collections of Magdeburg jury-court decisions already published form a considerable literature scattered through diverse books and historical journals of a more local nature.[94] Many more of these collections, however, are still unpublished.[95] A tremendous bulk of source material, amounting to thousands of individual decisions and hundreds of volumes of whole collections, is still resting in numerous archives all over Germany, Czechoslovakia, Austria, Hungary, Poland, the Baltic States, and Russia. It has as yet not even been opened to general research in legal history. Only those among the published collections of Magdeburg law which were current and widely used as lawbooks among medieval lawyers, such as the *Magdeburg-*

Breslauer Schöffenrecht and the *Magdeburger Fragen*, have received treatment by legal historians.[96] The causes for such neglect are obvious. This is the type of source material which, through its peculiar character, offers the greatest difficulties to proper handling by scholars: the number of individual documents, as well as of complete collections, is immense; they are widely scattered through many countries; moreover, the writing in these manuscripts is very hard to deal with, even for well-trained paleographers. Hence the bulk of this manuscript material has remained unknown, and even the known collections have not been satisfactorily utilized for research. Several attempts to solve the problem have been doomed to failure.[97]

For two full decades, from early 1915 until the end of 1934, the present writer endeavored to bring together for a legal-historical analysis and systematic survey all *collections* of Magdeburg jury-court decisions still in existence,[98] whereas previous efforts had been chiefly concentrated on collecting individual decisions only.[99] In spite of the considerable number and the great variety of types of these collections, this seemed to be the sole method of approach holding out a promise of success. Hundreds of manuscripts were studied, many of them carefully analyzed, either on the spot or in the writer's respective residences in Leipzig, Prague, and Halle, whither the materials had been sent by courtesy of the then owners. This work, already near its completion, was, however, abruptly halted shortly after the National Socialist regime had firmly established itself in Germany. In the course of the subsequent political events, all this writer's property was seized by the Nazi authorities. All his efforts to regain it after the German defeat remained unsuccessful. The results of years of painstaking labor could thus not escape a tragic fate. The writer's monograph on the *Oberhof* of Magdeburg, which had been announced for publication, will probably never appear in print.[100]

All the more fortunate, indeed, is the rescue of Magdeburg material pertaining to the legal history of the Jews. In the course of his general studies, the writer had always noted down and collected the jury-court decisions referring to Jews or to Jewish affairs. They amount to a respectable number of items, if one

takes into consideration the strict regulations of Jewish law prohibiting Jews from bringing their lawsuits before non-Jewish
courts. Picking out the decisions bearing on Jews from printed
material required the reading of hundreds, or rather thousands,
of cases, for there are no adequate indexes. Even greater labor
was demanded, for the same purpose, in scrutinizing the manuscript material of the thirteenth to the fifteenth centuries, with
its special paleographical difficulties, particularly if only photo-
stats were available.

Not only in number but also as far as the variety of their law
content is concerned, these *Schöffensprüche* represent a welcome
supplement, as interesting as it is important, to the universally
known and used sources of the medieval history of the Jews. The
material at hand is of great importance with respect to the legal
status and general culture of medieval Jewry and particularly its
relationship to non-Jewish authorities and Christian neighbors.
These documents disclose to a gratifying extent how the German
in his personal thoughts and feelings regarded himself in relation
to the Jew and how the medieval court brought the administration of law concerning Jews into agreement with the leading
ideas of the ruling legal philosophy of the time. The Magdeburg
decisions further reveal hitherto unknown data concerning the
settlement and economic activities of the Jews, their social standing and, above all, their legal status, in public as well as in private law, their actual treatment in matters of law, and their general place in German legal history.

In the present work an attempt is being made for the first time
to collect systematically all accessible Magdeburg jury-court decisions concerned with Jews or Jewish affairs and to expound and
evaluate their law contents historically, as well as juridically.
Decisions already in print, as well as others still unpublished,
will be included.

The method of presenting this material must differ from that
applied to the lawbooks, because of the dissimilarity in character of these two groups of legal sources. In the case of the lawbooks, a general knowledge of the history of each *Rechtsbuch* and
the genealogical relationship of the younger to the older among
these early products of legal literature seemed necessary for a

proper understanding of root, development, and dissemination
of every individual principle of medieval Jewry-law set forth in
them. The *Schöffensprüche*, on the other hand, disclose how these
principles were applied to individual cases and interpreted with
regard to particular situations or problems resulting from legal
practice. As the emphasis here is placed on the dogmatics of law,
it is sufficient for the student to know—besides the purely legal
aspects—that the individual decision under consideration is
found in an authentic collection and belongs to a definite period
and region. The history of the manuscript collection, in which
the cases and their decisions have come down to posterity, for the
most part very complicated and often no longer to be unraveled,
can remain in the background. Therefore, no separate enumeration and analysis will be devoted to these collections of *Schöffensprüche*, most of which contain only sporadic cases concerning
Jews.[101]

The fact that some collections were inaccessible to the author[102] and that other material was deliberately withheld by the
Nazi authorities[103] cannot materially impair the accuracy of the
legal-historical picture to be derived from the sources he did use.
It may, however, some day be supplemented, clarified or even
completed through further research, after access to European
archives has been restored.

In regard to original text and English translation, the same
method was followed as applied to the lawbooks. In the course
of discussing the *Schöffensprüche*, their substance is given in faithful translation, accompanied by precise citation of the original.[104]

The present study of jury-court decisions with regard to
Jewry-law is restricted to the *Oberhof* of Magdeburg and other
superior courts within the realm of the Magdeburg law. An inquiry into the judicature of other superior courts representing
different systems of municipal law in medieval Germany is a
separate task, going beyond the aims of this work.[105] Hence there
is no reference to decisions of courts outside the *Rechtskreis* of
Madgeburg.

Only one exception is made: it is in favor of the *Oberhof* of
Brünn (Brno), Moravia. Brünn was a center of southern Ger-

man, probably Viennese, law,[106] which was—at least temporarily—exposed to influences of Saxon and particularly Magdeburg law.[107] The *Schwabenspiegel* was here used as early as the beginning of the fourteenth century, and an original manuscript dating from this period is still in the municipal archives of Brünn.[108] The realm of Brünn law was, moreover, almost completely surrounded by court districts that stood immediately under Magdeburg law.[109] The *Oberhof* of Brünn, nevertheless, remained formally independent and developed a judicial practice and authority of its own. The numerous local courts under its legal guidance extended over a considerable territory, with a fairly large Jewish community.[110] Moreover, the decisions handed down by the *Oberhof* of Brünn enjoyed great esteem because of their juridical quality. Two voluminous collections have come down to us, both of which contain a respectable number of decisions concerned with Jews or touching on Jewish affairs.

Outstanding among them is the *Brünner Schöffenbuch*.[111] It is a lawbook compiled in the middle of the fourteenth century, probably in 1353, by the municipal clerk and notary, or *Stadtschreiber*, Johannes of Brünn, who held this office from 1343 to 1358.[112] He was a man well acquainted with the indigenous sources of German municipal law but also versed in the Roman and canon legal systems, which long since had begun to penetrate the various laws in central Europe. He allowed those foreign laws to some extent to enter the lawbook which he compiled from decisions (*sententiae*) handed down by the *Oberhof* of Brünn upon the request of numerous local courts in Moravia.[113] These pronouncements of the jurors at the superior court in Brünn were collected and systematically arranged under legal headings by Johannes and also subjected to editorial revision. The *Brünner Schöffenbuch* is written in Latin and includes, among its 730 decisions, 22 referring to Jews, who appear as plaintiffs or defendants. Eleven *sententiae* are gathered under the heading, "De judaeis," 11 are found under diverse titles.[114] Most of the cases related are of extraordinary interest from the point of view of legal history, as well as for the cultural history of medieval Jewry in general. In spite of the fact that a printed edition has been available since 1852, very little use has been made of these *Schöffensprüche*, even by Stobbe.

Another collection of similar importance was discovered only a few years ago and has not yet been published.[115] The decisions collected in the *Geschäften- und Bürgeraktenbuch* of the Moravian town of Ungarisch-Hradisch, east of Brno (Brünn), now in possession of the *Zemský Archiv* in Brno (Brünn), were directed from Brünn to Hradisch. They resemble the decisions in the *Brünner Schöffenbuch* but are even more original in character, because the questions of law submitted and the decisions or instructions returned were not subject to any editorial revision by a jurist. Hence even the names of the parties are often preserved. Nineteen cases treat of Jews.[116]

A third collection, smaller in volume and showing but few traces of editorial revision, is found in manuscript Cod. 12.472 of the Nationalbibliothek in Vienna. In this codex, twenty-seven jury-court decisions follow immediately upon the text of the *Brünner Schöffenbuch*, seemingly a sort of supplement to it and comprising new cases which were submitted to the *Oberhof* shortly after the *Schöffenbuch* had been completed. It is also possible, however, that they were compiled from documentary material not included in the lawbook or even that they belong to a later period. Be that as it may, their law content matches very well that presented in the *Schöffenbuch*. The decisions indicate as their place of destination Eibenschitz; one was sent to Moravian Kromau. Three of them concern Jews.[117]

Examination of this source material revealed its importance for purposes of comparison with the court decisions according to Magdeburg law. Thus it has been utilized to this end and will be referred to in the footnotes in English translation.[118]

III. Legal-historical Literature: A Critical Survey[119]

A. medieval *Remissoria* and *Glosses* on jewry-law

Literary preoccupation with the regulations of Jewry-law contained in the German lawbooks goes back as far as the Middle Ages.[120] Even in the very period when these lawbooks were originating, the practical importance of the subject was realized. This induced the leading jurists of the time to occupy themselves with the legal status of the Jews and to engage in discussions on its various aspects. Their works were mainly commentaries of different types on the lawbooks, and they gained wide use in the courts and among lawyers.

Several of the works mentioned in the preceding section as sources of medieval Jewry-law represent, at the same time, its earliest literary treatment. This treatment was determined primarily by practical considerations. This holds true for the commentaries (*Glosses*) to the *Landrecht* of the *Sachsenspiegel* and to the *Weichbild-Vulgata* as well as for the *Abecedaria* and the *Remissoria*. The literary-historical significance of the commentaries is generally recognized. The source-value of the *Abecedaria* and *Remissoria* must also not be underestimated. They represent noteworthy literary achievements, of course of a different character, despite the fact that they merely transmit material derived from other sources; for the authors put this material together in accordance with original methods and undertook an independent elaboration. Frequently the result was a presentation which must be regarded as an interesting attempt at welding together different sources of law into a unified legal system.[121] This was, of course, also accomplished in the commentaries, in which the combination and harmonization of Roman and canon law with the indigenous law of the *Sachsenspiegel* or *Weichbild* was the main goal.

The literary adaptations and discussions which Jewry-law underwent in these juridical works destined for legal practice are of great interest for the investigation of its historical development. That they originated still in the age of the lawbooks makes them all the more valuable for research. This applies in particular to the *Gloss* to the *Sachsenspiegel* by Johann von Buch, which was completed about one hundred years after the lawbook itself. Nevertheless, in utilizing this type of literary works for the purpose of interpreting the Jewry-law regulations in the *Sachsenspiegel*, great caution is required; for, like the language, the law content of the *Sachsenspiegel* can be explained only on the basis of the lawbook itself and not in accordance with the sense which later generations attributed to its regulations.[122]

B. THE *Judenrechtswissenschaft* OF THE SIXTEENTH TO THE EIGHTEENTH CENTURY

After the close of the medieval period, from the sixteenth to the eighteenth century an extensive literature of the "science of Jewry-law" (*Judenrechtswissenschaft*) was produced in the law schools of the German universities, particularly after the "reception of Roman law." The revival of the Jewry-law regulations of the Roman codes as binding and generally applicable rules made their adaptation and interpretation for practical purposes necessary. The science of canon law aided and the theological faculties of the universities participated in this work. The rise of Protestantism had, of course, a retarding effect on this development. Nevertheless, the number of books, essays, theses, and dissertations on the subject, augmented further by legal opinions issued by the leading law faculties or published by individual lawyers in their *Consilia*, amounts to very considerable volume. Of course, quotations and citations of medieval Jewry-law regulations are frequent in this literature.[123] But its orientation is completely that of the common law. In fact, these works are without significance for the early history of Jewry-law as presented in the lawbooks, and they contributed only to its replacement by Roman law rules. Although this vast literature, as yet hardly noticed, is well deserving a separate historical treatment, for the purposes of the present investigation it is not necessary to discuss it.[124]

C. NINETEENTH- AND TWENTIETH-CENTURY RESEARCHES ON THE JEWRY-LAW OF LAWBOOKS

1. JEWISH RESEARCH ACTIVITIES

During the nineteenth century, in spite of the rise and flourishing of research in medieval legal history in Germany, only slight attention was paid to the Jewry-law of the German lawbooks.

The principal scholarly interest of Jewish historians was held for long by the privileges granted to the Jews of the Rhenish cities, Speyer and Worms, toward the end of the eleventh century.[125] The contribution of those historians to the knowledge of medieval German Jewry-law as found in the lawbooks under consideration was extremely small. In his *Regesten zur Geschichte der*

Juden im fränkischen und deutschen Reich bis zum Jahre 1273, Julius
Aronius merely compiled the Jewry-law regulations of the
Sachsenspiegel, *Deutschenspiegel*, and *Schwabenspiegel*, translated
them into modern German, and added some bibliographical
notes.[126] A monograph on the relationship between the Jewry-
law of the lawbooks, the Rhenish privileges, and canon law has
been promised several times by Albert Dresdner, collaborator on
the *Regesten*, but to my knowledge, it has never been published.[127]
All Jewish historians, who have dealt with the subject since
then, down to the editors and collaborators of the *Germania
Judaica* have taken the data provided by Aronius as their basis.[128]
They simply reproduced the regulations concerning Jews in the
lawbooks, sometimes more and sometimes less completely, in
part not even correctly. The legal-historical literature on the subject has remained quite unknown to them. Research has not been
advanced through their works. Thus a description of this literary
production can in all fairness be omitted here. There are only two
exceptions.

George Caro, in his book, *Sozial- und Wirtschaftsgeschichte der
Juden im Mittelalter und der Neuzeit* ("Social and Economic History of the Jews during the Middle Ages and in Modern Times"),
treated the relation of protector and protected which grew up
between the king and the Jews during the Middle Ages and the
development of the royal prerogatives over the Jews (*Juden-
regal*).[129] In connection with this, Caro evolved independent
views on the pertinent legal conceptions in the *Sachsenspiegel*, to
whose author the theory of the Jews' "appertainment" to the
imperial chamber was still unknown. But the brief remarks in
Caro's work, which is concerned with economic rather than with
legal history, naturally did not suffice to solve the problem of
chamber serfdom or that of imperial and princely regality over
the Jews.

Thea Bernstein—the second exception—in her doctoral thesis,
Die Geschichte der deutschen Judeneide im Mittelalter ("History
of the Oaths for Jews in Medieval Germany"), made a noteworthy contribution to the history of the medieval Jewry oath
by devoting a special chapter to the oath formulas in the German lawbooks.[130] She traced their origin and development

through the centuries on the basis of comprehensive material, in part consisting of manuscripts. This careful investigation yielded interesting results, from the point of view of linguistic and cultural history. They are valuable and welcome as preliminary work for the legal-historical inquiry into the problem of the medieval Jewry oath.

Still another contribution, of the nineteenth century, must be mentioned, small but very interesting. As early as 1870, there appeared in an obscure publication a brief sketch, "Die rechtliche Stellung der Juden nach dem *Sachsenspiegel*" ("The Legal Status of the Jews According to the *Sachsenspiegel*"), by Emanuel Leser (1849–1914). Since its appearance, this article has been completely lost from sight.[131] Despite its popular presentation, the essay displays juridical knowledge and historical understanding. The author, for more than four decades professor of economic history at the University of Heidelberg, made no other excursion into legal history. Stobbe's book, which had appeared a few years earlier, is not referred to in his essay and does not seem to have been used. The author discusses in great brevity, but with good judgment, some of the Jewry-law regulations contained in the *Sachsenspiegel*. Besides this, he made a thought-provoking statement that lent his essay significance. He noted "the remarkable fact that the *Sachsenspiegel* interprets Bible passages in a manner to be regarded as peculiar to Jewish tradition." His conclusion, that Eike von Repgow may have come into official, and perhaps also unofficial, contact with Jews resident in his judicial district and may have learned those interpretations from them, was indeed deserving of careful consideration.

This observation, in connection with a conjecture of mine about the historical roots of the Josephus passage in the *Sachsenspiegel Landrecht*, III, 7, 3,[132] induced me to make an extensive study of two problems preliminary to the present researches: the significance of the Bible for the *Sachsenspiegel* and the possibility of the influence of Jewish thought on this lawbook. The results were published in my book, *Sachsenspiegel and Bible: Researches in the Source History of the Sachsenspiegel and the Influence of the Bible on Medieval German Law.*[133]

2. RESEARCHES BY GERMAN SCHOLARS

A glance at the researches so far enumerated reveals the fact that exceedingly few Jewish historians were interested in problems offered by the medieval lawbooks with regard to the Jews. The results of their investigations, moreover, were restricted to questions of a very limited scope. This situation, prevailing in Germany prior to 1933, is very regrettable indeed. Shortly after the establishment of the Third Reich, National Socialist pseudo-scientific propaganda launched, repeated, and defended a directly contradictory assertion: that German scholarship had left to the Jews the historical investigation of the Jewish question in general, and particularly in the field of legal history. The share of German scholarship, compared with the achievements of Jewish historians, it was emphasized, had been altogether insignificant.[134] This statement reversed the actual situation;[135] for, above all, Christian scholars—in fact, genuine and unbiased scholars—have treated extensively the problem of Jewry-law in the German lawbooks and have furthered it considerably. This can be gathered easily from the following survey of German legal-historical literature on the subject.

The first one in the nineteenth century to give careful attention to the Jewry-law regulations in the German lawbooks, especially the *Sachsenspiegel*, in a scientific presentation of German political and legal history, was Karl Friedrich Eichhorn.[136] The fact that his work was intended as a handbook for students rather than a detailed monograph set certain limits to his discussion of the subject. Nevertheless, he did not content himself with a mere reference to the pertinent passages of the *Sachsenspiegel* and with reprinting their wording, especially in his detailed notes to the chapter "Judenrecht." He also referred to the *Gloss* and the *Schwabenspiegel* and made suggestions as to the historical origin of individual rules.[137]

The Jewry-law of the German lawbooks was more comprehensively utilized in monographs by Otto Stobbe and Johannes E. Scherer on the legal status of the Jews in the Middle Ages.[138] These two authors, however, did not intend to discuss thoroughly the individual rules of Jewry-law found in the lawbooks or to expose their law content and character against the background of the general history of law. Stobbe endeavored rather to bring them in connection with the Jewry-law of the town laws, while Scherer compared them with the privileges granted to Jews in imperial or princely charters ("privileges"). Obviously, a valuable clarification was gained thereby for legal history. However, at the time that these two scholars wrote their works, neither source history nor textual criticism was sufficiently advanced to come to their assistance.

Later, there appeared a large number of comprehensive works and monographs in which one or another of the regulations of Jewry-law taken from the lawbooks was treated or mentioned. Most of them, if not all, were based on Stobbe's and Scherer's works. Such books are too numerous to be listed here. In the course of the presentation some of them will be referred to in the notes.

Special attention should be called only to the following treatises as the most noteworthy independent contributions to research in this field.

Karl von Amira, one of the foremost legal historians, who made the investigation of the illuminated manuscripts of the *Sachsenspiegel* his life's work, also contributed in an original and particularly valuable manner to the interpretation and understanding of the Jewry-law regulations in that lawbook. First, in his edition of the famous illuminated *Sachsenspiegel* manuscript of Dresden, he reproduced all illuminations picturing Jews.[139] In his voluminous commentary on this work, he then discussed all the pictorial representations of Jews.[140] In addition, Amira devoted a comprehensive study to the peculiar Jewish dress presented in the pictures.[141] Rich and widely scattered pictorial material for the history of Jewish garb was there gathered and discussed with great lucidity. The shape of the "Jewish hats" and their colors were given particular attention. Needless to say, the combination of art history and legal history proved especially fruitful.

Eduard Eichmann, in his essay "Die Stellung Eikes von Repgow zu Kirche und Kurie" ("Eike von Repgow's Attitude toward Church and Curia"), touched on the problem of the mutual relationship of canon Jewry-law and secular Jewry-law.[142] He deals with the passage in *Sachsenspiegel*, III, 2, concerning "clerics and Jews who bear arms and who are not shaven in accordance with their law." Although Eichmann's discussion is primarily concerned with the content of this passage from the point of view of canon law, it also sheds new light on the Jewry-law regulation contained therein.

The most specialized essay on the Jewry-law of the lawbooks was published by Karl Gottfried Hugelmann, in his "Studien zum Rechte der Nationalitäten im deutschen Mittelalter" ("Studies in the Law of Nationalities in the German Middle Ages"), under the subtitle: "Das Judenrecht der Rechtsbücher."[143] As the general title of his treatise reveals, the author views his problem through a modern political formulation of the question.[144] This is in complete contrast with all his predecessors. His point of departure is the old "alien-law" theory which runs through his essay like a red thread. He believes that "even the legal sources alone leave no doubt about the national element in medieval Jewry-law."[145] He goes even further and, from the national and religious diversity, also derives the racial dissimilarity of the Jews in the medieval period. In other words, Hugelmann's discussion results in a historical foundation of the modern doctrine of race. He finds that in the later Middle Ages Jewry-law was formulated in a manner "explicable only by a greatly exaggerated feeling of racial strangeness which expressed itself directly in physical aversion."[146]

Hugelmann's treatise was published as early as 1928. Unlike other works touching on the history of the Jewish question, which are similarly affected by modern political doctrines but have nothing to do with scholarship, this treatise was written by a scholar who previously (and later) has published recognized works on the history of canon and German law. His essay on the medieval Jewry-law, too, contains some correct observations and stimulating thoughts. It was seemingly not a product, but a forerunner, of National Socialist pseudo-scientific propaganda.[147] Nevertheless, its author's conclusions should not be shunned but given serious consideration. Its weaknesses, however, are so apparent that no unprejudiced critic can fail to notice them. In the first place, the author limited his investigations to the most important of the lawbooks. He did not trace at all the origin and textual and historical source relationships of the Jewry-law regulations in the individual lawbooks. Even the published source material by means of which he seeks to test the practical application of Jewry-law is altogether inadequate. Unprinted sources were not consulted at all. The literature which was drawn upon by the author is very scanty; not the slightest attempt toward completeness has been made.

But another fact weighs even more heavily. From the very outset of his investigation, Hugelmann succumbed completely to the dangers described above of a *gegenwartsnahe Fragestellung* and of the influence of modern political views. He did not even escape the pitfall of hyperhermeneutics. It is astounding to read in the work of a recognized scholar bold assertions without proof from the sources, to find conclusions remote from their solid basis and explanations contradicted by the clear wording of the sources. No wonder that the results are bound to be distorted. All this will have to be discussed and shown in detail in the course of the following investigation.

3. NATIONAL SOCIALIST RESEARCH

Hugelmann's essay carries us over to the researches in medieval Jewry-law under National Socialist auspices. Only two of their products concern the lawbooks and are worthy of mention.[148]

As early as 1902, Herbert Meyer, like Hugelmann a recognized scholar, in his book, *Entwerung und Eigentum im deutschen Fahrnisrecht* ("Disseisin and Property in the German Law of Chattels"), investigated the origin and legal significance of an old trade privilege accorded Jewish merchants, which is treated in *Sachsenspiegel*, III, 7, 4 and III, 7, 1, and also in other lawbooks: under certain conditions and legal precautions Jews could acquire property or security rights in stolen goods and were entitled to claim compensation if the object were reclaimed by its legitimate owner. For this privilege Meyer introduced the designation *jüdisches Hehlerrecht*, not derived from medieval sources, and tried to prove that this purely commercial privilege had its origin actually in talmudic law.[149] After 1933, when Meyer had enthusiastically joined the National Socialist ranks, it seemed desirable to him to revive his old theories in the service of political propaganda.[150] They had had, in fact, considerable influence on legal-historical literature and were accepted even by Jewish historians, although they had not remained uncontested. A refutation on the basis of careful re-examination from the general, as well as the Jewish, points of view was published only a few years ago.[151]

Another essay, Hans-Kurt Claussen's study, "Der Judeneid: Ein Beitrag zur Geschichte des Rechtsschutzes" ("The Jewry Oath: A Contribution to the History of Legal Procedure"), although not free from anti-Semitic remarks, must be considered a real contribution to scholarship.[152] Claussen offers a good survey and critical discussion of the oath formulas from the early medieval period up to the abolition of the special Jewry oath in the nineteenth century. His material, which was partly drawn from manuscripts and included the formulas of the Saxon and Swabian lawbooks, is arranged systematically. He subjected it to a careful philological and legal-historical analysis. For its reproduction of the several types of oath formulas, Claussen's study is a welcome supplement to Müllenhoff's and Scherer's collection of Jewry oaths.[153]

With the books and essays so far discussed, the list of contributions to the study of the Jewry-law in the medieval German lawbooks is exhausted.[154]

D. RESEARCH ON THE JEWRY-LAW OF COURT DECISIONS

Works which utilized medieval court decisions for the history of the Jews are extremely scarce. In spite of the fact that Stobbe and Hoeniger had already recognized the value of these sources for legal-historical research, they were almost totally neglected.[155] The only exception is Emanuel Forchhammer's essay, "Beiträge zur Geschichte der deutschen Juden mit besonderer Beziehung auf Magdeburg und die benachbarte Gegend" ("Contributions to the History of German Jewry, with Special Emphasis on Magdeburg and the Neighboring Regions").[156] The scope of Forchhammer's study is limited to central Germany and to the region of Magdeburg in particular. The author, who also consulted the northern German lawbooks, was fully aware of the importance of the jury-court decisions for the history of medieval Jewry.[157] He employed and interpreted a number of those that were available in print and treated particularly those contained in Friese-Liesegang's collection.

Forchhammer's presentation suffers, however, from two serious shortcomings. He was no jurist and thus had no understanding of the intricacies of legal-historical problems. Moreover, Forchhammer was decidedly biased against the Jews, although his essay was written in 1911, and he did not miss any occasion in the course of discussion to give vent to his anti-Semitic feelings.[158] While the reader is under the impression that the aforementioned author, Hans-Kurt Claussen, in his anti-Jewish utterances paid merely compulsory tribute to the political trend then current in Germany, there can be no doubt that Forchhammer's bias was determined by a deep-seated hatred of the Jews. This is all the more regrettable as his very detailed study, despite these shortcomings, is a fine specimen of good scholarship. It remained the only work which employed on a larger scale jury-court decisions for the history of the Jews.

E. MEDIEVAL GERMAN POETRY AND JEWRY-LAW

Finally, another kind of literary approach to medieval Jewry-law and its social and economic effects should not be overlooked, although it is not specifically legal-historical in character. German poetic literature of the thirteenth, fourteenth, and fifteenth centuries forms not only a true picture of the intellectual character of the epoch in which it was written but also allows us a clear insight into the actual social and economic conditions as well as into the attitude of the various classes toward one another and toward the problems of the day. The medieval "Jewish problem" or at least its subject, the Jew, turns up in this literature more frequently than one would be inclined to expect. Nevertheless, the role attributed to Jews in medieval German poetry has so far not been subject to specific scholarly inquiry.[159] Siegfried Stein's useful doctoral thesis, *Die Ungläubigen in der mittelhochdeutschen Literatur von 1050–1250* ("The Unbelievers in Middle High German Literature, 1050–1250"), treats of all unbelievers, including "Jews, heathen, and heretics," but offers extremely scanty material pertaining to Jews.[160] Erwin Gustav Gudde's thesis, *Social Conflicts in Medieval German Poetry*, is much more comprehensive in scope and also superior in the organization and evaluation of the source material gathered and worked up.[161] Here the Jewish problem, as it presents itself in medieval German poetry, has been well integrated in the study of the "social conflicts" in the Middle Ages. Gudde's valuable book came to this author's attention only after his researches and manuscript were practically completed. References could therefore be incorporated only in the notes. This slight disadvantage is, however, outweighed by the gain derived from the comparison of Gudde's and the author's findings. The former are in complete harmony with the results arrived at previously and independently in the present study. In fact, they find full confirmation in the poetical literature of medieval Germany and thus refute Hugelmann's assertion to the contrary, which was certainly not based on source material as comprehensive as had been assembled by Gudde.[162]

CHAPTER THREE

The Scope of Jewry-Law

I. TERRITORIAL RANGE

ONLY scanty information can be derived from general, as well as Jewish, sources about the settlement of Jews in the territories of Saxony and Thuringia during the early period of the second millennium. But their presence in the twelfth and the following centuries in these regions of central Europe has for long been a historically well-established fact. Their community must have counted a relatively considerable number of members. Jewish business activities are mentioned in the early *Mühlhäuser Reichsrechtsbuch*, and regulations concerning Jews and their relations to their Christian neighbors were included in the *Sachsenspiegel*. All this, together with its implications, offers support to the assumption that considerable economic importance was attributed to their commercial operations. As has been shown previously, it was this group of Jews living in Saxon-Thuringian territory for which the *Sachsenspiegel*'s Jewry-law was intended and to which it was applied.[1]

The existence of Jewish settlements may doubtless be assumed also in those territories outside of Eastphalia, where the other lawbooks originated. The status and legal relations of the Jews living there had likewise to be regulated. The regulation was accomplished by rules which either adopted or remodeled the *Sachsenspiegel*'s Jewry-law. The territory governed by each individual lawbook previously enumerated also determined the extent of the validity of its Jewry-law.

Some lawbooks, on the other hand, such as the *Livländischer Spiegel Land- und Lehnrechts*, did not pay any attention to Jews or regulations concerning their legal status. Because of the absence of Jews, voluntary or enforced, in the territories covered by such lawbooks, there was obviously no reason or opportunity for the insertion of provisions concerning Jews.

In this connection another problem arises concerning the territorial range of jurisdiction with regard to Jewry-law. Were these rules of the *Sachsenspiegel* and other lawbooks intended to be applied also to Jews who were territorial or local aliens (not to foreign Jews, that is, those alien to the empire)? In the absence of positive regulations on the subject, the question cannot be decided with certainty; but a conjecture suggests itself. An affirmative answer is possible because of two considerations.

First, as to the range of its rules, the *Sachsenspiegel* shows clear evidences of an incipient tendency to turn away from the pure "principle of personal law." True, this principle, under which each member of a national tribe carried his tribal law wherever he went, is basically still in effect. But a definite inclination toward the territorial principle, in the form of a "weakened" principle of personal law, can well be observed.[2] Law and jurisdiction are no longer considered as floating freely in space but, in certain respects, as projected upon a definite territory. The process of territorialization is in its early stages, however. It is possible to recognize clearly the existence of both principles side by side. Tribal law is still the standard law. But "the immigrant alien [*inkomen man*] may take possession of an inheritance in the land of Saxony according to the country's [territorial] law, and not according to the law [of origin] of the man, be he Bavarian, Suebian, or Frank."[3] The law of the land of origin is effective only with regard to certain legal relations. Second, as a rule, "in a village aliens are not bound to answer [to a charge in court] according to their particular village law, but according to common territorial law."[4]

It would be quite in line with these legal principles laid down in the *Sachsenspiegel Landrecht*, to declare its Jewry-law applicable also to alien Jews. This is borne out in particular by the consideration that the *Sachsenspiegel* provides legal regulations exclusively for the relations of Jews to their non-Jewish environment. Thus it is only logical to suppose that, in this respect, alien Jews should be subjected to the same laws as were their native coreligionists. The correctness of the train of thought followed here is also confirmed by the fact that the *Sachsenspiegel*'s Jewry-law received wide acceptance in the lawbooks in which municipal law was codified.[5]

II. PERSONAL REACH

The *Sachsenspiegel* speaks of "Jews" (*joden*) in several articles. In paragraphs 1–3 of Book III, article 7, the "Jew" (*jode*) is repeatedly placed in contrast to the "Christian" (*kersten man*).

There can be no doubt that, in contrasting Jews and Christians, the author of the lawbook had in mind to point out a religious distinction. According to medieval Christian ethics, God was regarded as the ultimate source of law. God created the world and man. God who is the beginning and the end of all things, as the opening passage of the *Textus Prologi*, a preface to the *Sachsenspiegel*, puts it, is also the beginning of all law. Eike von Repgow thus counts the temporal law established by the king as part of the law which has its origin in God. The state adopts religious aims for its own. Hence, Eike's state is a Christian state, a universal state of a secular-ecclesiastical nature. As can be seen, his general theory of law grows from the soil of medieval Christian ethics. With his demand for protection of the Christian world-order, Eike was also on religious ground. Accordingly, the maintenance of the Christian faith is demanded in his *Sachsenspiegel* (II, 13, 7), and the pope's right to excommunicate a heretical king is specifically recognized (III, 57, 1). The special protection extended to religious institutions (III, 57, 1; II, 66, 1) and to the clergy, "who are the masters of Christendom" (II, 66, 2), must be regarded as a duty of protection which the state took upon itself. The same applies finally to the close connection of outlawry and excommunication (*Acht* and *Bann*) (III, 63, 2) and of fines by secular and ecclesiastical courts (*gewette* and *bannbusse*) (I, 53, 4) as exposed in the lawbook.[6]

In fact, Eike succeeded in forging into a single indissoluble unity Christian ethics and secular law. When the *Sachsenspiegel* is viewed in the light of its author's world of thought, it is clear that he could have had none but a religious distinction in mind

when he contrasted Christian and Jew. The text of his lawbook
offers no grounds for any other interpretation.

Who now constituted the group of "Jews" contrasted with
Christians in the *Sachsenspiegel?* How are the persons defined to
whom its regulations of Jewry-law were applicable?

According to the medieval conception of law, Jews were those
professing the Jewish faith. Thereby they were united in a community and, by the peculiarities of their doctrines, worship, and
religious life, were separated from Christian society. While the
church community was made up of all baptized Christians, the
Jew stood outside the society of the Christian church and in religion was opposed to that communion. If he joined it by acceptance of baptism—a step taken but rarely by a medieval Jew
of his own free will—he definitely ceased to be a Jew. The fact
that, from the religious point of view, this apostate was considered as dead by his former coreligionists and was mourned as a
deceased person, can be left out of consideration.[7] The same applies to the attitude of the church. By the sacrament of baptism
the church conferred on the convert a distinctive mark that could
not be deleted (*character indelebilis*). According to the doctrine of
the Catholic church, the effects of baptism are indelible and
bring everyone who has been baptized into permanent membership in the church.[8] The church avenges apostasy with the severest punishments. Likewise according to the *Sachsenspiegel*, the
church communion formed a compulsory society organized on
the basis of personal membership. By law it was impossible to
leave it. A Christian who fell into unbelief was threatened with
the penalty of death at the stake (II, 13, 7).[9]

Jewry-law having reference to Jews was thus applicable to
those who were regarded as Jews in the conception of the medieval lawbooks. On the basis of the concept "Jew," clearly
formulated in the *Sachsenspiegel*, no question could arise in the
Middle Ages as to whether the regulations of Jewry-law should
apply also to converted Jews. From the viewpoint of Jewish life,
of Christian ecclesiastical law, and of secular state law, these
had ceased to be Jews. A return to Judaism was forbidden them
under penalty of death and, therefore, made legally impossible.
The applicability of Jewry-law to such persons would have been

utterly contradictory to the basic Christian conception of the
Sachsenspiegel. It must therefore be definitely excluded from the
range of possibility. This becomes evident also from other lawbooks, especially the *Schwabenspiegel*. To be sure, despite all legal
prohibitions, baptized Jews, particularly those baptized under
compulsion, sometimes reverted to their ancestral faith, even
with the emperor's permission.[10] This is a different story, however, and of no significance for the problem under discussion.

This question would probably not have been investigated here
in such detail if a different solution had not been suggested some
time ago. It was Karl G. Hugelmann who regarded as the "basic
problem of the Jewish question" in the Middle Ages the question
as to whether "everyone who was born a Jew or even everyone of
Jewish descent could appeal to the special rules of Jewry-law."[11]
From the *Sachsenspiegel* (III, 7, 1–3) that author could deduce
only "that with baptism the Jew ceases to be subject to the special regulations of Jewry-law." According to Hugelmann, this
is in agreement with our general knowledge of medieval Jewry-
law. But "despite the strong emphasis on the religious motive
[in the *Sachsenspiegel*]," he maintains, "baptism, unlike today, is
to be regarded also as a racial separation from Judaism, especially
because it effected necessarily the Jews' elimination from his
original legal and economic sphere."[12]

No doubt such a conception, derived from modern racial theories, was quite foreign to the author of the *Sachsenspiegel*, whose
lawbook offers no basis for it. Nor is the concept of a racial membership in Judaism or of a racial separation from it traceable in
other medieval sources.[13] The religious motive alone is strongly
emphasized. Therefore, no other factor can serve to explain that
Jewry-law was applicable to faithful Jews only.[14]

III. Extent as to Subject Matter

The Jewry-law of the *Sachsenspiegel* covers exclusively the legal
relations between Jews and their non-Jewish environment. In
each of its regulations this principle of limitation as to subject
matter discloses itself. The body of Jewry-law as a whole is also
evidence that it was the author's intention to restrict his rules
on the legal status of the Jews to the mutual Jewish-Christian

relations. Thus he composed merely a limited "code" of specific laws concerning Jews, whereas some compilers of other lawbooks assumed a different attitude.[15]

In view of this limitation, the question arises: What rules regulated those legal relations between Jews and Christians which were not covered by the *Sachsenspiegel*'s Jewry-law?

To answer it, the following conclusion is as logical as it is obvious: "The formulation of special regulations openly indicates that, in cases not covered by them, Jews in their relations to non-Jews were treated according to the rules applying to members of the German national tribes. In so far as no special provisions were made for Jews, they were judged according to the law of one of the German national tribes."[16]

This logically derived assumption can be raised to certainty, however, only if proof for its validity and correctness can be adduced from explicit regulations in the *Sachsenspiegel*. Since this has not been done hitherto, attention may be directed to three passages which offer such evidence.

1. In *Sachsenspiegel Landrecht*, I, 61, 4, this rule is stated: "Every man, except clerics, can be a spokesman according to *landrecht* in the land of Saxony, if no blame can be held against him on account of his legal status."[17]

It is difficult to render the conditional clause of the original text into English, but its meaning and legal significance are clear. Only such persons, whose standing in law could not be subjected to doubt, should be qualified to act in court as spokesmen. The several groups which were denied full legal standing, and therefore lacked the qualification for the office of spokesman, are listed in the *Sachsenspiegel* and designated as follows (I, 38, 1):

Kempen [professional (hired) champions] and their children, musicians [public entertainers], and all those who were born out of wedlock, and those who had to expiate or make restitution for theft or robbery, if convicted of such in court, or who redeemed their body, skin, or hair —all these are rightless.[18]

No mention of Jews is found in either of the *Sachsenspiegel* passages quoted here. From this it may be inferred that, in the question of qualification for the office of spokesman, Jews were treated on the same basis as Christians. The general rules of the

Sachsenspiegel applied to them, too. Hence they would lose that qualification only if their standing in law should be impaired by one of the general causes, through which Christians also would be disqualified.

Thus originally there was no discrimination against Jews in this respect. It remained still unknown to the illuminated *Sachsenspiegel* manuscript of Dresden of the middle of the fourteenth century. Jews came to be considered unfit to act as spokesmen only under the influence of Roman and canon law, later in the Middle Ages.[19] But this attitude, adopted in some lawbooks and even in two late manuscripts of the *Sachsenspiegel*, was not that of its author. This appears by an argument from major to minor and also from the content of the second passage to be discussed here.

2. In *Sachsenspiegel*, III, 70, 1, the following principle is laid down: "Where court is not held under royal ban, every man, on whom the blame of being rightless cannot be laid, can pass judgment on [and be a witness against] another, except a Wend on a Saxon, and a Saxon on a Wend."[20]

This principle is in agreement with a similar rule found in *Sachsenspiegel*, II, 12, 3, where the personal qualification for the ability of pronouncing judgment appears in a positive formulation reading thus: "every man . . . who enjoys full standing in law" (*iewelk man . . . der vulcomen is an sîme rechte*). The most important example for a court "not held under royal ban" is that of the margrave in the Marches, these being principalities of a somewhat independent political status.[21] The *Gloss* gives as an instance the March of Meissen. In such courts, thus, every man *vulcomen an sîme rechte* was capable of passing judgment and acting as witness.[22] Again reference is made to the aforementioned list of "rightless" persons (I, 38, 1). But neither there nor in the *Sachsenspiegel* articles discussed here (III, 70, 1; II, 12, 3) are Jews mentioned. This fact implies that they, too, were considered capable of passing judgment and acting as witnesses. For them, too, this qualification was dependent only on one condition, just as in the case of Christians: the Jew must not come under the group of "rightless" persons for one of the listed causes (I, 38, 1) but had to be *vulcomen an sîme rechte*. Hence this is another instance proving that *Sachsenspiegel* law in general, and not only its Jewry-law, was applicable to Jews.

The picture manuscripts confirm this interpretation in a very definite way.[23] Among the figures standing before the judge to pass judgment or bear witness, the pertinent illustration shows the unmistakable figure of a Jew, who can be seen by the side of a Frank and a Saxon. The picture manuscript of Heidelberg (of about 1300–1315) and that of Dresden (of about the middle of the fourteenth century) have corresponding representations on this theme. The Jew is clearly recognizable by his beard and pointed hat, which are the Jewish attributes in medieval paintings or pen drawings. In accordance with the text in the *Sachsenspiegel*, only the Wend occupies a separate position. He is seen at the far left of the beholder, turning away from the group of those capable of the judicial acts mentioned. Going, so to speak, his own way, he stands apart from them. By the gestures of his hands he indicates that he does not possess the same capacity of acting in court as the group of four men. These, in contrast to him, and among them the Jew, point with their forefingers to the judge, and, vice versa, the judge points to them, indicating that they are called upon to pass judgment or bear witness under his authority. The Jew's position is even nearest to the judge.

The picture manuscripts thus offer infallible proof that the Jews' capacity of passing judgment and acting as witnesses was not forgotten at the end of the thirteenth century and possibly up to the middle of the fourteenth century.

3. The third instance to prove that *Sachsenspiegel* law in general applied to Jews is also borne out by the Dresden picture manuscript. Its illumination to *Landrecht*, II, 71, 3, offers unquestionable proof that Jews, like all inhabitants of a judicial district, were under the obligation of *Gerichtsfolge*, which meant pursuing and capturing fugitive peace-breakers (*Gerüftsfolge*) and besieging a castle which had violated the peace (*Belagerungspflicht*).[24] In medieval Eastphalia all inhabitants of a certain judicial district formed a virtual peace association whose main duty consisted in the maintenance of peace within its boundaries. Membership in that political association carried with it *Gerichtsfolge* as a public duty. The pertinent provision reads: "Arms can legally be carried

in the pursuit upon *gerüfte;* by law all those shall participate in it who have come of age and are able to wield a sword unless prevented by a lawful excuse, with the exception of clerics, women, sextons, and shepherds.''[25]

Jews are again not mentioned in this text among those excluded. One may therefore surmise that they, too, were under the obligation of *Gerüftsfolge.* In fact, in the picture accompanying the quoted article in the *Sachsenspiegel* manuscript of Dresden, an armed Jew wearing his Jews' hat is clearly distinguishable in the group of armed men standing before a castle. Figures representing the excluded persons—a woman, a shepherd, a sexton, and a cleric—are shown passing by, their backs turned upon the scene to indicate that they have no part in it. Inclusion of the Jews in the obligation of *Gerichtsfolge* is quite evident.

The applicability to Jews of three important legal regulations in the *Sachsenspiegel* not included in its Jewry-law is thus firmly established. More instances to the same effect could be adduced.[26] From the very contents of that lawbook, it has now been proved beyond dispute that its general principles also were applicable (and were applied) to Jews in their relations to Christians.[27]

It deserves particular emphasis that the law of the *Sachsenspiegel* applies only to relations involving both Jews and Christians. To cover other spheres of law was not the author's intention.[28] His conception as expressed in his lawbook was rather as follows: For Jews, as non-Christians, in their relations to non-Jews there is a special law, historically explainable, which is partly favorable and partly unfavorable to them. In cases not covered by this law, they are treated in their legal relations to Christians on the same basis as the latter.

That this conception was really expressed in the *Sachsenspiegel* can still be seen from Johann von Buch's attitude in his *Gloss.* Nowhere is the application of the law in general limited to Christians only.[29] Non-Christians are also subject to it in so far as it has unlimited validity, only that they are sometimes placed in a less advantageous position.[30] Thus, with a reference to the Roman law (*Codex Justinianus* i. 5. 1), it is stated in the *Gloss* to *Sachsenspiegel,* III, 7, 1: "Know ye that Jews are in some respects under specific laws, in contrast to Christians, with reference to twelve subjects;[31] . . . Jews, heathen, and heretics shall not make use of all the special imperial privileges. . . ." The same tendency comes to the fore also in other regulations referred to in the *Gloss* (III, 7; III, 2). In this way the views originally expressed in the lawbook are evidently reflected there.

Nevertheless, the *Gloss* shows its own peculiar attitude toward the problem under discussion, indicating a development in a direction little favorable to medieval Jewry. In fact, a strong anti-Jewish tendency comes to light, which finds restriction not even through the limits of the law but seeks to bend the law according to the author's intentions. In this specific question, as in general, the glossator is completely under the influence of the doctrines of Roman and canon law. But he neither works up his sources sufficiently, nor is able properly to explain arising contradictions or to remove objections which suggest themselves. The interpretations offered by him remain self-contradictory, all of which can be gathered from a study of his method of reasoning.[32]

The glossator's proposition that all special imperial privileges (including the Saxon law embodied in the *Sachsenspiegel*) are not applicable to Jews, heathen, and heretics was derived from the *Justinian Code*. But the extent of its real relationship to and inclusion in the Roman law rule can easily be appraised through a comparison of the texts.[33] From the basis that he established, Johann von Buch pursues the following train of thought.[34] According to Saxon law, his argument runs, a Jew or a heretic may be convicted in all matters, while a Saxon may free himself by his oath. This right of a Saxon, he maintains, is based—according to *Sachsenspiegel*, I, 18, 2—on a special "imperial act of grace which was bestowed on Saxons alone." "Therefore Jews shall not use it, since they are no Saxon persons." In seeking a legal basis to support this discrimination against them, the glossator cites some passages from the Roman law code: "ff. de reg. iur. 1. privilegia [*Dig.*, 50, 17, 196]; ff. de censib. 1. etatem [*Dig.*, 50, 15, 3]; and ff. de lega. 2, 1. 2 in fi[ne] cum patronus [*Dig.*, 31, 1, 28]." But he is quite aware that his empty citations and contradictory arguments are weak. Therefore, he seeks to refute two objections which he raises and holds against himself. Of course, he does it in his own manner. First, he continues his argument, one could contradict this and assert that this is against the law, since it is written in the *Code, de Judaeis, l. Judei Romano* [*Cod. Just.* i. 9. 8], "that the Jews shall make use of the common imperial laws." In the glossator's opinion, this applies exclusively to those cases "in which Jews bring a lawsuit against someone before court or are sued by someone," this restriction being implied in that law. Furthermore, he continues to explain, the permission to use the "common imperial laws" does not mean that Jews should be allowed to avail themselves of "the land's privileges, despite the fact that they were living within it. In spite of that wording this cannot be understood in that way."

This interpretation obviously contradicts a thesis set forth elsewhere in Buch's *Gloss*. On *Sachsenspiegel*, I, 30, he declares himself undoubtedly in favor of the territorial principle regarding the extent of the validity of Saxon law (I, 30): "This *privilegium* [meaning the *Sachsenspiegel*] was given to the land, and not to the people."[35] Nor can that interpretation be reconciled with another proposition set forth by the glossator (III, 33, 5), according to which Saxon law is valid not only for Saxons but for everyone residing in the land of Saxony:

> Know ye that the Roman King gave this law to the Saxons so that everyone in the land of Saxony should live according to the law of the land and not according to the law of his origin, wherever he be from, as is written above in Book One, Article Thirty. For this privilege was given to the land of Saxony, and not to the people or persons who lived there at the time. For whatever privilege is given to persons, this perishes with them, as stated by the philosopher: "Omne ortum cum tempore simul et labascit cum tempore . . ." but whatever is given to a land, this remains forever.[36]

The contradiction was neither explained nor removed by the glossator. Nor was the other objection invalidated, that applicability of Saxon law to Jews could be derived from *Sachsenspiegel*, I, 30. The final solution of the problem offered by Buch sounds as contradictory and unsatisfactory as does his entire argument: "Hereupon we state: The law [I, 30] speaks only of Christians who are immigrants, and not of Jews. Also, the same law speaks of inheritance, and not of Jews' complaint or response."

It is evident that the legal ground of the *Sachsenspiegel* was abandoned by the glossator. In his interpretation of the lawbook he indulges in contradictions, just as he does in his interpretation of Roman law. His occupation with the foreign law unfitted him for a natural and unprejudiced consideration of the transmitted legal conceptions, without serving him as a means of training in the clear formulation of ideas. The glossator did not succeed in combining and harmonizing the two legal systems, the German and the foreign. His procedure is inexact, forced, and juridically unsatisfactory. It fits in well with his general manner of working. It reveals clearly how the way was prepared for the decline of the pure German law, which had reached a maximum of clearness and truth in the *Sachsenspiegel*. In contrast to it, an extralegal, anti-Jewish attitude gained ground in Buch's commentary and began to penetrate into the domain of law. A justification for this change was found in the foreign law. This was the method generally favored in later days. It quickly took possession of the entire domain of German law and for centuries divested it almost completely of its original character.[37]

CHAPTER FOUR

The Attitude of the Lawbooks to Jewry Privileges and to Jewish Law

I. The *Sachsenspiegel* in Relation to Older Jewry Privileges

IT HAS been demonstrated before that, with regard to Jews, the intention prevailed in the *Sachsenspiegel* to regulate their legal relations to Christians only. These relations were thus controlled by rules laid down in the lawbook as such and contained partly in its Jewry-law and partly in its general law. The *Sachsenspiegel* is distinguished from the other medieval German lawbooks by its clear and logical way of determining and limiting the subject matter to which its rules apply. Only in very rare cases are scattered references found in it which invoke or imply other law sources and their applicability to Jews.

Of such legal sources—obviously older than the *Sachsenspiegel* —the charters or privileges granted to Jews by the emperor or by territorial princes and the rules of Jewish law must be taken into consideration here. Were they known to, and utilized by, the medieval compilers of lawbooks, either in general or in some individual regulations? And, if so, what was their attitude and legal technique in employing this kind of matter, which was otherwise certainly foreign to them?

Some instances will clarify the problem. The royal prerogative of protecting the Jews—*Judenschutzrecht* or "Jewry protection"— was doubtless known to Eike von Repgow and to those of his successors who adopted his regulations pertaining to this right. In *Sachsenspiegel*, III, 7, 3, he offers his view on the institution of Jewry protection and its historical basis.[1] This passage must be studied in connection with the regulation (II, 66, 1) on the in-

clusion of the Jews in the king's peace, which has an old and
long history. The latter article is related to a similar clause found
in the Saxon Land Peace of 1221, which probably served Eike as
source.[2] There is another passage in the *Sachsenspiegel*, III, 7, 4
(2) (to be studied in connection with III, 7, 1), referring to an
old trade privilege which had been bestowed on the Jews as early
as 1090 by King Henry IV.[3] To be sure, one need not suppose that
Eike also had before him the wording of these or other privileges. Yet, from the related regulations found in his lawbook, it
is clear that he could not have been unacquainted with their content and the juridical tendency behind them.

In dealing with law matter contained in privileges, the author
of the *Sachsenspiegel* followed the same method that he generally
applied in codifying rules of customary law. He selected from his
material whatever he considered important and vital and incorporated it in his lawbook. "Thus he recorded the law and created law at the same time."[4]

It is no accident, indeed, that the German lawbooks originated
in the period when the power of territorial rulers began to spread
most widely. The national customary law was then imperiled by
new laws decreed by the princes. In the newly rising territories
the rulers created new conditions of life, and new conditions require new laws. Hence in many a land a desire may have been
felt to compile the old laws quickly, in order to be prepared for
any encroachment of the princely power in the sphere of the
customary law.[5]

The *Sachsenspiegel* is such a compilation of the good old law.
In reading and interpreting it, one must always bear in mind that
Eike von Repgow aimed at composing a code and not a legal
textbook.[6] As to rules of law contained in old royal privileges, he
took the same attitude as was observed toward old customary
law by the princes when they used it for their own new privilege
law. The old customary law was no longer considered valid as
folk law or territorial law but only as law of privilege because of
its adoption or recognition in the new privileges and within the
limits accorded therein.[7] Privilege law, in turn, found recognition in his "codification" only in so far as Eike accepted it and
embodied in his *Sachsenspiegel* its individual rules or principles as

independent regulations. This applies to the peace protection of the Jews in *Sachsenspiegel*, II, 66, 1, and to the old trade privilege in its modified form, in III, 7, 4 (2) and III, 7, 1.

Whenever reference is made to older sources of law, either explicitly or tacitly, this is not done for the sake of their general recognition as authoritative sources of law in force but merely to establish historically the validity of individual regulations adopted from the old law sources. The reference to "the old peace which the imperial might has established for the land of Saxony" in *Sachsenspiegel*, II, 66, 1, offers an example. Eike reserved for himself the liberty of choosing one or another of such regulations. At times he even felt free not to regard an actual legal status as a lawful status at all but to present his own juridical view on the subject.

As in other instances, well known and much discussed in legal-historical literature, this was done with regard to the aforementioned old trade privilege, in *Sachsenspiegel*, III, 7, 1. According to the principle set forth in Henry IV's Jewry privileges for Speyer and Worms, a Jew could claim compensation for the purchase price paid by him for an object that he had afterward sold, in case the buyer's right was disputed by a third person and the Jew was held responsible as warrantor (*Gewähre*).[8] Hence, every object, even if stolen from its lawful owner, when it had passed through Jewish hands could be recovered only upon compensation for the purchase price. But the *Sachsenspiegel* ruled out this regulation by declaring Jews incapable of being a Christian's warrantors unless they would submit to the rules of law applying generally to Christians, who were not favored by that trade privilege but were bound either to restore stolen goods unconditionally to their original owner or to pay full compensation to the purchaser, who had been ordered by court decision to restore the object to the claimant. Thus the trade privilege enjoyed by the Jews from olden times appears considerably modified in the *Sachsenspiegel*. The purely negative formulation of the rule implies a recognition of that old trade privilege, even if only to a very restricted extent. With a fine juridical technique, Eike in this case followed the direction prescribed for his work by himself, namely, to treat merely the legal relations between Jews and Christians. The passage reviewed here represents one of the rare and juridically interesting instances in which the codifier, though fully cognizant of the far-reaching import of the rules set forth, consciously pointed merely to their implications, without expounding them in full.

II. JEWRY PRIVILEGES IN OTHER LAWBOOKS

Among the German lawbooks here under consideration, the *Deutschenspiegel* completely shares the standpoint of the *Sachsenspiegel* in its legal-technical treatment and formulation of Jewry-law. This is not surprising, in view of the fact that the southern German translation of the *Sachsenspiegel* was the main source of the *Deutschenspiegel*. Obviously, there is no need to give separate consideration to those lawbooks which merely adopted the *Sachsenspiegel*'s Jewry-law.

The attitude of other lawbooks differs, however. In formulating their norms of Jewry-law, they leave room for the application of the rules of older Jewry privileges, which are referred to in several ways.

By the side of their own binding regulations, some lawbooks also offer the parties to a legal transaction the choice of deviating from them, i.e., by means of an explicit stipulation it can be agreed to apply privileged Jewry-law. In this way, later manuscripts of the *Schwabenspiegel* (W 214, 1; G 214, 1), and likewise the Freising lawbook (Maurer, I, 172; Knapp, 121), state: "If a Jew sells something to a Christian or has other dealings with him, he shall be the Christian's warrantor according to Christian law [*nach cristenlichem rechte*], unless the Jew makes a stipulation according to his [own] law [*nach sinem rechte*]."[9] The contrasting of "Christian law" and "his law," that is, the law of the Jew, naturally does not refer to the contrast of Christian to Jewish law, as has repeatedly been supposed.[10] What is meant is rather the rules of non-Jewish origin which, in this respect, are formulated one way for Christians and differently for Jews. In other words, Jews are permitted contractually to stipulate for themselves the application of that old trade privilege, which had been first granted them in the imperial charters of 1090 and later became customary law. They are accorded the right to choose

ernative, in spite of the fact that, as a matter of prin-
they had to share the duty of warrantorship with the
ians.

e *Schwabenspiegel* provided (in art. L 125; W 106; G 105, 2)
ther peculiar regulation. If the king intends to be absent from
German lands, he shall invest the Rhenish count palatine with
his supreme judicial authority. "And if he does not bestow this
authority on him, he cannot claim it by law." Furthermore, "he
[the king] shall also commend all his Jews who live in German
lands to his chancellor, that is, the Bishop of Mayence; and even
if he [the king] does not do this, he protects them nevertheless
according to law." The chancellor (*Reichserzkanzler*) thus had the
prerogative of taking the king's place in the exercise of general
Jewry protection, even if this peculiar right were not specifically
conferred on him.[11] The statement of this rule in the *Schwabenspiegel*, differing from that in the preceding passage, seems to
imply a recognition on the part of its author of the Jewry-law
regulation created by that privilege.

The Meissen lawbook goes even further—in fact, it goes
further than all the other lawbooks—and seems to have the
same point of view as the *Sachsenspiegel*. Where no provision is
made in the historically explainable Jewry rules, Jews are to be
treated on a basis of equality with Christians. This is particularly evident in the field of criminal law. Crimes and offenses of
Christians against Jews are to be punished in the same way as
when committed against Christians (III, 17, 31–33). Conversely,
a Jew is to suffer punishment like a Christian (III, 17, 38). In
court, Jews are treated like Christians (III, 1, 3; III, 17, 39, 48).
However, the principle of equal treatment of Jews and Christians is made subject to numerous exceptions, some being
privilegia odiosa, others *privilegia favorabilia*, for the Jews.

As has been mentioned before, the author of the *Meissener
Rechtsbuch* employed as sources for his lawbook various princely
charters granted to Jews. It is therefore natural for him to refer
to these privileges, which he did explicitly in a general statement
in the introductory article to his main section on Jewry-law (III,
17, 1). Although specifically referring to usury only, his theory
of the recognition and justification of princely Jewry privileges

allows generalization. Since Jews may not own real property in this country, the author explains, their position in law is formed differently from that of Christians. Emperors and princes in their good will favored them with *sunderlicheme rechte*, to compensate them under particular law.[12] This means, in fact, full recognition of privilege law.

According to the Meissen lawbook, this law is applicable to the legal relations of the Jews among themselves, especially regarding their relationship to their overlord or protector. Thus the lawbook includes legal relations of this kind within the sphere of its own regulations. In article III, 17, 30, it states: "If contention arises among the Jews, no one shall judge it except the overlord or his judge, to whom the Jews had subjected themselves."

Such disputes were to be settled according to a special law and before a separate court. The court thought of here is the non-Jewish court established by the protecting overlord of the Jews.[13] The author of the Meissen lawbook takes the existence, formation, jurisdiction, and function of such courts for granted, so that he excludes them from juridical treatment in his lawbook (III, 17, 2): "Of the Jews' established courts I do not wish to treat for, according to custom, they are governed by different rules in different lands."[14] Obviously, in this article the compiler of the lawbook could have in mind only the above-mentioned princely courts instituted for Jews under privilege law. By no means could one think here of autonomous Jewish courts, for their setup and practice was under Jewish law which could not have been different in various German lands.[15] Thus again princely privilege law is proved to have been recognized in its validity. This was also emphasized by implication when, in some lawbooks, transgressions of Jews are placed under the sanction of their "forfeiting Jewish law and all rights granted them by emperors and princes."[16]

To sum up the result of the preceding inquiry into the attitude of the medieval German lawbooks toward the law contained in Jewry privileges, it can be stated thus: The lawbooks adopted, and in some respects also modified, individual regulations of the law contained in older Jewry privileges, particularly those which in the course of time had come to be considered, in general, as customary law. Beyond that, the Jewry-law of the Jewry privileges attained recognition in the lawbooks in principle.

III. The Lawbooks and Jewish Law[17]

Jewish law, authoritative for the Jews' internal relations in the field of their religious as well as in that of civil activity, lay outside the scope of the lawbooks. Since their Jewry-law was limited to the Jewish-Christian relations, they had to take Jewish law into consideration only in so far as it could come within the range of practical applicability in the commercial or legal intercourse of Christians with Jews. Only then could the problem arise as to whether the validity of Jewish law and its administration by Jewish courts should be recognized. In the medieval German lawbooks this question was answered decidedly in the affirmative.

Eike von Repgow was cognizant of the existence of Jewish religious law. Ample evidence for this is found in *Sachsenspiegel*, III, 42, 4, where we read: "He also commanded that the seventh week be kept holy when He gave the Law to the Jews and to us the Holy Ghost." To give another example, Eike was well acquainted with the biblical regulations concerning the law of workers, and he emphasized the institution of the sabbatical year.[18] To be sure, those religious prescriptions which commanded the feelings and actions and the thought and life of the medieval Jew lay outside the realm of Eike's lawbook. In no other passage of his *Sachsenspiegel* did he refer to them. There is no reference to Jewish law, even in the passage where the Jews' oath is mentioned (III, 7, 4 [2]) and where such a reference perhaps could have been expected. Thus it follows from Eike's logic and methodology, as a matter of course, that he omitted a Jewry-oath formula from his *Spiegel*. But, on the other hand, this implies the recognition that Jews must take oaths in accordance with Jewish law.[19] It is explicit in Johann von Buch's *Gloss* on the *Sachsenspiegel*, where the applicability of Jewish law in this respect is expressly recognized: ". . . But the wording of the oath may well be as the law speaks of it: [for it says that] they shall swear according to their own manner, 22, *qu. 1.*, *c. movet* [*Decretum Gratiani*, c. 16, C XXII, qu. 1].''[20]

Logically, the later *Deutschenspiegel* and the original version of the *Schwabenspiegel* also did not include Jewry-oath formulas, whereas in some other lawbooks the Jewry oath occupies the center of the regulations concerning Jews.[21] This seems to indicate the transition from the supposedly original performance of the oath, strictly according to Jewish law, to that type of "Jewry-oath" ceremony which was often prescribed in medieval law sources and sometimes fashioned in a fantastic manner. With this in mind, one will understand why Johann von Buch, though by no means friendly toward the Jews, declared such a procedure "unlawful," while the *Weichbild* glossator considered it a "fantasy," adding that "the Jews' oath shall be respected in the same way as that of Christians."[22]

In the various lands of their settlement in the Diaspora the Jews were always able to maintain the rule of Jewish law and to preserve the functioning of Jewish courts. The oldest known charter issued to Jews in a municipal settlement on German soil —Bishop Rüdiger's privilege of 1084 for the Jews of Speyer—bestowed upon the Jewish court the right of exclusive jurisdiction in legal disputes between Jews.[23] It extended its competence even to lawsuits of Christian plaintiffs against Jewish defendants. Only if the Jewish court should regard itself unable to pass judgment, should the suit come for decision to the bishop or his chamberlain. Similar provisions were incorporated in Emperor Henry IV's privileges for the Jews of Speyer and Worms, in about 1090. Here the exclusive character of the Jewish courts' jurisdiction was pointed out with even greater distinctness: "Jewish litigants shall be convicted and judged by their equals and not by others . . . according to their own law."[24] Appeal to the imperial court was allowed only for *magnae causae*, dependent on the Jews' own free will.[25]

As to the lawbooks, it is most probable that, through the recognition of the law of Jewry privileges, the way was also paved for the recognition of Jewish law.

Among them, the Meissen lawbook is most explicit in recognizing Jewish courts and Jewish law. Although it takes for granted the functioning of princely courts established for Jews and considers the appeal of a Jew to his overlord permissible,[26] the rule is laid down that, except in certain criminal cases, "Jews shall not suffer judgment on any spot other than in the *Schule* or before the *Schule*."[27] Identical or similar provisions are found in several other lawbooks. A court decision, probably from the first half of the fourteenth century, offers two reasons for the exclusive competence of the Jewish court, one based on the recognition of Jewish law and the other probably taken from Roman-canon law: "Judei tamen, clerici et nobiles, quia proprios habent judices et actor forum rei sequi debet, coram eisdem judicibus sunt conveniendi."[28] Hence, Jews could be sued only in a Jewish court. The latter was thus competent even if the plaintiffs were Christians. The pertinent clause in the *Weichbild-Vulgata* (116, 1) was often referred to by other lawbooks: "No Christian may lay claim against a Jew unless he does it before the Jews' judge."[29] It is quite understandable that this far-reaching principle could not remain uncontested in medieval court practice.[30]

Still more instances of the recognition of Jewish law, explicit or implicit, are found in the Meissen lawbook. As previously mentioned, the receipt of stolen goods by Jews was put under the sanction of "forfeiting Jewish law and all rights granted them by emperors and princes."[31] That Jewish law is actually meant here and that only the second half of the clause refers to Jewry-law appears clearly from a preceding passage that carries this sanction: "They [Jews lending out money upon stolen goods] shall forfeit their legal standing among Jews as well as Christians."[32]

Furthermore, according to the same lawbook, cases involving bodily injuries or homicide between Jews were to be judged like those between Christians. Full recognition of Jewish law and Jewish courts is shown in the additional provision that such an offense should incur the penalty due according to Jewish law, in addition to that imposed by the general law: "What, in addition, is demanded by Jewish law, he [the Jewish transgressor] shall suffer afterward when he has suffered our judgment."[33]

The recognition of judgments pronounced by Jewish courts in accordance with Jewish law can also be proved from the legal practice under the law of Magdeburg.[34] One interesting instance may here suffice. A Jew, Moshe, applied to the municipal council of Breslau, where he resided, for a safe-conduct in order to be exempt, when traveling abroad, from any liability for debts of his home town. His application was rejected for the time being, "unless he were first absolved from the Jewish ban under which he is said to stand."[35] In other words, excommunication by a Jewish court was considered equal to *Verfestung* by a secular, or excommunication by an ecclesiastical, court. In another case related in the *Brünner Schöffenbuch*, from the middle of the fourteenth century, the Jewish court could, by virtue of superior legal reasoning, prevail even against the Christian court.[36] As a rule, the verdict of any lawfully instituted, recognized, and competent Jewish court was to be considered as *res judicata*.[37]

From all this it is evident that Jewish law and Jewish courts were, to a very considerable extent, recognized in medieval Germany. This also found expression in lawbooks as well as in court judicature. It is beyond doubt that, through this attitude of the Christian jurists and courts, the principles of Jewish law received noteworthy support and the authority of Jewish courts in Germany was considerably strengthened. This, in turn, was of great importance for the legal and social life of medieval Jewry; for the rules of German law operated strongly in favor of Jewish autonomy.

PART II

The Legal Status of the Jews

CHAPTER FIVE

The Status of the Jews in the Public Peace Law

I. The Jews under the King's Peace[1]

IN WHAT manner did the legal status of the Jews receive consideration and possibly even protection within the framework of public peace law in medieval Germany? This is the fundamental question the answer to which will in itself give a picture of the political status of the Jews in the medieval state (so far as such modern conceptions apply to those remote times). With this general consideration in mind, we may ask specifically: How did the author of the *Sachsenspiegel*, Eike von Repgow, guided by his knowledge of the actual conditions and by the desire to present and establish them from the legal point of view, record the conception of his time concerning the Jews? How did he think of legal questions of this kind in general and what, presumably, was his own attitude toward them?

The answer is found in various articles of the *Sachsenspiegel*, among which the following passage from *Landrecht*, II, 66, 1, is most significant:

Now hear ye the old peace which the imperial might has established for the land of Saxony with the consent of the good people [*gûden knechte*] of the land. On all days and at all times priests and clerics, girls and women, and Jews shall have peace for their possessions and their persons.

According to the *Sachsenspiegel*, a common peace had prevailed over the country from olden times, embracing all its inhabitants and protecting everyone against acts of violence. It is a reflection of the order of the law. In this sense, the order of the law is an order of peace, and law is peace, and peace law. By Eike von

Repgow's time, however, this common peace had long ceased to suffice in the empire. Violence was as rampant as if a general order of peace did not exist at all. The rise of a class of professional warriors, the knights, resulted in two serious evils in the Middle Ages—the robber-barons and private feudal warfare. The widespread practice of self-help led to intense legal insecurity. The establishment of a special system of peace protection proved necessary to guarantee the maintenance of law and order and thereby to attain the aim of the state. The *Sachsenspiegel* speaks of the "old peace which the imperial might has established for the land of Saxony." In the *Schwabenspiegel* (L 248; G 205) it is stated:

> Now hear ye the other peace which the imperial might has laid down and established in all the German lands with the consent of the princes and the masters and other wise people who were in those lands. On all days and at all times priests and all clerics, girls and widows, orphans and merchants, and Jews shall have peace for their persons and their possessions.

The authors of both lawbooks consider this peace, from the point of view of law, as something special. In addition to the common land peace (*gemeiner Landfrieden*), embracing all men and in force at all times, a special peace has been established and pledged. The special peace is an intensified peace, characterized by the idea that persons, places, and objects which are particularly exposed to acts of violence, such as Jews and clerics or, which, because of their nature, are considered inviolable, such as churches and cemeteries, shall enjoy stronger protection. In this sense, a special peace aims at legal equalization. In the conception of the *Sachsenspiegel*, the special peace was, under all circumstances, an inviolable peace, and its violation carried the penalty of death—a draconian sanction which best mirrors the gravity of the problem of law enforcement in this period.

A peak of legal insecurity was reached in Germany under King Henry IV (1056–1106). The beginning of the Crusades brought with it Jewish persecutions of unprecedented ferocity. The protection of the Jews, on the basis of charters granted up to that time by the kings to individuals or specific groups only, had proved entirely inadequate. The First Crusade introduced yet another problem. It made it clear that the Jews needed protection not merely as merchants or as residents but as non-Christians, exposed to the violence of Christian fanaticism and inadequately protected by the mere fact that they possessed a regular position in the social scheme.[2] The powerful rise of the idea of a promised and sworn land peace (*Landfrieden*), which was to become the cornerstone of law and order in the empire, was also to serve as a protection for the Jews. It was to become more effective in a new way.

Doubtless because of the persecutions during the crusade of 1096, the Jews were included among the persons specially protected in the Mainz Imperial Land Peace of 1103, the first of its kind. Along with the churches and clerics and merchants and women, the Jews also received general protection and security. Henry IV ordered peace to be sworn *aecclesiis, clericis, monachis, laicis: mercatoribus, mulieribus, ne vi rapiantur, Judeis.*[3] In the Swabian land peace of 1104 only *clerici, mulieres, mercatores et agricolae* were granted permanent peace protection.[4] Besides these persons, the Jews, *Judei, qui ad fiscum imperatoris pertinent,* were included in the special peace protection in Frederick I's land peace, established for two years in 1179.[5] This Rhenish-Frankish land peace is related to a Saxon land peace of 1221, proclaimed at Frankfurt, and to a Würzburg imperial land peace of King Henry (VII) issued in 1224, the so-called *Treuga Heinrici.*[6] Both contain similar clauses on the peace protection of the Jews.

Saxon Land Peace of 1221	Imperial Land Peace of 1224 (*Treuga Heinrici*)	*Sachsenspiegel*, II, 66, 1
Clerici, monachi, mulieres, moniales, agricole, iusti venatores, piscatores, Judei omni die et tempore firmam pacem habebunt in personis et in rebus.	Clerici, mulieres, moniales, agricole, mercatores, iusti venatores, piscatores, Judei omni die et tempore firmam pacem habebunt in personis et in rebus.	Alle dage unde alle tiet solen vrede hebben papen unde geistlike lüde, unde wif unde megede unde joden, an irme gude unde an irme live.

The wording of these passages shows clearly the textual relation of the regulation concerning Jews in the *Sachsenspiegel* to those in the land peaces mentioned. Furthermore, recent research has revealed even the sources of the *Sachsenspiegel* and has indicated that it made use of two different land peaces, namely, the Saxon land peace of 1221, and a lost land peace which, in period and content, stands between the Rhenish-Frankish land peace of 1179 and the *Treuga Heinrici* of 1224 and may have been Otto IV's land peace of 1208.

Thus in the *Sachsenspiegel* and in the lawbooks based upon it (Dsp., F 187; Schwsp., L 248; G 205, 1; *Freisinger Rechtsbuch*, I, 163; *Berliner Stadtbuch*, III, 16, 2) there appears a legal status, first met in the sources in 1103, which preserved its form firmly for more than one hundred and twenty years. Under this status the Jews are included among those persons especially in need of protection, the *homines minus potentes*.[7] Along with these, they belong to that great circle of persons who are awarded a special legal standing under the king's protection. The Jews are classed with women and the clergy as persons who cannot protect themselves. But it is to be noted that they are classed with groups which by no means lack freedom or general legal capacity. They are enveloped by their special peace and enjoy an enhanced legal protection.

This protection is remarkable from various points of view. First, it must be understood that the subject of the special legal protection is "the Jews." The regulations speak simply of the Jews; there is no limitation to individuals or communities. The legal protection, then, applies to the whole of Jewry, without differentiation, in the region where the regulation is valid. The persons and possessions of the Jews are placed under protection, enfolded in permanent, lasting peace. This peace, moreover, is different from the customary protection against feuds, in that it is valid not merely for a specified period of time or for definite days of the week, the so-called "limited days" (*gebundene Tage*). On the contrary, the Jews are to have peace "on *all* days and at *all* times." Every act of violence against an especially protected person means a particularly serious breach of the peace. This makes it an especially qualified offense (with aggravating circumstances), and it is more severely punished than is a crime committed against a person not included in the peace or one who enjoys only the general peace protection. The punishment, according to *Sachsenspiegel*, II, 13, 5 (Schwsp. L 174; G 148), is beheading.

II. The Jews' Right To Bear Arms

The general concept of *Waffenrecht* ("right of arms") and its basic elements as understood in the Middle Ages are of great importance for the understanding of the medieval status of the Jews.

The right to bear arms is based on the public-law status of an individual; in other words, it is a right which is dependent upon its holder's membership in a social group, be it a political body, a feudal society, or a judicial district. It is the honorific right of participation in certain institutions concerned with the use of arms, as developed by the legal system.[8] Five institutions of this sort constitute the essential elements of the right of arms: (1) the right to bear arms, which means the right to go about armed in time of peace, to travel armed, and to appear armed at court; (2) the right of military service (*Heeresrecht*), that is, the right to fight as a soldier in the army, which includes the right and also the obligation to take part in an aggressive war (*Heerfolge*), and to participate in a defensive war (*Landfolge*); (3) the right of self-help or the right of feud, which, however, applied also to persons incapable of bearing arms; (4) the right of combat, which was recognized in the medieval system of legal procedure, among other ordeals, as a means of proof (in this armed combat the destroying weapon was to overcome the malefactor with the help of the demons; the ordeal of combat was thus closely linked with the right of arms of the combatants); (5) the obligation of *Gerichtsfolge*, which meant carrying out court orders, including the duties of pursuing and capturing fugitive peace-breakers (*Gerüftsfolge*) and of besieging a castle which had violated the law of peace (*Belagerunspflicht*). This right and obligation, however, is only in a loose sense connected with the right of arms, for it was considered only as a form of judicial police service and, therefore, affected all inhabitants of the country, those capable, as well as those incapable, of bearing arms. All inhabitants of the judicial district, even those who had no freedom, were under this obligation.

The granting of the right of arms in the medieval state meant a prerogative to those thus endowed. Whoever possessed the right of arms was, in the legal sense, capable of bearing arms (*waf-

fenfähig). Permission to bear arms conveyed, in the view of the Middle Ages, a superior standing over those incapable of bearing arms. The man capable of carrying arms had full standing in law. Therefore, the right to bear arms was closely linked with the medieval concept of honor, since the right of arms was not extended to dishonorable persons. Hence, just as there are varying degrees in the conception of honor, so also were there various degrees within the right of arms. A person could be fully capable, half-capable, or incapable of bearing arms. Mere physical fitness to bear arms, however, in contrast with the legal capability, was of no significance as far as the law was concerned.

What, then, was the position of the Jews in regard to all these rights and obligations? Is it at all possible to speak of the *Waffenrecht* of the Jews in the Middle Ages?

It seems most appropriate to begin the discussion with a fact for which proof has already been adduced.[9] According to the *Sachsenspiegel* (II, 71, 3), Jews, like all inhabitants of a judicial district, were under the obligation of *Gerüftsfolge*, since they are not mentioned among those excluded from the duty of pursuit. Indeed, in a scene pictured in the illuminated manuscript of Dresden, dating from about the middle of the fourteenth century, an armed Jew wearing his Jews' hat is clearly distinguishable in the group of armed men standing before a castle. Like all other persons in this picture, the Jew also bears a weapon which, like the weapons of the other members of this expedition, was a halberd, not a sword. The duty of the Jews to take part in the *Gerichtsfolge* is thus firmly established.

In the *Schwabenspiegel*, this duty appears even clearer than in the *Sachsenspiegel*. This is interesting because the southern German lawbook generally gives evidence of a diminution of the legal status of the Jews, particularly with respect to their duty of *Gerichtsfolge*. In article L 253*a;* G 207, 4, the *Schwabenspiegel* states: "Clerics, women, sextons, shepherds, and Jews shall not participate in the pursuit personally; but they shall aid either by sending substitutes for themselves or by contributing materials toward it."

While, according to *Sachsenspiegel*, II, 71, 3 (Dsp., F 193), clerics, women, sextons, and shepherds are entirely exempt from the obligation of pursuit, these groups, according to the *Schwabenspiegel*, still have to render service to it, if not personally, then *mit liuten oder mit gute*, that is, by sending substitutes for themselves or by contributing materials. To the four groups named, the author of the *Schwabenspiegel* adds a fifth, the Jews, who, like the other groups, upon a call of *Gerüfte* or upon judicial summons must aid either by sending substitutes or by advancing material contributions for the pursuit. It is quite possible to interpret the latter clause as meaning a money contribution as well as a supply of weapons.

However, this duty is as weak a criterion for the establishment of the right of arms for any one class of people as is the right of self-help, because both affect those incapable, as well as those capable, of bearing arms. Nevertheless, this fact leads to an indirect conclusion on the question of the *Waffenrecht* of the Jews. If a Jew was in a position to arm himself and to act personally with a halberd, or at least to supply weapons instead of personal participation, then it is evident that the Jews were not prohibited by law from possessing arms. The case of the Jews is similar to that of the peasants. They also were obligated to serve the *Gerichtsfolge* as a judiciary police service; and it was even their express duty to keep weapons at home for this purpose.[10]

In the Hebrew literature of the Middle Ages, too, various interesting proofs are found as evidence that Jews were not prohibited by law from possessing arms. As early as the accounts of the Jewish persecution during the First Crusade, there is mention that the Jews possessed swords with which they took their own lives in order not to fall into the hands of their tormentors. In the anonymous report of the Darmstadt manuscript on the annihilation of the Jewish community in Mainz in 1096, we read: "When the sainted, God-fearing people saw that large crowd, they, old and young with Rabbi Kalonymos bar Meshullam at their head put on armor and outfitted themselves with weapons in their implicit faith in the Creator."[11] A battle took place between the Jews and the Crusaders under Emicho, in which the Jews were defeated.

In another encounter of a similar kind, however, the fortunes of war were favorable to the Jews, and they succeeded in repulsing the enemy. The report of Solomon bar Simson (*ca.* 1140) describes this battle at the mysterious place of שלא which is to be identified either with Halle on the Saale or with Prague, as follows:

> . . . the prince supported the Jews during the three days; he sent them a Duke with a body of a thousand swordbearing horsemen [to aid them]; besides, of the Jews living in the city of שלא, there were five hundred young men "that drew sword" and who would not turn their backs to the enemy. They "came upon the city unawares" and struck telling blows at the straying rabble [i.e., the crusaders] as well as the burghers themselves. Of the Jews only six were killed.[12]

In this connection, a passage in the work *Or Zarua* by Rabbi Isaac ben Moses of Vienna gains special significance. This scholar, generally called "Or Zarua" after his chief work, written probably between 1224 and 1250, was a younger contemporary of the author of the *Sachsenspiegel* and lived approximately between 1180 and 1250. He must have spent some time in Saxony, to which he refers twice as "our land." He describes an event which occurred about the time of the composition of the *Sachsenspiegel:*

> [For various reasons it is undesirable that Jews carry weapons on the Sabbath]. Therefore, our brothers in Bohemia do not act in accordance with the law who, on the eve of Sabbath [i.e., after sunset], take with them their swords and shields. Yet, sometimes, when they are in fear and they guard the city, perhaps it may be permitted [to carry arms]. [Reference to talmudic law, *Erubin* 45 a]. . . . Yet, a city situated on the boundary [of Palestine] is to be defended under all circumstances since its capture would make it easier for the enemy to conquer the entire country. The more so in our days living as we do among them [non-Jews]; it should be permitted to meet them with weapons even if they should only come to rob; because when they rob they also kill.[13]

Finally, notice may be taken of the account by Rabbi Eliezer ben Jehudah of Worms (*ca.* 1160–1230), describing the siege of Worms in February, 1201, in his work *Rokeaḥ:* "It happened once that great armies besieged Worms; then we allowed all Jews to carry *their* arms on the Sabbath."[14]

The Jews took up arms in self-defense and knew how to use them. This is clear and appears quite reasonable. All the occur-

rences mentioned are based on the fact that Jews were allowed to
—and, indeed, did—possess arms for defense. The decision of
Rabbi Isaac Or Zarua shows clearly that the right to bear arms
in general could not have been denied to the Jews under a threat
of punishment; for if the right to possess weapons and to go
about armed had actually been denied them under non-Jewish
law, then the situation described, with the religiolegal misgiv-
ings it created, could never have arisen. The conclusion reached
in the decision proves beyond the shadow of a doubt that, in
Rabbi Isaac Or Zarua's lifetime, Jews possessed and used arms for
purposes other than their military duties.[15] In another decision
by the same rabbi, we learn of Jews trading in arms and selling
them to non-Jews, which, in his opinion, was permissible.[16] The
possession of arms by Jews is also mentioned in the *Responsa* of
Rabbi Meir of Rothenburg (1220–93): armor and iron cuisses
which were pawned by Jews with Jewish creditors.[17]

The type of arms mentioned in the *Responsum* of Rabbi Isaac
Or Zarua is also noteworthy. Sword and shield were among the
chief weapons of the Middle Ages. The first was used for attack;
the second for defense. Peasants were prohibited by the imperial
land peace of 1152 from using such weapons; they had to manage
with bows and arrows, knives, and similar instruments.[18] Traveling merchants were allowed to carry swords only for purposes of
self-defense.[19] Whether Jewish traveling merchants enjoyed the
same privilege must remain undecided, since they are not mentioned in this imperial land peace of Frederick I. But Jews were
not forbidden to possess arms by the imperial land peace of
Mainz in 1103, in which they were mentioned for the first time.
Even in the thirteenth century, when the prohibition of Jews'
carrying arms was already established by law and had found its
way into the lawbooks, the violation of the arms prohibition by
Jews did not in itself involve any punishment, although it did
cause certain legal disadvantages for the transgressor. In the case
of the peasants, on the other hand, transgression of the arms
prohibition was followed either by forfeiture of the weapon or
by the payment of a fine. At the session of the Rhenish Land
Peace Confederation held at Worms in 1254, a regulation was
passed forbidding both Christians and Jews to support the ad-

versaries of the peace or the Confederation with arms or other supplies.[20]

Besides the Hebrew sources, German and other documents of the Middle Ages also offer evidence that not only did Jews possess arms and know how to use them but that in time of war they were called to military service and fulfilled their defense duty to the utmost. It will suffice to refer to the rich literature on the cultural and social history of the Jews in the Middle Ages.[21] Attention may be called, in addition, only to a passage in an obscure place. In Wolfram von Eschenbach's *Willehalm*, the queen, Willehalm's sister, emphasizes the duty of mourning those who had fallen in defense of the country "even if they were Jews."[22]

Two observations are to be emphasized. The duty of the Jews to defend city or country is deemed in medieval sources a general civic obligation of military service and not a special Jewish obligation.[23] The historical explanation for this probably lies in the fact that the municipal military duties were originally burdens attached to landownership, from which Jews, as is known, were not excluded during the first half of the Middle Ages.[24] As city dwellers, the Jews were subject to the same military duty as the burghers, a principle which a Regensburg document of 1251 states in these words: "cum hii, qui similem suscipiunt vitam, similem in legibus sentire debeant disciplinam."[25] If the Jews' military duty is so understood in the sources, then a conclusion concerning the legal content of their military obligation can also be drawn. Most probably, it was originally not different from the military duty of the ordinary burgher. The Jews—just like the citizens—were obligated not only to work on entrenchments and fortifications and to perform guard duty but also to take part in combat.[26] For confirmation of this, one need only refer to the example of the siege of Worms in 1201 and to similar cases, in which rabbinical decisions permitted carrying arms even on the Sabbath. Only in this way does the possession of arms by Jews and its lawfulness become plausible. For the hypothesis that the Jews were permitted to own arms solely in order to be able to defend themselves against violence is not a satisfactory one. The assumption that the Jews were subject to full military service is further supported by the fact that the sources repeatedly refer to

mounted Jews.[27] The Heidelberg and Dresden illuminated manuscripts of the *Sachsenspiegel* even show armed Jews on horseback
as illustration to Ssp., III, 2. If, as will be proved later, this picture does not show a war steed, still it reveals clearly that riding
was an activity which, according to the general opinion at that
time, Jews were entitled to carry on. It can be proved that, until
the beginning of the fourteenth century, keeping and supplying
horses was one of the duties of the Jews.[28] Another example appears in the clear wording of the Speyer Jewry privilege of 1084,
which has never been understood to mean anything other than
the obligation of the Jews for full military service. It states that
the Jews "vigilias, tuiciones, municiones circa suum tantum-
modo exhibeant ambitum, tuiciones vero communiter cum
servientibus."[29] A similar situation is found in Cologne and
Hameln.[30] In the present writer's opinion, an account in the
chronicle of the Erfurt monastery of St. Peter which describes
how the Jews, in 1309, together with the burghers, protected the
city against the attacks of the Landgrave of Thuringia,[31] cannot
be understood in any other way than as implying the Jews' full
military service.

These examples will suffice. They fully confirm the assertion
that from the eleventh to the thirteenth centuries the Jews had
the right to possess and to use arms and that they employed this
right to defend both their own persons and the cities in which
they lived. It has already been shown that they had the right of
self-help and that they were obliged to join the *Gerichtsfolge*.
Finally, it may be pointed out that the Jews originally had the
right, without restriction, of judicial combat; for even the decidedly anti-Jewish author of the *Schwabenspiegel*—as late as
the second half of the thirteenth century—recorded it as a duty
of a Jew to respond to the challenge of a Christian to judicial
combat.[32] According to the *Meissener Rechtsbuch* (III, 17, 44),
Jews were allowed to issue a challenge to judicial duel in actions
for deprivation of personal freedom.[33] Seen in this light, the occasional reports of the participation of Jews in tourneys and of
their own knightlike tournaments may not belong entirely to
the realm of fiction.[34]

The available sources indicate, then, that Jews were nowhere prohibited from bearing arms in the earlier centuries of the Middle Ages. Neither legally nor actually were they deprived of the right to possess and use weapons. On the contrary, unquestionable evidence from the sources has established that their participation in all the five institutions which form the elements of the medieval concept of the "right of arms" was originally unrestricted. This participation, moreover, was in some cases not voluntary but obligatory. It was not a burden placed upon the Jew because he was a Jew but a general obligation imposed upon Jews as well as on all other members of a territorial or social unit. From the point of view of legal history, this means nothing less than that the Jews originally possessed the *Waffenrecht*, the full right to bear arms.[35]

This result is not at all in conflict with the general picture that the history of civilization has formed of the Middle Ages. To be sure, in general, the Jews were not knights or men-at-arms but almost always merchants and traders. Making a livelihood was their external concern; the study of the Torah and the observance of the religious commandments was their task in life. The difference, however, between the Jewish and the Christian city dweller was not great on that account. The latter's life also was strongly influenced by his religion; the church entered into almost every sphere of his activity. The burgher of the medieval city, too, was a merchant and not a soldier by profession. But, in an hour of danger threatening the community from without, all inhabitants had to stand together for their common defense. This was changed only when, in the twelfth century, the building of castles—the homes and strongholds of the knights—spread far and wide. Universal military service was abolished; from then on, the call to arms concerned only the class of knights. For the other classes the right to bear arms was either withdrawn or restricted.

All this developed in accordance with the changing customary law. Thus it is intelligible that, according to the medieval German lawbooks, only vassals and liegemen were capable of and subject to military service.[36] The great social and legal developments and changes in the twelfth century combined with political events and economic transformations to influence essentially the legal status of the Jews, too. Here the change followed the path of the general development. It was not a matter of any sudden revolutionary legal enactments but—despite spasmodic catastrophes—of a slow and steady development taking its course on the basis of custom.

III. The Jews' Exclusion from Bearing Arms[37]

As in the land-peace laws, so in the *Sachsenspiegel* and the law-books based upon it the Jews appear merely as one of several groups whose particular need for protection was recognized by the law and guaranteed by their inclusion in the king's special peace. The *Sachsenspiegel* (II, 66, 1) extends the special peace to priests and clerics, women, and Jews. The *Schwabenspiegel* (L 248; G 205, 1) adds two more groups, namely, orphans and merchants. The latter lawbook offers the following motivation for the special peace being granted to these classes (L 248; G 205, 2): "The persons mentioned before are singled out for a special reason; namely, they must not bear arms; that is why all of them shall enjoy perpetual peace." The *Sachsenspiegel* (III, 2), on the other hand, states the following principle: "Those who are included in the king's daily peace shall bear no arms."

Both lawbooks, then, proceed from the premise that persons granted peace are incapable of bearing arms. Arms prohibition and the special peace are closely linked. While the *Sachsenspiegel*, however, considers the prohibition as a consequence of the special peace, the *Schwabenspiegel* reverses the principle and declares that such persons enjoy the peace because they are unable to bear arms. Both are correct. It is necessary to take into consideration the various groups of persons involved. Women were always unable to bear arms and therefore particularly exposed to danger. Thus the king placed them under a special peace. Clerics, on the other hand—according to secular law—as well as peasants and merchants, were capable of bearing arms. They were placed under the arms prohibition only through their inclusion in the special peace.

What can be said of the Jews in this respect? While the legal status of clerics, women, and peasants has already been adequately explained, a solution of the problem with regard to the

Jews has not yet been attempted. In the modern literature of legal history only one author has approached this question in the following remark: "I cannot say whether the prohibition of the Jews from bearing arms goes back to their status as serfs of the king—*servi nostri* as they are referred to in the Jewry privilege of Frederick II in 1236—or to other considerations."[38] With respect to the particular period, namely, that of the composition of the *Sachsenspiegel* (1221-24), which concerns us primarily, the first alternative must be eliminated; for in this lawbook the concept of the so-called "chamber serfdom," that is, of the Jews as the only *servi camerae imperialis*, does not appear. Thus the investigation must turn to other considerations in order to clarify the problem of the arms prohibition and the special peace for the Jews.

An explicit prohibition of the Jews from bearing arms in medieval German law occurs, to the present writer's knowledge, for the first time in the *Sachsenspiegel*, III, 2: "Clerics and Jews who bear arms and [clerics][39] who are not shaven in accordance with their law, if an act of violence is committed against them, they shall be compensated like laics; for those who are included in the king's daily peace shall bear no arms."

The *Deutschenspiegel* (FE 198) took over the passage word for word from the *Sachsenspiegel*. In the *Schwabenspiegel* (L 255; G 210) the article is formulated thus (similarly in *Freisinger Rechtsbuch*, I, 168): "Priests and Jews who are not shaven in accordance with their law, if anything is committed against them, they shall be compensated like laics; and if they bear arms, a sword or a long knife, or other weapons, . . . then the same rule holds."

Chapter 484 of the Glogau lawbook of 1386 contains the following regulation: "Priests and Jews shall not bear arms, for the sake of peace which was obtained for the Jews from the Emperors Titus and Vespasian."

The medieval lawbooks, as is known, are records of customary law, aiming to give a comprehensive account of the whole body of law in force at the time of their composition. Hence there can be no doubt that, at the end of the first quarter of the thirteenth century, when the *Sachsenspiegel* was composed, the prohibition of the Jews from bearing arms was a valid legal regulation in Saxony. The range of its validity was greatly extended when the *Sachsenspiegel* law spread north, south, and east over Germany and penetrated far beyond the borders of the empire. In view of this fact, the later inclusion of the Jews in full military duty in time of war must be considered as a temporary exception from the arms prohibition. But such prohibition makes sense only if using weapons was previously lawful; and deviations therefrom in times of danger merely signify the temporary return to the original status of the Jews' full capability to bear arms and liability to military service. The historical development that effected this change and limited considerably the original full rights of the Jews to bear arms can be traced rather clearly.

The prohibition of the Jews from bearing arms as found in *Sachsenspiegel*, III, 2, represents the conclusion of a development which extends over a period of approximately one hundred and twenty years. It runs a course similar to a certain extent to the history of the exclusion of the peasant class from bearing arms. It goes back to the year 1103, when, for the first time, the Jews were placed under a qualified peace protection along with other social groups. The consequence of the peace protection was the ban on carrying arms. The Jews, like all other groups of protected persons, were legally guarded from any attack through their inclusion in the imperial land peace of Mainz. Since a Jew could not be attacked (from the point of view of law) and therefore needed no self-protection against a breach of the law, he had no need of weapons. Rather, the law protected him with its provision of peace, the breach of which was subject to heavy penalties. On the other hand, the Jews themselves were not to use any weapons for attack. They were denied the active, as well as the passive, right of feud by virtue of their having been placed under the king's peace. The Jews, like the other groups included in the special peace protection, were deprived of every opportunity of "breaking" the peace lawfully. Therefore, they also lost the right to carry arms. Whoever stands within the peace does not need any weapons. The law affords better protection than a weapon does.

As in the case of the peasants, however, explicit prohibitions to bear arms were imposed on the Jews only in a comparatively late period. The conclusion emerges that only a very gradual development led to that result, manifestly because the protecting arm of the law did not suffice to afford immediate and continuing full protection. Fifty years of comparative quiet passed after the slaughter of the First Crusade before, in the middle of the twelfth century, popular passions were once more stirred up against the Jews. It is striking that the contemporary accounts of Jews taking refuge in the keeps and fortresses during the Second Crusade do not mention their being armed—as do the reports of the First Crusade. The Jewish persecutions in the middle of the twelfth century, on the other hand, make it clear why, from then to the prohibition in the *Sachsenspiegel*, the possession and use of arms played, according to rabbinical *Responsa*, a not inconsiderable role among Jews. This, in turn, sheds light upon the fact that to the author of the *Sachsenspiegel* the formulation of the arms prohibition against the Jews appeared obviously as indicated.

The legal form of the arms prohibition in the *Sachsenspiegel* and the *Deutschenspiegel* reveals unique characteristics and therefore deserves special consideration. According to *Sachsenspiegel*, III, 2, and *Deutschenspiegel*, 198, the persons particularly protected enjoy the increased legal protection held out to them only on condition that they themselves bear no arms. The king's peace is broken and a severe breach of the peace in the narrower sense is thus perpetrated, only when violence is done to *unarmed* priests or Jews. If, on the other hand, the priests or Jews were armed, they lost the special protection. The reasoning of the regulation is as follows: whoever disregards the duties imposed upon the class to which he belongs, shall not enjoy its privileges; he cannot have it both ways. To lay claim to a special right, like augmented legal protection collateral to the arms prohibition, and yet, at the same time, to make use of the general right to bear arms is repugnant to healthy moral and social feeling.[40] The disadvantage involved in the enjoyment of the strengthened protection by the king's peace is the renunciation of self-help, the ban on carrying arms. By violating this prohibition, the Jew—as well as the priest—forfeits the special king's peace. From the fact that the king's peace is the foundation of the legal status of the Jews

in general, one would logically conclude that, as soon as the Jew
had forfeited the king's peace, he would forfeit peace altogether.
The *Sachsenspiegel*, nevertheless, does not draw this conclusion; it
says exactly the contrary: that the Jew, like the cleric, upon forfeiting the king's peace passes under the peace of the common
laity. Should a priest or a Jew *bearing arms* be wounded or killed,
then the crime is no longer a qualified one but merely an ordinary
offense, punishable according to the folk law. It is only the general folk peace that is then broken, not the legally qualified special peace. For this type of breach of the peace, the priest or Jew
can demand no other satisfaction than any layman not under special peace protection. Whoever protects himself with the weapons he carries thereby renounces the protection offered by the
special peace. Indeed, even more, it amounts to provocation; and
the provoker has no title to special legal protection. If, on the
other hand, the conditions demanded for the efficacy of the augmented peace protection are fulfilled, then it retains its force in
full. Although this can be gleaned indirectly from the contents
of the regulation in *Sachsenspiegel*, III, 2, this legal conclusion is
explicitly set forth by the *Sachsenspiegel* in III, 7, 3, 1: "Should a
Christian slay a Jew or commit a crime against him, he shall be
judged because of the king's peace which he has broken on
him"[41] (cf. Dsp., 208; Schwsp., L 260; G 214, 5). Naturally, the
peace-protected persons had to refrain from any punishable act,
any crime or breach of the peace. "Should a Jew slay a Christian
or commit a crime against him and be caught in the act, he shall
be judged like a Christian [unprotected by the special peace]"
(Ssp., III, 7, 2; Dsp., F 208; Schwsp., L 260; G 214, 4). Through
his crime the Jew placed himself outside the sphere of the king's
peace.

This equal legal treatment of priest and Jew might appear surprising at first glance. In illustrating article III, 2, the Heidelberg
and Dresden illuminated manuscripts of the *Sachsenspiegel* show
the scope of the arms prohibition by picturing the affected persons, mentioned in the text. According to the general arms prohibition in *Sachsenspiegel*, II, 71, 2, no other weapon than the
sword shall be carried within the reach of the sworn peace
(*binnen gesworeme vrede*); whoever bears other arms is outlawed by

means of the *Reichsacht* as a violator of the peace. The protected priest and Jew must carry no weapons at all; especially not the sword and the knife. Thus the *Schwabenspiegel* (L 255; G 210; similarly *Freisinger Rechtsbuch*, I, 168) characterizes this violation as follows: "and if they carry arms, swords, or long knives or [other] weapons" (*unde fuerent si wafen, swert oder langue messer oder geweffen*). In the illuminated manuscripts of the *Sachsenspiegel*, the priest and Jew are pictured on horseback and carrying long swords at their sides. When Karl von Amira said "they are mounted in order to make an even more martial appearance,"[42] he overlooked the fact that the pictures show not the typical war steed, but the usual riding horse with the traveling saddle.[43] Thus the illustrator has correctly shown that "journeying" people (*wegefährtige Leute*), priests and Jews traveling, are being considered here. Otherwise, the carrying of a sword would have been forbidden under penalty, as seen in the last clause of *Sachsenspiegel*, II, 71, 2 (Dsp., F 191). In addition, the illustrator could have pictured the priest and the Jew in full battle attire, but he has failed to do so. The cleric is distinguished by his tonsure; the Jew, pictured with a beard, wears a colored pointed Jews' hat. The striking gestures, pointing at each other, suggest that they both stand under the same principle of law.[44] Having transgressed the arms prohibition, they have forfeited the qualified legal protection of the king's peace and are protected only within the scope of the general folk peace.

This was the only consequence of infringing the arms prohibition and was the same for both classes. It thus carried with it only legal disadvantages, quite considerable for the transgressor, although no immediate punishment was inflicted upon him. In this respect the cleric and the Jew were treated legally in the same manner. They both belonged to groups of the population which, in certain spheres of life, were by legal cognizance not under the general legal regulations, but the clerics under canon law, the Jews under Jewish law. By the decrees of a number of church councils, clerics were forbidden to carry arms—in fact, those who bore weapons or went about armed were to be punished by the loss of their sacerdotal order and, under certain conditions, were even to be excommunicated.[45] Jewish law knows no such arms prohibition. Only the use of weapons on the Sabbath entailed restrictions (Mishna, *Shabbat*, 6. 4), which occasioned the discussions and decisions of the rabbis mentioned above. But there was no general arms prohibition in Jewish law. This led to the result that the position of the Jews in the practical application of the right to bear arms was essentially different from that of the clerics. They were obliged to participate in the *Gerüftsfolge*, while the clerics, unlike the other classes of the population, were exempt from performing the duty of pursuit with the sword (Ssp., II, 71, 3; Dsp., F 193).[46] Furthermore, the legal status of the Jews was different also from that of the peasant class, which was likewise under the arms prohibition. According to article 12 of the imperial land peace of 1152, the transgression of the arms prohibition by a peasant was punished by the confiscation of the weapon or the payment of a fine (*Busse*) of twenty *solidi*.[47] The *Sachsenspiegel* as well as the *Deutschenspiegel* and the *Schwabenspiegel* provide no like sanction for the transgression of the arms prohibition by a Jew. Thus, despite the arms prohibition, the Jews still retained the right to possess and carry weapons unpunished, though not without incurring certain legal disadvantages. The factual side of this development and its causes have been discussed previously. The legislative reasoning behind it may have been similar to that expressed in article 13 of the imperial land peace of 1152, in which merchants were permitted to carry a sword, but only for their protection.[48]

It would be wrong, however, to draw the conclusion that, by reason of the juridical imperfection of the arms prohibition in the *Sachsenspiegel*, the Jews were spared the effects which in the Middle Ages any restriction of the right to bear arms could not fail to entail, both legally and socially. The *Sachsenspiegel* gives clear evidence of the original legal equality of the Jews by naming them along with the clerics in *Sachsenspiegel*, III, 2, and by treating them equally in the sphere of secular law, with regard to the bearing of arms. Here, as very often in his presentation of the medieval law, Eike von Repgow views the obsolescent and the nascent as equally present and actual.[49] He is like a wanderer between two worlds. He strives to retain the old, and at the same time includes the seeds of the new. In the *Sachsenspiegel*, the old legal equality of the Jews still comes to light in more than one respect. Their inclusion in the king's peace is surely referable not only to the political causes previously mentioned but also to economic reasons. If, in *Sachsenspiegel*, II, 66, 1, the Jews, together with the clerics and the tools of the peasants along with the mills and the public highways, are placed under special protection, then assuredly the consideration of the Jews' utility value to the body economic had not been without weight—acknowledgment of it is still explicit in *Sachsenspiegel*, III, 7, 4. According to the regulation of the *Sachsenspiegel*, everything pertaining to the maintenance of productive economic life was placed under a special dispensation of the king's peace. Even then, however, the onset of a retrograde tendency is discernible. One of its starting-points within the domain of law is undoubtedly the restriction on the right to bear arms. Just as the exclusion of the Jews from the right of feud through their inclusion in the land peace had the inevitable, even if slowly evolving, consequence of their subsequent exclusion from the right to bear arms, so the restriction on the Jews' right to carry arms could not help reacting on their legal and social status.

The deprivation of the right to bear arms necessarily altered the Jews' position in regard to their military duties. From about the middle of the thirteenth century onward, Jews were employed as a rule only for entrenchment work and guard duty, thus rather performing *operae serviles*. For the discharge of such duties, the Speyer privilege of 1084 had authorized substitution by their *servientes*.[50] Less and less did it become customary to employ Jews as warriors proper. Even personal guard duty was, first occasionally and finally as a rule, compounded for a money contribution.[51] Only exceptionally, in emergencies, were Jews called upon for service at arms. Depreciation of the legal status of the Jews must needs carry in its train deterioration of their social position. Concomitantly, there were at work other weighty factors, which will be discussed later.

Attention has already been called to the fact that in the Middle Ages the right to carry arms was closely connected with the concept of honor. This relationship is evident also in those cases in

which the right to bear arms affected the Jews. It must be considered a diminution of the status of the Jews when the right to
judicial combat is granted to them, in *Meissener Rechtsbuch*, III,
17, 44, only upon substitution of a hired fighter (*kemphe*).[52] To
substitute a professional fighter was, as a rule, permitted only to
clerics, because of the provisions of canon law concerning irregularity, and to such persons who could not themselves wield
arms because of their youth, old age, or illness. The *Schwabenspiegel* (L 260; G 214, 5) had still granted the Jews the right and
duty of entering personally into judicial combat. Despite this,
the southern German lawbook excluded them from fulfilling the
duty of *Gerichtsfolge* in person, just as was the case with clerics,
women, sextons, and shepherds (L 253a; G 207, 4). Within
feudalism and feudal law, the clerics played a prominent role,
whereas Jews were entirely excluded. The principle of equal
treatment by the law of priests and Jews, *papen unde jüden* (Ssp.
III, 2), was maintained in the second half of the thirteenth century only as a matter of formal law. Its social-legal content, however, had changed. The feudal development, based on exaggerated ideas of honor attached to arms and martial occupation, had
changed the traditional concept of honor and produced an entirely new stratification of society.

All this found particular expression in the field of the right of
arms; nor could it fail to affect considerably the status of the
Jews. It would be erroneous to raise the objection that to the
medieval Jew professional soldiership and the right to bear arms
could never have meant anything of moment. It may have been
so when all went peaceably. But that is not the point. What is at
issue are the criteria which the surrounding world applied to the
Jews in assigning them their legal and social status within society. The economic activity of the Jews was still considered
useful—in certain respects, even indispensable—and therefore, in
the interests of the public peace and the maintenance of the economic order, a special protection was extended to the Jews.
There can be no doubt, however, that, beside the motive of
Jewry protection, another motive, namely, the diminution of
honor within the domain of the right of arms, came into play
with equal force. The restriction on the right to bear arms repre-

sented by no means only a protective regulation for the Jews who enjoyed the king's peace. The right to carry arms, which legally placed its possessor on an equal footing with the entire free population, was no longer compatible with the socially diminished honor of the Jew. The restriction on the Jews' military service and their exclusion from the right of combat, expressed not only protective considerations but also depreciatory intentions, in consequence of the diminution of honor. Limitation or denial of the right to bear arms meant a most serious diminution of a man's honor. The Jew gradually sank into an inferior position within the social order. There is no more impressive evidence of this development than Johann von Buch's remark in his *Gloss* on the *Sachsenspiegel*, III, 2, written about 1325: "Note here a great difference: weapons are forbidden to priests and clerics for their own honor; and forbidden to Jews for their ignominy."[53]

This was the attitude expressed about one hundred years after the composition of the *Sachsenspiegel*, in which Jewry-law received a just and unprejudiced treatment. The development, there only germinal but already discernible, had been accomplished in these hundred years. At the end of the fourteenth century it no longer occurred to the illustrator of the Görlitz manuscript (Varia 1) of the *Sachsenspiegel* to picture the Jew mounted or armed, in his illustration accompanying the passage (III, 2).[54] In the beginning, the idea of protection was predominant also in Jewry-law as it was in the development of the peasant law in Germany; from the middle of the thirteenth century onward, the idea of the diminution of honor gained more and more ground. Jewry protection, maintained until then by the inclusion of the Jews in the king's peace in consideration of the public peace and in the interests of the economic order, had to change its juridical character at the moment when its objects were no longer considered as full-fledged members of society.

CHAPTER SIX

Medieval Theories about the Status of the Jews

I. Chamber Serfdom and Medieval German Legislation

IN THE present writer's opinion, the development described in the preceding chapter contains the legal-historical roots of the *Kammerknechtschaft* or "chamber serfdom" in Germany. For decades, research has been attempting to unravel the complete history of this institution which is indicated in medieval sources by such designations as *servi camerae nostrae* or *unsir kamerknechte*, and is known in the pertinent literature by the name of "Jewish serfdom."[1]

The development of this "complicated and, in its legal nature, not easily definable status of German Jewry in the later Middle Ages"[2] is to be traced neither solely to the "alien law," as suggested by Johannes Scherer, Eugene Täubler, and Ismar Elbogen, nor exclusively to the Christian theological view of the Jewish Diaspora, which branded the adherents of the defeated synagogue as a pariah people, as Fritz Baer has pointed out. Independently, rather, and on an entirely different path, the development of *secular* law in Germany led to a similar estimation and status of the Jews, and thus prepared the way for the concept which later crystallized in the legal institution of chamber serfdom.

The *servitudo camerae*, in its final legal form which developed only at the summit of the Middle Ages, signifies the complete "appertainment" of the Jews, with their persons and possessions, to the imperial chamber. Rudolph I's mandate of December 6, 1286, concerning confiscation of the property of fugitive

Jews gives clear insight into the legal concept of this relationship.

Cum universi et singuli Judei, utpote *camere nostre servi, cum personis et rebus suis omnibus specialiter nobis attineant vel illis principibus*, quibus iidem Judei a nobis et imperio in feodum sunt concessi, dignum et justum est ac utique consonum racioni, ut, si aliqui Judeorum huiusmodi facti profugi sine nostra sive domini sui speciali licencia et consensu se ultra mare transtulerint, ut se a vero dominio alienent, de illorum possessionibus, rebus et bonis omnibus, tam mobilibus quam inmobilibus, ubicunque ea reperiri contigerit, *nos vel domini, quibus attinent*, licite intromittere debeamus ac ea non immerito nostre attrahere potestati.[3]

The aforesaid development in secular law has its factual and legal basis in the arms prohibition imposed upon the Jews. In the early Germanic and medieval German conception, the arms prohibition applied to the unfree and to serfs. It was extended to monks and clerics as God's servants, *servi Dei*, owing, among other factors, to considerations of propriety. By using weapons, the cleric would also have incurred the risk of irregularity.[4] As the preceding discussion has shown, the arms prohibition for Jews was based upon other presuppositions and had for them socially and legally more unfavorable effects. Characteristic among these effects were the restriction of their military duties to *operae serviles* and the later substitution of a money contribution for these duties. In this, their inferior social position found clear expression. The exclusion of the Jews from the right of arms was the result of their reception into the king's protection, while the loss of the right to bear arms lowered their legal as well as their social standing and made them completely dependent upon their protector. It was as obvious as it was logical that the Jews, barred from the right of arms, reduced to merely subordinate services in the army, socially degraded, and legally at a disadvantage, should come to be considered outright serfs, *servi*, and that rule over them should be assigned to their protector, the king. Indeed, this conclusion was drawn completely by medieval political practice and the medieval doctrine of law. The Jews had been transformed from agents in the economic and legal life, endowed with full rights and worthy of protection, to objects of the economic policy in need of protection, general and legal. The

extent of the rights granted to them became dependent on and
determined by the benefits accruing to the holder of power from
his tolerating them. Therewith was engendered at the same time
the idea of a political Jewish question, something which had not
existed before.

The conformity between political and theological thought and
the harmony between the secular and the ecclesiastical concepts
of law with regard to this significant problem naturally increased
the weight of the doctrine of "Jewish serfdom." From the point
of view of historical research, however, both spheres of law must
be studied separately, in order to discover and describe accurately
the course of the development and, in particular, to analyze correctly the mutual influence of theology and political doctrine, of
ecclesiastical and secular legislation.

In considering the imperial Jewry legislation of medieval Germany, special attention must be directed to a fact which has not
received proper appreciation in the discussion of the history of
the *Kammerknechtschaft*. This fact lies in the field of legislative
technique and directs the historical inquiry into spheres from
which new light can be thrown on the development and character of this legal institution.

It is known that, from Carolingian times until the end of the
eleventh century, individual Jews or distinct groups of Jews
were granted protection by the king in the legal form of charters
(privileges). From 1103 on, the legal protection of the Jews became the subject of imperial land-peace legislation and later also
of territorial land-peace legislation. From the point of view of
legal history, this fact signifies a fundamental change in the form
of Jewry protection. It was elevated from the sphere of special
laws of privilege to the general public peace law. The most important land-peace laws which show this transformation, the
constitutiones pacis, have been enumerated and discussed in the
preceding chapter. From 1103 on, the Jews were included in the
king's protection on a par with other groups who, under the law,
were considered particularly exposed and therefore in need of
special protection. This legal development lasted for a period of
about a hundred and twenty to a hundred and thirty years; and

the results were summarized in the *Sachsenspiegel* (II, 66, 1) at the
end of the first quarter of the thirteenth century.

No regulation concerning the Jews is found in Frederick II's
Constitutio Moguntina, the great imperial land peace of 1235,
which surpassed all its predecessors in significance and remained
supreme throughout the thirteenth century. The considerable
number of later land-peace laws down to the Eternal Land Peace
of 1495 no longer contain regulations on the king's peace and
the protection of the Jews.

Beginning with the *Constitutio Moguntina*, the land peaces
sought, for the most part, to supplement the traditional customary law and, in particular, to create a well-reasoned criminal
law and procedure of evidence. In this tendency a motive for the
elimination of Jewry protection from the legislative program
cannot possibly be found. Even the Frankfurt land peace of
Frederick III in 1442 unmistakably recalls the wording of the
protective clauses in the older land-peace laws, in that, in articles
7 and 8, it places under special protection "all clerics, . . . also
pilgrims, country travelers, merchants, . . . churches, and cemeteries" (*all geistlich lewt, . . . auch pilgrim, lantfarer, kaufleut, . . .
kirchen, kirchhofe*).[5] Here also, however, as in the Mainz land
peace of 1235, the Jews are not mentioned.

Seemingly, the only exceptions are the land-peace confederations formed for the protection of law and order by the Rhenish
cities in the dreadful days of the great interregnum. Like the
land-peace laws of the twelfth century, they included the Jews
in their peace among other groups particularly in need of protection, the *innocentes*.[6] The *Confoederatio pacis Rhenana*, founded on
July 13, 1254, in Mainz, in which Köln, Worms, Speyer, Basel,
and other cities took part besides Mainz, was the broadest of all
in scope. Without restriction, it expressly granted clerics and
Jews the protection of the land peace. The return to the model of
the old land-peace legislation by the Rhenish confederation finds
its justification in the fact that all these confederations represented exceptional legal measures taken by German *cities* for the
maintenance of public order and law at a time when the imperial
authority was powerless. Emergency demands emergency laws.
What, then, was more obvious than to return to the old and tried
land-peace law? Thus, the exception does not violate but rather

confirms the rule observable in the course of historical development that, from the imperial land peace of Mainz in 1235, Jewry
protection was eliminated from the land-peace legislation of the
Holy Roman Empire and its territories.

If the historical development at this point should not be considered as showing a fundamental change in imperial legislation,
such change comes clearly into view in the year 1236. On the
request of *universi Alemannie servi camere nostre*, Frederick II confirmed the old Jewry privilege of Worms *universis judeis Alemannie*
and extended its validity to cover all Jews within the territories
of the empire and the domains of the dynasty in Germany,
omnibus judeis ad cameram nostram immediate spectantibus.[7] For the
first time, the Jews were referred to as *servi nostri*, and this designation remained in use from then throughout the Middle Ages.

As is now generally agreed, the expression *servi camerae* appears
in Germany for the first time in Frederick II's privilege of 1236.
What legal-historical significance attaches to this imperial privilege? In view of the traditional conservatism of medieval legislation, the apparently sudden, yet fundamental, change in the
legislative technique in the sphere of Jewry protection—this return to the privilege form—demands an explanation. What relationship has this change to the development and nature of the
very legal institution of chamber serfdom, which it concerns? By
probing these questions, the core of the problem posed by medieval chamber serfdom in Germany may be laid open.

The discussion and clarification of the history of chamber serfdom has suffered chiefly from two shortcomings. First of all, the
wording of Frederick II's privilege of 1236 was taken for an expansion and generalization of the privilege of Worms so as to
include all German Jews in the imperial Jewry protection. This
so-called "extension of the chamber serfdom to all Jews in the
Empire" (Elbogen, Schiffmann) was given an entirely unjusti-
fied prominence. From this underlying idea there was construed a
sharp contrast between "special" and "general" chamber serfdom. A supposedly exact historical scheme of the development
in Germany was drawn thus: *Kammerknechtschaft* of the Jews of
Worms—general chamber serfdom—chamber serfdom of individual communities and individual Jews.

Furthermore, an important difference in the terminology of the documents has been overlooked, and *Kammerknechtschaft* was, throughout, the only term used in the literature.[8] In the documents before 1236, the only designations used with reference to the Jews were: *ad cameram nostram attineant* (Worms privilege of 1090, and its confirmation in 1157); *ad fiscum imperatoris pertinent* (Frederick I's land peace of 1179); *ad imperialem cameram dinoscuntur pertinere* (Regensburg Jewry privilege granted by Frederick I in 1182); *ad nostram et imperii cameram spectare noscuntur* (Regensburg donation deed of 1233). All these are significant legal documents, the wording of which had been carefully weighed and precisely composed in the imperial chancellery.[9] Therefore, if the technical expression *servi camerae nostrae* was introduced for the first time in 1236, the Jews being pointedly designated as *servi nostri*, that undoubtedly discloses the precise formulation of a new legal institution—chamber serfdom. The prior development had already come to an end in 1235 with the omission of Jewry protection from the land peace of Mainz.

In view of these observations, the stages of development assumed for the history of chamber serfdom by Eugene Täubler and Sara Schiffmann prove to be untenable.[10] One may speak of the *Kammerknechtschaft* of the Jews in Germany in a technical sense only from the year 1236 on.

Moreover, still other reasons may be adduced for refraining from laying down any such rigid developmental sequence. Above all, the mode of expression in the documents—that the Jews *ad cameram nostram (imperialem) attinent* or *pertinent*—should be neither misunderstood nor overlooked, nor yet overrated. It was not used exclusively with reference to Jews, as was the designation *servi camerae*, but in other documents refers particularly to churches.[11] The term *ad cameram attinere* contains nothing more than a reference to an immediate legal relationship of the *attinentes* or *pertinentes*, institutions or persons, to the emperor or king, with the exclusion of all intermediary powers. Such a direct protective relationship to the emperor is found in the privilege granted by Henry IV to the Jews of Worms about 1090, as well as earlier in the charters of protection extended to individual Jews by Louis the Pious, to which the former can be traced. In the Carolingian formulae the clause referring to protection and payments is extended equally to Jewish and Christian grantees.[12] Imperial "Jewry protection" in Germany saw its greatest expansion, in point of territory, time, and the number of persons affected, not so late as 1179 or 1236, but as early as 1103, when the Jews were included in the imperial land peace of Mainz. Thus the contrast between special chamber serfdom (or chamber pertinence), on the one hand, and general chamber serfdom (or chamber pertinence), on the other, also vanishes, and, with it, its importance as a determining factor in the history of chamber serfdom ascribed to it heretofore in literature.

The way is thus cleared for an unprejudiced investigation of the documentary source material; and this will become a suitable basis for a fair appreciation of the entire legal-historical development. In order to view properly the significance of Frederick II's privilege of 1236, three phases must be differentiated in the legal development of Jewry protection.

II. Three Phases in the Legal Development of Jewry Protection

A. SPECIAL RIGHTS GRANTED TO JEWS BY PRIVILEGE FROM THE CAROLINGIAN PERIOD TO THE END OF THE ELEVENTH CENTURY

The privilege was the basic legal form in the Middle Ages for conferring rights and establishing prerogatives which deviated from the regular order of law.[13] According to the great canonist, Gratian (ca. 1140), the privilege is "a special law established for individuals, which bestows upon its recipients a favor not issuing from the common law."[14] In other words, the privilege establishes a *jus speciale*, a law of exception, for a particular individual in place of the universally valid common law, the *jus commune*. This medieval juridical analysis of the concept of the privilege is not confined to canon law but applies to the secular law of privilege as well.[15]

Even in late Carolingian times, royal decrees of all sorts are explicitly called *privilegia*. The Carolingian formulae of charters of protection for Jews, handed down in a collection from Louis I's times, the *Formulae imperiales*, also belong in this category. They are charters of protection, *cartae mundeburdii, tuitionis, defen-*

sionis, by which Jews were taken under the special guardianship of the king.[16] These formulae show that the grantee commended himself to the *munt* of the king: "in manibus nostris se commendavit, et eum sub sermone tuitionis nostre recepimus ac retinemus."[17] In others, expressions are used such as: *sub nostra defensione, sub mundeburdo et defensione nostra suscepimus.*[18]

This protection, which reveals a relationship to the *tuitio* of the late Roman and Ostrogoth empires, arises from the legal act of commendation and bestows certain prerogatives. But—and this is fundamental for the considerations to follow—it represents by no means a legal institution characteristic of, and applied exclusively to, Jews. On the contrary, individual churches, clerics, freemen capable of bearing arms, women, and merchants as well could receive the special protection of the king.[19] Royal charters of protection have been preserved through which non-Jewish private persons and Christian ecclesiastical institutions were admitted to the king's special protection. Their wording and contents do not differ in the legally important fundamentals from the documents for Jewish grantees.

Every charter of protection contains three basic clauses, namely, (1) the protective clause, granting inclusion in the king's protection; (2) the peace ban clause, which forbids doing any harm to the protected person; and (3) the complaint clause, *jus reclamandi*, by which the protected person could invoke immediate royal jurisdiction. The idea that the law and charters of Jewry protection were used as models for the protection of Christian merchants has had to be dismissed since Michael Tangl's penetrating paleographic investigations of those documents.[20] From the comparison of the wording and the content of the Carolingian formulae of charters of protection for Jews and non-Jews (no detailed account can be given here)[21] there arises the unambiguous conclusion that in all cases the legal conditions are of the same kind and the legal regulations similar. In their application to Jews they were modified in certain respects only, with regard to their religious distinctions. Under Louis the Pious the charters of protection and the immunity formula were adapted to the needs of the church and the *servi Dei*.[22] With respect to the Jews, consideration of their religion was also a legis-

lative necessity because, according to the capitulary of Charlemagne in 802, the general oath of loyalty included the fulfilment
of religious duties, which could not apply to them.[23] In general,
however, from the privilege formulae, no difference in legal position can be made out between Jewish and non-Jewish bene-
ficiaries. In either case they are designated as *fideles:* their relationship to their protector is founded on fidelity. The king binds
himself to grant protection, *quamdiu nobis fideles extiterint,*[24] the
grantee pledges certain services or payments such as a freeman
can render. By commendation and reception in the king's protection and jurisdiction, no change in the grantee's personal status
is effected. Neither a lack of freedom needs to be assumed as
antecedent, nor the creation of any type of servitude as conse-
quent to this legal transaction. Not even the obligation to make
certain payments to the royal chamber resulting from the protection could justify a contrary interpretation. The legal term used
for this duty in the charter formulae—*partibus palatii nostri fideliter deservire*—applies to Jewish as well as to non-Jewish grantees.[25]
The amount of the payments to be made to the king was defined
by established custom for certain types of protection; for Jews
it was one-tenth, for Christian merchants one-eleventh, of, probably, their profit.[26]

These observations now supply positive proof for the conclusion which was supported hitherto only by the negative indication of Tangl's textual emendation in the charter formulae: no
typical law of Jewry protection existed in the Frankish realm.
From the legislative point of view, the king's protection was, as
such, abnormal because it placed the individual outside the ordinary operation of the law. But there was no qualitative, let alone
discriminating, difference in the granting of charters of protection to Jews as compared with the privileges for non-Jews. For
both of them merely a *jus speciale* was created, which exempted
them from the rule of the *jus commune.* The charters of protection
for Jewish grantees constitute merely special laws for individuals,
or a number of individuals—individual privileges, so to speak.
But no collective regulation of the status of a whole social group
(*jus singulare*) was intended.[27] Therefore, this is not a genuine
type of specific Jewry-law which, in the strictest sense, means

laws enacted for the Jews collectively as a separate social group, by which their legal status in general was determined.

The legal-historical significance of the privileges issued to the Jews in the second half of the eleventh century in the Rhenish cities of Speyer and Worms,[28] cannot be regarded differently. As it is uncontested in the literature that these privileges of about 1090 must derive from a Carolingian model because of their archaic wording, it cannot be doubted that they are identical in their legal character with their predecessors. It is surely no accident that the Rhenish Jewry privileges come just at the time when city privileges appear in Germany as a new category of constitutional documents, of which Henry IV's charter for Worms in 1074 is the earliest example.[29]

The much-discussed question of whether the Jewry privileges of Speyer and Worms were granted to the individuals named as the grantees or to their Jewish communities may be answered thus: they were granted and were applicable *de facto* to the entire Jewish population residing there.[30] Legally, to be sure, they were not granted to the "community" because, at that time, no such thing, Jewish or Christian, existed as a legal body but was only beginning to take form. The Jews were merely one of various groups of the city population whose status necessitated special legal regulation, in their case because of a religious difference. Therein lay nothing derogatory from either the social or the legal point of view. Only a few years prior to the charters under consideration, Bishop Rüdiger of Speyer, in enlarging his city, had stated that "he expected to enhance a thousandfold the dignity [significance] of his city by gathering there also Jews."[31] In the medieval cities there were other groups, too, which possessed special charters which gave them a position different from the rest of the population.[32] For instance, a hundred years later in the region of German colonization in the East, we find the Jews being granted the same rights as those of the national groups of Germans and Latins.[33] If in the *Wormatiense* of 1090 their special status is described by the expression *ad cameram nostram attineant*, this signified merely their direct relationship to the king, with the exclusion of all intermediate powers—a sort of *Reichsunmittelbarkeit*, not in any way personal dependence or even a social diminution of their status. No change had occurred in the legal condition of freedom which the Jews enjoyed in Carolingian times.[34] Documents from the years 965, 973, and 1004 tell of a merchants' community, a community of *negotiatores et judei* in Magdeburg, and of *judei et mercatores* in Merseburg, where traders and Jews formed the only free community, while the rest of the population was composed of *liti, coloni,* and *servi.*[35] If evidence for the freedom of the Jews of Speyer and Worms is needed at all, it is provided by the different, frequently quoted regulations of the Rhenish Jewry privileges, especially article 12, whose legal-historical significance so far has not been taken into consideration. In this article the Jews are declared capable of submitting proof in lawsuits merely by taking an oath and producing witnesses—which was the right of freemen. On the other hand, while the ordeals of the hot iron and of hot and cold water usually applied to the unfree, they were declared inapplicable to Jews.[36] The general principle prevailing in the realm of municipal law, *Stadtluft macht frei* ("city residence confers freedom"), could have meant no betterment for the Jews but at most a legal guaranty of their status.

Despite all the conditions set forth, the Rhenish Jewry privileges signify still another stage in the course of the development of the Jews' legal status in medieval Germany. The type of individual privilege underwent amplification in the form of general privilege (*privilegium generale*), that is, a special law governing a number of persons of the same kind, but which, because of the regional restriction, cannot as yet be regarded as *jus singulare,* embracing a class as a whole. By the repeated bestowal of privileges of the same kind, a *jus singulare* for all Jews might have evolved in contrast to the *jus generale.* This tendency toward an organic development parallel to that of medieval municipal law was, however, suddenly interrupted by the events of the year 1096.

B. GENERAL JEWRY PROTECTION OF THE LAND-PEACE LEGISLATION
FROM THE IMPERIAL LAND PEACE OF MAINZ (1103) TO THE
DEATH OF EIKE VON REPGOW (*ca.* 1233)

During the Middle Ages law was considered a part of the divine world order. Customary law was still predominant.[37] In the beginning, royal authority abstained from establishing general regulations and contented itself with merely creating special laws by the bestowal of privileges. Thus the Roman-German empire produced only few regulations by way of legislation. One of its most important spheres was the land-peace law. The historical significance of the *constitutiones pacis*, which have been aptly called "imperial laws in the form of treaties," lies in their establishing the preconditions for a system of public criminal justice, in contrast to the older times, in which complaint was entertained only upon the plea of the person injured. More and more, the land-peace legislation directed its attention to the general protection of the public good against injury, especially of the lives of the population. The prosecution of heinous crimes was no longer carried on in the interests of the victims only; instead, the crime was now considered as an offense against the whole society. It was to be expiated by criminal punishment and no longer by pecuniary penalty. With the rise of sanctions applied by public authority, especially through the imposition of the death penalty, the penal law of the earlier Middle Ages, originally of a more private character, was gradually transformed by the land-peace legislation into a more public penal system, which finally developed into the "criminal law" (*Kriminalrecht*) of the later Middle Ages, more conformable to the modern concept.[38]

As late as the second half of the twelfth century, a medieval chronicler, Provost Burchard von Ursberg (*ca.* 1177–1231), a trustworthy witness of the conditions of his time, reports as a *mos Teutonicorum*, that they "sine lege et ratione voluntatem suam pro jure statuunt . . . et omnem justitiam detestantur et odio habent."[39] From this can be gathered what the legal significance must have been when Henry IV included the protection of the life and property of the Jews in the reform of the penal law initiated by him. The imperial land peace of Mainz, which was sworn to in 1103 for a period of four years by the nobles of the land, placed the protection of the Jews on a new legal basis. Its wide extension with respect to territory, time, and persons affected has been discussed in the preceding chapter. On the other hand, the reinforcement of the public guaranty of the legal protection granted was, without doubt, of no less importance.

While the privileges were considered as revocable and could be forfeited, the land peace was issued with the co-operation of the nobles of the empire and for a comparatively longer period of time. This procedure offered a legal safeguard against arbitrary change in the regulations once enacted. That is why the assistance of the *gûden knechte* or "the princes and masters and other wise people of the land," respectively, in enacting the land-peace law is emphasized in the *Sachsenspiegel* as well as in the *Schwabenspiegel*. There can be no doubt that it was the direct purpose of the king to establish a Jewry protection more effective in both substance and form than was the older law of privilege; for this protection guaranteed by law was the peak and conclusion of a preceding series of protective measures in favor of the Jews. As early as the disastrous year 1096, Emperor Henry IV, while in Italy, issued an appeal to the princes, bishops, and counts, and especially to Duke Godfrey of Bouillon, to protect the Jews against the crusaders. Upon his return to Germany, in 1097, he allowed Jews, previously baptized by force, to return to their paternal faith—and this in contradiction to the express rules of canon law. In 1098, the emperor made an investigation in Mainz concerning the property of the Jews slain there.[40] The peak of imperial efforts to protect the Jews was finally attained in 1103, when every offense against their lives and possessions was placed under the sanction of criminal punishment (death penalty). Jewry protection thus became interrelated with the general intervention of the state in the prosecution of crimes. It thereby attained in every respect the widest extension and the strongest guaranty ever bestowed upon the Jews by the medieval state. The *Sachsenspiegel* in its Jewry-law reflects this legal situation.

What, then, is the relationship of the general Jewry protection of the land-peace legislation to the older law of the Jewry privileges? In the literature they are either equated (Fischer) or insufficiently differentiated (Elbogen). In particular, it has been maintained that "the protection of the land peaces refers only to the life and property of the groups mentioned therein, while the protection of the privileges goes much further and secures, for instance, even freedom of movement, freedom of trade and exemp-

tion from merchandise duty."[41] Quantitatively, the contrast
ought not to receive too much emphasis; for the protection of
life and property is fundamental and, accordingly, was incorporated into the Carolingian formulae for charters of Jewry protection as well as into the Rhenish Jewry privileges. Moreover,
it is characteristic of the development of law during the Middle
Ages that a strong legislative and executive power, able to initi-
ate the new and invalidate the old, was lacking. Thus it was
that in times of change, as in the twelfth and thirteenth centuries, the old persisted by the side of the new, and the abolition
of the old was effected only in the measure in which the innova-
tions became more and more cogent.[42] This was also true of the
law of the Jewry privileges. While the land peaces were limited
to a few years' duration only, still the privileges remained in
force along with them. The privilege of Worms, for example, was
confirmed in 1157 by Frederick I. The sources indicate, indeed,
that Jewry protection by privilege was to be brought into organic connection with the legal land-peace protection. Only thus
is the fact to be understood that in Frederick I's Rhenish-Frankish land peace of 1179—for the first time in the history of land-
peace legislation—the Jews are designated as persons, *qui ad
fiscum imperatoris pertinent*. This designation, up to that time used
only in Jewry privileges, must have passed from the privileges
into the text of the land peace. Since at that time and even later
the Jews were still enumerated together with other persons in
need of protection, yet having full legal capacity, there can be
no idea of either a limitation of their freedom or a diminution of
their legal status.[43]

The regulations of Jewry protection in the land peaces, like
those of the privileges, represent merely a *jus speciale* in the sense
discussed previously. The difference in the juridical view is a
qualitative one. The form of a sworn treaty or of an imperial law,
in which the land peaces appear, objectifies the Jewry protection
to the greatest possible extent. The penalties inflicted for offenses
against Jews no longer are fines but criminal (body) punishments.
If the legal development could have been completed in this direction, undisturbed by religious, political, and social influences, it
would have taken place within the framework of the general

penal law and would have kept pace with it. The result would have been that the law of Jewry protection finally would have become nothing other than a special norm of the general penal law. In Saxony this tendency was fostered by the endeavor of the *Sachsenspiegel* to present the penal provisions of the land peaces as belonging to the general penal law. In the domain of the law of Jewry protection, however, the course of organic development was once more broken off prematurely.

C. THE CHAMBER SERFDOM OF THE JEWS FOLLOWING FROM FREDERICK II'S JEWRY PRIVILEGE OF 1236

The Jewry privilege of Frederick II, issued in 1236, was directly preceded by political events of anti-Jewish character, just as had been the case with the new regulation of the law of Jewry protection in 1103. At the end of 1235 the blood accusation was raised for the first time in Germany. Charges of ritual murder, together with Jewish persecutions at Lauda and Fulda,[44] had shown that even the land-peace guaranty of the life and property of the Jews was insufficient, bearing out Burchard von Ursberg's assertion that the land-peace laws—the only laws the Germans had—were not properly obeyed.[45]

The regulation of the law of Jewry protection by Frederick II appears retrogressive in two respects, in form as well as in substance.

Through the return to the privilege form, the legal protection of the Jews, as in Carolingian times, was put completely under the control of the emperor. On the other hand, the guaranties of definite duration and of augmented checks against alteration, which were bound up with the legal form of the sworn land peace or imperial law, lapsed accordingly. The protection of Jewish life and property was removed from the frame of the protection by general penal law. The factor of arbitrariness again gained greater weight in its regulation.

In content, to be sure, it was once more the old privilege of Worms with its well-known provisions, that was to determine the legal status of the Jews. But the situation had undergone an essential change through the conception and designation of the Jews as *servi camere nostre*. For its understanding, a glance at the general legal development will prove rather instructive. The provisions of punishment for murder, robbery, arson, and the like, contained in the land peaces, had gradually become common law. These provisions were supposed to be universally known and therefore did not have to be incorporated in the Mainz land peace of 1235.[46] This was not so with the provisions for the passive Jewry protection, which are likewise missing from the *Constitutio pacis Moguntina*. Not the passive, but the active Jewry protection as wielded by the emperor had become part of the common law. In his letter of justification to Pope Gregory IX, Frederick II, in September, 1236, refers with emphasis to the fact that "the Jews in the empire and in his [southern Italian] kingdom, according to common law, were directly subject to his authority."[47] This is plainly an authentic interpretation of the expression *servi camere nostre* which had been used a few weeks before in his Jewry privilege.

This conception stands in direct contrast to that dominant heretofore. The older privileges and the land-peace legislation presupposed the freedom of the Jews and their direct relation to the emperor, without intermediaries. When, in 1236, this relation underwent transmutation in the sense of *servitus camerae*, the freedom of the Jews became juridically nullified by implication, although one must not think of outright servitude in the narrowest sense of the term but, for the time being, only of personal and economic dependence in the legal sense. A sort of dependence, to be sure, had existed within certain limits even prior to 1236. But a fundamental change in the legal concept was effected and officially documented by Frederick II's Jewry privilege; and the later development had its starting-point here. The regulation of Jewry protection and of their legal status no longer treats the Jews as merely one of several individually privileged groups, such as women, merchants, and clerics or city dwellers and different only in religion, as was the case previously. Now the Jews were officially declared to be a special class of the population, for which the single phrase *servi camerae* created an all-inclusive special law. This special law embraced without exception all persons of like kind, namely, the Jews, as a unified, socially closed group. They constituted a body for whose members neither place of settlement nor profession nor any other non-religious criterion had any weight. They were Jews, and nothing but Jews.

Thus the content of their privilege represents a special law governing the entire class. It has become a *jus singulare* for Jews. This was not only in contrast to the *jus generale* but also eliminated its original validity for Jews. It is "Jewry-law" proper, in the specific sense of the word, carrying with it a deterioration of the Jews' legal status.

Frederick II's Jewry privilege is therefore not to be regarded as progress, as has been the hitherto prevailing opinion, but as a regression in the development of the medieval law of Jewry protection.

III. Chamber Serfdom and the Theologic-juridical Concept of *Servitus Judeorum*[48]

So far the discussion has centered on the significance of the break with the past and the changes in the German legislation affording protection to the Jews first manifested in the basic imperial decree of 1236. The underlying causes and the course taken by this development still call for historical analysis. But an attempt to trace historical processes such as the genesis of the *Kammerknechtschaft* to a *single* root must always lead astray. It is bound to show that the investigator is either blind to the manifoldness of the forces at work, or overrates one motive at the expense of others, or else that he goes in for untenable generalizations. The correctness of this contention will be substantiated by the endeavor to elucidate the motives that combined to produce the institution of chamber serfdom of the Jews.

In the main, development of the *servitus camerae* in medieval Germany may be traced back to three motivations: one constitutional and political, the second social (bound up with the contemporary stratification in classes or "estates"), and the third theologic-juridical.

The first of these is imbedded in the imperial policy regarding the Jews. On the basis of painstaking research, the attempt has been made to integrate that policy in the interplay of forces of the Middle Ages in general.[49] Among scholars unanimity now prevails on the fundamental ideas. The Jewry policy of the Ghibelline age was dominated by the tendency to put the Jews into a definite relation to the state (i.e., the sovereign). "The policy of Emperor Frederick II had for its single aim to turn even the smallest force to the advantage of the state and to let nothing be wasted." Where Frederick II could carry through his governmental organization without material resistance, as in Sicily, integration of the Jews in the structure of the state was actually accomplished. In Germany, however, forces of resistance, too strong to be overcome, were already in being—above all, the growing power of the princes and the cities, which worked against the centralizing forces—hence measures for the recovery of alienated prerogatives of the crown and for the rigorous employment of such as had been retained; hence, also, the endeavor to achieve the general integration of the Jews by means of establishing their close dependence, legally and economically, on the emperor and his chamber. In so far as the imperial Jewry policy seems to exhibit contradictions, these are to be interpreted in the light of the fact that, at any given time and place, the real political power complex was always the sole decisive developmental factor. The imperial policy regarding the Jews was made subservient to imperial policy as a whole. To achieve that end, politically, legally, and economically, the institution of chamber serfdom was organized.

This process could be carried through the more readily, since the change in the legal and social status of the Jews had created favorable conditions for that imperial policy. Here is where the deterioration, legal and social, of the position of the Jews coincides with their deprivation of the right to bear arms, without which the blood accusation also would not have been put forward so easily. The second motive, that of social status, is becoming effective. Its historical development and significance, touched upon previously, will be discussed extensively in Part IV of this book.

Since imperial protection of the Jews derives ultimately from their separate religious position, the name and the ideological history of the *servitus camerae* leads finally to the third element, the theologic-juridical root. The unity of state and church, which found such striking expression in the two-swords doctrine of the *Sachsenspiegel* (I, 1), remained merely a theoretical postulate throughout the Middle Ages. The incessant tension between the two powers affected the treatment of the Jews also. Again and again, on the part of the state as well as of the church, there emerged the conviction that the Jewry policy belonged to the disputed border domains. The "autonomous Jewry policy" of the secular rulers[50] was thus constantly contending with the unequivocally formulated principles of the Jewry policy of the church. Often the latter left its mark, even where the state had its own way. It is a challenging task, therefore, to retrace the ecclesiastical influence on the formation of the concept of chamber serfdom.

It has been well known for a long time that the conception of the so-called "serfdom of Jewry," *servitus Judeorum*, had already been formulated by the theologians of late antiquity.[51] According to Christian doctrine, the Jewish people were condemned to eternal servitude as just punishment for their rejection and crucifixion of the Savior. But, in accordance with God's precept, they should not be killed; instead, they should be preserved, like Cain, in a life that is worse than death. A remnant of them should be scattered over the world and, through their scriptures as well as through their bodily existence, serve as an external witness (*testimonium veritatis*) for Christendom to the fact that the prophecies concerning Christ had by no means been fictitious. Finally, the conversion of the Jews might be a prelude to the Last Judgment. But until the very last day they were to remain in political servitude, in a state of submission and patent inferiority.

This was the doctrine of the Fathers of the church in extending toleration to the Jews because they had to perform a special function in the church's historical task. Augustine (354–430) already considered the Jews as servants of the Christians in the Christian state: "The elder shall serve the younger."

Major serviet minori [i.e., Esau to Jacob; with reference to Gen. 25:23] id est prior natus populus Judaeorum posteriori nato populo Christianorum. . . . Ecce Judaeus servus est Christiani. . . . Et hoc manifestum est et implevit orbem terrarum.[52]

It is probably no accident that these sentences were written only a few years after the Jews within the Roman Empire had been excluded by Emperor Honorius from all military service—an interesting parallel, perhaps, to the historical development that took place eight hundred years later.

The ecclesiastical doctrine of *servitus Judeorum* remained unchanged and prevailed through the centuries to follow. It gained real importance in the era of the First and Second Crusades.[53] This conception occurs in Rodulphus Glaber (middle of the eleventh century)[54] as well as in Rupertus Tuitiensis (died in Deutz near Cologne, in 1135); it is found in Peter the Venerable of Cluny (1094–1156) and in Bernard of Clairvaux (1091–1153),[55] down to Thomas Aquinas (1225–1274).[56] There is no great difference in thought, reasoning, or formulation. All the authors declare the Jews to be serfs of Christian princes: *judaei christianis principibus subjecti sunt.*[57] By the early Church Fathers and medieval theologians this serfdom was originally conceived in a purely spiritual sense. But from the middle of the thirteenth century onward—most probably under the strong influence of the then rising power of Roman law reinforced by feudal law—the concept of spiritual overlordship was replaced by the juridical scheme of private ownership.[58]

The assumption is quite obvious that there is a direct connection between the Christian theological doctrine and the legal and political concepts of the Middle Ages. This assertion, however—plausible as it may be—will always suffer from vagueness unless certainty is established concerning the connecting links.[59]

It is striking, indeed, that, to the present writer's knowledge, no explicit reference to the ecclesiastical concept of *servitus Judeorum* is found either in the laws or in the secular legal literature of medieval Germany prior to 1237.

Notoriously, no period of history exhibits such a deep-seated contradiction between positive law and legal theory as do the Middle Ages.[60] Medieval theory and the common sense of justice would not, to be sure, acknowledge the existence of that contradiction. They tried either to resolve it theologically or—likewise on a theological basis—to deny validity to the contradictory positive law. This theoretical attitude and method is found also in the outstanding German jurist of the Middle Ages, Eike von Repgow. From the author of the lawbook that, for the first time in medieval legal literature, presents a systematic account of Jewry-law, it was clearly to be expected that he would take a definite stand toward the problem of *servitus Judeorum*. This is true for Eike von Repgow even more than for any other medieval jurist; for he knew the Bible thoroughly and was widely conversant with the historical and theological writings as well as with the literature of secular and canon law of his time. In the *Sachsenspiegel* he drew on land-peace laws and tapped canon law and theological sources, including the works of Isidore of Seville.[61] Even more, in one of the most interesting among the articles of his *Sachsenspiegel* (III, 42), he searchingly discussed, from both the philosophical and the theologic-historical point of view, the problem: Is servitude legally justifiable?[62] What, then, would have been more obvious than a similar discussion of the theological concept of the *servitus Judeorum*, in the same work, to accompany his account of the regulations of Jewry-law? Yet not even a mention is found in that Saxon lawbook of the serfdom of the Jews, either of the *Kammerknechtschaft* or of *servitus Judeorum*. This fact alone gives telling evidence that up to the time of Eike's death (*ca.* 1233)—until which time he had continued work on the *Sachsenspiegel*[63]—the theological concept of the *servitus Judeorum* cannot have exercised direct influence on secular law in Germany.

All the more important, then, is the motivation which Emperor Frederick II, in his privilege for the city of Vienna, 1237, appended to the clause excluding Jews from public office: "Faithful to the duties of a Catholic prince, we exclude Jews from public office so they will not abuse official power for the oppression of Christians; for, of old, imperial authority has imposed *perpetual servitude* upon the Jews, as punishment for their crime."[64]

Two reasons are advanced for the exclusion of Jews from office. Within the domain of the secular law of Germany the two are met here for the first time. The first, preventing oppression of Christians by Jewish officials, originates, indeed, in Roman law[65] but recurs in papal decretals and decrees of church councils.[66] The second is no other than an explicit reference to the theological doctrine of *servitus Judeorum*. It will scarcely be going astray to suspect in this argument, heretofore unusual in an act of secular legislation, one of the motives which were causative in the formulation of the legal concept of chamber serfdom. What had taken clear shape for the first time in the Jewry privilege of 1236 is grounded in 1237—notably enough again in the form of an imperial *privilegium—expressis verbis* on the theologic and canon-law argument.

These dates having been obtained, the inquiry becomes centered on the external incentive for the "reception" of the theological doctrine of *servitus Judeorum* into the imperial legislation. Undoubtedly, the fact that Jewry protection was eliminated from the Mainz Imperial Land Peace of 1235 has a part therein. Most likely the grounds for the negative attitude of the imperial enactment toward the Jews are to be found in the circumstance that at that time a different regulation of Jewry protection was contemplated, such as was actually accomplished in the year 1236.[67] But where are we to look for its cause, considering that the theological conception had not yet gained any visible influence on secular legislation and legal doctrine, as has been demonstrated before?

The connecting link—to anticipate the final result—is the ecclesiastical legislation. The term *perpetua servitus* makes its first appearance in the official documents of the church in the epistles of Innocent III. In the decree of this pope to the archbishop of Sens and the bishop of Paris of July 15, 1205,[68] the expression is used repeatedly, the servitude of the Jews is most sharply emphasized and related to their guilt for Christ's death. At the same time, the doctrine, until then conceived only theologically, acquires a political coloring, probably not unintentionally. Whoever studies the text of this papal decretal cannot fail to gain the impression that its idea content, and perhaps even its wording, had decisively influenced Frederick II in excluding the Jews from office in his Vienna privilege of 1237. This opinion was, in fact, put forward by Johannes Scherer and George Caro, though, unfortunately, without adequate substantiation.[69] It thus met with rejection, for which not the shadow of a proof was adduced.[70] Yet various reasons may be brought forward which make that assumption appear very probable.

The correspondence in thought and wording between the papal decretal and the Vienna imperial privilege has already been pointed out. It must also not be overlooked that in the first half of the thirteenth century the attitude of the church toward Judaism contributed materially to widening the chasm between Christians and Jews. The name of every one of the popes who reigned in that period—Innocent III (1198–1216), Honorius III (1216–27), Gregory IX (1227–41)—recalls an anti-Jewish program.[71] Two peaks are reached by the Fourth Lateran Council (1215), with its separation policy that culminated in the dress regulations and prohibition of public office for Jews, and by Pope Gregory IX's accusations against the Talmud (1239), which led to the well-known disputation and mass burning of Talmud manuscripts at Paris (1240–42). The papal decretals went into every country, and the conciliar decrees were valid for the whole of Christendom. There is no doubt that ecclesiastic propaganda turned the Jewish question into a problem of international importance. Nor did it remain without effect in Germany, where in the year 1235 regulation of the legal status of the Jews was due. The papal decrees were, of course, not unknown in the imperial chancellery.

Yet this general argument might appear too slight, if its weight were not augmented by an accessory event, which hitherto has been entirely overlooked. Assisted by Raymundus de Penafort, Pope Gregory IX, from earlier compilations and his own decretals, arranged a new codification of church law, which was to supersede all *Compilationes antiquae* and go into force as the sole official collection of decretals beside the *Decretum Gratiani*. It was in 1234 that the pope promulgated this *Liber Extra*, which became an integral part of the *Corpus juris canonici*.[72] In this, Gregory's, collection of decretals was incorporated the previously mentioned decretal of Innocent III in which the theological doctrine of *servitus Judeorum* had for the first time found admission into papal legislation.[73] It would hardly go too far to contend that the fact of publication as well as the content of the new collection of decretals presently became known to the imperial chancellery.[74] Indeed, it is not improbable that the emperor himself had been preoccupied with the idea of a similar codification of the laws of the empire. It is reported at least that, in 1235, the English poet, Henry of Avranches, an ardent admirer of Frederick II, adjured him to win everlasting renown by publishing a *Summa* of the vast mass of scattered imperial laws which should be a companion to the pope's collection of decretals published a year before.[75]

Therewith, the missing link in the chronology of events is supplied, and the circle of proofs simultaneously closed. When the bull *Rex Pacificus* proclaimed to the world, on September 5, 1234, the promulgation of a new papal code, only the law schools of Paris and Bologna were in possession of authentic texts. In the case of every medieval code and lawbook, one must reckon with a time interval between issue or composition and its becoming generally known—a "dissemination period," as it were. As to Gregory's collection of decretals, its dissemination period appears to throw more light on why, at the promulgation of the Mainz land peace on August 15, 1235, the regulation of the Jews' legal status was provisionally postponed. The subsequent modification of secular Jewry-law then drew advantage from the new papal legislation. On the well-prepared legal soil of Germany the theological conception of *servitus Judeorum*, canonized by incorporation in the papal code, could win influence on the legislative formulation of the *servitus camerae* in 1236. And in 1237 the whole theologic-historical trend of thought was taken over into an imperial privilege. This "reception" is to be regarded less as an institutional process than as a spiritualized process of adaptation to and equalization with the orientation of canon law.

If any doubt should still be left concerning the source of the justification for the office-holding prohibition in Frederick II's Vienna privilege, it would be dispelled by the fact that not only this one but also another reason had been advanced: avoidance of the oppression of Christians by Jewish officeholders, *ne sub pretextu prefecture opprimant Christianos*. The formulation of the latter motivation can derive only from canon law and cannot have been borrowed—a notion that might still be entertained—from the Justinian Code.[76]

Finally, one can also dispose of a last possible objection. The question could be raised: How was it that precisely Frederick II took over from Gregory's code theologic and canon-law ideas of

far-reaching importance and incorporated them in the secular law
—he who, almost throughout his entire reign, was engaged in the
most embittered warfare against the pope? The answer is simple.
The emperor warred against the wearer of the tiara, not against
the church and her institutions. In his battle with Gregory,
Frederick emphasized that again and again.[77] The admission of
theological ideas and principles of canon law into the imperial
legislation in a politically important border region between the
secular and the ecclesiastical powers was without doubt a saga-
ciously conceived fighting instrument of the emperor's policy; for
in this way he brought home to his contemporaries most impressively that his battle was not aimed at the church and her principles but was directed solely against a personal enemy. Moreover, the ecclesiastical idea was refashioned in an imperial sense.
In the Vienna privilege the imperial authority was quietly pos-
ited solely and exclusively in place of the *Christiani* and the
merely mediating *Christiani principes*.

IV. Eike von Repgow's View of Royal
Jewry Protection[78]

Before continuing to trace the far-reaching influence of the
theological doctrine and canon-law legislation on the development of secular law, we must return for a moment to the *Sachsenspiegel* which, as stated, knows still nothing of chamber serfdom. This fact seems scarcely explicable on any ground other
than that in Eike von Repgow's lifetime the legal concept of
chamber serfdom had not yet acquired definite form.[79] It is not
difficult to divine what attitude the author of the *Sachsenspiegel*
would have taken toward this legal institution if it had entered
the practical sphere in his day or if he had been acquainted with
the fundamentals of its legal nature. Undoubtedly, he would
have rejected it. In his opinion any type of servitude contradicted
the concept of the divine nature of law and was thus basically
unrighteous and therefore illegal.[80] "In truth, serfdom has its
origin in compulsion and captivity and unrighteous force, which
in olden times was regarded as unlawful custom and now wants
to be held for law" (Ssp., III, 42, 6). Thus Eike expressly refused
to place the origin of servitude on a justifiable legal foundation.

The protagonist of law and justice, who even had found impressive words of condemnation for the crusaders' atrocities perpetrated on the Jews,[81] was not blind to the peculiarity of the actual status of the Jews and their complete dependence upon the possessors of power. He presented his historical interpretation of the subject in *Sachsenspiegel*, III, 7, 3: "Should a Christian slay a Jew or commit a crime against him, he shall be judged because of the king's peace which he has broken on him. It was Josephus who gained this peace for them from King Vespasian after having cured his son of the gout."

This passage, which must be studied in connection with the regulation in *Sachsenspiegel*, II, 66, 1, previously discussed, on the inclusion of the Jews in the king's peace, presents an explanation of the genesis of the royal prerogative of Jewry protection as well as of the legal status of the Jews. Their legal security rested, according to the *Sachsenspiegel*, upon the king's Jewry protection. Both the king's overlordship and the rights of the Jews originated in Roman times. After the conquest and destruction of Jerusalem, the surviving Jews became slaves of Emperor Vespasian, finally losing all their rights. Nevertheless, Vespasian showed them his favor and granted them legal protection. This was a reward for the medical skill of Flavius Josephus, who had cured the imperial prince Titus of the gout. The former was supposed to have benefited his coreligionists by extracting this concession from the grateful emperor. Therefore—this is the inference to be drawn—the German kings, who considered themselves the successors of the Roman emperors, continued to favor the Jews and protect their rights. In this conception, referring back to the Roman victory over the Jews, as bold as it is ingenious, the author of the *Sachsenspiegel* saw the cause for the Jews' particular legal position.

From the *Sachsenspiegel* this so-called "Josephus passage" was taken over unaltered into the more recent lawbook, the *Deutschenspiegel* (F 208, 3), and in a different version, into the *Schwabenspiegel* (L 260; W 214; G 214, 2, 3). The problem of the historical origin of this tale has only lately been cleared up. In the last analysis Eike's historical construction, most probably, originates in the rabbinical legend of Vespasian's having been

healed by Rabban Johanan ben Zakkai (first century of the
Christian era), reported in the Talmud, *Gittin*, 56a–b. The tale
of Josephus' healing arts and Titus' gout is found in the so-called
Historia Miscella of Landolfus Sagax (*ca.* 1000). The same story,
with full details, occurs also in Jacobus de Voragine's *Legenda
Aurea* (composed between 1263 and 1273), one of the most famous
hagiographical works of the Middle Ages, and in a Copenhagen
fifteenth-century manuscript collection of early legends. Both
Landolfus and Jacobus de Voragine took it probably from one of
the later versions of the *Vindicta Salvatoris*, a widely known cycle
of apocryphal stories dealing with the expiation of Christ's
crucifixion, composed before the end of the tenth century. Eike
von Repgow very likely drew the Josephus story from one or two
intermediary sources.[82]

So much for the source and history of the Josephus passage.
What is of primary concern here, however, is the political bearing of the tale, and the significance for legal history of the theory
of royal Jewry protection presented in the *Sachsenspiegel;* for with
Eike von Repgow begins a new chapter in the history of the
ancient legend.

According to the *Sachsenspiegel*, Josephus interceded with Vespasian on behalf of his fellow-believers, the survivors of the destruction of the second Temple, and succeeded in obtaining their
inclusion in the king's peace. Thus a legend originally entirely
untendentious is made the basis of a historical argument. What,
then, was the purpose underlying the insertion of the Josephus
legend into the Saxon lawbook? According to older as well as recent research, it was to present a secular justification of the emperor's claims over the Jews in the competition between secular
and ecclesiastical authority during the twelfth and thirteenth
centuries.[83]

To answer the question properly, one must take into consideration Eike's general attitude to the problem of the relationship
between emperor and church. It was in this period that the
struggle for supremacy between emperor and church reached its
climax and was carried on by both sides with a deep sense for its
historical implications. In this conflict of opposing opinions,
however, one must not look for Eike in either the imperial or the

church camp, in so far as these represent political-partisan op-
positions.[84] In his lawbook he takes sides neither for nor against
the pope, neither for nor against the emperor. Characteristic of
the way in which he viewed the relation between the secular and
ecclesiastical powers is his formulation of the two-swords doctrine, which he put at the head of the *Sachsenspiegel* (I, 1). The
spiritual power should help the secular power when such help is
needed, and vice versa.[85] In a word: Eike is always "more jurist
than politician." Now it would certainly not be compatible with
this characteristic of Eike, long since scientifically established,
to assume that "the Josephus legend recorded in the *Sachsenspiegel* had to fulfill the function of a *secular* justification by which
the emperor became independent of the church in this particular
matter" (namely, in his prerogative of Jewry protection). No
plausible reason is discernible which could have necessitated, in
those days, such an advocacy against the church of an imperial
right which had been exercised on German soil from Carolingian
times.[86] More truly, Eike aimed at no more than presenting a
legal-historical explanation of the emperor's overlordship over
the Jews and their claims to rights and legal protection.[87] This is
the only reason why he refers to the Roman emperor (characteristically he calls him *king* Vespasian)[88] whose historical and
legitimate successor, the German *king*, granted to the Jews the
protection of his peace, just as, long before, his Roman predecessor had done after the conquest of Jerusalem. Thus the historical
continuity was established. In a similar manner Eike, in the
Textus Prologi to the *Sachsenspiegel*, referred to the Emperors Constantine and Charlemagne as the great lawgivers. It is common
knowledge that in the Middle Ages the German kings regarded
themselves as rightful successors of the Roman imperators, that
the medieval empire was considered the continuation of the Roman, and that imperial laws—particularly in the reign of Frederick II—were incorporated as *Authenticae* in Justinian's *Corpus
juris*.[89] Eike von Repgow was not only a learned theologian and
great jurist but also a historian of rank (he composed the *Saxon
World Chronicle*, the first universal history in the German language). If, then, for the historical elucidation of the imperial
law of Jewry protection he makes use in his lawbook of a current

contemporary political conception, which in the course of time became an established dogma, this does not by any means reveal antichurch partisanship in favor of the emperor. Rather does the *Sachsenspiegel*, in regard to the contemporary juridical-political theory, prove to be what its author meant it to be: a mirror of the law of his day. Accordingly, Eike's explanation of the imperial law of Jewry protection can be regarded only as a purely secular forerunner of Frederick's conception of chamber serfdom. Eike himself, however, must not be considered an imperial partisan standing against the church. His theory has nothing to do with the theological doctrine of *servitus Judeorum*.

The same conclusion must be drawn from yet another consideration. The church, for theological reasons, was prompted to plead for the *preservation* (not protection) of the Jews, but in a state of serfdom. Secular law, in Eike's times, however, was not in accord with this conception. Therefore, the latter could not find expression in the *Sachsenspiegel*, which, like the lawbooks of the Middle Ages in general, treats only of the law of freemen.[90] There is no doubt that the Jews also are considered freemen in the judgment of the lawbook; for they were classed in the land peaces of 1221 and 1224 and consequently also in the *Sachsenspiegel* with groups lacking neither freedom nor general legal capacity, and they were even mentioned along with the "masters of Christendom," the priests (Ssp., II, 66, 2). This interpretation alone renders the introduction of the Josephus legend intelligible. It would lose its meaning if one were to assume that inclusion in the king's peace did not mean annulment of serfdom but only protection in case of violence.[91] Such an interpretation is in direct conflict with the whole spirit of the Jewry-law of the *Sachsenspiegel* and, more particularly, in manifest contradiction to Eike's emphatically expounded doctrine of the illegality of every species of unfreedom, "which originated from capture, captivity, and the unrighteous exercise of power."

In this rejection of unfreedom as a basis of law (cf. Ssp., II, 7; III, 41, 1) there also lies the explanation of why the myth of the sale of the Jews surviving the subjugation of Jerusalem, which in later lawbooks like the *Schwabenspiegel* (L 260; G 214, 3) came to be cited as historical justification of chamber serfdom, gained no admittance into the *Sachsenspiegel* or the *Deutschenspiegel*. Yet this narrative, which ultimately goes back to the account of Flavius Josephus in his *Bellum Judaicum*,[92] was not only known to Eike in its original nontendentious version but was even reproduced in chapter 44 of his second great work, the *Saxon World Chronicle (ca.* 1230), where he also tells of Josephus' imprisonment, his prophesying to Vespasian and being set free, and, indeed, explicitly names Josephus and Hegesippus as his authorities.[93] In the *Sachsenspiegel* there was no room for this legend. First of all, there was no occasion for a legal justification of chamber serfdom, since this concept was not yet in existence. Furthermore, Eike proceeded from different tendencies in his lawbook and his world chronicle. In the latter he described the course of world history, of transient events, as they had actually taken place, seen in the light of the state of knowledge at that time. In his lawbook, on the other hand, Eike treated of what endures, of the universally valid, which may, indeed, be obscured temporarily by actuality but whose claim to validity cannot be permanently eliminated.[94] To Eike, the historian and good Christian, the sale of the Jews after the fall of Jerusalem "thirty for one penny, as they had sold Christ for thirty pennies," was a historical fact that had its proper place in his world chronicle. For Eike, the protagonist of the loftiest ideals in the law, on the other hand, it was impossible to acknowledge a state of slavery issuing from capture in war as a lawful status and to declare it, on the basis of the law of retaliation clearly reflected in that story,[95] as law continuing in force.[96] Therefore, for this reason, too, the myth of the sale of the Jews found no place in the *Sachsenspiegel.*

The Josephus legend had no purpose other than to explain historically and to found juridically the existing state of the law, the royal overlordship over the Jews and their legal status. That this could not be done in the light of the historical-theological doctrine of *servitus Judeorum* but only in the light of the biblical-philosophic conception of man created in the image of God—in Eike's view the ultimate and profoundest reason for men's freedom—was a matter of course to the author of the *Sachsenspiegel.* In his *Sachsenspiegel* (III, 42) he himself demonstrated, with impressive reasoning and profound interpretation of the Bible, that on this point there was no antithesis between secular and divine law.[97]

This is the real importance and the fundamental cause of the introduction of the Josephus legend into the *Sachsenspiegel*. Its Josephus passage mirrors, indeed, the conception of the greatest medieval German jurist and theoretician of law of the legal status of the Jews in his day.

V. FROM THE *Sachsenspiegel* TO THE *Schwabenspiegel*

The history of ideas is largely dependent on source history. It is not often that the state of medieval sources permits tracing chronologically and step by step the progress and propagation of an idea that has proved determinative in legal theory and practical lawmaking. One such happy exception is the history of the doctrine of *servitus Judeorum* in Germany from the middle to the end of the thirteenth century. A rare favor of fortune has preserved a number of documents from which especially the influence of the theological and canon-law doctrine on the political formation and the juridical support of chamber serfdom can be clearly perceived, up to the point of the mutual conjunction of the two trends of thought. The decisive stages of the development fall within the half-century between the composition of the *Sachsenspiegel* (1221–24), to which chamber serfdom and *servitus Judeorum* are equally unknown, and of the *Schwabenspiegel* (ca. 1275), in which the theological tenets and the juridical doctrines inseparably interpenetrate. That this synthesis of ideas was one of the greatest and, for the political fortunes of the Jews, most fateful achievements of Christian theology in the Middle Ages, is obvious.

How the theological doctrine was fitted into the frame of the contemporary juridical ideas and how the latter were employed for reinforcing the former is best shown in the development of the textual transmission of Eike's *Saxon World Chronicle* (*Sächsische Weltchronik*).

Whereas formerly all versions of this work were supposed to be by one and the same author,[98] it is now securely established that each of the three is by a different hand and that A must be given

priority in age over B and C.[99] In version A of the *World Chronicle*
(*ca.* 1230–31) the story of the sale of the Jews after the fall of
Jerusalem, "thirty for a penny, as they sold Christ for thirty
pennies"—not contained in the *Sachsenspiegel*—is related, on the
authority of Josephus and Hegesippus, still without ulterior
tendency, merely as a fact of history (chap. 44).[100] Just as Eike
was impartial as a jurist, so as a historian he related the facts only
as they presented themselves to him, "with restrained objectivity." No conflict with the Jewry-law of the *Sachsenspiegel* is
encountered in the original of the *World Chronicle*. This character
of the historical account of the sale of the Jews is in no way altered in the B recension (chap. 46), which already shows additions and interpolations by its redactor. In this connection, it is
worth noting that this version was composed in 1237, the very
year in which Frederick II in his privilege to the city of Vienna
had appropriated the doctrine of *servitus Judeorum* in its full scope.
The practical consequences flowing from chamber serfdom, promulgated by the emperor as early as 1236 and reaffirmed in
1238,[101] are thrown into relief by the tax register of German cities
in 1241, where the first instance of a regular imperial tax levied
on the Jews is encountered.[102] About the same time, however,
there is Berthold of Regensburg (1210–72), who in his sermons,
on the one hand, still wholly adheres to the purely theological
point of view of the Jews' predestination to the *testimonium veritatis* and, on the other hand, follows in Eike's footsteps when he
pleads for protection of the Jews, "because the emperors have
admitted them to their peace."[103]

The first occurrence of different ways of thinking within historical literature is found in version C of the *Saxon World Chronicle*, which was composed at Lüneburg between 1237 and 1251.
It probably had a cleric for its compiler. He provided Eike's
work with extensive interpolations and, in particular, worked in
many legends. One of the additions bears on the religious history
of the Jews, another on the history of their legal status. The first
group of interpolations (chap. 81) refers to the well-known disputation under Pope Sylvester I[104] and here calls for no more than
brief mention; it is symptomatic of the author's attitude toward
the Jews. This reveals itself once more with complete clearness in

the second group of interpolations, in connection with the story of the sale of the Jews after the destruction of Jerusalem. In the C version (chap. 44), namely, Eike's traditional "historical" account[105] undergoes a tendentious interpretation. Through recourse to the juridical views of medieval Germany, the enslavement of the Jews by the Roman conqueror is brought into relation with the Jews' legal status in the thirteenth century.

In [den juden] wart verdelt echt unde recht, erve unde eigen, dat se oc eigen scolden wesen immer mer. Sus wrach godes viant godes anden.

"[By a sentence of outlawry] they [the Jews] were deprived of status and rights, of hereditary possessions and property, so that they also should be bondsmen henceforth. Thus the enemies of God suffered for the offense against God."

The interpolator here endeavors to account for the condition of complete rightlessness of the Jews subsequent to the destruction of Jerusalem and for the enslavement of the survivors in accordance with the legal conceptions current in his own time, when complete rightlessness could be lawfully brought about only by a sentence of outlawry, namely, pronouncement of the ban. He assumes, therefore, that those historical events had led to the sentence of permanent outlawry (*Oberacht*) being passed on the Jews, whereby they were deprived of all personal rights and all property. This was the genesis of their servitude: it had begun with the fall of Jerusalem and was to endure forever. "Thus the enemies of God suffered for the offense against God." The idea of retaliation is employed twice: first, in the sale into slavery and, second, in the eternal perpetuation of the enslavement.

The compiler of version C gleaned the material for his additions to the *Saxon World Chronicle* from a number of different sources. He no longer refers to Josephus and Hegesippus for authentication of the story of the sale of the Jews, as version A had done. Its wording in C points to the tradition of the Fathers of the church.[106] There is but a slight possibility that the tendentious amplifications were derived from the *Annales Palidenses* (–1182; composed in the second half of the twelfth century).[107] Who was the actual originator of the conception that the political dependence of the Jews about the middle of the thirteenth century has its root in the sale of the Jewish captives after the

destruction of Jerusalem and the application of the law of retaliation, is a question which apparently will have to be left un-
answered. Whether it was the Lüneburg ecclesiastic himself, the
redactor of C—readily conceivable, for all the additions in C betray the clerical touch—or someone in the unidentified sources
from which the Lüneburg cleric borrowed, the outstanding fact
remains that in the field of secular literature it has been version
C of Eike's *World Chronicle* which brought into relation the
theological doctrine of *servitus Judeorum* with the political and
legal dependence of German Jewry and even gave a strictly juridical exposition of the theological thesis.

Just as the *Sachsenspiegel* was an epoch-making lawbook, so
likewise was the *Saxon World Chronicle* an epoch-making historical book. Its great importance and influence in the thirteenth
century can be recognized from its wide dissemination, as well as
from the fact that it was brought up to date several times
through medieval continuations. Best of all, however, its importance is illustrated probably by the different revisions it underwent in the course of time, from the angle of different political
tendencies. Hence its influence on the theoretical views regarding
the legal position of the Jews in Germany must not be under-
rated. It should be borne in mind, of course, that theology, too,
in its old track, continued vigorously at work in this direction
and that the steady advance of Roman law produced the same
trend. Thus secular legislation as well as legal literature was directed unequivocally into a course the development of which
moved ahead consistently.

An isolated regressive exception is represented by the land-
peace confederations of Rhenish cities—particularly the *Con-
federatio pacis Rhenana* of 1254—which, on the subject of Jewry
protection, resort again to the old model of land-peace legislation. The use of this law-form, due to the political emergency,
naturally left no room for the conception of chamber serfdom.[108]
How far the latter, however, jointly with the theory of *servitus Judeorum*, was making headway everywhere, may be seen
from the peace confederation formed under the lead of the archbishop of Mainz in 1265 between ecclesiastic and secular princes
and cities in the region of the Rhine, Main, and Lahn.[109] True,

it also makes use of the form of the land peace, whose protection is explicitly extended to the Jews; but their unqualified inclusion here is no longer in the old manner. The peace is to serve "omnibus hominibus secundum jus et conditionem ac consuetudinem necnon honorem cuilibet debitum et antiquitus observatum, immo eciam et Judeis." The explanation of why the Jews were included in the circle of persons to be protected runs as follows:

Since lawless folk in the cities—without obedience[110] to the Lord as a reminder of Whose passion the church tolerates the Jews, and without deference to the empire to whose chamber, as well known, they pertain —are prone to create disorder and to insult them, sometimes even inhumanly and pitifully slay them, it is ordained that whoever in such manner transgresses against Jews shall be punishable as one having broken the public peace.

With regard to legal history, this provision is most interesting because all the motives behind the Jewry protection of the thirteenth century are clearly discernible in it. First of all, one is struck by the diminution of honor. Unlike previously, the Jews are not simply put on one level with the persons who by right, condition, custom, and honor are traditionally entitled to claim protection but "even the very Jews" are taken under the peace protection ("*immo eciam et Judeis*"). Two legal grounds are set forth equivalently for the grant of Jewry protection: the ecclesiastical theory and the doctrine in imperial law of chamber serfdom, a juridical argument unique in the history of land-peace legislation; and, as if to bring out the contrast between the prevailing state and the legal ideal aimed at by the land peace, there is added: "Et ne . . . discordia oriatur, sed quilibet prelatus, clericus, nobilis, miles, mercator, burgensis, ruris cultor et judeus gaudeat suo jure pariter et honore. . . ."

It is a belated revival of the old endeavor to incorporate Jewry protection in the frame of the public penal law. In 1265 such an attempt was doomed to futility. This becomes readily intelligible on consideration of the circumstance that the old land-peace law of the twelfth century assumed the equality of the Jews with the other protected classes, their mutual freedom and equal treatment, whereas by the middle of the thirteenth century the doctrines of *servitus Judeorum* and chamber serfdom were making marked headway. The future belonged not to the equality of rights but to the chamber serfdom of the Jews.

An important milestone in this development is represented by the southern German lawbook, the *Schwabenspiegel*. At the time that it was composed (*ca.* 1275) chamber serfdom of the Jews was already manifestly a fully developed legal institution, in concept and validity simply taken for granted (L 260; G 214, 3). In order to do full justice to the treatment which the problem received in that lawbook, it should be borne in mind that the author of the *Schwabenspiegel* was an ecclesiastic of markedly papal orientation. This comes clearly to light at the very opening of his *Spiegel* in the curialistic presentation of the doctrine of the two swords. The author utilized German law as well as Roman and canon-law sources and also drew on medieval literature, particularly the sermons of Berthold of Regensburg and the writings of David of Augsburg. By this fact alone his attitude toward the Jews is unambiguously established. Of Eike's sense of justice there is no trace in him. On the whole, the *Schwabenspiegel* is a diffuse, uncritical compilation by a man not profoundly versed in the theory and philosophy of law. This characteristic is shown particularly in the treatment of the problem under discussion.

Like Eike in the *Sachsenspiegel*, the author of the *Schwabenspiegel* also seeks to explain historically the peculiarity of the Jews' legal status and their rights and privileges. But his attitude, unlike that of his greater predecessor, is not purely theoretical and scholarly and hence objective, but narrowly political and partisan and hence outspokenly anti-Jewish. The *Sachsenspiegel*'s Jewry-law regulations are augmented, accordingly, by the addition of numerous others deriving from canon law and thus unfavorable to the Jews. The *Schwabenspiegel* does, indeed, still recognize the protection of the Jews by the king's peace (L 260; G 214, 3, 5). Its author, however, no longer sees in the king's peace the source of the freedom and rights of the Jews—which had been Eike's view—but merely the historical cause for tolerating and protecting them in a state of servitude. In as far as he finds the Jews to have any rights (*gnaden und rechte*), such "favors and rights" appear to him as resulting from acts of grace or from encroachments by the Roman kings, the former not being in accord with canon law. In one place (L 261; G 214, 7) he states explicitly that "the kings have given them in contravention of law": "das hânt in die künige gegeben *wider recht.*"

In the *Schwabenspiegel*, chamber serfdom figures as a recognized legal institution. This is, of course, in direct contradiction to Eike's teaching of the unlawfulness of servitude (Ssp., III, 42, 3–6), which passage is completely incorporated in the southern German lawbook (Schwsp., L 308; G 256, 4–7). But the Franciscan friar of Augsburg has a way of easily brushing aside whatever scruples may arise from that contradiction. He takes his stand on the existing facts and, in order to arrive at recognition of the servitude as a general legal institution, states summarily (L 68, 308; G 57, 2): "We know from Holy Writ that no one ought to be in bond. Yet such has come to pass by violence and coercion, so that it is lawful now that there are bondmen."[111]

Besides, the *Schwabenspiegel* finds yet another historical-theological reason for the chamber serfdom of the Jews, namely, the sale of the captive Jews after the conquest of Jerusalem. But here, too, the author of the southern German lawbook puts things aright very simply. Without looking for any juridical justification that would conform to the contemporary point of view in matters of law (as was still done in version C of the *Saxon World Chronicle*), he traces the origin of chamber serfdom to the circumstance that, as he says, Titus had assigned the surviving Jews to the chamber of the Roman king as bondmen, whereby the Roman king at the same time had become protector of the Jews.

It was the Roman kings who gave the Jews this right. Whatever favors and rights are in possession of the Jews were gained for them by Josephus from King Titus. This occurred at the time of the conquest of Jerusalem. Josephus then provided food for the surviving Jews. Three times eighty thousand Jews were besieged in Jerusalem, of whom one third died of starvation, another was killed and the last third was fed by Josephus. These were offered for sale, and were sold, thirty for one bad penny. They were given by King Titus to the chamber of the Roman kings as servants, and therefore they shall be servants of the Empire and the Roman king shall protect them [Schwsp., L 260; G 214, 3].[112]

The ecclesiastical author of the *Schwabenspiegel* contented himself with that historical exposition. He did not even find it necessary to insert a reference to the theological interpretation resting on the idea of retaliation, as set forth in the C version of the *Saxon World Chronicle* and the approximately contemporary *Legenda Aurea* (*ca.* 1263–73) by Jacobus de Voragine.[113] Yet the clerical profession of the author of the *Schwabenspiegel* and his familiarity with the writings on theology and canon law of his time exclude the possibility that the theological conception, which also represented the official teaching of the church, could have been unknown to him.

Since in the view of the *Schwabenspiegel* the Jews are not freemen but bondmen—*eigen, des riches knechte*—there was *per se* no room in the southern German lawbook for Eike's Josephus legend. It is, in fact, absent from the passage corresponding to *Sachsenspiegel*, III, 7, 3, namely, *Schwabenspiegel*, L 260; G 214, 5, which is differently composed. But its author did not want to relinquish the Josephus passage after all. So he summarily divested it of its true meaning and its connection with the king's peace. Only to prevent its dropping into the void, it was made to do duty for a historical explanation of certain preferences accorded to the Jews in the medieval law of evidence (L 260–61; G 214, 2, [5], 6, 7). This meant, in fact, destroying such historical context as had been reached by literary tradition.[114] The theological doctrine of *servitus Judeorum* had established itself in the domain of secular law and had become an important support of chamber serfdom in theory and practice, as shown, for instance, by the approximately contemporary utterances of Thomas Aquinas (1226–74).[115]

Within the domain of imperial law, the concept and legal content of chamber serfdom were laid down exactly in Emperor Rudolph I's mandate of 1286 concerning the confiscation of the possessions of fugitive Jews.[116] Here the secular conception of chamber serfdom in its final form found definite and clear expression. There was no longer any need of appending a historical-theological expository argument, as there had been in the time of Frederick II.

It is all the more interesting and instructive, then, that, until even the end of the fourteenth century, legal doctrine in its attitude toward the problem of the Jews' legal status did not abandon historical-theological arguments. The fate of the Josephus legend mirrors the course of development. Through the victorious advance of the idea of *servitus Judeorum* and the practical organization of chamber serfdom as an established legal institution, Eike's interpretation of the Josephus legend had lost its meaning. It is logical, therefore, and evidence of the juristic acumen of their authors, that the Meissen and the Prague lawbooks of the fourteenth century, which reproduced *Sachsenspiegel*, III, 7, 3, omitted the Josephus legend.[117] Other German jurists of the thirteenth and fourteenth centuries were not so circumspect or understanding. The *Weichbild-Vulgata*, adopting in its article 177 the relevant passage of the *Sachsenspiegel*, carried with it also the unaltered Josephus legend.[118] Others again were even more inconsistent, inasmuch as they took over textually the *Sachsenspiegel*'s Jewry-law inclusive of the Josephus legend, yet added, more or less circumstantially, the theological doctrine of *servitus Judeorum*, thus showing that they had lost all understanding of Eike's conception. That is the procedure of the Dutch *Sachsenspiegel* in articles 16 and 65. It points out that "God has scattered the Jews unto all the ends of the world, to give testimony of their ancient sins."[119] The *Berliner Stadtbuch* of 1397 enlarges on the Jewry-law of the *Sachsenspiegel*, textually carried over, including the Josephus legend, in an introductory article designed to set forth a circumstantial theological explanation of why the Jews were tolerated at all in Christendom.[120]

While legal theory in its treatment of the status of the Jews could not free itself of juridical hesitation, the practical procedure of the state, rigorously and with inexorable logic, had, by the middle of the fourteenth century, already carried chamber serfdom to the final stage of its development. Early in 1342 Emperor Louis the Bavarian decreed that "every Jew and every Jewess who is a widow, and those who are twelve years of age and worth twenty florins, each and every one shall give annually a florin as tribute on their bodies, which shall then accrue to the Empire against its expenses, and in return for which he [the emperor] will all the better protect the Jews."[121] This so-called *guldin pfenning* ("gold penny") is the first regular imperial poll tax imposed on the Jews in the Middle Ages.[122] "Whoever pays tribute on his person, be it to the emperor, the territorial ruler, or a private protector, is no longer completely free'' (Stobbe). In a request for legal instruction submitted to the jury court of Magdeburg late in the fourteenth or some time in the fifteenth century, the then current opinion of the Jews' legal and actual status is thus reflected: "As subjects of the princes, Jews enjoy no rights except those bestowed on them by the princes.''[123]

That by this time chamber serfdom meant personal unfreedom is beyond doubt. The fate of the Jews had touched nadir. Slowly and consistently their legal status had been transmuted from the freedom of the Carolingian period to overt bondage. The circumstance that in the course of the following centuries the designation *guldin pfenning* was altered into body tax or Jewry protection tax signified no essential difference in the juridical conception. It was only the victory of the ideal of liberty in the nineteenth century that turned the Jewish chamber serf into a free citizen.

PART III

Specific Jewry-Law and Its Application

CHAPTER SEVEN

Jews under Magdeburg Jury-
Court Jurisdiction

I. Introductory Remarks

THE lawbooks, as the earliest "scholarly" treatises on medieval German law, proved the most authentic sources for
obtaining a true picture of the basic ideas and theoretical foundations of the Jewish status and, generally, of Jewry-law in the
Middle Ages. The legal-historical evolution of these basic ideas
as presented in Parts I and II must now be checked against, and
supplemented by, another important aspect of the problem under
consideration: the specific application of Jewry-law in judicial
practice.

Did the principles set forth in the lawbooks by the experts in
law of medieval times find expression in the practice of the courts?
Was the reality of law in conformity with the norms of law?
As German juridical language puts it so well: "Entsprach die
Rechtswirklichkeit der Normwirklichkeit?" What was the ac-
tual treatment at law accorded to the Jews in the numerous
"supreme-court" decisions handed down during the Middle
Ages?

These are the problems, not yet touched by research, to be
studied in detail in Part III of the present work. The proper answers to the many questions arising in the diverse fields of law—
penal, civil, procedural, and administrative—must be derived
from the court decisions or case material, which, in turn, require careful comparison with the principles of law laid down in
the pertinent regulations, often very detailed, of the lawbooks.

The function and significance of the "supreme court," the
Magdeburg jury court, in medieval Germany, and of the "su-

perior courts" of Halle, Leipzig, and Dohna, flourishing at different periods, as well as the reach of their jurisdiction extending over wide territories inside and outside Germany have been outlined in Part I. Hence the discussion can turn immediately to the individual problems involved.

II. Jews under Jewish Courts

In the Middle Ages the Jews were, for the most part, inhabitants of the cities. Hence, in general, they were subject in their relations with non-Jews to municipal laws and statutes, unless they were favored by exemptions or endowed with privileges of an individual or collective character establishing special regulations for them.

As is well known, Jewish law and Jewish courts were permitted and even explicitly recognized as authoritative instruments for regulating internal legal relations among the Jews. According to the principles of medieval Jewish law, the jurisdiction of these Jewish courts was both compulsory and exclusive for Jewish litigants.[1] It was at a synod at Troyes, about 1150, that Rabbi Jacob ben Meir Tam (1100–1171) and other rabbinic authorities, with the assent of a large group of northern French and possibly western German rabbis, decreed, under the penalty of excommunication (herem), "that no man or woman, related or unrelated, may bring a fellow-Jew before Gentile courts or exert compulsion on him through Gentiles, be they prince or common man, superior or lower official, except by mutual agreement made in the presence of proper witnesses."[2] After the issuance of Rabbenu Gershom's (960–1028) Takkanah against polygamy, this was probably the only rabbinical ordinance that was universally accepted by all Jewish communities throughout France, Germany, and elsewhere. This ban covered even a declaration of intention to bring suit against a fellow-Jew before a non-Jewish court. The prohibition of recourse to secular (Christian) courts by Jewish litigants was re-emphasized by the German rabbinical synods of the thirteenth century.[3]

The efforts of medieval rabbis to keep litigations between Jewish parties before Jewish tribunals were motivated by religious reasons, by the fear of injustice from non-Jewish courts,[4]

and by the desire to strengthen Jewish judicial power and autonomy. This attitude "reaffirmed the eternity and inviolability of
the divinely instituted Jewish law and, hence, the sovereignty of
the Jewish community." It was therefore logical as well as liberal for the rabbis to permit Jewish litigants to bring their lawsuits before non-Jewish courts only upon mutual agreement.

This explains why the medieval court decisions under consideration include none dealing with a litigation to which both
parties were Jews. There is, in fact, not a single instance of a
Jew's bringing suit against a fellow-Jew in a non-Jewish court,
not even as the result of mutual agreement or of a Jewish defendant's refusing to appear before a Jewish court.[5]

Some of the thousands of medieval court decisions handed
down to posterity deal with litigations involving Jews. In every
one of these cases, however, one party, either plaintiff or defendant, is non-Jewish.

III. Jews before Non-Jewish Courts

In the medieval system of procedural law the right of Jews to
submit their litigations for decision to non-Jewish courts represents nothing unusual. That right is explicitly recognized in the
Regulae juris (J 169): "Jews may lay complaints and defend
themselves according to Magdeburg law." Such cases are reported in the sources.[6] Jews were also entitled to bring a lawsuit
before a superior court by way of appeal; *Freisinger Rechtsbuch*
(Knapp, 263): "If a sentence is pronounced in court upon a Jew,
he may well appeal it, be it that he has a *volchman* or not."

On the medieval principle that the defendant's residence is decisive for the competence of the court,[7] the Jewish court claimed
and sometimes had exclusive jurisdiction, namely, in cases in
which the defendants were Jews. This was clearly recognized and
pointed out in the pertinent regulations of several medieval German lawbooks. Hence it could happen that a Christian plaintiff
was compelled to seek justice against a Jew before the latter's
own court, which had jurisdiction even over a Christian. "When
a Christian lays a complaint against a Jew, the Jew betakes himself before his [own] judge to reply [to it]; likewise does the Jew
[in a complaint] against a Christian."[8] This principle, however,

did not remain uncontested in medieval court practice. As early as the fourteenth century the *Scheppin* ("jurors") of Magdeburg issued an authoritative, restrictive interpretation:

> . . . furthermore, you ask us: when a Christian has a complaint against a Jew, whether he [the Jew] should respond before *gehegter bank* [duly inaugurated session of the Christian court], the Jews saying that they are to answer nowhere except before their *schule;* and what the law is thereon.
>
> Thereupon we *scheppin* of Magdeburg pass judgment: If a Christian accuses a Jew *vor gehegten dinge*, the Jew must respond to the accusation as a Christian would have to do, confess or deny. If he makes denial, he shall be directed to take an oath before his *schule*. . . .[9]

Thus Jews were declared obligated to respond to a charge by Christians in a Christian court just as Christians were bound to do. Only when they had to take an oath, such oath was to be taken at their *schule*. This is why Caspar Popplaw, the author of the Breslau lawbooks, *Der Rechte Weg* and *Remissorium*, expressed doubts in recording that rule, while the Jews naturally persisted in demanding its recognition and application. But, while the judicial interpretation mentioned offered no argument, the Magdeburg jury court reasoned in another decision that "Jews who seek justice in your court, must [also] respond there, if they are lawfully required to do so."[10]

IV. Jews and the *Oberhof* of Magdeburg

All this, however, does not apply directly to the immediate jurisdiction of the Magdeburg jury court or the other superior courts in Saxon territory. They were not courts of appeal in the modern meaning of the term, implying the general right of a formal appeal from the decision of a local court to a superior tribunal or supreme court. Instead, the *Oberhöfe* or "superior courts" were called upon to pass judgment or impart legal instruction solely in difficult or doubtful cases, not necessarily decided previously by a lower court. They were called upon not only when this seemed desirable to one or both of the litigants but particularly when the local-court authorities desired to seek legal information in order to relieve themselves of responsibility. Yet responsibility still remained with them, since they were not bound to accept and pronounce the requested decisions of the superior court as their own. However, hardly any deviation from a Magdeburg court decision is recorded in the history of this supreme tribunal in medieval Germany. Its pronouncements came into force similarly, when they were accepted by private applicants who had agreed to abide by its judgment.[11] By their juridical quality these judgments were, as a rule, raised to the level of precedents for future legal practice.[12]

Hence, it could easily happen—and, indeed, did happen—that cases involving a Jewish party came from local courts for decision before superior courts of Magdeburg law. In accordance with the general custom in resorting to superior courts—the so-called *Zug an den Oberhof*—this could be effected on the initiative either of the local court or of the non-Jewish litigant or upon mutual agreement between both litigating parties. In most of the cases the application for a Magdeburg jury-court decision was actually made in this way. The Magdeburg jurors, or *Schöffen*, in general, considered themselves "obligated to hand down a decision to anyone petitioning them for it."[13] Consequently, they also upheld this right in favor of Jews. In a specific case it had been contested in a local court, whereupon, as late as 1524, the *Schöffen* of Magdeburg decided: "By appealing to the higher court [of Magdeburg] against the illegality of the court-order, the Jew [Isaac] did not incur any fine or penalty."[14]

There is also indubitable evidence that Jews, like non-Jews, as private individuals, enjoyed and actually used the right of applying directly to the Magdeburg *Oberhof* for legal instruction or authoritative decision on a given law matter. Two such cases are recorded at the beginning of the fifteenth century, the applicant in both being a certain Margkart, an otherwise unrecorded Jew of Naumburg on the Saale River.[15] Margkart's claim for repayment of a loan made by him to a citizen of Naumburg had been refused by the latter's heirs. He thereupon turned to the jury court of Magdeburg, stated and explained his case in writing in the customary way, attached a copy of the promissory note in his possession, and asked for authoritative instruction: "Hirumb bethe ich uch, mich rechtes zcu berichtene." The *Schepphin zcu*

Magdeburg complied with his request, their reply opening with this clause:

> Unsern gruss zuvor. Margkard jode, du hast uns gefraget umbe recht in deszin wortin.

> "Greetings first. Jew Margkard, you have asked us to state the law, in these words."

The substance of the decision seems to have called for further explanation. Margkart once more turned to the Magdeburg jurors, addressing them as "Ersamen wyszen hern unde gunstigen vorderer" ("Honorable wise lords and gracious patrons"), referring to his previous application and their first legal instruction. The requested explanation, which was granted, began with this phrase:

> Unsern gruss zuvor. Wisse, jode, du fragest uns abir umbe recht in deszin worten.

> "Greetings first. Know, oh Jew, you again asked us to state the law in these words."

A third instance is recorded as late as the end of the fifteenth or the beginning of the sixteenth century. The Jew Abraham, living in the court district of Leitmeritz, submitted a hypothetical law case to the *Schöffen* of Magdeburg and asked for their legal opinion. It was sent to him through the mediation of the local *Oberhof* of Leitmeritz. The introductory clause read as follows: "Jew Abraham, as you have written to us . . . and asked us to state the law upon this application [*Schrift*], we, the jurors of Magdeburg, state the law upon this application which was sent to us."[16]

It is well known that the Magdeburg *Schepphen* placed such introductory clauses at the head of the original application, as a rule written on parchment. The text of the decision, usually much briefer than the application which included the *status causae et controversiae*, was then inscribed at the bottom of the document in the space provided by the applicant for this purpose.[17]

All told, there is no doubt that the applications to the Magdeburg jury court, as recorded in the decisions under consideration, represent the original wording of Margkart's and Abraham's petitions. Whether they were drawn up by these Jews personally

or by an adviser versed in legal practice remains an open question.[18] However, this much is sure: Jews as well as non-Jews enjoyed the right to apply to the Magdeburg jury court for legal
instruction or decision on a given law matter.

In all probability it is due only to the loss of a great number of
Magdeburg court decisions and to the impossibility of employing, at present, the complete manuscript material in existence
that not more documentary evidence can be adduced for that
fact. But it is clear from the decisions of superior courts administering Magdeburg law that, in addition to the cities known to
have had a Jewish population, Jews resided in places not heretofore known as harboring Jewish communities or individuals,
such as Guben, Schweidnitz, Sagan, Reichenbach, Zerbst, and
Naumburg. For this reason, too, it is safe to suppose that the
superior courts of Saxon law were called upon to decide more
cases affecting Jews living under their jurisdiction than are found
in the preserved documentary sources.[19]

As to the form and content of the applications for superior-
court decisions by Jews and of the legal instructions handed
down to them, no divergence from the standard type is generally
observable. Only the introductory clauses mentioned above reveal a deviation. The customary form runs:

Unseren fruntlichen gruss zuvor; besonders guten frunde; ir habt uns
umbe recht gefragit in sulchen worten.

"Friendly greetings first; very good friends; you have asked us to state
the law in these words."

In the opening salutation addressed to a Jew the attribute,
"friendly," *freundlich*, and the formula, "very good friends," are
missing. Moreover, the second person singular, *du*, is used to
address Jews, instead of *ir*, the second person plural, as in other
cases. It is an open question whether the use of the singular must
necessarily be interpreted as an expression of disesteem for
Jews[20] or whether this deviation from custom was only a social
and legal differentiation, perhaps generally applied, arising from
the applicant's status. It is worth noting that in the text of the
two first-mentioned decisions Jews as well as non-Jews are addressed in the second person plural—and this in spite of the fact
that the identity of the Jewish applicant must have been known

to the jurors both from his application and from the inclosed copy of the promissory note or other documents. Although in the beginning and first half of the fifteenth century the social position of the Jews in Germany was already considerably impaired, the Magdeburg court members did not allow themselves in their official pronouncements to refer to Jews in a derogatory manner. In a request for legal instruction, the local court of Eisleben once called the Jewish litigant involved an *unsaligen joden*, meaning an "unblessed, evil, or godless Jew." The Magdeburg *Oberhof*, however, in its decision spoke in a manner which was then appropriate and even dignified, merely of the "Jew Aaron."[21]

So far as can be thus determined from external forms or from recognizable principles in the administration of legal instructions or law decisions, no discriminatory treatment seems to have been meted out to Jewish applicants. Whereas in local courts, at times, Jewish litigants had to pay twice the usual fees,[22] no such discrimination seems to have been practiced at the *Oberhof* of Magdeburg. True, this is merely an *argumentum e silentio*, no positive evidence to the contrary being available. However, the sources would hardly have been silent had Jews been subjected to special treatment in the matter of court fees.

There are many more questions that might be asked with regard to the jurisdiction over Jews of the superior courts administering Magdeburg law. Unfortunately, in many respects the sources leave us in the dark. What is of greater importance, the administration of justice to Jewish litigants by the Magdeburg and other superior courts can be clarified, to a certain extent, for the different fields of law. Here, too, however, the sources do not offer information on all problems and questions which the legal historian would like to pose, specifically with regard to Jews. Hence the presentation to follow cannot extend systematically over all individual fields of law but must be confined to the subjects treated in the superior-court decisions. Although combined with and supplemented from the regulations of the lawbooks, it will nevertheless still remain somewhat fragmentary.

CHAPTER EIGHT

Penal Law[1]

I. PROTECTION OF JEWS

A. PROTECTION OF LIFE

THE limitation in quantity of source material at hand is only one reason for the fragmentary character of the following chapters on the legal status of the Jews in the diverse branches of Magdeburg law. Other reasons, of a qualitative nature, also make themselves felt at times. This fact becomes immediately apparent when one turns to the judicial activity of the Magdeburg *Oberhof* in the field of penal law.

From numerous Magdeburg *Schöffensprüche* it is well established that the infliction of capital punishment lay outside the jurisdiction of this high court. Since the jurors lacked the privilege of the "*Blutbann*," as a matter of principle they declined to pass judgment on crimes punishable by death and likewise, though on different grounds, on the kind and degree of criminal punishment.[2] Such decisions generally rested with the provincial or territorial rulers and local authorities, respectively. But the *Schöffen* of Magdeburg by no means renounced criminal jurisdiction altogether. Many *Schöffensprüche* offer ample evidence that they did not refuse legal instruction or decision on juridical problems of criminal procedure or of penal law connected with civil-law questions.

This legal situation had a particular bearing on the Jews. Their lives and possessions were under the special protection of the land-peace laws. The special relationship of the Jews to the emperor and to territorial rulers emphasizes strongly the exclusive jurisdiction of these princes in all cases of criminal offenses against Jews. It is therefore safe to assume that no such case was

179

ever brought before, or decided by, the *Oberhof* of Magdeburg. The Jews' protection in the domain of criminal law was tightly bound up with their status under public peace law.[3] Thus the Magdeburg Law Instruction for Görlitz of 1304 included in its paragraph 118, articles III, 7, 2, and 3 of the *Sachsenspiegel*, the latter referring expressly to the king's peace (II, 66, 1): "Should a Christian slay a Jew or commit a crime against him, he shall be judged because of the king's peace which he has broken against him."[4] "Jews are under the protection of the old imperial peace," is the formula recurring in all Saxon lawbooks, including *Abecedaria* and *Remissoria*, as late as the fifteenth century.[5] They refer unanimously to the pertinent article of the *Sachsenspiegel* (II, 66, 1), which had been borrowed from land-peace laws. Some of the lawbooks bolster the traditional theory of the king's peace extended to the Jews with quotations from Roman law, at that time gaining recognition among German lawyers.[6] Other lawbooks, such as the *Meissener Rechtsbuch*, III, 17, 31 (cf. 32, 33), laid down the following rule: "If a Christian inflicts bodily injury on a Jew, the Christian shall lawfully be punished as if he had inflicted the injury on a Christian, by virtue of the special peace accorded the Jews by emperors and princes." Thus the principle set forth in *Sachsenspiegel*, III, 7, 3, was still in full force: every act of violence against a Jew constituted a particularly serious breach of the king's peace. Transgressions of this kind, as a rule, did not come under the jurisdiction of town law.

It must be borne in mind that, for the first time, the penalties in the land-peace laws for offenses against Jews are no longer fines but criminal (bodily) punishments in the severest cases; even the death penalty, in the form of beheading, was imposed.[7] This principle was adopted by the Saxon lawbook. The practice of criminal law appears to have been in conformity with the regulations of the *Sachsenspiegel*. In the Dresden illuminated manuscript, on the plate illustrating III, 7, 2, and 3, a Jew (first figure from the left) is shown being murdered or one of his hands being cut off by a Christian (second figure). At the right, the offender (the fourth figure, identical with the second, both showing the same color in the Heidelberg manuscript) is being

"judged," that is, on the count's (fifth figure) order he is be-
headed by the executioner (third figure).[8]

The substitution of criminal punishment for fines offers the
explanation for the striking fact that, in the *Sachsenspiegel* (III,
45) and in Magdeburg law (LSchSprS., 9), the Jews—although
considered freemen and under the same protection as Christians—are not mentioned in the lists of those persons whose
Wergeld is fixed and differentiated in grade in accordance with
their legal and social standing.[9] Owing to the character of the
Wergeld in these legal systems as *Totschlagsbusse* (amends for
homicide consisting of a fine comprising both compensation and
punitive damages), this type of penalty could be applied only if
criminal (bodily) punishment was considered unsuitable.[10] The
omission of the Jews from the *Wergeld* list would then mean that
substitution of a fine for the death penalty was no longer permitted in cases of a capital offense against them. In fact, the
further general development of medieval penal law was here
anticipated with regard to the Jews. In the course of the thirteenth century, criminal punishment, including the death penalty, became universal and obligatory after the model of the
land-peace legislation. Thus the institution of *Wergeld* became
gradually extinct in Saxon law, and it remained altogether foreign to the southern German lawbooks.[11]

B. PROTECTION OF HUMAN DIGNITY

Unlike some other groups, the Jews were *not expressly excluded*
from among those entitled to lay claim to a *Wergeld* or a *Busse*
of a fixed amount. In the light of the previous explanations, this
fact has no bearing on the *Wergeld* problem. The picture changes,
however, if attention is directed to the *Busse*.

A *Busse*, again a fine, was due to the injured person in the case
of lesser offenses. It was intended to conciliate the injured person
and to penalize the offender through a money payment.[12] Just as
in other cases not covered by special rules of the *Sachsenspiegel*
Jewry-law, the principle that the general regulations set forth in
the lawbook were applicable to the Jews in their relation to non-
Jews may also have applied to the *Busse*.[13] This would mean that
Jews were entitled to claim the same *Busse* as that provided by

law for non-Jews. The question of the status of the Jews in relation to the groups enumerated in *Sachsenspiegel*, III, 45, as entitled to *Busse* offers no difficulty. Magdeburg law at an early
period relinquished the gradation of *Wergeld* and *Busse* according
to origin and social standing as differentiated in the *Sachsenspiegel*. It knew only one uniform *Busse* of thirty shillings, which
was granted in the *Sachsenspiegel* (III, 45, 1) to the upper class of
freemen. The result would be that Jews were considered equal to
non-Jews in their title to *Busse* for lesser offenses: the general
Busse of thirty shillings was also due to Jewish persons. They
had the right to claim it.

This theoretical conclusion derived by interpretation from the
Sachsenspiegel finds corroboration in a Magdeburg *Oberhof* decision
of the fourteenth century handed down to the *Scheppen* of Stendal.[14] "A Jew and a Jewess . . . complained against a Christian
that he had beaten them brown and blue and inflicted on them
bloody wounds. The Christian man came and confessed it." The
Magdeburg decision reads: "He shall give them their *Busse*, to
the Jew thirty shillings as *Busse*, to the Jewess half a *Busse*, that
is fifteen shillings."

The amounts adjudged here to the Jewish claimants correspond
to those generally applied under Magdeburg law. Thirty shillings are the *Busse* due to a municipal councillor, a *Ratmann*,[15] or
a member of a local jury court, a *Schöffe*.[16] They represent, moreover, the *Busse* to be paid to the upper class of freemen, the
schepenbâre lûte, according to the *Sachsenspiegel* (III, 45, 1), and
generally to citizens.[17] The *Busse* to be paid to women was one
half of that accorded to men.[18]

The *Busse* for verbal injuries inflicted on Jews was set at the
level of the reduced *Busse* for bodily injury to (Jewish) women.[19]
The amount forfeited in such cases seems of less importance when
compared to the actual maintenance of the principle that legal
protection must be extended to the Jew. A case decided by the
Schöffen of Magdeburg at the end of the thirteenth or in the beginning of the fourteenth century offers an interesting illustration. "A Jew sued a Christian for having called him a *hurnson*, a
whoreson. That the Christian confessed. He [the Jew] obtained
this decision: Since he [the defendant] pleaded guilty in a duly

inaugurated session of the court, he shall pay him [the Jew] the
Busse."[20] The Christian, however, resorted to *Urteilsschelte*, a
kind of appeal, declaring: "Inasmuch as all the world calls the
Jews whoresons, I did right by him, and need not pay a *Busse* to
him, and have done no wrong." But he was not permitted to
escape with this excuse. The reference to the alleged universal
custom in itself sheds light on the social status of the Jews,
which must already have been in a stage of decline. In the fifteenth century a Magdeburg decision for Aschersleben held that
the reproach of "evil-doing or acting in a Jewish manner" leveled against a Christian represents a transgression punishable by
a *Busse.*[21] The fairness to the Jew expressed in the first court decision is thus all the more worthy of appreciation.

Another case reported from the town of Zeitz, where a refugee
peasant from the vicinity had broken into and robbed a Jewish
home, shows that, even during the Hussite war, protection and
justice were not denied the Jews.[22]

Hence, it is no surprise to find such regulations as the following in the lawbooks:

If a Christian inflicts bloody wounds on a Jew, or beats him with a
club or his fists without causing such wounds, or wrongs him with
unseemly words, he shall suffer at law as if he had done it to a Christian.[23]

Everyone, be he Jew, heretic, or heathen, may and shall bring suit for
any grief or injury inflicted on him by anyone (Ssp., III, 7, 3, and 2;
C. *qui accusare* [*non*] *possunt, l. si crimen* [*Cod. Just.* ix. 1. 10]; *IV q. VI
omnibus* [*Decretum Gratiani*, c. 2, C. IV, qu. 6]).[24]

According to *Meissener Rechtsbuch*, III, 17, 45, "every Christian
shall, by day or by night, hasten to help stop any outrage threatened or perpetrated against a Jew or Jewish home." Neglect of
this obligation was punishable by a fine of thirty shillings. The
same lawbook placed kidnapping of Jewish children under the
death penalty (MRb., III, 17, 42).

There was only one exception to this general rule. The Jews
forfeited their legal claim to protection under penal law if they
suffered corporeal injuries in transgressing specific laws which
they had to obey. This was the case, for instance, if they violated
the prohibition against bearing arms, showed themselves in pub-

lic on Good Friday, reviled the Christian religion, or engaged in proselytizing and, in consequence, were injured or killed.[25] Even in such cases, however, the law required the Christian offender to adduce evidence through six witnesses "that he committed it [the homicide] for the sake of his faith; only then shall he go without punishment."

C. PROTECTION OF RELIGIOUS INSTITUTIONS AND RIGHTS

Medieval penal law did not restrict its protection to Jews as individual members of society. It extended protection also to their religious institutions and thus to the Jewish community as such, even if indirectly; for synagogues and cemeteries were communal property in Saxon lands.[26]

Flinging stones at the *Judenschule* was punishable by a special *Busse* payable to the (Christian) court: "Whoever wantonly flings [stones] into or at the *Judenschule*, shall pay to the court the *Busse* prescribed therefor, according to law."[27]

With the reception of Roman law in medieval Germany, its provision "that synagogues must not be torn down by violence," found general acceptance, as pointed out in Johann von Buch's *Gloss* to *Sachsenspiegel*, III, 7, 1.

The *Meissener Rechtsbuch* (III, 17, 36) places any disregard or violation of the sanctity of a Jewish cemetery under *frevelsrecht*, meaning "criminal penalty." Already under land-peace law and, accordingly, in the *Sachsenspiegel* (II, 66, 1) cemeteries in general were the objects of special protection. Jewish cemeteries were probably included. Robbing Jewish graves was punished by a fine of ten pounds of gold or, in case of inability to pay, by the death penalty.[28] Provisions concerning the protection of graves are cited again from Roman law, *Cod. Just.* ix. 19. 4 in particular. There is no record, however, of any actual violations which were prosecuted in local courts and submitted for decision to the *Oberhof* of Magdeburg.

Certain religious rights of the Jews also enjoyed protection under secular law. According to the Meissen lawbook (III, 17, 28), no Christian debtor was entitled to force his Jewish creditor to return pledges "on his holiday." It seems that this prohibition implies the right of the Jewish creditor, without risk of material

loss, not to accept payment of debts on the Sabbath. The prohibition is, however, a *lex imperfecta* from the point of view of
penal law, carrying no penalty for its violation. Yet it was sufficient to state the illegality of any act of compulsion with reference to the given situation. Transgressing the prohibition by
violence or other compulsion fell under the sanction of breaking
into a man's home (cf. MRb., III, 17, 45).[29]

II. Transgressions by Jews

A. GENERAL RULES ON PROSECUTION AND PUNISHMENT

Crimes committed by Jews were punishable under the same
rules and in the same manner as those committed by Christians.
This is the basic principle that is found in medieval German
town laws as well as in the lawbooks. It governs all regulations
on criminal acts by Jews and is best represented in the *Sachsenspiegel* (III, 7, 2): "Should a Jew slay a Christian or commit a
crime against him and be caught in the act, he shall be judged
like a Christian."

Through his crime the Jew placed himself outside the sphere of
the king's peace. He "shall be judged like a Christian," unpro-
tected by the special peace. This rule recurs in the same or similar
wording in Dsp. F 208; Schwsp. L 260, G 214, 4; Glogau Rb.
483.[30] It has a threefold implication. First, the penalty for homicide committed by a Jew is beheading, according to the general
rule in Ssp. II, 13, 5 (Schwsp. L 174; G 148, 11), applicable in
this special case, too. Second, the term "crime" or *ungerichte* includes cases of felony only, namely, such as were punishable not
merely by a *Busse* but by loss of life or limb, for instance, robbery,
rape—both under death penalty (Ssp. II, 13, 5)— or bodily injuries, under penalty of the loss of one hand (Ssp. II, 16, 2).[31]
Third, the delinquent must be caught in the act, as the *Gloss* to
the *Weichbild-Vulgata* explains the case of so-called "handhavingness" so well: *ab er yn hanthaftiger tad begriffin wirt*.[32] Only when
the condition of being apprehended in the act is fulfilled are prosecution, procedure, and punishment under criminal law possible.
Deutschenspiegel (F 208), in its interpolation, *oder daz man erzeugen
mach*, opens up an alternative, namely, that lawfully adduced
evidence could be substituted for the specification of *handhaftige*

Tat. These are the main regulations representing, so to speak, a medieval criminal code for Jews.

From a simple *argumentum a majori ad minus* it is obvious that the principle applied to crimes designated *ungerichte* or felonies was also applicable to minor offenses punishable merely by a *Busse*. The *Meissener Rechtsbuch*, III, 17, 38 (cf. 39) expressly draws this conclusion and presents it in a very broad formulation:

(38) In all matters in which a Jew becomes subject to a *Busse*, he shall suffer *Busse* like a Christian.

(39) Every Jew shall come before the court if called or bidden there. If he fails to do so, he must pay a *Busse* like a Christian.

The *Meissener Rechtsbuch* stands alone among the lawbooks in extending the principle under consideration to crimes perpetrated by a Jew against another Jew, thereby somewhat restricting Jewish autonomous jurisdiction (III, 17, 40):

Should a Jew beat or wound or slay another Jew, that shall be judged as between Christians. What in addition is demanded by Jewish law, he shall suffer afterward, when he has suffered our judgment.

It is well known in the history of criminal law that, beginning in the late Middle Ages and up to the seventeenth century, punishments were imposed on Jews which differed considerably from those fixed by law and applied to Christian delinquents.[33] They intensified the medieval system of penalties, cruel enough as it was. The motives of ridicule and degradation received especial emphasis. When hanged on the gallows, for instance, a Jew was suspended by the feet, instead of by the neck. It became customary to string up two vicious dogs by their hind legs beside him, to make the punishment more ignominious and painful. This latter intensification was, however, also applied to Christian offenders. It does not seem to be in its very origin a particularly "Jewish execution."[34] In some provinces a Jewish thief hanged by the neck would have a Jews' hat filled with boiling pitch placed on his head.[35] Fines for an offense against judge or court, called *Gewette*, were imposed on Jews in larger amounts than on Christians. At times Jews were expected to pay their fine in a certain quantity of pepper.

Such intensifications in punishment, it seems, found no basis in

Saxon law. The illustrations which accompany the text of the *Sachsenspiegel* in the illuminated manuscripts demonstrate best the correctness of this statement. The picture illustrating *Sachsenspiegel*, III, 7, 4, shows a Jewish offender (third figure from the left) brought into court; in the picture in the Heidelberg manuscript his hands are bound crosswise in front of him. The plaintiff (fourth figure) points with his right hand to the ecclesiastical objects found with the Jew, a vessel and a book; with left forefinger raised, he calls for attention. At the left of the picture the Jew is being "judged as if a thief," that is, he is hanged like any thief in accordance with *Sachsenspiegel*, II, 13, 1. Theft, the typical contemptible offense, was subject to the penalty of the gibbet, the typical degrading punishment. The Jew is hanged, however, not upside down by his feet but by the neck, like any thief; his hands are bound behind him. The execution of a Jewish thief is in no way different from that of a Christian thief, as pictured in the illustration of *Sachsenspiegel*, II, 13, 1, except for the pointed hat worn by the Jew. With respect to the manner of hanging, the Oldenburg illuminated manuscript of 1336 shows the most archaic representation: the Jew's trunk is bared, his hands bound across his back; his eyes are covered. The Dresden and Heidelberg manuscripts clothe the Jew in the penitent's shirt, as universally used; the Heidelberg manuscript fetters his hands in front, the Dresden manuscript leaves his eyes uncovered.[36] All manuscripts are alike in showing the Jew hanged by the neck; none of them pictures him accompanied by dogs.

The only reference to punishments of the degrading type described, namely, to an increased *Gewette*, is found in *Meissener Rechtsbuch*, III, 17, 48. But here it is explicitly stated that such discrimination against Jews is applied only in the imperial court, whereas "in all other secular courts the Jew pays the same *Gewette* as a Christian." Purgoldt's *Rechtsbuch*, in its corresponding article, VIII, 68, for the sake of clarification states that "the Jew has not to pay more than any Christian man."

A regulation of 1399 is worth noting in this connection. Treating of brawls between Jews and Christians, it stipulates that only the guilty individuals and not the entire Jewish community may be held responsible.[37] This provision would make it appear that such responsibility had been placed on the community either in general or in certain cases; but no such instance is recorded.

In the execution of criminal punishment during the Middle Ages churches and cemeteries played an important role as sanctuaries, from which criminals or debtors could not be forcibly taken without sacrilege.[38] Such places did not afford asylum, however, in numerous cases of crimes of a graver character than misdemeanors, namely, of *ungerichte*. Besides, in the cities, there prevailed a general tendency to restrict or completely to abolish the right of sanctuary, in the interest of regular administration of justice. Since asylum must be considered a religious institution of the church, anchored in canon law, the denial of this privilege to Jewish transgressors, found already in Roman law (*Cod. Just.* i. 12. 1), was quite natural. In the medieval sources considered. here, there is no case in which the right of asylum was declared applicable to a Jew.[39] Hence the rule, "church asylum does not protect Jews," as pointed out in Caspar Popplaw's *Remissorium* to his *Summa, Der Rechte Weg* (2), with reference to Buch's *Gloss* on *Sachsenspiegel*, II, 10, is in full accord with Roman and canon as well as German law: "Know ye, that the church and the cemetery protect and secure from capture all transgressors. . . . But excluded therefrom are five sorts of persons. The first are Jews. . . ."[40] In medieval Germany, exclusion of the Jews from the right of asylum does not appear to have been an intentional measure of discrimination. Their admission found even an advocate, if theoretically only. Heinrich der Teichner, a medieval "meistersinger" who wrote from about 1340 to 1375, devoted a lengthy poem to the problem of asylum and its legal justification, found already in the "book of Herr Moises." Here he championed the idea that no one, not even "Jews, heathen, murderers, and heretics," should be excluded from the right of asylum.[41] Only after the reception of Roman- and canon-law principles into the German legal system was the exclusion of Jews strongly emphasized.

B. INDIVIDUAL CRIMINAL OFFENSES

Criminal cases involving Jews are rather few in the Magdeburg jury-court decisions. Yet the material at hand is sufficient to show that the general principles transmitted in the lawbooks and discussed previously, were applied impartially to Jewish transgressors.

First should be mentioned a decision, referred to above, which proves the equality of Jews with non-Jews as far as fines for minor injuries are concerned. The Jew Zcadagk, who called a Christian woman a "hungry harlot" (*eyne hongeriche kotze*) was sentenced to pay the insulted Christian the ordinary *Busse* of fifteen shillings due to women, and to the judge the regular *Gewette*.[42]

Other cases and legal problems arose from the activity of Jews in moneylending and pawnbrokerage. Besides their significance for legal history, they reveal the temptations and risks to which the medieval Jewish trader was exposed in almost the only field left open to him.

Fraudulent appropriation by a Jewish moneylender of an object intrusted to him in pledge was regarded as theft, if the object were found in his locked room.[43] This is again an application to Jews of a general rule in medieval penal law, which treated the embezzlement of property in trust simply as theft and placed it under the severe penalty generally imposed for this crime.[44]

A decision of a basically similar type was handed down from Magdeburg to the local court of Cracow in Poland, some time in the fourteenth century. Here counterfeit money worth over six *groschen* had been found in the possession of an unnamed Jew. The case was submitted to the *Oberhof* of Magdeburg.[45] A general principle, pointed out in Ssp., II, 26, 2; Schwsp., L 192, G 165, 3; MRb., IV, 17, 8, and also adopted by Magdeburg law (BlM., II, 5, 9), held that a person found in possession of counterfeit coins beyond a certain amount was to be regarded and judged as a counterfeiter; for it must be assumed that he is aware of the fraudulence of the coins and yet means to put them into circulation. His punishment was the loss of one hand.[46] The decision concerning the Cracow Jew reads accordingly: "Judge him as a counterfeiter."

In contradistinction to both these law cases, in which Jews figured merely as common offenders, a particularly Jewish issue now presents itself. As early as Carolingian times, secular legisla-

tion—probably in support of similar prohibitions by the church
—sought to prevent church property from falling into Jewish
hands, in order to avoid the possibility of its being dishonored
or desecrated.[47] In the *Sachsenspiegel* (III, 7, 4) neither purchase
nor acceptance in pledge of chalices, books, or vessels of church
provenance was specifically prohibited to Jews.[48] Yet they were
threatened with the severe penalty for theft if such objects were
found in their possession and they could not prove their unobjectionable acquisition. Similarly, as in the case of the possession of
counterfeit coins, the mere keeping of *res sacrae* by a Jew carried
the implication that they had been illegally acquired. This constituted a crime, regardless of the keeper's knowledge or intention. This legal conception of *Sachhehlerei* recurs repeatedly in the
lawbooks[49] and was also maintained under Magdeburg law.[50]
The prohibition of purchase or acceptance in pledge of stolen
goods in general, and particularly of sacred vessels, vestments,
or books, was upheld and stressed also by rabbinical authorities,
individual leaders as well as rabbinical synods, "because of the
dangers to be feared from such acquisition."[51] Hence acceptance
of such goods was considered illegal from both the Jewish and
the Christian points of view. It might be owing to this circumstance that no actual case of such nature was brought for decision
before the Magdeburg *Schöffen*, as far as can be judged from the
Schöffensprüche in the collections available.

In the ascending scale of transgressions under discussion we
have now reached the category of capital crimes. Here the fact
must be recorded that no case of murder or homicide by Jews occurs in the extant annals of the *Oberhof* of Magdeburg. In fourteenth-century Stendal, some Jews were brought to trial on the
accusation of having inflicted *kampfwürdige* wounds on a Christian.[52] Wounds which, according to ancient law, could be vindi-
cated in the ordeal of combat were considered *kampfwürdig*. They
had to be "a man's fingernail deep and as long as the longest
joint of the middle finger," that is, such as would cripple or
even cause death.[53] The infliction of bodily injuries of this type
was punishable at a *minimum* by the loss of one hand, and at a
maximum by the death penalty.[54] The *Oberhof* of Magdeburg was
asked by the local court of Stendal for an opinion as to "where

the Jews should defend themselves with [the testimony of] Christians or Jews against the accusation of the infliction of wounds, before the synagogue on Moses's books [*vor der joden scole*] or [*vor dem hegheden dinge in den ver scaren*] before the ordinary court in its proper place of session." The decision handed down to the court of Stendal held that the Jews should "exculpate themselves before the synagogue with six oath-helpers according to their Jewish law." The jurors confined their decision to the questions of procedural law, since it was the constant practice at the Magdeburg *Oberhof* not to pass judgment on capital crimes.[55] In the case of Jews, too, the Magdeburg jurors followed their general practice of refraining from the imposition of criminal punishment for bodily injuries.

A retrospective glance over the criminal cases analyzed here reveals beyond doubt that the traditional method, generally applied and in no way differing from the ordinary routine, was used by the *Oberhof* of Magdeburg also in cases involving Jewish litigants. Since this high court had no functions at all in the general administration of municipal affairs, there also was no temptation for its jurors to take advantage of accidental criminal offenses by Jews for the pecuniary benefit of their city.[56]

There now remains to be considered one more broad field in the realm of medieval penal law, namely, that created by the attitude of the church toward Judaism and the Jews.

C. OFFENSES AGAINST CHRISTIANITY

1. USURY

In medieval law, ecclesiastical as well as secular, and particularly in Magdeburg law, a special situation prevailed with regard to usury. This is not the place for a general discussion of the history of usury in the Middle Ages,[57] or even for that aspect of it which appertains specifically to the Jews[58]—a subject which is not yet completely elucidated, despite a voluminous literature. It must suffice here to recall only some historical aspects of usury which are of basic importance.

A twofold meaning attaches to the terms *wuocher* (*wûcher*) and *gesuch* as used synonymously in medieval German law sources.[59] They originally designate products of the soil or proceeds of pecuniary value accruing to a person from legitimate labor or trade. But the practice of charging illicit or excessive interest on moneys lent and the proceeds from such credit activities are also called *wûcher*. The original meaning of a legitimate gain was extended to illicit or excessive profit only through the influence of the ecclesiastical theory of "usury." This doctrine of the medieval church, in its most stringent formulation, condemned every practice by which more was received than had been paid out, irrespective of how the excess may have been effected.[60] This theory was vigorously enforced in canon law, its application extended from the clergy to Christian laymen, and then also applied to every kind of usurer, including Jews and "foreigners," particularly the Lombards or Caorsins, these two groups being the principal moneylenders of the Middle Ages. Usury was even officially identified as a form of heresy.

The church did not, in principle, make any exception in favor of the Jews. The long evolution of her attitude on this point was marked by much vacillation, owing to the varying requirements of different periods and regions. In the end, the canons issued by the Third and Fourth Lateran Councils in 1179 and 1215, particularly canon 67 of the decrees of 1215 (c. 18, X, *de usuris* 5, 19),[61] referred to by later church councils, such as the provincial synod at Breslau in 1267,[62] attained universal validity and application. In her final position the church tolerated usury by Jews to a certain extent, excluding them from any intercourse with Christians only if they extorted "heavy or immoderate interest" (*graves immoderatasve usuras extorserint*) and until proper restitution had been made. This seems to imply that Jews were allowed to make a moderate profit from moneylending, which could therefore be considered as legitimately acquired but could not well be so described explicitly. It remained with the church, through the ecclesiastical courts and judges, to determine the limits of "moderate" profit and to establish in each individual case whether or not "heavy or immoderate interest" had been "extorted."[63] This basic attitude of the church, which remained unchanged in principle to the end of the Middle Ages, must be taken into account here because of its bearing on the attitude of the medieval lawbooks and of the Magdeburg court toward the problem of "usury" by Jews.

In the Middle Ages almost all important church laws—quite naturally—exerted an influence, directly or indirectly, on secular law. The failure of the church doctrine concerning usury, including usury by Jews, to find a commensurate repercussion in the medieval German lawbooks is therefore all the more conspicuous. In fact, none of the northern German lawbooks of the thirteenth and fourteenth centuries, including the *Sachsenspiegel*,[64] make any mention of usury at all.[65] It is significant that Johann von Buch's commentary, the *Gloss* to the *Sachsenspiegel*, herein as elsewhere strongly influenced by Roman- and canon-law doctrine, was the first northern German lawbook to adopt the ecclesiastical theory by taking over even the canon-law wording, without, however, mentioning usury by Jews.[66]

Conversely, the *Meissener Rechtsbuch*, composed between *ca.* 1357 and 1387, is silent on usury practiced by Christians and deals only with usury by Jews (III, 14, 3; III, 17, 1, 9, 11, 25, and 26). This lawbook was widely used in Meissen, Silesia, Bohemia, Moravia, and Poland—all countries with a large Jewish population. Drawing in its Jewry-law regulations, on numerous princely privileges granted to Jews in these countries, its author aimed at a reconciliation of the canon-law principle with the necessities of medieval economic life. Thus he advanced a theory of his own regarding Jewry privileges to justify the abnormal legal situation of the Jews with respect to usury (III, 17, 1): "By divine law no Jew shall take usury. Yet their position in law is differently formed, because they may not own real property in this country; and have been favored by emperors and princes in their good will so that they be compensated under particular law."

This theory was readily accepted by the lawbook of Walter Ekhardi, *Neun Bücher Magdeburger Rechts* (*ca.* 1400).[67] Later, the town clerk of Eisenach, Johannes Purgoldt, who at the beginning of the sixteenth century composed a lawbook for court use, elaborated on that doctrine in a manner remarkable both historically and juridically (VIII, 31).

It is written in the third book of Moses, chapter 25 [v. 37], that God spoke thus: Thou shalt not give thy money to thy fellow-man upon usury, nor thy produce. By God's law no Jew shall take usury from Jews, nor from Christians. But God has permitted them to take it from the heathen, when He spoke: Ye shall take no usury from any human being except from strangers, since the heathen are strangers to God and worship strange gods, that is, idols; Christians do not do that, they worship the immortal eternal God, the same as the Jews. Now, however, their [the Jews'] position in law is differently formed, because they may not own real property in this country, nor own hereditable possessions, from which they are excluded. And if they had such property, people would damage it; if they work in handicrafts, the guilds and master artisans would not tolerate it, and they would not be received into their associations, and the people would not let them work; if then, they engage in trading, no one would like to buy from them. And therefore must they thus engage in usury, and this is their excuse. But the Christian usurers have no such excuse, since they do it from their greed and their abandoned malice.[68]

The statement on usury in the *Sachsenspiegel Gloss* was adopted with some modification by the *Berliner Stadtbuch* of 1397 (III, 18). The first paragraph in this article is the only provision among all the lawbooks to state explicitly: "In these lands the Jews take usury without punishment by the church."[69] And in Purgoldt's lawbook (VIII, 85) we read further:

The written law [*beschreben recht*] states that their *wücher* should be moderate. Should they surpass, however, the limits assigned to them by the princes or municipalities in whose territory they live, then the secular court or the municipal council shall inflict punishment for their transgressions.

All told, it remains a fact—strange as it may seem at first glance—that the *Sachsenspiegel* and the older lawbooks of northern Germany take no cognizance of usury and are silent on usury by Jews in particular. This naturally has not remained unnoticed in earlier research.[70] Max Neumann was, however, the only scholar who, more than eighty years ago in his excellent *History of Usury in Germany*, tried to get to the bottom of this problem.[71] He suggested several possible reasons for the silence of the lawbooks on usury by Jews: (1) incompleteness of the manuscript transmission of the pertinent medieval sources; (2) reluctance to lay down rules of law for an unlawful practice, tolerated though it was even by the church; (3) local differences in customary law; and (4) absence of Jews from the northern German territories, particularly the cities, until the late Middle Ages.

Most of these explanations can easily be discarded. Our present secure knowledge of the manuscripts of medieval German law-books and the Jewry-law contained therein, as presented in Part I of this book, must be considered sufficient proof to dispose of the first point. The third is refuted by the very passage adduced in its support, namely, *Meissener Rechtsbuch*, III, 17, 2. As quoted by Neumann, its wording, *von der juden gesatczten gesuche beschrebin ist nicht*[72] ("nothing is ordained concerning the Jews' established usury"), contradicts the fact that, actually, usury by Jews is treated extensively in this lawbook. It rests, moreover, on a scribe's mistake not found in the better manuscripts, including the oldest of 1387. The passage reads correctly: *Von der jodden besaczten gerichte beschribe ich nicht*[73] ("of the Jews' established courts I do not wish to treat"). Neumann's last reason, although acceptable for single town or territorial laws, does not lend itself to generalization. This is disproved by the *Sachsenspiegel* and other lawbooks, which present an elaborate system of Jewry-law, although they are silent on usury by Jews.

The remaining explanation, his second, has the greatest plausibility. Precisely the same attitude seems here to come into view in secular law as was noticed in ecclesiastical legislation. Although this assumption appears quite obvious, no proof has been adduced in its support. But there must be a connecting link.

Two Magdeburg jury-court decisions in cases of usury by Jews may offer the missing clue. In one, the Jewish moneylender, Schalam, sues the heirs of his debtor for a certain amount which, as was mutually agreed, should remain on *gesuch* after the debt-or's default.[74] In the second case the Jewish creditor, Kussil, is sued by his debtors for the release of some pledges he is holding against their debt of twenty marks plus "eight marks *wûchir*."[75] The decisions handed down are identical in law content: "It does not behoove us to pass judgment on usury" (*gesuch und wûcher*); and "On usury we pass no judgment." The attitude manifested here conforms completely to a principle generally established at the *Oberhof* of Magdeburg. It is pointed out in numerous deci-sions, sometimes with even greater clarity.[76] We may cite, for instance, a *Schöffenspruch* which reads: "What is or is not to be considered usury, to recognize and decide, that belongs in the province of the ecclesiastical power, and not in ours."[77] The uncontested competence of the ecclesiastical courts as to "what should be considered usury," was thus explicitly acknowledged by the Magdeburg jurors. To decide this question was regarded a matter of canon law, even where Jews were concerned. The canon-law concept of usury was practically dominant, and the field of usury by Jews was to a great extent surrendered by secular jurisdiction to that of the ecclesiastical courts.

This legal maxim, as constantly applied at Magdeburg, was, however, restricted to the criminal-law aspect of the problem. It did not include in its scope questions of civil law involved, on which the *Schöffen* of Magdeburg did not refrain from passing judgment. In both Jewish law cases under consideration the *Schöffen* declared the debtors obligated to pay to their creditors the borrowed principal plus the sum (*gesuch, andir gelt*) which orally or in writing they had promised to pay in case of default: ". . . since Walman has made an agreement with him [the Jew Schalam] that, after the date, the money shall remain on interest [*uff das gesuch sal stehin*]." Hence, to claim or pay a compensation for the actual loss suffered by the lender through default of the borrower in meeting financial obligations (*damnum emergens*) was not considered usury as such, provided that such payment was contractually agreed upon in advance by the parties. Such interest for default, when the borrower failed to repay the money at the time appointed, was not even condemned by the church.[78] Even some lawbooks declared it permissible, provided only that it was stipulated by mutual agreement.[79]

Two interesting observations arise from these decisions and their legal implications. First, the Magdeburg *Oberhof*, in refusing to pass judgment on usury by Jews, adhered to its general rule applied in all cases of usury. Thus the *Schöffen* avoided conflict with both secular and canon law, neither exempting Jews from a prohibition to which Christians were subject nor, on the other hand, discriminating against them in any way.[80] Second, in strictly separating the criminal-law issue from the civil-law problems involved (to speak in present-day law terms), a way was cleared for doing justice also to the necessities of professional moneylending. While the contemporary canonists and

scholastics clung to the traditional doctrines, irrespective of the
varying needs of changing times, the *Schöffen* of Magdeburg
wisely recognized the growing demand for money in the national
economy, caused by an immense increase in commercial activity
from the twelfth and thirteenth centuries onward. Thus they
showed a better understanding of the emergence both of loans
for commercial purposes and of a social need for professional
moneylending which to a large extent was serving the interests
of the borrower. By leaving the decision on how to define the
criminal transgression of "usury" to the ecclesiastical judges,
they proved at the same time that they already knew and appre-
ciated the distinction between a reasonable and an unreasonable
return on money loaned. In other words, the differentiation of a
socially necessary and useful trade from antisocial criminal practices did not escape them. Through this liberal attitude, based
on reason and observable also in other fields of their judicature,[81]
the *Schöffen* of Magdeburg manifested a pronounced unwilling-
ness to promote by their forensic interpretation of law any retrograde developments. This attitude was also determinative for
their stand on usury in Jewish lawsuits.

2. BLASPHEMY, CONVERSION, APOSTASY

If the church placed usury under the jurisdiction of ecclesiastical courts, it is all the more understandable that she regarded the
immediate protection of the Christian faith and its dogmas, symbols, ceremonies, and followers against possible violation by
unbelievers as her manifest duty and special privilege. Nearly all
Europe was christianized at the crest of the Middle Ages. The
Jews were the only remaining group living among Christian
peoples and yet not attached to the church. Although the endeavor to win them over never ceased, popes and church councils, for self-protection, drew a sharp line of demarcation by
means of strict ecclesiastical Jewry legislation.[82] The attitude of
the medieval state and law was patently determined by the
church. There is no need to refer to all the pertinent articles in
the *Schwabenspiegel*, whose clerical author plainly adopted the
church policy and regulations concerning Jews in his lawbook,

which was of great general influence and even dominance in southern Germany. The following may suffice as an illustration:

With regard to these laws and to other laws concerning Jews, the jurisdiction belongs to ecclesiastic and secular judges. If one fails, the other shall act. The ecclesiastic judge may excommunicate the secular judge for failure to pass judgment. Whichever Jew transgresses these laws, the secular judge shall punish him with as many lashes as this book says [L 174; G 148]. Or either court may fine him pennies in such measure as will not be overly severe [*Schwabenspiegel*, L 262; G 214, 13].

Even Eike von Repgow, the author of the *Sachsenspiegel*, who cannot be identified with either the imperial or the church camp, in his formulation of the two-swords doctrine (I, 1), propagates the thesis that the secular arm must reinforce the spiritual. No wonder, therefore, that the entire jurisdiction over specific matters of canon Jewry-law was left completely to the church authorities. Except for the regulations in the *Schwabenspiegel*, mentioned above, and consequently also those in the *Freisinger Rechtsbuch* (Maurer, I, 173; Knapp, 122), none of the German lawbooks dealt with this particular segment of medieval Jewry-law. No superior-court decision dwells on it. Only the late *Regulae juris* offer a brief survey of the legal principles and rules involved. They are in part taken directly from canon law and supported by reference to Roman law. Even quotations from the *Sachsenspiegel* are not missing at times, in order to adduce support from Saxon law, too, though this was possible only by way of analogy.

a) Blasphemy.—As a rule, neither the church nor the medieval state in Germany interfered with the Jewish religion as practiced in the synagogue and taught in Jewish schools and academies. No book-burnings of the type enacted during the Talmud persecution in thirteenth-century France are recorded in medieval Germany. It seems that the view of Alexander of Hales (about 1170–1245) that "secret blasphemies" were not subject to prosecution still prevailed.[83] But blasphemies perpetrated in social intercourse with Christians or otherwise publicly, causing public scandal or indignation, naturally called for punishment and preventive measures. The author of the Stendal *Gloss* on the *Sachsenspiegel* (III, 7, 2) derives his legal reasoning, an *argumentum a minori ad majus*, from late Roman law:

If then a crime committed by a Jew against a Christian is punishable, much the more so, if he blasphemes God, he shall be penalized by lawful process through the secular power. And since God is great and venerable above all, injury to Him should be considered the greater. . . . Hence it is graver to violate the eternal than the temporal majesty. . . . Wherefore such a blasphemer not undeservedly is to suffer punishment in head and life through the secular power, according to the imperial law which, among other things, says: If then blasphemies committed against men are not left unpunished, all the more fit it is that he who blasphemes God Himself suffer punishment. . . . This concerning the lawful penalty holds in the secular jurisdiction. In the ecclesiastical jurisdiction, however, such a blasphemer shall be punished with a pecuniary or temporal penalty.[84]

The profanation of sacred objects and open insults against the Christian faith were similarly dealt with by canon law. Hence the secular law also forbade Jews to purchase or accept in pledge sacred vessels, vestments, or books.[85] Transgression of similar prohibitions such as that against appearance in public on Good Friday, reviling the Christian religion, or engaging in conversionist activities, besides subjecting them to the appropriate penalties, deprived them of the protection under penal law which was otherwise guaranteed.[86] As every Christian was bound to sacrifice his life for his faith if it were dishonorably attacked, so he would be acquitted in case he slew a Jew, heretic, or heathen in active defense of his faith.[87] The general principle is thus pointed out in the *Regulae juris*, J 155: "No Jew shall defame our Law. If he did so and were found guilty, he should be burnt. *C. de judeis et celicolis, l. ultima* [*Cod. Just.* i. 9. 18]; Ssp., II, 13, 7."

b) Conversion.—While in the early centuries of the Middle Ages Jewish proselytizing activity may still have been pursued to some extent, particularly in France, the situation in Germany in the age of the lawbooks here under consideration, seems to have been quite different. The problem of Jewish conversionist activities among Christians in the Middle Ages has been touched only slightly by research.[88] So much, however, seems to emerge from non-Jewish as well as Jewish sources, scanty as they are: the Jews of this period were hardly possessed of great "conversionist zeal" and were even careful to avoid such an attitude. Otherwise, much more documentary material, theological discussions, and canon-law regulations would be available with reference to this question. It is significant that not even the *Schwabenspiegel* devotes an article to the subject, though its clerical author was well acquainted with the trends and tendencies current in church policy and legislation of his day. Buch's *Gloss* to *Sachsenspiegel*, III, 7, 1 and the *Regulae juris*, which were leaning on it, both strongly influenced by Roman and canon law, state a unique rule that proves the assertion set forth.

Buch's *Gloss* to *Sachsenspiegel*, III, 7, 1:

No Jew shall convert a Christian to his faith; if he does it, it costs his life; *C. de jude., l. judeos* [*Cod. Just.* i. 9. 11]; *C. ne sanctum bapti. ite., l. ulti.* [*Cod. Just.* i. 6. 3]; *C. de apost., l. penulti.* [*Cod. Just.* i. 7. 5]; *C. ne christi. manci., l. judeus* [*Cod. Just.* i. 10. 1].

Regulae juris, J 164:

No Jew shall convert a Christian if he values his life; *ut C. de judeis, l. judeos* [*Cod. Just.* i. 9. 11]; [*C.*] *ne christianum mancipium hereticus, l. judeus* [*Cod. Just.* i. 10. 1].

Cussiel of Breslau is the only Jew mentioned in the sources as actively engaged and apprehended in proselytizing activities. He is said to have secretly circumcised and sent abroad a Christian boy, in 1434, and also to have converted a Christian woman to Judaism.[89] He was imprisoned but not executed. The municipal court was content to pardon him in exchange for his freeing the city of Breslau of a debt of 800 marks due him.

c) Apostasy.—The medieval lawbooks were much more concerned with Jewish converts to Christianity than with Jewish proselytizing activities. Two legal aspects entered the picture: first, protection of the new members of the church against personal injury and financial damage inflicted by their former coreligionists; second, protection of the church against desertion by her newly acquired members through open or clandestine reversion to Judaism. In both cases regulations of criminal law, both ecclesiastic and secular, came into action.

Pope Gregory the Great (590–604) renewed for medieval Christendom the old prohibition of the Christian Roman Empire against forced baptism of Jews and elucidated the problem of conversion to Christianity in this general statement:

It is necessary to gather into the unity of the faith those who are at variance with the Christian religion, through kindliness, benignity, admonition, and persuasion, so that what the sweetness of the sermon and removal of the terror of the Judge to come could achieve in leading to belief, should not be undone by threats and terrors.[90]

This, then, was the official position of the church. The same principle was proclaimed by Popes Alexander III (1159–81) and Clement III (1187–91), was embodied in Innocent III's (1198–1216) *Constitutio pro Judeis* of 1199, and was repeatedly enunciated by the popes of the thirteenth century.[91] It was expounded also in an impressive exposition by Thomas Aquinas (1225–74),[92] and found direct acceptance in the *Schwabenspiegel* (L 262; G 214, 8) (cf. *Freisinger Rechtsbuch*, Maurer, I, 173; Knapp, 122, II): "No one shall force the Jews into the Christian faith; if one can bring them to Christianity with good words, one shall do that readily."

Johann von Buch, in his *Gloss* to *Sachsenspiegel*, II, 66, 1, propagates the same idea, with an even more persuasive note, theologically as well as juridically:

[Know ye] as God waited for our own conversion from sheer goodness, so we too should justly await their [the Jews'] conversion in gentleness; for one shall compel no one by force to the service of God [and the faith unless he had previously been a follower of the faith].[93]

In Purgoldt's *Rechtsbuch* (VIII, 60) we read:

No one shall force the Jews into the Christian faith, for it is written: God shows mercy to whom he wants to do so; and to whom he does not want to show mercy, he remains obstinate in unbelief. God does not want anyone to be blessed by Christianity without his own will. One shall persuade the Jews to the faith, but one shall not force them into it by threats.

A similar idea perhaps underlies the prohibition against kidnapping Jewish children, which was placed under severe penalty in *Meissener Rechtsbuch*, III, 17, 42.[94]

Once a Jew was baptized, however, even if by force, he had to remain faithful to Christianity, according to canon law[95] as well as to the precept in the *Schwabenspiegel*, L 262; G 214, 8:

If a Jew turns Christian, and again would abandon the faith, the ecclesiastic as well as the secular court shall compel him to abide by it. . . . Be it even that they had been compelled to receive baptism, yet they shall remain steadfast in their Christian faith. This is because no one can be deprived [rid himself] of baptism once received.

In Purgoldt's *Rechtsbuch* (VIII, 60) a similar reasoning is found:

If a Jew should be forced to become a Christian, and received baptism, he should be forced to abide by the faith lest Christ's name be profaned. This is the rule according to ecclesiastical law.

The addition *expressis verbis* of the theological and canon-law reasoning in the *Schwabenspiegel* reveals most clearly the strong influence of the church doctrine on this lawbook. Indeed, in its regulation protecting the converts' rights of property and inheritance the *Schwabenspiegel*, in a special clause of article L 262; G 214, 12, directly refers to canon law (c. 5, X, *de judeis* 5, 6): "If it happens that a Jew receives baptism, he may rightfully hold his property and inheritance. This is permitted to him by the writing entitled *Decretalis*."

It is well known that the Jews, in self-defense and to prevent apostasy, used to dispossess and disinherit apostates. Their right to do so was recognized by secular law as early as 1090 in the privileges granted to the Jews of Speyer and Worms, which stated in article 7: "Just as they [the apostates from Judaism] abandoned the law of their fathers, so let them also abandon their possessions."[96]

Hence the aforementioned clause in the *Schwabenspiegel*, recurring only in the *Freisinger Rechtsbuch* (Maurer, I, 173; Knapp, 122, II) and missing from all northern German lawbooks, meant in fact a protection of the convert's economic interests. This was in accordance with canon law.[97] However, no penalty was placed on Jews for noncompliance with the requirements of that clause or even for directly preventing an apostate from exercising the privilege thus granted to him.

Besides, protection was also extended to the person and feelings of the converted Jew. Bodily or verbal injuries inflicted on him by his former coreligionists were heavily penalized. In the most serious cases the penalty was death by burning at the stake; even the "accomplices" of the offending Jew were to be subject to such punishment. The choice of this form of punishment, generally reserved for heretics and apostates, shows clearly that a

similar juridical qualification was attributed to the offenses in
question. But on this point not even the *Schwabenspiegel* resorts to
such juristic overrefinement, which was left to Buch's *Gloss* to
Sachsenspiegel, III, 7, 1, and to the *Regulae juris*, where under
J 152 the point is similarly stated, though without reference to
the *Gloss:* "Jews who revile a baptized Jew or inflict an *ungericht*
on him, if brought to court and convicted thereof, according to
law, shall rightfully be burned, the Jew and all his abettors
(*C. de judeis et celicolis, l. judeis*) [*Cod. Just.* i. 9. 3]."

As mentioned before, in the Middle Ages and particularly from
the thirteenth century on, the specific punishment for heresy and
apostasy was death by fire.[98] Although the medieval church considered heresy a purely ecclesiastical delict (*delictum mere ecclesiasticum*), in its prosecution she invoked the assistance of the
state, in view of the fact that the penalties available to her were
deemed inadequate. It was the Fourth Lateran Council which, in
its third canon, later incorporated in the canon-law code (*Corpus
juris canonici*, c. 13, X, *de haeretics* 5, 7), promulgated extensive
regulations concerning heretics and imposed on the secular
powers as a particular duty "to exterminate all heretics from the
lands under their jurisdiction to the best of their ability [*pro
viribus exterminare*]." Secular legislation quickly responded.
Within two and a half decades, laws in various countries placed
heresy under the penalty of death at the stake, thus greatly in-
tensifying the severity of the punishments previously inflicted.
In 1231 Pope Gregory IX expressly approved the death penalty
for heresy and decisively promoted its general introduction (cf.
c. 15, X, *de haereticis* 5, 7).[99]

Accordingly, death at the stake had to be the penalty for denial of the Christian faith by a convert, which means, of course,
also for the return of a baptized Jew to his ancestral faith. The
Schwabenspiegel explicitly takes this stand in article L 262; G 214,
8: "And if he [the baptized Jew] denies the Christian faith, and
will not cease therefrom, he shall be burnt as a heretic."[100]

Relapse into, or reversion to, Judaism is thus equated with
ordinary heresy and subjected to the same punishment as that
provided in *Schwabenspiegel* (L 174; in G 148, 12 missing) for a
heretical (*ungeloubig*) Christian. This implication, apparent from

the *Schwabenspiegel* (*ca.* 1275), obviously has its basis in older church legislation, which had arrived earlier at that specific conclusion. It was Pope Innocent III who, in his letter to the archbishop of Arles in 1201, clearly stated that even those who under direct or indirect compulsion had accepted baptism had become members of the church and thus were to be compelled to the observance of the Christian faith. True, the Pope had not explicitly ordained the application of legal sanctions and penalties to enforce obedience. But this consequence was implied in his reasoning and actually drawn by the Fourth Lateran Council of 1215, which called upon the bishops to take the necessary steps. It therefore stands to reason that backsliding Jewish converts fell under the group of "other heretics of whatsoever designation" (. . . *et alios, quibuscunque nominibus censeantur*) who were to be first excommunicated and then extradited for punishment to the secular authorities, according to Pope Gregory IX's decretal of 1231 (c. 15, X, *de haeret.* 5, 7). In 1267, relapse into Judaism was, in fact, explicitly equated with heresy by Pope Clement IV in his bull *Turbato corde*, later confirmed by several popes. This was done only after the foundation of the Papal Inquisition which brought all violations of the faith before its tribunal.[101]

The author of the *Regulae juris*, in his article J 157 repeating the rule of *Schwabenspiegel*, article L 262; G 214, 8, though in a different wording, refers to *Sachsenspiegel*, II, 13, 7, which is thus interpreted by him as including relapse into Judaism of a baptized Jew (J 158; cf. J 163). In view of the variant manuscript readings in the pertinent article, it is open to doubt, however, whether the Saxon lawbook considered heresy at all as a distinct crime within the realm of secular law. The reference in the *Regulae juris* would support this interpretation, although the term *Ketzer* ("heretic") does not occur in the *Sachsenspiegel*.[102] Be this as it may, there is no regulation in the *Sachsenspiegel* placing return to Judaism by a baptized Jew in the same category with heresy. Such questions were of no concern at all to Eike von Repgow. The compiler of the fourteenth-century *Prager Rechtsbuch*, on the other hand, though following *Sachsenspiegel*, II, 13, 7, went much beyond his model when he stated in article 34: "He who is an unbeliever, who is not a Christian, or who engages in sorcery, shall be burned."

3. ILLICIT SEXUAL RELATIONS AND MARRIAGES

Since the Council of Elvira, at the beginning of the fourth century, the medieval church had endeavored, through increasingly vigorous sanctions, to prevent sexual relationships between Jews and Christians.[103] It was, however, only under the influence of the measures taken by the Fourth Lateran Council against heretics that the fines and corporal punishment previously imposed for such transgressions[104] were replaced in secular legislation by the penalty of death at the stake.[105]

This entire historical development is reflected in one of the most drastic provisions of medieval German Jewry-law, incorporated in *Schwabenspiegel*, L 322; G 272, and taken over literally in *Freisinger Rechtsbuch* (Maurer, I, 204; Knapp, 123) (cf. *Reg. jur.*, J 163): "If a Christian lies with a Jewess, or a Jew with a Christian woman, they are both guilty of superharlotry [*uberhure*], and they shall be laid one upon the other and be burned; for the Christian has denied the Christian faith."[106]

In other Jewry-law articles of the *Schwabenspiegel*, discussed previously, explicit references to canon law supplied hints as to their proper interpretation. Here the additional clause justifying the severe penalty offers the clue to a correct juridical understanding, although that clause refers only to the Christian transgressor.[107] The severity of the punishment would not seem justifiable if this were to be regarded merely as a rigorous measure to segregate Christians from Jews. Furthermore, the ordinary penalty for superharlotry (*uberhure*) in the *Schwabenspiegel* (L 174; G 148, 11) is beheading. Hence, the juristic qualification of the crime as "denial of the Christian faith"—that is, heresy or unbelief (*ungelouben*) in the case of the Christian—must be considered the sole reason for inflicting such a drastic punishment as death by fire. The same punishment was simultaneously imposed, *per analogiam*, on the Jewish offender. Thus sexual relations of whatever nature between Christians and Jews were considered by the Christian world in those days as at least suspect of heresy.[108] The justification of the severe penalty imposed in the *Schwabenspiegel* on the Christian offender places this assertion, for the sphere of secular law, beyond doubt.

There is, however, another juridical difficulty, which must not be overlooked. The clerical author of the *Schwabenspiegel* in his zeal for Christianity applies the penalty, generally reserved for heresy and apostasy by Christians, equally to both transgressors, Jew as well as Christian. He could claim for himself the liberty of resorting to such a juridical analogy in view of the fact that his *Spiegel* was intended to serve the purposes of secular law, and this, in turn, was supposed to reinforce the canon-law rules, particularly in the cases under consideration and for crimes actually perpetrated. Such a consideration might have appeared to him sufficient justification for extending the penalty for heresy to Jews also.[109]

The argument of the church at the Fourth Lateran Council had been different. Jews and heretics were differentiated and considered two distinct groups.[110] As far as heretics were concerned, the church was in a position to induce the secular authorities to effect the ecclesiastical punishment through secular penalties, culminating in death by fire in the case of heresy. For Jews, who were not considered as heretics under canon law, different means had to be chosen. The church had to apply preventive measures to forestall illicit sexual relations of a supposedly heretical nature, between Jews and Christians, and thereby simultaneously to prevent the latter from committing heresy. It was thus quite in line with its general antiheresy policy that the Fourth Lateran Council resorted to a measure of exceptional severity against the Jews and decreed

that Jews and Saracens of both sexes in every Christian province and at all times shall be marked off in the eyes of the public from other peoples through the character of their dress, [in order] that through error Christians [may not] have relations with the women of Jews or Saracens, and Jews or Saracens with Christian women.[111]

This is not the place to go into the details of the history of the distinctive garb imposed on the Jews in the thirteenth century by the church and consequently also by secular legislation. A discussion of the pertinent regulations in the lawbooks must be deferred at the moment. Attention should be directed merely to one characteristic fact. While the *Sachsenspiegel* makes no mention of any compulsory distinctive garb for the Jews, its southern German counterpart contains, in connection with and in addition to its antiheresy provisions, the following article (L 262; G 214,

10): "The Jews shall wear pointed hats; thereby they are marked off from the Christians, so that one shall take them for Jews."[112] Once more the influence exerted by canon law on the *Schwaben-spiegel* comes clearly to the fore.

It is conspicuous that none of the widely disseminated German lawbooks contains a prohibition against intermarriage between Jews and Christians. Undoubtedly this is due to the obviously illicit character of such alliances in the view of the church. An explicit prohibition is first found in Buch's *Gloss* on *Sachsenspiegel*, III, 7, 1, with particular reference to the Roman law principles established in *Codex Justinianus* i. 9. 6 and 7. The prohibition of intermarriage was taken over into the *Remissorium* to Caspar Popplaw's *Summa, Der Rechte Weg* (19; cf. *Reg. jur.*, J 162): "Between Jews and Christians there must be no marriage under penalty of death."

In Purgoldt's lawbook alone (VIII, 104) provisions are embodied concerning children originating from illicit sexual relations between a Jew and a Christian woman:

If a Jew commits a transgression by lying with a Christian woman, and she gives birth to a child, the child shall not remain with the father. It is to be baptized, and its Christian mother shall educate it. Should she die, another Christian shall educate it. The secular court or municipal council shall direct and compel the Jew to reimburse them for the cost of the child's education until it will be able to care for itself. This is law according to ecclesiastical law, *landrecht, wichpildsrecht*, and also municipal law [of Eisenach]. The Jew is responsible to the ecclesiastical as well as to the secular court.

From this regulation it is apparent that the penalty of death at the stake for illicit sexual relations between Jews and Christians had become obsolete in Purgoldt's time (about 1500).

There are no decisions by the Magdeburg jury court in actual cases covered by the prohibitions treated in this subsection.

CHAPTER NINE

Civil Law[1]

I. Civil Law and Jewry-Law

THE title of the present chapter, covering a wide range of the
subject matter under consideration, must not lead the reader
to expect a full exposition, even if only in outline, of the status of
the Jews in the various fields of what today is called "civil law."
As in the preceding chapter, the scope of this inquiry is subject
to some inherent limitations.

Two facts must be borne in mind. First, the strict separation
of, and differentiation between, public and private law, as developed early and significantly in ancient Roman law, remained
foreign to medieval German law.[2] It was only by a slow and
gradual process that the differentiation began to emerge in the
later centuries of the Middle Ages. This development must not be
lost sight of, since the categories of Roman and modern law are
applied in this inquiry merely as a methodological expedient of
legal-historical research.

Furthermore, though Jews had close contacts with their Christian surroundings within the realms of constitutional, criminal,
and procedural law, in the field of civil law the points of contact
were very limited; for Jewish internal relations, above all those
touching on religious matters, were governed by Jewish law.
This was to a certain extent recognized and, as a rule, not interfered with by the authorities of the medieval state.[3] Hence extensive branches of law, such as the law of persons, family law, including the law of marriage and divorce, and the law of inheritance, were automatically withdrawn from non-Jewish influence.

In the field of civil law, special Jewry-law could thus develop
only in connection with the commercial and other business trans-

actions which brought Jews into contact with the Christian population. For such legal relationships, however, the common rules of the prevailing law ordinarily came into action, as has been previously established.[4] Hence the area within which specific Jewry-law could operate was restricted to those situations which demanded exceptional regulations for the Jews, deviating from the general rule. Again, only those situations that attracted the greatest attention from the points of view of commercial life and legal practice found treatment in the lawbooks or consideration by the superior courts of law.

These, then, are the limitations which determine the several aspects of civil Jewry-law to be presented in this chapter.

II. Ownership of Real Property

From lawbooks as well as from the Magdeburg jury-court decisions no clear picture emerges of the right of Jews to acquire and own real property. Synagogues and cemeteries seem to have been legally their property, as can be gathered from the protection against violation which the law extended to these places of worship and sanctity.[5]

The fact that private possession of real property is mentioned only very rarely in the law sources does not necessarily imply, however, that Jews were entirely barred from such ownership. Documents of a type different from those under consideration testify to the contrary.[6] There is even a comparatively late decision of the *Schöffen* of Leipzig which attests to the fact that, as late as the fifteenth century, real property could lawfully be acquired and transferred by a Jew.[7] Real estate, originally belonging to a Christian, Hans Lasicz of Eilenburg, was adjudged by the local court to a Jew, Jordan, son-in-law of a well-known Jew of Leipzig, Abraham. Judge and jurors acknowledged that "the Jew may sell it, give it away or pledge it as security." Thereupon the Jew transferred his property with all the rights acquired, again in court, to a non-Jew, George Lindmann. In the course of a lawsuit, occasioned by the original owner's refusal to surrender the *gewere* ("possession"), both transactions were confirmed as lawful acts, and their validity was upheld by the superior court of Leipzig. Two related lawsuits were decided by the *Schöffen* of Magdeburg, also in the first half of the fifteenth century. They confirmed the pledge of warranty given by some Jews who, in a similar way as in the Lasicz case, had acquired houses from non-Jews and resold them afterward to Christian purchasers.[8]

The only lawbook of the thirteenth and fourteenth centuries which excludes Jews from ownership of real property is the *Meissener Rechtsbuch*, though it otherwise displays much understanding and concern for the legal problems of the Jews. In its article III, 17, 1, the privilege of the Jews to engage in usury is explained and excused on the ground that "Jews are not allowed to own real property in this country."[9] Documentary evidence to the contrary from the same country and period shows, however, that no universal validity attached to this rule at the time.[10] Moreover, the Stendal *Gloss* to *Sachsenspiegel*, III, 7, 1, in Latin, sometime before 1434, states the obligation of a Jew who acquires a house from a parishioner to continue to pay the annual tithes which the church had received prior to the change of ownership.

The scarcity of information in the law sources, which furnish the basic principles of Jewry-law and record the law cases in which it was applied, forces upon the observer the impression that Jewish ownership of real property could have been of no great legal importance in Germany. The prohibition against acquisition and ownership of real estate by Jews must have gained ground only gradually. In practice, enforcement of this prohibition probably varied locally, prior to its universal adoption late in the Middle Ages.

III. Acquisition of Movable Property

Incomparably greater importance than to real property was evidently attached to the acquisition and ownership by Jews of movable objects. Telling proof of this assertion is furnished by the bare fact that, within the Jewry-law regulations of the *Sachsenspiegel*, the model for most of the other medieval German lawbooks, the only provision not dealing with the Jews' status in constitutional and criminal law is devoted entirely to the acquisition and ownership of movables and the rights and obligations flowing therefrom. This subject, therefore, rightly deserves, together with the law of pledge and of moneylending contracts— all three showing a close interconnection commercially as well as legally—to take principal place in the present chapter.

Sachsenspiegel, III, 7, 1, states the following rule: "A Jew must not be a Christian's warrantor [*gewere*] unless he is willing to respond [to assume the defense] by taking the Christian's place."

Eike von Repgow continues in article III, 7, 4, which is closely related to the regulation in III, 7, 1, as follows:

> If a Jew purchases or accepts in pledge chalices or [church] books or garments for which he has no warrantor: if such should be found in his possession [*gewere*], he shall be judged as a thief. What a Jew buys of other things, unconcealed and not stolen, in the light of day, and not behind locked house doors, if he can prove this with two witnesses, he shall obtain on his oath his pennies thereon, which he had spent therefor or put out thereon, although it was stolen; if he lacks the witnesses, he loses his pennies.

We may begin with the last clause, which deals in particular with the acquisition by Jews of movable objects both as property and as security. It contains, in a modified and very restricted form, the old trade privilege accorded Jewish and Lombard merchants as early as the eleventh century, for which—very arbitrarily and without any support from medieval sources, either Jewish or German—the designation *jüdisches Hehlerrecht* was introduced into the literature of legal history.[11] As mentioned before, this subject achieved prominence in the pseudo-scientific and anti-Semitic propaganda of National Socialist Germany.[12] The hypothesis was advanced that the purely commercial privilege, intended to protect commercial intercourse and the security of common trade, had its origin in Jewish-talmudic law of a particularly criminal character. This entirely unfounded theory has been critically examined and refuted elsewhere.[13] Not a shadow of scholarly proof has been adduced either for the talmudic origin of this principle or for its intentional or general application in a criminal way by medieval Jewry. Hence there is no need to dwell further on this point, and the reader interested in the controversy may be referred to the pertinent literature.

The following discussion can thus be limited to what the lawbooks and the Magdeburg court decisions have to contribute to the problem. Aside from the immediate aim of this presentation, it will yield additional proof for the refutation of the *Hehlerrecht* theory with all its implications. Even this simple consideration leads to that end: a tribunal of the authority and reputation universally attributed to the *Oberhof* of Magdeburg in the Middle Ages would never have lent its support to improper practices, least of all if they were indulged in by Jews. In fact, it was this self-same high court which fully indorsed and enforced all regulations concerning the Jewish trade privilege under consideration, the so-called *jüdisches Hehlerrecht*, as set forth in the *Sachsenspiegel*, and thus made these rules genuine Magdeburg law.

The *Sachsenspiegel* rules regulating acquisition of ownership of movables applied in general to all legal transactions aiming to establish property rights. Jews were not excluded. They were accorded a special position only in one single respect. Under certain conditions and legal precautions they could acquire property or security rights even in stolen goods, whereas non-Jews in such cases were bound by law to restore them unconditionally to their original owner, if he claimed his lawful possession. Jews, in such instances, were entitled to claim compensation to the extent of the price they had paid for the object now reclaimed by its legitimate owner.

This trade privilege was bestowed on the Jews as early as 1090 in the Jewry privileges of Henry IV for Speyer and Worms: "But if a stolen object should be found with them, if the Jew says that he has bought it, he shall testify on oath, in accordance with his law, how much he has bought it for, and he shall receive just as much and shall restore the object to the owner."[14]

Certain points in this concise—for the legal historian perhaps too concise—formulation caused much controversy and discussion. Was good faith on the part of the Jew in connection with the purchase a requirement for his claim to compensation? Did the oath to be taken by him have to cover merely the amount of the purchase price, or had it to cover his good faith in the transaction, too?

The formulation in the *Sachsenspiegel* is not open to any such doubts or controversies. The privilege accorded to the Jews ap-

pears here in a very definite and considerably restricted form.
First, Jews are absolutely barred from buying or accepting in
pledge certain articles, such as chalices, church books, or sacred
vestments;[15] for a Jew incurs the penalty for theft, that is, death,
if such sacred objects are found in his possession and he is unable
to prove lawful acquisition. This alone was a far-reaching restriction as to subject matter. Yet it did not go far enough to
assure the prevention of improper practices. Hence, second, even
with respect to this restriction as to permissible objects, another
precaution was taken, still stricter and more comprehensive.
The German principle of "publicity" was introduced. Even for
permitted objects the Jew may claim compensation only if they
are *unverholen unde unverstolen*, and the purchase is made "in the
light of day and not behind locked house doors."[16] In other
words, *bona fides* on the part of the Jew must be established beyond objection. And, finally, a third precaution: in order to be
entitled to compensation, the Jew is required to prove the lawfulness of his acquisition, including his good faith in the purchase, by means of an oath to be taken by himself and two supporting witnesses.

Through such precautions, all points which had been objectionable to medieval commercial and legal practice in their progressive development and were revived only by the modern theorists of the so-called *jüdisches Hehlerrecht* for vicious exploitation
had already been eliminated in the *Sachsenspiegel*. In fact, its
formulation provided the strongest protection which the law
could possibly extend to the owner of stolen property.

What, according to *Sachsenspiegel* law, still remained to the
Jew of his once far-reaching trade privilege must be considered a
modest—though practically by no means unimportant—remnant. The Jew could establish the amount of the reclaimed purchase price by oath. If he could not produce proof for the legality
of his purchase, in accordance with the requirements set forth in
Sachsenspiegel, III, 7, 4 (2), he forfeited his claim to compensation
completely, but nonetheless could not be regarded as a thief. It
is self-evident that these privileges represent very obvious concessions for the sake of effective protection of commercial life.

Such concessions could be made by the author of the *Sachsen-*

spiegel without any scruples, in view of the fact that, in addition
to all the precautions enumerated, he introduced still another
restrictive regulation. This new restriction bears on the Jew's
role in the legal procedure invoked by the dispossessed owner of
stolen property, who seeks to recover the objects alienated from
him. According to the regular procedure in medieval German
law, the holder in whose possession the stolen object was found
had to prove its lawful acquisition, to escape the blame of being
the thief himself. If he could name the former possessor, from
whom he had obtained the object, this warrantor (*Gewähre*) had
to take the place of the purchaser as defendant. Now the warrantor had to prove his right of possession and lawful acquisition. This procedure was repeated until finally that former possessor who was unable to prove lawful acquisition was identified
as the thief. A Jew, always privileged under the provisions of
Sachsenspiegel, III, 7, 4 (2), to claim compensation for the purchase
price paid by him, would interrupt this line of gradual regression
in the prescribed process of law. To avoid this undesired consequence resulting from his—though restricted—trade privilege,
this further restriction was added in *Sachsenspiegel*, III, 7, 1: "A
Jew must not be a Christian's warrantor unless he is willing to
respond [to assume the defense] by taking the Christian's place."
This meant, in fact, the most rigorous legal protection of the
public against any possible inconvenience arising from the trade
privilege of the Jews. Every one buying from a Jew had to be
aware that he made this purchase at his own risk. He would lack
a warrantor recognized by law and thus could never recover the
purchase price, if the goods turned out to be stolen goods. If the
Jew, on the other hand, wanted to escape the economic disadvantage resulting from this prohibitory rule, he was compelled
to take upon himself the obligation of functioning as a regular
warrantor—as any Christian would have to do—in a possible
lawsuit for recovery of goods which turned out to be stolen
goods. In other words, the Jew was indirectly compelled to
renounce his trade privilege.[17]

Eike von Repgow must be credited with having discovered
this ingenious solution of a most difficult legal problem. He gave
equally thoughtful consideration to the needs of commerce, to

the protection of the public, and to the traditional trade privilege of the Jews. By not abolishing the latter in its entirety, yet restricting and conditioning it, he indicated the line of development which a wise lawgiver would elect.

Considerations of this kind, however, did not concern the compilers of later lawbooks. Eike's way of settling the problem was reversed by them, so that the Jews were deprived outright of their traditional trade privilege. Its negation was to be the common rule, though the Jew might be allowed to deviate from this rule by means of an explicit stipulation. The strict negation provided already in the older *Schwabenspiegel* manuscripts (L 260) found a different formulation in a later group of *Schwabenspiegel* manuscripts (G 214, 1) through insertion of the stipulation clause. The clerical author of the southern German counterpart of the *Sachsenspiegel* made no attempt to hide the pronounced anti-Jewish trend revealed by this reversal of his Saxon model.

If a Jew sells something to a Christian or makes another transaction with him: he shall be the Christian's warrantor according to Christian law, unless the Jew makes a stipulation according to his own law.[18] If the Christian denies this, the Jew shall convict him with three Christians [*Schwabenspiegel*, L 260; G 214, 1].

If a Jew buys goods taken by theft or robbery, he must respond [assume the defense] like a Christian. And what he denies, he shall be convicted of like a Christian.

And if a Jew gives a loan against goods taken by theft or robbery, and should the one to whom they belong claim them, he [the Jew] shall return to him his goods according to law like a Christian. This is the law. Yet they [the Jews] have acquired a better law [privilege]; this the kings have given them in contravention of the law:[19] so that they thence lend on goods taken by theft or robbery. They shall do this, however, in broad daylight, publicly before their doors, in the street. And if he who had owned them [the goods] comes to recover them according to law: one shall return to him [the Jew] the principal and no interest. If, however, he made a loan thereon clandestinely, he must restore them [the goods] without compensation [*Schwabenspiegel*, L 261; G 214, 7].

The *Schwabenspiegel* regulations, adopted by the *Freisinger Rechtsbuch* (Maurer, I, 172; Knapp, 121), with only slight changes taken from later manuscripts, go into much detail on the modification in the legal status of the Jews, as do other lawbooks with their respective rules and comments.[20] The state of the law was that outlined here. The *Remissorium Wolrab* probably went furthest with the following brief and unconditional rule: "Jews are bound to restore stolen goods purchased by them, without compensation."

I need not further pursue all the minor problems involved and their individual ramifications. One point only perhaps deserves particular mention. Some of the lawbooks state directly and unmistakably both the reason and the aim of the continued maintenance on a restricted scale of the Jewish trade privilege, even under changed economic conditions. Johann von Buch, the glossator of the *Sachsenspiegel*, explains article III, 7, 1 thus *in extenso:*

A Christian who admits the purchase must take recourse to a warrantor; this the Jew must not do, as he [Eike von Repgow] says here, since he [the Jew] retains his pennies in the stolen goods. This is for the following reason: that one may find and recover one's lost goods all the more readily. Therefore, it was granted to the Jews not to be warrantors to anyone for their sales. Hence they may buy stolen goods; therefore one also supposes that they were stolen goods.[21]

The picture of the legal situation briefly outlined above may well be clear. As it is drawn from the theoretical regulations in the lawbooks, it needs only to be checked against the reality mirrored in pertinent decisions of the Magdeburg jury court or other superior courts of Magdeburg law. The following cases from legal practice are available. They testify to the fact that Magdeburg law had adopted the principles of the *Sachsenspiegel* (III, 7, 1 and 7, 4), as appears also from article 118 in the Magdeburg-Görlitz Law Instruction of 1304.[22]

Hempil Czigilheym found his stolen horse in the house of another Christian, from whom he claimed his property in court. A Jew, whose name is not given, also laid claim to the horse, with the assertion that "the horse belonged to him, he had lent his money on it and had openly taken it as security, hence the horse was still his." The lawsuit was submitted to the *Manschaft der Donyschen Pflege*, the superior court of Dohna, which issued the following decision:

Since the Jew sets forth in his answer that the horse claimed at law was his and still is, and he had publicly made a loan thereon: if the Jew with two supporting witnesses, one a Jew and one a Christian, can prove that he lent his money on the horse unconcealed in the light of day and not behind locked house doors, he shall obtain on his oath his pennies thereon, which he had spent therefor or put out thereon, although it [the horse] was stolen. If he lacks the witnesses, he loses his pennies, if Hempil Czigilheym can testify according to law with two witnesses to the stolen horse being his.[23]

Comparison of the wording of this decision with that in *Sachsenspiegel*, III, 7, 4 (2), reveals a striking conformity.

Two cases decided by the Magdeburg *Oberhof* give evidence that Jews actually took upon themselves the obligations of warranty, as provided in *Sachsenspiegel*, III, 7, 1—and this even with regard to immovable property. In the first suit three Jews sold some real estate, obtained from their debtor, to a citizen of Naumburg under obligation of warranty. The new proprietor, sued by the original owner for compensation for damage suffered through the sale, had recourse to the Jewish sellers. Although these declined to take full responsibility for certain procedural neglects of the plaintiff, they nevertheless offered to return the purchase price, plus expenses for repairs—all this only on account of their stipulation of warranty. The Magdeburg jurors decided accordingly.[24] In a very similar case, three Jews, Canold, Meyger, and Czadagk, probably identical with the first mentioned, were compelled by a court decision to fulfil their promise of warranty made *in gerichte und in geheite bang*.[25]

IV. LAW OF PLEDGE

A. EXTENSION OF THE JEWS' TRADE PRIVILEGE TO THE LAW OF PLEDGE

In granting or recognizing the Jews' trade privilege treated in the preceding section, the Rhenish Jewry privileges as well as the *Sachsenspiegel* specify merely acquisition of property by purchase of stolen goods, while later law sources deal only with the acceptance of such goods in pledge. This difference has caused some controversy among writers on the subject.[26]

There can be no doubt that the trade privilege as formulated in

Sachsenspiegel, III, 7, 4 (2), was extended to the acceptance in pledge of stolen goods. The best proof is *Glogauer Rechtsbuch*, 477, whose wording is very similar to, though not identical with, the *Sachsenspiegel* passage. The term in the latter *kouft* ("buys") is there replaced by *leyhet uff phand* ("gives a loan on pledge"). *Meissener Rechtsbuch*, III, 17, 11 and 25, also offers telling evidence.[27]

That privilege naturally had particular importance for the Jewish moneylending business with respect to pledges given and received as security. In the absence of public credit institutions, the Jews were considered and recognized as—so to speak—substitutes for these. They were often even expressly compelled by the authorities to lend their money against adequate security in the form of pledges.[28] There is nothing in the sources under consideration to indicate that that trade privilege was restricted to the acceptance of pledges alone. The rules developed by *Sachsenspiegel* and Magdeburg law for the acquisition of property by Jews simply operated analogously in their application to the acceptance of pledges. However, some special regulations concerning the acceptance of goods in pledge and the obligations flowing therefrom, peculiar to Jews and deviating from the general rule, must be considered.

B. TRAFFIC IN PAWNED GOODS

For a better understanding, one point must be called to mind first. The pledging of goods was of paramount importance in connection with the petty moneylending trade. A man in need of money could naturally obtain a loan more easily and quickly if he could offer some pledge, even if its monetary value covered the loan only partially. The holding of pledges, on the other hand, brought to the Jewish as well as the Christian creditor two great advantages, strengthening his economic and commercial position. First, he had in his hands an object which represented a monetary value and to this extent security for the eventual payment of the debt; for in case the debtor failed to redeem his pledge, this became the creditor's property. Through selling, repawning, or otherwise disposing of the pawned object, the creditor could secure quick satisfaction for his claim. Second, possession of a pledge placed him in an advantageous position in legal proceedings with respect to the evidence for his claim. The pledge enabled the creditor to establish the amount of the debt due him by simply taking an oath.[29] The various points involved produced a multitude of legal regulations covering traffic in pawned goods.

In particular, the "publicity" principle, pointed out in *Sachsenspiegel*, III, 7, 4 (2), was applied analougously to the acceptance of goods in pledge. It was especially stressed in Magdeburg law, as shown in the following passage:

If a Jew gives a loan on such a pledge in the light of day before a sworn man [an official], the juror [*schepffe*] inspecting it and seeing the money counted: upon his [the juror's] testimony in court according to law, the Jew obtains the money lent on the pledge, and keeps his honor[30] [that is, he is not regarded as a thief].

The prohibition against Jews' accepting sacred chalices, books, or vessels has already been discussed in another connection. Suspect articles of another kind, such as wet or blood-stained garments, were also included in such interdictions, which were extended, moreover, to arms. In the interest of the defense of the country or city, arms, too, were not to be sold, pawned, or accepted in pledge, except with the consent of the city council.[31]

Owing to the conditions of commerce and traffic prevailing in the Middle Ages, the Jewish moneylender could not be legally obligated to inquire into the origin of the goods or his debtor's right to them:[32]

A Jew may lend on pledges brought to him of whatever kind; he is not obligated to inquire about them, unless he cares to do so; except, as pointed out previously, for mass vestments, bloody or wet garments [*Meissener Rechtsbuch*, III, 17, 24].[33]

According to the principle of medieval German law, "hand must warrant hand" (*Hand muss Hand wahren*), the owner of a movable, which was contractually intrusted to another person, had no claim against a third party to whom the object had passed later. The rightful owner could always proceed against his bailee only, because the agreement was made with him alone.[34] From him he might possibly obtain damages but could not reacquire the object. In a case brought before the *Schöffen* of Magdeburg, a man had intrusted to a carter some goods, part of which the latter pawned with a Jewish moneylender.[35] The owner sued to recover the alienated article from the moneylender. The Magdeburg jury court held in its decision that the owner "had no claim against the Jews but against him to whom he had intrusted the object. The Jew is 'nearer' [privileged] [upon his oath] to retaining his pledge." Thus the Jewish moneylender was protected in the possession of a *bona fide*, and hence rightfully acquired, pledge even if it was misappropriated from the owner.

Naturally, Jews were not supposed to give loans to or accept pledges from suspicious persons or under circumstances liable to give rise to suspicion:

> Jews shall not give loans at night, neither before sunrise, nor after sunset. Jews shall not give loans to persons of ill repute, such as thieves or robbers. If they should give them loans clandestinely and the stolen or robbed goods be found in their possession, they must restore them without compensation and pay a fine. They become outlawed among Jews and Christians [*Meissener Rechtsbuch*, III, 17, 3; cf. III, 17, 4].[36]

If such goods were concealed by a Jew and later discovered in his house, he was to be considered a thief himself and to lose his standing at law among Jews as well as among Christians.[37] There was also a general rule that no forfeited pledge should be pawned with Jews without the owner's consent.[38]

C. PLEDGE AND DEBTOR'S PERSONAL LIABILITY

As a result of the historical development of legal duty and liability (*Schuld und Haftung*) in German law, forfeiture played a characteristic role in the regulations concerning the law of pledge. In case of the debtor's default the pawned object was left to the creditor for his satisfaction. In disposing of the pledge, he might obtain a sum in excess of the debt, whereas he had to shoulder the loss if he realized less than the amount of the loan, no personal recourse to the debtor being possible. In other words, liability for an obligation was absolutely restricted to the object which had been given as pledge ("real liability," *reine Sachhaftung*).[39]

This general configuration in the German law of pledge obviously bore also on the legal situation of the Jewish pledgee.

As to the value of the pawned object and its relation to the amount of the debt, the *Meissener Rechtsbuch* offers clear regulations, which also comprise the problem of personal liability on the part of the debtor.[40] Two types of loan contracts entailing pledges are differentiated (III, 17, 16): those under which an object is simply given in pledge, *ein phand, do nicht zcu gelobet ist,* without any accessory promise of personal liability by the debtor; and those under which a pledge is given with an additional obligation of personal liability by the debtor, *ein phand, darzue gelobit ist.*

In the first instance the Jewish creditor has recourse only to the pawned object and has no right to sue his debtor for payment of the difference between the value of the pledge and the amount due. He must offer the object to his debtor for redemption in the presence of witnesses and thereafter make public summons in court three times. After the third proclamation the object becomes his property.[41] If it should yield an amount less than that of the loan, the creditor has no additional claim against his debtor (III, 17, 15). If, on the other hand, the object should yield proceeds in excess of the loan, the gain must of necessity go to the creditor. This arrangement corresponds exactly to the general German law of pledge.

In the second instance, the Jew can recover the deficiency in amount from the debtor (III, 17, 16), who had expressly pledged his responsibility. The same rule applies when a Christian, after contracting personal responsibility, refrains from redeeming a pawned object because it has deteriorated and hence lost value (III, 17, 19; Purgoldts Rb., VIII, 72). On the other hand, the Jewish creditor is obligated to turn over to his debtor any amount realized on the pawned object in excess of the loan.[42]

D. DETERIORATION AND DESTRUCTION OF PAWNED OBJECTS

There remains a final problem concerning pawned property: who bears the risk of deterioration or accidental destruction of the pledge?[43]

The general rule is stated in *Sachsenspiegel*, III, 5, 4: "What one lends or gives in pledge to anyone, he [the holder] shall return undamaged or give compensation for it according to its value."

This means that the pledgee is always liable for *culpa* as well as for *casus*, that is, liable for deterioration, lessened value, or destruction of the pawned object, whether through his negligence or through accident. According to medieval German law, the risk thus had to be borne by the creditor in possession of the pledge, Christian or Jew.

For the Jewish creditor, a special rule is found in *Meissener Rechtsbuch*, III, 17, 17: the Jew is liable for *culpa;* he must pay compensation but may deduct the amount of his loan.[44] In this lawbook (III, 17, 18) and similarly also in Purgoldt's *Rechtsbuch* (VIII, 71) a legal device was provided in order to eliminate disputes on the condition of pawned articles and the creditor's liability which could possibly arise. Before accepting objects as pledges, the Jewish creditor was supposed to "examine them carefully as to whether they were damaged by moths, mice or rats." If, in his opinion, such damage was found, it had to be ascertained by means of three witnesses, two Jewish ones and one Christian according to the Meissen lawbook, or two Christian ones and one Jewish according to Purgoldt's *Rechtsbuch*. If this precaution was taken and later a dispute should arise, the Jewish creditor was entitled to prove by taking an oath that the objects had been in a defective condition previously, that he had established this fact through witnesses, that he had informed the debtor of it, and that he had taken good care of the pledges. His liability was restricted merely to additional damage caused by his negligence. While such proceedings were customary law in Saxony, Meissen, Thuringia, and Hesse, a different custom prevailed in Eisenach, as Johannes Purgoldt tells us. Here a Jewish creditor was privileged in any case, without taking any precaution beforehand, to obtain release from any liability by taking an oath that "he had taken good care of the pledges, in such a manner as if they were his own."

In the event of accidental destruction of a pledge the sources take into account the fact that other belongings of the creditor perished together with it. Here medieval lawyers seem to have been in disagreement. A Magdeburg *Oberhof* decision makes the Jewish holder of the pledge liable to its owner and is thus completely in accord with the general principle.[45] *Meissener Rechts-*

buch, III, 17, 12, on the other hand, permits the Jew in case of
conflagration or theft to take an oath "on the books of Moses"
and thus free himself from any obligation and responsibility:
"The Jew loses his pennies and the Christian his [pawned] object."[46] The fact that the holder's own belongings had perished
together with the pawned objects was considered proof to establish that he had exercised the necessary care required by law.
The corollary was the presumption that the pledgee was innocent
of offense: he was permitted to take an oath of purgation in order
to be relieved of any liability or obligation of restitution. Which
of these two courses was more favorable to, and which more to
the disadvantage of, the Jewish pledgee depended on the value of
the pledge and its relation to the amount of the loan.

V. LAW OF CONTRACT

A. JEWISH MONEY TRADE IN HISTORY

Jewish moneylending in the Middle Ages has been the subject
of penetrating research by numerous scholars, who have approached it from the point of view of general economics, as well
as particularly of Jewish history.[47] Even the Hebrew source material, chiefly medieval rabbinic *Responsa*, has been worked up
with regard to this problem, a phenomenon as rare as it is remarkable.[48] To be sure, in the scholarly evaluation the role
played by Jews in the medieval money trade still wavers, distorted by partisan favor or prejudice ("von der Parteien Hass und
Gunst verzerrt"). It cannot be the task of this presentation to
plow this field again deeply or even only to sum up the results
of previous research. What can be attempted is merely a modest
contribution from the domain of legal history, completely neglected in this sector since the days of Stobbe.

The primary intention of the medieval lawbooks is to regulate
traffic in, and the law of pawning and accepting, pledges. They
show, however, hardly any concern for the juridical features of
moneylending contracts, their various clauses, the obligations
of the debtors, and the privileges of the creditors. Nonetheless,
all these had to meet certain legal requirements to guarantee the
validity and eventually the lawful enforcement of the contracts
and special stipulations involved. In the Middle Ages, actual

care for all this was left to commercial and legal practice, just as under some modern systems of law. True, relevant instances have been produced by previous research from deeds of indebtedness and from narrative sources. Arguments of the opposing parties in actual lawsuits and the pertinent court decisions, however, have remained almost unused in the literature until now. And yet, they can add indubitable illumination to the facts already known and thus offer a new contribution from the field of legal history.

In summing up a careful study of this voluminous source material—not restricted to Jews but yielding a comparatively rich harvest for the history of legal techniques in the Jewish moneylending trade—one general observation forces itself on the historian. It is the conclusion that, contrary to the prevalent notion that Jews enjoyed a virtual monopoly in moneylending, Christian trade in money played a far from negligible role in the economic life of medieval Germany.[49] Detailed evidence for this assertion would amount to an independent monograph far beyond the limits of this work. This historical observation, however, must be pointed out before the legal details concerning Jewish moneylending are presented. Other misrepresentations by anti-Semitic writers on the subject will find correction automatically through the data drawn directly from the sources.

B. INDEBTEDNESS TO JEWS

It is self-evident that documents of indebtedness containing a written promise to pay a stated sum to a Jewish creditor, either at a specified date or on demand, were drawn up and delivered only if the loan amounted to a considerable sum. Petty loans, most probably, were usually given against pawned objects of appropriate value, so that it was unnecessary to draw up formal bonds or promissory notes. Amounts ranging from 8 Hungarian florins plus 4 old *Schock Groschen*[50] up to 200 marks[51] are recorded as objects of lawsuits. Most frequently a fixed total sum is stated. Sometimes the principal is given and, in addition, the rate of interest in case of default, the currency lent and to be repaid also being specified.[52] The rate of interest is that customary in money transactions between Jews and Christians, 2 pennies per pound per week.[53] Since the pound was worth 240 pennies

(*pfennige*), this amounted to 104 pennies a year, or 43⅓ per cent.
At times the rate is even higher, approximating 65 per cent. It
is well known that such rates of interest were common in medieval times; they were recognized and imposed judicially on
Christian debtors by the *Oberhof* of Magdeburg.[54]

Burghers, obligated either individually or jointly, appear most
frequently as debtors.[55] In one instance it is the municipal council
of the town of Guben (Lower Lausitz),[56] in another, the council
and community of Frankenstein which are indebted to Jews, *alz
selpschuldigir mit gesamptir hand*.[57] Bartholomew Risted, *Schöffe* in
the municipal court of Eisleben, was a debtor of the Jew Aaron.[58]
Among the debtors are often found personages of knightly
rank,[59] *edle herren, ritter und knechte;*[60] a prince's chamberlain;[61]
even Duke Ruprecht of Liegnitz must be counted among them.[62]

In the entire source material under consideration, reaching up
to the fifteenth century, there is not even a single instance proving or even indicating indebtedness of peasants to Jews. True,
Jewish moneylenders were—as were most Jews in the Middle
Ages—city dwellers and carried on their business in the towns.
Yet, in the same way that knights and princes enter the picture
as parties to loan contracts with Jews, peasants would also appear in the sources if they had been customers of Jews in any considerable number. It can, therefore, by no means be accidental
that not even a single case of this sort has come to light.[63]

C. PROMISSORY NOTES

1. MONEYLENDING BY JEWS AGAINST PROMISSORY NOTES

In an age which in legal matters adhered almost excessively
to prescribed forms, the bond or promissory note, if properly
executed, provided the best evidence in an eventual lawsuit. It
was therefore an item of particular concern in effecting a loan
contract. Such documents could even play a decisive role in
legal disputes. They were themselves often the main objects of
contention between debtor and creditor. The original documents
were therefore referred to, produced, and read in the courts and
sometimes even employed by the *Schöffen* of Magdeburg as the
basis of their decisions.[64] Exact copies were inserted in, or appended to, a request for a decision by the *Oberhof* of Magdeburg.

Hence they appear likewise in superior-court decisions. In this way the customary wording of promissory notes, interesting in many respects from the point of view of legal history, has come down to posterity,[65] while only a few of the originals have survived through preservation by the litigants.[66]

This very obvious fact, requiring no further explanation, that only a few originals of promissory notes in favor of Jewish creditors have survived from the Middle Ages, apparently induced the excellent historian of Jewish economic life, George Caro, to believe that promissory notes originally played a very minor role in Jewish moneylending in medieval Germany.[67] He supposed that it was even impossible for Jews to lend money otherwise than on security. Promissory notes, he surmised, came into use by Jewish creditors in Germany only comparatively late in the Middle Ages. In view of the documentary material adduced here and the conclusions to be drawn from it, this hypothesis must now be definitely abandoned.[68]

2. THE DEBTOR'S PRINCIPAL OBLIGATIONS

Juridical exactitude and cautiousness in wording such documents of indebtedness are not surprising. They find expression in several clauses having historical interest for an understanding of the legal relationships involved.

First, as to the designation of debtor and creditor: the individual debtors, or several debtors jointly, assumed obligation for payment not only for themselves as personal and principal debtors (*selbschuldigen*) but also for all their heirs.[69] The binding clause, strengthened in the case of several joint debtors, by the added phrase, *mit gesampter hand*, points to the personal and principal obligation of each of these main debtors in the loan contract, in contradistinction to that of accessory sureties, *burgen*, who sometimes assumed additional obligations.[70]

In principle, medieval German law sources (*Sachsenspiegel*, I, 6, 2), and particularly those of Magdeburg law, considered all contractual obligations of the main debtor, in case of his death, as an integral part of his estate;[71] the *Sachsenspiegel*, however, added the restriction that the deceased debtor must have enjoyed and left to his heirs some *wederstatinge*, that is, some equivalent benefit. Nevertheless, the explicit extension of liability to the debtor's heirs was not a superfluous clause in promissory notes in favor of Jews; for even the more progressive laws subsequent to the *Sachsenspiegel* made exceptions from the principle mentioned, in order to exclude from transmission to the debtor's heirs obligations carrying a stipulation of interest or violating the prohibition of usury. In a lawsuit involving 210 florins the superior court denied to a Jew any claim against his debtor's widow and heirs, since the latter had not been included in the promissory note either as principal debtors or as sureties.[72] True, in this decision the *Oberhof* stood by the restrictive interpretation of the legal principle as found in the *Sachsenspiegel*. Despite the fact that, in the later Middle Ages, the heir was considered in general liable for the debts of the deceased, to the extent of the entire estate, Jewish creditors still preferred to have in their hands an explicit stipulation, black on white. The records of medieval lawsuits disclose that even in such cases their claim to prompt payment from the heirs did not remain uncontested, on the ground of a different interpretation of the laws of inheritance.

The stipulation of indebtedness *mit gesampter hand* represents another precaution taken for similar reasons. Thereby all co-debtors were bound to fulfil the assumed obligation *in toto*, each individual being liable for the total amount of the debt.[73] Those debtors who fulfilled their obligation toward the common creditor became thereby themselves creditors of the others, whose default had caused their responsibility for the full amount to become effective. Hence, all debtors were responsible for one another. The Jewish creditor was entitled to sue them jointly or individually, the liability of all continuing until the debt was paid in full. It must also be noted that, in the cases under consideration, this type of obligation in favor of Jewish creditors is extended to the debtors' heirs, although the latter had not been consulted, while the sureties limited their obligation to their own persons alone.[74] This procedure finds its explanation in the principles of the medieval German law of inheritance. While, as has been mentioned, the full liability of heirs for the debts of the deceased was finally recognized with only few exceptions, debts resulting from obligations of guaranty (*burge*) were not capable of being imposed on the heirs by way of transfer through inheritance.

3. THE CREDITOR'S CLAIM

The promissory notes incorporated in the Magdeburg jury-court decisions being considered here identify the Jewish money-lender, his wife, and heirs as creditors: "Abraham vom Hayne, Perlin, his wife, Jews, residing in Naumburg, and all their heirs, or whoever holds this letter by their free will and consent";[75] or: "Junger and Kanold, Jews, residing in Naumburg, their wives and all their heirs, and whoever holds this letter by the free will of the aforenamed Jews and with their consent."[76]

The formulation of this clause must be explained again through the respective rules prevailing in medieval German law in the era of the lawbooks. There was a rule that, without the debtor's consent, a creditor's contract-claim resulting from an obligation in his favor was not freely transferable to a third person.[77] Furthermore, in case of the principal creditor's death, a collision between the rules of the Jewish law of inheritance and those of the German law could arise, if the hereditary succession were to be contested or disputes resulting from such obligations should be brought before non-Jewish courts. It was therefore in accord with the prevailing legal situation to take precautions in the promissory note and make wives and heirs of the principal creditors co-claimants with full title. The same purpose was served by the "clause of attorney," which reserved to the Jewish creditor the right of indorsing the promissory note to a third person. Each of these claimants was to derive an original and entirely independent title from the document and the original contract.

The clause of attorney, or indorsement clause, seems to have sprung from an urgent need in medieval and particularly in Jewish money trade. Loans were often made for long terms, while the economic and legal situation of the Jews was not infrequently subject to rapid change. Thus it was a legitimate desire on the part of Jewish creditors to be able to respond to the needs of pressing present conditions by immediately transferring their monetary claims to other persons, without the debtors' co-operation. The maker of the instrument promised performance under certain circumstances to some third person, still unknown, who might be the holder of the promissory note but was not a party to the original contract. Thus promissory notes of Jewish creditors could have become easily negotiable securities, which could have led to a remarkable development in economic life. Medieval commercial as well as legal practice in Germany, however, interpreted the wording of such clauses in a very restricted sense and required from the indorsee proof that "he holds the promissory note by the free will of the other Jews, to whom the letter was also made out," as a Magdeburg decision once laid down.[78] Such an attitude, which was by no means confined to Jewish promissory notes or creditors alone,[79] had precisely the opposite effect of the original aim of these transfer clauses. This is evident from the case, already cited, of Kussel, a Jew of Kalish, who, as the holder of such a promissory note, brought the debtor to trial in an extraordinary court (*Gastrecht*) in a Silesian town. Instead of obtaining his money quickly, in accordance with the accelerated procedure of such courts provided by German town law for foreigners, he had to wait for an adverse Magdeburg *Oberhof* decision.

4. CLAUSES FAVORING THE CREDITOR

Legal disadvantages might easily arise for the Jewish creditor from formal defects in instruments of indebtedness. Hence other appropriate clauses were required to insure his protection. The insertion of such clauses, not unusual also with Christian creditors, must be regarded as fully justified in the case of Jews. Most of them were little versed in matters of German law and legal formalities, even if they were able to read or write German. Furthermore, it is a fact proved by the group of documents under consideration, and others as well, that the debtors tried to evade their obligations to their Jewish creditors by all possible means. Hans Glogaw, citizen of Naumburg, figuring as debtor in all these cases, offers a particularly striking example. Hence it was altogether legitimate for Jewish moneylenders to try to forestall any potential objections or arguments by anticipating them through protective clauses.

A clause found in all these promissory notes reads: "As long as the Jews hold this letter, no one shall take this letter from them by an oath or recourse to any other objection, nor shall he allege payment of the debt."[80] The underlying tendency is clear. In one case this clause was fully upheld by the Magdeburg jurors.[81] Hans Glogaw maintained in court that he had paid his debt ten years earlier. At that time, he asserted, Abraham had been unable to find the letter of indebtedness whereon he now claimed payment once more. The Magdeburg decision is remarkable. It expressly recognized the validity of the clause appealed to by the Jew Abraham and literally quoted in the *Schöffenspruch*. Glogaw was ordered to stand by his promise and to pay in accordance with the letter. Only after this was done and the promissory note redeemed, could he sue Abraham for improper practices, provided that he could produce satisfactory evidence.[82]

In another decision Hans Glogaw, truly ingenious in finding legal excuses for refusal to pay his debts, also had his contention rejected. Yet the Magdeburg *Oberhof* declined expressly to uphold the validity of that clause because the authenticity of the debtor's seal was contested.[83] Here there come into play the strict medieval laws concerning seals, which will be discussed later. The same attitude was taken by the *Schöffen* with regard to an error in the date of a letter.[84] Prior contractual elimination of objections to errors in fundamental essentials of legal instruments was also refused recognition in Magdeburg. The underlying reason which prevented the *Oberhof* from accepting that clause in the last-mentioned cases is again a strict adherence to rigid formalism: errors in such formalities as sealing or dating legal documents, which were essential for their validity, should always be placed beyond the possibility of contest and never be open to legalization by general protective clauses. Hence such clauses, when applied to certain essentials of legal deeds, were considered *pro non scripto* and were thus not binding on the debtor.

In another instance Hans Glogaw took refuge in the fact that his co-debtor's seal was missing from the letter.[85] The Jewish creditor, on the other hand, pointed to the following clause in the promissory note: "Should there be some omission or defect in this letter or seal, this shall not be prejudicial to the Jews." The court decision did not explicitly touch on the validity of that clause, but favored the Jews, since Glogaw's seal was found intact on the letter.

As can be seen from these instances, the actual value of such and similar clauses was doubtful, if the debtor was unable or unwilling to fulfil his obligation. It is safe to assume, therefore, that debtors of Glogaw's caliber, in seeking loans again and again, were not sparing with additional and even more stringent protective clauses, in order to impress their Jewish creditors with the alleged security of their loans. In order to deprive themselves in advance of excuses of any kind, particularly for eventual delay or failure of payment, they pledged themselves, for instance, in this manner:

And we, the aforementioned personal debtors and sureties, shall be obligated and are willing to cover and pay the aforementioned money, principal and interest [wūcher], messengers' fees, letter-money, traveling and living expenses, such as might arise,[86] in ready money or in good pledges, as will satisfy the Jews, without recourse to an ecclesiastic or secular court, [payment to be made] in the city of Naumburg or within a circuit of seven miles, in whatever town they claim payment from us. No lord's service, request or order shall impede us therefrom, and nothing shall be found therein that may be injurious to the aforementioned Jews regarding their aforementioned money, be it of ecclesiastic or secular jurisdiction.[87]

To any legal-minded observer it must be surprising indeed that, even in view of such documentary promises, debtors were brazen enough to deny their obligations entirely or to throw doubt on their lawful origin. In one case Hans Glogaw took refuge in the assertion that the ancient Germanic form of making a solemn vow by hand and mouth (mit hand und mund) had not been observed: "I have not sworn to the debt, neither with my mouth nor my hand; and I have also not become personally liable for it to the Jew."[88]

The Magdeburg jurors, however, denied this plea and declared that merely stating the obligation in writing sufficed for its validity.

5. SEALS ON PROMISSORY NOTES

The strict adherence to prescribed traditional forms in medieval German law made the seals of principal debtors and sureties a most important essential of promissory notes. To be complete and valid, every such document had to contain the terms and conditions, written by hand, and the seals, attached by their rightful owners. Both content and seals were necessary essentials, according to Magdeburg law. Just as obligations entered into by word of mouth were in medieval German law considered definitely binding (*ein Mann, ein Wort*), so likewise was an obligation created by the written word.

The validity of this strict principle was explicitly extended to Jewish creditors in one of the aforementioned Magdeburg decisions:

> If Abraham the Jew possesses a promissory note, sealed with your seal, of such a tenor as the letter inserted in your request [for law instruction] shows, the letter must be observed and interpreted in accordance with its words; and the Jew must not forsake the clauses, even if they be against the law, and you cannot free yourself by your denial and your personal oath of the debt and promissory note to the Jew.[89]

This was indeed a remarkable decision, strictly upholding the validity of a lawfully executed document. It bluntly rejected Hans Glogaw's plea that "the Jew should forsake all articles and clauses which were against the law, and should content himself in court with what was lawful."

In this generalized form, however, that principle was not adhered to by the *Schöffen* of Magdeburg, as was pointed out before. They established, besides, another principle against which certain clauses and rights, reserved in promissory notes in favor of Jewish creditors, could not stand: objections against defects in some essentials (seal, date) were always to be given consideration and hence could not be contractually eliminated in advance.[90]

Except for cases of this kind, a promissory note lawfully executed was a strong weapon in the hands of a Jewish creditor. As long as the letter of indebtedness remained in his (or his heirs') possession, the presumption was that the debt still remained unpaid:[91]

> If a man puts in pledge to a Jew promissory notes with his own seal appended, and the Jew asserts, claims, and requests that the bonds be redeemed, whereas the debtor maintains that they had [already] been

redeemed: he must prove this against the Jew with two supporting witnesses [*selbdritte*], and it shall be one Jew and two Christians who bear witness. Therefore every one should beware, if he redeems his promissory notes, to bring along a Jew [or to make it public, so that he may remain unharmed] [*Meissener Rechtsbuch*, III, 11, 4 (1); cf. Purgoldt's Rb. VII, 97].

If a Jew dies with promissory notes in his possession which might well have been redeemed, his heirs cannot prove more with them than what is attested according to the wording of the bond, if one does not want to get back the promissory notes. If one claims, however, that they were redeemed, it must be proved with two supporting witnesses [*selbdritte*] that the debt had been paid [*Meissener Rechtsbuch*, III, 11, 5; cf. Purgoldt's Rb., VII, 99].

It was commonly assumed that if the debt had been paid, the document would have been returned to the debtor, or a properly executed receipt would have been made out, which could invalidate the letter of indebtedness. Therefore, a specific kind of qualified evidence was required.

In a lawsuit between the Jew Moshe and one Bartusch Koslig, the former claimed payment on a promissory note in his possession, probably received from the original creditor, a Jew named Ychel of Reichenbach. Koslig, however, exhibited a *quitancia*, according to which Bishop Conrad of Breslau as an arbiter had previously settled a dispute between the parties and Ychel had freed his debtor from all obligations. The decision of the Magdeburg jurors stated that the original promissory note was invalidated by the *quitancia* resulting from that arbitration. The bond had become "*tot, crafftlos und machtlos*, so that no Jew should benefit from it henceforth."[92]

Besides previous payment of the debt, there were also other objections through which promissory notes could become invalidated while still in the possession of Jewish creditors. One of them—the defectiveness of the instrument as to date or seal—has been mentioned. Absence or faultiness of one seal, however, did not affect the obligation of those debtors whose seals were intact.[93] Even if the letter as such should be invalidated, debtors could be held responsible by their Jewish creditors on the basis of their obligational promises alone.[94]

Another objection frequently made against Jewish creditors—
and not only by Hans Glogaw—was fraud, particularly fraudulent use of the seals attached to the instrument.[95] The assertion
would run that a seal was affixed to the promissory note "not of
the debtor's own will or knowledge, [but] by fraud" (*an mynen
willen und wissentschaft, mit betriklichkeyd*). While the first-mentioned objection was directed against openly visible defects in
the document, the reproach of fraudulent manipulation (*falsch-
eid*), affecting the letter only indirectly, was leveled against
the alleged forger, the Jewish creditor. The frequency of such
reproaches is bound to arouse some suspicion.[96] Such legally important instruments as seals must have been well secured by their
owners and would hardly be easily accessible for fraudulent use
by Jewish moneylenders.[97] Be this as it may, the *Oberhof* of
Magdeburg had a feeling for facts as well as for law and met this
objection in a way which was constantly applied in its decisions
and adopted also by the *Oberhof* of Dohna. Since no open defects
are visible in the document, the *Oberhof* reasoned, the debtor cannot evade his obligation by denying it on his personal oath only.
He must rather take a qualified oath supported by two witnesses
who can testify to his own credibility. Even by this procedure he
can void merely the legal instrument as such, but by no means
the obligation involved. For the latter he must obey a call to
court, just as for any claim not resting on specific forms. Only if
he again succeeds in taking an oath supported by two witnesses,
has the debtor "redeemed his seal, invalidated the letter, and no
obligation to the Jew on account of the debt."[98]

A legal effect similar to that produced by duly sealed promissory notes—in fact, even stronger—was attained by entering
Jewish loan contracts in the official municipal register, the
Stadtbuch, or in the court records, the *Gerichtsregister*. Several instances of this kind are mentioned in court decisions from Magdeburg, Leipzig, and Dresden.[99] In medieval law such entry in
official records of public authenticity constituted unimpeachable
evidence. Accordingly, this principle operated also in favor of
Jewish creditors. In all cases in which they had been able to avail
themselves of this means of strengthened evidence, the superior
courts decided unfailingly in their favor. It could, however, also

serve as evidence against them. The Meissen lawbook (III, 11, 4 [2]) and Purgoldt's *Rechtsbuch* (VII, 98) contain regulations to this effect. Actual or alleged loss of a promissory note by a Jewish creditor provided such an opportunity. The creditor's obligation upon payment to return the bond to his debtor was then replaced by the duty to have the payment of the debt entered into the *Stadtbuch* or *Gerichtsregister*, whereby the promissory note would be invalidated.

All the instances from medieval law and judicature testify to the correctness of Caro's general statement: "Jewish moneylending was far from being a business quite free of risks and troubles."[100] On the other hand, the Magdeburg court decisions in lawsuits by Jewish creditors give ample proof that the medieval supreme court of Germany did not use a double yardstick in administering justice but afforded the Jews, too, fair judgment in accord with its own high judicial and moral standards.

D. CONTRACTUAL ENFORCEMENT OF MONEY OBLIGATIONS

Liability for debt and enforcement of payment are legally in close connection. As a rule, medieval German law intrusted enforcement of contractual obligations to the courts; but it was no infrequent phenomenon in civil-law relations that, by contractual agreement between the parties, the rightful claimant was left to demand recognition and enforce fulfilment of obligations due him, by his own competence. The lawfulness of contracts aiming at private distraint for nonperformance of obligations was recognized. The debtor was then subject, in his person as well as in his property, to such contractual constraint to perform his obligation, under pain of personal or pecuniary disadvantages in case of continued nonperformance. The history of the medieval law of contract in Germany shows how the tendency to make the debtor's liability more stringent by means of voluntary stipulations of various kinds was made to serve a twofold purpose: first, to reinforce the debtor's liability through the contractual inclusion of additional objects subject to seizure by the creditor; second, from the very beginning to facilitate and guarantee to the fullest possible extent enforcement and final realization of his claims by the creditor. Thus a whole system of contractual means developed to enforce fulfilment of obligations, particularly those arising from loan contracts.[101] It was often difficult for creditors, even for Christians, to claim and recover their money, especially from debtors of rank, such as knights, church or secular dignitaries, princes, or kings. Even when courts of law had decided in favor of the creditors, it sometimes remained difficult or impossible to translate the court's decree into reality. Hence the attempt to facilitate enforcement of legal obligations extra-judicially by means of indirect pressure on the debtor's person or property, when direct satisfaction appeared doubtful or impossible of attainment.

All this applies generally to the creditor-debtor relation in the Middle Ages; the Jewish moneylender was obviously in a far more precarious situation than was his Christian colleague.[102] He was often dependent on circumstances or chances entirely beyond the reach of his personal influence. Thus he stood in even greater need of contractually insuring in advance the enforcement and fulfilment of his rightful claims. It is necessary, therefore, to inquire how far Jewish creditors could avail themselves of, and were benefited by, this system of indirect enforcement of contractual obligations, which was so highly developed and widely employed in medieval law.

That pledges were extensively used to guarantee to Jewish creditors security and realization of their monetary claims has been shown and discussed at length. The same applies to the function of sureties for debts in loan contracts between Jewish moneylenders and their Christian customers.[103]

Two other legal means of contractually reinforcing the security of loans are *Pfändungsklausel* and *Schelmenschelten*. They were frequently employed by non-Jewish creditors. The source material under consideration reveals no trace of their use specifically by Jewish claimants.

The first-mentioned "seizure clause" or *Pfändungsklausel* accorded the creditor the contractual right of extra-judicial seizure of the debtor's person or property if he should fail to pay his debt at the time agreed on.[104] Thus the creditor was *ab initio* empowered and entitled to seek satisfaction from his debtor "by his own force." He could do this without prior legal procedure and without any other recourse to public authority. This was indeed a strong protection of the creditor's claim, assigning to him the same legal position as if he had obtained valid legal title to execution issuing from a court of law. In fact, the creditor's position was even stronger, since, in using this right of self-exercised execution, he was freed from the necessity of resorting to any judicial assistance.

From the silence of Saxon law sources on the application of the seizure clause in favor of Jewish creditors, the conclusion does not necessarily follow that this convenient legal instrument was denied to Jews. Indeed, it seems not beyond the range of possibility that the contrary conclusion may be drawn from the *argumentum e silentio;* for we know from other sources that the seizure clause was legally permitted to, and even regularly employed by, Jewish creditors.[105]

The same may be true, though to a lesser degree, of the second clause, the stipulation of *Schelmenschelten*. This contractually conceded to the creditor the debtor's permission, in case of default, to attack his honor publicly in word and picture; the defaulter was to be derided in lampoons and defamatory caricatures and proclaimed a rogue or *Schelm*.[106] The legal tendency behind the "rogue clause" in loan contracts was to intensify the debtor's liability and, by indirect pressure, to prompt him to meet his obligations more quickly. "The honor of the debtor was forfeited to the creditor by his inability to pay, and could publicly be offered for sale and thrown away."[107] The injured creditor would compose a *Scheltbrief* full of defamation and insult, designating the defaulting debtors or sureties as lawbreakers and without honor. The satirical posters expressive of this practice picture the debtors in shameful and humiliating situations, particularly undergoing execution, as on the gallows, on the wheel, at the stake, or in the pillory. The mere threat embodied in the contract clause often proved effective, and its influence naturally grew more coercive when actually executed.

Very few of such *Scheltbriefe* or *Schandgemälde*, destined as they were for temporary use, have survived from the Middle Ages. Among the scarce satirical pictures of this kind preserved, one in the Munich State Archives was directed by the Jewish merchants, Saydro Straubinger and Isaac of Regensburg, against their defaulting debtor, Hans von Judmann zu Affeking.[108] Two more cases reported from the domain of Magdeburg law[109] offer indubitable proof that Jews in Germany enjoyed the right to make use of this powerful means of forcing debtors to meet their obligations.[110]

Another means of contractual enforcement of obligations, widely employed in medieval Europe, was the stipulation of a special kind of custody, called *Einlager* in Germany.[111] The debtor or his sureties or both took upon themselves the obligation, in case of failure to pay at the stated date, "to ride, men and horses," to an inn or another place agreed on and to remain there until payment of the debt in full. The legal idea underlying this agreement was again to exert indirect pressure on the debtor. Not only would he voluntarily deprive himself of his freedom, but the steadily mounting charges for the keep of "men and horses" would increase the burden of his indebtedness.

It is well known, even from rabbinic literature, that the promise of *Einlager, Leistung*, or *Einreiten*, was frequently incorporated in promissory notes in favor of Jewish creditors.[112] According to southern German sources, such voluntary confinement of Christian debtors was not to be effected in the homes of Jewish creditors, and in Christian inns only if the Jewish creditor paid the charges himself.[113] This was, of course, contrary to the basic idea of this means of indirect pressure on the debtor and entirely frustrated its aim. Neither the *Sachsenspiegel* (II, 11, 3) nor Magdeburg law nor even the *Wiener Stadtrechtsbuch* (art. 138), all well acquainted with the *Einlager*, mention such restrictions to the disadvantage of Jewish creditors. In one instance the Magdeburg jurors handed down a decision unequivocally upholding the right of a Jewish creditor to demand that his defaulting Christian debtor fulfil his *Einlager* promise.[114] "If Cussel the Jew has proved this, Nassengneff shall be obligated to perform the *Einlager* and not to be relieved of it, unless it be by the aforementioned Jew's permission." From this *Schöffenspruch* it may be safe to assume that under Magdeburg law no restriction frustrating the aim of this legal institution was imposed on Jews. If any such restriction had been applied at all, surely it would have been mentioned in that decision as a deviation from customary legal practice.

One more means of contractual enforcement of debt obligations must finally be considered—next to the seizure clause perhaps the most potent of all: *Schadennehmen*. The debtor empowered his creditor in case of default "to borrow an equivalent amount from Christians or Jews at the debtor's 'damages' [charge]" ("das geld auf des schuldners schaden nehmen unde awsgewinnen czu cristen ader in juden"). The creditor unable to obtain the amount due from his debtor was contractually entitled to assume an obligation for ready money with a Christian or Jewish moneylender, adding the expense to the defaulting debtor's burden. The contract of *Schadennehmen* and its execution offer problems of extraordinary interest from the viewpoint of the legal, as well as the economic, history of the Jews in the Middle Ages. They have been discussed extensively by the present writer in a monographic essay.[115] In medieval Germany and central Europe the *Schadennehmen* clause was not customary in promissory notes issued to Jewish creditors.[116] Frequently, however, Jews played an important role in this legal relationship as the intervening "new creditors." Their loans afforded to the original (Christian) creditor immediate satisfaction of his unpaid claim. A detailed discussion of all the problems involved would far exceed the limits of this work. The reader is referred to the aforementioned monograph, which can here be supplemented merely by new observations on the basis of sources not accessible to the writer in 1912.

From the lawbooks[117] as well as from jury-court decisions[118] it is evident that the prescription of *Schadennehmen* was frequently employed and acted upon in the medieval money trade. Thirty-six years ago, in studying a large number of documents of indebtedness, the present writer was struck by the fact that the pertinent contract clauses most frequently named Christian moneylenders in the first place: "super dampna debitoris recipere apud christianos vel judeos."[119] Sometimes first place was given to the Caorsins, the well-known merchants of Cahors, who, from the thirteenth century on, engaged in money and loan transactions throughout Europe.[120] In one document Jews were even expressly excluded as possible creditors.[121] At that time no plausible explanation suggested itself for this strange circumstance. It has now been illumined by two Magdeburg *Schöffensprüche*, both of which settled disputes, of common occurrence between debtor and original creditor, over the "damages" or expenditures resulting from the *Schadennehmen* transaction. The first decision still sounds obscure unless recourse is taken to the second. To prove that "the damages are honest and customary," the original creditors were ordered "to prove such damages with two witnesses and to take an oath by the Saints that they were unable to obtain [the money] *nearer*," (". . . tzu den heiligen behalden, das sie das nicht nehir bekomen konden").[122] In the second case, very similar to the first one, the original creditor, upon the debtor's contractual promise "schaden czu cristen ader czu joden darumbe czu lidene," had borrowed the money from Jews. He was ordered by the Magdeburg jurors to prove with two witnesses "that he had been unable to obtain the money nearer than from the Jews" (". . . daz her geldes nicht neher wenne czu den joden bekomen konde").[123] The second decision renders the first understandable. In executing the stipulation of *Schadennehmen*, the original creditor was legally bound, on pain of loss of his claim to reimbursement for his "damages" (expenditures), to apply for a loan to Christian moneylenders first, and only if unsuccessful there was he permitted to take recourse to Jews. In other words, Christian moneylenders were officially given preference, and their Jewish colleagues were permitted to function only as substitutes, as far as *Schadennehmen* was concerned. The reason for this rule is not given in the decisions. Money was hardly obtainable at a lower rate of interest from Christian moneylenders than from Jewish ones. At all events, the fact stands out that Christians were officially recommended to the public as moneylenders. This offers telling proof that Christian moneylenders were far from unknown in medieval Germany.[124]

There can be no doubt that the stipulation of *Schadennehmen* was legally recognized in the domain of *Sachsenspiegel* and Magdeburg law as a contractual means for enforcement of obligations. Purgoldt's *Rechtsbuch*, VIII, 10, contains a regulation to this effect: in the absence of an explicit stipulation of *Schadenneh-men* in writing or by word of mouth, no creditor may invoke this legal institution unless he obtains permission to do so by due process of law. In case of contractual stipulation, however, recourse to *Schadennehmen* can always be taken without any prior legal procedure in court.[125] In view of the fact that Jews were very efficient moneylenders, this meant—though indirectly only —official support and legalization of their loan business and money trade. Once *Schadennehmen* was stipulated in the loan contract, the law even compelled the creditor to resort to it. The *Schöffen* of Magdeburg once even denied any claim to compensation for loss sustained through default, on the ground that the creditors had not lived up to the stipulation of *Schadennehmen*, since they had omitted to cover the default by borrowing the sum from ''either Christians or Jews.''[126] In such cases *Schadenneh-men* was the only lawful means for enforcing the performance of money obligations. It is therefore not at all surprising but rather consistent that the claims of Jewish creditors originating from transactions connected with *Schadennehmen* were, as a rule, upheld by the Magdeburg jury court.[127]

CHAPTER TEN

Criminal and Civil Procedure[1]

I. COURT AND PARTIES

A. GENERAL PRINCIPLES OF JUDICIAL PROCEDURE

IN THE period of the lawbooks, procedural law in Germany was still dominated by the basic ideas and principles which had prevailed in the Frankish realm. True, by the thirteenth and fourteenth centuries, great changes were taking place, in particular the gradual differentiation and separation of criminal and civil procedure. Yet the struggle for the individual's rights remained throughout the Middle Ages a contest between opposing parties, with the plaintiff the aggressor and the defendant under attack. The law compelled no one to institute action in court. The state put its judicial machinery into operation only on the plea of a suitor. Once instituted, the parties to a suit carried it out in court in person, orally and publicly. Judicial decision originally represented no more than legal instructions to the litigants, an explanation of prevailing law. The court procedure was under the direction of a judge whose duty it was to apply and see to the enforcement of the ruling folk law. It was also his duty to inquire into the pertinent law through his assessors, the *Schöffen*, who thus served as advisers to the judge. But the judge's pronouncement alone endowed their legal opinion with the authority of law. This explains the lofty conception of the judicial function which permeated medieval law and literature and culminated in the idea that earthly judges are God's vicars.[2]

Medieval life brought Jews into various contacts with non-Jewish courts of law, to whose jurisdiction they were subject to a large extent. This was explained at length in the seventh chapter.[3] While Jews were there dealt with as litigating parties, here the question arises as to whether they were capable of taking any part in medieval judicature.

B. JEWS AS JUDGES IN NON-JEWISH COURTS?

The problem of whether Jews were capable of active judicial functions in non-Jewish courts has been touched on previously in connection with a discussion of a passage in the *Sachsenspiegel* (III, 70, 1).[4] From this article and its illustration in the illuminated manuscripts the fact was established that, in the thirteenth century and probably up to the middle of the fourteenth, Saxon law considered Jews capable of passing judgment on everyone and also, in general, of acting as witnesses. This must not be understood, of course, in modern terms. Thus there is no instance of Jews being appointed or functioning as judges in purely non-Jewish courts within the domains of territorial or municipal law. This would have been contrary to the entire medieval concept of a society dominated by religious and class consciousness.[5]

Nonetheless, the recognition of the Jews' capacity to act as judges was not merely theoretical. Jews were actually called to judgeships and did perform judicial functions affecting the interests of non-Jewish litigants. This occurred where mixed courts of law composed of Jewish and Christian assessors were established to handle legal disputes between Jews and Christians.[6] It might happen, moreover, that a Christian plaintiff had to seek justice against a Jew exclusively in the latter's court, where, under certain circumstances, a Christian could even be made to stand trial.[7] There was, finally, the possibility of the voluntary appointment by litigating parties of a court of arbitration, which might put a Jew in a position to pass judgment on a Christian litigant.[8]

These instances show that the qualification of Jews for judicial functions carried with it some important legal implications. Apparently, these were clearly recognized by the authors of the *Deutschenspiegel* and the *Schwabenspiegel*, for both, concurrently discriminating against Jews, deprived them of this capacity. These lawbooks enumerate the disabilities rendering one incapable of being a judge as follows (Dsp., FE 77, 2; Schwsp., W 71, L 86, G 71, 2):

In the judge the following things shall not be (which I will enumerate here. He shall not be a perjurer). He shall not be outlawed [by the secular authority] nor excommunicated [by the church]. He shall also be neither a Jew nor a heathen nor a heretic. He shall also be the child of a proper marriage. He shall not be lame either in hands or feet. . . . Whichever of these things attaches to a man, he cannot be a judge according to the law.[9]

In an addition to Johann von Buch's *Gloss* on *Sachsenspiegel*, I, 55, 1, a catalogue of disqualifications for the appointment to judgeships was compiled, of which the following section is pertinent here: "Know ye, the judge shall not be a perjurer nor outlawed [by the secular authority] nor excommunicated [by the church] nor a Jew nor a heretic nor a heathen."[10]

As is well known, the king was the supreme judge in medieval Germany.[11] Hence he, too, had to meet the requirements laid down by law for all judges. It was the compiler of the *Schwabenspiegel* alone—in this case not in conformity with, and going beyond, the *Deutschenspiegel* (F 295)—who found it necessary explicitly to exclude Jews from eligibility to the kingship. Article W 102, G 101, 3 reads: "The princes shall not elect [as king] a lame or leprous man, or one who is excommunicated or outlawed, or is a heathen or a Jew or a heretic."[12] With the inclusion of Jewishness as a disqualification for the throne, the author of the *Schwabenspiegel* outdid not only Eike von Repgow,[13] but even Pope Innocent III, who in his bull, *Venerabilem*, mentioned as disqualifications only heresy, sacrilege, tyranny, imbecility, perjury, or descent from persecutors of the church.[14] There is not the slightest doubt that no practical significance could ever have attached to this strange provision. Yet it is an interesting reflection of the exclusion of Jews from the judicial office. That the southern German lawbook alone added this to its other anti-Jewish regulations is illuminating in itself.

No other restrictions with regard to the performance of judicial functions by Jews are found in the lawbooks. The reason is obvious: such functions were neither generally open to Jews nor were they desired by them.

C. JEWS AS PARTIES TO LITIGATIONS

The question of whether Jews were capable, according to the lawbooks and Magdeburg jury-court practice, of bringing their lawsuits to trial before non-Jewish courts or of applying to superior courts for law instruction, was discussed extensively above, in chapter seven.[15] No evidence is discernible in the law sources under consideration that Jews were excluded in general or on special grounds from these procedural activities. There are no provisions in medieval secular law corresponding to those embodied in the *Decretum Gratiani* and other canon-law sources, by which all non-Christians—pagans, apostates, schismatics, heretics, and Jews—were not admitted to the role of plaintiff and prosecutor against Christians.[16] Attempts to introduce such a provision were made only after Roman and canon law had gained strength in Germany. It was evidently due to this influence that Johann von Buch, in commenting on *Sachsenspiegel*, I, 30, endeavored to deprive Jews of the right to act as plaintiffs or defendants in Saxon courts of law.[17] In that article, he maintains, the lawbook says:

Every man [who had] immigrated to the Saxons' land shall have Saxon law, be he Bavarian, Frank, or Swabian, etc. Thus you might perhaps think that a Jew who had come into the land of Saxony could also make use of the Saxon laws, as said heretofore in book one, article thirty. But if he had Saxon law, would he also have the right to take an oath in court? Hereupon we say, that the law speaks only of Christians who are immigrants, and not of Jews. Also, the same law speaks of inheritance and not of Jews' complaint or response.[18]

Even a man of Johann von Buch's caliber had difficulty in harmonizing his reinterpretation of Saxon law with the principles of Roman and canon law, after which he was striving. Roman and canon law were themselves in conflict on the point at issue. The contradictary points of view, which naturally could not fail to become manifest in the *Sachsenspiegel Glosses*, called for reconciliation. The Stendal *Gloss* to III, 7, 3, refrained from such an attempt and contented itself with merely quoting *Cod. Just.* i. 9. 8, the well-known imperial constitution, which prescribed that all legal actions by Jews belonged in the Roman

courts and had to be dealt with in accordance with Roman law.[19]
Johann von Buch, on the other hand, who was also not ignorant
of this regulation, found a way out of the difficulty (in his comment on III, 7, 1) by contrasting *einiges landes privilegia*, the
"privileges of one land," with the *gemeine Keyserrecht*, "common
imperial laws."

If, however, someone were to object and say that it is unjust [*sc*. the
Jews' exclusion from Saxon-law privileges] because it is written in the
Codex [*Justinianus*] that the Jews shall make use of the common imperial
laws, as [pointed out in] *C. de judaeis, l. judaei Romano* [*Cod. Just*. i. 9. 8];
let him know that the *leges* are to be understood with reference to
whether they [the Jews] sue someone or are sued by someone.

To be sure, this interpretation by Johann von Buch is in agreement with the rule of Ssp., III, 7, 3, that a Christian perpetrating
a crime against a Jew was to be prosecuted and punished. From
this it follows necessarily that the Jew was entitled to invoke
the aid of a non-Jewish court. In the glossator's own opinion,
however, this interpretation and the legal situation flowing
from it were in conflict with canon law. In the *Decretum Gratiani*,
c. 25, C. II, qu. 7, it is stated explicitly: "Pagans, heretics or Jews
cannot sue Christians." Johann von Buch was familiar with this
precept: "It is there written, Jews, heathens, and heretics may
not censure or denounce a Christian to the courts. If they cannot
censure him, one does not pass judgment on him: for where
there is no plaintiff, there is also no judge and no judgment."

This result of juridical argumentation, in accord with canon
law only, naturally could not satisfy our glossator, since its
contradiction of Saxon, as well as of Roman, law principles was
manifest. In his urge to reconcile all the legal systems involved,
he had to resort—as he usually did on such occasions—to a
somewhat artificial and forced interpretation. He even offered
two explanatory arguments. Both of them, however, are of little
juridical persuasiveness in the given legal situation. First, an
argument against self-defense unauthorized by law: "The law
says: If someone has a cause against a Jew, he shall make his
complaint to the judge; for no one shall be his own judge [*Cod.
Just*. i. 9. 14]." Second, an argument designed to remove the obstacle presented by canon law:

If they [the Jews] are not allowed to sue [in court], also no judgment can be passed on him [the Christian transgressor]? Decide thus then and say: They may not lay charges for what is inflicted on others; but what wrong they suffer themselves, of that they may well complain [*Cod. Just.* ix. 1. 10 and 19; *Decr. Grat.*, c. 2, C. IV, qu. 6].

This means that even Johann von Buch, despite his earnest endeavors and despite the existing regulations of canon law, did not succeed in excluding the Jews from the right to appear as plaintiffs or defendants in Christian courts.

As a matter of fact, this right was never subjected to doubt by the *Schöffen* of Magdeburg and of other superior courts of Magdeburg law, who decided numerous cases in which one of the litigants was Jewish and who even accepted direct applications from Jews for legal instruction.[20] They also explicitly declared Jews to be obligated to respond to charges by Christians in Christian courts, thus restricting to this extent the jurisdiction of the otherwise recognized Jewish courts.[21] Not even letters of protection granted by a prince to individual Jews or the fact that they belonged to the imperial chamber were, according to the Magdeburg *Oberhof*, to have any bearing on the jurisdiction of the ordinarily competent courts. We have two cases of this kind in which the Jews involved appear to have pleaded for their exemption from trial in the ordinary courts and for the transfer of the law matters to princely or imperial jurisdiction, respectively.[22] In both cases the Magdeburg jurors rejected these pleas and declared the Jews obligated to take their suits to the ordinary courts and to abide by their decisions.

The actual participation of Jewish plaintiffs and defendants in the court procedure and in the various phases of procedural law will be discussed later.

D. JEWS AS SPOKESMEN AND WITNESSES

In the Middle Ages court procedure was characterized by an almost overrefined formalism, developed in the most minute detail. For all who attended a court session, particularly for the litigants, this formalism, with its specialized techniques and its technicalities, came to be defined as *vare* or *gefahr*, indicating the ever present hazard of error in speech or act and the serious consequences which this might entail. Nonobservance of the mere verbal formalities could result in loss of a suit, since the principle of *ein Mann, ein Wort* left no room to repair the damage. Therefore, the legal institution of spokesmen, *vorsprecher* or *vorreder*, was widely employed and played an important role in medieval court procedure. These spokesmen pleaded for the litigants, the latter reserving the right to disavow the appointed *vorsprecher* under certain conditions and to correct their legal actions (right of *Erholung* and *Wandelung*). The spokesmen acted upon the instruction and in behalf of the parties present in court. At the same time, they functioned as their counsel.[23]

The legal qualification for the office of spokesman was, in principle, in line with that for juror or witness. Hence, in accordance with the foregoing discussion of the Jews' qualification for the office of judge, they could not have been legally excluded as spokesmen. They are not included among those unfit to be *vorsprecher*, either in article I, 61, 4, or in I, 38, 1, of the *Sachsenspiegel*. Nor were Jews included among those barred from spokesmanship by Magdeburg law. A decision in the *Magdeburger Fragen* (*ca.* 1386–1400), interpreting the *Sachsenspiegel* law very liberally, considers not even foreign citizenship, residence in another dominion, or lack of immovable property under the jurisdiction of the court as impediments to being *vorsprecher*.[24] Here again a special Jewish disability is not mentioned. Only two late manuscripts of the *Sachsenspiegel*, dating from the second half and end, respectively, of the fourteenth century, substituted for the words "every man [may act as spokesman . . .]" in *Sachsenspiegel*, I, 61, 4, the words "every Christian man."[25]

It is most probable, then, that it was only under the influence of Roman and canon law (*Cod. Just.* i. 4. 15; ii. 6. 8; i. 9. 18; i. 5. 12) that Jews came to be considered unfit to act as spokesmen later in the Middle Ages. It will be remembered that the authors of the *Deutschenspiegel* (FE 77, 2) and *Schwabenspiegel* (L 86; W 71; G 71, 2), as well as the unknown author of an addition to Johann von Buch's comment on *Sachsenspiegel*, I, 55, 1, declared Jews unfit for a judicial position. Consequently, the *Deutschenspiegel* (FE 78, 1) and *Schwabenspiegel* (L 87; W 72; G 72, 1) declared the rules valid for judges applicable also in regard to the requirements for the office of spokesman. In Buch's *Gloss* to *Sachsenspiegel*, I, 60, Jews were also regarded as incapable "of being spokesmen of a man and of standing in court against a Christian," like heretics and unbelievers.[26] Legally the same result was effected by a slightly different stand, taken in the *Richtsteig Landrechts*, II, 4, and in the *Blume des Sachsenspiegels*, article VII. Neither of these lawbooks refers to Roman or canon law, but both exclude Jews from spokesmanship just as they do clerics, who are explicitly disqualified even in the original text of the *Sachsenspiegel* (I, 61, 4). However, while Nicholas Wurm's *Blume des Sachsenspiegels* treats Jews on an equal footing with clerics (art. VIII), perhaps *per analogiam* from *Sachsenspiegel*, III, 2, *Richtsteig Landrechts* creates a group of persons unfit for the office of spokesman, comprising "clerics, Jews, women, and rightless folk."

Still another conclusion must be drawn from this discrimination against Jews, namely, that a Jew could not act in court as *vorreder* even for a fellow-Jew. In its section on legal procedure the *Zwickauer Rechtsbuch*, I, 15, 3, plainly states: "No Jew shall be spokesman in court."

Thus the Jew was barred from aiding and counseling another Jew present in court. But he was well able by virtue of an attorney-clause in a promissory note personally to plead the cause of an absent coreligionist, either on the basis of his own independent right[27] or merely under a mandate.[28]

The exclusion of Jews from the office of spokesman in general did not deprive them of the privilege of employing a *vorsprecher* as legal aid and adviser in court. In his lawsuit against Nitcze Nassengneff, the Jew Kussel of Kalish, himself acting in behalf of another Jew by virtue of a clause of attorney, pleaded *durch seinen forreder*.[29] It must be assumed that this spokesman was a Christian. At the end of the fourteenth century and in the beginning of the fifteenth, in fact, "whether a Jew may employ a Christian as spokesman against another Christian" was something not self-understood. An explicit decision of the *Oberhof* of Magdeburg was needed to make this right legally indisputable.[30]

There is still more evidence for the correctness of the surmise that the Jews' exclusion from the office of spokesman must have

taken place late in the legal development: Jews were not barred
from being witnesses, a legal qualification discussed in the
sources concurrently with that for the office of judge. The interpolation of the words *unde tüch sin* ("and to be witnesses") in
Sachsenspiegel, III, 70, 1, proves that, at the end of the thirteenth
century, the legal opinion which admitted Jews as witnesses
without restriction, was as yet uncontested.[31] In legal disputes
over the "damages" from *Schadennehmen*, common between
debtor and original creditor (both usually Christians), the immediate Jewish creditor was perforce a witness par excellence
and, as such, could play an important role in the lawsuit. As
late as the end of the fourteenth century or the beginning of the
fifteenth, in a lawsuit of this kind decided by the *Oberhof* of
Magdeburg, a Jew acted, in fact, as a witness of decisive importance.[32] No objection to his qualification was raised by either of
the Christian litigants. Johann von Buch, in his *Gloss* to *Sachsenspiegel*, III, 7, 1, again and typically referring to Roman- and
canon-law regulations, attempts to set forth the thesis that
Jews are not to be admitted as witnesses against Christians.
This is the glossator's argument:

> No Jew may be a witness against a Christian, although a Christian
> may well be a witness against a Jew. Although this is contradicted by
> the *decretales* in other places, and also by the *leges*, yet know ye, that
> they [the Jews] are indeed admitted as witnesses at times, but only in
> minor matters, such as in minor purchases, or when they themselves
> purchase something.[33]

Not even von Buch's labored—though neither unbiased nor unambiguous—consideration of the issue amounted to more than
a restrictive interpretation of the Jews' right to act as witnesses
in court. Even in lawsuits between Christian litigants, their
testimony was not entirely excluded. The restriction remained
mere theory, as did others of Buch's teachings.[34] That it found
no recognition in court practice can be seen from the case cited
before, in which a Jew effectively testified with reference to an
entire *hoff und vorwerk*, real property of doubtless more than
merely "minor" value.[35]

II. Order of Judicial Procedure

A. BASIC IDEAS AND TYPES OF PROCEDURE

In civil and criminal procedure Jews were subject, under the law, to the same treatment as that which Christians received. Clear evidence for this fact can be gathered from almost innumerable provisions in the lawbooks and from actual proceedings, recorded in numerous court decisions. According to *Meissener Rechtsbuch*, III, 1, 3, the oath of office prescribed for the judges' executive officers or bailiffs included a clause providing that "in all matters they would lawfully treat the poor as the rich, foreigners as all people, Jews as Christians." As a rule, Jews were neither granted privileges nor subjected to discrimination. Exceptions to this rule can be observed only in so far as the religious or social issue came into the picture, when actions at law involved Jewish rites and customs. This was so, above all, in the law of evidence, and particularly when an oath had to be taken by Jewish parties.

In view of this state of things it seems appropriate to confine the discussion here to illustrating merely the treatment of Jewish litigants through individual law cases. The law of evidence and the Jewry oath will be discussed more fully later in separate sections.

In spite of the growing tendency to strengthen law enforcement, particularly in the realm of criminal law, the principle of "no suitor, no judge" (*kein richter, kein kläger*) remained dominant almost throughout the Middle Ages. Action had to be taken in court by those who deemed their rights to have been infringed. The actual or alleged offender had to obey the summons and to assume his defense. Hence Jews, too, had to appear and actually did appear before municipal courts, as plaintiffs or defendants in civil-law matters as well as in criminal cases. A great variety of legal causes underlying and necessitating actions in court have been presented in the preceding discussions of criminal and civil law. Unlike ancient Roman law, in differentiating actions under medieval German law the aim of an action, not its legal *causa*, was considered the determinative factor. Thus actions were differentiated according to the nature of the plaintiff's objective.

When criminal punishment was demanded, it was a penal action; and it was a civil action when performance of an obligation was sought. Mixed actions could pursue both aims or begin with one and later change to the other.[36] The rigorous formalism observed largely determined the substantiation of the claim and the quality, production, and weight of the instruments of evidence, and thus also considerably influenced the ultimate judicial decision itself.

This means that strict observance of a great number of procedural formalities was as important as was the presence of a lawful and well-substantiated claim.

B. INITIATION OF PROCEDURE AND THE PARTIES' DUTIES

When Jews wished to bring their civil claims into court (concerning debts or movable or real property), two ways of asserting their rights were available. The plaintiff could simply state his claim without referring to a specific legal cause underlying it. This was a "simple action" (*schlichte klage*), which could be defeated by the defendant's oath.[37] If the plaintiff, however, did not wish to run the risk of such a rejection, it was necessary for him to substantiate his claim and action by propounding the specific legal cause which would establish the defendant's obligation. The latter, of course, also had the right of presenting relevant facts to disprove his opponent's claim. The procedure of producing and weighing evidence, with its complicated rules, then had to set in to prepare the suit for judicial decision.

From among the many lawsuits discussed in the preceding chapter the litigation of the Jew Abraham against John Trochtil may be singled out.[38] The Magdeburg court decision in this case offers a vivid illustration of how the Jew could freely challenge his opponent in court with manifold legal inquiries and how the latter, in accordance with the order prescribed by procedural law, had to follow up and respond to each individual charge or question. Naturally, when the Jew was the defendant, he was bound to act in a corresponding manner. Again a single example may suffice.[39] This is another decision of the Magdeburg jury court in which the underlying legal principle was distinctly set forth as follows: "If a Christian brings an action against a Jew in a duly inaugurated court session [*vor gehegten dinge*], the Jew must respond according to the action as a Christian would have to do, confess or deny."[40]

Once a trial was opened in court, neither party could eliminate himself by substituting another person. A decision to this effect was handed down by the *Schöffen* of Leipzig in favor of the Jew Jordan.[41] His opponent, N. Limar, surety for a Christian debtor, was not permitted to leave the defense of the case to the latter after once having caused the Jew to produce the promissory note in evidence.

To institute legal proceedings in criminal cases, as a rule, the formal cry for help, the hue or *gerüfte*, was an essential part of the procedure. This was to achieve for the aggrieved individual the publicity requisite to free his act of self-protection from the suspicion of unlawful aggression.[42] The most effective penal action was that based on a handhaving crime (*handhafte tat*), namely, when the transgressor was caught *in flagrante delicto*. In the case of handhavingness the hue must have been raised and the wrongdoer caught either while perpetrating a crime or in flight from it. The complaint then had to be supported by corporeal evidence of the fact. All these legal requirements had been met by a Jewish plaintiff in a case of handhaving theft which came to Magdeburg for final decision. There the legal process pursued by the Jew to establish his claim is described as follows:

> You have consulted us: Outside the regular court session, a Jew appeared before the judge, ourselves [*sc.* the *scheppen*], and before our burghers, with a Christian on whose back was tied more than two marks in our money. And the Jew laid complaint against the thief and the country, that he had stolen his rightful goods and that he had thereupon raised his hue. The Christian then responded that he was not guilty of it. Thereon the Jew has requested [the court] to inquire into the law: Since he [the defendant] stands there with the *mainour* [the stolen thing] tied to his back, was not he [the plaintiff] "nearer" to produce the proof. Thereon the law was stated by our burghers that the Jew is nearer to produce proof than he [the defendant]. This was decided with the assent of the *scheppen*.[43]

In the special procedure of handhavingness, which took place outside the regular court session, the main means of the normal procedure, namely, the oath of purgation, was denied to the defendant caught in the act and immediately brought to trial. The injured party, on the other hand, had the privilege of convicting the accused by his oath with a certain number of "helpers" asserting his credibility. This was the procedure followed here, which is all the more remarkable in view of the fact that the punishment for handhaving theft, according to medieval penal law, was death.[44]

If, conversely, the Jew happened to be in the role of defendant, it was his duty also to meet all the requirements of procedural law. For instance, in the procedure of *Anefang* ("hand-laying"), prescribed for the purpose of recovering stolen goods from the present possessor,[45] a Jew, like any other defendant, was obliged to clear himself of any suspicion of theft by producing adequate proof of honest acquisition, particularly of purchase "in the light of day and not behind locked house doors."[46] Needless to say, every Jewish defendant had to obey a court summons. If he was not a resident of the town or was considered untrustworthy, another Jew had to pledge himself for the defendant's appearance in due time.[47]

Even the part of plaintiff carried with it definite procedural obligations, noncompliance causing certain legal disadvantages. Upon the defendant's request, the plaintiff was bound to pledge the *gewere* or *klagengewere*, that is, to guarantee formally that the action in its present form would remain the only one brought into court regarding his claim.[48] According to Magdeburg law, the defendant in every trial was entitled to refuse to answer the complaint until the guaranty of *klagengewere* was given. This actually happened in a case involving a Jewish party, as late as the beginning of the fifteenth century. It was "Moshe, Jew of Sagan," who is reported "thereupon to have performed the *were* and sworn to it according to the Jewish oath and law."[49] The performance of the *klagengewere* by the Jew in person clearly testifies to the fact that he was considered in possession of full capacity for legal action under procedural law (*Prozessfähigkeit*). For women, for instance, guardians were required to perform the *were* because of their restricted capacity for legal action.[50] In another case a Jewish woman lost her otherwise rightful claim for the sole reason that she had neglected to protest in court against another claimant's action, as prescribed by law.[51]

The medieval German law of judicial procedure did not, in general, develop the possibility of passing judgment by default against a party wilfully disobeying the summons or order of the court. Nonetheless, such contumacy caused disadvantages and fines for the disobedient. With particular reference to Jews the *Meissener Rechtsbuch*, III, 17, 39, stated: "Every Jew shall come before the court if summoned or ordered. If he does not do it, he must pay a fine [*busse*] like a Christian."[52]

C. COURT DECISION AND ARBITRATION

Patently there was neither a need nor an occasion in the law sources under consideration to particularize the permanent binding force of court decisions in its bearing on Jewish litigants. These were under the legal obligation, just as were all others, to respect the judgment pronounced and live up to its legal and factual contents. On the other hand, execution of judgment was also awarded in favor of Jews.[53] As to the decisions of Magdeburg and other superior courts, the problem of their legally binding force, which lies quite beyond this investigation,[54] offers no special aspects with regard to Jewish parties. Furthermore, just like all other applicants for legal instruction, they were entitled to *läuterung*, an elucidation of the *Oberhof*'s decision, customarily handed down in the form of a new decision.[55]

Although the normal procedure for Jews was to pursue their litigations with Christians in the general courts, still another way was open to them, as well as to others, to settle legal disputes, and particularly cases of civil law. By the common consent of the parties in dispute, one or more men of repute could be chosen to decide the legal differences between them. The contending parties pledged themselves to abide by the decision of the arbitrators.[56] True, in medieval law arbitration did not necessarily mean a decision based exclusively on equity but could very well include the application of the valid law and traditional legal customs. Yet, compared to the solemnity and stringency of the regular court procedure, the way here was open to a more liberal interpretation of law and custom and, above all, to less strictness in the proceedings owing to the predominance of writing, replacing here the otherwise merely oral proceedings. Hence by mutual agreement Jews as well as non-Jews would refer their claims to arbitrators, to *zunleute und entscheitleute noch innehald des entscheitbriefs*.[57] This practice gained ground particularly in the later part of the Middle Ages. This way of obtaining an authoritative decision, for various reasons generally favored in that period, must obviously have been expedient and desirable for Jews in particular.

The customary number of arbitrators was four (sometimes only two), no chairman of this collegium being mentioned in the sources. These likewise contain no restrictions concerning either persons or subject matter, whence it is safe to assume that Jews were not excluded from acting as arbitrators.[58] Unfortunately, in most of the known cases the arbiters' names are not given. In one case of 1396, however, it is explicitly stated that "Hannes Domnic and Lazarus the Jew have amicably and in a friendly way arbitrated all disputes between Czenke Domning and Joseph Jew of Schweidnitz concerning 723 ducats payable at Venice."[59] Sometimes arbitration was effected by a single arbitrator, who was expected to submit the case to an *Oberhof* and then merely to pronounce its decision as his own judgment. Bishop Conrad of Breslau seems to have been much sought after as arbitrator in the first half of the fifteenth century. It is very improbable, of course, that he consulted a superior court. The *Oberhof* of Magdeburg, on the other hand, upheld the bishop's decision by arbitration, in an *entscheyt und suneliche richtunge*, between the Jew Ychel of Reichenbach and Bartusch Koslig.[60]

In view of the fact that an arbitrator actually possessed authority and jurisdiction equivalent to, or even surpassing, that of a judge, the cardinal problem of arbitration is the attitude of the state toward compromises and arbitrators' decisions. No distinction was made between Christian and Jewish parties. Private arbitration was fully recognized in medieval Germany.[61] This means that the parties were entitled to bring their legal differences before arbitrators instead of before the ordinarily competent courts. Once they had compromised on this procedure, they had to abide by it. The decision rendered was to be "observed fully and faithfully." The *Oberhöfe*, as a rule, refused to review cases which had been arbitrated. In other words, arbitration constituted a final decision, for Jewish and Christian parties.

D. EXTRAORDINARY FORMS OF PROCEDURE

Some special types of criminal and civil procedure in which Jews participated actively or passively have already received consideration in the preceding pages. These include the procedures in a handhaving crime, of *Anefang*, and in the case of contumacy. There is also evidence that Jews—though exempted from their jurisdiction[62]—were summoned before those secret and ill-famed tribunals which, under the name *Vehmgericht*, developed a peculiar and particularly cruel procedure, wrapped in mystery, and exercising great power all over Germany from the end of the twelfth century to the middle of the sixteenth.[63]

From the point of view of the actual application of the law to Jews litigating with non-Jews, some other types of extraordinary procedure also deserve attention.

Medieval municipal law, in order to promote traffic and commerce, extended to foreigners certain special privileges in deviation from the regular order of civil and criminal procedure. Special courts for aliens, the so-called *Gastgerichte* or "guest courts," were instituted for the duration of regularly recurrent fairs.[64] *Gast* was the legal term for any person not domiciled in a given city or within its jurisdiction and therefore ordinarily not subject to the municipal courts. The *Gastgerichte*, which were intended to settle legal disputes between aliens in this sense (*Gäste*) and between aliens and citizens (*Bürger*) or residents (*Einwohner*), provided a specially accelerated form of procedure according to simplified legal rules. Along with all other foreign merchants, Jews were allowed to share fully in the advantages of *Gastgericht* and *Gästerecht*. That this was, in fact, an important privilege is clear from the broad meaning of the term *Gast*. Throughout the German realm everyone was legally considered a foreigner or *Gast* when he was outside the town of which he was a citizen or resident, even though he were only a short distance from it. "Alien" Jews, then, were entitled as plaintiffs to invoke the jurisdiction of the *Gastgericht* and were also subject to these extraordinary courts in the role of defendants. This fact is explicitly stated in an early decision of the *Schöffen* of Magdeburg, incorporated in the lawbook, *Magdeburger Fragen*, I, 2, 13: "Aliens and residents [*geste adir umbsessen*], laymen and Jews, who seek justice in your court, must [also] respond there, if they are lawfully required to do so."

Another Magdeburg *Schöffenspruch* decided the case of the Jew Kussil of Kalish who "as a *gast* in a Silesian town summoned his debtor Nitcze Nassengneffe to its *gastrechte*[65] and brought action against him for money debt."[66] In this suit, however, the accelerated procedure did not make for a quick decision, because of the restrictive interpretation of the clause of attorney contained in the relevant instrument.[67] But this is a different story.

In close connection with the *Gästerecht*, medieval German law developed the special procedure of seizure or *Arrest*.[68] Seizure of a defaulting debtor's person, individual belongings, or entire possessions served, first of all, the purpose of bringing him to court for ordinary legal proceedings. Thus with the court's aid he could be compelled to perform his obligations to the creditor; otherwise satisfaction would be secured by execution. Hence the procedure of *Arrest* was a very effective means of legal security or distraint.

Two cases decided by the *Schöffen* of Leipzig give evidence that seizure was applied on behalf of Jewish creditors. In both cases objects belonging to a Christian debtor and in the possession of a third person were seized in favor of the Jewish claimant: in one case it was a horse, in the other an amount of money.[69] In a third case, decided by the jurors of Magdeburg, seizure of an allegedly defaulting debtor took place upon the instigation and in favor of a Jewish claimant, Samuel of Prague.[70]

Often neither the person nor the belongings of a foreign debtor who had failed to obey a court summons or to perform his legal obligations were available for seizure in the creditor's place of residence. Then relatives or fellow-citizens of the defaulter visiting there could be held responsible and subject to arrest instead of him. This was actually done in favor of the above-mentioned claimant, Samuel of Prague. However, as early as the twelfth and thirteenth centuries, this widespread institution of arrest in reprisal was recognized as harmful to commerce and was considered illegal.[71] Only the debtor himself and not a fellow-citizen could be exposed to seizure when sojourning in a foreign city.[72] An exception to this rule took place, however, when justice was denied to a creditor by a foreign court. Then not only the *Gast*-debtor but all his fellow-citizens were subject to arrest.

Another kind of personal liability for foreign obligations was also enforced by way of seizure. Private individuals, whether citizens or merely inhabitants, including Jews, when sojourning in cities outside of their own, were held responsible by foreign creditors particularly for communal debts or other claims against their home town. The traveling merchant, Christian as well as Jewish, had to be cognizant of his liability, in his person and merchandise, to seizure in reprisal, for the municipal debt of his home city. Such liability and exposure to arrest were customary and originally even unrestricted under Magdeburg law[73] and could be removed only by formal grants of exemption, extended to individuals or entire municipalities by means of individual letters of privilege or intercommunity treaties. The latter often made reciprocity a requirement for their operation. Only in rare instances were Jews explicitly excluded from the safe-conduct extended for that purpose to entire cities.[74] On the other hand, safe-conduct was sometimes granted to Jews on request with regard to the communal debts of their home city. It did not apply, of course, to their own private obligations. In 1433 the following letter of safe-conduct was issued in Breslau:

Canald and Isaac, a Jew called Ico, of Kalis, are to have safe-conduct this whole year, so that no one can trouble them or take action against them on account of the communal debts of the city of Kalis; but for their own debts they have no safe-conduct.[75]

In the course of further development individual liability for municipal debt became more and more restricted. According to the practice of the Magdeburg jurors, unrestricted responsibility could attach only to the members, present or past, of the town council. The rest of the citizens and inhabitants, including Jews, were freed from any comprehensive liability for communal debts, provided that they had duly paid their current taxes and were not otherwise indebted to their city. They could be held responsible by foreign creditors of their home town only in so far as they themselves were indebted and liable to their own municipality. In other words, Magdeburg law in its further development generally limited liability for communal debts to the community's outstanding claims. Jews benefited from this easement of liability equally with non-Jews. What remained was an inescapable minimum required by law as well as by equity.[76]

It is significant indeed that personal liability for municipal debts and other communal obligations was imposed upon the Jewish inhabitants of a city on exactly the same grounds as those applied to Christian citizens and other inhabitants. The several hypotheses concerning the juridical basis of this liability as a general civic obligation need no extensive discussion in this connection.[77] As far as Jews are concerned, they were evidently regarded as belonging to the municipal community, economically as well as legally. Thus they too were supposed to share in the common responsibility for municipal debts and other obligations.

III. LAW OF EVIDENCE[78]

A. PROBLEMS AND PRINCIPLES

Any attempt to investigate the principles governing the law of evidence in litigations between Jews and Christians and to uncover the underlying ideas is bound to suffer from two serious difficulties. First, the Jewish issue is a complicated problem in itself. Second, it is made still more complex by the fact that the legal historian finds himself here generally on unsafe ground, for the scholarly disputes over the leading principles which dominated the medieval law of evidence in Germany are still unresolved.

This much, however, seems clear and beyond controversy. The old doctrine, once uncontested but later sharply attacked, remains unshaken and is still dominant. This doctrine holds that, as a rule, the defendant was "nearer" (privileged) to prove innocence by purgation. The cause for this "purgation privilege" in favor of the defendant, however, is much disputed. Two scholars of renown advanced the theory that the greater probability and credibility inherent in one party's assertion was the decisive criterion.[79] This position—although presented with great acumen and persuasiveness—was vigorously opposed by scholars of no less repute.[80] In this still unsettled controversy, evidence given by Jewish parties in "mixed" litigations played a not altogether unimportant role. It was pointed out that the ascertainment of the truth by means of proof requires two elements in the party liable or entitled to produce evidence: knowledge of the facts involved and honesty in testifying. Hence certain groups of persons and types of facts lacking these qualities had to be singled out and placed under a special law of evidence.[81] Accordingly, the Jews as a group of inferior legal status were not to be accorded by law equal credibility with Christians. This had already been indicated in Visigothic law by this play on words: "Profanum etenim satis est infidelis fidem fidelibus anteponere."[82] The latter, therefore, found themselves in an advantageous position with regard to the rules of evidence: Jews were not permitted to testify as witnesses against Christian litigants. There were, however, according to the law sources in question, numerous exceptions to this rule. Another advocate of the theory of "greater probability and credibility," on the contrary, rejected entirely evidence by Jewish parties in mixed lawsuits as pertinent support for this doctrine: "The principle governing the allocation of proof can emerge only from lawsuits between *Volksgenossen*."[83] This reasoning evidently employs as its foundation the old theory of alien law, in this generality long outdated as a valid argument. None of the arguments set forth by these authors seems convincing to the present writer or even capable of bearing out the inherent implications. Far from resting on a solid foundation of source material, each of these suppositions represents no more than a *petitio principii*.

For the present investigation, as far as Jewish parties are concerned, there is no need to link the problem of evidence in mixed litigations with the search for the definite general principle underlying the medieval law of evidence in Germany. It appears more appropriate to the subject matter to restrict the discussion to the issue of Jewry-law. If the results thus obtained should throw some light also on the broader problem, so much the better.

As to the role of the Jews in the medieval law of evidence, Magdeburg law is very explicit. The following general and basic rule was laid down in the *Magdeburg-Breslauer Systematisches Schöffenrecht*, in the middle of the fourteenth century (III, 2, 38):

On a Jew's suit for money or *ungericht*. If a Jew brings suit against a Christian man for money, the Christian man may void it by attesting to his innocence with one hand on the Saint; for about money no Jew's oath is permissible against Christian persons, and no Jew may convict a Christian man about money. But about *ungerichte*, as *campirwunden*, *lemde*, and homicide, a Jew may convict a Christian man, the peace-breaker, in handhavingness, just as a Christian man could do, with the support of six Christian witnesses. Such is the law.[84]

The principle set forth here is as clear as is the legal reasoning behind it. A Christian can free himself from a money suit brought against him by a Jew by taking a single-handed oath of purgation, that is, without helpers. This is undoubtedly an advantageous privilege which he enjoys over the Jewish claimant. As far as money claims are concerned, Jews are incapable of convicting a Christian either by taking an oath or by adducing proof through witnesses. That this rule is restricted to money claims only is placed beyond any doubt by the words *umme gelt*, "for money," repeated no less than three times in that regulation. One manuscript has this variant reading: "No Jew may take an oath about money." The law imposes no such limitation on the Jew if his claim does not originate from money transactions. In suing for serious crimes, *ungerichte*, perpetrated against him, the Jew is placed by the law on an equal footing with any Christian: he may convict "his peace-breaker" with six Christian witnesses.

For the civil lawsuit the emphasis laid on the claim to money makes these facts clear: with regard to their money transactions, Jews were not considered trustworthy, from the point of view of economics; or unbiased or credible enough to give evidence in their own affairs, from the point of view of legal procedure, on account of their difference in faith. But this discrimination was not entirely the result of religious prejudices. There were other trades in medieval economic life which by their very nature marked those engaged in them with a similar stigma. It was generally taken for granted, to mention only the best-known among the numerous examples,[85] that in the miller's trade cheating supplied the main substance of business profit.[86] In the same way, Jews were stigmatized in society on account of their "usurious" trade. Hence it was, in addition to the religious, above all, social, discrimination which also effected a procedural disadvantage for the Jewish party; for it must be borne in mind that the litigating parties still played a dominant role in medieval legal procedure, including the law of evidence. The plaintiff produced evidence to the defendant (not to the judge or to the law), while the latter likewise proved his innocence or lack of obligation to the plaintiff. The means of proof and the procedure of evidence were strictly unilateral and formal. The law merely determined which kind of proof should be admitted, how it should be presented and how evaluated, in order to be binding also for the adversary.[87] From this angle it is intelligible that a social motive could thus gain some influence in the sphere of civil procedure.

In the realm of criminal law, too, the system of *Wergeld* and *Busse* was dominated from the very outset by the gradation according to origin and social standing of the injured persons, as differentiated in *Sachsenspiegel*, III, 45. This differentiation, however, was relinquished by Magdeburg law at an early period and replaced by one uniform penalty, without discrimination against Jews.[88] Little wonder that, consequently, Magdeburg law did not know any discrimination in the sphere of criminal procedure either. No difference existed between a Christian and a Jewish plaintiff in convicting "his peace-breaker" because of a serious crime, an *ungericht*, such as *campirwunde*, *lemde*, or homicide.

A brief digression seems in place here. It is interesting to note that, in article III, 2, 39, exactly corresponding in structure and wording to III, 2, 38, the *Magdeburg-Breslauer Schöffenrecht* extended to Christian women a legal treatment identical with that accorded to Jews:

If a woman brings a suit against a [Christian] man for money, the man is "nearer" to voiding it [by swearing a single-handed oath] than is the woman to convicting him; for no woman may convict a man about money. But for *ungerichte* such as *campirwunden*, *lemde*, or homicide she may convict "her peace-breaker" in handhavingness, as a man may do, with the support of six male witnesses.[89]

This was, quite as in the case of the Jews, also due to a difference in social standing. It is well known that, according to *Sachsenspiegel* and Magdeburg law, women could claim only half the *Wergeld* and *Busse* accorded to men.[90]

To return again to *Magdeburg-Breslauer Schöffenrecht*, III, 2, 38: the Jew was, on the other hand, not to enjoy any privilege over his Christian neighbor on account of his religious difference. The Jew, too, had to produce proof, "with six Christian men as witnesses," and was not permitted to employ coreligionists for that purpose (similarly, the Christian woman could convict a man only by male witnesses).

The question immediately arises as to whether this seeming disadvantage was meant and is to be regarded by implication as a discrimination against the Jew. The requirement to produce six Christians as witnesses as such need not necessarily imply any discrimination against the Jewish plaintiff. One must remain aware of the very narrow local conditions generally prevailing in medieval society. These were also instrumental in shaping the rules of law and determinative for the principles of legal practice. It seems possible and indeed more probable that a Jew would be attacked or injured outside the Jewish quarters, while traveling or attending to his business, than in the midst or presence of quite a number of his fellow-believers. Jewish witnesses, therefore, as seems very plausible, might commonly not even have been available. Hence, in general, recourse to Christian witnesses was necessary. This reasoning the writer found supported by the following argumentation presented in *Schwabenspiegel*, L 260; G 214, 4:

If a Jew slays a Christian or commits other serious crimes, he shall be judged as is a Christian man. And if the Jew makes denial and if Christians and Jews have seen it, there shall be at least one Jew as witness. And if it was thus that no Jews were present, proof shall be adduced by Christian men alone. This however is not the law except when a Jew commits a crime.[91]

Furthermore, there can be no doubt that in medieval procedural law the standard evidence was produced by Christian male witnesses. This general practice could be made to serve discriminatory tendencies only if it was used to deny the admission of Jewish witnesses for a Jewish litigant.

The cases decided by the *Oberhof* of Magdeburg, which will be discussed in the two following subsections, may perhaps throw more light on the problem here discussed.

B. CRIMINAL PROCEDURE

According to *Sachsenspiegel* and Magdeburg law, crimes committed by Jews were punishable under the same rules and in the same manner as those committed by Christians.[92] This parallel treatment applied also to criminal procedure, including the law of evidence. The rule that a Jew may convict "his Christian peace-breaker" with six Christian witnesses, as enounced in the *Magdeburg-Breslauer Schöffenrecht*, III, 2, 38, thus represents merely a logical application of the general principle.

In criminal procedure, obviously, the law required a greater number of oath-helpers or witnesses than in civil cases. As a rule, they had to number six, whether in behalf of the defendant or of the plaintiff. This was generally the largest number of witnesses permissible and necessary according to Magdeburg law: the malefactor caught in handhaving crime was convicted by the plaintiff *selbsiebent*, that is, with six witnesses.[93] The same rule applied for a murderer who was apprehended later. Hence a Jew needed six Christian witnesses to convict a Christian,[94] just as the Christian did to convict a Jew. When indicted, a Jew had to accomplish his exculpation in the same way as a Christian. According to a Magdeburg court decision, the Jew was supposed to have the assistance of six Christians and could not get by with swearing a single-handed oath.

As David Jew is sued by the dean with the testimony of reputable persons, David Jew must free himself and prove his innocence with as many Christian witnesses as he is sued with, and he cannot accomplish this with his single denial. And that he is the emperor's chamber serf and belongs to his chamber, that cannot be of aid to him here. But in the measure that he is sued by the dean, in that measure must he acquit himself, as has been ruled before. However, David Jew must not suffer the testimony of more than seven witnesses. This is the law.[95]

This corresponds fully with the general rules of Magdeburg law.[96]

In a case decided by the Magdeburg court in the first half of the fifteenth century, the Jewish plaintiff demanded purgation by ordeal from a Christian who had broken into his house and stolen twenty *schock* worth of gold and silver. "He [Heinrich Kreczschmar] should not be allowed to take a single-handed oath of purgation, but should carry a hot iron or put his arm up to the elbow in a kettle of boiling water, because of his [previous] restitution of stolen goods and because of his illegitimate birth."[97] The Jew seems to have been well informed of the pertinent regulation in the *Sachsenspiegel*. According to article I, 39, those who had lost their full legal capacity by once committing robbery or theft were not permitted to free themselves by taking a single-handed oath of purgation, in case of relapse. Instead, they had to perform one of three acts: to carry a hot iron, to plunge an arm up to the elbow into boiling water, or to defend themselves in combat. The Jew or his counselor seems also to have been aware that, according to Magdeburg law, judicial combat was permitted and even required in cases of infringement of domestic peace, under two conditions. The peace-breaker must have been caught *in flagrante delicto* and be seeking exculpation, or, in the event that he had been killed, the demand must be made by his kindred.[98] Since both these conditions were absent in the case under consideration, judicial combat was out of the question.[99]

The Magdeburg jurors did not decide this case in favor of the Jew. In accordance with their constant practice of refusing recognition to the ancient *ordalia*, which the church condemned, they rejected his demand for proof by ordeal, although it was based on the *Sachsenspiegel*.[100] The decision from Magdeburg required the kind of evidence that the alleged restitution of stolen goods by the accused robber might demand. If he had not been convicted of this act in court, he was to be allowed to take a single-handed oath of purgation; but if convicted, he alone was not to be considered trustworthy, and hence his testimony was to be reinforced by six witnesses. In other words, neither the defendant's illegitimacy nor the plaintiff's being a Jew determined the quality of proof in any respect.

Recourse by a Jewish plaintiff to ordeals by fire and water,

obsolescent generally as early as the thirteenth century and locally even earlier, brings to mind the exemption of Jews from such
ordalia in Carolingian charters of protection[101] and in the privileges of Speyer and Worms of about 1090.[102] To the present
writer's knowledge, there is no mention of these ordeals in the
Saxon or related law sources. Only very few references to judicial
combat as an ordeal, found in medieval lawbooks, concern
Jews.[103] According to *Schwabenspiegel*, L 260; G 214, 5, in criminal
procedure generally "no Jew's [challenge to] combat can be
issued against a Christian"; but it was the duty of a Jew to respond to the challenge of a Christian.[104] On the other hand, the
Jew in the role of plaintiff was entitled to issue a challenge to
duel in an action for deprivation of personal freedom. The pertinent provision in *Meissener Rechtsbuch*, III, 17, 44, in accordance
with older Jewry privileges, does not require the Jew to duel in
person. He is allowed to substitute a "*kempfe* whom he may procure with his money." The legal reason underlying this exemption does not appear from the sources.[105]

In fact, the problem of judicial combat seems not to have occupied any superior court in connection with Jews. This is probably due to the general trend of developments in the law of evidence. By the first half of the fifteenth century, judicial combat
as a means of evidence had generally become as obsolete as the
ordeals of hot iron or boiling water, rejected by the *Schöffen* of
Magdeburg in the decision previously mentioned.[106] Furthermore, by that time the prohibition against Jews' bearing arms
had long been in force.[107] But no general prohibition of judicial
combat between Jews and Christians, such as appears in the
thirteenth- and fourteenth-century codes of Aragon and Na-
varre,[108] is discoverable in German law sources. The ordeals of
hot iron and boiling water had hardly any significance at all for
procedural evidence in relation to Jews. This may have been, to
some extent, an aftereffect of the early exemption of the Jews
from this kind of ordeal. Besides, these ordeals, as employed in
judicial practice, were performed with the assistance of the
church. The accompanying Christian ritual by itself made the
ordeals by fire and water nonapplicable to Jews, for religious
reasons alone.

Religious reasons, on the other hand, were responsible for a flagrant discrimination against the Jews—the only open and apparently deliberate disregard of lawful right in the criminal procedure of the medieval lawbooks. Though merely of local significance and theoretical import, this regulation stands out as an intentional reversal of a fundamental rule of the *Sachsenspiegel* and of Magdeburg law. That regulation is found in the municipal lawbook of Salzwedel, of the early fifteenth century, representing a compilation of the contents of two charters of 1273 and 1278, and of excerpts from the *Sachsenspiegel Landrecht*.[109] While articles III, 2 and III, 7, 1 of the latter were taken over in paragraphs 77 and 83, 1, respectively, with insignificant changes, *Sachsenspiegel*, III, 7, 2 was completely reversed in the Salzwedel lawbook, paragraph 83, 2. It reads as follows:[110]

Salzwedel Lawbook, § 83, 2	*Sachsenspiegel*, III, 7, 2
Should a Jew assault a Christian or kill him, the Jew may not make any reply, he must suffer in silence what the law appoints, for he has no claim on Christendom and is God's persecutor and a murderer of Christendom.	Should a Jew slay a Christian or commit a crime against him and be caught in the act, he shall be judged like a Christian.

This is indeed a remarkable case of the penetration of religio-political sentiments and reasoning into the realm of law. Such a negation of the ideals of justice which permeate medieval secular law is as rare in the law sources under consideration as its occurrence is striking.

C. CIVIL PROCEDURE

In the sphere of civil procedure in litigations between Jews and Christians, particular importance attached to the law of evidence. It was governed by a variety of rules which were, at times, even differently interpreted by the Magdeburg "supreme court."

In cases of simple action or *schlichte klage*, without specification of particular legal grounds or presentation of witnesses, a Jew, just like any other defendant, was able to withstand the plaintiff by taking a single-handed oath.[111] "Abraham the Jew shall take an oath on Moyses' books in his synagogue that he is innocent of the charge laid against him by Hans von Czemen, so help him God and the Jewish Law."[112]

This right of the Jews was upheld by the Magdeburg and Leipzig superior courts up to the second quarter of the fifteenth century. It was only Johann von Buch who, on particularly weak grounds derived from Roman law, sought to deprive the Jews of that privilege in his *Gloss* to *Sachsenspiegel*, III, 7, 1, under No. 12: "According to Saxon law a Jew or a heretic may be convicted in all matters, while a Saxon may free himself by his oath."[113] This standpoint was not accepted universally, not even in the practice of Saxony.

In the case of substantiated actions, when witnesses were offered, Jews as plaintiffs as well as defendants were permitted and, in fact, obligated to produce evidence through witnesses. As to the details, however, it seems that judicial practice on this point in Germany was far from uniform.

The number and qualification of witnesses necessary to support civil claims of or against Jewish parties were prescribed in several lawbooks. The Saxon *Landrecht* has a regulation only in connection with the old trade privilege of the Jews, in III, 7, 4. There the Jew is required to prove the lawfulness of his acquisition of property by an oath with two supporting witnesses. No specific qualification as to the religion of his witnesses is given. In the related case treated in *Schwabenspiegel*, L 260; G 214, 1, the Jew is supposed "to convict his Christian adversary with three Christians." The requirement of Christians as witnesses in this case is probably due to the involvement of criminal law, since failure to prove lawful acquisition necessarily raised the question of theft. "If one would convict a Jew," *Schwabenspiegel*, L 260; G 214, 2, continues, "one must have for it at least one Jew who is supposed to have been present," a privilege extended, incidentally, to Jews even in criminal law (L 260; G 214, 4).[114] In other lawbooks, too, provisions concerning evidence in mixed litigations occur frequently. A Christian needs one Jewish and one Christian witness to convict a Jew, according to *Weichbild-Vulgata*, art. 135, 2. The same rule applies when a Jew seeks to convict a Christian defendant (art. 135, 3).[115] An identical regulation is found in the Glogau lawbook, chapter 481. The *Meisse-*

ner Rechtsbuch, III, 17, 20, requires two Jews and one Christian as witnesses for a Christian against a Jew and, accordingly, two Christians and one Jew as witnesses for a Jew to convict a Christian.[116]

Under Magdeburg law evidence could be presented by means of two or six witnesses, *selbdritt* or *selbsiebent*. The larger number was required only in certain juridically difficult cases. Against substantiated actions Jews usually had to defend themselves with two witnesses, one Christian, one Jewish. This rule was applied by the *Schöffen* of Magdeburg,[117] as well as those of Dohna,[118] the latter interpreting even *Sachsenspiegel*, III, 7, 4, to the effect that one Jew and one Christian were satisfactory. It seems that Jews could also be convicted through *eynem fromen unbeschulden cristen und eynem unverlumethen joden*.[119]

In other decisions evidence *selbdritt*, that is, supported by one Jewish and one Christian witness, as offered or demanded by the Jewish litigant, was explicitly refused by the Magdeburg jurors. Hasze, a Jewish inhabitant of the city of Zerbst, for instance, claimed an amount of money from Andrew Litzow, father of his deceased debtor. His offer to prove his claim by the testimony of a Jew and a Christian burgher of Zerbst, together with the latter's wife, was rejected. Instead, Hasze was ordered to produce evidence of his claim "nach doder hand sulff sevende mit cristen unde joden, de men van getugnisse nicht vorleggen mag, alse recht is," that is, with six respectable witnesses, Jewish and Christian. "According to Magdeburg law, the Jew cannot produce the evidence with one Christian and a Jew."[120] The reason why Hasze had to provide the maximum number of witnesses admissible under Magdeburg law is obvious: such evidence was always required *nach toter hand*, namely, in disputes over the legal relations or obligations of deceased persons.[121] In another lawsuit, also decided in Magdeburg, the testimony *nach toter hand* (with six supporting Christians) was imposed on the defendants in favor of the Jewish plaintiff.[122] In yet another case the *Schöffen* of Dresden saved the Jewish claimant from that onerous procedure, to which he had objected, by recognizing an official document of the burgomaster and council of the city of Meissen as sufficient and unimpeachable evidence.[123] It is patent that in all these decisions the question of whether Jewish witnesses should be admitted was not the issue. In the suit of the Jewish moneylender, Hasze of Zerbst, in which evidence with six supporting witnesses was substituted for the usual "mixed" proof *selbdritt*, the acceptability of Jews as well as Christians was made quite explicit.

There is, however, another group of jury-court decisions in which the rejection of mixed evidence *selbdritt*, particularly the rejection of Jewish witnesses, is conspicuous.

The first case is as follows: A Christian suing a Jew, Zcadak, for satisfaction for verbal injury allegedly inflicted on his wife, offers two Christian witnesses. The Jew denies the charge and refuses to submit to the evidence offered by the plaintiff; he thus becomes bound to offer two witnesses on his side. "The Jew Zcadak asks to have the law stated: since she [the plaintiff's wife] is a Christian and he a Jew, should he not equitably convict by means of one Jew and one Christian, or what is the law?"[124] This inquiry evidently referred to the practice prevailing in Saxon and Magdeburg law as previously described. The jury court decided:

Hereupon we, the *Schöffen* at Magdeburg, state the law: Since the Jew says no to the charge, he may exculpate himself according to law; and Herman Gerwer must not convict him thereof. In particular, since the Jew says that he did not submit to Herman's witnesses, he shall exculpate himself with two Christian witnesses.

In other words, the Jew must support his oath of purgation with two Christian witnesses in order not to lose his case. He is not permitted to have recourse to mixed evidence.

The second such case involved one Bartholomew Risted, juror of the municipal court of Eisleben, who was sued for debt by the Jew Aaron and advanced the defense of *res judicata*. He had been cleared of this claim, he contended, in a previous court suit involving his wife. Legal instruction from Magdeburg was requested on behalf of the Jew by the municipal court of Eisleben "whether he [Risted] should do that by himself [i.e., take a single-handed oath on the *res judicata*] or *selb anderer* [with the support of others, namely], with two Christians and one Jew, or what is the law thereon?"[125] The *Schöffen* of Eisleben in judicial fairness thus admitted that the Jew might be entitled to have one of his fellows among his opponent's witnesses. It was doubtless Aaron himself who had made this suggestion.[126] It, too, was rejected by the *Oberhof* of Magdeburg:

> If he [Risted] can prove this with the testimony of the court or that of two reputable Christian men, . . . according to the law, then he is not obligated to answer yes or no to Aaron the Jew with a greater number of witnesses; and he also need not prove his case with any Jew according to Magdeburg law. Such is the law. Sealed with our seal.

It is characteristic of medieval jury-court decisions—in contradistinction to the judgments of modern courts—that they do not set forth the specific reasons for the ruling.[127] Although the legal ideas and positive rules on which the pronouncements were based can often easily be grasped, sometimes the decisions raise enigmatic problems of historical interpretation. This applies particularly to the two preceding *Schöffensprüche*. The generalization drawn from the first decision alone, that "the Jew as defendant appears to have no right to demand of the Christian plaintiff that he select witnesses from among people of his own [the Jews'] group,"[128] does not seem justified. *Weichbild-Vulgata* and *Meissener Rechtsbuch*, for example, adopted a contradictory regulation.[129] The exiguous basis of only two lawsuits actually decided in Magdeburg calls, therefore, for an individual and more conservative interpretation.

In the first case, involving compensation for a verbal injury, the Magdeburg jurors followed their routine in matters of criminal law: Jews were to support their oaths with Christian witnesses only. In the second case, too, the *Schöffen* adhered to their customary practice. Evidence by the court of the original trial makes an oath and supporting witnesses unnecessary. Likewise, adding a Jew to the usual number of two (Christian) witnesses, thereby changing the proof *selbdritt* into a proof *selbviert*, has no basis in Magdeburg law. Nor did it appear suitable to the *Oberhof*, or perhaps even admissible, to abide by the testimony *selbdritt*, but to replace one of the Christian witnesses with a Jew.

An impartial examination of the legal situation must lead to the conclusion that no expressed or inherent anti-Jewish tendency comes to light in these decisions. Nevertheless, there is a reflection on the Jews. Their putative right, again and again pressed in the courts, to mixed evidence as a precondition for conviction in any lawsuit was by no means recognized in the judicature of Magdeburg. Furthermore, the fact that Jews were actually excluded from convicting their Christian debtors by oath and from presenting supporting witnesses of their own faith in criminal matters—even though arising from social considerations—casts a shadow over the legal status of the Jews. On the other hand, it must not be forgotten that in other cases Magdeburg law allowed Jews, as plaintiffs[130] as well as defendants,[131] to bring witnesses from among their coreligionists and thus to employ mixed evidence.

There can be no doubt that the legal requirement of mixed evidence, as such, was indeed an important concession and privilege in favor of the Jews. It is also clear from the sources that, in Germany in the period of the lawbooks, considerations of a purely religious nature were basic.[132] This becomes particularly manifest in the multitude of regulations on the Jewry oath, interlocked with the problem here discussed. No mention is made, moverover, of national "otherness" with reference to the Jews in the legal sources here expounded.[133]

In concluding this section it should be pointed out that in certain civil-law proceedings, typical of actions involving Jews, the latter enjoyed a decidedly privileged position with regard to the law of evidence.

To a creditor, Jew as well as Christian, "holding a pledge" meant, first of all, the possession of an object appropriate for securing the discharge of the debtor's obligation. Beyond that, a pledge in the creditor's hand improved his legal position also with regard to the evidence for his claim. Special importance attached to the latter because of the customary law, widespread in medieval Germany, which made it possible for a debtor to disavow an obligation on oath and thus to exclude the creditor from any means of convicting him.[134] To guard against the legal prejudice inherent in such a contingency, every creditor, the Jew in particular, was very anxious to secure a pledge or a promissory note from his debtor or to have the loan contract entered in the municipal register, the *Stadtbuch*, or in the records of the competent court, the *Gerichtsregister*. Duly sealed promissory notes or entries in official records naturally supplied unimpeachable evidence.[135] But even the mere possession of a pawned object enabled the creditor to establish the existence of the debt and its amount by his single-handed oath.[136] Moreover, the Jewish creditor had the right to establish by oath the amount of interest due him.

Meissener Rechtsbuch, III, 17, 9 (cf. III, 17, 26; Purgoldts Rb., VIII, 74):

When a Christian has pawned a pledge to a Jew, if the Christian says, it is not so much, and the Jew says, it is more: the Jew has the preference of proof by the pledge and his oath. This being performed, the Christian shall then redeem the pledge [in the amount of] principal and interest.[137]

Meissener Rechtsbuch, III, 17, 25 (cf. also 9, 13):

. . . [the Jew] may recover his principal with the interest which he is to prove by the same oath. . . .[138]

Jewish creditors were similarly favored, though indirectly, in the execution of contracts of *Schadennehmen*.[139] The original creditor's oath, supported by two witnesses, was sufficient to prove the "damages" or expenses arising from such contracting loans with Jews.[140] According to the Vienna lawbook, the Jewish creditor "had to testify on his good faith and upon his Law that he had made the loan in this amount and on this day at the debtor's charge."[141]

The same principle as applied here operated, furthermore, in the old trade privilege accorded Jewish merchants, who were able to claim compensation to the extent of the purchase price paid for stolen goods or of a loan made on them, on reclamation by their legitimate owners. Under certain conditions, the Jew could establish the amount involved, by his oath.[142]

One need scarcely emphasize that no special *favor Judaeorum* lay at the bottom of all these procedural regulations which worked out in favor of Jewish moneylenders. Rather was it well considered *favor commercii* that had to be served by the rules of the law of evidence even when they affected Jews. In fact, some of them applied equally or in a similar way to Christian creditors, under identical conditions.[143]

D. THE JEWRY OATH[144]

I. A BRIEF HISTORY OF THE MEDIEVAL JEWRY OATH

In a presentation of the medieval law of evidence in its reflection and effect upon the Jews, the Jewry oath deserves special attention.

By "Jewry oath" (*juramentum Judeorum*) we understand the oath that Jews had to take to establish proof in lawsuits with Christians. Its form and content as well as the accompanying ceremonial offer many points of interest to the historian and sociologist. An extensive investigation of its history, its linguistic development, and its legal significance, long a desideratum, would go far beyond the frame of this study, which must concentrate on the pertinent regulations in the lawbooks and jury-court decisions. Of its earlier history only the phases necessary for a better insight into its development in the age of the lawbooks can here be briefly touched on.

The taking of an oath by a Jew was performed always in accordance with the rules of Jewish law. This was a principle recognized in the legislation of almost all the countries in which fate had scattered the Jewish people after the loss of their political independence. The best means to assure non-Jewish courts and parties that Jews would consider their oaths legally binding seemed to be to permit them to comply with the precepts of Jewish law in this solemn juridical act.

As early as the Visigothic period in Spain, the sources refer to a special oath of abjuration required of converts to Christianity. It exhibits the characteristics which, for centuries after, were preserved as essential elements of the Jewry oath, namely, the solemn invocation of God; the enumeration of certain miraculous events from biblical history in which the omnipotence of God is especially manifest; and the curse to discourage perjury. The Visigoths were apparently the first to use a special Jewry-oath formula; the Frankish empire evolved more and more elaborate formulas in its own legislation. Three oath texts, drawn up in Latin, are preserved from late Frankish times. Their relationship to the Visigothic formula is obvious. In some manuscripts they are traced to Charlemagne, but they must have been composed at a somewhat later date, since they do not conform to the authentic Carolingian capitularies.

Jewry-oath formulas written in German are first found in the twelfth century. They are the so-called "Erfurt Jewry oath"[145] and the Jewry oath of Görlitz.[146] Both may derive from an unknown formula, which certainly goes back to the Carolingian oaths. These, in turn, have their ultimate origin probably in old Jewish formulas. Evidence of this may be seen in the abundance of biblical events enumerated in the Jewry oaths, in the many curses and punishments taken from the Old Testament, and in the fact that special emphasis was placed upon the retention of the Hebrew form of the name of God, even in the German oath texts. The Jewry oath of Görlitz, therefore, must be representative of the oldest German form, for it contains the word *Adonai*, as the designation of God. This does not occur in the Erfurt oath but appears as early as the Carolingian formulas. Thus the archetype of the Erfurt and Görlitz Jewry oaths is the model for the style and composition of the Jewry oaths so frequently found in thirteenth- and fourteenth-century German municipal statutes and lawbooks. The German oath formulas can be divided into three groups: the Rhenish-Westphalian, the Saxon, and the Swabian. In the present investigation only the second and third group are to be considered.

The Jewry oath represents a typical combination of Jewish law and medieval Jewry-law. Upon examining the contents of the oath formulas customary in medieval German law, one cannot fail to notice the fact that Jewish and German elements are here linked together. The appeal to God, the mention of the divine laws, the inclusion of the biblical punishments and curses against perjurers, and, finally, the solemnity of the symbolic ceremony are, no doubt, essentially Jewish. The Germanic conception of the oath, however, was not materially different from the Jewish. In the common Germanic word, *Eid*, in all probability the basic meaning *ligamen* is expressed, that is, making liable or responsible. According to Germanic law, every oath represented a "conditional self-denunciation" (*bedingte Selbstverfluchung*).[147] The person taking an oath staked his salvation or property on the truthfulness of his words and thus secured for them absolute credence; for, by this solemn act of self-surrender, he delivered himself to the avenging arm of the gods, later the Christian God, if he committed perjury. The penal clauses of some early medieval documents contain similar curses, to apply in the event of breach of contract. Some of them resemble those in the Jewry oaths.

The Jewry-oath ceremonial, too, combined elements of Jewish and Germanic law. According to Jewish law, the person taking an oath is obliged to stand and hold or touch the Torah.[148] In the Christian era the old German oath was taken upon the cross or relics or the Bible or some other sacred book. According to old German custom, the opposing party and, in later development, the judge held out a staff to the person taking the oath. The latter touched it with his hand, and, at the same time, the administrator of the oath recited the oath formula, clause by clause, to the person to be sworn. The German legal term, *den Eid staben*, originates from this procedure. Aside from its technical significance, this phrase means merely reciting the oath formula. Under German law the Jewry oath is also recited to the Jew by the *Eidstaber*, and the Jew must either repeat it or affirm it by saying "Amen." The *Eidstaber* may be either a Christian (sometimes he was a clergyman) or a Jew.[149] The fact that the oath formula assumes a metrical and, occasionally, even a rhymed form is to be attributed to this German practice of reciting the Jewry oath to the person who had to be sworn.

2. THE JEWRY-OATH FORMULAS IN THE LAWBOOKS

With this summary presentation of the history and legal significance of the Jewry oath in mind, we can now turn to the relevant regulations in the lawbooks and court decisions.

The *Sachsenspiegel* contains no Jewry-oath formula, although this lawbook was the first to include a systematic presentation of medieval Jewry-law. As previously explained, this omission is due to its author's attitude toward Jewish law, which he regarded as entirely outside the realm of his *Spiegel*.[150] The lack of an oath formula here obviously accounts also for the absence of any such formula in the *Deutschenspiegel*. Nor, probably, did the original version of the *Schwabenspiegel* include a Jewry oath. It is only in the fuller version, the second group of *Schwabenspiegel* manuscripts, originating in the eighties of the thirteenth century, that a Jewry-oath formula is included in the corpus of the lawbook.[151] This Jewry oath, in what was probably its original form, reconstructed from the principal manuscripts,[152] reads in translation as follows:

This is the Jews' oath, as they shall swear it, and everything that belongs to their oath. He shall stand on a sow's skin, and his right hand shall lie in a book up to the wrist; and that shall be the five books of Moses. And he who administers the oath to him shall speak thus:

About the goods for which this man sues against thee, that thou dost not know of them nor have them, nor hast taken them into thy possession, neither thyself nor thy servants, buried in the earth nor hidden beneath walls nor under lock.

So help thee God, who created heaven and earth, valleys and mountains, wood, foliage and grass, that was not before;

So help thee the Law that God wrote with His hand and gave to Moses on Mount Sinai;

And so help thee the five books of Moses;

And that, so thou eatest something, thou wilt become defiled all over, as did the king of Babylon;

And that sulphur and pitch rain upon thy neck, as it rained upon Sodom and Gomorrah;

And that the same pitch pour over thee, which at Babylon poured over two hundred men or more;

And that the earth swallow thee as it did Dathan and Abiram;

And that thy clay never mingle with other clay, and thy dust never mingle with other dust, in the bosom of Abraham;

So art thou true and right.

And so help thee Adonay; thou art true in what thou hast sworn.

And so that thou wouldst become leprous like Naaman: it is true.

And so that the scourge would have to come upon thee as it came upon the Israelites as they passed through Egypt: it is true what thou hast sworn.

And so that the blood and the curse ever remain upon thee which thy kindred wrought upon themselves when they tortured Jesus Christ and spake thus: His blood be upon us and upon our children: it is true.

So help thee God, who appeared to Moses in a burning bush.

It is true, the oath thou hast sworn:

By the soul which on doomsday thou must bring to judgment.
Per deum Abraham, per deum Isaac, per deum Jacob: it is true.
So help thee God and the oath which thou hast sworn. Amen.

This *Schwabenspiegel* Jewry oath (L 263; G 215) represents one
of the fullest formulas known in medieval law sources. It is found
in most of the "long" manuscripts, particularly in the Donaueschingen, Zürich, and Munich codices of the last two decades of the thirteenth century.[153] From this fact one must draw
the conclusion that it was incorporated early into the lawbook,
which was composed about 1275. Most of the manuscripts in the
aforementioned group, including the Munich codex, have, in
addition, a second oath formula of a simpler and more archaic
character. It is restricted to the punishments of Sodom and
Gomorrah, Dathan and "Abyron" (Abiram), Lot's wife, and
Naaman's leprosy, to which the leprosy of Maria (Miriam,
Moses' sister) is added.[154]

With the *Schwabenspiegel* itself, its Jewry oath found wide dissemination. It was also adopted by Ruprecht of Freising's lawbook (1328)[155] and by the *Frankenspiegel* (*ca.* 1328–38),[156] additional facts indicating still further dissemination.

Jewry-oath formulas are found in several late *Sachsenspiegel*
manuscripts, too. From the manuscript transmission as such it
is clear that they represent only later additions; for their texts
are not embodied in the lawbook proper but appear only as separate and independent appendixes, added, as a rule, at the end to
the *Landrecht*.[157] No doubt, these oath formulas owe their insertion to the needs of juridical practice. Nevertheless, they were
always regarded as extraneous additions, for which there was no
place within the *Sachsenspiegel* text. This applies in particular
to the *Sachsenspiegel* edition printed from manuscripts in 1516 at
Augsburg. Here one longer and one shorter oath formula are
inserted between *Richtsteig Landrechts* and the *Lehnrecht* of the lawbook.[158] Only research based on a comparative study of all pertinent manuscripts and primary editions of the *Sachsenspiegel* (derived again from manuscripts) will allow us to establish the filia-
tion of the manuscripts and the genealogical relationship among
the various versions of these oath formulas. No final results can
be expected from the restricted source material now at hand. Yet

a critical analysis will permit at least a grouping of the different oath formulas on the basis of their texts and thus perhaps provide new insight into the problem.

For this purpose there remains to be mentioned, in addition to the *Schwabenspiegel* and the *Sachsenspiegel* formulas, a third group of Jewry oaths: the various versions of the formula transmitted at the end of the *Weichbild-Vulgata*, which itself is encountered first in the Berlin manuscript of 1369.[159] It recurs, nearly identical in text, in the almost contemporaneous Meissen lawbook.[160] There are also shorter and somewhat different versions in other *Weichbild* manuscripts and old editions, but these need not be included in the present inquiry.[161]

In all three groups the unabbreviated text contains the words of the *Eidstaber* directed to the swearing Jew in the second person. The content clearly reveals the three essential elements of the medieval Jewry oath: the mention of God as the Creator of the world, who has made "heaven and earth" and, especially "the leaves and grass" *ex nihilo;* the miracles of the Old Testament, which both call to mind God's sovereign omnipotence and strengthen the belief in God and his power; the several curses and imprecations, should the swearer commit perjury. The text of the oath is sharply divided into these three elements of thought.

In wording and composition as well as in thought content and legal connotation, all formulas, naturally, show a resemblance to the oldest German Jewry oaths. But they are much expanded versions which differ in many details from their archetypes. Hans von Voltelini has compiled almost completely and examined in detail the manifold miracles as well as the curses and punishments from the Bible, which appear frequently in the medieval Jewry-oath formulas.[162] While in the oaths under consideration the miracles are rather briefly mentioned, the curses, on the other hand, are, with few exceptions, recited at length. Even more, they include several clauses which are peculiar to them and do not appear in the familiar formulas. These and other singular features offer valuable clues for critical analysis.

First, the introductory clause referring to the *thema probandum:* The *Weichbild* group, in its longer as well as its briefer form, is couched in very general terms and has no particular specification of proof in mind: "Of what this man accuses thee, of that thou art innocent." The *Schwabenspiegel* formula is more specific on this subject: "Of the goods about which this man accuses thee, that thou hast them not nor knowest, nor ever hadst received them into thy power, nor that thy servant had buried them under the earth, nor hidden within walls, nor shut behind locks."

It is obvious that this clause can refer only to *Schwabenspiegel*, L 261; G 214, 7. The Jew is supposed to take an oath of purgation against the charge of having bought goods taken by theft or robbery. It will be remembered, furthermore, that Jews were obligated to "be the Christians' warrantors" according to *Schwabenspiegel* law, whereas the *Sachsenspiegel* ruled: "A Jew must not be a Christian's warrantor."[163] All this offers ample proof that the *Schwabenspiegel* formula fits well into the framework of this lawbook, factually as well as juridically.

With regard to the *thema probandum*, the oath formula appended to some *Sachsenspiegel* manuscripts and editions combines the *Weichbild* version with that found in the *Schwabenspiegel*. Furthermore, another feature in the *Sachsenspiegel* oath formula is striking. It refers to the curse which, according to Matthew 27:25, the Jews had taken upon themselves when they demanded of Pilate the crucifixion of Jesus. This very clause, though in an expanded version, is found only in the *Schwabenspiegel* and the oath formulas derived from it. All these indications make it safe to assume that the *Schwabenspiegel* formula served as the model for the *Sachsenspiegel* Jewry oath, which latter appeared only in late manuscripts and editions.[164] The reference to the New Testament story also renders it very probable that the *Schwabenspiegel* oath was composed by a churchman, just as were the Erfurt and Donaueschingen Jewry oaths.[165]

The *Sachsenspiegel* formula also concurs with the *Swabian Mirror* in requiring the Jew to stand on a pigskin while taking the oath. It includes, moreover, a clause which does not appear in any other of the oath formulas in manuscript or print collected by the present writer during many years. This is the reference to the Jewish eschatological concept implied in the curse that the perjurer "never shall come to Jerusalem," that is, never shall be admitted into the messianic kingdom.[166] More detailed observations concerning the textual form of the *Sachsenspiegel* Jewry oath must be left to monographic treatment in the future. In the Augsburg edition of the *Sachsenspiegel*, the text of the oath has this clause immediately after the designation of God by the Hebrew name: "Constantine the King ordained that the Jews take this oath." Obviously no historical weight can be attached to such an authentication, trading as it did on the lack of historical sense so common in medieval times.

The oath formulas are preceded or followed by more or less detailed instructions concerning administration of the oath. These offer interesting information about the ceremonial accompanying the Jewry oath.[167]

According to all the formulas, the oath is administered by an *Eidstaber*. The *Schwabenspiegel* prescribes that the Jew is to stand on a sow's skin; according to the *Sachsenspiegel* formula, the swearer must be barefooted, and the hide, on which he is to stand, must come from an animal that had brought forth young during the past fortnight.

The skin shall be cut open along the back and spread on [displaying] the teats; on it the Jew shall stand barefooted and wearing nothing but nether garment and a haircloth about his body.[168]

This fantastic ritual, both offensive and degrading to the Jews, is explicitly disapproved in the *Glosses* on *Sachsenspiegel* (III, 7, 1) and *Weichbild-Vulgata* (art. 137, ed. 1557), both of the fourteenth century. Johann von Buch declares this procedure "unlawful" (*unrecht*), and the *Weichbild* glossator considers it a "fantasy" (*fantasey*), adding that "the Jews' oath shall be respected in the same way as that of Christians."[169] Both these medieval authors reflect the influence of the canon law (*Decretum Gratiani*, c. 16, C. XXII, qu. 1) which recognizes that the Jew in taking an oath appeals to the true God (*judei juraverunt per Deum verum*).

The Meissen lawbook (III, 17, 46) and the *Weichbild* formula prescribe similar proceedings, which are more elaborate in point of costume, corresponding to ancient German judiciary custom:

. . . So he shall swear on the *Rodal* and shall have on a gray coat, without shirt, on the bare skin, and two gray leg-coverings without feet, and a hat moistened with lamb's blood, thereon he shall stand, and a pointed hat on his head.

Here the bloody "hat" is an obvious mistake for the pigskin still fresh from slaughter, as proved by other manuscripts.[170]

Another ritual is introduced by an Oxford (Bodleian) manuscript of the *Weichbild-Vulgata*, in which the ceremony is described as follows:

He shall be turned toward the rising sun; barefoot he shall stand on a stool, he shall have on his cloak, and a Jew's hat. For every failure [to repeat the oath formula correctly] up to the third he loses a *vierdunc*. At the fourth, he forfeits standing [in court].[171]

The *mantel* which the swearer is here supposed to wear seems not to have been the ordinary cloak but the garment with fringes, the *tallit*, worn, according to Jewish custom, at prayer. Illuminations in medieval manuscripts sometimes depict Jews thus attired, their heads covered with the Jews' hat.[172]

The Glogau lawbook requires of the swearer "that he shall stand facing the sun and raise two fingers."[173] Facing the sun while taking the oath evidently implies that the perjurer is not worthy of God's light. This accords completely with the curse that the perjurer may be swallowed up by the earth "that swallowed Dathan and Abiram." Both these features are unmistakably reminiscent of the ancient ordeal element inherent in the oath. Earth and sun, being sacred to all ancient peoples, also had an important role in their systems of legal evidence. Very conveniently for the Jewry-oath ritual, the requirement of facing the (rising) sun corresponded to the Jewish custom of turning toward the east (or Jerusalem) while at prayer.

The Jewry oath could be administered either within or in front of the synagogue or at the regular meeting place of the (Christian) court.[174] It seems that the lawbooks regarded the synagogue as the proper and regular place for this ritual. The Latin version of the *Weichbild-Vulgata* makes this statement: "Judaeus, si promittat jus, seu juramentum alicui, id in congregatione seu schola eorum facere eum oportet."[175]

In lawsuits involving minor amounts the oath could be performed in front of the synagogue.[176] In such cases the swearing Jew had to grasp the chain (or ring) locking the synagogue door.

This was most probably a symbolic substitute for the Sacred
Books, the Torah, which within the synagogue he would have
held in his hands; for the Torah was not accessible, since the
synagogue was shut outside of service hours and the Jews were
certainly not anxious to open it for this ceremony. An oath on the
Torah was not considered requisite in minor matters, and every
effort was made to avoid it.

In lawsuits involving greater sums—according to the Meissen
lawbook, III, 17, 46, more than 50 marks—the oath had to be
taken in the synagogue, upon the Torah or *Rodale* itself.[177] This
seems to have been the general rule. "A Jew must not come out
of the synagogue [where head-covering was prescribed by Jewish custom] without a Jews' hat"; this statement, found at the
end of the oath regulations in the *Weichbild* and the Meissen lawbook, gives further evidence that the oath was taken predominantly in the synagogue.[178] Although the *Schwabenspiegel* has no
corresponding regulation, other law sources from southern Germany indicate that the same procedure was customary in this
region. Here, too, as a rule, the synagogue was deemed the most
appropriate place for the oath ceremony.[179] In the synagogue an
authentic copy of the Sacred Scriptures was available, namely,
the scroll used by the Jews in their services. Thus, no doubt could
be entertained of its genuineness.

It seems, however, that sometimes the oath ceremony was held
at the regular meeting place of the (Christian) court. Judge and
jurors then faced the problem of securing a genuine copy of the
Pentateuch. The binding character of the oath depended on the
sanctity of the Torah used, which therefore had to be genuine
and unobjectionable in every respect. The original Hebrew text
was required, and no translation could be substituted for it. The
fact that the *Weichbild* Jewry-oath formula and another one,
probably of Magdeburg provenience, include an additional oath
affirming the genuineness of the Torah[180] makes it safe to assume
that in the domain of Saxon law, too, the Jewry oath was at
times taken in the Christian court.

The law contents of the oath formulas, though differing in
the various versions, are, for the most part, in accord in basic
essentials. Sometimes different oath formulas were provided for

minor and for more important law matters, as in the Meissen lawbook (III, 17, 46): in lawsuits involving less than 50 marks a less elaborate ("simple") oath had to be taken on the "Book of Moses," not otherwise specified, while in lawsuits of over 50 marks the full oath must be sworn upon the Torah in the hallowed form of the scroll. Another differentiation is found according to whether suit was brought under municipal or under territorial law, and a different oath formula was prescribed for either case, as recorded in Purgoldt's lawbook.[181] Finally, consideration for Jewish sentiment also led to a simplification of the oath formulas by the elimination of particularly offensive clauses, such as the reference to the Jews' self-denunciation upon the delivery of Jesus in the shorter *Sachsenspiegel* and *Weichbild* formulas. Hence the difference between the briefer forms and the full versions.[182] The omission of such objectionable passages and of some of the curses from the long series could not but enhance the solemnity, seriousness, and rigor of the oath. It seems that in certain cases the text was generally abbreviated. This is probably why the *Weichbild Gloss* deems it fit to emphasize the statement that "each clause of the oath is taken severally for the whole of the oath, in the matters in which Jews are accused."[183]

3. THE JEWRY OATH IN MAGDEBURG LAW PRACTICE

Despite the fact that the so-called "*Sachsenspiegel* Jewry oath" is related to the *Schwabenspiegel* formula and most probably derived from it, the differentiation of Saxon and Swabian oath formulas may still be retained. One must only bear in mind that the Saxon formulas and practice are not to be traced to the *Sachsenspiegel* but originated in the texts and regulations found in the various versions of the *Weichbild-Vulgata*. True, the *Sachsenspiegel* oath formula and the "fantastic" ceremonial accompanying it were introduced and disseminated also in the province of Magdeburg law. This is true particularly of the domain of the Bohemian crown, where Saxon law entering from the north came into collision with Swabian law coming in from the southwest.[184] Nevertheless, and quite naturally, the law of the Saxon *Weichbild*, which had originated in Magdeburg or Halle, and especially its Jewry-oath regulations were adopted in the wide realm of Magdeburg law.

Decisions handed down by the *Schöffen* of Magdeburg or other jury courts of Magdeburg law throw light on the legal practice in this special field of the medieval law of evidence. From these impeccable sources clear insight can be gained as to which of the elaborate requirements in the Jewry-oath formulas and in the oath ceremonial found application in actual legal life.

First, one may note that the brief oath formula from the *Weichbild-Vulgata* is incorporated in some manuscript collections of Magdeburg jury-court decisions, such as those of Naumburg[185] and Tovačov.[186] The *Summa*, "*Der Rechte Weg*," a lawbook compiled in Breslau in the fifteenth century and consisting of about sixteen hundred Magdeburg jury-court decisions, includes the Jewry-oath formula typical of Silesia. It requires the swearer to stand on a stool and to wear a *tallit* and the Jews' hat while performing the ceremony.[187] If local *Willkür* ("statute") or custom adopted such standard formulas, occasion could hardly arise to resort to the *Oberhof* of Magdeburg, which, moreover, would not have passed on such statutory law.[188] Other cities under Magdeburg law, in which no such legal standardization of the Jewry oath had yet been effected, would send their requests for law instruction to the *Schöffen* of Magdeburg, who readily responded on the various points in question.

It is conspicuous indeed that, according to the extant *Schöffensprüche*, the Magdeburg jurors never referred to the *Weichbild* Jewry oath, either directly or by implication. The procedure and formula which they prescribed for the taking of an oath by a Jew, in several decisions replying to inquiries of provincial courts, were far different from those presented and studied earlier in this chapter. In contradistinction to the numerous threats and curses which these heaped upon the swearer, the manner of administering and taking an oath recommended by the *Schöffen* of Magdeburg was simple and dignified. Their decision in response to a query from the local court of Eisleben is typical. It reads as follows:

Hereupon we, the *scheppen* at Magdeburg, state the law: The Jew shall take his oath in public before the synagogue, so that the plaintiff may hear and see it, and he shall put his whole hand into Moses' book and shall swear that he is innocent of the matter, so God help him and his Law. This is the law.[189]

The essentials for meeting the requirements of legality as laid down in this ruling recur in other decisions bearing on the Jewry oath.[190] The swearer is supposed "to name the plaintiff's claim and to say that he is innocent of the matter, so God help him and his Law." This was the standard formula constantly recommended by the Magdeburg jurors. Nowhere is there any reference to degrading ceremonies accompanying the taking of the oath. The only formal act to be observed by the swearer was to place his hand in Moses' book during the ceremony.[191] The act of swearing had to take place either in the synagogue or in front of it. The municipal jurors of Stendal at one time explicitly raised the question as to where the oath should be taken, whether "before the synagogue upon Moses' books or before the *hegheden dinghe* in the court place." The *Schöffen* of Magdeburg in their decision favored the first alternative.[192] The oath had to be in accordance with Jewish law, *nach erme jodeschen rechte*,[193] but uttered in the German language and solemnly, "so that the plaintiff may hear and see it."[194] According to a Magdeburg decision sent to the local court of Stendal in 1331, an oath *selbsiebent* had to be sworn in this way:[195] first, by the Jew "with his own hand"; then the six oath-helpers had to follow, not, however, all together, as otherwise customary under Magdeburg law,[196] but in groups of three. The underlying reason for this departure from the usual procedure was probably the special emphasis laid on a distinct pronunciation of the oath formula by all the swearers.

It was, again, concern for law and justice that held first place in the considerations of the *Schöffen* at the high court of Magdeburg. In the problems offered by the Jewry oath, just as on other occasions, they recognized with juridical sagacity the crucial point, namely, how to obtain the most reliable evidence of the truth. Therefore, they did not indulge in elaborating complex and degrading oath formulas. The application of these, on the other hand, by local courts that favored them, was not barred, because of the broad formulation that the *Schöffen* of Magdeburg chose for their decisions. Yet the latter's judicial acumen pointed in a direction which others failed to follow.

CHAPTER ELEVEN

Administrative Law

I. Administrative Jewry-Law; Its Concept and Character

IN SOME of the preceding chapters it has been stressed that, for one reason or another, the subject matter was not susceptible of exhaustive presentation. This applies with increased force to the present chapter, though for somewhat different reasons arising from the particular nature of its subject matter.

Again, as a methodological expedient, a modern category is employed here, namely, that of "administrative law." The term as such calls for a historical explanation. In Continental jurisprudence the idea of administrative law is based on the differentiation of civil and criminal justice from other functions of government. The body of law controlling the exercise of governmental powers in matters of police, revenue, and public services is usually designated as "administrative law."[1] The corresponding terms in the German legal phraseology are *Polizei* and *Polizeirecht*.[2]

The idea of *Polizei*, or the task of providing for the general welfare, is an outgrowth of communal self-government. The autonomy of the medieval cities, developed early, is the origin and starting-point of modern city administration and public welfare policies. It was in the medieval cities that markets, weights and measures, and trade in food were first placed under systematic regulation. Municipal control gradually expanded over an ever wider area of social activities: industrial production (particularly the craftsmen's guilds), commerce, traffic, building, sanitation, public safety, and social welfare in general. Taxation and matters military constituted other important branches of *Polizei* in the medieval city. If one takes into consideration the economic regimentation, sumptuary laws, moral restrictions, and all the regulations of social conditions resulting from the comprehensive competence claimed by the medieval municipality, it becomes clear that the municipal *Polizeirecht* reached deeply into the private life of every city dweller.

The Jews, though city dwellers, were, in principle, not subject to the administrative competence of the municipalities where they resided. They were chiefly dependent on the "town lords," who granted extensive self-government to the Jewish communities. But, their legal recognition, on the one hand, and the fact of their territorial inclusion in the cities, on the other, affected their relationship with the municipal authorities and their status under administrative law. The internal organization and authority of the Jewish communities rested, of course, predominantly on Jewish law. The jurisdiction of the Jewish courts, taxation, and the entire internal Jewish *Polizeirecht* were based from the earliest times on the principle of self-government. The pertinent provisions were incorporated in the charters of the Jewish settlements. While the Jewish communities were thus dependent on the charters granted them by the town lords, it was only in the nature of things that their internal life had to undergo a measure of adjustment to the surrounding frame of the general municipal administrative law. On the other hand, the medieval "state" did not, as a rule, interfere in internal Jewish affairs. The authority of municipal administrative law over the Jewish community was thus quite restricted. It bore only on those legal aspects which the Jews presented as a community within the larger community, a Jewish city within the Christian city, or as individuals in their immediate contacts with the Christian inhabitants.

The field of specific administrative Jewry-law was thus very small. Basically it extended merely to the physical and legal foundations of the communal settlement of Jews, that is, to their quarters and religious institutions and also to taxation, inasmuch as the Jews were required to pay municipal taxes in addition to their financial obligations to the emperor and town lord and in addition to internal Jewish taxes.

It was only with reference to these points that an "administrative" Jewry-law in the true sense of the term could develop. Only scant traces of it are found in the German lawbooks, for obvious reasons. In matters affecting the construction and maintenance of the Jewish quarters in general and of the religious institutions in particular, such as synagogue, community house, slaughter-house, ritual bath, or cemetery, the individual local conditions were decisive. The same is true of municipal taxation. Hence it is not surprising that most of the regulations concerning these subjects were of too local a character to find a place in the medieval lawbooks, which did not usually take account of local peculiarities.

The same explanation will account, if not quite completely, for the absence of administrative Jewry-law from the collections of Magdeburg jury-court decisions. Another course of reflection, however, may well suggest a concurrent reason. In disputes with the municipal authorities in matters of administrative law the Jews were obviously not on an equal footing with their opponents. They were manifestly the weaker party. This was, it seems, the fact, even if only on psychological grounds. The Jews obviously could not but seek to maintain peaceable relations with the Christian world surrounding them. Hence they would not care, or even dare, to impugn the municipal authority by bringing their suits before the *Schöffen* of Magdeburg for decision. The latter not infrequently rendered judgment in cases involving administrative law, e.g., on admission to craft guilds or on the simultaneous pursuit of two different trades.[3] Christian citizens, and even municipal authorities, did not hesitate to take such disputes before the Magdeburg jurors, who would, in fact, sometimes adjudicate against the guilds or municipal authorities. No analogous instance of a Jewish claimant is recorded. The Jews apparently preferred to acquiesce in the administrative ordinances and orders of the Christian municipal authorities. Thus no pertinent jury-court decisions were handed down.

In view of this situation, all the more weight attaches to the material on administrative Jewry-law embodied in the lawbooks. The mere fact of its incorporation in them testifies to its general validity and importance.

The scantiness of such regulations is compensated for by a

comparatively large body of noteworthy legal rules of a restrictive and anti-Jewish character. They are enumerated under twelve consecutive heads in Johann von Buch's *Gloss* on *Sachsenspiegel*, III, 7, 1, and in the *Remissoria*, indicating that the legal treatment of Jews was different from that of Christians in many respects. "It shall be borne in mind that the Jews are treated legally in a particular manner chiefly on twelve subjects."[4] The most important among these rules are first encountered in the *Schwabenspiegel* (L 262; G 214, 9–11). Many of those differentiations go back to the ancient codes of Roman law.[5] True, these restrictions had been adopted, multiplied, and propagated by canon law. They represented an essential part of medieval ecclesiastical legislation and practice. It was, however, only by consequence of their incorporation into German secular law that these rules and principles of alien origin gained universal validity and the character of genuine administrative Jewry-law. They will be discussed hereafter, together with the original German law matter.

II. Jewish Quarters and Religious Institutions[6]

The absence from the leading lawbooks of any regulation on the construction or maintenance of separate Jewish quarters in the medieval German cities has been a puzzle to many historians. A variety of explanations has been suggested, differing in accordance with the individual scholar's general conception of the position of the Jew in medieval society. In the main, two contradictory theories were put forward as possible solutions of the problem. One held that, at its inception, the medieval Jewish settlement was under legal compulsion imposed from without and thus, from the very beginning, formed a "ghetto" in the term's narrowest meaning. The other theory offered a somewhat more subtle explanation for the silence of the lawbooks. It assumed that Jewish custom coincided with external compulsion and so promoted residential segregation. This self-segregation was, moreover, interpreted as convincing evidence of a Jewish "feeling of national strangeness" (*Gefühl völkischer Fremdheit*). And it was also the ghetto, it was held, which, in turn, prevented this strangeness from wearing off.[7]

Both these hypotheses were launched *cum ira et studio* rather than on the basis of penetration into the available sources. Both must be discarded; for a more recent inquiry, scholarly and calm, has probed the question of the Jewish quarter, the *Judenstadt* or *Judengasse*, merely as part of the problem of the history of medieval city planning, and has arrived at more plausible results.[8] There can no longer be any doubt that the separation of the Jewish from the general settlements in medieval cities had its origin in the free will of the early Jewish settlers and by no means in compulsory measures imposed on them. Such measures would be absolutely contradictory to the alluring conditions of settlement offered at times to Jewish immigrants, such as those included in the old Rhenish Jewry privileges.

Various factors contributed to make a separate and closed settlement desirable to the Jewish pioneers in Germany and elsewhere. First of all, there were religious reasons, such as convenient access to synagogue, school, bathhouse, hospital, etc. The desire for common prayer and communal activities made dwelling close together imperative. There were, furthermore, economic reasons which spontaneously suggested a closed settlement for the Jewish merchants in the neighborhood of the market place. This corresponded also to a universal medieval custom. Those who plied the same trade or business used to live and work in the same neighborhood. Just as the butchers or shoemakers occupied a street or section of their own, so the Jews lived together in a *vicus judeorum, inter judeos, apud judeos,* or in a *Judengasse.*[9] Finally, in addition to general topographical and social reasons, there were also legal reasons for establishing a closed Jewish settlement in a certain locality. It guaranteed better and prompter protection by the town lord. Inclosure within walls or behind a gate was at first considered a particular favor by the Jews. Closed quarters also made much easier the regulation of Jewish life, including the collection of taxes and the administration of justice, in particular. All these developments flowed quite naturally from the basic conditions of the Jewish settlements as established by the town lords in their charters. Within these—so to speak—"constitutional" limits the religious and social, legal and economic, life of the Jews could unfold freely. Therefore, no occasion was offered to incorporate relevant general regulations or restrictions in the lawbooks.

As early as the second half of the thirteenth century these comparatively favorable conditions underwent a change, with a growing trend toward deterioration. It was Pope Innocent III who, particularly at the Fourth Lateran Council of 1215, sought to elaborate the old and traditional church policy toward the Jews. Various drastic measures aiming at a strict social segregation of the Jews were revived in 1215 and were enforced more and more intensively in the decades following that ecumenical council.[10] It is doubtful whether the segregation of the Jews in a separate quarter was demanded in Mayence as early as 1233 as has been maintained.[11] But in 1267 the provincial council of Breslau adopted a more specific resolution, valid for the entire archdiocese of Gnesen:

Since the Polish country still is a young plantation in the body of Christendom, in order that the Christian populace be not the more easily infected by the superstitions and the depraved mores of the Jews dwelling among them; and in order that the Christian religion be more easily and quickly implanted in the hearts of the faithful in these parts: we strictly prescribe that the Jews dwelling in this province of Gnesen shall not have their habitations intermixed among the Christians, but shall have their houses either contiguous or adjoining in some segregated location of a city or village; in such manner that the quarter of the Jews be separated from the communal dwellings of the Christians by a fence, a wall, or a moat. We prescribe, moreover, that Christians as well as Jews whose houses are intermingled be compelled in the appropriate way by the diocesan bishop or the temporal lord to effect their sale or exchange according to the arbitration of honorable men. If this separation shall not have been effected before the next feast of Saint John the Baptist, then the diocesan bishop as well as the temporal lord shall know that they are thenceforward interdicted from entering the church, if they have failed to exercise their jurisdiction or interdict against the recalcitrants.[12]

This policy of the church could, of course, not remain without influence on secular law. The competition of Christians engaged in trade and convenience in levying municipal taxes on Jews were additional factors supporting the enforced segregation of the Jews. It is difficult to determine exactly the time when the

original intention of protecting the Jews in settlements of voluntary seclusion was replaced by that of compulsion and discrimination. It certainly was a process which differed in detail in the
various localities but which extended from the thirteenth to the
end of the fifteenth century. From a Magdeburg jury-court decision of the first half of the fifteenth century it is clear that Jews
then still enjoyed lawful long-term residence in houses rented
from Christian owners.[13] The legal problem as to whether a
Christian could rent his house to a Jew was discussed in Johannes
Purgoldt's lawbook, at the beginning of the sixteenth century, as
follows (Book VIII, art. 99):

> There is also a question: May a Christian rent his house to a Jew ac-
> cording to law? Thereto the learned answer saying: This may well be
> done according to the law, in order to separate them from the Chris-
> tians.

Little wonder, therefore, that Purgoldt's is also the only German
lawbook to include strict ghetto regulations, in Book VIII,
article 102:

> Their houses shall be separated from those of the Christians, and [all
> of them] shall be together, and ropes shall be drawn across the street.

This signifies, indeed, the final step in the development.
Whether the protection which was extended by penal law, in the
Meissen lawbook, to synagogues and cemeteries was caused by
this change in the character of the Jewish closed settlement must
remain an open question.[14] Another regulation concerning the
construction and repair of synagogues seems to point in this direction. It is the revival of the ancient prohibition that "the
Jews may build no more new synagogues; but they may repair
the old ones. Also no one may make forcible entry into their
synagogues."

This prohibition, revived from the *Theodosian Code* by Popes
Gregory the Great in 598 and Alexander III in 1179,[15] makes its
first appearance on German soil in Johann von Buch's *Gloss* on
Sachsenspiegel, III, 7, 1 (3).[16] Explicit reference is made there to
Roman and canon law: *C. de judaeis et coelicolis, l. in synagoga et
l. ultima,* § *illud* [*Cod. Just.* i. 9. 4 and 18 (1)]; *45 distinct. c. qui
sincera* [*Decretum Gratiani*, c. 3, D. 45], and *Extra de judaeis, el. 1*
[c.3. (cf. also 7), X, *de judaeis*, 5, 6]. The same passage was also

included in later lawbooks.[17] And a *Sachsenspiegel* manuscript from the fourteenth or fifteenth century has an addition to *Land-recht*, III, 8, "concerning the *Busse* of a Jew who builds a synagogue without the consent of his lord."[18] It is hardly open to doubt that only the growing influence of canon and Roman law was responsible for the fact that this ancient regulation, maintained, of course, by the church, now also made its way into the secular law of Germany.

III. Dress Regulations[19]

Early in the thirteenth century many European countries, including England, France, Spain, and Sicily, had to deal with the problem of special Jewish costume and distinguishing marks. In 1215 the Fourth Lateran Council, one of the most important ecumenical councils, which exerted a lasting influence on Christian faith and life all over the world, ordained in canon 68 of its decrees:

In some church provinces a difference in dress distinguishes the Jews or Saracens from the Christians, but in certain others such a confusion has grown up that they cannot be distinguished by any difference. Thus it happens at times that through error Christians have relations with Jewish or Saracen women, and Jews or Saracens with Christian women. Therefore, that they may not, under pretext of error of this sort, take recourse to excusing themselves in the future for the excesses of such accursed intercourse, we decree that such [Jews and Saracens] of both sexes in every Christian province and at all times shall be marked off in the eyes of the public from other peoples through the character of their dress. Particularly, since it may be read [in Num. 15:37–41] that this very law has been enjoined upon them by Moses.[20]

The motives for this stringent measure cannot receive detailed discussion here. It must suffice to point out that it was completely in line with the general tendency of Pope Innocent III's Jewry policy and legislation.[21] His desire to mark off the Jews, expressed as early as 1204, presaged the later prescription of a distinctive Jewish garb.

The secular powers of Europe quickly responded to the pope's call. In England, Spain, Sicily, and some parts of France, Jewish assimilation in garb had progressed so far by 1215 that the secular authorities, in order to eliminate the confusion decried in the precept of the Lateran Council, had to take drastic measures; and they did so almost immediately. Already by 1217, the Jews were under the obligation of wearing badges of peculiar shapes and colors to distinguish them from Christians.

In central Europe, on the contrary, and in Germany in particular no explicit mention of the yellow or red wheel as a Jew badge is found prior to the fifteenth century. This is readily understandable, since in these central European countries the Jews were otherwise differentiated from the Christian population and thus easily distinguishable to the eyes of their Christian neighbors. The distinction was effected, first, by their beards, unshaven in accordance with Jewish ritual law, but no less by their peculiar head-covering, the "horned hat," which they wore of their own free will, according to an old local tradition, whereas their coreligionists in northern France, for example, used to go about bareheaded. The older form of the "Jewish hat," *pileus cornutus*, was conical and low, without a brim or with only a very narrow brim. The top often bent over, making the "horn" of the *pileus cornutus*. From this original several different types developed.

These traditional marks of Jewish distinctiveness, adhered to voluntarily, though to some extent imposed by Jewish law, implied no diminution in the Jews' legal rights or even social status. The Middle Ages were a period of the greatest variety and differentiation in social classes or "estates." Differences in costume were brought about by differences in class, means, profession, and other factors: "Clothes made the man." Everyone's position, from beggar to king, was easily recognizable from his clothing. The dress of clerics and professional men was prescribed by tradition, that of the laboring and agricultural classes was dictated by considerations of convenience. Medieval literature throws into relief this unswerving loyalty to custom by designating the costumes of the several classes as "conforming to law."[22] Members of one and the same social group were knit together the more closely by their identical garb, a sort of symbolic bond.

This applies to the Jews no less than to all other groups in medieval society. From the point of view of the world which

surrounded them, the Jews, as a distinct group, were in no different position, in this respect, than all others. This becomes evident from numerous illustrations in medieval manuscripts, representing Jews and members of other classes of the population in
their distinctive attire, yet on the same footing and without dis-
paragement of the Jew. In the illuminated manuscripts of the
Sachsenspiegel, Jews are pictured side by side with soldiers in full
accouterment, with Franks and Saxons standing before the
judge, and also with clerics, each type clearly identified by costume, mark of distinction, or symbolic attribute, the Jews by
their beards and pointed hats.[23] No pejorative connotation is
implied in these pictorial representations of Jews, as can be
gathered also from the well-known miniature of the Jewish minnesinger, Süsskind von Trimberg, in the Manesse manuscript,[24]
who is pictured in fashionable dress, though with beard and
pointed hat, standing before the bishop [of Constance?] and
other dignitaries.[25]

The wearing of the "Jewish hat" was made obligatory, however, from the second half of the thirteenth century onward. The
transformation of a traditional custom into an obligation was
effected in Germany, too, in response to the numerous regional
church councils which, time and again, called for the strict enforcement of the Lateran conciliar decrees.[26] The laws required,
in particular, that Jews must wear the hat on leaving the synagogue and when taking an oath.

No provision of this kind is found in the *Sachsenspiegel*. But
the *Schwabenspiegel*, in article L 262; G 214, 10, lays down the
rule that "the Jews shall wear hats that are pointed," so as to be
marked off from the Christians.[27] At the end of its description of
the ritual and procedure of the Jewry oath, the *Weichbild-Vulgata*
(second half of the thirteenth century) states: "A Jew must not
come out of the synagogue without a Jewish mitre."[28]

The same regulation recurs in the Meissen lawbook (III, 17,
47), which also prescribes that the Jew, when taking an oath,
has to be dressed in a particular manner and "has to wear a
pointed hat upon his head" (III, 17, 46).[29] Johannes Purgoldt's
lawbook, from the beginning of the sixteenth century, mentions (VIII, 85) the fact that "in some countries such as Italy,

where Rome is situated, the Jews must wear clothes different from those of the Christians." Among all the German lawbooks, that of Purgoldt has the most elaborate regulations concerning Jewish dress, extending even to footgear.[30] Article 102 of Book VIII makes the following prescriptions:

In all respects the Jews shall be different, in their dwellings, clothes, and other things. Their houses shall be separated from those of the Christians, and all of them shall be together, and ropes shall be drawn across the streets. Their clothes shall also be different from the clothes of the Christians; males shall not wear *kogeln* but higher hats of felt. So writes Pope Innocent the First [*sic!*]. Moreover, it is also written in the *Weichbildrecht* that no Jew shall walk from his *shul* ["synagogue"] or from his house into the street without hat. Men shall also wear boots and go without wooden shoes; the women covered with veils, and with wide "head windows" on their cloaks, and without wooden shoes. That they now go about differently is a sign that to the princes Jewish gold is dearer than the honor of God or Holy Christendom.

The reference in this regulation to Pope Innocent III speaks for itself. This passage, moreover, clearly testifies to the ideological connection between the Jewish garb and the ghetto in their historical development. There is a striking parallel, socially as well as legally, between these two means of discrimination against the Jews. Living together in separate quarters of the medieval cities originated, just as did their typical attire, in religious precepts or needs and in established social traditions and to a certain extent also in considerations of occupational convenience. As long as garb and ghetto represented voluntary institutions not subject to any compulsory regulation from outside, no diminution in legal or social status attached to them. The moment that garb and ghetto were made compulsory by ecclesiastical or secular legislation, the status of the Jews underwent a change. Their relegation to restricted dwelling places and to wearing a prescribed garb implied their prohibition from living in the ordinary ("Christian") quarters and from wearing the common costume. The inevitable consequence was not only discrimination against them legally but also the beginning of their degradation socially. The initial phase in the development of the ghetto as well as of a special Jewish garb in Germany came in the second half of the thirteenth century and at its end. While the hat remained there the principal mark of distinction throughout the fourteenth century, it was chiefly due to the activities and influence of the papal legate and philosopher, Nicholas of Cusa, and of the fanatical Franciscan preacher, John of Capistrano, that the wearing of a distinctive badge, the *gelber Fleck*, instead of the Jewish hat, was finally enforced in the course of the fifteenth and sixteenth centuries.

IV. RESTRICTION ON SOCIAL INTERCOURSE BETWEEN JEWS AND CHRISTIANS[31]

It is well known that Innocent III's activities as pope were largely concerned with the two problems of reviving and propagating the orthodox faith and firmly establishing the political power of the papacy. In connection with the first, his pontificate is famous for the Albigensian Crusade, launched by him in 1207 to extinguish that heresy. His management of the second problem marks one of the high points of papal influence over the secular powers. Christendom, he maintained, was not only a moral unity but a visible concrete world-state under clerical guidance; although it was governed by territorial rulers, yet each part and the whole must recognize the supremacy of the Roman See and the plenitude of power held by Peter's successor, the representative of Christ.[32]

The regulation of relations with the small number of Jews then living among Christian peoples was entirely in line with this conception. To preserve the purity of the true faith, all groups of unbelievers were to be strictly separated from the flock of the faithful. It is not accidental that, in his letter of January 16, 1205, to the king of France, Innocent III called for the "elimination of the heretics," after re-emphasizing a number of preventive measures against the Jews decreed by the Third Lateran Council.[33] Thus Pope Innocent III initiated no basically new legislation with regard to the Jews: he merely elaborated on the traditional church policy or sought to enforce older decrees by drastic measures. On July 15, 1205, he reformulated the theological doctrine of the "eternal servitude" of the Jews, until then conceived only theologically, but now with a political coloring.[34]

Viewed in this light, the general tendency of Pope Innocent's

Jewry legislation becomes more understandable. The segregation of Jews from Christian society was intended to prevent those close contacts which might seduce Christians to forsake the true faith. For a long time the church had been unsuccessful in this endeavor. Social intercourse and cordial relations persisted between followers of both religions up to the thirteenth century, naturally not without occasional temporary interruptions. Hence the separation now had to become even stricter than it had been in the past. The anti-Jewish laws enacted by the Christianized Roman Empire and later by the church were to be scrupulously observed. Thus the repression of the Jew might serve as a warning example to those vacillating Christians who might be tempted to succumb to the religious influence of this or any other infidel group. Such were the motives for the re-enactment of several anti-Jewish measures: Jews must not employ Christian servants or nurses; Jews must not exercise power over Christians or oppress them under the pretext of public office, hence they shall be excluded from holding public office; they must not appear in public on Good Friday ("on the days of lamentation and the Passion of the Lord"); they must not erect new synagogues, engage in usury, commit blasphemy, etc. Most of these precepts were endowed with the authority of the Fourth Lateran Council (*canones* 67, 68, and 69) and later incorporated in the *Corpus juris canonici*.[35] Little wonder, therefore, that secular legislation could not escape their influence, particularly in view of the fact that these restrictions and prohibitions were constantly reiterated and re-emphasized by numerous provincial councils.

It would require much more space than is here available to describe in full the reflection of all these church laws in secular legislation. Among the medieval German lawbooks the *Schwabenspiegel* was the first to mirror this trend. Apart from its other Jewry-law regulations mentioned in the course of this presentation, it contains the following articles quite in line with the canons of the Fourth Lateran Council:

9. Christians are forbidden to eat in the company of Jews any food prepared by them; nor shall they invite any [Jews] to a wedding or conviviality. No Christian shall bathe together with Jews. On Holy

Thursday afternoon they [Jews] shall have their doors and windows shut; also they shall not go into the street. This is to last until the coming of Easter day.

11. The Jews shall not have Christians with them in service, to eat their bread and food. These [Christians so serving] are excommunicated [L 262; G 214].

The incorporation in the most influential southern German lawbook of these regulations, still foreign to its northern German model, was no doubt due to the fact that its clerical author was well acquainted with the ecclesiastical [legislation. He wished to assert its authority also in the realm of secular law. About fifty years later these regulations recur with slight differences, in some respects more complete and elaborate, in Johann von Buch's *Gloss* on the *Sachsenspiegel:*[36]

Know ye that four things are forbidden to the Jews. Firstly, no Christian shall take meals with them, nor again they [Jews] with Christians . . . nor shall Christians take service with them. . . . With the pagans, however, we may do so [but not with an excommunicated Christian]. . . . Secondly, Jews shall hold no public office [or command] over Christians. . . . Thirdly, no medical care [medicine] shall be taken from among them. Fourthly, they shall not go abroad on Good Friday, nor keep their doors or windows open [III, 2].

2. Secondly, no Jew shall have Christian bondsmen or bondswomen, and if he has, whoever will may take them from him but shall give twelve shillings for each one. Thereupon, the Christian may keep them or set them free, as is his will.

4. Fourthly, whichever Christian is servant to a Jew is excommunicated.

5. Fifthly, on Good Friday, Jews shall not show themselves in the streets, nor leave doors or windows open [III, 7, 1].

The original text includes references to the pertinent canon-law precepts. Their acceptance in other lawbooks clearly shows how widespread their penetration into secular law finally became.[37] Naturally, however, no medieval jury court ever engaged in deciding actual cases arising from these regulations.

V. TAXATION[38]

As is well known, levying taxes on their Jewish subjects was the easiest and most profitable way for territorial rulers, town lords, and municipal authorities to tap almost inexhaustible sources of financial aid. In addition to the general taxes imposed on the Jews, ordinary and extraordinary, there were taxes on private property as well as synagogues and schools, taxes in commutation of personal defense service, taxes for safe-conducts, burial taxes, etc. In spite of this multiplicity of taxes, for reasons previously set forth, no regulations on the taxation of Jews are found in the older of the medieval German lawbooks, prior to the second half of the fourteenth century. Even in the later law sources only two passages treat of special problems of taxation.

One, in the Meissen lawbook, III, 17, 35, states the rule that Jews shall not be assessed for safe-conducts or transit tolls in any way differently from Christians: "According to the law a Jew, be he living or dead, shall pay no other duty or toll than a Christian. If the collectors force more from them, that is robbery."[39]

The other passage, in the Stendal *Gloss* on *Sachsenspiegel*, III, 7, 1 (prior to 1434), is not so favorable to the Jews.[40] It is concerned with the payment of the customary tithes from urban real property to the local church authorities. Canon 67 of the Fourth Lateran Council had established the rule that Jews must continue to pay to the church the same taxes on real property which they had acquired as had been paid by its former Christian owners.[41] This precept was reiterated by the provincial Council of Breslau in 1267.[42] It was also adopted by the Stendal *Gloss* on the *Sachsenspiegel*. But a restrictive interpretation, favorable to the Jews, was added here. A Jew's obligation to continue payment should not include voluntary offerings but be limited to obligatory dues only:

You are to know that, if a Jew acquires the house of a parishioner, he must pay to the church as much as it used to receive annually from the parishioner and family dwelling there, and to that extent such Jew is obligated. But such Jew is not required to make voluntary offerings that do not arise from necessity.

PART IV

General Aspects of Medieval Jewry-Law

CHAPTER TWELVE

The Medieval Conception of the Jew and His Destiny

I. Religious Difference

IT IS an old truism that the conditions of every age are mirrored in its laws. Hence a survey of the laws—their aims, the ways and means whereby they seek to realize these aims, their success or failure, and their relation to past, present, and future laws— furnishes a panorama of the age to which they owe their genesis. Law, as a pillar of every social community, has always occupied a central position in the history and destiny of peoples.

This applies particularly to medieval Jewry-law and its effect on the scattered remnants of the Jewish people. Jewry-law reflects the basic ideas which determined the medieval conception of the Jew and reveals the solution which the Middle Ages found for its "Jewish problem." The colorful mosaic assembled in the preceding pages from medieval legislation, legal doctrine, and judicial practice discloses, in the final analysis, the main factors that were operative in shaping the destiny of medieval Jewry. The presentation to follow is thus exclusively concerned with the general, that is, *non-Jewish*, aspects of the Jewish problem and destiny in the Middle Ages.[1]

It has long been recognized that medieval man was dominated by a unitary order. Law, ethics, religion, art, and language formed one harmonious whole. Religion and law, in particular, were linked most closely. This synthesis found expression, profoundly reasoned religiously as well as philosophically, in the representative German lawbook of the Middle Ages, the *Sachsenspiegel*. Poetic literature reflects the same view. According to medieval poetry, law is the true faith, true Christianity, the Christian life, true justice.[2] Little wonder, therefore, that the difference in the Jews' religion impressed itself forcibly on the medieval mind. Early Christian theology had laid the foundation well, and throughout the Middle Ages this difference, with all its implications, was constantly emphasized in the Christian doctrine.[3] It occupied a most conspicuous place also in the domain of medieval law.

It is safe to assume that it was the religious difference of the Jews which, from the very beginning up to the later centuries of the medieval period, constituted the main, if not the only, reason for their different legal treatment. This is to be noted as early as the Carolingian formulae of protective charters which, when applied to Jewish grantees, were modified in consideration of their religion.[4] While the medieval state, as a rule, granted the Jews full self-government and did not interfere in matters of religion, Jewish religious law found recognition in Jewry privileges, in legal theory, and in judicial practice.[5] A special oath formula was prescribed and prepared for Jews.[6] Even if often derogatory in wording and sometimes degrading in ceremonial, it yet took account of the Jewish religious requirements for a binding oath. More, excommunication inflicted by a Jewish court was respected and upheld by the Christian authorities; and punishment of Jewish transgressors according to Jewish law was reserved to the Jewish court after the penalty due under secular law and imposed by the Christian court had been executed.[7] Finally, attention should also be drawn to the legal protection extended to religious institutions such as synagogues and cemeteries.[8]

All the instances adduced—and they could easily be multiplied —testify clearly to the correctness of the assertion that it was their religious difference, above all, which made the Jews conspicuous to the world around them and caused their special treatment in law.

Modern research in the history of law has generally recognized religious difference as the main motivation for the particular legal status of the Jews in the Middle Ages.[9] Another theory, however, propounded by and prevailing among German historians of law,[10] regarded medieval Jewry-law as an outgrowth of the original Germanic "law of aliens" (*Fremdenrecht*), thus laying particular emphasis on the national "otherness" of the Jews[11] and relegating the religious difference more or less to the background. An interpretation in racial terms, occurring only sporadically prior to 1933 could not prevail, until then, among scholars, either in Germany or elsewhere.[12]

The doctrine, however, that the Jews, considered religiously as "nonconformists" and ethnically as aliens, were throughout the Middle Ages subjected to the "law of aliens" and legally treated under this aspect, once most effectively championed by the historian of law, Johannes E. Scherer, still holds sway in all fields of general[13] as well as Jewish history and sociology.[14] Weighty scholarly objections notwithstanding,[15] two versions of the alien-law theory are widely disseminated. They even reach into the sphere of modern legislation and politics, bolstered up by some hypocritical concepts in the legal philosophy of early National Socialist rule.[16] The more specific of the two versions of that doctrine is still confined to the history of law and to the original determination, with all its implications, of medieval Jewry-law as an offspring of the ancient Germanic "law of aliens."[17] The other version, in contradistinction, broadens the underlying idea and its historical function, thereby trying to overcome the patent shortcomings of the original theory by means of an ethnic-sociological interpretation and adaptation. The medieval Jew is conceived of as "an alien without a motherland," the Jewish community as "a corporate body of a unique kind consisting of a group of permanent 'aliens,' essentially living apart from corporate Christian society."[18]

However the alien-law theory may be reinterpreted or modified—by the assertion that the Jews were subjected to some kind of alien law or were regarded socially as a type of "aliens" or appeared, for one reason or another, to medieval man as strangers—the nationalist tinge will always remain. Thus the problem reduces itself to the inquiry as to whether medieval "nationalism" came into play, socially and legally, in the relationship of Christian society toward the Jews. In other words, did considerations of national otherness enter demonstrably into the legal and political thinking of medieval man with regard to the Jews?

There is no doubt that in the Middle Ages a feeling of unity in culture and destiny, a realization of common bonds, developed—though slowly—in each of the countries of Europe. The concept of nationality and the idea of nationalism come to the fore in medieval sources in one form or another. Language and law played an important role in this evolution. Scholarly inquiry, historical and sociological, into this intricate process is still in its incipient stage.[19] As to medieval Germany, this much can safely be said: national sentiment and the fatherland idea developed with exceeding slowness. The Germans almost always thought of themselves either in a tribal sense, as Saxons, Franks, Swabians, Bavarians, etc., or as citizens of the Holy Roman Empire. National self-consciousness never developed among them as among the French and English.[20] The sense of an all-embracing national law, in particular, was weak in medieval Germany.[21] Practically no Reich legislation existed from the tenth to the twelfth century; and even later the central legislation was restricted to land-peace laws, to the regulation of constitutional problems and of such matters as concerned the relationship of state and church.[22] None of the great medieval lawbooks undertook a systematization of universal German law. Legal unification in Germany was in the end accomplished by Roman, and not by German, law. It was, only and above all, the Germans' coming into contact, peaceably or otherwise, with foreign peoples, and all the ensuing contrasts and conflicts, that in the Middle Ages awakened and gradually strengthened some kind of national consciousness among them. German colonization in the East in the thirteenth and fourteenth centuries and the ensuing clash with the Slavic peoples offer the best example of this development.[23]

Was the German-Jewish contact of similar character, and did it lead to analogous consequences in the spheres of legal and political relations?

The answer to both these questions must be in the negative. None of the factors determining German-Slavic relationship (including hatred) were operative between Germans and Jews. Historically, their meeting was, from the very beginning, not that of two different peoples. It was only individual Jews or small numbers of them that first entered Christian society. Even if the largest Jewish communities in medieval Germany are taken into consideration, one could hardly speak of a consolidated "national minority." The language issue, a factor of decisive importance in the process of national evolution—in fact, the paramount object of contention, legal, social, and political[24]—was nonoperative in the case of the Jews living in German territory. They were not bound together as a linguistic (national) community by a common tongue that could have been considered foreign from the German point of view. Long before, the Jews had given up Hebrew as their vernacular; they knew and employed the German language of their native province.[25] They even used it for annotating and translating single parts and books of the Scriptures. Hence considerations of language could not be determinative in any respect in the German-Jewish relationship. This was different, for example, in the case of the Wendish Slavs on German soil, whose region of settlement at one time extended westward to the Elbe and the Saale rivers, but whose political independence ended in the thirteenth century.[26]

It is, moreover, an interesting phenomenon in the history of the medieval roots of nationalism that the language and laws of "minorities" (national as well as religious)—to speak in modern terms—were given thoughtful consideration and equitable recognition by the conquering or dominant people within the realm of the national law, once national consolidation of the law was attained.[27] This applies, in particular, to the language, law, and jurisdiction of the Wends in German lands. According to the *Sachsenspiegel* (III, 70, 71), the use of their language and law was not only permitted in German courts but even prescribed to a certain extent. The fact that Jewish law, too, was recognized in medieval Germany within certain limits must be explained from a different angle, however, as was previously demonstrated.[28] National issues were evidently not involved here, but only a religious one.

In the Middle Ages no more than in our day was it the aim of legal policy to perpetuate national "minority" differences within a national body. According to *Sachsenspiegel*, III, 71, 2, once a Wend had sued, responded, or rendered decision in the German language, he forfeited his right henceforth to employ his Wendish language in court. This means that, notwithstanding all toleration, tacit or explicit, legal policy tended toward the assimilation of foreign elements.

Accordingly, no differentiation of nationality took place before the courts in the old territories of the German Reich. "Where court is held under royal ban . . . jurors and judges shall pass judgment on every man, be he German or Wend" (Ssp., III, 69, 1, 2). In the Marches, however, at the frontier, the national contrasts and the consciousness of national difference seem to have persisted longer. Although here, too, Germans and Wends were subject to the same jurisdiction, a differentiation was made according to the defendant's nationality. As a rule, no Wend could pass judgment on or bear witness against a Saxon, and vice versa (Ssp., III, 70, 1). In other words, judicial functions could be performed only by a fellow-member of the same nation, as far as Germans and Wends were concerned. It is conspicuous, indeed, that no analogous restriction applied to the Jews, who were not excluded from passing judgment on, or acting as witnesses for or against, Saxons. It is a notable fact that, accordingly, in the medieval illuminations to the pertinent passage in the *Sachsenspiegel* (III, 70, 1), among the persons standing before the judge, a Jew is found in a group with Frank and Saxon, while the Wend has to stand separate and aloof from that group.[29] There is no doubt that the Jew was not regarded as belonging to a different or alien nation, as the Wend doubtless was.[30]

In spite of this remnant of legal disability, reminiscent of their national difference, the assimilation of the Wends was virtually accomplished by the end of the fourteenth century and the first half of the fifteenth.[31] A comparison of their final situation with that of the Jews brings to light a most remarkable point. While neither language nor general law nor social considerations placed any obstacle in the way of a full assimilation of the Jews, such assimilation was never accomplished. For the medieval Jew it was attainable only through conversion to Christianity.[32] No better evidence than this could be adduced as additional proof that the medieval mind did not understand the "Jewish problem" in terms of nationalism but exclusively under the aspect of religion. While the former conception is not specified at all in medieval sources of law, the latter everywhere comes clearly into view, directly as well as indirectly.

⌊That the contrast between the Jews and the Christian world was principally based on religious and not on nationalistic grounds⌋can readily be gathered also from extra-legal sources. The Germanic-Slavic hatred, based on nationalistic feelings and independent of religious contrasts, again offers a good example. In the *Vita Sturmii*, dating from the beginning of the ninth century, Eigil, fourth abbot of Fulda, mentions Slavs bathing in the river Fulda and the bathers' smell being most repulsive to him.[33] In the beginning of the twelfth century, German historiographers described the Slavs as lacking human qualities and even explicitly designated them as dogs, emphasizing their contempt derived from national aversion, which was felt with like intensity on the other side.[34] No similar motivation can be inferred from medieval allusions to the Jews, prior to the persecutions in the late Middle Ages. Only then could this sort of animadversion grow into anti-Jewish agitation and polemics; and even at that time there was no reference to a national, but merely to the religious, difference of the Jews.[35] According to medieval German poets (Freidank, Walther von der Vogelweide, Reinmar von Zweter, and others), God had created all men, Christians as well as Jews and pagans, and was worshiped by all of them.[36] The Jews who lived before Jesus had been very dear to Him. Even the contemporary Jews were, in this literature, called nothing worse than condemned, miserable, unfortunate, unbelieving, or unfaithful Jews, with reference to their religious position.[37] The sole ground for antagonism against them was their refusal to recognize Christ and to accept his teachings.[38] No mention is made of any national or racial difference⌊In short, in the view of the Middle Ages, the religious distinction was the dominating factor that determined the political and legal situation of the Jews.[39] There is no trace of a conscious national antipathy or opposition toward them as an alien element or group.[40]⌋

II. CONSIDERATIONS OF RACE[41]

While rudimentary concepts of nationality and nationalism in some form or another are found as early as the Middle Ages,

there was hardly room or need for any expression of "race relations" (in the refined present-day meaning of the term) as distinguished from national or political divergencies.

Internationally, the crusades brought Europe into contact
with various Moslem and Arab peoples. There was, however,
scarcely any real race antipathy between Nordics and Arabs.[42]
Within the boundaries of the Holy Roman Empire of the German Nation,[43] only two "minorities" existed to which "racial"
difference from the general populace could possibly be ascribed:
the remnants of the conquered Wendish Slavs and the Jews.

Speaking in modern terms, there can be no doubt about the
racial distinction between the Wendish Slavs and the Saxon Germans. Their ancient political and national antagonism found
mention in the *Sachsenspiegel*[44] and, about a hundred years later as
a historical reminiscence, in Johann von Buch's *Gloss* on that
lawbook.[45] There is, however, no trace in legal sources of any
enmity between Wends and Saxons on purely racial grounds. Reliable evidence for just the opposite is found in the gradual assimilation of the Wends to, and their absorption by, the Germans in
whose midst they lived. The Wendish inhabitants of German
cities, little by little, were endowed with rights equal to those of
the German burghers. In the thirteenth century there were in
Stendal two *consules* and, in the period from 1175 to 1338 in Lü-
beck, thirteen councilmen of undoubtedly Wendish stock.[46] Wendish descent was thus in medieval Germany by no means an obstacle to rising to a socially higher or even the highest group.
And this in spite of the legal disability of the Wends in the territories of the eastern Marches, according to *Sachsenspiegel*, III, 70,
1, a disability which did not apply to Saxons, Franks, and even
Jews.[47] A Magdeburg lawbook of the middle of the fourteenth
century characteristically speaks of two parties to a lawsuit
"both of whom are of Wendish *Art*,[48] yet who are no Wends."[49]
Here the process of assimilation and absorption of the Wends
seems to have reached completion.[50] Little wonder, therefore,
that, at the end of the fourteenth century and in the first half of
the fifteenth, the use of the Wendish language in court, formerly
guaranteed by law, was finally abolished.[51] So far-reaching an acceptance of a racially different minority in various spheres of le-

gal and social life is unthinkable under the rule of modern racial doctrines of the National Socialist type. It is, therefore, safe to assume that the treatment of the Wends in medieval Germany did not follow the pattern of the modern race theory. It was their difference in nationality which was, for long, conspicuous to the German mind.

Compared with the Wends, the legal status and treatment of the Jews show similarities as well as dissimilarities. Both Wends and Jews had no definite territory of their own, no closed region of settlement of any considerable extent, within medieval Germany. In the cities, the foremost dwelling places of Jews, the German burghers were numerically far predominant, the numbers of Wends and Jews small compared with the general populace. While the Wendish language found consideration at law to some extent, Hebrew is not mentioned as the language of the Jews which, indeed, it was not even among themselves, and certainly not in their intercourse with Christians.[52] Jews were not excluded from passing judgment on, or bearing witness against, anyone, while Wends were restricted in this regard.[53] Wendish law and legal custom were respected within certain limits and even extended to non-Wends.[54] The same principle applied to Jewish law as well.[55] The most conspicuous difference of a basic nature between the two groups was the religious one. The Wends were Christians, the Jews had remained outside the church. From the point of view of a slowly developing national consciousness, the Wends were thought of as belonging to a different or alien nationality, while in the attitude toward the Jews no such trend became explicit.[56] Although Wends were regarded as of foreign nationality, their social and legal assimilation was gradually accomplished. The Jews, on the other hand, even though not classed in the same category and, under Saxon law, better off in some respects than the Wends, did not attain assimilation even locally, in individual communities. Only individuals desirous of being fully accepted became merged in the Christian world around them. Embracing Christianity was the only road to this goal.

All these facts emerging from the historic-sociological comparison of Wends and Jews are self-explanatory. In the medieval treatment of neither group were considerations of race (in the modern meaning of the term) of any weight.

Prior to the year 1933, the predominance of the religious factor in all avenues of medieval life was universally recognized. Even in Germany there were then but a few scholars who placed some emphasis on "race" as a determining factor in the medieval evolution, particularly with regard to the Jews.[57] Their opinion could not prevail, however, in the then unbiased world of scholarship.[58] It was left to the National Socialist era of pseudo-science to claim that the modern concept of race was already known to the Middle Ages, that the antithesis of races was recognized then, and that, besides religious and economic causes, one must look for the element of racial distinction as an important reason for the special legal treatment of the Jews, particularly at the close of the Middle Ages.[59] No convincing proof for this assertion has been brought forward as yet from the wide domain of medieval legislation, legal doctrine, or judicial practice. Scholarship, therefore, may pass over unfounded theories concocted for purposes of political propaganda. However, *semper aliquid haeret*. More, those doctrines begin to receive support, be it even unintentionally, from among Jewish scholars.[60] Thus certain general impressions of medieval conditions are propagated that cannot stand up under critical inquiry into the sources. It seems, therefore, appropriate to call attention to a few striking examples of evidence to the contrary.

First, in the thirteenth and fourteenth centuries Jews were admitted to citizenship in Worms (and probably in other Rhenish and German cities, too) under almost the same conditions and forms as Christians.[61] No racial discrimination is observable. Like the Wends, Jews, too, were able to reach even the highest rank in the municipal hierarchy. However, as the several recorded cases reveal, conversion to Christianity was an indispensable condition.[62] Once this step was taken by a Jew and he became a full-fledged member of the church, from the legal point of view he was subject to no discrimination whatever, least of all on racial grounds.[63] Special or intensified punishments intended for Jews under secular law were immediately voided by baptism, which freed even criminals from such discrimination.[64]

It will be remembered that the *Schwabenspiegel*, in which the influence of canon law was most pronounced, imposed the penalty of death by fire on Christians and Jews convicted of mutual sex relations.[65] Is this perhaps a medieval regulation against "race defilement"? The southern German lawbook itself answers the question unmistakably through its juridical qualification of the crime as "denial of the Christian faith," namely, heresy or unbelief, *ungelouben*, in the case of the Christian. This explains the severe penalty imposed on the Christian offender and, *per analogiam*, extended also to the Jew.[66] Only considerations of a religious nature are involved here. Not the slightest trace of racial ideas is discoverable. Ambrosius had already disapproved of marriages of Christians with "gentiles, Jews, or the foreign-born, i.e., heretics," on the ground that "primum in conjugio religio quaeritur."[67]

There is another fact which does not allow for interpretation in racial terms. In medieval law sources, converts from Judaism are, as a rule, designated explicitly as former adherents of the Jewish faith. This was done partly to call special attention to their merit in embracing Christianity and in permanently separating themselves from the "Jewish superstition." Partly, however, it was done for reasons of caution, since the religious trustworthiness of proselytes never remained above suspicion in Christian, particularly ecclesiastical, circles. This comes to light clearly from sources at hand extending over a century and a half.[68] None of these has any connection with, or implications of, racial origin.[69] It was exactly the same suspicion of infidelity in matters of faith which was raised against new converts of dubious sincerity in Spain after 1391 and throughout the fifteenth century.[70]

The church did not think in terms of racism. A decision issued by Pope Alexander III to the Bishop of Tournay (1167–81) and incorporated in the *Corpus juris canonici* gives clear evidence of this.[71] A prebend-seeker of Jewish descent, who had been rejected by the local bishop, appealed successfully to the papal throne. "You shall not lower him because of his Jewish descent," read the papal decision. It is evident that the bishop was prompted by mistrust of a convert rather than by racial prejudice.[72] Considerations of race were, of necessity, incompatible with the universalist conception of the church. They were decidedly antithetical to the Christian religion and to the constant teaching of the church.

As is well known, medieval secular law was considerably influenced by the Christian Weltanschauung. Its legal philosophy was anchored in Christianity. *Sachsenspiegel* law, for centuries dominant in central Europe and influential even beyond its boundaries, offers a good example. The concept that God is the source and limit of all law permeates the *Sachsenspiegel*. Its entire legal system is subordinated to the one great idea of God. Even the good old law inherited from the forefathers can maintain itself only in so far as it does not conflict with Christian law and Christian faith.[73] Modern sociologists hold that states were founded upon conquest and migration and that, in organizing society, the conquering race constituted itself the ruling class, while the conquered were relegated to servile status, race therefore becoming a factor of social superiority; and this doctrine, with all its implications, was not unknown to the author of the *Sachsenspiegel*. But his own train of thought did not follow the path of racial theory. Indeed, he unmistakably rejected the essence of that doctrine. Servitude, to him, is unlawful. It has its source in might and not in right. It originated in capture, in the unrighteous exercise of power. Despite such an origin, servitude became customary. But it remained unrighteous custom and therefore unlawful, for it contradicted the concept of the divine nature of law and of the divine likeness of man. A victor may establish a state on the basis of his power, but he cannot rightfully deprive a human being of freedom. The boundary line of freedom drawn by God may not be violated.[74]

The racial concept and doctrine have no foundation in medieval law, either ecclesiastical or secular. Race was no factor in the medieval attitude toward, and legal treatment of, the Jews.

III. The Jews' Function in the Medieval Economy

The results of this investigation into medieval law sources, and of their critical evaluation, are in complete agreement with prevailing opinion, even of those scholars who have not attacked the problem specifically from the point of view of legal history. Only two representative authorities need be quoted, the one a recognized historian of medieval economy, the other a fine historian and sociologist, the former Jewish, the latter Christian. In his standard work on the social and economic history of the Jews in the Middle Ages, published thirty-nine years ago, George Caro stressed religion as the most important factor governing the relationship of the Jews to their neighbors: "Religion caused social grouping; in determining the ways of life and thought, it erected a separating wall between those who were otherwise equals."[75] And, thirty years later, James Parkes, in his sociological analysis of the Jewish situation in the medieval community, arrived at this conclusion: "The Jews lived the lives of ordinary townsfolk, shared in the privileges and responsibilities of their fellows, and were distinguished from them only by their religion."[76] It was their difference in religion, too, that for centuries determined the Jews' status in medieval law.

Law and religion, however, though of paramount importance, are only two realms of a people's cultural self-expression. As history shows, other factors sometimes gain powerful influence and divert the trend of evolution. In fact, the several motives that come into play are almost inextricably interwoven. Yet the historian must try to disentangle them to the greatest possible extent by discovering their chronological sequence and unraveling the functional relationships in their interplay, if he would answer these questions: How is it that at about the middle of the fourteenth century the Jews suffered cruel persecution in all German cities and elsewhere, in spite of their favorable treatment in judicial practice and legal doctrine? How is it that after the second half of the fourteenth century their social and legal status took a decided turn for the worse? How is it that secular Jewry legislation in the late Middle Ages changed its traditional attitude toward the Jews? Had religious fanaticism, temporarily aroused during the Crusades, then become a permanent feature of European society? How was this effected despite the legal and political security extended to the Jews even after those catastrophes?

The key to a solution of all these problems seems to lie in the function which destiny had assigned to the Jews in medieval economy. There is a fairly informative literature on the Jews' role in medieval economy,[77] although rich source material still awaits scholarly investigation. For the present discussion attention should be directed, above all, to the facts and observations concerning the economic activities of the Jews as they present themselves in the legal sources, particularly in the lawbooks and jury-court decisions produced in medieval Germany.

It was, no doubt, as itinerant merchants that many of the Jewish pioneers entered Germany in the early centuries. In the Carolingian era "Jew" and "merchant" were used as almost interchangeable terms. The economic structure of the early medieval town, still markedly agrarian in complexion, did not allow any considerable place for commerce.[78] According to St. Thomas' teachings, the ideal was a self-sufficient city. Only when the ideal of self-sufficiency was not attainable and the city had an abundance of wares, should merchants be admitted.[79] Here was the opportunity for Jewish merchants to perform a necessary economic function. Indeed, they developed a kind of "guardianship" over trade and laid the foundations of settlements which later assumed a permanent character. The growth of the mercantile spirit and enterprise in Europe, particularly in the cities, from the period of the Crusades onward, tended to displace the Jews from their favorable position. Another factor which worked to accelerate this development was that the merchant guilds, permeated by Christian ideas in their economic and social activities, did not admit Jews and thus excluded them from the privileges which these mercantile corporations enjoyed. The new field of activity, as well as the new economic function, which offered itself to the Jews in the twelfth and thirteenth centuries was moneylending. In the precapitalistic era the Jew was again a pioneer whose financial operations were needed and welcome in spite of—or, better, because of—the ecclesiastical condemnation and the canon-law restriction on usury by Christians. From lending money on interest and on the security of articles of personal property, there developed automatically the trade of pawnbroking. This, in turn, led to trade in secondhand goods, which had to become the Jews' main occupation in the course of the fifteenth century, after their displacement from moneylending by early capitalism.

It is in the role of moneylender and pawnbroker that the Jew is chiefly active during the period of the lawbooks. True, he was not yet entirely excluded from ownership of real property. Lawbooks and court decisions, however, are particularly concerned with regulating his trade in money and pawned goods. Its usefulness in medieval economic life was fully recognized by law.[80]

Turning from the general to the specific, again, certain achievements in the field of commercial technique are observable, which were originally initiated by Jews, only later becoming a common practice in economic life. This refers, in particular, to the Jews' old trade privilege of lawful acquisition of property from nonowners and to the extension of the underlying principle to the law of pledge,[81] universally operative to this very day in the traffic with, and law of, pawned goods. Another example, from the law of contracts, of no less importance for economic and legal technique, is the promotion by Jews of the use of promissory notes and the insertion in them of the "clause of attorney,"[82] a noteworthy step in their development into negotiable securities. The medieval mind was not always cognizant of the progressive character and economic usefulness of such trends and developments in economic and legal life, as one may see from the stand of the Magdeburg *Oberhof* against free transfer of contractual claims by means of negotiable bonds.[83] On the other hand, the *Schöffen* of Magdeburg showed a full grasp of the growing demand for money in the national economy and thus of the social need for professional moneylending.[84] It was owing to this insight and foresight that the Jews could avail themselves of all possible means for the legal enforcement of their money claims against tardy debtors, even of such drastic methods of private execution as the *Schelmenschelten* or issuance of defamatory lampoons and caricatures against defaulters.[85] In fact, the Jews were often compelled by the authorities to lend their money, against adequate security, and were officially commended for and supported in their loan business.[86]

Such activities, recognized as economically needed and useful,[87] could not fail to integrate the Jews into the economic and

legal community of their residence. This process occurred automatically. The liability of Jews for municipal debt offers a good
illustration of the way it worked.[88] The foreign creditors of a
city took its Jewish inhabitants for citizens of that city in order
to subject them or their property to seizure in reprisal for outstanding claims. This, in turn, had a reaction on the legal status
of the Jews in their home town. Since they were exposed to
liability for municipal debt, they could not but be included in
letters of privilege or intercommunity treaties concerning safe-
conduct and exemption from arrest in reprisal. In other words,
they had to be recognized as members of the local economic community for which they had to assume responsibility.

The strength of the Jewish position was, however, instantly
shaken when Christian elements appeared ready to share or take
over their function in the economic life. In such competition the
Jew had to suffer from obvious disadvantages. For this phenomenon, too, a striking example is found in the judicature of the
Magdeburg high court. When the stipulation of *Schadennehmen*
was to be executed for the enforcement of money obligations,
Christian moneylenders were officially given preference under the
law.[89] The creditor was bound, under pain of legal disadvantages, to turn first to Christian moneylenders for recovery.
Only in the absence of Christian creditors were Jews permitted
to function in their place. The plain tendency was, first, to re-
press the Jewish moneylender and, finally, to displace him entirely from this trade. This telling example now leads us to considerations of a general nature.

The previous observations, general as well as specific, derived
from medieval law sources, seem to offer unquestionable confirmation of a widely accepted theory which was advanced in
1875 by the distinguished German historian of economics, Wilhelm Roscher.[90] His doctrine, in its original or some modified
version, has since become almost a common possession of numerous branches of modern research. It has been successfully applied
to the economic history of the Jews in central Europe, and its
validity has been proved also for the eighteenth and nineteenth
centuries.[91] Roscher sought an explanation of the fact that "in
the first and cruder half of the Middle Ages the Jews, as a rule,

were better treated than in the second and otherwise more refined period." His solution, summarized in his own words, reads as follows:

> In those days the Jews satisfied a great economic need, something which, for a long time, could not be done by anyone else, namely, the need for carrying on a professional trade. Medieval policy toward the Jews may be said to have followed a direction almost inverse to the general economic trend. As soon as peoples become mature enough to perform that function themselves, they try to emancipate themselves from such guardianship over their trade, often in bitter conflict. The persecutions of the Jews in the later Middle Ages are thus, to a great extent, a product of commercial jealousy. They are connected with the rise of a national merchant class.[92]

This theory suggests several implications—political, national, and social—and thus is open to different interpretations. It was soon combined with the conception of the Jews as foreign nationals and strangers ethnically (although not as aliens politically).[93] Widely accepted, even by authors of outspoken anti-Semitic inclination,[94] it was conjoined with racial theories.[95] Modern racial anti-Semites, however, had to forsake their former adherence to Roscher's doctrine, since it no longer fitted into their scheme.[96] It was opposed by Jewish scholars because of its emphasis on the rise of nationalism as the foremost factor in the development of anti-Jewish feeling, as well as for other reasons.[97] One prominent Christian author objected to that theory for methodological reasons and because of his claim that usury by Jews (besides religious fanaticism and national antipathy) was the outstanding cause of anti-Jewish phenomena, while a German "national commerce," in his opinion, is traceable far earlier than the Crusades.[98]

All controversies among scholars notwithstanding, the kernel of Roscher's doctrine received ample support through subsequent Jewish research[99] and recent studies in the general field of economic history.[100] It cannot be expected, however, in the present author's opinion, to offer a direct explanation for the phenomena of hatred and persecution or the deterioration of the legal status of the Jews in the Middle Ages. The core of Roscher's theory, not brought out with full emphasis in his own formulation, can be apprehended only through our better insight into the historic-economic developments gained from modern research. It is the observation of an economic phenomenon recurring from the early Middle Ages up to this very day. The Jews, through their talents and activities, have in every age and in every type of economy fulfilled an economic function. They were needed and used for certain pioneering activities (trade, money-lending, pawnbroking, etc.). This need existed as long as the majority of the population had either no interest in, or no ability for, such economic services. As soon as they learned to satisfy this need themselves, the mission of the Jew was finished. Displacement from his position in the economic life followed sooner or later; he had to look for other opportunities to perform pioneering functions in new fields, but again only until the majority group should once more move into them. This is an endlessly recurring process, an endless curve of ups and downs. In contradistinction to Roscher, I would call it an "economic phenomenon" rather than a "law of history," similar economic conditions, events and developments producing similar effects. It is the explanation only for the Jews' function in medieval economy. And this was but one among several factors, though a key factor behind the fundamental change in the legal status of the Jews in the late Middle Ages.

IV. THEOLOGICAL, PSYCHOLOGICAL, AND SOCIAL FACTORS

A. INTRODUCTORY REMARKS

Owing to Roscher's doctrine in its original formulation, two schools of opinion opposed each other for a long time in the attempt to analyze and lay bare the ultimate causes of medieval hatred and persecution of the Jews. For the one the true motive was religious hatred culminating in the era of the Crusades; the other emphasized economic rivalry or jealousy, which reached its peak later and directly caused the expulsions of the fifteenth century. In his re-evaluation of facts and opinions, James Parkes took a middle stand,[101] and this in spite of his conviction that the only difference between the Jews and other groups was exclusively a religious one.[102] As to the Crusades, he maintains that "the mob fell upon the Jewries and massacred, burnt and pillaged

with a mixture of religious and economic fury."[103] "It is only by
an artificial separation of inextricably interwoven motives that
it is possible for a historian to say that the hatred of the Jew was
exclusively religious or *exclusively* economic. As a complete explanation either is untrue by itself."[104]

One can fully agree with this view. The proposed synthesis of
religious and economic hatreds alone, however, offers no deeper
insight into the decline in the legal status of the Jews from the
second half of the fourteenth century onward. One must rather
be cognizant of the fact that *several* causative factors were intertwined in the history of medieval "anti-Semitism," in the same
way as in almost every historical development. Among them,
the psychological and social factors and their concatenation
with the religious, economic, legal, and political factors must
be given careful consideration. The psychology of the masses deserves particular attention in the search for an explanation of the
origin and growth of popular hatred of the Jew in the Middle
Ages.[105]

B. THE JEW AS A DELIBERATE UNBELIEVER

The roots of all popular hatred of the Jews, of course, can be
traced back to their difference in religion. After the Christianiza-
tion of western and central Europe and the fierce suppression of
heresy, the Jews remained the only exception to the universal
homogeneity in faith. But they were no heretics. They had
neither committed apostasy from Christianity, nor did they pro-
fess a faith which might represent a deviation from the orthodox
Christian religion or a revolt against it. Rather had they remained steadfast, from the very beginning, in their own religion,
different from Christianity. They were neither heathen nor
heretics but had persisted in remaining outside the church.[106]
"Moreover, the Jew knew the Scripture, he lived among Christian people, he was not ignorant of Christianity." Under this
religious aspect, the Jew appeared, of necessity, to the medieval
Christian mind as something more than an ordinary unbeliever,
namely, "a *deliberate unbeliever*. He was one who, knowing the
truth, refused to recognize it." According to this historic-
psychological analysis, which was put forward with convincing

arguments by Cecil Roth,[107] the Jews appeared "deliberately to reject Christianity, while realizing to the full the implications of their attitude." Possessed of such a mentality, they were in many circles held not to be rational beings, thinking or acting like other humans. This was the medieval conception of the Jew, "as a deliberate miscreant rather than as a mere unbeliever." A similar analysis was also given by James Parkes: The Jew whom the early church displayed before its adherents "is not a human being at all. He is a 'monster,' a theological abstraction, of superhuman and cunning malice, and more than superhuman blindness. He is rarely charged with human crime, and little evidence against him is drawn from contemporary behaviour, or his action in contemporary events."[108]

The most sagacious theory is bound to remain mere theory if not supported by ample evidence from the sources. Such evidence is actually available here. A wealth of illustrative documents, assembled by Roth, A. Lukyn Williams,[109] and Joshua Trachtenberg,[110] raises the conception of the Jew as a deliberate unbeliever, as a creature of a different (not human) nature, inspired and instigated by Satan's own majesty, to a concretely apprehended image in the medieval mind. Only against the background of such a mentality, indeed, is a reasonable explanation possible of the popular beliefs current in the late Middle Ages, such as that the Jews had tails, that they were distinguished from the rest of mankind by a bloody flux and a peculiar odor which disappeared automatically on the administration of the waters of baptism. In this way specific demonic attributes and functions were ascribed to the Jews.

Two questions emerge from these considerations. First, did the conception of the Jew suggested by this psychological analysis prevail universally throughout the Middle Ages, and was it dominant in all strata of medieval society? Second, did this conception actually originate in a popular prejudice or anti-Jewish sentiment among the broad masses, or was it, perhaps, only instilled from above into a populace more or less prepared and ready to accept and develop it further, wittingly or unwittingly?

The conception of the Jew as a deliberate unbeliever was not a universal expression of the medieval mentality, though it must have been widespread among the less educated and the wholly uneducated classes. A "Gregory the Great, or St. Bernard of Clairvaux, or Thomas Aquinas, obviously thought differently. More than one Pontiff and scholar of the Middle Ages, indeed, went out of his way to teach that the Jews were men like any others, and should be treated as such. Clearly, this was intended to controvert the popular view of the Jew."[111] Instances of such an attitude can easily be adduced also from the field of law. One need only recall the appeal, on the basis of Christian ethics, "to respect the Jews' humanity, and not their unbelief," as pointed out in the preamble to King Venceslas II's charter for the Jews of Moravia promulgated about 1283.[112] The same ideological attitude is also found in Middle High German poetic literature. Heinrich der Teichner, who wrote from about 1340 to 1375, insists that all are God's children and that non-Christians, including Jews, should enjoy the protection of the law. He thinks that it is better not to convert the Jews because they soon would become heretics. The Flemish poet, Jan van Boendale (de Clerk), who wrote in the first half of the fourteenth century, shows the same attitude. "It always seems to me," he emphasizes, "that they are human beings like us and have also come from Adam."[113] Moreover, the field of law—legislation, legal doctrine, and judicature—is almost free from notions emanating from the conception of the Jew as a deliberate unbeliever. The literature in this field did not, as a rule, originate in circles given over to that belief. Only slight traces are discernible, for instance, in the careful adaptation—by clerics—of the Jewry oath to the requirements of Jewish law, since otherwise, it was held, a binding oath could not be obtained from these "unbelievers."[114] Another example, in the fields of criminal law and procedure, is the conception and formulation of the various offenses against Christianity.[115] Little wonder, therefore, that the southern German lawbooks, *Schwabenspiegel* and *Wiener Stadtrechtsbuch*, strongly influenced by ecclesiastical views, took into account even the anti-Jewish sentiment universally current in the lower ecclesiastical circles in the period of their composition.[116]

From these examples the judicious reader may also deduce the answer to the second question. In general, there is no basic anti-

Jewish sentiment of the Christian masses expressed in secular customary law, juridical literature, or legal practice, as attested by all northern German lawbooks without exception. On the contrary, instances of an outspokenly friendly attitude are not missing, even in the late fourteenth and fifteenth centuries. The numerous regulations in the lawbooks prohibiting social intercourse between Jews and Christians[117] are proof enough that their relations were amicable. In a quarrel between two Jews one of them is reported to have boasted to a Jewish witness of his friendly relations with members of the city council, on whose assistance he could rely.[118] In another lawsuit between Christian parties, which came for decision before the *Oberhof* of Magdeburg, reference was made to a Jew "of whom I know nothing but what is likable and good."[119] Such utterances gain weight because they are evidently free expressions, made publicly in court, of popular sentiment in favor of Jews. In this connection the memorable assistance extended by Christian burghers in the Rhenish cities to the Jewish victims of the Crusades comes immediately to mind.[120] Apart from mob actions, hostile sentiments break through only on occasions which have theological implications. Medieval secular belles-lettres reveal a similar phenomenon. In Middle High German poetry—that of Wolfram von Eschenbach (*ca.* 1170–1220), for example—no hostile feelings against the Jews found expression, although reference is made explicitly to their trades and pawnbroking.[121] The Jews are berated only for rejecting the Redeemer and persistently refusing to accept his teachings.[122] Again the theological aspect of the deliberate unbeliever comes into play.

The religious-theological origin of this conception is so obvious that doubt can hardly be cast on it.[123] If additional evidence is needed, it is supplied by the various instances mentioned previously, in which popular belief and superstition led to the crassest and most preposterous distortions, almost incomprehensible to the modern mind. It is, however, not suggested here that all these distortions and their fateful consequences were instigated, officially or unofficially, by the church, although in numerous cases members of the clergy evidently took an active part. The conception as such of the Jew as a deliberate unbeliever, born and nurtured on theological grounds, could very well arouse among the lower classes and uneducated masses all the instincts of superstition and hatred against the Jews.

When viewed in this light and with the limitations implied, it may be correct to state that "anti-Jewish prejudice originated among the classes, not among the masses; that medieval history displays no deep-seated, natural animosity, but at the most a latent suspicion which needed fanning from above if it was to blaze forth into a destructive conflagration."[124] Yet, in the long run, such conflagrations, even of the dimensions of the First Crusade, were less harmful to the existence and survival of the Jews than was the steady decline in their social status. The conception of the Jew as a deliberate unbeliever doubtless contributed considerably to this process. It was, however, only one of the factors instrumental in bringing about that result.

C. THE JEW AS A USURER

Another factor of no less importance and consequence was the conception of the Jew as usurer.[125] He was, again, conceived of as a *deliberate* sinner who transgressed the precepts against usury laid down in the Bible as well as in canon law. It is again a theological argument that comes into the picture. Small wonder that churchmen, even if by no means hostile to the Jews, such as Bernard of Clairvaux, are the first to raise their voices against usury by blaming the Jews.[126] True, the same passage in Bernard of Clairvaux's letter to the clergy and people of eastern France (1146), against persecuting Jews during the Second Crusade, voices complaints against Christian usurers also, no less bitter and emphatic than those against Jewish usurers. The latter, however, seem to have impressed themselves much more deeply on the popular mind. The complaints against usury by Jews became more frequent in Germany in the course of the thirteenth century.[127] In fact, although only in Germany, the terms "Jew" and "usurer" became almost identical, as the terms "Jew" and "merchant" had formerly been. Unfortunately, research has not yet delved adequately into the causes of these complaints, whether they originated from economic facts and experiences with Jewish moneylenders or were brought about, to some extent at least, by anti-Jewish propaganda. It is quite obvious, of course, that the psychological factor contained in the creditor-debtor relationship played a role not to be underestimated. Furthermore, the conception of the Jew as deliberate unbeliever must certainly also have been of some moment in the theological deliberations on usury and in the popular attitude toward trade in money carried on by Jews.

In Middle High German poetic literature up to 1250, where at times mention is made of Jewish traders, moneylenders, and pawnbrokers, Jews are not accused either of commercial dishonesty or of usury.[128] The attitude in the spheres of applied law and legal literature is particularly characteristic. The canon-law concept and prohibition of usury were dominant, of course, and extended their influence also to secular law. Decisions on such issues were thus regarded as pertaining to the ecclesiastical jurisdiction exclusively, to which they were referred and left.[129] The *Sachsenspiegel* and all the older lawbooks of northern Germany, being accounts of traditional customary law, do not mention usury at all. In Eike von Repgow's time, no doubt, the economic activity of the Jews was still considered useful.[130] The *Schwabenspiegel*, on the other hand, composed by a clerical author, accepted the canon-law regulations on usury.[131] And as late as 1328 Ruprecht of Freising, leaning on the *Schwabenspiegel*, very significantly embodied Bernard of Clairvaux's condemnation of usury in the text of his lawbook.[132] This fact reveals how the theological and canon-law conception of the Jew as a deliberate transgressor (usurer) was disseminated and found its way even into secular law.

The continual complaints against Jewish moneylenders, coming from all classes of the medieval population, particularly in the fourteenth and fifteenth centuries, necessarily made the Jew an unpopular figure.[133] This is reflected also in the poetic literature of the time. Muscatblüt, a polemic poet who wrote during the first part of the fifteenth century, attacked the Jews violently and persistently. In his opinion every moneymaker had to wear a Jews' hat so that he should be recognized in all countries. Michael Beheim, a Swabian weaver and court poet who wrote in the middle of the fifteenth century, directed a whole cycle of thirty-two poems against the Jews; and, in a similar manner, Hans Schnepperer, called "Rosenblüt," scorned Jews living on usury.[134]

The fact that the Jews' services could not be dispensed with did not reduce the ever growing intensity of popular sentiment against Jewish business activities. True, some circles recognized the social need for professional moneylending as a requirement arising from contemporary economic conditions. This refers, for instance, to the *Schöffen* of Magdeburg, who, from the legal point of view, extended justice to the Jews in lawsuits arising from their commercial transactions or to town councils which readmitted Jews for financial reasons after their expulsion. However, they could not prevail against the public attitude toward the Jews. There was little or no understanding among the broad masses of contemporary economic changes and their requirements. The greatest obstacle to a universal recognition of the necessity of more modern economic methods was, however, the fact that theology and canon law conducted an almost permanent crusade against usury and usurers. Hence, there is some truth in the remark that usury secured for the Jews official protection at the price of public detestation. The continuous deterioration in popular estimation, derived from the Jews' main profession, even if it was not accepted universally, was bound to affect their social reputation seriously. This, in turn, reacted unfavorably on their status in law. By the middle of the fourteenth century, Jews were not considered capable of convicting a Christian, when money claims were in litigation, by taking an oath or adducing proof through witnesses.[135] This legal discrimination was evidently motivated by a depreciatory social evaluation, originating in the conception of their untrustworthiness in the money trade.

D. THE JEW AS A PERSON IN NEED OF PROTECTION[136]

But it was not the Jews' difference in religion and economic activity alone that impaired their social reputation and consequently affected their standing in law. Transformations and influences of a different type, but to the same effect, were operative in the sphere of law itself. No theological doctrines came into play here.

The impulse originated directly in an act of secular law, intended as a favor for the Jews in order to guarantee their services to economic life under the protection of the law. This act was their inclusion (for the first time in 1103) in the particular peace protection, extended in land-peace laws to several groups which were recognized as useful, worthy, and in need of special protection, such as women, merchants, and clerics. These groups were by no means lacking in freedom or general legal capacity. The same is true of the Jews. They were in need of special protection as non-Christians, who, shortly before their official acceptance among these groups, had been exposed to the violence of religious fanaticism during the First Crusade. Their protection, universal, permanent, and of special legal qualification, became a tradition in German customary law. Thus it was taken over into the foremost German lawbook, the *Sachsenspiegel*. Here (*ca.* 1221–24), however, this privilege is accompanied by an important restriction, foreshadowing a fateful legal and political development—their exclusion from bearing arms, a right they had previously possessed without limitation. With the *Sachsenspiegel* law this prohibition spread over almost all Germany and central Europe.

The ban on carrying arms was a consequence of the protection afforded by the special peace. Augmented legal protection, it was held, renders the use of arms superfluous. This restriction, originating from purely legal and moral considerations, affected first the legal status of the Jews. Their exclusion from full military duties, from judiciary police service, and from judicial combat followed as logical concomitants. Depreciation of their legal status resulted in a deterioration of their social position, also; for within medieval society exaggerated ideas of honor attached to arms and martial occupations. Limitation or denial of the right to bear arms, therefore, meant a most serious diminution of a man's honor, hence also of the Jew's honor. He was not considered an equal any longer by those in whose midst he lived and on whose respect he depended. This gradually deteriorating position within the social order is best characterized in Johann von

Buch's *Gloss* on the *Sachsenspiegel* (*ca.* 1325): "Weapons are forbidden to the Jews for their ignominy." The contrast to priests and clerics, with whom the Jews shared the arms prohibition is most conspicuous. In Buch's opinion, weapons were forbidden to priests and clerics "for their own honor." Both groups, clerics and Jews, still united under one and the same legal rule, were now strictly separated in social estimation.

The criteria which the surrounding world applied to the Jews in assigning to them their value and position within society had fundamentally changed. The original idea of protection was pushed more and more into the background. From the middle of the thirteenth century onward, the idea of diminution in honor gained ground. The Jew gradually sank into an inferior position within the social order.

E. THE JEW AS A SERF OF THE IMPERIAL CHAMBER[137]

According to ancient Germanic as well as medieval German law, the privilege of bearing arms meant full status in public law. This applied also to the Jews, who, from the Carolingian period on, had been placed legally on an equal footing with the entire free population. The prohibition against bearing arms, on the other hand, stigmatized the unfree and the serfs. Extended to priests and clerics as God's servants, *servi Dei*, for considerations of propriety or canon law, the arms prohibition did not affect their legal or social status. In their case the arms prohibition held "for their own honor."

The situation was different with regard to the Jews. Although their exclusion from the right of arms was caused by a legitimate reason, their reception into the king's protection, it had a profound and lasting effect on their status. Politically, they became completely dependent upon their protector. Reduced to merely subordinate services in the army and in defense work, to *operae serviles*, and relegated to a position of legal and social inferiority, they were soon considered serfs, *servi*, and rule over them was assigned to their protector, the king. True, one must not think outright of servitude in the narrowest sense of the term. In the beginning the change in their status amounted to personal and economic dependence in the legal sense. Political practice and

legal doctrine, however, subsequently completed the process by
which the Jews' original freedom was finally transmuted to
bondage. From free agents in the economic and legal life, endowed with full rights and considered as worthy of protection,
they became objects of the economic policy, in need of general
and legal protection. The extent of the rights granted to Jews
was dependent on, and determined by, the benefits which those
in power expected to derive from tolerating them. The full
course of this development, out of which the concept of a political Jewish question was born, is comprised in the term *Kammerknechtschaft*, "chamber serfdom."

The complex genesis of this medieval legal institution may
be traced to three motivations. The first is of a constitutional
and political character. It has its factual and legal basis in the
land-peace protection extended to the Jews and in the arms prohibition imposed on them in consequence, with all the disadvantages resulting from these measures. The development was
decisively influenced, on the other hand, by the general policy
prevailing during the Ghibelline age of establishing a definite
relation between the Jews and the state. This was effected
through their close dependence, politically, legally, and economically, on the emperor and his chamber.

The second motive, of a social nature, is bound up with the
contemporary stratification of society in classes and the medieval
concept of honor resulting from the feudal organization. This
motive was permanently in operation and, in fact, concurred
with all other motives, whether as cause or as consequence.

The third motive is theologic-juridical. It owes its force to the
interpenetration of state and church in the Middle Ages, despite
all the antagonism between these two great powers. The theological doctrine of *servitus Judeorum* ("the servitude of the
Jews"), already formulated by theologians of late antiquity,
found "reception" in the imperial legislation. According to the
Christian doctrine, the Jewish people had been condemned to
eternal servitude as just punishment for their rejection and crucifixion of the Savior. But God's precept did not require their extermination. They should be preserved, like Cain, in a life worse
than death. They should be scattered over the world and,

through their scriptures as well as their very existence, serve as an eternal testimony (*testimonium veritatis*) to the truth of the prophecies concerning Christ. Finally, their conversion might be a prelude to the Last Judgment. But until the very last day they were to remain in political servitude.

This doctrine of the Church Fathers remained unchanged and prevailed through the medieval centuries. There is a direct connection between the Christian theological doctrine and the legal and political concepts of the Middle Ages. The connecting link is the ecclesiastical legislation. It is no mere accident that the doctrine of *servitus Judeorum*, incorporated in 1234 in Pope Gregory IX's canon-law code, *Liber Extra*, with a political coloring, won a decisive influence on the legislative formulation of *servitus camerae*, in 1236, and was taken over in its entirety in an imperial privilege of 1237.

Once adopted by secular legislation, the theological doctrine was quickly fitted into the frame of contemporary juridical theory. In contradiction to the *Sachsenspiegel*'s teaching of the unlawfulness of servitude, chamber serfdom already figures in the *Schwabenspiegel* as a recognized legal institution. Yet, for a long time, legal theory could not free itself of juridical hesitation in its treatment of the status of the Jews. The practical procedure of the state, on the other hand, rigorously and with inexorable logic, carried chamber serfdom to the final stage of its development in the middle of the fourteenth century. After the imposition of the first regular imperial poll tax on the Jews in 1342, chamber serfdom meant personal unfreedom, beyond doubt. Politically and legally, the tragic fate of the Jews had reached fulfilment.

F. THE JEWS' POSITION WITHIN THE SOCIAL ORDER

After analyzing and evaluating the several factors operative in medieval thought and life, little effort would seem required to determine the position of the Jews in medieval society. True, it was now the religious, now the economic, now the legal, and then again the political, factor which pressed into the foreground and bore heavily upon the Jews' destiny. A critical analysis, however, ought not to concentrate exclusively on periods of great crisis alone, such as the First Crusade or the Black Death, although proper consideration must also be given to the phenomena caused by them, particularly to those of basic importance and lasting effect. In other words, the forces which produced relative equilibrium in the medieval status of the Jews and those which evoked evolutionary or revolutionary effects must be studied with equal care.

As far as law and public order are concerned, it can hardly be denied that public authority was restored in a comparatively brief time, even after the disturbances and massacres of the First Crusade. Legal protection of the Jews was then put on an even firmer basis than before. It took about one hundred and thirty years (1103–1236) before the steady development was reversed; a tendency toward a general decline set in only in the middle or second half of the thirteenth century. How did the several factors work together to bring about gradually such results?

A brief glance at the motivating forces in the social history of the medieval cities, the main dwelling places of the Jews, will prove informative. Here, the economic, social, and political structures—besides other factors—were most intimately connected.[138] In the final analysis, however, it was neither the occupational (commercial or trade) organization nor the form of the municipal government which was decisive for the particular structure of society in the medieval commercial cities. It was rather the dynamics imparted to these cities by co-operation and antagonism of those different forces. Such commercial cities, in their social structure, were quite different from those of a more agrarian character, without commerce and export trade and with an age-old stability of economic conditions. The principle for the social organization within the commercial community derived from the sphere of social order. The position of the individual within society was determined by the social valuation put upon him by public opinion.

This standard of valuation was also applied to the Jew. In his case, too, the most important determinant was the concept of social "honor." This concept itself was the product of crystallization from a number of different constituent elements. Once the crystallizing process had come to a provisional standstill, the social factor, in turn, acquired great force in influencing and re-shaping the original elements and the dynamics of their opera-tion—above all, the functioning of economy, law, and politics. This process of evolution worked in an uninterrupted cycle. At times the foundations were shaken by sudden changes. At those moments the development was, of course, driven in a different direction. The various factors involved operated in all kinds of combinations. In previous chapters it has been demonstrated, for example, how, in 1103 as well as in 1236, the new regulations concerning Jewry protection were preceded by political events directed against the Jews and how those legal changes, again, were instrumental in bringing about essential alterations in the social and economic status of the Jews.

It seems, however, that one factor, although of paramount importance in modern history and in the development of na-tional as well as international law, was not operative in creating the general atmosphere or in shaping the conception of the Jew in the Middle Ages. "Nationalism," in the modern meaning of the term, did not in any way influence the destiny of the medie-val Jew. Nationalism was, in particular, neither a cause for, nor an expression of, religious intolerance toward so inconsiderable a minority. The possible implication in this sense of Roscher's doctrine, emphasized more by his interpreters than by himself, has been dismissed above.[139] Evidence has also been adduced to indicate that the Germans did not think of the Jews in terms of nationhood or nationality, either collectively or individually.[140] Furthermore, it has been pointed out that in Germany national sentiment and the fatherland idea came into folk consciousness only through a slow process of evolution.[141] True, there is ob-servable a tendency toward national consolidation, above all with regard to the German language.[142] It reached a peak in the thirteenth century in the secular literature of *Minnegesang*, the homiletic literature of the church, the legal literature of the lawbooks, and the historical literature of the chronicles—all written in German. These "prenationalistic" tendencies in me-dieval Germany were, however, of only a weak nature and by no means aggressive in character. Their role as a means of defense against the impact of foreign influences is a logical consequence of their historical origin. It was the contact with Slavs on the eastern frontier that first awakened and later strengthened some kind of German national consciousness in the Middle Ages. And it is entirely in accord with this historical role that the "nationalistic" conflicts, born of international antagonisms, lost their intensity in a consolidated national atmosphere. Justice now exercised its tempering influence. According to the *Sachsenspiegel* (III, 70, 71), the use of a Slavic language and of foreign law was not only permitted on German soil but even prescribed to a certain extent.[143] This refers to the language, law, and jurisdiction of the Wendish Slavs. As far as the law was concerned, no Wend was to suffer any wrong because of the fact that he could speak only his mother-tongue. Thus no tendency is visible on the part of the victors to annihilate the conquered people or even to deprive it of its own law, language, and culture. It is beyond question that, in this primitive medieval stage of development, "nationalism" did not bring forth intolerance.

This applies to the Jews in particular. Jewish law and jurisdiction were, within certain limits, recognized in medieval Germany.[144] The constant reissuance of church laws against intermarriage between Jews and Christians, against employment of Christian servants by Jews, and against Jews and Christians taking meals together indicates clearly that there was no national hatred against Jews among the people.[145] The medieval mind did not view the "Jewish problem" in terms of nationalism, and the legal situation of the Jews differed considerably from that of the Wends. If nationalism, as understood in the Middle Ages, had logically presupposed or entailed intolerance, the Jews would not have escaped this intolerance. The medieval intolerance toward the Jews, culminating, finally, in Jew-hatred, was caused by other factors. The historical and psychological explanation of the several causes and their interaction leaves no room for medieval nationalism as an additional factor. The chronological coincidence between the emergence of prenationalistic trends and a deterioration in the legal status of the Jews must not distort historical insight. The latter development is satisfactorily explained otherwise. Furthermore, thirteenth-century "nationalism" in Germany had in the end not even so much defensive force and inner consolidation as to withstand the inroads of canon and Roman law, not to mention the effects of humanism and the Renaissance. From the intra-national aspect as presented here, Germany's national-political status within the empire underwent no considerable change in the fourteenth and fifteenth centuries, even up to the period when, in international relations, medieval national consciousness was transformed into modern political nationalism.[146] Again, the coincidence of this phase in the international development of early nationalism with Jewish persecutions and expulsions from German cities does not suggest necessarily a relationship of cause and effect. There is no evidence in the sources for a deep connection between the processes of national unification and the growth of religious intolerance toward the Jews in medieval Germany.[147] This is not, however, the place to show how, conversely, the growth of late-medieval nationalism was decisively fostered by religious intolerance.

In contradistinction to the absence of nationalism as a powerful factor in intra-national relations, the *religious* factor, particularly in its theological aspect, holds a vastly predominant position in all spheres of medieval thought and in all strata of medieval life. This is a fact established beyond the slightest doubt. The dynamic influence of the theological factor on the other factors co-determinative for the social status of the Jews can hardly be overrated. The doctrine of the Jews as rejectors and killers of the Savior, the theological conception of the Jew as deliberate unbeliever and deliberate usurer, will quickly come to mind. It will also be remembered how the theologic-juridical concept of *servitus Judeorum* gained entrance into political thought and secular legislation and aided considerably in shaping the concept of chamber serfdom.[148]

The social status and popular conception of the medieval Jew were by no means definitely determined, nor had they taken final shape, in the period of the First or Second Crusade. From the days when Otto Stobbe laid the groundwork for all research in the legal and social history of the Jews in central Europe,[149] the First Crusade has come to be considered the turning-point in medieval Jewish history and particularly in medieval Jewish-

Christian relations. It is held to have determined the situation of the Jews in the whole of Europe. This view can be maintained only if properly interpreted in a way that finds full support in the sources.

It is true that the horrifying experiences of that world-shaking, religiopolitical enterprise left a deep and lasting impress on both Jews and Christians.[150] But no sudden change followed after the First Crusade. The line of development, instead, extended over centuries, finally to reach a low point, marked by the actual decline and gradual extermination of the German-Jewish community during the last century and a half of the Middle Ages. All this was effected by the dynamic combination of the several factors enumerated and discussed above. This entire process has, indeed, its origin and point of departure in events and developments connected with the First Crusade. But it must be understood as a slow evolutionary process rather than a sudden revolutionary event. Furthermore, one must be aware of the fact that the motives for the First Crusade were of a purely religious-political character, not religious-economic in nature. Its consequences, of course, cut deeply into the economic life of all Europe, producing fundamental changes. These economic changes could not fail to effect incisive repercussions also on the role of the Jews in the European economy. But this was only a secondary aftereffect, although fateful in character and developing into a factor of the first magnitude.

The consequences of the First Crusade on the status of the Jews found a powerful expression in politics and in law. The impact of the changes in these fields on the Jews is second only to the massacres themselves—which, of course, provoked these changes. It was after the massacres that the idea of the need of special protection for the Jews first entered the public consciousness, and it first found legal expression in the Imperial Land Peace of Mainz, in 1103. There the dynamic interplay of all the factors enumerated took its point of departure.

The second element, which was always active in the medieval "Jewish question," was religious zeal and fanaticism. True, it was not born in the era of the Crusades, and it reappeared after centuries with, perhaps, even greater intensity. But in those days religious fanaticism for the first time reached a peak in the whole of Europe. Church and state were and remained powerful political confederates, notwithstanding the incessant tensions between them. The two-swords doctrine, requiring their mutual support, did not work in favor of the Jewish status. Even the rivalry in the disputed border domain of Jewry policy was not to the advantage of the Jews. For theology developed into a forceful weapon, reaching deeply even into the domain of political theory and practical politics. The ecclesiastical formulation of the two-swords doctrine in the opening chapter of the *Schwabenspiegel* (L *Prooemium;* G 1, 4) is the most representative expression in secular law of the all-embracing aspirations of theological doctrine and of the political aims of the church.

Thus it was only logical and completely in line with the ideological setting that theological conceptions became a dominant factor in the medieval attitude toward the Jews. Christian theology penetrated and permeated all phases of medieval life and thought. Through the marvelous organization of the church it became the most powerful means of propaganda and the most successful instrument in shaping public opinion. The late-medieval conception of the Jew thus fell entirely under the influence of theological thinking. Theological doctrines gained an overwhelming influence on the social evaluation of the Jew within medieval society. Fostered by all the other factors, the final product was "contempt and hatred which had sunk so deeply into the public consciousness that not even the highest authorities of Church and State were able to meliorate it."[151] Such was the popular picture of the Jew in large sections of Germany and central Europe during the second half of the fourteenth century and in the fifteenth. The centuries-old process of cultural and social adaptation of the Jews was slowly reversed into one of progressive dissimilation and gradual elimination from German culture and society.

Gone were the tolerance and mutual interest expressed in common religious and social observances; gone, too, was the cordiality of personal association and of business dealings. In their place came suspicion and distrust, mutual fear and loathing, to poison the inescapable contact between Jew and Gentile, thrust together as unwilling neighbors by their common physical and psychical environment.

This transformation did not take place universally or simultaneously all over central Europe. But, once popular sentiment had adopted such an attitude, the way was cleared for outlawing the Jew. This was done gradually and regionally only.¹⁵² The invention of the host-desecration fable, the revival of the myth of image-mutilation, the spread of the ritual-murder legend and of blood accusations, the charges of poisoning the wells, become intelligible from this angle. The role played in this process by the universal intensification of superstition, the belief in demons and the devil, and the growth of the witch-cults has been recently demonstrated by Joshua Trachtenberg so impressively that a reference to the wealth of source material assembled in his book may suffice.¹⁵³

Popular literature and the graphic arts, developing greatly and broadening their suggestive influence upon the masses after the invention of printing, aided the current anti-Jewish tendencies considerably. It was in this stage of development that the Jew became a favorite subject of chronicles and legends, poems, folk tales, folk songs, folk plays, mystery, miracle, and morality plays, ecclesiastical as well as secular.¹⁵⁴ These presented him in the light in which he was viewed from the aspect of theology, and the masses were stimulated to see him in the same way. The mass production and dissemination of broadsides for religious and political propaganda added another feature. The broadside —the "intellectual scourge" of the Reformation era—in all fields of its activity successfully employed exaggeration and hyper-exaggeration, characteristic of this type of literature and of the pictorial representations accompanying it.¹⁵⁵ The Jews were a very welcome object. Caricature, that powerful weapon in influencing and shaping public opinion, soon seized upon the Jews, their appearance, and their actual or alleged activities. This is the origin of anti-Jewish pictorial propaganda. It is no mere accident that "Jewish noses" appear in one of the woodcuts by Michael Wohlgemuth in Schedel's famous *Weltchronik* (1493), which depicted the alleged ritual murder at Trent of 1475.¹⁵⁶ There is no connection between this type of artistic production and the legitimate pictorial representations of Jews in the illuminated manuscripts of the thirteenth and early fourteenth centuries. In the latter, Jews are pictured in different social settings, appearing even before emperors and high church dignitaries. In spite of their Jewish attributes, that is, the characteristic beard and hat, their apparel, carriage, and gestures, completely dignified, show them to have been far from debased in the conception of the Christian artists. This may readily be seen by a mere glance at the well-known picture of Josephus before Vespasian in a Fulda manuscript of the twelfth century;[157] the much-reproduced picture of the Jewish minnesinger, Süsskind of Trimberg, before the bishop of Constance,[158] in the Manesse codex of the thirteenth century; or the representations of Jews in the Heidelberg and Dresden *Sachsenspiegel* manuscripts from the fourteenth century.[159] The conception of the Jew in these and hundreds of illuminated manuscripts of the Middle Ages differs considerably from that in the fifteenth and the following centuries. The conception and its expression in literature and art had undergone a fundamental change.

There can be no doubt that theological doctrine was a factor of the first magnitude in the transformation of the popular attitude toward the Jew in the late Middle Ages. It overshadowed all other factors, indeed, and subjected them, sooner or later, to its psychological and sociological influence. The consequences are widely visible and indisputable. Nevertheless, they do not justify the full acquittal of the medieval population as was attempted in more recent discussions of the subject: "One can hardly blame the populace . . . for failing to discern the distinction between the theological Jew and the actual Jew, or for reacting violently upon the clearly implied suggestion of this delineation."[160] Such reasoning does not take fully into consideration the dynamic interaction of all contributing factors. Among them, the receptivity and reaction of the medieval masses and their active response directly corresponded to the creativeness and activity of medieval theology. None of the psychological and social factors in operation is negligible, from the point of view of historical analysis and evaluation. After all, the medieval period was not yet ripe for the ideals of enlightenment and tolerance.

CHAPTER THIRTEEN

The Jews in Medieval Law

I. UNDER GERMAN LAW

ANALYSIS and evaluation of the several factors that shaped the medieval conception and destiny of the Jews still leave a complex problem for discussion and solution. This problem lies in the field of law and is as puzzling as it is important to the historian of law. The discrepancy between the favorable legal status and treatment accorded particularly to the Jew in legal doctrine and judicial practice and his constantly declining social estimation calls for a historical explanation. How is it that for centuries medieval law maintained its position regarding the Jews against all those powerful influences of a religious-theological, political, economic, and social character? How is it that for centuries anti-Jewish motives and tendencies failed to win access to the realms of legal doctrines and judicial decisions?

The answer to these questions derives from the medieval German concepts of law, justice, and the state.

The fundamental ideas of law and justice—what we may call the medieval German "philosophy" of law—found emphatic expression in the Prologue and Introduction to the *Sachsenspiegel*.[1] According to Eike von Repgow, law has its source in God and is designed to regulate the social life of man. Law is based on God's will. The court of law is God's mouthpiece. The human judges are God's viceroys. The divine origin of law is manifested in the order of the universe. "God is Himself law, hence He loveth law." "God is Himself just, He is justice itself." If God is law, then every legal infraction is a sin, and every sin a legal infraction. The world of law is, at the same time, the world of morality. Justice is one of the cardinal virtues, according to the medieval moral code.

In the medieval German concept of the state, the law stood above the power of every ruler.[2] It was the state's function to maintain and to defend the "good old law." This faith in the immutability of legal norms encountered in Christianity a spiritual attitude which asserted that the consciousness of moral obligations was rooted in the individual human personality. Hence, devotion to the old divine law was both a legal and a moral duty. Law, not made by man, could not lawfully be altered by man, not even by the king. Altering it meant, indeed, an unlawful infringement of the law.

The judge took God's place on earth. This held for the supreme judge, i.e., the emperor and king, as well as for every lower judge or juror. Their highest task and duty were "to strengthen Right and to weaken Wrong" ("das Recht zu stärken und das Unrecht zu kränken" [Ssp., III, 54, 2]).[3] This ideal was cherished particularly at the supreme court of Magdeburg. Under Magdeburg law every judge and juror had to take an oath of office. The wording of such an oath is transmitted in a Cracow manuscript from the first half of the fourteenth century:

I swear to God and my lord, the king, and the court, now that I have been chosen, that I shall obey the judge according to law, and shall render right judgment to people poor and rich in the country, and shall administer the *scheppen*'s office according to the German law, as well as I can and know the law so as to be supported, and shall not forfeit it [the office] for any cause, neither favor nor gift. So help me God and the Saints.[4]

Of the innumerable admonitions and references to the lofty ideals and duties of the office of judge, recurring in Magdeburg court decisions of daily routine, the following may be quoted: ". . . The judge shall help everyone to obtain justice, if it is asked of him."[5]

The conception of the equality of all men before God led to that of equality of all men before the law. In so far as the Jews were subject to the general courts, they, too, benefited from the unalterable application of the basic ideas of the philosophy of law, which always remained the guiding principles in judicial practice. Hence legal disputes affecting Jews were decided according to the same principles and in the same manner as were those of Christian parties. In the considerable number of legal decisions issued from the twelfth to the fifteenth century by the Magdeburg *Oberhof* and other superior courts of Magdeburg law the jurors never let themselves be carried away by prejudice against a Jew to the point of perverting the law.[6] Even in matters of etiquette, such as addressing Jews, or of legal formalities, such as drafting an appropriate oath formula for Jews, the *Schöffen* of Magdeburg were guided, above all, by the desire to uphold law and justice. Theirs is the most honorable record among all medieval authorities with regard to the treatment of the Jews. Law was to remain law, justice to remain justice, even where Jews were concerned. They granted the Jews, too, law and justice.

Most of the medieval German theoreticians of law, like the author of the *Sachsenspiegel*, Eike von Repgow, came from the ranks of the jurors or lay judges. Small wonder, therefore, that with very few exceptions they remained true to the ideals of law and justice in assigning the Jews a place in their systematizations of the law. To be sure, legal doctrine had to take into account the changes in their legal status originating from political factors, such as inclusion of the Jews in the land-peace protection, the prohibition against their bearing arms, their designation as serfs of the imperial chamber, etc. The problems of public law and legal status deriving from such issues were neither ignored nor particularly emphasized in the lawbooks but were presented and discussed objectively and with juridical fairness. In legal doctrine the Jew was considered a *Rechtsgenosse* and was treated as such—not as an equal in every respect, it is true, but still on the basis of fellowship. The special regulations for Jews meant that, except for these regulations, Jews in their relation to Christians were subject to the same rules as were their Christian fellows.[7]

The status of the Jews under public law was naturally most exposed to political repercussions. But, after the storms of the Crusades, peace was restored again gradually, the Jews were allowed to return to their homes, the Jewish communities recovered, and new communities could arise. The commercial talents of the Jews proved indispensable for the growth of cities. In many instances Jews entered into a permanent legal relationship with the cities. Up to the middle of the fourteenth century, the law content of the municipal rights and duties of the Jews was almost identical with that of Christian citizens. The Jews were actually designated as citizens, and the rights of citizenship conferred on them were not essentially different from those enjoyed by Christian city dwellers.[8] The Jews had the right of domicile, enjoyed legal protection of life and property, were entitled to acquire real property and mortgages in all parts of the city, and were permitted to dwell among the other citizens. Their activity in trade and industry was scarcely subject to legal restrictions, and Jewish craftsmen were to be found in many places. Jews, like the Christian citizens, were subject to the cities' taxes and military requirements. But, in accordance with medieval conceptions, not yet enlightened by modern ideals of the rights of man and of citizens, the law governing Jewish city dwellers showed one distinction: Jews could not exercise political rights in the medieval urban community and were thus also excluded from public office. This meant little, however, to the medieval Jew; for, on the other hand, the Jewish community had complete autonomy in governing its own internal and external affairs, including the administration of justice. Even their direct relationships with the king were not impaired.

Surveying the attitude toward the Jews of medieval law in its various functions, namely, legislation, judicature, and legal doctrine, one may make the following statement: medieval law was conscious of the peculiar position of the Jews as a separate religious entity. But it took into consideration and tried to understand the unique situation and requirements of the Jews imposed by their religion. The high moral conception of law, justice, and judicial office made it impossible to tamper with the rights of the Jews by a conscious perversion of the law.

Furthermore, medieval law in general was of an outspokenly static nature, not flexible or easily changeable. It was the "good old law," much of whose authority rested on its ancient and traditional character as customary law. The Magdeburg law and the judicature of the *Oberhof* of Magdeburg in particular show— as did Saxon law generally—a strong aversion to change and a strict adherence to tradition. This can readily explain the circumstance, strange as it may seem at first glance, that the legal status of the Jews, and particularly their treatment under Magdeburg law, could for long remain unaffected by all the changes which their political, economic, and social status had to undergo. The fact that, despite their declining fortunes, the Jews were still entitled to, and actually able to seek and obtain, justice in the courts of law, particularly in the supreme court,[9] strengthened not only their own morale but also their position in a world which became more and more hostile toward the "enemies of Christianity." It was indeed a notable achievement of law and justice in the "Dark Ages"—and of the Magdeburg judicature above all—to impede the decline of medieval Jewry.

II. The State's Policy toward the Jews

Still another aspect deserves consideration. Though predominantly in the domain of politics, the state's policy had strong repercussions in the sphere of law and thus on the conception of the Jews in medieval law.

The policy of the medieval state toward the Jews[10] was motivated and characterized by an inner contradiction arising out of the discord between theory and reality. From the Carolingian era to the end of the Middle Ages, the state was conceived of as *one* great universal empire encompassing all Christendom. In its structure, spiritual and secular views were embodied in the same way as the soul is united with the body in the individual man; for Christendom constituted *one* flock, *one* body, with Christ as its mystic head, king, and shepherd. "It is an all embracing corporation (*universitas*), which constitutes that Universal Realm, spiritual and temporal, which may be called the Universal Church (*ecclesia universalis*), or, with equal propriety, the Commonwealth of Mankind (*respublica generis humani*)" (Gierke). According to theological doctrines and canon law, the Jews had rejected and crucified the Savior and were therefore justly condemned to eternal servitude and a life of misery. Hence the medieval state, subordinate to the omnipotence of the church, could not extend its protection to a religious conviction different from, and opposed to, the true faith. Medieval society, bound together by the church and highly organized in estates, corporations, and guilds, refused admittance to the Jews as unbelievers, and finally excluded them from all legitimate occupations.

But, on the same basis of Christianity, theology and philosophy and legislation and legal theory just as clearly taught another doctrine: that Christian charity commands respect for the human dignity of the Jew also and forbids carrying the first major premise to its strict logical conclusion. The political discord thus created is best reflected in the following Preamble to King Venceslas II's charter for the Jews of Moravia promulgated about 1283–1305:

Because of the crime once committed by their fathers against our Lord Jesus Christ, the Jews are deprived of the protection of their inborn rights and condemned to eternal misery for their sin. Although they are like us in the form of human nature, we are severed from them by our holy Christian faith. So Christianity teaches us to cast off our harshness, and to wait with our treasure for them; for we must respect their humanity and not their unbelief.[11]

These contradictory views called for reconciliation, especially with respect to the necessities of medieval economic life. The institution of Jewry protection, which accorded the Jews legal security and thus integrated them legitimately into the state, was the compromise solution. This was the formula which enabled the possessors of political power to admit the Jews, with certain restrictions, as a constituent part of the medieval state and to incorporate them as active participants in the economic life. At the same time, however, the Jews were on sufferance, tolerated for the benefits derived from them, particularly those accruing to the state treasury. In return for these benefits, the medieval state, represented by emperor, king, town lord, or municipal council, guaranteed them favorable living conditions through the grant of basic rights and even privileges.

But too much emphasis should not be laid on a specific scheme of political, legal, or social organization as the foundation for integrating the Jewish community into the medieval community at large and for the Jewish status in the Middle Ages. From the point of view of public law, it is held, "the Jewish group was considered as but a corporate body like other bodies within the corporate structure of medieval society." As such the Jews, according to this opinion, enjoyed a particular status of their own, especially privileged and with a peculiar system of rights and duties.[12]

The corporate structure of medieval society, in fact, presented almost insurmountable difficulties to the integration of the Jews in the medieval state because of the latter's Christian character. Yet this corporate structure accounts for the final organizational form of the medieval Jewish community.[13] This final form, however, is of much less importance than are the legal basis of its origins and the historical evolution, with its bearing on the process of integration.

When, in 1084, Bishop Rüdiger of Speyer, in enlarging his city, decided to invite Jewish settlers, he did not envisage the immediate founding of a Jewish community as a corporate body like others but merely stated that he would like to "gather there also Jews."[14] The later Jewish community grew only from within. When between 1170 and 1200 the Jews in Worms decided to rebuild their original synagogue of 1034, they did it after the model and in the architectural style of the Christian cathedral in that city,[15] reflecting the current fashion of their environment. When they organized an executive board of their community, they again followed a Christian model, that of the municipal council of their city.[16] In medieval documents, moreover, the head of the Jewish community is designated as *magister Judeorum* or *Judenmeister*, doubtless in imitation of the municipal *magister civium*. The designation "Jewish bishop," *episcopus Judeorum* or *Judenbischof*, also found in the sources, clearly shows another analogy, with a religious implication.[17]

These examples could easily be multiplied.[18] They offer proof that the corporate structure of medieval society served only as an obvious external model for the organizational form but cannot be regarded as the direct source and basis of the political and legal status of the Jews, whether favorable or unfavorable. Developmentally the Jewish "corporate bodies" do not represent phenomena analogous to the craftsmen's guilds or other medieval corporations. Rather did their legal and political status develop from that sum total of basic rights, privileges, and duties, accorded them or imposed on them by the holders of political power. It constituted a charter which allowed a Jewish community to arise and to develop communal self-government. It was an internal evolution which may have been aided to some extent by the traditions of ancient Jewish community law.[19] This evolution took place within the Christian community, whose laws applied also to the Jews, except where special regulations were provided for them. Those special regulations, however, were broad and inclusive enough to enable the Jews to carry on their own life and to adjust it to the Christian world surrounding them. By subjecting them to the rules of the common law, the state, in turn, was given an opportunity to take a hand in this process. This is the way in which the integration of the Jews in medieval state and society must be understood historically.

The laws governing this complex process were not dictated by a definite political attitude. Medieval legislation concerning the Jewish status was of great "elasticity and adaptability." That is why medieval Jewry-law has been aptly described as "a law of privilege composed of accidental and heterogeneous favors and restrictions."[20] The controlling factors were, as a rule, the will and interest of those in power and the time, place, and special circumstances. Jewry-law, its content, enactment, curtailment, and abrogation, were thus conditioned by these ever changing elements. The consequence, quite naturally, was a state of permanent instability, perhaps not unwelcome to medieval dynamics.[21] While factors of various kinds were operative in the formation of the political and legal status described, its origin and motivation lay, above all, in the religious difference of the Jews from the surrounding world.

III. Influence of Canon Law

By means of Jewry legislation of varying forms, the medieval state had succeeded in adjusting its relationship to the Jews and finding a legal *modus vivendi* for them. As previously demonstrated, their social status largely depended on the content and development of the state's legislation concerning them. It was, however, also influenced by extra-legal factors, and, conversely,

it reacted again upon the legal status. But all this still fails to
account fully for the decided turn for the worse which secular
Jewry-law took in the later part of the Middle Ages. An additional and important clue for understanding this phenomenon is
to be found in the general development of German law in that
period. The decisive feature was the interruption of its natural
evolution through the adoption of canon and Roman law.

With regard to the Jews, the church—the other chief political
power of the Middle Ages, dogmatically bound, unlike the
state—was not in a position to provide by law a *modus vivendi* on
similar lines. The Jews' integration into the organizational
structure of the church could be effected only by conversion:
extra ecclesiam nulla salus. The path of canon Jewry-law was thus
strictly prescribed by Christian dogmatics and the teachings of
theology. It was the responsibility for the rejection and crucifixion of the Redeemer that was to rest like a curse on the Jews
of all lands and generations.[22] Never once, from the early days
of Christianity, did the church cease preaching that the Jewish
people must not be completely destroyed but preserved to the
end of days. They were needed for a double purpose: to prove by
their very existence as eternal witnesses (*testimonium veritatis*)
that the Christian teachings were true; and to prove, by their
ultimate conversion, the actual triumph of the church. Thus, for
the sake of both prestige and better "testimony," they should
be kept in a state of submission and overt inferiority. The specific
canon laws concerned with the Jews were a natural corollary of
this Christian philosophy which pervaded all public life in the
Middle Ages. True, the Jews were not to be molested or oppressed;
but, as unbelievers, they were to be segregated from the flock of
true believers as much as possible, in order to protect the Christian religion and its adherents from any danger of harmful influence. The religion of the Jews was not recognized, yet it was
tolerated for apologetic and other reasons. But their synagogues
were to be simpler and lower than the local churches. They
should not erect new houses of worship, should abstain from
blasphemy, were not to employ Christian servants or nurses,
were not to exercise any power over Christians or oppress
them under the pretext of public office. They should not inter-

fere with Christian rites, and particularly not appear in public on Good Friday. They had to refrain from any social intercourse with Christians, such as eating, drinking, and bathing in their company, even if this were not prohibited by state law. To enforce the laws of segregation and also to prevent mistakes leading to intercourse, the Jews were to be marked off by distinguishing dress or other visible signs. The institution of compulsory ghettos was to become the cornerstone of this edifice of ecclesiastical Jewry legislation. Only its main points can be mentioned here; numerous others have had to be omitted.[23]

The attitude of the church toward the Jews and the effect of canon Jewry-law on the Jewish status and destiny in the Middle Ages have for long intrigued Jewish and Christian scholars alike.

Among Jewish historians there are two schools of opinion, representing two extremes of sociological evaluation. The one puts the full blame for "the definite relegation of the Jews to an inferior social and political status" on the church's "policy of degradation."[24] "The voices raised in defense of the Jews [by some of the popes] were weak compared to the power of official Church theory and local Church practice which made for their degradation." According to the other school, church and synagogue,

overtly representing two hostile principles, . . . the two institutions nevertheless complemented one another. . . . The Church . . . insisted upon that kind of limited toleration which alone made it possible for the Jews to survive the successive waves of persecution. Fairness also essentially permeated the relations between the Church and the Jews. Despite its all-embracing claims for supremacy, despite its overt attempts to penetrate all domains of public and private life, the Church imposed upon itself limitations in regard to Jews which are truly remarkable. . . . There was a basic unity of thinking which converted all conflicts into a struggle between brethren rather than a war between strangers.[25]

A Catholic historian of repute, earnestly endeavoring to attack the problem with scholarly calmness, does not see the historical picture in so bright a coloring.[26] He blames the Jews for their mistakes and likewise the Christians for their vehemence. He sides with Bernardin of Feltre (1439–94) who, in one of his sermons about 1491, said: "One must do no injustice to the Jews and must not kill them; on the other hand, they must observe the canon laws, but they do not do this." In his opinion, religious and theological reasons in particular were above all responsible for the strict Jewry legislation of the church and the persecution of the Jews. The religious steadfastness of the Jews, he adds, "strengthened their faith and raised their community spirit and separated them all the more from the Christians and the Christian religion, so that the very opposite was attained of what the church then sought to attain."

In seeking to probe the problem dispassionately and objectively, the following facts must first be established. From the point of view of the church, her practical policy regarding the Jews and the entire body of her Jewry legislation were but the logical results of the basic dogmas and doctrines of Christian theology. This was a course prescribed by necessity, religious as well as political. The church framed and pursued her Jewry policy as an integral function of her earthly mission. All this was justifiable for the ecclesiastical conception of the "Jewish question." Obviously, it is not within the province of legal history to pass judgment on this conception. Historical criticism cannot fail, however, to point out an inherent weakness in the policy of creating permanent barriers between Christians and Jews. The whole Jewry policy of the church was purely negative. It lacked any constructive idea as to how the Jews were to be kept alive in the state of humiliation to which they were doomed until their ultimate conversion.[27] The often reissued papal bull of protection, *Constitutio pro Judaeis*,[28] notwithstanding, the church never made any legal guaranty which would have entitled the Jews to claim definite rights of status. Even if the "concessions"[29] granted them under legal sanctions were violated, the canon law did not admit Jews to the part of plaintiff or prosecutor against Christians.[30] This characteristic negative feature in her Jewry policy is readily explicable from the universalistic aspirations of the church. If she had been the sole political power to determine the destiny of the Jews, the trump cards would perhaps have actually remained in her hands. There were, however, competitive aspirations of the state which made

themselves felt with greater or lesser intensity
legislation, consequently, became a challenge to
method whereby an equilibrium between these t
powers was attained is connected with anothei
problem which must be discussed first.

The effect of church policy and legislation on r
cannot be passed over in silence. The papal dec
every country, and the conciliar decrees were valid ... ... whole
of Christendom. Even if they did not immediately influence the
state's Jewry legislation (in the long run, however, they in-
evitably did), they nevertheless seriously affected the status of
the Jews; for, as a rule, medieval Christians, both individually
and collectively, would not openly incur the ecclesiastical sanctions extending even to excommunication and interdiction.
Thus the effects of canon Jewry legislation were promptly felt
by the Jews, who were made to suffer from their full force. Their
economic and social position was adversely affected and their
life made miserable indeed by the canonical Jewry laws.

There is also no doubt that ecclesiastical propaganda encompassing the Christian world soon transformed the Jewish question into a problem of international importance. The church
laws in their all-embracing authority were not restricted to the
forum ecclesiasticum alone. They were constantly reiterated and
reinforced by provincial councils and local synods. Ecclesiastical
courts jealously watched over their enforcement. Thus they
could not fail to impress themselves also upon secular legislation, which either adapted itself to the canon-law requirements
or directly adopted the church regulations. Through this "reception" of canon law into secular law, heresy was placed under
the penalty of death at the stake;[31] temporary relapse into, or
reversion to, Judaism by a convert was equated with ordinary
heresy;[32] sexual relations between Christians and Jews were
punished by death by fire;[33] a distinctive dress was made obligatory for Jews; and their inclosure in the ghetto became compulsory.[34] Even the medieval "supreme court" of Magdeburg
could not escape the powerful impact of the unyielding rules of
canon law. The latter's dominant concept of usury was recognized by the *Schöffen*, who explicitly acknowledged the com-

tence of the ecclesiastical courts to decide "what should be considered usury": "This belongs to the province of the ecclesiastical power, and not to ours."[35]

Small wonder that canon-law rules concerning the Jews also found their way into the medieval lawbooks. While the *Sachsenspiegel* (*ca.* 1221–24) is still free from such influence, its southern German counterpart, the *Schwabenspiegel* (*ca.* 1275), stands out as an example of the extent to which canon Jewry-law was adopted into the system of secular law. Eike von Repgow's original systematization of secular Jewry-law appears here considerably enlarged, revised, and supplemented on the basis of canon Jewry-law, for the first time introduced into a medieval German lawbook (L 262, 322; G 214, 8–13, 272). Not even a direct quotation from Gregory IX's collection of decretals, *Liber Extra*, and its section, *de judeis*, is missing (L 262; G 214, 12). The legal doctrines concerning the status of the Jews also betray patently theological and canon-law conceptions. *Servitus Judeorum* and chamber serfdom, both unknown to the author of the *Sachsenspiegel*, are, in the *Schwabenspiegel*, valid concepts which are simply taken for granted.[36] Here the theological tenets and the juridical doctrines are inseparably intertwined. This synthesis of ideas, accomplished by the clerical author of the *Schwabenspiegel* with much skill and logical consistency (though not with juridical acumen and critique), represents one of the greatest achievements of Christian theology and canon law in the Middle Ages.

Theological aspects entered and powerfully affected the picture from other angles also. The realm of religion naturally felt their impact first, in the shape of the doctrine of the Jew as a deliberate unbeliever.[37] The economic sphere was impregnated by the doctrine of the Jew as a usurer.[38] No less was the impression on the domain of secular law, on the political formation and the juridical support of the concept of chamber serfdom, produced by the theological doctrine of the perpetual servitude of the Jews and the canon-law concept of *servitus Judeorum*.[39] Emperor Frederick II's charter for the city of Vienna (1237), excluding Jews from public office, refers explicitly to this theologic and canon-law argument. One year earlier, in the universal

Jewry privilege of 1236, the Jews had, for the first time, been designated *servi camerae nostre.*

The famous two-swords doctrine in the *Sachsenspiegel* (I, 1) taught that the secular arm should reinforce the ecclesiastical when such help was needed, and vice versa. In the sphere of Jewry-law, it seems, this theoretical principle found an ideal practical realization. The support extended by the state to the church in this field was, moreover, for the most part voluntary, although at times motivated by political expediency. The impress on all aspects of the Jewish status can hardly be overrated. That it was by no means a favorable influence can also hardly be denied. It was, above all, the canon-law regulations which, directly or indirectly, erected an insurmountable wall between the Christian and the Jewish elements in the city population. This attitude found expression also in contemporary poetry, which directly refers to those regulations of canon law.[40]

Secular law provided a legal *modus vivendi* for the Jews by granting them basic rights of their own and thus assigned them, at least in some measure, a status of legal security, despite all implicit hazards, including the usual limitation in time of the charters granted. Both rights and status were denied them under canon law, which could not possibly integrate Jews into the realm of the church. Here the "enemies of the Cross" (*inimici crucis*)[41] were merely tolerated on humanitarian grounds and were to be preserved for theological reasons. But they had no legally established, protected, or enforcible claim to such toleration. The more the secular Jewry-law yielded to canon law and the more canon Jewry-law penetrated the state's laws, the more were the latter exposed to and dominated by the purely negative Jewry policy of the church. Accordingly, the status of the Jews under secular law was destined for gradual deterioration. But the church did not attain the most important, ultimate goal of her Jewry legislation—conversion of the Jews to Christianity.[42]

IV. The Reception of Roman Law

The penetration and reception of canon Jewry-law into all branches of secular law—legislation, judicial practice, and juridical doctrine—was a slow process, only gradually completed.

The most significant feature of this evolution is the fact that laws and regulations were adopted one by one or in small groups. Through their incorporation into the system of secular law, their purely canon-law contents gained the strong validity of state law, being no longer restricted solely to the *forum ecclesiasticum*. Originally, however, there was in Germany no reception *in toto* of the rules of canon Jewry-law, either in tendency or in result. Hence legislation and judicature still retained ample opportunity to find a way out of the dilemma when particular regulations of the canon Jewry-law were too much in conflict with the customs and needs of everyday life, as in the case of moneylending on interest by Jews.[43]

This phase of the legal evolution underwent a fundamental change, though also only gradually, by the so-called "reception of the Roman law." This historically significant process set in very early in the Middle Ages and made itself felt particularly in central Europe.[44] It has often been compared with the Renaissance or with humanism because of the external similarity of these phenomena of revival of ancient civilization. But the reception of the Roman law had its peculiar causes and followed its own paths. The final victory of the foreign over the native law was prepared and facilitated by the lack of uniformity and the disintegrated character of medieval German law. The resulting insecurity, which was felt in many legal spheres and was particularly onerous in the application of the law, called for a remedy. Such a remedy could not be expected either from the legislative activity of the weak empire or from German jurisprudence, which was only in the beginning of its development. Thus the idea could gain ground that Roman law could claim validity on German soil, since the medieval Holy Roman Empire was considered to be the continuation of the ancient Roman Empire, whose laws had never been abolished. This argument was obviously vague in conception and rested on very weak grounds juridically. Nevertheless, it promoted and effected the actual penetration of the Roman law into the German legal system.

The church, which had early incorporated many principles of Roman law into her system of canon law, was the first to transmit the ideas and institutions of ancient Rome to the medieval world. Among these were anti-Jewish laws, some of them enacted by the christianized Roman Empire, such as that the Jews must not erect new synagogues, own Christian slaves, etc.

The interest in Roman law received a new and decisive stimulus from the rediscovery of the Roman law codes and the subsequent revival of their study in northern Italy at the end of the eleventh and in the twelfth centuries. A renaissance of Roman law set in, with its center in Bologna, and continued to the middle of the thirteenth century. The flourishing schools of the glossators and commentators of Roman law attracted students from all Europe, particularly from Germany, who on their return propagated and disseminated their new knowledge in their respective homelands. Thus, in the fourteenth century, Roman law ideas began to penetrate deeply into German legal thought. A literature sprang up intended to harmonize the native law with the Roman and canon legal systems and to popularize the foreign concepts of law throughout Germany. This adoption or reception of Roman law comprised Justinian's codification, the *Corpus juris civilis*, in its original form and its original contents, *in complexu*. First restricted to juridical thought and literature, it gradually outgrew the "theoretical" stage and, in the fifteenth century, became transformed into a powerful movement, striving for the general adoption of Roman law principles and rules in all avenues of legal life, the "practical reception" of Roman law.[45] The final result was an almost complete victory of the foreign over the autochthonous German law, a victory officially recognized for the first time by the legislation of the Holy Roman Empire in the *Reichskammergerichtsordnung* of 1495.

The conception of the immediate validity and applicability of Justinian's *Corpus juris civilis* on German soil naturally included its anti-Jewish laws. With regard to Jewry-law, the difference in approach and method between the author of the *Schwabenspiegel* and the glossator of the *Sachsenspiegel*, Johann von Buch, is characteristic of the entire development. The former merely enlarged and elaborated on the *Sachsenspiegel*'s Jewry-law by incorporating some of the canon-law rules and introducing ecclesiastical views.[46] Johann von Buch, though commenting on the *Sachsen-*

spiegel Jewry-law (II, 66; III, 7, 1), which was still untouched by Roman or canon Jewry-law, adds under twelve consecutive heads a complete and well-arranged catalogue of the anti-Jewish regulations from Roman and canon law.[47] This was indeed a peculiar comment, for all its principles were foreign to the work commented upon. It is, moreover, accompanied by full citations from the Roman and canon codes, whose uncontested validity and direct applicability *in complexu* on German soil are taken as a matter of fact. Johann von Buch was not a cleric but was of knightly rank and a judge at the court of the Elector of Brandenburg. In 1305 he had devoted himself to the study of Roman law in Bologna.[48] When he undertook a harmonization of the Saxon with Roman and canon law in his *Gloss*, according to the methodology of scholasticism, as a jurist he was doubtless aware of the incompatibility of the *Sachsenspiegel*'s Jewry law and that of the alien codes. Nevertheless, he forcibly incorporated the latter *in toto* in his system of laws, thus being compelled to deny to the Jews certain fundamental rights which they undoubtedly had enjoyed under *Sachsenspiegel* law—for instance, the general applicability to Jews of the rules of Saxon law.[49] It is obvious that through such an attitude the firm legal basis of the Saxon code was abandoned by its glossator. In his attempt to justify his stand juridically, he was bound to become involved in contradictions, as in his interpretation of Roman law. In fact, there was no juridically legitimate basis for harmonizing the just and fair Jewry-law of the *Sachsenspiegel* with the outspokenly anti-Jewish rules found in the *Corpus juris civilis* and *Corpus juris canonici*. The actual basis was nothing else than the very reception of the Roman and canon laws, which was, of course, taken for granted by the learned jurists (not by the lay jurors) of those days.

In the place of the nonexisting juridical grounds, extra-legal reasons now had to be substituted. This was done without any scruples, as can be seen from the instance adduced, in which the enjoyment of Saxon law was denied to the Jews. For the first time in the history of medieval German jurisprudence, anti-Jewish sentiments penetrated the domain of law in the guise of legal reasoning. One will remember that, under Roman and

even under canon law, professing Jews were not considered heretics and legally not placed in the same category with them.[50] In
his *Gloss* on *Sachsenspiegel*, III, 7, Johann von Buch, having no
deep insight into the subtleties of Roman and canon law, equates
Jews (heathens) and heretics, contrasts them with "Saxon persons," and consequently excludes them from the enjoyment of
the *privilegium*, that is, Saxon law.[51] He, like most of his Romanizing contemporaries, was not beyond adorning his juridical
theses and conclusions with numerous citations from the foreign
law, though they were not pertinent and, in some cases, even
contradictory from the point of view of juridical logic. This su-
perficiality and lack of juridical criticism are characteristic not
only of Johann von Buch but also of the era of the reception of
the Roman law in general. In fact, its introduction and adoption
were considerably facilitated and accelerated by this uncritical
attitude among lawyers. This method was far different from that
of the great jurists of northern Italy, such as Bartolus or Baldus,
whom their German disciples sometimes quoted and tried to imi-
tate, without ever being able to reach their level. Their juridical
genius prevented those true jurists from adopting such methods
and from being misled in the application and interpretation of
the laws concerned with Jews.[52]

It seems that, before and for some time even after the invention
of printing, the commentaries, *Consilia*, and other casuistic writings of the great Italian jurists had generally not had wide dissemination or decisive influence in Germany, particularly not as
regards Jewry-law.[53] As a rule, no reference to such literature is
found in the several glosses on the *Sachsenspiegel*'s Jewry-law.[54]
German jurists rather adhered to the legal texts proper, represented by the Roman and canon-law codes and to the *Glossa
ordinaria*.[55] They followed the path broken by their master,
Johann von Buch, whose method they imitated faithfully. Extra-legal sentiments of an anti-Jewish character were much more
in accord with the anti-Jewish Roman laws than with the interpretations, at times quite liberal, of the Italian glossators and
commentators of Roman law.[56] That attitude, fostered by the
growing anti-Jewish sentiments and popular superstitions in
Germany, became from then on more and more rooted in the Ger-

man legal literature. It was only in the course of the sixteenth and the first half of the seventeenth centuries, particularly due to the humanists, that Italian jurisprudence gained lasting influence on German law and jurisprudence.[57]

A few striking examples deserve to be pointed out. In the *Regulae juris "Ad decus"* (end of the fourteenth century), an alphabetical register of medieval German law arranged according to subject matter, under the rubric *Juden* and in the midst of the usual provisions of Jewry-law, there appears a paragraph (J 158) concerning heretics and another (J 159) on the punishment of sorcerers,[58] with no explicit reference to Jews. The alphabetical sequence (in German, *keczer* for "heretic," and *czauberer* for "sorcerer") did not suggest the inclusion of these paragraphs in the section on Jews. The apparent digression can be accounted for only on the assumption that the compiler believed paragraphs on heretics and sorcerers belonged under the general heading "Jews."[59] Another compiler of a *Remissorium* appended to the *Sächsisches Weichbild* took pains to insert in the gloss on article 137, and accordingly, in his section *Juden*, a paragraph stating only this: "All Jews in buying and selling in general act fraudulently."[60]

One cannot simply dismiss this attitude of the Romanizing German jurists as a negligible expression of a perhaps personal anti-Jewish bias; for, first, they were the legal theoreticians and practitioners trained in the foreign laws, who were destined to prepare and shape the future German law for centuries to come. Second, this attitude of the German jurists gained crucial importance, since it determined the spirit in which the task of dogmatically adjusting and harmonizing German law with the adopted foreign legal systems was carried out.

One more example, unparalleled in legal history and matched only by the National Socialist legislation for the extermination of the Jews, will suffice as evidence. At the same time, it will demonstrate how Roman law was misinterpreted and misused by these jurists to serve Jew-baiting politics. In the aforementioned *Remissorium, Regulae juris "Ad decus,"* the author propounds an elaborate theory concerning the property of Jews who might be slain in a pogrom. The topic is discussed in six paragraphs (J 142–46, 148), under the common heading "Concerning Jews Slaughtered in a City" (*Von juden, di man yn eynir stat sleet*). The term *slachtung*, used in paragraph 145, is translatable only by the word "pogrom."[61] If a pogrom occurs, it is ruled, no one shall be allowed to appropriate Jewish possessions, "because the Jews with their possessions belong to the Reich chamber." One is obligated to hand over their property to the city council and to take an oath that he has no more of it, under penalty of death and confiscation of property. During the pogrom (*in der slachtung*) no Jew is allowed to donate or intrust his possession to a Christian for safekeeping, and no Christian shall accept such goods under severe penalties: (148) "The property of Jews, movable or immovable, is forfeited property and falls to the Reich chamber, when one kills them."

Such juridical acumen and refinement put the old conception of chamber serfdom on a new legal basis. The support adduced from canon and Roman law is, however, shaky and insubstantial. That Jews are forbidden to associate with Christians and to have Christian servants is one pillar borrowed from canon 26 of the Third Lateran Council (1179), later incorporated in Gregory IX's decretals;[62] the general rights and claims pertinent to the *Fiscus* in Roman law, the other pillar.[63] The conclusions drawn from these laws were naturally neither implied nor provided for in the canon and Roman codes. The method of our author is clear. It is as unscrupulous and lacking in true scholarship as was the form of procedure first introduced and systematically developed by his predecessor, Johann von Buch. In medieval German law there existed the legal institution of chamber serfdom. In political practice it was not only needed for purposes of taxation but also utilized in case of pogroms. Emperor Charles IV was an ardent promoter of Roman law in German and in Bohemian legislation. Anticipating pogroms in Nuremberg and Frankfort, early in 1349, he had been brazen enough to enter into legal agreements with the respective city councils, in which he transferred to them the rights of the crown in the possessions of the Jews eventually to be slain.[64] Evidently this aspect of rights derived from chamber serfdom was eminently practical and important.

The jurists' was the task to find support in the rules of canon and Roman law.[65]

This was the method generally employed by the legal theoreticians and practictioners of law in Germany during the era of the reception of Roman law. The influence of Roman law was particularly effective in those legal domains in which the medieval development of German law had reached a phase close to that of the Roman codes and in cases where similar legal institutions existed in both law systems. Fostered by the general trend of the "reception era" and the idea of the subsidiary or even primary validity of the Roman law code in Germany, the temptation was great to adopt mechanically institutions or individual regulations from the Roman legal system. This is exactly what happened to a great extent in the field of medieval Jewry-law. The decades following the era of the Black Death, with its repercussions on the political and economic status of the German Jewish community, were particularly receptive to such developments. The prohibition of gifts or bequests by Christians in favor of Jews and vice versa[66] and the intensification of the death penalty for Jewish delinquents[67] are only two of a host of instances awaiting scholarly investigation. Still another may be pointed out because of its paramount importance. It was under the strong influence of the rising power of Roman law that the ecclesiastical idea of spiritual overlordship over the Jews, as conceived by the early Church Fathers and medieval theologians, was replaced by the juridical scheme of private ownership.[68]

On the basis of Roman law, German legal doctrine and legislation in the later Middle Ages thus participated in the general trend to deprive the Jews not only of their legally recognized status but also of the recognition of their human dignity. The anti-Jewish Roman legislation as laid down in the *Justinian Code*, now recognized as law of universal validity in the empire, was an important factor in the deterioration of the legal status of the Jews.[69] This fact, so far overlooked by modern research, is borne out by the comprehensive *Judenrechtswissenschaft*, the science of theoretical Jewry-law, which developed with the progressing secularization of legal instruction in the German universities from the sixteenth to the eighteenth century, and concerned

itself with the Romanized Jewry-law in force a
extraordinarily rich literature resulting from th
which Jews obviously could not share) and extenc
riod of three hundred years, is completely domi
man law.[70]

But the same fourteenth and fifteenth centuries
foundations were laid for the developments describ
nessed something of a miracle, which puzzled historians: the
Schöffen of Magdeburg still wielded the scepter of justice in the
old traditional way, strictly observing the rules of the *Sachsenspiegel* and respecting the principles of Magdeburg law and met-
ing out justice in fairness even to the Jews. They remained steadfast in their loyalty to the traditions and ideals of German law.
In one case, late in the fourteenth century or sometime in the
fifteenth, a lower court, already reflecting the influence of the
Roman law conception of the *princeps legibus solutus*, raised the
following question:

. . . whether the prince shall maintain the peace and rights of the
Jew which he had promised, pledged and guaranteed in a deed to him,
since as subjects of the princes, Jews enjoy no rights except those bestowed on them by the princes?

The decision of the *Oberhof* of Magdeburg nevertheless read as
follows:

If a prince bestows on a Jew peace for a time in a deed, he shall keep
the Jew's peace against any unlawful force, both for himself and his
people.[71]

The *Schöffen* of Magdeburg still adhered to their traditional
ideals of justice and judicial office, sanctified by a constant judicature extending over centuries. Never would they surrender
these ideals, to which they owed, and still owe, their reputation.
They knew only their municipal law and the traditional German lawbooks and remained unperturbed by the Roman law, to
which they would not submit voluntarily.[72] The trend of the
time, however, was against them. The future was not theirs but
fell to the more "modern" jurists trained in and propagating
Roman law. The fate of the *Oberhof* of Magdeburg and of the old
traditional German law, including Jewry-law, was sealed.[73]

With the doom of German law and the victory of Roman law in Germany, the way was also open for the reception of Roman Jewry-law *in complexu*. Its principles and the doctrines of the Roman law jurists could penetrate and conquer the judicature. What was not fully achieved by canon law was accomplished by the reception of Roman law:[74] the legal degradation of the Jews, from which they were redeemed only after centuries through their emancipation.

NOTES

NOTES

1. There is no modern, authoritative monograph on the general history of the Jews in medieval Germany. The pertinent sections in the well-known comprehensive presentations of Jewish history by Heinrich Graetz, Simon Dubnow, and George Caro are, to say the least, not up to date now. To replace them with a competent volume—a great desideratum of historical research—is a task in itself, far beyond the scope of this study, which is restricted to a very limited field. The specific purpose of the present investigation does not require more than a brief restatement of the historical facts and developments. For more details see Ismar Elbogen, "Deutschland," *Germania Judaica*, ed. I. Elbogen, A. Freimann, H. Tykocinski (Breslau, 1934), pp. xvii–xlviii; Elbogen, "Deutschland," *Encyclopaedia Judaica*, V (Berlin, 1930), 971–90; Elbogen, *Geschichte der Juden in Deutschland* (Berlin, 1935); Adolf Kober, "Aus der Geschichte der Juden im Rheinland," *Rheinischer Verein für Denkmalpflege und Heimatschutz*, 1931, Heft 1 (Düsseldorf, 1931), pp. 11–39; Alexander Pinthus, *Die Judensiedlungen der deutschen Städte: Eine stadtbiologische Studie* (doctoral thesis, Technische Hochschule Hannover, 1931); published also under the title, "Studien über die bauliche Entwicklung der Judengassen in den deutschen Städten," *ZGJD*, II (1930), 101–30, 197–217, 284–300.

2. Cf. the cartographical description, "Jüdische Siedlungen im Rheingebiet bis zum Jahre der grossen Judenverfolgung 1349," prepared by the Institut für geschichtliche Landeskunde der Rheinlande in Bonn, in Kober's above-mentioned article, facing the title-page. Unfortunately, no similar maps are available to illustrate the historical development of the Jewish settlements in the other parts of central Europe and Germany in particular. One must resort to the *Germania Judaica*, although the pertinent historical-geographical data are not easy to survey in that alphabetically arranged work. Cf. also Erich Keyser, *Bevölkerungsgeschichte Deutschlands* (Leipzig, 1938), pp. 228–40; this book is anti-Semitic, contains, however, an unbiased survey of the history of the Jewish settlement in medieval Germany with a valuable compilation of statistical data.

3. See below, pp. 138 f.

4. Cf. H. J. Zimmels, *Beiträge zur Geschichte der Juden in Deutschland im 13. Jahrhundert, insbesondere auf Grund der Gutachten des R. Meir Rothenburg* ("Veröffentlichungen der Oberrabbiner Dr. H. P. Chajes-Preisstiftung an der israelitisch-theologischen Lehranstalt in Wien," Vol. I [Vienna, 1926]); Herbert Fischer, *Die verfassungsrechtliche Stellung der Juden in den deutschen Städten während des dreizehnten Jahrhunderts* (Gierke's "Untersuchungen zur deutschen Staats- und Rechtsgeschichte," Heft 140 [Breslau, 1931]).

5. A. Neubauer and M. Stern, *Hebräische Berichte über die Judenverfolgungen während der Kreuzzüge* (Berlin, 1892); Siegmund Salfeld, *Das Martyrologium des Nürnberger Memorbuches* (Berlin, 1898); cf. Fischer, *op. cit.*, pp. 37-53; Samuel Steinherz, "Kreuzfahrer und Juden in Prag (1096)," *JGJC*, I (1929), 1-32; Sarah Schiffmann, *Heinrich IV und die Bischöfe in ihrem Verhalten zu den deutschen Juden zur Zeit des ersten Kreuzzuges* (University of Berlin Ph.D. thesis [Berlin, 1931]); also in *ZGJD*, III (1931), 39-58, 233-50; James Parkes, *The Jew in the Medieval Community: A Study of His Political and Economic Situation* (London, 1938), pp. 59-89.

6. Cf. Robert Hoeniger, *Der schwarze Tod in Deutschland: Ein Beitrag zur Geschichte des vierzehnten Jahrhunderts* (Berlin, 1882); Johannes Nohl, *Der schwarze Tod: Eine Chronik der Pest 1348-1720* (Potsdam, 1924), pp. 239-73; also "Schwarzer Tod," in *Jüdisches Lexikon*, V (Berlin, 1930), 298-301; Siegbert Neufeld, *Die Juden im thüringisch-sächsischen Gebiet während des Mittelalters* (Halle a.S., 1927), pp. 6-16.

7. Cf. Ellen Littmann, *Studien zur Wiederaufnahme der Juden durch die deutschen Städte nach dem Schwarzen Tode* (University of Cologne Ph.D. thesis [Breslau, 1928]), some chapters also in *MGWJ*, LXXII (1928), 576-600; Hans Lichtenstein, "Zur Wiederaufnahme der Juden in die brandenburgischen Städte nach dem Schwarzen Tode," *ZGJD*, V (1934), 59-63.

8. Cf. Willy Andreas, *Deutschland vor der Reformation: Eine Zeitenwende* (2d ed.; Stuttgart and Berlin, 1934), pp. 375-79; and the chronological survey of the expulsions from central Europe from the twelfth to the sixteenth century in *Encyclopaedia Judaica*, II, 985 f.

9. Guido Kisch, "Research in Medieval Legal History of the Jews," *Proceedings of the American Academy for Jewish Research*, VI (1934-35), 234-44; G. Kisch, "Jüdisches Recht und Judenrecht: Ein Beitrag zur wissenschaftlichen Grundlegung für eine Rechtsgeschichte der Juden," *Festschrift für Dr. Jacob Freimann* (Berlin, 1937), pp. 94-105 (in both articles numerous bibliographical references). Cf. also G. Kisch, "Jewry-Law in Central Europe—Past and Present," *Journal of Central European Affairs*, II (1943), 396-422.

10. For details see below, pp. 135 ff. and 305 ff.

11. Cf., e.g., Wilhelm Weizsäcker, "Die Fremden im böhmischen Landrechte des 13. und 14. Jahrhunderts," *ZRG*, XLV (1925), 209.

12. Cf. Hermann Rudorff, *Zur Rechtsstellung der Gäste im mittelalterlichen städtischen Prozess* (Breslau, 1907); for more bibliographical data on this subject, see below, chap. x, n. 64.

13. See below, pp. 257 ff. and 306 ff.

14. In the historical literature the adjective "Jewish" is used with various meanings, partly technical, partly nontechnical, sometimes in a general and comprehensive, sometimes in a very special, restricted sense. Thus one speaks of "Jewish history" and means by this, at one time, the history of the Jews and, at another, only its investigation and presentation by Jewish historians. One speaks, for example, of Jewish law and thinks of the Bible or the Talmud, and then again of Jewish law of privilege as comprising a sum of rights granted the Jews by kings or princes in the form of charters. Often the literary treatment of the matter is as confused and confusing as is the terminology. For instances see G. Kisch, "Jüdisches Recht und Judenrecht," pp. 96 f., n. 2; and his "Research in Medieval Legal History of the Jews," pp. 236 f., n. 12. Therefore, the strict terminological distinction of "Jewish law" and "Jewry-law" is here suggested. All the more so since the term "Jewish law" is correctly apprehended and applied in the medieval law sources with hardly any exception to this rule (cf. G. Kisch, "Relations between Jewish and Christian Courts in the Middle Ages," *Louis Ginzberg Jubilee Volume* [New York, 1945], p. 211; also below, pp. 102 f.).

15. Cf. Harold Steinacker, "Über die Entstehung der beiden Fassungen des österreichischen Landrechtes," *Jahrbuch des Vereins für Landeskunde für Niederösterreich* (1916-17) (Vienna, 1917), p. 261, quoted in Fritz Kern, "Recht und Verfassung im Mittelalter," *Historische Zeitschrift*, CXX (1919), 39; also Fritz Kern, *Kingship and Law in the Middle Ages* (Oxford, 1939), pp. 175 f., from which the translation of the German original is taken.

16. On the legal form of "privilege" see below, pp. 135 f.

17. For a survey of privileges conferred upon Jews in various countries see Selma Stern, "Judenprivilegien," *Jüdisches Lexikon*, III (Berlin, 1929), 439-42; cf. also Otto Stobbe, *Geschichte der deutschen Rechtsquellen*, I (Braunschweig, 1860), 572-73; Stobbe, *Die Juden in Deutschland während des Mittelalters in politischer, sozialer und rechtlicher Beziehung* (Braunschweig, 1866), pp. 294-307; Adolf Kober, "Die deutschen Kaiser und die Wormser Juden," *ZGJD*, V (1934), 134-51; Max Freudenthal, *ZGJD*, IV (1932), 83-100; Parkes, *The Jew in the Medieval Com-*

munity, pp. 391–404. On the overlapping of the imperial, territorial, and municipal rule over the Jews see G. Kisch, "Die Rechtsstellung der Wormser Juden im Mittelalter," *ZGJD*, V (1934), 125 f. (pp. 6 f. of the reprint); Karl Frölich, *ZRG*, LII (1932), 428.

18. Feudal law (*Lehnrecht*) had obviously no room for Jewry-law, as Jews were not integrated into the feudal hierarchy.

19. See below, pp. 70 ff.

20. It need not be pointed out that canon Jewry-law offers a separate vast field to scholarly investigation (see also below, chap xiii, n. 23).

21. Until now, no uniform terminology has been developed for the description of the subject here under consideration. For the reasons pointed out above (n. 14), the designation "legal history of the Jews" here suggested, awkward as it may be, is preferable to all other formulations using the adjective "Jewish."

22. Karl Friedrich Eichhorn, *Deutsche Staats- und Rechtsgeschichte* (4 vols.; Göttingen, 1808–23), *Vorrede*, reprinted in the subsequent editions (fifth ed.; Göttingen, 1843–44), I, xiii; cf. also Ulrich Stutz, "Die Schweiz in der deutschen Rechtsgeschichte," *Sitzungsberichte der Preussischen Akademie der Wissenschaften*, 1920, p. 92.

23. On Eichhorn's role in German legal history see Ernst Landsberg, *Geschichte der deutschen Rechtswissenschaft*, III, sec. 2 (Munich and Berlin, 1910), Textband, 253 ff.; Ferdinand Frensdorff, "Das Wiedererstehen des deutschen Rechts: Zum hundertjährigen Jubiläum von K. F. Eichhorns Rechtsgeschichte," *ZRG*, XXIX (1908), 1–78; Rudolf Hübner, "Karl Friedrich Eichhorn und seine Nachfolger," *Festschrift Heinrich Brunner zum 70. Geburtstag dargebracht von Schülern und Verehrern* (Weimar, 1910), pp. 807–38. For bibliography on Savigny see Landsberg, *op. cit.*, III, sec. 2, Textband, 186 ff., and III, sec. 2, Notenband, 94; cf. Guido Kisch, "American Research in Medieval Legal History," *Jurist*, II (Washington, D.C., 1942), 214, n. 1.

24. Eichhorn, *op. cit.* (fifth ed.), II, secs. 297, 350, and *passim;* Eichhorn, *Einleitung in das deutsche Privatrecht mit Einschluss des Lehenrechts* (fifth ed.; Göttingen, 1845), secs. 80–82, pp. 236–49.

25. On Eduard Gans see Landsberg, *op. cit.*, III, sec. 2, Textband, 354–69, Notenband, pp. 166–70; Siegfried Ucko, "Geistesgeschichtliche Grundlagen der Wissenschaft des Judentums," *ZGJD*, V (1934), 24 ff.

26. Gans, "Gesetzgebung über Juden in Rom nach den Quellen des römischen Rechts," in Leopold Zunz's *Zeitschrift für die Wissenschaft des Judentums*, I (Berlin, 1823), 95–113, 231–76. (This volume, which remained the only one of this journal, had already been published in two issues, in 1822). Gans promised a continuation of this study, which did

not appear, however. His essay escaped the attention of his excellent biographer, Ernst Landsberg (see above, n. 25), but was mentioned in I. Elbogen, "Ein hundertjähriger Gedenktag unserer Wissenschaft," *MGWJ*, LXVI (1922), 93.

27. To fill the chronological gap between Gans and Stobbe, a two-volume work should not be left unmentioned, although it pursued pre-eminently apologetic purposes in behalf of Jewish emancipation in Austria, namely, *Die Juden in Österreich vom Standpunkt der Geschichte, des Rechts und des Staatsvorteils*, inspired and anonymously published (Leipzig, 1842) by Joseph von Wertheimer, protagonist of Jewish emancipation in Austria. Wertheimer was, however, not the author of the first (historical) part. For a characteristic of this book see Alfred Francis Pribram, *Urkunden und Akten zur Geschichte der Juden in Wien*, I (Vienna and Leipzig, 1918), clvii f.

28. On Otto Stobbe (1831–87), who was professor of German legal history in the universities of Königsberg, Breslau, and Leipzig, see Emil Friedberg, *Otto Stobbe* (Berlin, 1887); Ernst Landsberg, *op. cit.*, III, sec. 2, Textband, 891–94, Notenband, 375–76, with bibliography; E. Landsberg, "Otto Stobbe," *Allgemeine Deutsche Biographie*, XXXVI (Leipzig, 1893), 262–66; Guido Kisch, "Otto Stobbe und die Rechtsgeschichte der Juden," *JGJC*, IX (1938), 1–41.

29. Stobbe, *Geschichte der deutschen Rechtsquellen* (2 vols.; Braunschweig, 1860–64).

30. Originally published in Braunschweig in 1866, it has been re-printed twice; the (last) "third edition," of course unrevised, appeared in Berlin in 1923. All editions are, long since, out of print and practical-ly unobtainable. The critical reviews, which appeared upon the original publication, are listed in Friedberg, *op. cit.*, p. 37. Among them, only the review by Konrad Maurer is worth mentioning because of its scholarly discussion of several problems involved (see *Kritische Viertel-jahrsschrift für Gesetzgebung und Rechtswissenschaft*, IX [1867], 564–81; cf. also G. Kisch, "Otto Stobbe und die Rechtsgeschichte der Juden," pp. 8–10).

31. Karl Gottfried Hugelmann, *Historisches Jahrbuch der Görresgesell-schaft*, XLVIII (1928), 582, n. 36: "Stobbe bietet überhaupt meines Erachtens bis heute die übersichtlichste Orientierung über die ein-schlägigen Tatsachen, allerdings mit einer für die Juden sehr günstigen Beurteilung."

32. Ismar Elbogen, *ZGJD*, VII (1937), 65: "Stobbes Buch ist noch heute Stab und Stütze des jüdischen Historikers, weil die Forschung nur wenig über es hinausgekommen und in den rechtsgeschichtlichen

Untersuchungen das Problem des Judenrechts kaum berührt worden ist."

33. Wilhelm Grau, "Die Judenfrage als Aufgabe geschichtlicher Forschung," *Deutsches Volkstum, Monatsschrift für das deutsche Geistesleben*, XVII (1935), 669: "Bemühungen wie die von Otto Stobbe ergaben ein gutes Bild von der rechtlichen Lage der Juden im mittelalterlichen Deutschland, blieben aber vereinzelt. . . ." The author was, of course, under obligation to add: ". . . und stiessen zur eigentlichen Problematik nirgends vor" (cf. Grau, *Die Judenfrage als Aufgabe der neuen Geschichtsforschung* [Hamburg, 1935], p. 12).

34. On the sources and methods of German legal history see the voluminous systematic works on German legal history and German private law enumerated in the appended Bibliography; in addition, see especially Claudius Freiherr von Schwerin, *Einführung in das Studium der germanischen Rechtsgeschichte und ihrer Teilgebiete* (Freiburg i.Br., 1922).

35. For a brief consideration of this material and its significance for research in the legal history of the Jews, including bibliographical references and methodological suggestions, see G. Kisch, "Research in Medieval Legal History of the Jews," pp. 252–58. Until now, this vast and important historical material has aroused comparatively little interest among scholars. Only a close collaboration of Jewish-theological and legal-historical specialists will be able to bring the varied problems in question nearer to a satisfactory solution.

36. Cf. the stimulating essay by Hans Fehr, "Mehr Geistesgeschichte in der Rechtsgeschichte," *Deutsche Vierteljahrschrift für Literaturwissenschaft und Geistesgeschichte*, V (1927), 1–8; equally apt, though somewhat too subtle, is the exposition by Herbert Meyer, in his *Recht und Volkstum* (Weimar, 1933), pp. 30 f.; more recently, Heinrich Mitteis, *Vom Lebenswert der Rechtsgeschichte* (Weimar, 1947). Also instructive are the conception and organization of a noteworthy work by Helmut Hillmann, *Das Gericht als Ausdruck deutscher Kulturentwicklung im Mittelalter: Ein geistesgeschichtlicher Versuch* ("Deutschrechtliche Forschungen," ed. Guido Kisch, Vol. II [Stuttgart, 1930]).

37. For a more detailed discussion of this situation see G. Kisch, "Research in Medieval Legal History of the Jews," pp. 257 f. and n. 60, pp. 268 f. and n. 85, where some examples are mentioned from the more recent literature; cf. Otto H. Stowasser, "Zur Geschichte der Wiener Geserah," *VSWG*, XVI (1922), 104–18; G. Kisch, *VSWG*, XXIV (1931), 470–77; G. Kisch, "Ein neues Urkundenwerk zur Geschichte der Wiener Juden," *ZGJD*, IV (1932), 47–50.

38. See Guido Kisch, "American Research in Medieval Legal His-

tory" (cited above, n. 23), pp. 214–47; G. Kisch, "A Decade of American Research in Medieval Legal History," *Progress of Medieval and Renaissance Studies in the United States and Canada* (Bull. 17 [1942]), pp. 27–34; cf. *Seminar: Annual Extraordinary Number of the Jurist*, I (Washington, 1943), 1–2. Cf. also the recent pleas for the recognition of the history of thought as a separate field of research by Paul O. Kristeller and Philip P. Wiener, in *Journal of the History of Ideas*, VII (1946), 360–73.

39. Stobbe, *Die Juden in Deutschland während des Mittelalters*, *Vorrede*, p. vi.

40. On inapplicable and unapplied regulations of medieval privileges in general see Guido Kisch, *Die Kulmer Handfeste: Rechtshistorische und textkritische Untersuchungen* ("Deutschrechtliche Forschungen," ed. G. Kisch, Vol. I [Stuttgart, 1931]), pp. 48–54.

41. This will be done, e.g., with regard to the Wends (cf. below, pp. 312 ff.).

42. Cf., e.g., below, pp. 87 f. and n. 19, 159 ff., and 277 ff.

43. For a detailed discussion of this problem see G. Kisch, "Otto Stobbe und die Rechtsgeschichte der Juden," pp. 19 f.

44. The contrary opinion was previously held by some German legal historians, who maintained that there was some direct borrowing from Jewish law because of certain scanty traces of the latter allegedly found in Jewry-law (cf. Schwerin, *Einführung in das Studium der germanischen Rechtsgeschichte*, p. 38, n. 10). The so-called *Jüdisches Hehlerrecht*, a frequently cited example for such influence, however, has no basis in Jewish law at all, as has been proved by recent researches (see below, pp. 211 ff.). Nor are there otherwise traces of any adoption of post-biblical Jewish law discoverable in medieval German law, not even in the field of commercial law. Cf. Paul Rehme, "Geschichte des Handelsrechts," in Victor Ehrenberg's *Handbuch des gesamten Handelsrechts*, I (Leipzig, 1913), 114, 132, 170 f., especially 171: "Weitere Einwirkungen des Rechtes der Juden auf das mittelalterliche deutsche Recht sind, wie schon hier betont werden möge, nicht nachgewiesen und haben auch kaum stattgefunden." F. Ashe Lincoln ("The Legal Background to the Starrs," in Herbert Loewe, *Starrs and Jewish Charters Preserved in the British Museum*, II [London, 1932], lvii–lxxiv; also published separately [London, 1932]) discussed two different problems: (1) the adoption, in the general law practice, of principles of non-Jewish law originally intended for the Jews alone ("the laws of the Jewry") and (2) the penetration of ideas of Jewish law into English law through Jewish influence and usage. The problem of whether Jewish legal con-

cepts and practices actually influenced non-Jewish scholars and legal systems in the Middle Ages to a considerable degree calls for further investigation. On this subject see Guido Kisch, *Sachsenspiegel and Bible: Researches in the Source History of the Sachsenspiegel and the Influence of the Bible on Mediaeval German Law* (Notre Dame, Ind., 1941). In Spain and England the familiarity of Christian lawyers with Jewish law "must have made a permanent impression upon the legal thinking of many an influential non-Jewish judge," according to S. W. Baron ("The Jewish Factor in Medieval Civilization," *Proceedings of the American Academy for Jewish Research*, XII [1942], 24, n. 38); cf. also F. Ashe Lincoln, *The Starra: Their Effect on Early English Law and Administration* (London, 1939), esp. pp. 132–45, who in this book follows the same paths as in his aforementioned article. Sir William Holdsworth, in his Foreword to Lincoln's book, merely remarks: ". . . it may well be that his theory is correct."

45. The suggested collaboration of Jewish-theological and legal-historical specialists (above, n. 35) notwithstanding, Jewish law and Jewry-law must be studied and presented separately. In a historical presentation of Jewry-law, Jewish law (just as Roman or canon law) should be referred to only if contacts are actually traceable or definitely demonstrable. While Stobbe was guided by wise discrimination in this respect (cf., e.g., *Die Juden in Deutschland während des Mittelalters*, pp. 160 f.), Scherer went too far in often merely listing parallels from Jewish law, although they had no specific relation to, or relevance for, the subjects under consideration (cf., e.g., J. E. Scherer, *Die Rechtsverhältnisse der Juden in den deutsch-österreichischen Ländern* [Leipzig, 1901], pp. ix, 227, 286).

46. This is also a problem still much in need of an exhaustive monographic study (cf. G. Kisch, "Research in Medieval Legal History of the Jews," p. 244, n. 24; and G. Kisch, "Jüdisches Recht und Judenrecht," p. 105, n. 14; Baron, *op. cit.*, p. 42, n. 67; Isaac Herzog, *The Main Institutions of Jewish Law*, I [London, 1936], 24–32). For an interesting case of possible penetration of German law into a medieval work on talmudic law see Hans Fehr, "Deutsches Recht und jüdisches Recht," *ZRG*, XXXIX (1918), 314–18.

47. Cf. Fritz Baer, *Galut* ("Bücherei des Schocken Verlags," No. 61 [Berlin, 1936] and English translation, "Schocken Library," No. 2 [New York, 1947]), *passim;* Selma Stern, "The Jew in the Transition from Ghetto to Emancipation," *Historia Judaica*, II (1940), 102–19.

48. Ismar Elbogen, for some time the leading German-Jewish historian, devoted an extensive review article to this writer's first publica-

tions on the subject and welcomed these researches, "die unsere Kenntnisse in einem dem jüdischen Historiker nur schwer zugänglichen Gebiete wesentlich bereichern. . . . Der Dank für die Fortsetzung wird umso heisser sein," he continued, "je rascher sie erfolgt und das ganze Gebiet erschliesst"; Elbogen, " 'Judenrecht' als wissenschaftliche Disziplin," ZGJD, VII (1937), 65-71; similarly, Ludwig Feuchtwanger, "Neue Forschungsaufgaben für die Geschichte der Juden im Mittelalter," Jahrbuch für jüdische Geschichte und Literatur, XXX (Berlin, 1937), 123 f.: "Was Kisch als richtige Arbeitsmethode fordert, ist ohne Einschränkung richtig, auch die Lücken, die er zeigt, müssen aufgefüllt werden"; Feuchtwanger, "Die Erforschung der Rechtsgeschichte der Juden," Jüdische Rundschau, XLIII, No. 66 (August 19, 1938), 4: "Guido Kisch gebührt das Verdienst, auf eine dringende jüdische Forschungsaufgabe unter Beherrschung eines Riesenmaterials aufmerksam gemacht zu haben"; cf. also Louis Rabinowitz, The Ḥerem Hayyishub: A Contribution to the Medieval Economic History of the Jews (London, 1945), pp. 104 f. Researches in medieval Jewry-law have been recently included in the research program of the American Academy for Jewish Research (cf. Proceedings, XI [1941], xi f., and subsequent volumes).

49. This subsection, in its original version, was first published in 1936 when National Socialist pseudo-scholars were beginning to instil anti-Semitic propaganda into German research. It was then intended to take exception against their methods. In order not to imperil the author's relatives in Germany, it had to be cautiously worded, and, in the argumentation, he had sometimes to choose a roundabout way. Extensive quotations from the works of renowned scholars, such as Gierke and Schmoller, seemed to serve this purpose best. The author saw fit not to eliminate but merely to revise and aptly annotate this section.

50. On the idea, origin, and development of Wissenschaft des Judentums see Ismar Elbogen, "Ein Jahrhundert Wissenschaft des Judentums," Festschrift zum fünfzigjährigen Bestehen der Hochschule für die Wissenschaft des Judentums in Berlin (Berlin, 1922), pp. 101-44; Elbogen, "Zum Begriff 'Wissenschaft des Judentums,' " 49. Bericht zum sechzigjährigen Bestehen der Hochschule für die Wissenschaft des Judentums in Berlin (Berlin, 1932), pp. 33-41; cf. Elbogen, "Neuorientierung unserer Wissenschaft," MGWJ, LXII (1918), 81-96; Ucko, "Geistesgeschichtliche Grundlagen," ZGJD, V (1934), 1-34; Fritz Bamberger, "Zunz's Conception of History," Proceedings, XI (1941), 1-25; Luitpold Wallach, "The Scientific and Philosophical Background of Zunz's 'Science of Judaism,' " Historia Judaica, IV (1942), 51-70; Wallach, "The Beginnings of the 'Science of Judaism' in the Nineteenth Century," ibid.,

VIII (1946), 33–60; cf. Salo Baron, "M. Jost the Historian," *Proceedings*, I (1930), 7–32; Baron, "Levi Herzfeld: The first Jewish Economic Historian," *Louis Ginzberg Jubilee Volume*, pp. 75–104. For a survey of, and bibliography on, modern Jewish historiography see G. Kisch, "Research in Medieval Legal History of the Jews," pp. 230–34.

51. Immanuel Wolf, "Über den Begriff einer Wissenschaft des Judentums," *Zeitschrift für die Wissenschaft des Judentums*, I, Heft 1 (Berlin, 1822), 24; cf. Ludwig Feuchtwanger, "Zur Geschichtstheorie des jungen Graetz von 1846," in his edition of Heinrich Graetz's *Die Konstruktion der jüdischen Geschichte*, ("Bücherei des Schocken Verlags," Heft 59 [Berlin, 1936]), pp. 103, 102, where the quoted sentence is ascribed to Zunz.

52. For a detailed discussion see Salo W. Baron, *A Social and Religious History of the Jews*, II (New York, 1937), 31; III, 5 f., n. 6; 42 f., n. 27; 104 f., n. 14; cf. also Baron, "The Jewish Factor in Medieval Civilization," pp. 35 f., n. 54.

53. Maurer, *Kritische Vierteljahrsschrift für Gesetzgebung und Rechtswissenschaft*, IX (1867), 579: "Auf eine Apotheose oder auch nur Rechtfertigung des mittelalterlichen Judenrechtes ist es natürlich mit diesen Gegenbemerkungen ganz und gar nicht abgesehen; aber so einfach liegt dessen Verkehrtheit doch meines Erachtens nicht zu Tage, dass die Berufung auf blinden Fanatismus einerseits und duldendes Martyrium andererseits zu deren Erklärung genügen könnte, vielmehr will mir scheinen, als ob hier ein tief tragischer Konflikt zwischen der national-religiösen Auffassung des Judentums und der ebenso national-religiösen Gestaltung unseres germanischen Föderativstaates sich abspiele, welcher, da beiden sich gegenüberstehenden Prinzipien nur eine relative Berechtigung zugestanden werden kann, eben nur in dem Untergange beider, beziehungsweise der Entkleidung beider von der ihnen anklebenden Einseitigkeit seine endliche Lösung finden konnte und kann"; cf. Maurer, *ibid.*, pp. 574, 578; and below, chap. xiii, n. 12.

54. Cf. the announcement of the program by Wilhelm Grau, in his book, *Antisemitismus im späten Mittelalter: Das Ende der Regensburger Judengemeinde 1450–1519* (Ph.D. thesis of the University of Munich [Munich, 1934]), p. vii, and in the article cited above (n. 33), later reprinted as a separate booklet under the title, *Die Judenfrage als Aufgabe der neueren Geschichtsforschung* (Hamburg, 1935). This program was to be developed scientifically in specially founded and richly endowed research institutes for *Judentumskunde*, that is, for the study of the Jewish question, one in Munich under Grau's direction, one in Berlin, another in Frankfort-on-the-Main—merely agencies of Joseph Goebbel's Minis-

try for Propaganda. Numerous books, collections of essays, booklets, and articles were published and disseminated in many countries, among them the *Forschungen zur Judenfrage* (9 vols.; Hamburg, 1937–44). Even German scholars of reputation did not hesitate to join the "research" staff and to lend authority to these publications through their names. On the "Nazification" of Jewish history in general see Isidore S. Meyer, "History into Propaganda: How Nazi 'Scholars' Are Rewriting Jewish History," *Menorah Journal*, XXVI (1938), 51–74; Bernard D. Weinryb, "Nazification of Science and Research in Nazi Germany," *Journal of Central European Affairs*, III (January, 1944), 373–400; Weinryb, "Nazification of Jewish Learning," *Jewish Review*, III (1945), 25–54; Weinryb, "Political 'Judeology' in Nazi Germany," *ibid.*, III (1945), 107–37. Weinryb's studies are chiefly concerned with the misuse of research institutions and methods for the purposes of political propaganda in Hitler's Germany. But the refined Nazification of medieval legal history and its propagandistic abuse has not yet been made the object of detailed study. It was exposed as early as 1938 by this writer in *Historia Judaica*, I (1938), 66–72, and *JGJC*, IX (1938), 37–41, upon the publication of the periodical, *Deutsche Rechtswissenschaft*, Vol. II (1937), Heft 2. It remained untouched, however, in the otherwise meritorious books by Max Weinreich, *Hitler's Professors: The Part of Scholarship in Germany's Crimes against the Jewish People* (New York, 1946) and Frederic Lilge, *The Abuse of Learning: The Failure of the German University* (New York, 1948).

55. In the Jewish camp, where a reaction could be voiced openly only in the early days of the National Socialist rule, two views opposed each other. The one pointed to the German historical tradition recognizing "two powers as the highest ideal in the sense of Wilhelm von Humboldt: the Jewish moral law, and the great German tradition of a historical outlook. In Ranke's sense, it would bend its efforts toward objective clarification; in Treitschke's sense, it would stand wholeheartedly on the side of Judaism" (so Fritz Friedländer, "Der Wille zur Objektivität," *Central-Vereins-Zeitung*, XIII [Berlin, 1934], No. 47, 2; cf. Friedländer, "Ein Charakterbild in der Geschichte," *ibid.*, XIV [1935], No. 45, 1 f.). The other assumed that "the old picture of the history of the Jews in Germany would no longer suffice," thereby giving recognition to the recent "transformation of the historical picture." Thus it closely approached the anti-Jewish point of view, its ideas led logically "to the same conclusions," although "out of opposite motives" and with a "different outlook" (so Ludwig Feuchtwanger, "Verändertes Geschichtsbild," *Jüdische Rundschau*, XL, No. 86 [Berlin,

1935], 2). This view was, however, later attenuated in Feuchtwanger, "Jüdische Geschichte aus den neuesten Geschichtswerken über die Anfänge des Christentums," *Bayerische israelitische Gemeindezeitung*, XII (1936), 152, and in Feuchtwanger, "Neue Forschungsaufgaben für die Geschichte der Juden im Mittelalter," *Jahrbuch für jüdische Geschichte und Literatur*, XXX (Berlin, 1937), 95 ff. This discussion was abruptly halted due to the political development in Germany following the November pogrom of 1938.

56. Some of these writings can be identified as of National Socialist character from Adolf Jürgens, *Ergebnisse deutscher Wissenschaft: Eine bibliographische Auswahl aus der deutschen wissenschaftlichen Literatur der Jahre 1933–1939* (Essen and New York, 1939), including, however, literature of the pre-Nazi period published in 1933. For a better protection of research, the compilation of a historical bibliography of all Nazi publications concerning the Jews would be a worth-while undertaking. Then every book or article could easily be identified and, if cited at all, should be marked as "anti-Semitic." For the time being the "Index of Persons and Institutions" in Weinreich, *op. cit.*, is useful for this purpose.

57. Only two German historians may be mentioned as illustration, Johannes Haller and Willy Andreas. Haller's pamphlet, *Über die Aufgaben des Historikers* ("Philosophie und Geschichte," Heft 53 [Tübingen, 1935]) deserves reading in full. Indeed, it will be impossible then to escape the persuasive power of his profoundly thought-out conclusions. They are equally masterly in the balance and unerring aim of historical judgment. Cf. Andreas, *Deutschland vor der Reformation: Eine Zeitenwende* (2d ed.; Stuttgart and Berlin, 1934), Preface, p. 3: "Thus may the Germany of the later Middle Ages also demand that it be not measured merely by that which had preceded it or that which happened later. It must be understood by itself, from the conditions of its own life, from its own peculiar character. This, however, is possible only if the historian faces all forces, even those which are not sympathetic to his Weltanschauung or religious attitude, with the will to unshakable justice." Interesting also are the remarks on the significance of cultivating scholarship of a nonpolitical character for national education in Aloys Fischer, *Über Sinn und Wert geschichtlicher Bildung in der Gegenwart* ("Münchener Universitätsreden," Heft 24 [Munich, 1932]).

58. Cf. the thought-provoking work by Ulrich Noack, *Geschichtswissenschaft und Wahrheit, nach den Schriften von John Dalberg-Acton, dem Historiker der Freiheit, 1834–1902* (Frankfort-on-the-Main, 1935); cf. G. Kisch, *Bayerisch-israelitische Gemeindezeitung*, XII (1936), 147; G. Kisch, "Research in Medieval Legal History of the Jews," pp. 232 f.; Hans

Fehr, "Rechts- und Staatsphilosophie der Gegenwart," *Die Tatwelt*, XI (1935), 222.

59. Cf. Graetz, *Die Konstruktion der jüdischen Geschichte* ("Bücherei des Schocken Verlags," No. 59 [Berlin, 1936], with a *Nachwort*, "Zur Geschichtstheorie des jungen Graetz von 1846," by Ludwig Feucht-wanger; Israel Rabin, "Stoff und Idee in der jüdischen Geschichts-schreibung," *Festschrift zu Simon Dubnows siebzigstem Geburtstag* (Berlin, 1930), pp. 41–56; I. Elbogen, "Historiographie," *Encyclopaedia Judaica*, VIII (1931), 107–15; additional references in G. Kisch, "Research in Medieval Legal History of the Jews," p. 233, nn. 6 and 7. More recent attempts at a clarification of the present state of knowledge are Salo W. Baron's "Emphases in Jewish History," *Jewish Social Studies*, I (1939), 15–38; and Morris R. Cohen's "Philosophies of Jewish History," *Jewish Social Studies*, I (1939), 39–72.

60. G. Schmoller, *Deutsches Städtewesen in älterer Zeit* ("Bonner staatswissenschaftliche Untersuchungen," Heft 5 [Bonn and Leipzig, 1922]), p. 1; cf. also p. v f.

61. *Ibid.*, p. 1.

62. J. Huizinga, *Wege der Kulturgeschichte* (Munich, 1930), p. 13. The entire first chapter of this work entitled, "Aufgaben der Kulturge-schichte," offers interesting vistas. No English translation is available.

63. Adolf von Harnack, *Die Aufgabe der theologischen Fakultäten und die allgemeine Religionsgeschichte* (2d ed.; Giessen, 1901), pp. 8 f.: "Die his-torische Methode allein ist konservativ; denn sie sichert die Ehrfurcht— nicht vor der Überlieferung, sondern vor den Tatsachen—und macht der Willkür ein Ende, Blei in Gold und Gold in Blei verwandeln zu wollen."

64. Haller, *op. cit.*, pp. 29 f.: "Ist uns die volle Objektivität versagt, so soll der Wille zur Objektivität um so stärker, das Streben nach ihr um so unverdrossener sein. . . . Die wahre Historie fordert Ehrfurcht und Bescheidenheit und mehr als alles andere Ehrlichkeit und lautere Wahrheitsliebe."

65. For details and bibliographical material on this problem see G. Kisch, "American Research in Medieval Legal History," *Jurist*, II (1942), 220 ff.

66. Otto Gierke, *Das deutsche Genossenschaftsrecht*, II (Berlin, 1873), 1–6. Only excerpts from this four-volume work are available in English translation (cf. Otto Gierke, *Political Theories of the Middle Age*, trans-lated with an Introduction by Frederic W. Maitland [Cambridge, 1913]; O. Gierke, *Natural Law and the Theory of Society 1500–1800*, translated by Ernest Barker [2 vols.; Cambridge, 1934]).

67. It is needless to point out here the patent contrast to the unscru-

pulousness and servility of such leading legal historians in National Socialist Germany as Herbert Meyer, Rudolf Ruth, and others to political-propagandistic aims (above, n. 54). For the sake of fairness this should not be overlooked by American scholars. Charles McIlwain, in his own works much indebted to Gierke, changed his judgment about this great scholar after the outbreak of National Socialism, with which Gierke had obviously nothing to do, since he died as early as 1921 (cf. C. H. McIlwain, "Medieval Institutions in the Modern World," *Speculum*, XVI [1941], 279 f.).

68. Gierke, *Das deutsche Genossenschaftsrecht*, II, 5 f.

69. Von Schwerin, *Einführung in das Studium der germanischen Rechtsgeschichte*, pp. 119, 124; cf. Guido Kisch, *Die Kulmer Handfeste: Rechtshistorische und textkritische Untersuchungen*, pp. 35–40.

70. Gotthelf Bergsträsser, "Zur Methode der *Fiqh*-Forschung," *Islamica*, IV (1930), 285–86: "The German jurist forgets too easily that his conceptual systematic legal thinking is not something absolute and generally valid, that, in fact, it is lacking in the entire Anglo-Saxon world. In relation to a foreign legal system, such as the Islamic, for example, which should be viewed in a purely cognitive way, such a position is quite impossible; carried to its logical conclusion, it must lead to a situation where the one who describes the elements of Islamic law, constructs something altogether new which never existed in Islam itself." Cf. also Walther Schönfeld, *ZRG*, L, kanon. Abt. XIX (1930), 686; Alfred Hübner, "Vorstudien zur Ausgabe des Buches der Könige," *Abhandlungen der Gesellschaft der Wissenschaften zu Göttingen, phil.-hist. Klasse*, 3. Folge No. 2 (Berlin, 1932), p. 115.

71. For examples see G. Kisch, *Proceedings of the American Academy for Jewish Research*, VII (1935–36), 87 f. This, of course, does not refer to some excellent scholars such as Karl von Amira, Ulrich Stutz, or Hans Fehr. Particularly fine understanding for the world of medieval thought and feeling is shown in Otto von Gierke, *Johannes Althusius und die Entwicklung der naturrechtlichen Staatstheorien* (3d ed.; Breslau, 1913), pp. 60–64 (translated into English as *The Development of Political Theory*, by Bernard Freyd [New York, 1939]); J. Huizinga, *The Waning of the Middle Ages: A Study of the Forms of Life, Thought, and Art in France and the Netherlands in the XIVth and XVth Centuries* (London, 1924); Jacob Wackernagel, *Die geistigen Grundlagen des mittelalterlichen Rechts* ("Recht und Staat in Geschichte und Gegenwart," Heft 62 [Tübingen, 1929]); F. M. Powicke, *The Christian Life in the Middle Ages* (Oxford, 1935).

72. Herbert Meyer, *Recht und Volkstum* (Weimar, 1933), pp. 31, 9; cf. also Franz Stadelmeyer, "Otto von Gierke und unsere Zeit," *Monats-*

schrift Hochland, XXXIII, Heft 6 (1936), 518-29. While Herbert Meyer was quickly converted to national socialism, Stadelmeyer, a Catholic author, as late as the fourth year of Nazi rule, tried to propagate the idea of "Back to Gierke" as a prophylaxis against eventual excesses of the Nazi interpretation of law.

CHAPTER TWO

1. The best information regarding the German lawbooks of the Middle Ages, on their transmission in manuscripts, on the editions, and the literature is offered in Gustav Homeyer, *Die deutschen Rechtsbücher des Mittelalters und ihre Handschriften* (3d ed. by Conrad Borchling, Karl August Eckhardt, and Julius von Gierke; Weimar, 1931, 1934); cf. the reviews by G. Kisch, *ZRG*, LII (1932), 377-83; LV (1935), 376-79. Cf. Otto Stobbe, *Geschichte der deutschen Rechtsquellen*, I (Braunschweig, 1860), 286-446; Karl von Amira, *Grundriss des germanischen Rechts* (3d ed.; Strasbourg, 1913), pp. 60-72; Richard Schröder and Eberhard Freiherr von Künssberg, *Lehrbuch der deutschen Rechtsgeschichte* (7th ed.; Berlin and Leipzig, 1932), pp. 718-32, 1061-63; Heinrich Brunner, *Grundzüge der deutschen Rechtsgeschichte* (8th ed. by Claudius Freiherr von Schwerin; Munich and Leipzig, 1930), pp. 109-17, 123-29; Cl. Freiherr von Schwerin, *Grundzüge der deutschen Rechtsgeschichte* (Munich and Leipzig, 1934), pp. 125-32, 134-38; Wolfgang Stammler, *Die deutsche Literatur des Mittelalters: Verfasserlexikon*, I-III (Berlin and Leipzig, 1933-43), *passim;* Fritz Kern, *Kingship and Law in the Middle Ages* (Oxford, 1939), p. 168.

2. Cf. Stobbe, *op. cit.*, I, 287, n. 2; Ferdinand Frensdorff, "Beiträge zur Geschichte und Erklärung der deutschen Rechtsbücher. IV. Der rechtshistorische Gehalt der *Sachsenspiegel*-Vorreden," *Nachrichten der Königlichen Gesellschaft der Wissenschaften zu Göttingen, phil.-hist. Klasse*, 1921, Heft 2, pp. 132, n. 2, and 147; also Fr. W. von Rauchhaupt, *Geschichte der spanischen Gesetzesquellen* (Heidelberg, 1923), p. 110 and n. 174. According to medieval opinion, the "Mirror" reflects an idealized picture (cf. Wilhelm Wackernagel, *Kleinere Schriften*, I [Leipzig, 1872], 132).

3. Cf. Guido Kisch, *Literarische Wochenschrift*, I (1925), 532; cf. Karl August Eckhardt, "Rechtsbücherstudien. I-III," *Abhandlungen der Gesellschaft der Wissenschaften zu Göttingen, phil.-hist. Klasse*, N.F., XX, No. 2 (1927), XXIII, No. 2 (1931); Dritte Folge, No. 6 (Berlin, 1933).

4. Fritz Kern, "Recht und Verfassung im Mittelalter," *Historische Zeitschrift*, CXX (1919), 19 f.: "Für das Mittelalter dagegen ist, wie gesagt, 'Gesetzesrecht' nichts als Gewohnheitsrecht, aufgezeichnet, damit seine an sich stets vorhandene unbegrenzte Geltung vor dem

Vergessenwerden gesichert sei" (this passage was omitted in the English translation of Kern's essay, on p. 161); Kern, *Kingship and Law in the Middle Ages*, p. 169: "In the Middle Ages, on the other hand, the law that is, was regarded as identical with the law that ought to be" (German original, p. 30: "Der mittelalterliche Rechtsgedanke aber setzt ja das Recht, das ist, gleich mit dem Recht, das sein soll").

5. Lawbooks compiled of decisions of jury courts or based on collections of such decisions will not be included here. They will be treated in connection with the Magdeburg jury-court decisions to which they belong with regard to their genesis.

6. The original texts in the medieval languages are reproduced in full in a separate volume, Guido Kisch, *Jewry-Law in Medieval Germany: Laws and Court Decisions Concerning Jews* ("Texts and Studies," ed. by the American Academy for Jewish Research, Vol. III [New York, 1949]).

7. For a full description and bibliography of each individual lawbook see Homeyer, *Die deutschen Rechtsbücher des Mittelalters und ihre Handschriften*, and the other works on the history of medieval law sources cited above, n. 1. More recent relevant literature, not yet listed in these works, will be added in the notes to the following enumeration, subsequent to the editions used.

8. Editions used: Carl Gustav Homeyer, *Des Sachsenspiegels erster Teil oder das Sächsische Landrecht, nach der Berliner Handschrift vom Jahre 1369 herausgegeben* (3d ed.; Berlin, 1861); Karl August Eckhardt, *Sachsenspiegel Land- und Lehnrecht* ("Monumenta Germaniae Historica: Fontes Juris Germanici Antiqui," N.S., Vol. I [Hannover, 1933]). A modern critical edition of the *Glosse* to *Sachsenspiegel Landrecht* is lacking. The following sixteenth-century editions were used: *Sachsenspiegel* with *Glosse* (ed. Augsburg, 1516), described in Homeyer, *Sachsenspiegel Landrecht* (3d ed.), p. 70, No. 15, and pp. 75 f., No. 4; *Sachsenspiegel, auffs newe vbersehen mit Summariis vnd newen Additionen . . . vnd an den glossen vnd Allegaten vielfeltig gebessert, . . . durch Christoff Zobel*, ed. Georgius Menius (Leipzig, 1560). Illuminated manuscripts: Karl von Amira, *Die Dresdener Bilderhandschrift des Sachsenspiegels*, Vol. I: *Ausgabe* (2 parts; Leipzig, 1902); Vol. II: *Erläuterungen* (2 parts; Leipzig, 1925–26). For full bibliography and a survey of the present state of knowledge concerning the *Sachsenspiegel* see Guido Kisch, *Sachsenspiegel and Bible* ("Publications in Medieval Studies," Vol. V [Notre Dame, Ind., 1941]), pp. 3–20, 173–75, 180–84 (*Sachsenspiegel* Bibliography). The following summary is based on this presentation. To the *Sachsenspiegel* Bibliography the following items are to be added: p. 181 ("*Sachsenspiegel* Editions"): J. J. Smits, "De Spiegel van Sassen of zoogenaamde

Hollandsche Sachsenspiegel," *Nieuwe Bijdragen voor Regtsgeleerdheid en Wetgeving*, XXII (1872), 5–72, 169–237; B. J. L. Baron de Geer van Jutphaas, *De Saksenspiegel in Nederland* (2 vols.; 's Gravenhage, 1888); p. 182 ("Eike von Repgow and the *Sachsenspiegel*"): Malcolm Letts, "The *Sachsenspiegel* and Its Illustrators," *Law Quarterly Review*, XLIX (October, 1933), 555–74, a summary survey of contents and illustrations of the *Sachsenspiegel*; Karl Bischoff, "Zur Sprache des Sachsenspiegels von Eike von Repgow," *Zeitschrift für Mundartforschung*, XIX (1943–44), 1–80; Erich Molitor, "Der Gedankengang des Sachsenspiegels: Beiträge zu seiner Entstehung," *ZRG*, LXV (1947), 15–69; Erika Sinauer, "Studien zur Entstehung der Sachsenspiegelglosse," *Neues Archiv der Gesellschaft für ältere deutsche Geschichtskunde*, L (1935), 475–581; Erik Wolf, *Grosse Rechtsdenker der deutschen Geistesgeschichte* (Tübingen, 1939), pp. 1–34; p. 184 ("Source-History of the *Sachsenspiegel*"): Hans Rost, *Die Bibel im Mittelalter: Beiträge zur Geschichte und Bibliographie der Bibel* (Augsburg, 1939), pp. 292–95, a survey of the *Sachsenspiegel* articles which show biblical influence; Sten Gagnér, "Sachsenspiegel und Speculum ecclesiae," *Niederdeutsche Mitteilungen*, III (1947), 82–103.

9. *Sachsenspiegel*, Rhymed Preface, ll. 151–53:

> Diz recht hân ich selbe nicht irdâcht,
> iz habent von aldere an unsich gebrâcht
> Unse gûten vorevaren.

10. In his other work, the *Saxon World Chronicle*, Eike offered the advice that only *"achtbare warheit"* should be laid down in historical works:

> Swer so leve vorebaz,
> swaz dan gesche, der scrive daz,
> unde achtbare warheit.
> Logene sal uns wesen leit.
> Daz ist des van Repgouwe rat.

Cf. Karl Zeumer, "Die Sächsische Weltchronik: Ein Werk Eikes von Repgow," *Festschrift Heinrich Brunner zum 70. Geburtstag* (Weimar, 1910), p. 136.

11. Cf. Hans Fehr, "Die Staatsauffassung Eikes von Repgau," *ZRG*, XXXVII (1916), 133; Frensdorff, "Beiträge zur Geschichte und Erklärung der deutschen Rechtsbücher. IV. Der rechtshistorische Gehalt der *Sachsenspiegel*-Vorreden," *Nachrichten der Königlichen Gesellschaft der Wissenschaften zu Göttingen, phil.-hist. Klasse*, 1921, Heft 2, pp. 132 f., 137, 139; "V. 1. Die Rechtsbücher und die Königswahl," *ibid.*, 1923, pp. 79 f.

12. Cf. Raimund Friedrich Kaindl, "Zur Geschichte des deutschen Rechts im Osten," *ZRG,* XL (1919), 275 f.; Wilhelm Weizsäcker, "Das deutsche Recht des Ostens im Spiegel der Rechtsaufzeichnungen," *Deutsches Archiv für Landes- und Volksforschung,* III (1939), 52 ff.; also the maps by Dietlinde von Künssberg, "Heimat und Umwelt des Sachsenspiegels," and "Der Sachsenspiegel und seine Tochterrechte," Appendixes to Hans Christoph Hirsch, *Eike von Repgow: Der Sachsenspiegel (Landrecht) in unsere heutige Muttersprache übertragen und dem deutschen Volke erklärt* (Berlin and Leipzig, 1936).

13. On Johann von Buch and his *Gloss* see Emil Steffenhagen, "Die Entwicklung der Landrechtsglosse des Sachsenspiegels," *Sitzungsberichte der kaiserlichen Akademie der Wissenschaften in Wien, phil.-hist. Klasse,* Vols. CXIII (1886), CXIV (1887), CXXXI (1894), CXCIV (1922), and CXCV (1923); Erika Sinauer, "Studien zur Entstehung der Sachsenspiegelglosse," *Neues Archiv der Gesellschaft für ältere deutsche Geschichtskunde,* L (1935), 475–581; G. Kisch, "Juridical Lexicography and the Reception of Roman Law," *Seminar,* II (1944), 60, n. 31. In Stammler's *Die deutsche Literatur des Mittelalters: Verfasserlexikon,* there is no article on Johann von Buch. On Nicholas Wurm and his *Gloss* see Hugo Boehlau, *Nove Constitutiones Domini Alberti d.i. der Landfriede vom Jahre 1235 mit der Glosse des Nicolaus Wurm* (Weimar, 1858), pp. xxi ff.; Guido Kisch, *Leipziger Schöffenspruchsammlung* ("Quellen zur Geschichte der Rezeption," Vol. I [Leipzig, 1919]), p. 87*, n. 4; Emil Steffenhagen, *Die Landrechtsglosse des Sachsenspiegels* ("Akademie der Wissenschaften in Wien, phil.-hist. Klasse, Denkschriften," Vol. LXV, Abh. 1 [Vienna, 1925]), pp. 15, 32, n. 184. On the Stendal *Gloss* see Steffenhagen, *ibid.,* pp. 15 f.; Steffenhagen, "Die Entwicklung der Landrechtsglosse des Sachsenspiegels," *Sitzungsberichte der kaiserlichen Akademie der Wissenschaften in Wien, phil.-hist. Klasse,* C, Heft 2 (Vienna, 1882), 887–934; CXIV, Heft 2 (Vienna, 1887), 701 f.

14. Cf. *Germania Judaica,* ed. I. Elbogen, A. Freimann, H. Tykocinski (Breslau, 1934), article "Sachsen," pp. 313–17; on Thuringia an article is missing from the *Germania Judaica,* but the spreading of Jewish settlements in Thuringia from the first third of the thirteenth century onward is mentioned in Elbogen's article, "Deutschland," *ibid.,* pp. xix f.

15. Cf. Julius Cahn, "Ein Wetterauer Dynastenbrakteat mit hebräischer Umschrift," *Zeitschrift für Numismatik,* XXXIII (1923), 100 ff.

16. Cf. Herbert Meyer, *Das Mühlhäuser Reichsrechtsbuch aus dem Anfang des 13. Jahrhunderts* (2d ed.; Weimar, 1934), pp. 69–71.

17. Cf. "Erfurt," *Germania Judaica,* pp. 98 f.

18. Cf. A. Lewinsky, "Regesten zur Geschichte der Juden in der

Provinz Sachsen während des Mittelalters," *MGWJ*, XLIX (1905), 746 ff.; Siegbert Neufeld, *Die Juden im thüringisch-sächsischen Gebiet während des Mittelalters*, Vols. I (Berlin, 1917) and II (Halle a.S., 1927); Arthur Süssmann, *Das Erfurter Judenbuch (1357-1407)* (Leipzig, 1915), pp. 110 ff.; cf. also the pertinent articles in *Germania Judaica*, especially on Sachsen, Meissen, Elbe, Saale, Erfurt, Halle, and Merseburg.

19. Siegbert Neufeld, "Jüdische Gelehrte in Sachsen-Thüringen während des Mittelalters," *MGWJ*, LXIX (1925), 283-95. In the well-known work of Rabbi Isaac ben Moses of Vienna, *Or Zarua*, written between 1224 and 1250, a responsum is included which concerns Jewish mint masters and their employees (Vol. II, fol. 1*b*, §2); cf. Cahn, *op. cit.*, p. 101.

20. Meyer, *op. cit.*, art. 45, 8, p. 170.

21. That they were apparently almost unrestricted in their commercial activities was recognized even by an author like Karl G. Hugelmann (see below, pp. 77 f.), who writes in *Historisches Jahrbuch der Görresgesellschaft*, XLVIII (1928), 578: "In many of the later regulations of the South-German law the motif is obvious, namely, to protect the Christians from being economically harmed by Jews. The *Sachsenspiegel*, which lacks all traces of any such tendency, differs sharply in this respect."

22. Ludwig Weiland, *Sächsische Weltchronik* ("Monumenta Germaniae Historica, Deutsche Chroniken," Vol. II, Sec. I [Hannover, 1876]), chap. 191, p. 179: "It volgede oc en grot here eneme moneke, de was Peter geheten. Se voren umbeschedenlike; se slogen alle de Joden in allen steden, dar se se vunden."

23. Editions used: F. L. A. Freiherr von Lassberg, *Der Schwabenspiegel oder Schwäbisches Land- und Lehenrecht-Buch nach einer Rezension vom Jahr 1287 mit späteren Zusätzen* (Tübingen, 1840); Wilhelm Wackernagel, *Der Schwabenspiegel in der ältesten Gestalt mit den Abweichungen der gemeinen Texte und den Zusätzen derselben*, Part I: *Landrecht* (Zürich and Frauenfeld, 1840); Heinrich Gottfried Gengler, *Des Schwabenspiegels Landrechtsbuch* (2d ed.; Erlangen, 1875). Cf. Ludwig Rockinger, "Die handschriftliche Grundlage der Ausgabe des kaiserlichen Land- und Lehenrechts," *Abhandlungen der Königlich Bayerischen Akademie der Wissenschaften, phil.-philol. u. hist. Klasse*, Vol. XXVI, No. 5 (Munich, 1913), with bibliography of Rockinger's voluminous researches on the *Schwabenspiegel*, on pp. 8 f.; Ernst Klebel, "Studien zu den Fassungen und Handschriften des Schwabenspiegels," *Mitteilungen des Österreichischen Instituts für Geschichtsforschung*, XLIV (1930), 129-264.

24. Cf. Weizsäcker, "Das deutsche Recht des Ostens im Spiegel der

Rechtsaufzeichnungen," *Deutsches Archiv für Landes- und Volksforschung*, III (1939), 55 f.

25. On the Jews in southern Germany at the time of the composition of the *Schwabenspiegel* see *Germania Judaica*, articles "Bayern," pp. 22–24; "Regensburg," pp. 285 ff.; "Augsburg," pp. 14 f., and *passim;* cf. also articles "Österreich," pp. 256 ff., and "Wien," pp. 397 ff.

26. On Berthold of Regensburg's and David of Augsburg's attitude toward the Jews see Julius Aronius, *Regesten zur Geschichte der Juden im fränkischen und deutschen Reiche bis zum Jahre 1273* (Berlin, 1887–1902), No. 757, pp. 318–20; George Caro, *Sozial- und Wirtschaftsgeschichte der Juden im Mittelalter und der Neuzeit*, I (Leipzig, 1908), 453; Moritz Güdemann, *Geschichte des Erziehungswesens und der Kultur der Juden in Frankreich und Deutschland* (Vienna, 1880), pp. 133, 140, 146; Peter Browe, *Die Judenmission im Mittelalter und die Päpste* (Rome, 1942), pp. 33, 91. On David of Augsburg and Berthold of Regensburg, cf. Gustav Ehrismann, *Geschichte der deutschen Literatur bis zum Ausgang des Mittelalters*, Part II: *Die mittelhochdeutsche Literatur, Schlussband* (Munich, 1935), pp. 415–19; Stammler, *Die deutsche Literatur des Mittelalters: Verfasserlexikon*, I, 404 f., 214 ff.

27. For details see below, pp. 159 ff.

28. The present analysis of author and sources of the *Schwabenspiegel* leaves no room for a purely economic-historical interpretation of the anti-Jewish character of its Jewry-law as offered by Hugelmann, above, n. 21. According to him, the protection of the Christian population against harmful business conduct of Jews was the motif of these anti-Jewish laws. Thus the full responsibility for the necessity of their issuance would fall upon the Jews. This hypothesis finds, however, no specific support in the sources.

29. Cf. Von Amira, *Grundriss des germanischen Rechts* (3d ed.; Strasbourg, 1913), p. 63. The clerical author of a formerly unknown medieval lawbook attempted to revise the *Sachsenspiegel* with an ecclesiastical tendency by inserting sections from the *Schwabenspiegel*. However, the work breaks off at Ssp., II, 26, so that the Jewry-law remained untouched (cf. Theodor Goerlitz, "Ein bisher unbekanntes Rechtsbuch als Beitrag zur Geschichte des Sachsenspiegels," in *Oberlausitzer Beiträge: Festschrift für Richard Jecht* [Görlitz, 1938], pp. 49–54).

30. Edition used: Friedrich Ortloff, *Das Rechtsbuch nach Distinctionen nebst einem Eisenachischen Rechtsbuch* (Jena, 1836). This is the only edition of this lawbook in existence. For the time of its publication, one hundred and twelve years ago, the editor did excellent work indeed, which, however, does not satisfy the demands of modern scholarship. Prior to the war a new critical edition, to be based on all manuscripts avail-

able, was being prepared by Professor Wilhelm Weizsäcker in Prague (cf. Weizsäcker, "Zur Geschichte des Meissner Rechtsbuchs in Böhmen und Mähren," ZRG, LVIII [1938], 584 ff.). It was to include the oldest manuscript so far known, found in a codex of the Nationalbibliothek in Vienna, No. 2680 of the year 1387 (Homeyer, Rbb., No. 1144), which had not been used by Ortloff. In the oldest manuscripts so far studied by Weizsäcker the main body of Jewry-law regulations (III, 17) has proved to be fairly consistent, although individual articles are missing in certain manuscripts (see, e.g., Weizsäcker, "Zur Geschichte des Meissner Rechtsbuchs," pp. 592 [III, 17, 42], 603 [III, 17, 33]). My collation of the text of the Vienna manuscript has produced only five variant readings not yet included in Ortloff's apparatus of variants.

31. Homeyer, *Die deutschen Rechtsbücher*, p. *38. According to a recent hypothesis, the years 1344–56 are supposed to be the probable date of the composition of the Meissen lawbook; cf. Wilhelm Weizsäcker, "Der Böhme als Obermann bei der deutschen Königswahl," in *Festschrift Ernst Heymann . . . zum 70. Geburtstag am 6. April 1940 überreicht von Freunden, Schülern und Fachgenossen*, I (Weimar, 1940), 208. This earlier date was contradicted, however, by Karl August Eckhardt (*ZRG*, LXI [1941], 286).

32. Magdeburg *Schöffenspruch* ("jury-court decision") for the town of Eisleben, undated, presumably from the beginning of the fifteenth century; Hermann Grössler, "Sammlung älterer nach Eisleben ergangener Rechtsbescheide des Magdeburgischen Schöppenstuhls," *Zeitschrift des Harzvereins für Geschichte und Altertumskunde*, XXIII (1890), 178 f., No. 13: ". . . süllet ir wissin umme das buch Distinctiones, das wir da nicht von halden, wen das nicht bestetigt ist von pawesen ader von keysern, und ist körczlich uffkomen, daz man nicht enweyss, wy daz zcu houffe gesaczt, und ouch menigerleye und vele artikele heldt, dy wedder unse alde beschrebene und bestetigede recht sin." Cf. also Kretschmann, *Geschichtsblätter für Stadt und Land Magdeburg*, XXVI (1891), 335.

33. On Jews in the march and city of Meissen from the tenth to the thirteenth century see *Germania Judaica*, article "Meissen," pp. 225 f.; Alfred Leicht, "Die Judengemeinde in Meissen," *Mitteilungen des Vereins für die Geschichte der Stadt Meissen* (1890), pp. 1–33; on Jews in Thuringia, see above, p. 37; in Silesia, *Germania Judaica*, article "Breslau," pp. 63 f.; in Bohemia and Moravia, *Germania Judaica*, articles "Böhmen," pp. 27 ff. and "Mähren," pp. 171 ff.; Bertold Bretholz, *Quellen zur Geschichte der Juden in Mähren vom XI. bis zum XV. Jahrhundert (1067–1411)* (Prague, 1935); Bretholz, *Geschichte der Juden in Mähren im Mittelalter*, Part I: *Bis zum Jahre 1350* (Brünn and Prague, 1934).

34. For Meissen Rb., III, 17, 3–4, cf. Ssp. Ldr., III, 7, 4; for MRb.,

III, 17, 31–33, cf. Ssp. Ldr., III, 7, 3; for MRb., III, 17, 38, cf. Ssp. Ldr., III, 7, 2; for MRb., VI, 2, 2, cf. Ssp. Ldr., II, 66, 1; for MRb., VI, 2, 6, cf. Ssp. Ldr., III, 2.

35. Cf. Ortloff, *Das Rechtsbuch nach Distinctionen*, pp. xxix and 475–85; cf. Stobbe, *Die Juden in Deutschland während des Mittelalters in politischer, socialer und rechtlicher Beziehung* (Braunschweig, 1866), pp. 294–307; Ernst Theodor Gaupp, *Das schlesische Landrecht* (Leipzig, 1828), p. 41.

36. Cf. Günther Ullrich, "Zu den Quellen des Meissner Rechtsbuches," *Deutschrechtliches Archiv*, I (1940), 87–96; also below, n. 112.

37. Cf. Hugelmann, *Historisches Jahrbuch der Görresgesellschaft*, XLVIII (1928), 575 f., 582, where, however, he overlooked the regulation in MRb., III, 17, 47; Guido Kisch, "Relations between Jewish and Christian Courts in the Middle Ages," *Louis Ginzberg Jubilee Volume* (New York, 1945), pp. 210 ff.

38. Editions used: Julius Ficker, *Der Spiegel deutscher Leute: Textabdruck der Innsbrucker Handschrift* (Innsbruck, 1859); Karl August Eckhardt and Alfred Hübner, *Deutschenspiegel und Augsburger Sachsenspiegel* ("Monumenta Germaniae Historica: Fontes Juris Germanici Antiqui," N.S., Vol. III [2d rev. ed.; Hannover, 1933]). Cf. Eckhardt, "Rechtsbücherstudien." I. "Vorarbeiten zu einer Parallelausgabe des Deutschenspiegels und Urschwabenspiegels," *Abhandlungen der Gesellschaft der Wissenschaften zu Göttingen, phil.-hist. Klasse*, N.F., XX, No. 2 (Berlin, 1927), 80 f., 89, 94, 110; Hans Lentze, "Die Kurzform des Schwabenspiegels," *Sitzungsberichte der Akademie der Wissenschaften in Wien, phil.-hist. Klasse*, Vol. CCXVII, Heft 3 (Vienna, 1938); E. Klebel, *Deutsches Archiv für Geschichte des Mittelalters*, IV (1940), 256 f.; H.-K. Claussen, *ZRG*, LIX (1939), 559 ff.

39. Eckhardt and Hübner, *op. cit.*, p. 145, note to art. 73, 3; cf. Eckhardt, "Rechtsbücherstudien," I, 94.

40. The German text reads: "Ez sol chein christen gesuch nemen noch pfant auf den schaden setzen, niwan an die juden."

41. Editions used: *Sechsisch Weichbild, Lehenrecht und Remissorium* (*gedruckt zu Budissin durch Nicolaum Wolraben, 1557*), accompanied by the *Gloss;* Jacob Friederich Ludovici, *Das Sächsische Weichbild* (Halle, 1721); Wilhelm von Thüngen, *Das Sächsische Weichbildrecht nach dem Codex Palatinus Nro. 461* [von 1504] (Heidelberg, 1837); A. von Daniels, *Dat buk wichbelde recht. Das sächsische Weichbildrecht nach einer Handschrift der königl. Bibliothek zu Berlin von 1369* (Berlin, 1853); A. von Daniels and Fr. von Gruben, *Rechtsdenkmäler des deutschen Mittelalters*, Vol. I: *Das Sächsische Weichbildrecht, Jus municipale Saxonicum, Weltchronik und Weich-*

bildrecht in [C]XXXVI Artikeln mit der Glosse (Berlin, 1858). Cf. Paul Laband, *Magdeburger Rechtsquellen* (Königsberg, 1869), pp. 108–11.

42. Laband, *op. cit.*, pp. 109–11.

43. The original German: "Von der juden rechte ist gesprochen in dem lantrechte, daz der *Sachsenspigel* genant ist, in dem dritten buche in dem sebinden articulo; darum wil ich hy nicht davon schryben." This insertion has even eluded the most detailed treatment of the *Sächsisches Weichbild* in the Berlin-Steinbeck manuscript, by Emil Steffenhagen, "Die Entwicklung der Landrechtsglosse des Sachsenspiegels. I," *Sitzungsberichte der Kaiserlichen Akademie der Wissenschaften in Wien, phil.-hist. Klasse*, XCVIII (1881), 47–83, especially 79–83.

44. Cf. Homeyer, *Die deutschen Rechtsbücher*, p. *54; G. Kisch, *Leipziger Schöffenspruchsammlung* (Leipzig, 1919), Einleitung, p. *97.

45. *Gloss to Sächsisches Weichbild*, ed. Budissin (1557), fols. cvi–cvii; ed. von Daniels and von Gruben, pp. 436–38 (not identical).

46. Cf. Homeyer, *Die deutschen Rechtsbücher*, pp. *12–*15.

47. Of them, the *Löwenberger Rechtsbuch*, of the first half of the fourteenth century, influenced by Frankish law, and preserved in a single manuscript in the Staatsarchiv of Breslau (Homeyer, Rbb., No. 195), was not available to the author. On the *Richtsteig Landrechts* see below (p. 54), in sec. 10; on the *Abecedaria* and *Remissoria*, see in sec. 19 (pp. 60–62).

48. Cf. Ernst Theodor Gaupp, *Das Schlesische Landrecht oder eigentlich Landrecht des Fürstentums Breslau von 1356 an sich und in seinem Verhältnisse zum Sachsenspiegel dargestellt* (Leipzig, 1828), pp. 173 f., 175, 176; Theodor Goerlitz, "Die Breslauer Rechtsbücher des 14. Jahrhunderts," *ZRG*, LIX (1939), 155 ff.

49. Otto Meinardus, *Das Neumarkter Rechtsbuch und andere Neumarkter Rechtsquellen* ("Darstellungen und Quellen zur schlesischen Geschichte," Vol. II [Breslau, 1906]), pp. 95 ff.

50. B. J. L. Baron de Geer van Jutphaas, *De Saksenspiegel in Nederland* (2 vols.; 's Gravenhage, 1888), II, 129, 136, 140.

51. J. J. Smits, "De Spiegel van Sassen of zoogenaamde Hollandsche Sachsenspiegel," *Nieuwe Bijdragen voor Regtsgeleerdheid en Wetgeving*, XXII (1872), 33–35, 191–92.

52. Carl Gustav Homeyer, *Des Sachsenspiegels zweiter Teil nebst den verwandten Rechtsbüchern*, II: *Der Auctor Vetus de beneficiis, das Görlitzer Rechtsbuch und das System des Lehnrechts* (Berlin, 1844), 23 ff.

53. On this Homeyer, *ibid.*, p. 56; Richard Jecht, "Über die in Görlitz vorhandenen Handschriften des Sachsenspiegels und verwandter Rechtsquellen," *Neues Lausitzisches Magazin*, LXXXII (1906), 225 f.

54. Gustav Adolf Tzschoppe and Gustav Adolf Stenzel, *Urkunden-sammlung zur Geschichte des Ursprungs der Städte und der Einführung und Verbreitung deutscher Kolonisten und Rechte in Schlesien und der Oberlausitz* (Hamburg, 1832), p. 473.

55. Friedrich Georg von Bunge, *Über den Sachsenspiegel als Quelle des mittleren und umgearbeiteten livländischen Ritterrechts* (Riga, 1827), pp. 113 f.; Bunge, *Altlivlands Rechtsbücher* (Leipzig, 1879), p. 20.

56. Cf. Anton Buchholtz, *Geschichte der Juden in Riga bis zur Begründung der Rigischen Hebräergemeinde im Jahre 1842* (Riga, 1899), p. 1.

57. Editions used: Georg Ludwig von Maurer, *Das Stadt- und das Landrechtsbuch Ruprechts von Freysing nach fünf Münchener Handschriften* (Stuttgart and Tübingen, 1839); Hermann Knapp, *Das Rechtsbuch Ruprechts von Freising (1328)* (Leipzig, 1916). Knapp's edition is impaired by serious shortcomings, however; cf. Edward Schröder's critique in *Göttingische Gelehrte Anzeigen*, CLXXIX (1917), 317–20. The synoptic tabulation in Knapp's edition (pp. 144 f.) facilitates identification of individual articles in the antiquated edition of the *Freisinger Rechtsbuch* by L. Westenrieder (Munich, 1803). Only after the typesetting of this volume had begun did the new and critical edition of the Freising lawbook become available to the author: Hans-Kurt Claussen, *Freisinger Rechtsbuch* (Weimar, 1941). While it was impossible to change the citations given according to Knapp's edition, the new numeration of Claussen's edition could still be inserted in the following tabulation of the Jewry-law regulations, which are contained in that lawbook.

58. Cf. Hermann Knapp, "Das Rechtsbuch Ruprechts von Freising (1328) in seiner Bedeutung als strafrechtliche Quelle des Mittelalters," Goltdammer's *Archiv für Strafrecht und Strafprozess*, LXI (1914), 219–26, 233, 240 f., 245, 251, 253; also Moritz Güdemann, *Geschichte des Erziehungswesens und der Kultur der Juden in Deutschland während des XIV. und XV. Jahrhunderts* (Vienna, 1888), pp. 141–44, 159, 177.

59. See below, chap. viii, n. 64, and chap. xii, n. 134.

60. Edition used: Hermann Wasserschleben, *Sammlung deutscher Rechtsquellen*, I (Giessen, 1860), 1–79. Cf. Theodor Goerlitz, *ZRG*, LIX (1939), 147, 152; LXIV (1944), 319–26. In deviation from the methodological principle stated above (chap. ii, n. 5), the *Glogauer Rechtsbuch* is included here, since its Jewry-law is, for the most part, derived from older lawbooks. For the same reason, the same method was applied in listing and describing the Glogau lawbook in Homeyer, *Die deutschen Rechtsbücher*, p. *33.

61. Editions used: E. Fidicin, *Historisch-diplomatische Beiträge zur Geschichte der Stadt Berlin*, Part I: *Berlinisches Stadtbuch* (Berlin, 1837); references to this edition are to the pages, and on each page the para-

graphs are numbered; P. Clauswitz, *Das Berlinische Stadtbuch aus dem Ende des XIV. Jahrhunderts* (Berlin, 1883). Since the newer and better edition by Clauswitz is difficult to procure, Fidicin's edition was still included in the following synoptic table.

62. See above, p. 49, sec. 6.

63. See below, chap. viii, n. 69.

64. Ed. Fidicin, p. 149, 3; ed. Clauswitz, III, 14; see below, chap. vi, n. 120. Cf. Joseph Seeboth, *Das Privatrecht des Berliner Stadtbuches vom Ende des 14. Jahrhunderts* ("Einzelschriften der Historischen Kommission für die Provinz Brandenburg und die Reichshauptstadt Berlin," Vol. II [Berlin, 1928]), p. 10.

65. Partial edition by Hans Planitz, "Das Zwickauer Stadtrechtsbuch," ZRG, XXXVIII (1917), 321–66. Only after typesetting of this volume was almost finished, did the new, complete edition become available to the author: Günther Ullrich and Hans Planitz, *Zwickauer Rechtsbuch* (Weimar, 1941). The passage, I, 15, 3, is reproduced there as III, 1, 15, par. 4, on pp. 184 f. One more regulation concerns the Jews, I, 6, 1: "Meat from cattle slaughtered by Jews shall not be offered for sale in the butchers' stalls but shall be put in front of the slaughterhouses. Whoever sells anything of such meat [in the butchers' stalls], . . must pay [a fine of] five shillings in pennies of full weight to the [municipal] council, if he is apprehended with such meat."

66. Homeyer, *Sachsenspiegel Landrecht* (3d ed.; Berlin, 1863), I, 61, 4; see also below, p. 248.

67. Carl Gustav Homeyer, *Der Richtsteig Landrechts nebst Cautela und Premis* (Berlin, 1857). This lawbook contains only one more regulation concerned with Jews, in 13, 7, being the well-known statement from Ssp. Ldr., I, 7, 1.

68. There is no modern edition of this lawbook. The quotation of its sources in the text (above, p. 54) is from an epilogue in the Königsberg manuscript (Homeyer, Rbb., No. 592) (cf. Max Neumann, *Geschichte des Wuchers in Deutschland* [Halle, 1865], p. 69, n. 1). The tabulation of the text rests on the comparative tables and corresponding passages in Ortloff's edition of the Meissen lawbook (pp. 774–78): "Vergleichung der von Poelmann herausgegebenen Distinctionen mit dem Rechtsbuch nach Distinctionen." The variant readings are also listed in Ortloff's edition. According to the survey offered there, the following identities could be established: MRb., III, 17=Poelmann, IX, 15; MRb., V, 5, 3 = Poelmann, VIII, 11, 3; MRb., VI, 2, 2=Poelmann, VI, 14; MRb., VI, 2, 6=Poelmann, VI, 20, 3; MRb., III, 1, 3; III, 14, 4; IV, 42, 22; and IV, 46, 12, seem to be missing in Poelmann.

69. Edition used: Emil Franz Rössler, *Das altprager Stadtrecht aus dem*

XIV. Jahrhundert ("Deutsche Rechtsdenkmäler aus Böhmen und Mähren," Vol. I [Prague, 1845]). Cf. W. Weizsäcker, "Das deutsche Recht des Ostens im Spiegel der Rechtsaufzeichnungen," *Deutsches Archiv für Landes- und Volksforschung*, III (1939), 61.

70. Cf. Homeyer, *Sachsenspiegel*, II, 1, pp. 33 f., No. 79; H. G. Ph. Gengler, *Deutsche Stadtrechte des Mittelalters* (Nuremberg, 1866), pp. 394-407.

71. For details see below, p. 268.

72. Hugo Boehlau, *Die Blume von Magdeburg* (Weimar, 1868). The *Blume des Sachsenspiegels*, the other work of Nicholas Wurm, which is still unpublished, also belongs to the end of the fourteenth century (possibly 1397) (cf. Jecht, "Über die in Görlitz vorhandenen Handschriften des Sachsenspiegels" [above, n. 53], pp. 243-49; Homeyer, *Der Richtsteig Landrechts*, pp. 355 ff., one chapter referring to Jews).

73. Herbert Meyer, *Das Mühlhäuser Reichsrechtsbuch aus dem Anfang des 13. Jahrhunderts, Deutschlands ältestes Rechtsbuch* (2d rev. ed.; Weimar, 1934); cf. H. Meyer, *Hansische Geschichtsblätter*, LIX (1934), 1-27.

74. See below, pp. 239 ff.

75. Heinrich Maria Schuster, *Das Wiener Stadtrechts- oder Weichbildbuch* (Vienna, 1873).

76. On the Jewry-law of Frederick II's privilege for the Jews of Vienna of 1238, see J. E. Scherer, *Die Rechtsverhältnisse der Juden in den deutsch-österreichischen Ländern* (Leipzig, 1901), pp. 135-72. Schuster (*op. cit.*, p. 39) proved that the borrowings from the *Schwabenspiegel* were originally not intended or included by the author of the Vienna lawbook. Because of the character of this lawbook's Jewry-law as described above, its regulations need not be considered here.

77. Schuster, *op. cit.*, p. 41. Hugelmann, *Historisches Jahrbuch der Görresgesellschaft*, XLVIII (1928), 581.

78. Hermann Ernst Endemann, *Das Keyserrecht nach der Handschrift von 1372* (Kassel, 1846).

79. Cf. Homeyer, *Die deutschen Rechtsbücher*, p. *29; Karl August Eckhardt, *Frankenspiegelstudien* (Witzenhausen, 1923), pp. 12, 15.

80. Edition used: Friedrich Ortloff, *Das Rechtsbuch Johannes Purgoldts nebst statutarischen Rechten von Gotha und Eisenach* (Jena, 1860). Cf. Ortloff, *Das Rechtsbuch nach Distinctionen*, pp. liv-lxii.

81. Guido Kisch, "Juridical Lexicography and the Reception of Roman Law," *Seminar*, II (1944), 59 f.

82. Elsewhere (VIII, 102) Purgoldt remarks after enumerating the various dress regulations valid for Jews: "That they now go about differently, is a sign that to the princes Jewish gold is dearer than the honor of God or Holy Christendom."

83. For a full quotation and translation of this article see below, pp. 193 f.

84. On *Abecedaria*, *Remissoria*, and *Vocabularia* in general see Homeyer, *Die deutschen Rechtsbücher des Mittelalters und ihre Handschriften* (2d ed.; Berlin, 1856), pp. 57–61; Homeyer, *Die deutschen Rechtsbücher* (3d ed.), pp. *55–*57; Erika Sinauer, *Der Schlüssel des sächsischen Landrechts* (Gierke's "Untersuchungen zur deutschen Staats- und Rechtsgeschichte," Heft 139 [Breslau, 1928]), pp. 188 ff.; Guido Kisch, "Juridical Lexicography and the Reception of Roman Law," pp. 51–81.

85. Cf. Sinauer, *Der Schlüssel des sächsischen Landrechts*, pp. 99 f., 258.

86. Cf. Homeyer, *Des Sachsenspiegels Erster Teil oder das Sächsische Landrecht* (3d ed.; Berlin, 1861), pp. 116 f.; G. Kisch, "Zwei Sachsenspiegel-Vokabularien," *ZRG*, XLIV (1924), 311; G. Kisch, "Juridical Lexicography and the Reception of Roman Law," pp. 63 f., n. 38; of different opinion, Sinauer, *Der Schlüssel des sächsischen Landrechts*, pp. 188 f.

87. Cf. Theodor Goerlitz, "Der Verfasser der Breslauer Rechtsbücher *Rechter Weg* und *Remissorium*," *Zeitschrift des Vereins für Geschichte Schlesiens*, LXX (1936), 195–206; Goerlitz, *ZRG*, LVII (1937), 752 f. The Jewry-law regulations of the three *Remissoria* mentioned above are published for the first time from the manuscripts in G. Kisch, *Jewry-Law in Medieval Germany*, pp. 118–34.

88. Edition used: *Sechsisch Weichbild, Lehenrecht und Remissorium auffs new an vielen orten, in Texten, Glossen und derselben allegaten, aus den warhafftigen glossen Keiserlicher und Bepstlicher Recht, und also den hauptquellen, mit fleis anderwerts corrigiert und restituiret* (gedruckt zu Budissin durch Nicolaum Wolraben 1557). Cf. Homeyer, *Sachsenspiegel*, II, 1, pp. 41 ff.; and for the text, G. Kisch, *Jewry-Law in Medieval Germany*, pp. 135 f.

89. There is no comprehensive monograph of recent date on the history and dissemination of Magdeburg law in general and the significance of the Magdeburg *Oberhof* in particular, as can be seen from the bibliography up to 1932, in Schröder and von Künssberg, *Lehrbuch der deutschen Rechtsgeschichte* (7th ed.; Berlin and Leipzig, 1932), pp. 741–44 and 1063 f. The only general survey, though outdated in many respects, is found in Ferdinand von Martitz, *Das eheliche Güterrecht des Sachsenspiegels und der verwandten Rechtsquellen* (Leipzig, 1867), pp. 1–79; cf. also Stobbe, *Geschichte der deutschen Rechtsquellen*, I, 276 ff., 421 ff.; II, 63 ff.; Adolph Stölzel, *Der Brandenburger Schöppenstuhl* (Berlin, 1901), pp. 233 ff., 246 ff., 248 ff.; Max Dittmar, "Der erste Versuch zur Wiedererrichtung des magdeburgischen Schöffenstuhls nach dem 10./20. Mai 1631," *Geschichtsblätter für Stadt und Land Magdeburg*, XXX (1895),

158-61. The sketchy essays by Walter Möllenberg, *Eike von Repgow und seine Zeit* (Burg b.M., 1934), pp. 80-86, 126 f., and by Fritz Markmann, "Zur Geschichte des Magdeburger Rechtes," in *Magdeburg in der Politik der deutschen Kaiser*, pub. by the city of Magdeburg (Heidelberg and Berlin, 1936), pp. 81-128, are based on secondary sources only and offer no original research. Such research on various problems involved here is, however, embodied in the following works: Albert Brackmann, *Magdeburg als Hauptstadt des deutschen Ostens im frühen Mittelalter* (Leipzig, 1937), pp. 67-73; Guido Kisch, "Das Recht am Zeitzer Mühlgraben," *Jahrbuch "Sachsen und Anhalt,"* V (Magdeburg, 1929), 302 ff.; Walter Becker, *Magdeburger Recht in der Lausitz* ("Deutschrechtliche Forschungen," ed. G. Kisch, Vol. III [Stuttgart, 1931]) (the reviews of the last-mentioned book by R. Jecht, *Neues Lausitzisches Magazin*, CVII [1931], 207, and by R. Lehmann, *ZRG*, LII [1932], 461 ff., are written from a one-sided viewpoint of local history, while its achievements for legal history are rightly valued by P. Rehme, *Deutsche Literaturzeitung*, 1933, pp. 424 f., and E. Wohlhaupter, *Kritische Vierteljahrsschrift für Gesetzgebung und Rechtswissenschaft*, XXVI [1933], 159 ff.); Helmut Hillmann, *Das Gericht als Ausdruck deutscher Kulturentwicklung im Mittelalter* ("Deutschrechtliche Forschungen," Vol. II [Stuttgart, 1930]); cf. G. Kisch, *Speculum*, XIV (1939), 39, n. 1. See also Heinrich Felix Schmid, "Das deutsche Recht in Polen," in *Deutschland und Polen: Beiträge zu ihren geschichtlichen Beziehungen*, ed. Albert Brackmann (Munich and Berlin, 1933), pp. 64-80; H. F. Schmid, *ZRG*, L, kanon. Abt. XIX (1930), 359, n. 2; Wilhelm Weizsäcker, "Die Ausbreitung des deutschen Rechtes in Osteuropa," in *Staat und Volkstum*, ed. Carl von Loesch, II (Berlin, 1926), 549-67; Weizsäcker, "Eindringen und Verbreitung der deutschen Stadtrechte in Böhmen und Mähren," *Deutsches Archiv für Landes- und Volksforschung*, I (1937), 95-109; Weizsäcker, "Das deutsche Recht des Ostens im Spiegel der Rechtsaufzeichnungen," *ibid.*, III (1939), 58-60, 62 ff., 71-73; Weizsäcker, "Leitmeritz als Vorort des Magdeburger Rechts in Böhmen," *Neues Archiv für sächsische Geschichte*, LX (1939), 1-23; Fritz Markmann, "Zur Geopolitik des Magdeburger Rechts," *Zeitschrift für Geopolitik*, XII (1935), 384-93; Theodor Goerlitz, *Die Oberhöfe in Schlesien* (Weimar, 1938); Gertrud Schubart-Fikentscher, *Die Verbreitung der deutschen Stadtrechte in Osteuropa* (Weimar, 1942), esp. pp. 57-379. A map showing the dissemination of the Magdeburg law over Europe, "Die Verbreitung des deutschen Stadtrechts nach dem Osten," is appended to the work, *Magdeburg in der Politik der deutschen Kaiser;* cf. also Markmann, *op. cit.*, pp. 385, 391.

90. The problem posed in this heading has not been treated pre-

viously, in spite of the fact that Otto Stobbe has already pointed out in his *Die Juden in Deutschland während des Mittelalters*, p. vi: "Gerade die Urkunden und *Schöffensprüche* sind die unzweideutigsten Quellen [*sc.* for the legal status of the Jews in the Middle Ages]"; similarly also Robert Hoeniger, in Geiger's *ZGJD*, I (1887), 66. Both authors themselves, however, made only scant use of these sources. As to the *Schöffensprüche* as a source of legal history in general, see Guido Kisch, "Schöffenspruchsammlungen als Quelle der Rechtsgeschichte" (Christian Friedrich Kees Memorial Lecture delivered at the University of Leipzig on February 2, 1918) (unpublished, manuscript in the writer's possession); G. Kisch, "Schöffenspruchsammlungen," *ZRG*, XXXIX (1918), 346–65; G. Kisch, "Schöffensprüche als historische Quellen," *Niederdeutsche Mitteilungen*, IV (Lund, Sweden, 1948), 50–58; from the older literature, Ernst Theodor Gaupp, *Das alte Magdeburgische und Hallische Recht* (Breslau, 1826), pp. 166–84.

91. Aronius, *Regesten*, Nos. 129, 133, 140; Siegfried Rietschel, *Markt und Stadt in ihrem rechtlichen Verhältnis* (Leipzig, 1897), pp. 53, 55, 58; Moritz Güdemann, *Zur Geschichte der Juden in Magdeburg* (Breslau, 1866), pp. 7 f.

92. Cf. above, p. 50.

93. This tendency was one of the main reasons why, as early as the Middle Ages, the Magdeburg *Schöffensprüche* were compiled by local court authorities, with the aim put so well in MS Breslau, J 5, fol. 1: "zu nutcze und stewre der hernoch komenden herren und schepphin, das sie ire houpte nicht dorffen mwhen und denn der gleich snelle mogen hirynne finden beschrieben" ("for the benefit and guidance of later gentlemen and jurors so that they need not fatigue their heads and may here quickly find similar [decisions] written down"); cf. Hugo Böhlau, "Aus der Praxis des Magdeburger Schöffenstuhls während des 14. und 15. Jahrhunderts," *ZRG*, O.S., IX (1870), 1.

94. For bibliography see Wilhelm Theodor Kraut, *Grundriss zu Vorlesungen über das deutsche Privatrecht* (6th ed. by F. Frensdorff; Berlin and Leipzig, 1886), pp. 55–57; Kisch, *ZRG*, XXXIX (1918), 346–48; Hillmann, *op. cit.*, pp. ix ff.; Becker, *op. cit.*, pp. ix ff.; and the Bibliography at the end of this volume.

95. Only a few are listed in Carl Gustav Homeyer, *Die deutschen Rechtsbücher des Mittelalters und ihre Handschriften* (3d ed.; Weimar, 1931–34), where emphasis is laid mainly on the lawbooks based on Magdeburg law; cf. Kisch, *ZRG*, LII (1932), 381 f.; Paul Gülland, *ZRG*, LX (1940), 278 ff.

96. Paul Laband, *Das Magdeburg-Breslauer systematische Schöffenrecht*

aus der Mitte des 14. Jahrhunderts (Berlin, 1863); Jacob Friedrich Behrend, *Die Magdeburger Fragen* (Berlin, 1865); Ferdinand von Martitz, "Die Magdeburger Fragen," *Zeitschrift für Rechtsgeschichte*, XI, O.S. (1873), 401–31; Emil Kalužniacki, "Die polnische Rezension der Magdeburger Urteile und die einschlägigen deutschen, lateinischen und czechischen Sammlungen," *Sitzungsberichte der kaiserlichen Akademie der Wissenschaften zu Wien, phil.-hist. Klasse*, CXI (1886), 113–330; Weizsäcker, "Das deutsche Recht des Ostens im Spiegel der Rechtsaufzeichnungen," p. 72.

97. Cf. Karl von Amira, *ZRG*, XXIII (1902), 281 ff.; Hubert Ermisch, *Neues Archiv für sächsische Geschichte und Altertumskunde*, XL (1919), 426. In the early eighteen-seventies the late Geheimrat Professor Ferdinand von Martitz, of the University of Berlin, prepared a collection of Magdeburg *Schöffensprüche* not referred to by either von Amira or Ermisch. It was, however, neither completed nor published. The considerable material consisting of transcripts and notes from manuscripts —some of these lost in the meantime—are now in the possession of the author, to whom they had been presented by Professor von Martitz shortly before he died.

98. Cf. G. Kisch, "Schöffenspruchsammlungen," *ZRG*, XXXIX (1918), 348; G. Kisch, *Leipziger Schöffenspruchsammlung* (Leipzig, 1919); G. Kisch, "Schöffensprüche als historische Quellen" (above, n. 90), p. 52.

99. Cf. Erich Liesegang, "Bericht über eine zur Herstellung eines Verzeichnisses der Magdeburger Schöffensprüche im Auftrage der königl. bayrischen Akademie der Wissenschaften im Jahre 1889 unternommenen Reise," *ZRG*, XVI (1895), 281–300; Victor Friese and Erich Liesegang, *Magdeburger Schöffensprüche*, I (Berlin, 1901); cf. the extensive reviews by Karl von Amira, in *ZRG*, XXIII (1902), 281–88; and Richard Behrend, in *Göttingische Gelehrte Anzeigen*, CLXV (1903), 671–87.

100. In 1937 the city of Magdeburg founded an Institute for the History of Magdeburg Law ("Institut zur Erforschung des Magdeburger Rechts") (see communication of the Municipal Archives of Magdeburg, *ZRG*, LIX [1939], 670; Schubart-Fikentscher, *Die Verbreitung der deutschen Stadtrechte in Osteuropa*, p. 73). Nazi scholars took up and continued the writer's research, adopting his editorial principles, naturally without reference to his earlier work. Three volumes of *Schöffensprüche* were published, which are listed below in the Bibliography. In 1945, in the course of the war, the Institute, its library, and materials were destroyed. Cf. G. Kisch, "Schöffensprüche als historische Quellen," pp. 50–58.

101. An exception could perhaps have been made for those collections

which had emerged as lawbooks, such as the *Magdeburg-Breslauer Schöf-fenrecht* or the *Magdeburger Fragen* (see above, n. 96). But this was not done for the sake of uniformity in the presentation.

102. (1) Manuscript from the beginning of the fourteenth century in the Municipal Archives of Brünn, Moravia (Homeyer, No. 213); a copy of the contents of the *Schöffensprüche* in this volume, fols. 18–19: "Hie hebt sich an von klagen und von urteile," written many years ago by Otto Stobbe and now in the writer's possession, shows the following headings: "15. Ob ein man auf den andern claget, das er erlanget habe in den juden mit allen rechten hundert schock grossen und mer; 21. Das ein jude claget gegen einen cristen umbe hauptgut." (2) Manuscript collection of Magdeburg jury-court decisions sent to Merseburg (1424–52), in the Stadtbibliothek of Merseburg, Germany (Homeyer, No. 788).

103. (1) Collection of jury-court decisions, probably of the fifteenth century, discovered in the Altertumsmuseum of Torgau, Germany, after a long search by the writer (Homeyer, No. 1111a); an inadequate description of this codex was published by Martin Granzin in ZRG, LIV (1934), 244 ff. (2) In 1875 a manuscript collection of jury-court decisions of Magdeburg, Leipzig, and Halle for various Thuringian towns (compiled in 1474) was discovered by the late librarian of the Reichsgerichtsbibliothek in Leipzig, Professor Karl Schulz, in Poessneck, Thuringia. It is not in Homeyer and remained completely unknown and unpublished. In 1915, because of his advanced age, Professor Schulz abandoned his plan of publishing this manuscript, which was then deposited in the Forschungsinstitut für Rechtsgeschichte, located in the University Library of Leipzig. For many years the writer prepared editions of both manuscripts under the auspices of the aforementioned Forschungsinstitut für Rechtsgeschichte. In April, 1933, owing to Hitler's access to power, he was barred from further use of these codexes, whereby his work was bound to be frustrated. A complete transcript of the Poessneck manuscript remained with the original codex in possession of the Leipzig Forschungsinstitut.

104. All jury-court decisions dealing with Jews or Jewish affairs are reproduced in full in G. Kisch, *Jewry-Law in Medieval Germany*, pp. 137–242.

105. On *Oberhöfe* outside the territory of Magdeburg law see Schröder and Künssberg, *op. cit.*, pp. 739, 744 ff.

106. Cf. Weizsäcker, "Eindringen und Verbreitung der deutschen Stadtrechte in Böhmen und Mähren," pp. 104, 107.

107. Cf. Weizsäcker, "Zur Einführung des Magdeburgischen Rechtes

in Mähren," *Prager Juristische Zeitschrift, Wissenschaftliche Vierteljahrs-schrift*, II (1922), 79–85.

108. It is Homeyer, No. 213; cf. Weizsäcker, "Das deutsche Recht des Ostens im Spiegel der Rechtsaufzeichnungen," *Deutsches Archiv für Landes- und Volksforschung*, III (1939), 55. See also below, chap. x, n. 9.

109. See Weizsäcker, "Eindringen und Verbreitung der deutschen Stadtrechte," map, facing p. 104.

110. The latter extended over twenty and probably more localities (cf. Bretholz, *Geschichte der Juden in Mähren im Mittelalter*, I [Brünn, 1934], 118, 121).

111. Edition used: Emil Franz Rössler, *Die Stadtrechte von Brünn aus dem XIII. und XIV. Jahrhundert* (Prague, 1852).

112. Cf. Julius Weiske, "Bemerkungen über das Brünner Schöffenbuch privat- und prozessrechtlichen Inhalts," *Zeitschrift für deutsches Recht und deutsche Rechtswissenschaft*, XIV (1853), 113 ff.; Emil Ott, "Das Eindringen des kanonischen Rechts, seine Lehre und wissenschaftliche Pflege in Böhmen und Mähren während des Mittelalters," *ZRG*, XXXIV, kanon. Abt., III (1913), 71 ff.; Gertrud Schubart-Fikentscher, *Das Eherecht im Brünner Schöffenbuch* (Stuttgart, 1935), pp. 1–17; Schubart-Fikentscher, "Das Brünner Schöffenbuch: Beiträge zur spätmittelalterlichen Rechts- und Kulturgeschichte," *Deutsches Archiv für Geschichte des Mittelalters*, I (1937), 457 ff.; Schubart-Fikentscher, "Neue Fälle zum Brünner Recht," *ibid.*, III (1939), 430–96; Schubart-Fikentscher, "Römisches Recht im Brünner Schöffenbuch," *ZRG*, LXV (1947), 86–176; Weizsäcker, "Das deutsche Recht des Ostens im Spiegel der Rechtsaufzeichnungen," p. 61. For older bibliography see Bertold Bretholz, *Quellen zur Geschichte der Juden in Mähren*, p. xx, n. 1; Otto Peterka, *ZRG*, LVIII (1938), 426 f., n. 2.

113. Cf. Emil Ott, *Beiträge zur Rezeptionsgeschichte des römisch-kanoni-schen Prozesses in den böhmischen Ländern* (Leipzig, 1879), pp. 174–76; E. Ott, "Das Eindringen des kanonischen Rechts," *ZRG*, XXXIV, kanon. Abt., III (1913), 71 ff.; Schubart-Fikentscher, *op. cit.* (above, n. 112); Miroslav Boháček, *Římské právní prvky v právní knize brněnského písaře Jana* ("Traits of Roman Law in the Lawbooks of John the Clerk of Brünn"; in Czech) ("Práce ze Semináře Českého Práva na Karlově Universitě," No. 9 [Prague, 1924]); Boháček, "Ještě k římskoprávnímu obsahu brněnské právní knihy" ("Additional Information on the Roman Law Content of the Brünn Lawbook"; in Czech), *Sborník prací z dějin práva Československého*, I ("Práce ze Semináře Českého na Karlově Universitě," No. 15 [Prague, 1930]), 39–49.

114. The decisions referring to Jews are Nos. 14, 19, 93, 241, 306, 313,

337, 430–41, 537, 544, 664, in Rössler's edition. All the decisions are summarized in German in Bertold Bretholz, *Quellen zur Geschichte der Juden in Mähren vom XI. bis zum XV. Jahrhundert (1067–1411)* (Prague, 1935), No. 40, pp. 18–29. In the footnotes Bretholz offered some textual emendations of the Latin text on the basis of the original manuscript. His translation, however, does not always render the Latin accurately. Another summary of these decisions with a brief discussion is found in Bretholz, *Geschichte der Juden in Mähren im Mittelalter*, I, 135–50.

115. For more details see Bretholz, *Quellen zur Geschichte der Juden in Mähren*, pp. xx–xxii.

116. They were published in condensed form, only in a German translation, by Bretholz (*ibid.*, Nos. 204, 205, 211, 215, 280, 298, 314, 326, 329, 338, 343, 366, 367, 369, 370, 387, 400, 419, 441).

117. The entire collection was published by Gertrud Schubart-Fikentscher, "Neue Fälle zum Brünner Recht," *Deutsches Archiv für Geschichte des Mittelalters*, III (1939), 430–96. The decisions concerned with Jews are Nos. 19a–c, pp. 492 f.

118. The Latin text is reproduced in G. Kisch, *Jewry-Law in Medieval Germany*, pp. 243–61.

119. See also the appended Bibliography at the end of this volume.

120. The literature concerned with the Jewry-law in the medieval jury-court decisions will be discussed separately, below, pp. 79 f.

121. On *Remissoria* in general see above, pp. 60 ff.

122. Cf. Eduard Eichmann, *Historisches Jahrbuch der Görresgesellschaft*, XXXVIII (1917), 741.

123. Cf., e.g., Johannes Jodocus Beck, *Tractatus de juribus Judeorum: Von Recht der Juden* (Nuremberg, 1741), p. 469.

124. Cf. Georg Landauer, "Zur Geschichte der Judenrechtswissenschaft: Hinweis auf ein Kapitel aus der Rechtsgeschichte der Juden," *ZGJD*, II (1930), 255–61; Jean Juster, *Les Juifs dans l'empire Romain*, I (Paris, 1914), xiii f., n. 1; also, below, pp. 362 f. A bibliography of the *Judenrecht*, particularly in the second half of the eighteenth century, is included in Volkmar Eichstädt, *Bibliographie zur Geschichte der Judenfrage*, Vol. I: *(1750–1848)* (Hamburg, 1938), pp. 159–64 (with anti-Semitic annotations).

125. Cf. R. Hoeniger, "Zur Geschichte der Juden Deutschlands im frühern Mittelalter," Geiger's *ZGJD*, I (1887), 65–97, 136–51; cf. G. Kisch, "Die Rechtsstellung der Wormser Juden im Mittelalter," *ZGJD*, V (1934), 123 f. (pp. 4 f. of reprint).

126. (Berlin, 1887–1902): No. 458, pp. 200 f. (*Sachsenspiegel*); No. 667, pp. 277 f. (*Deutschenspiegel*); No. 771, pp. 327–31 (*Schwabenspiegel*).

This remark, however, is not intended to detract from Aronius' merit in compiling his *Regesten*. This work, though long outdated, is still indispensable. The voluminous source material concerning medieval Jewry in central Europe, dispersed in innumerable source books and collections of a general nature, urgently demands scholarly attention. Many years ago, some fine projects were launched by Eugen Täubler, aiming at the compilation of a new medieval *Urkundenbuch*. Unfortunately, they remained projects. Cf. Eugen Täubler, "Plan für die Bearbeitung eines Urkundenbuches zur Geschichte der Juden im Mittelalter," *Mitteilungen des Gesamtarchivs der deutschen Juden*, IV (1913), 1-30; Täubler, "Urkundliche Beiträge zur Geschichte der Juden in Deutschland im Mittelalter," *ibid.*, pp. 31-62; Täubler, "Das Forschungsinstitut für die Wissenschaft des Judentums," *Korrespondenzblatt des Vereins zur Gründung und Erhaltung einer Akademie für die Wissenschaft des Judentums*, I (Berlin, 1920), 15-18. At present, one may hardly count upon relief for some time to come.

127. Cf. Aronius, *Regesten*, No. 458, p. 201; Geiger's *ZGJD*, V (1892), 298.

128. So, for instance, Ismar Elbogen, "Deutschland," in *Germania Judaica*, p. xxv; H. Tykocinski, "Sachsen," *Germania Judaica*, pp. 314-17. An uncritical discussion may be found in K. Sidori (=Isidor Kaim), *Geschichte der Juden in Sachsen mit besonderer Rücksicht auf ihre Rechtsverhältnisse* (Leipzig, 1840), pp. 7-10.

129. (Leipzig, 1908; 2d unrev. ed.; Frankfort-on-the-Main, 1928), pp. 401-3, 419 f.

130. Ph.D. thesis of the University of Hamburg (1922), pp. 46-62. The thesis is available in a typescript copy only, in the Preussische Staatsbibliothek in Berlin. A brief excerpt appeared in print (Königsberg i. Pr., 1922).

131. "Wissenschaftliche Beilage" to No. 8 of the *Israelit*, XI (1870), 149 f.

132. G. Kisch, "A Talmudic Legend as the Source for the Josephus Passage in the *Sachsenspiegel*," *Historia Judaica*, I (1939), 105-18; cf. below, pp. 153 ff.

133. "Publications in Medieval Studies," Vol. V, ed. Philip S. Moore and published by the University of Notre Dame (Notre Dame, Ind., 1941).

134. So, for the first time, Wilhelm Grau, "Die Judenfrage als Aufgabe geschichtlicher Forschung," *Deutsches Volkstum*, XVII (1935), 668 f., and *Die Judenfrage als Aufgabe der neuen Geschichtsforschung* (Hamburg, 1935), pp. 12 f.; in agreement, Eugen Wohlhaupter, *Historische Zeitschrift*, CLIV (1936), 107; Herbert Meyer, *Deutsche Rechtswis-*

senschaft, II, No. 2 (1937), 97: "Die neuere Geschichte der Juden ist—in stillschweigendem Übereinkommen—fast ganz ihnen allein als Arbeits-feld überlassen worden"; similarly, Rudolf Ruth, *Deutsche Rechtswis-senschaft*, II, No. 2 (1937), 111, with special reference to the medieval legal history of the Jews; cf. also Walter Frank, *Historische Zeitschrift*, CLXII (1940), 565. In a truly pseudo-scientific manner, Grau supported his thesis by reference to the present author's bibliographical essay, "Dissertationenliteratur zur Geschichte der Juden aus den Jahren 1922–1928," *ZGJD*, III (1931), 117–23, in which, of course, Jewish as well as Christian authors were listed (cf. G. Kisch, *Proceedings*, VII [1935–36], 118, n. 113; Kisch, "Otto Stobbe und die Rechtsgeschichte der Juden," p. 33, n. 55).

135. In 1937 this writer exposed the actual situation and adduced bibliographical support for his assertion in his last contribution to the *Savigny-Zeitschrift für Rechtsgeschichte*, LVII (1937), 714–17. It was a book review which was published upon invitation and instance of the editor, Ulrich Stutz, the well-known historian of canon law, who was opposed to national socialism. This review article was promptly contradicted, of course with no documentation, by George A. Löning, *ZRG*, LVIII (1938), 257, n. 2, after the editorship of the *Savigny-Zeitschrift* had passed out of the hands of Stutz.

136. See above, chap. i, n. 24.

137. Eichhorn, *Deutsche Staats- und Rechtsgeschichte*, Vol. II (5th ed.; Göttingen, 1843), § 350, pp. 612–14.

138. On Stobbe's work, *Die Juden in Deutschland*, see above, pp. 12 ff. J. E. Scherer, *Beiträge zur Geschichte des Judenrechtes im Mittelalter mit besonderer Bedachtnahme auf die Länder der österreichisch-ungarischen Monarchie*, Vol. I: *Die Rechtsverhältnisse der Juden in den deutsch-österreichischen Ländern* (the only volume published; Leipzig, 1901); cf. the critical reviews of this work by Ernst Bruck, *ZRG*, XXIII (1902), 320; Max Eschelbacher, *MGWJ*, XLVI (1902), 388–94; Arnold Luschin von Ebengreuth, *Historische Zeitschrift*, XCII (1904), 132–35.

139. Karl von Amira, *Die Dresdener Bilderhandschrift des Sachsenspiegels*, Vol. I: *Ausgabe* (2 parts; Leipzig, 1902).

140. *Ibid.*, Vol. II: *Erläuterungen* (2 parts; Leipzig, 1925–26), see Register, *s.v.* "Juden." Cf. also Ulrich Stutz, *ZRG*, XLVII (1927), 685–95.

141. *Op. cit.*, II, Part I, 35–40.

142. *Historisches Jahrbuch der Görresgesellschaft*, XXXVIII (1917), 746–57.

143. *Historisches Jahrbuch der Görresgesellschaft*, XLVIII (1928), 565–85.

144. He starts out with this declaration (p. 585): "Let us now turn to a problem indeed more familiar to the modern law of nationality, to the treatment under medieval German law of a foreign racial [*völkischen*] individuality, namely, that of Jewry."

145. Hugelmann, *ibid.*, p. 585, n. 40: "Ich glaube, dass schon die juristischen Quellen, denen allein dieser Aufsatz gewidmet ist, an dem nationalen Element im Judenrecht keinen Zweifel übrig lassen. Der Eindruck dieses Elementes verstärkt sich, wenn man nichtjuristische Quellen heranzieht, z.B. die poetische Literatur; dem in dieser Beziehung von Stobbe, S. 163, Beigebrachten wäre Konrad von Würzburg beizufügen."

146. Hugelmann, *ibid.*, p. 579: ". . . so erfahren dafür die privilegia odiosa eine—vielfach bis zum Gehässigen gesteigerte—Ausgestaltung, welche schlechterdings nur durch ein sogar übersteigertes, in geradezu physischer Abneigung sich äusserndes Gefühl völkischer, rassischer Fremdheit erklärt werden kann" (cf. also Hugelmann, *ZRG*, LVIII [1938], 216).

147. It seems appropriate here to note some data of the author's career. Hugelmann was professor of legal history and canon law at the University of Vienna until 1935. He was very active in politics and for some time held the position of vice-president of the Austrian *Bundesrat*. At that time he became an exponent of national socialism and had to flee to the Third Reich as early as 1935. There he was immediately elevated to the presidency (*Rektorat*) of the University of Münster, Westphalia.

148. Mention should be made here of the fact that a special issue of the law journal, *Deutsche Rechtswissenschaft*, ed. Karl August Eckhardt, Vol. II, No. 2 (1937), was entirely devoted to the history of Jewry-law in Germany; for criticism see G. Kisch, *Historia Judaica*, I (1938), 66–72; *JGJC*, IX (1938), 37–41; also above, chap. i, n. 54.

149. Herbert Meyer, *Entwerung und Eigentum im deutschen Fahrnisrecht: Ein Beitrag zur Geschichte des deutschen Privatrechts und des Judenrechts im Mittelalter* (Jena, 1902); cf. the critical review by Max Eschelbacher, *MGWJ*, XLVII (1903), 181–92; cf. H. Meyer, "Entgegnung," *MGWJ*, XLVII (1903), 382 f.; Eschelbacher, "Nachwort," *MGWJ*, XLVII (1903), 384; also Konrad Beyerle, *ZRG*, XXIII (1902), 344–48.

150. H. Meyer, "Das Hehlerrecht der Juden und Lombarden," *Forschungen zur Judenfrage*, I (Hamburg, 1937), 92–109; H. Meyer, "Das jüdische Hehlerrecht," *Deutsche Rechtswissenschaft*, II (1937), 97–111.

151. G. Kisch, "The 'Jewish Law of Concealment,'" *Historia Judaica*, I (1938), 3–30; Boaz Cohen, "The So-called *jüdisches Hehlerrecht* in the Light of Jewish Law," *Historia Judaica*, IV (1942), 145–53.

152. *Deutsche Rechtswissenschaft*, II, No. 2 (1937), 166–89.

153. K. Müllenhoff and W. Scherer, *Denkmäler deutscher Poesie und Prosa aus dem VIII.–XII. Jahrhundert*, II (3d ed.; Berlin, 1892), 465–74.

154. It is perhaps worth mentioning that in a selection of important regulations from the lawbooks prepared for schools and popular use, Jewry-law is not missing; Hans Fehr, *Aus deutschen Rechtsbüchern* ("Voigtländers Quellenbücher," Vol. XXXIII [Leipzig, (1912)]), pp. 74–79; cf. Eberhard Freiherr von Künssberg, *Der Sachsenspiegel: Bilder aus der Heidelberger Handschrift* ("Insel-Bücherei," No. 347 [Leipzig, (1935)]), pictures Nos. 13, 80, 83. Books and periodicals published in Germany during the years of war 1939–45 were available to the author only to a limited extent.

155. See above, chap. ii, n. 90. The Magdeburg jury-court decisions concerning Jews published in Friese-Liesegang, *Magdeburger Schöffensprüche*, I (Berlin, 1901), were listed and excerpted by the editors in their "Sachregister," *s.v.* "Juden," pp. 809 f.

156. *Geschichtsblätter für Stadt und Land Magdeburg*, XLVI, No. 1 (1911), 119–78; No. 2, 328–408.

157. Forchhammer, *ibid.*, pp. 374–76.

158. Cf., e.g., Forchhammer, *ibid.*, pp. 122 ff., 369, 373, 389, 408.

159. It is different as far as French medieval literature is concerned; cf., e.g., David Strümpf, *Die Juden in der mittelalterlichen Mysterien-, Mirakel- und Moralitäten-Dichtung Frankreichs* (Ph.D. thesis, University of Heidelberg [Ladenburg a.N., 1920]); Manya Liftschitz-Golden, *Les Juifs dans la littérature française du moyen age* (New York, 1935).

160. Ph.D. thesis, University of Heidelberg (Berlin-Wilmersdorf, 1933).

161. "University of California Publications in Modern Philology," Vol. XVIII, No. 1 (Berkeley, Calif., 1934). It is regrettable that some of Gudde's references are not accurate.

162. See above, n. 145.

CHAPTER THREE

1. See chap. ii, pp. 37 f.

2. Cf. Hans Fehr, "Die Staatsauffassung Eikes von Repgau," *ZRG*, XXXVII (1916), 169 f., 201 f., 237; K. G. Hugelmann, "Studien zum Recht der Nationalitäten im deutschen Mittelalter. I. Die deutschen Stämme im *Sachsenspiegel* und in anderen Rechtsquellen des 13. Jahrhunderts," *Historisches Jahrbuch der Görresgesellschaft*, XLVII (1927), 280–83; see also below, nn. 35, 36.

3. Ssp., I, 30: "Jewelk înkomen man untveiet erve binnen deme lande zu Sassen nâch des landes rechte unde nicht nâch des mannes, her sî Bayer oder Swâf oder Franke." Cf. the Latin version in Zobel's *Sachsen-*

spiegel edition (Leipzig, 1560): "Quilibet advena in percipienda haereditate succedit non secundum suae personae, sed secundum iura terrae Saxoniae, cujuscunque etiam sit, Bavariae, Franciae, vel Sueviae nationis." Cf. E. Th. Gaupp, "Einige Bemerkungen über Stammrecht, Territorialrecht, Professiones juris," *Zeitschrift für deutsches Recht und deutsche Rechtswissenschaft*, XIX (1859), 163–66; H. Fehr, *Die Tragik im Recht* (Zürich, 1945), pp. 26 f., 100, n. 2.

4. Ssp., III, 79, 2: "Nichên ûzwendich man nis och plichtich in deme dorphe zu antwordene nâch irme sunderlîcheme dorphrechte, mêr nâch gemeyneme lantrechte, . . ."

5. On this, see chap. ii, pp. 64 f. Another problem is presented by the question of whether *Sachsenspiegel* law in general, in so far as it was not Jewry-law in particular, was applicable to Jews. This problem will be touched in discussing the extent as to subject matter of the validity of Jewry-law, in Sec. III of this chapter. There, too, is the place for considering the passage in the *Gloss* on Ssp., III, 7, 1, dealing with this question.

6. Guido Kisch, *Sachsenspiegel and Bible* (Notre Dame, Ind., 1941), pp. 117–25; Fehr, *ZRG*, XXXVII (1916), 161–64, 217–21; cf. also Alfred Hübner, *Vorstudien zur Ausgabe des Buches der Könige* (Berlin, 1932), pp. 115–26.

7. This custom has, however, no foundation in Jewish religious law. It is traced back to Rabbenu Gershom of Mainz (960–1028) (cf. Simon Bernfeld, "Apostasie," *Encyclopaedia Judaica*, II, 1218 f.).

8. Cf. Emil Friedberg, *Lehrbuch des katholischen und evangelischen Kirchenrechts* (5th ed.; Leipzig, 1903), pp. 260 f., 303; Albert M. Koeniger, *Katholisches Kirchenrecht* (Freiburg i.Br., 1926), pp. 113 ff., 283, 285 ff.

9. For an extensive discussion of the punishment of heresy according to the *Sachsenspiegel* and other lawbooks see below, pp. 203 f.

10. Cf. *Annales S. Disibodi* (1097): "Judeis de preterito anno vel coacte baptizatis, legem et ritus judaizandi concedit." Aronius, *Regesten zur Geschichte der Juden* (Berlin, 1887–1902), Nos. 203–4 (1097–1098), pp. 93 f.; Otto Stobbe, *Die Juden in Deutschland während des Mittelalters* (Braunschweig, 1866), pp. 166, 267 f.; Moritz Güdemann, *Geschichte des Erziehungswesens und der Kultur der Juden in Frankreich und Deutschland* (*X.–XIV. Jahrhundert*) (Vienna, 1880), p. 140.

11. Hugelmann, *Historisches Jahrbuch der Görresgesellschaft*, XLVIII (1928), 570 f.: "Nun ergibt sich aber die weitere Frage, unter welchen Voraussetzungen die Besonderheiten des Judenrechts anzuwenden sind; mit anderen Worten, wer als Jude gilt. . . . Dass sich nur der im Reiche

Sasse upphe den Wend." The addition in brackets corresponds with the original wording in Ssp., III, 70, 2; it is found in manuscripts later than 1270.

Ssp., II, 12, 3 reads: "Bûten kuninges banne mût iewelk man uber den anderen urtêl vinden unde urtêl schelden, der vulcomen is an sîme rechte, um alsô getâne sache, die man âne koninges ban richten mach."

21. *Gloss* on Ssp., III, 70, 1. Cf. also Karl G. Hugelmann, "Die Rechtsstellung der Wenden im deutschen Mittelalter," *ZRG*, LVIII (1938), 250 ff.

22. On the problem of "Jews as judges in non-Jewish courts" see below, pp. 243 f.

23. See the illustrations reproduced from the Heidelberg and Dresden picture manuscripts in Guido Kisch, *Jewry-Law in Medieval Germany: Laws and Court Decisions Concerning Jews* (New York, 1949), p. 50. Cf. Karl von Amira, *Die Dresdener Bilderhandschrift des Sachsenspiegels*, II (Leipzig, 1925–26), Part II, 95; E. Freiherr von Künssberg, *Der Sachsenspiegel: Bilder aus der Heidelberger Handschrift* (Leipzig, 1935), picture No. 13, and p. 19. On the illuminated manuscripts of the *Sachsenspiegel* in general see above, p. 36; cf. Rudolf Kötzschke, "Die Heimat der mitteldeutschen Bilderhandschriften des Sachsenspiegels," *Berichte über die Verhandlungen der Sächsischen Akademie der Wissenschaften, phil.-hist. Klasse*, Vol. XCV, No. 2 (Leipzig, 1943).

24. See the reproduction in G. Kisch, *Jewry-Law in Medieval Germany*, p. 90. In the Heidelberg manuscript the figure of the Jew is missing. On the same subject see also below, pp. 112 f.

25. Ssp. II, 71, 3: "Wâphen mût men wol vûren, swenne men deme gerûchte volget; deme sollen durch recht volgen alle die zu iren jâren comen sîn, alse verre daz se swert vûren mugen, is ne neme ine echt nôt, sunder paphen unde wîph unde kerkenêre unde herden."

26. This is confirmed by many court decisions which are to be discussed in Part III; cf., e.g., Stendal UB. XXVII, 1, in confirmation of the applicability of Ssp., III, 45, 1, to Jews (below, p. 182); LSchSprS., No. 500 (below, p. 209).

27. An argument following the train of thought pursued in the preceding discussion was, interestingly enough, employed in an actual law case, probably dating back to the thirteenth century and related in the *Brünner Schöffenbuch* (of about 1353) (Emil Franz Rössler, *Die Stadtrechte von Brünn aus dem XIII. und XIV. Jahrhundert* [Prague, 1852], No. 432, p. 203). A Jew had been convicted of theft and put to death by the municipal court of Brünn. The governor of Moravia, thereupon, protested to the jurors: "quod judaeum, qui fuisset servus camerae domini

Marchionis, contra justitiam suspendissent." In defense of their legal decision and its subsequent execution, the jurors pointed out that a law not exempting anyone must be applicable to everybody, including Jews. The principle set forth here found recognition, although it was questionable in this specific case, viewed in the light of the concept of *servitudo camerae*. The pertinent passage reads:

"Ad quod jurati responderunt, quia moti jure civitatis judaeum patibulo tradidissent. Scribitur enim in privilegio jurium civitatis sic: 'Quicumque in alio furto deprehensus fuerit, quod sexaginta denarios valet, suspendium patiatur, et infra.' Et quia nullus fur excipitur a poena suspendii in verbis praescriptis, ideo jurati plenum jus habent, omnem furem, et maxime cum furto captum vel de furto confessum, cum in dicto privilegio auctoritate regia confirmato hoc ipsis non sit prohibitum, suspendendi. In hoc enim nomine infinito 'quicumque' omnis fur includitur, et *nullus* fur excipitur. In qua juratorum responsione ipse contentatus nullam de judaei suspensione fecit ulterius mentionem."

28. Thus one cannot read anything else into the *Sachsenspiegel* without leaving the solid ground of the textual basis of the lawbook. This is done, however, by Hugelmann's assertion in *Historisches Jahrbuch*, XLVIII (1928), 580, that the limitation to Jewish-Christian relations "offers further proof that the memory of the Jews as aliens in the empire had not yet disappeared." Nor is his statement accurate "that all the lawbooks regulate, like the *Sachsenspiegel*, only the relations of Jews and Christians to one another." On this see below, pp. 99 f. Nor is it proper to derive the conclusion, as Hugelmann does on p. 570, that "the Jews were not regarded as a group parallel to the German national tribes nor placed in a legal position on the same basis with them." Such trains of thought were quite foreign to Eike von Repgow. Cf. also above, pp. 77 f.

29. See *Gloss* to the *Textus Prologi.*

30. Cf. Karl Schilling, *Das objektive Recht in der Sachsenspiegelglosse* ("Freiburger Rechtsgeschichtliche Abhandlungen," Vol. II [Berlin, 1931]), p. 56; cf. G. Kisch, *ZRG*, LII (1932), 383–88.

31. *Gloss* Ssp., III, 7, 1 (ed. Augsburg, 1516): ". . . unde schalt weten dat yoden wat sunderlikes rechtes hebben wan cristen lüde in twelverleie saken." Zobel's ed. (Leipzig, 1560): ". . . das man dabey mercken soll, das an den jüden etwas sonderlichs rechtens ist, und dasselbige stehet fürnemlich in zwölf stücken."

32. This is not the only instance of this kind found in Buch's *Gloss* (cf. Schilling, *op. cit.*, pp. 51, 54; Kisch, *ZRG*, LII [1932], 386).

33. *Cod. Just.* i. 5. 1: "Imp. Constantinus A. ad Dracilianum. Privile-

gia, quae contemplatione religionis indulta sunt, catholicae tantum legis observatoribus prodesse oportet. Haereticos non solum his privilegiis alienos esse volumus, sed et diversis muneribus constringi et subici.''

34. *Gloss* to Ssp., III, 7, 1, under No. 12.

35. *Gloss* to Ssp., I, 30: ''. . . id privilegium is gegeven den lande unde nicht den lüden.''

36. Ssp., III, 33, 5: ''Der koning sol ouch richten um eigen nicht nâ des mannes rechte, wan nâ des landes, [dâ iz inne liget].'' The translation of the text of the *Gloss* to III, 33, 5 follows Zobel's edition (Leipzig, 1560). In the Augsburg 1516 edition the passage reads: ''Wen dy koningk het so den Sassen or recht gegeven dat ein ichlick het ymme lande tu Sassen des landes recht, unde nicht syn angeboren recht, he sy van wanne he sy, *supra, libro I, arti. XXX.* Wan dat privilegium is gegeven deme lande van deme ryke, unde nicht den lüden, dy do leveden. Wan dat privilegium, dat den lüden gegeven wert, dat vorgeit met den lüden, *ut [Decretum Gratiani],* VII, qu. 1, c. *petisti.* Unde dar umme dat yt deme lande gegeven is, dar umme blivet yt ewichliken, *ut [Decr. Grat.],* XVI, qu. 1, c. *hinc est.* . . .''

This argumentation was adopted in Reg. jur., J 165, and Bocksd. Rem., 5, 7. Cf. also above, n. 2; Schilling, *op. cit.,* p. 67.

37. See also below, pp. 357 ff.

CHAPTER FOUR

1. For a detailed discussion see pp. 153 ff.

2. For a detailed discussion see pp. 109 f. In comparing the Jewry privileges of 1090 with the *Sachsenspiegel's* Jewry-law only one vague, yet possible, similarity suggested itself: Worms privilege, art. 2 (Geiger's *ZGJD,* I [1887], 138): ''Si quis vero contra hoc edictum nostrum eos in aliquo inquietare temptaverit, in graciam nostram reus sit''; cf. Ssp. Ldr., III, 7, 3: ''Sleit ouch die kersten man eynen joden, men richtet uber ine durch des kuninges vrede, den her an ym gebrochen hât.''

3. Its origin in old imperial privilege law has already been recognized by K. F. Eichhorn, *Deutsche Staats- und Rechtsgeschichte,* II (5th ed.; Göttingen, 1843), p. 613, n. *f:* ''Dies Recht ist ohnstreitig aus dem Privilegium irgend eines deutschen Königs herzuleiten.'' For a detailed discussion see pp. 212 ff.

4. So Hans Fehr, ''Die Staatsauffassung Eikes von Repgau,'' *ZRG,* XXXVII (1916), 132 f.

5. Cf. Hans Fehr, *Schweizerischer und deutscher Volksgeist in der Rechtsent-*

wicklung ("Die Schweiz im deutschen Geistesleben," Vol. XLIV [Frauenfeld-Leipzig, 1926]), p. 74.

6. See above, chap. ii, n. 11.

7. For a detailed discussion see Guido Kisch, *Die Kulmer Handfeste, rechtshistorische und textkritische Untersuchungen* ("Deutschrechtliche Forschungen," ed. G. Kisch, Vol. I [Stuttgart, 1931]), pp. 40–47.

8. The text of art. 6 of the charters for Speyer and Worms is reproduced below, chap. ix, n. 14.

9. Cf. pp. 215 ff.

10. So by Heinrich Gottfried Gengler, *Des Schwabenspiegels Landrechtsbuch* (2d ed.; Erlangen, 1875), p. 176, n. 82; and Hugelmann, *Historisches Jahrbuch*, XLVIII (1928), 573.

11. On this prerogative of the *Reichserzkanzler*, cf. Stobbe, *Die Juden in Deutschland während des Mittelalters* (Braunschweig, 1866), p. 46; Eugen Nübling, *Die Judengemeinden des Mittelalters, insbesondere die Judengemeinde der Reichsstadt Ulm* (Ulm, 1896), p. 26; also Georgius Wilhelmus Hoscher, *Dissertatio historico-juridica de statu judaeorum hodierno in Germania* (Mainz, 1764), pp. 12 f.

12. Cf. pp. 193 f.

13. This is quite clear from the text. A corresponding interpretation can also be derived from the more detailed article 120 (8) in King Venceslas II's charter for the Jews in Moravia, a confirmation (about 1283–1305) of King Přemysl Otakar II's Jewry privilege of 1268, which had been used by the author of the Meissen lawbook. Its text reads:

"Ist daz die juden under in selben ein chrieg oder ein urleug machent oder ein gevecht, da schol sich der statrichter nichtes nicht um an nemen, noch im czu recht an czien, sunder dem chunich oder dem herczogen oder marchrawen oder dem hauptmanne oder dem chamerer dez reiches wehalten; der ainer schol iz richten, und der schuldick czeucht sich an den chunich oder herczogen, daz wiert den selben czu gerichte wehalten."

See E. F. Rössler, *Die Stadtrechte von Brünn aus dem XIII. und XIV. Jahrhundert* (Prague, 1852), p. 369; Bertold Bretholz, *Quellen zur Geschichte der Juden in Mähren vom XI. bis zum XV. Jahrhundert (1067–1411)* (Prague, 1935), p. 11, No. 16; cf. also Stobbe, *op. cit.*, p. 145; E. Forchhammer, "Beiträge zur Geschichte der deutschen Juden mit besonderer Beziehung auf Magdeburg und die benachbarte Gegend," *Geschichtsblätter für Stadt und Land Magdeburg*, XLVI (1911), 378 and n. 368.

14. On the textual transmission of this passage see p. 195.

15. This obvious consideration eluded even Stobbe, *op. cit.*, p. 141, who regarded MRb., III, 17, 2 as referring to Jewish autonomous courts

and to the application of Jewish law. Hugelmann (*op. cit.*, p. 580) not only accepted this erroneous interpretation but extended it also to MRb., III, 17, 30, which does not make sense at all in view of the text (cf. above, n. 13). Forchhammer (*op. cit.*, p. 377 and n. 363), in contrast to the aforementioned authors, seems to have understood MRb., III, 17, 2 correctly.

16. So MRb., III, 17, 4; cf. Purgoldts Rb., VIII, 88: ". . . he forfeits rights and privileges granted the Jews by emperors, kings and also by princes, and thus becomes rightless." Cf. also Johannes G. Ullmann, *Das Strafrecht der Städte der Mark Meissen . . . während des Mittelalters* ("Leipziger rechtswissenschaftliche Studien," Heft 34 [Leipzig, 1928]), p. 80.

17. Guido Kisch, "Relations between Jewish and Christian Courts in the Middle Ages," *Louis Ginzberg Jubilee Volume* (New York, 1945), pp. 201–25, esp. pp. 208–13.

18. For an extensive discussion of this see G. Kisch, *Sachsenspiegel ana Bible* (Notre Dame, Ind., 1941), pp. 117 ff., esp. pp. 140 f., 156 ff.

19. G. Kisch, "A Fourteenth-Century Jewry Oath of South Germany," *Speculum*, XV (1940), 331 f.; also G. Kisch, "Studien zur Geschichte des Judeneides im Mittelalter," *Hebrew Union College Annual*, XIV (1939), 434 ff. Moreover, that this was merely the logical, specific application to the Jews of a general principle of medieval law appears clearly from the following decision of the Jury Court of Brünn:

"Homo nobilis, et militaris, et clericus ordinatus, quamvis respondeant pro debitis in judicio civili, tamen, si jurare debent et petunt, ad judices proprios puta nobiles ad provincialem, et ordinatus ad canonicum, quod coram eis jurent, more solito remittantur" (*Brünner Schöffenbuch*, ed. Rössler, No. 452, p. 211).

Obviously, there is no basis for Hugelmann's assumption (*op. cit.*, pp. 571, 579) that "in individual cases the application of national-Jewish law was permitted Jews even in their relations with non-Jews"; on the so-called *jüdisches Hehlerrecht*, to which he refers in particular, see pp. 211 ff. Long before, Andreas Heusler (*Institutionen des deutschen Privatrechts*, I [Leipzig, 1885], 152) refused to consent to such an interpretation.

20. *Gloss* on *Sachsenspiegel*, III, 7, 1 (ed. Augsburg, 1516), fol. 131r; ed. Zobel (Leipzig, 1560), fol. 332v; the addition in Zobel's edition is put in brackets. For a detailed discussion on this passage see p. 282 and chap. x, n. 169.

21. For details on the Jewry oath of the medieval lawbooks see pp. 277 ff.

22. See p. 282.

23. Aronius, *Regesten zur Geschichte der Juden* (Berlin, 1887–1902), No. 168, p. 70: "Deinde sicut tribunus urbis inter cives, ita archisynagogus suus omnem judicet querimoniam, que contigerit inter eos vel adversus eos. At si quam forte determinare non potuerit, ascendat causa ante episcopum civitatis vel ejus camerarium" (cf. Stobbe, *op. cit.*, pp. 143 f.; Scherer, *Die Rechtsverhältnisse der Juden in den deutsch-österreichischen Ländern* [Leipzig, 1901], pp. 251, 254 ff.).

24. Aronius, *op. cit.*, No. 170 (Speyer), p. 73, par. 14: "Quod si Judei litem inter se aut causam habuerint discernendam, a suis paribus et non aliis convincantur et judicentur. Et si aliquis eorum perfidus rei alicujus inter eos geste occultare voluerit veritatem, ab eo, qui ex parte episcopi preest synagoge, juxta legem suam cogatur, ut de eo quod queritur verum fateatur."
Similarly, *ibid.*, No. 171 (Worms), p. 76, par. 14.

25. Aronius, *op. cit.*, No. 171 (Worms), p. 76, par. 14: "Si autem de magna causa inculpati fuerint, inducias ad imperatorem habeant, si voluerint."

26. MRb., III, 17, 30 and 2; cf. above, p. 99.

27. MRb., III, 17, 41.

28. *Brünner Schöffenbuch*, No. 14, ed. E. F. Rössler, *Die Stadtrechte von Brünn aus dem XIII. und XIV. Jahrhundert* (Prague, 1852), p. 10; Brünn SchB., No. 441, p. 207 (below, chap. x, n. 6).

29. Cf. Glogau Rb. 478; Stobbe, *op. cit.*, pp. 255 f., n. 133; also Hugo Boehlau, *Die Blume von Magdeburg* (Weimar, 1868), II, 2, 45. Similarly, Reg. jur., J 129: "As to Jews, whoever wants to try them, shall try them before their own judge"; Bocksd. Rem., 9: "*Jude:* Where shall one sue a Jew: say, before his judge." The passage in Wb., 116, 1 was given too narrow a meaning by Hugelmann, *op. cit.*, p. 573.

30. Rem. RW., 17: "*Jude:* Jews shall be tried before their judge, and a Jew shall defend himself under him, in his synagogue." The author of this *Remissorium*, Caspar Popplaw of Breslau, however, expressed his own doubt in this rule by adding *in margine:* "*dubito*" (cf. p. 174).

31. MRb., III, 17, 4 (cf. above, p. 99).

32. MRb., III, 17, 3; cf. Purgoldts Rb., VIII, 87. Hugelmann (*op. cit.*, p. 575) describes this sanction inaccurately in speaking only of "Verlust seiner Privilegien."

33. MRb., III, 17, 40 (cf. Stobbe, *op. cit.*, p. 255, n. 132a).

34. Cf. also G. Kisch, "Relations between Jewish and Christian Courts in the Middle Ages," p. 212, n. 31.

35. Manuscript G 5, 28, of the Stadtarchiv of Breslau, Germany, p. 91

(cf. also 64) (*anno* 1431): "Mosshe (de Brega) non debeat habere conductum, nisi prius fuerit absolutus a banno judaico, quo dicitur esse innodatus." Cf. Theodor Goerlitz, "Die Haftung des Bürgers und Einwohners für Schulden der Stadt und ihrer Bewohner nach Magdeburger Recht," *ZRG*, LVI (1936), 159.

36. *Brünner Schöffenbuch*, ed. Rössler, No. 306, pp. 139 f.; for its discussion see G. Kisch, "Relations between Jewish and Christian Courts in the Middle Ages," p. 213.

37. For a detailed discussion see G. Kisch, *ibid.*, pp. 215 ff.

CHAPTER FIVE

1. G. Kisch, "The Jewry-Law of the *Sachsenspiegel*," in *Occident and Orient: Gaster Anniversary Volume* (London, 1936), pp. 307–11, with bibliography; Hans Fehr, "Das Waffenrecht der Bauern im Mittelalter," *ZRG*, XXXV (1914), 168 f.; Fehr, "Die Staatsauffassung Eikes von Repgau," *ibid.*, XXXVII (1916), 144–46; Richard Schröder and Eberhard Frh. von Künssberg, *Lehrbuch der deutschen Rechtsgeschichte* (7th ed.; Berlin, 1932), pp. 712–18, with bibliography; Wolfgang Schnelbögl, *Die innere Entwicklung der bayerischen Landfrieden des 13. Jahrhunderts* (Heidelberg, 1932), pp. 42 f., 50; Rudolf His, *Das Strafrecht des deutschen Mittelalters*, I (Leipzig, 1920), 4, n. 6; 6 ff., 17 f., 238 ff.

2. James Parkes, *The Jew in the Medieval Community* (London, 1938), p. 106; cf. the wording of the introductory clause in Frederick I's *privilegium* of 1182 to the Jews of Regensburg, which probably originated from an earlier charter by Henry IV, in Julius Aronius, *Regesten zur Geschichte der Juden im fränkischen und deutschen Reiche bis zum Jahre 1273* (Berlin, 1887–1902), No. 314*a*, p. 139: ". . . officium est imperatoriae majestatis nostrae et juris equitas atque rationis hortatio, ut unicuique fidelium nostrorum, non solum christianae religionis cultoribus, verum etiam a fide nostra discolis ritu paternae traditionis suae viventibus, quod suum est, equitatis examine conservemus et consuetudinibus eorum perseverantiam et tam personis eorum quam rebus pacem provideamus."

3. *MG, Constitutiones*, I, 125, No. 74; Karl Zeumer, *Quellensammlung zur Geschichte der deutschen Reichsverfassung in Mittelalter und Neuzeit*, I (2d ed.; Tübingen, 1913), 2, No. 3; Aronius, *op. cit.*, No. 210.

4. *MG, Constitutiones*, I, 614, No. 430; Zeumer, *op. cit.*, I, 3, No. 4. The Jews are not mentioned; Schnelbögl (*op. cit.*, p. 43), however, erroneously assumes that they are included.

5. *MG, Constitutiones*, I, 381, No. 277; Zeumer, *op. cit.*, I, 20, No. 16; not in Aronius; Täubler, *Mitteilungen des Gesamtarchivs der deutschen*

Juden, IV (1914), 45. The Third Lateran Council of 1179, c. 22 (*Corpus juris canonici*, c. 2, X, 1, 34), "renewed" the regulation that "presbyteri, monachi, conversi, peregrini, mercatores, rustici, euntes et redeuntes, et in agricultura existentes, et animalia, quibus arant et quae semina portant ad agrum, congrua securitate laetentur" (cf. Eduard Eichmann, "Die Stellung Eikes von Repgau zu Kirche und Kurie," *Historisches Jahrbuch der Görresgesellschaft*, XXXVIII [1917], 751).

6. *MG, Constitutiones*, II, 394, No. 280, and 399, No. 284; Zeumer, *op. cit.*, I, 46, No. 42, and 48, No. 43; cf. Aronius, *op. cit.*, No. 422, p. 428; Karl August Eckhardt, "Rechtsbücherstudien. II. Die Entstehungszeit des Sachsenspiegels und der Sächsischen Weltchronik," *Abhandlungen der Gesellschaft der Wissenschaften zu Göttingen, phil.-hist. Klasse*, N.F., XXIII, No. 2 (Berlin, 1931), 56–71.

7. The problems of legal history involved here are inadequately treated by Herbert Fischer, *Die verfassungsrechtliche Stellung der Juden in den deutschen Städten während des dreizehnten Jahrhunderts* (Breslau, 1931), pp. 1–3; Karl Gottfried Hugelmann, "Studien zum Recht der Nationalitäten im deutschen Mittelalter," *Historisches Jahrbuch der Görresgesellschaft*, XLVIII (1928), 566 f.; Ismar Elbogen, *Germania Judaica*, pp. xxii f. Nevertheless, these presentations offer useful vistas from a general historical point of view. The only noteworthy discussion with regard to legal history is found in Ferdinand Frensdorff, "Beiträge zur Geschichte und Erklärung der deutschen Rechtsbücher. II," *Nachrichten der K. Gesellschaft der Wissenschaften zu Göttingen*, 1894, pp. 30–35. For Spain, where, up to the thirteenth century, the Jews were also included in the land-peace legislation of Catalonia and Aragon, the problems still await adequate treatment; the pertinent laws are mentioned in Eugen Wohlhaupter, *Studien zur Rechtsgeschichte der Gottes- und Landfrieden in Spanien* (Heidelberg, 1933), pp. 104, 135.

8. Cf. Hans Fehr, "Das Waffenrecht der Bauern im Mittelalter," *ZRG*, XXXV (1914), 111–211; also Eichmann, *op. cit.*, pp. 746–57; Schnelbögl, *op. cit.*, pp. 95–109; and Frensdorff's essay cited in n. 7.

9. See above, pp. 89 ff.

10. For instances see Fehr, "Das Waffenrecht der Bauern im Mittelalter," p. 153. As to the duty of the Jews to take part in the *Gerichtsfolge* (Ssp., II, 71, 3) see above, pp. 89 ff.

11. A. Neubauer and M. Stern, *Hebräische Berichte über die Judenverfolgungen während der Kreuzzüge* (Berlin, 1892), pp. 179 and 94; p. 182: ". . . the one fell upon his sword and died, the other slaughtered himself with his sword or knife"; cf. also I. Elbogen, "Hebräische Quellen zur Frühgeschichte der Juden in Deutschland," *ZGJD*, I (1929), 41.

12. Neubauer and Stern, *op. cit.*, pp. 137 f.; cf. Samuel Steinherz, "Kreuzfahrer und Juden in Prag 1096," *JGJC*, I (1929), 16 ff.; *Germania Judaica*, pp. 508–12.

13. *Or Zarua*, II (ed. Žitomir, 1862), fol. 40b, No. 13; this passage is very often quoted in the literature, but its important last sentence is always omitted. Fischer (*op. cit.*, p. 104, n. 1) assumes that the underlying event occurred in the twenties or thirties of the thirteenth century.

14. Aronius, *op. cit.*, No. 358a; H. J. Zimmels, *Beiträge zur Geschichte der Juden in Deutschland im 13. Jahrhundert insbesondere auf Grund der Gutachten des R. Meir Rothenburg* (Vienna, 1926), pp. 10 and 98, n. 177; Fischer, *op. cit.*, pp. 101 ff., 188 ff. For another reference to Jews engaged in actual battle see David M. Shohet, *The Jewish Court in the Middle Ages* (New York, 1931), p. 17, n. 5; cf. also Irving A. Agus, *Rabbi Meir of Rothenburg: His Life and His Works as Sources for the Religious, Legal, and Social History of the Jews of Germany in the Thirteenth Century*, I (Philadelphia, 1947), 56, n. 5.

15. That this was by no means a matter of course becomes clear from a comparison of the medieval with the Jewish situation in Germany on the tenth of November, 1938. Then, only a few days before hundreds of synagogues were burned throughout German lands and the property of the Jews pillaged, nor their lives spared, all weapons found in the possession of Jews were taken from them. Later, an "Ordinance forbidding Jews to own arms" (carrying a penalty up to five years' imprisonment) was published in the *Reichsgesetzblatt* of 1938 (I, 1573) under the date of November 11. This regulation, however, is not mentioned in the chapter concerning the Jews in Johannes Heckel, *Wehrverfassung und Wehrrecht des Grossdeutschen Reiches*, I (Hamburg, 1939), 131–34.

16. J. Kahan, "Or Sarua als Geschichtsquelle," *JGJC*, IX (1938), 53, and 86, n. 72. The Jews' right to trade in arms was also recognized under general (non-Jewish) law, as is clear from a decision of the jury-court of Brünn, Moravia, rendered to the town of (Hungarian) Hradisch in 1368 (Bertold Bretholz, *Quellen zur Geschichte der Juden in Mähren vom XI. bis zum XV. Jahrhundert* [*1067–1411*] [Prague, 1935], No. 204. 4, p. 80). Purgoldt's *Rechtsbuch* is the only lawbook that contains a prohibition against Jews' accepting arms as pledges for loans (VIII, 91): "Guns, harness, foils, cross-bows, rifles, and other armor serve for the protection of the population in the cities: therefore Jews shall not accept them as pledges for loans."

In Wolfram von Eschenbach's (*ca.* 1170–1220 or 1237) poetical work, *Willehalm*, Nos. 195, l. 12—197, l. 3, Princess Irmenschart advises Ren-

newart and the army to secure their arms equipment from a Jew of Nar-
bonne; see Karl Lachmann, *Wolfram von Eschenbach* (6th ed.; Berlin and
Leipzig, 1926), No. 195, ll. 12–15:

> "Einen juden von Narbôn
> liez dâ diu fürstinne Irmenschart:
> der solte gein der hervart
> bereiten des marcgrâven diet."

No. 196, ll. 8–11:

> "daz galt im gar des juden hant
> durch des marcgrâven êre.
> er bôt im dennoch mêre,
> harnasch, ors und lanzen starc."

No. 197, ll. 1–3:

> "Sus wart bereitet Rennewart
> und manic anderr gein der vart.
> allez von des juden hant."

As late as 1495 the Portuguese government conferred special privileges
upon Jewish armorers from Spain (cf. Fritz Baer, "Probleme der jüdisch-
spanischen Geschichte," *Korrespondenzblatt der Akademie für die Wissenschaft des Judentums*, VI [Berlin, 1925], 9).

17. Zimmels, *op. cit.*, pp. 57 and 113, n. 383; cf. also below, p. 219.
18. *MG, Constitutiones*, I, 195 ff., No. 140; Zeumer, *op. cit.*, I, 8, No.
9, art. 12: "Si quis rusticus arma vel lanceam portaverit vel gladium,
judex, in cujus potestate repertus fuerit, vel arma tollat vel viginti
solidos pro ipsis a rustico accipiat."
19. *MG, loc. cit.*, and Zeumer, *op. cit.*, art. 13: "Mercator negotiandi
causa provinciam transiens gladium suum sue selle alliget vel super
vehiculum suum ponat, ne unquam laedat innocentem, sed ut a praedone
se defendat."
20. Zeumer, *op. cit.*, I, 90, No. 71, art. 2 (Aronius, *op. cit.*, No. 602):
"Item constituimus, quod nulli domino, paci resistenti et nobis con-
juratis . . . arma vel aliqua subsidia exhibeantur, sive a christianis sive
a judeis."
21. Heinrich Graetz, *Geschichte der Juden*, VI (4th ed.; Leipzig, n.d.),
230; Moritz Güdemann, *Geschichte des Erziehungswesens und der Kultur der
abendländischen Juden*, I (Vienna, 1880), 137 f.; III (1888), 164 f.;
A. Berliner, *Aus dem Leben der deutschen Juden im Mittelalter* (Berlin,
1900), pp. 25 ff., with the older bibliography, pp. 130 f.; Israel Abrahams, *Jewish Life in the Middle Ages* (London, 1896), pp. 377 ff.; George
Caro, *Sozial- und Wirtschaftsgeschichte der Juden im Mittelalter und der*

Neuzeit, I (Leipzig, 1908), 95, 177 f.; II (1920), 185 f.; Emanuel Forchhammer, "Beiträge zur Geschichte der deutschen Juden mit besonderer Beziehung auf Magdeburg und die benachbarte Gegend," *Geschichtsblätter für Stadt und Land Magdeburg*, XLVI (1911), 177 f.; Zimmels, *op. cit.*, pp. 36 f., 97 f.; Fischer, *op. cit.*, pp. 98–106; Elbogen, *Germania Judaica*, p. xxxiv; Parkes, *op. cit.*, pp. 187, 260 f. Cf. also M. Ginsburger, "Les Juifs et l'art militaire au moyen âge," *Revue des études juives*, LXXXVIII (1929), 156–66; Isidor Fischer, " 'Streitbare' Juden im Mittelalter," *Festschrift Armand Kaminka zum siebzigsten Geburtstage* (Vienna, 1937), pp. 33–37.

Only one single impressive document may be quoted here, not referred to elsewhere as yet. It is King Alphonso XI's (of Castile) letter to Pope Clement VI of July 25, 1342, asking in behalf of the Jews of Seville for permission to use their lately erected synagogue. The following reason is advanced: ". . . judei sunt summe necessarii, quia contribuunt in necessitatibus civitatis necnon aliquotiens exeunt una cum christianis adversus Saracenos et se exponere morti non formidant" (Fritz Baer, *Die Juden im christlichen Spanien*, I, Part 2 [Berlin, 1936], 163, No. 167; cf. 333, No. 320 [*anno* 1466]).

22. Lachmann, *Wolfram von Eschenbach*, No. 180, ll. 23–27:

> "nu lât se alle juden sîn,
> die durh den trûregen bruoder mîn
> iwer lant ze werne sint verlorn:
> wort ie triwe an iu geborn,
> ir sult durch triwe klagen sie."

Cf. Siegfried Stein, *Die Ungläubigen in der mittelhochdeutschen Literatur von 1050 bis 1250* (Ph.D. thesis, Heidelberg; Heidelberg, 1933), p. 75; cf. also Gertrud Goetz, *Die Idee der sozialen Nothilfe in der Dichtung Wolframs von Eschenbach* (Ph.D. thesis, Freiburg i.Br.; Schramberg, 1936), pp. 27, 39 ff., and *passim*.

23. Cf. Richard Koebner, *Die Anfänge des Gemeinwesens der Stadt Köln* (Bonn, 1922), pp. 446 f.; Fischer, *op. cit.*, pp. 106, 148.

24. Cf., e.g., charter of 1285 for the city of Schweidnitz, Silesia, in G. A. Tzschoppe and G. A. Stenzel, *Urkundensammlung zur Geschichte des Ursprungs der Städte . . . in Schlesien und der Oberlausitz* (Hamburg, 1832), No. 78, p. 403: "Judei vero de suis hereditatibus cum civitate nulla servitia facere debent seu solutiones, nisi ad vigilias et ad muros atque ad alias firmitudines civitatis."

25. *Regensburger Urkundenbuch*, Vol. I ("Monumenta Boica," Vol. LIII, N.S. Vol. VII [1912]), No. 78; Siegmar Bromberger, *Die Juden in Regensburg bis zur Mitte des 14. Jahrhunderts* (Ph.D. thesis, Berlin Univer-

sity; Berlin, 1934), p. 35; Fischer, *op. cit.*, pp. 105, 99, n. 3. Cf. also Berthold Altmann, "Studies in Medieval German Jewish History," *Proceedings*, X (1940), 38 f.

26. This was already the prevailing opinion in the older literature dealing with this problem, such as Aronius, *op. cit.*, No. 185, p. 87; No. 358*a;* Caro, *op. cit.*, I, 177 f. Siegmund Keller's contradictory remarks in *Vierteljahrschrift für Sozial- und Wirtschaftsgeschichte*, X (1912), 188, were refuted by S. Steinherz, *JGJC*, I (1929), 17 f. Fischer (*op. cit.*, pp. 98–106) collected and discussed the material available in non-Jewish sources on the military service of the Jews in German cities during the thirteenth century. The outcome is the following statement: "Military service, that is, the threefold liability to entrenchment work, guard duty, and combat in war, does not *de jure* apply to the Jews dwelling in cities, for, according to the imperial law governing them, they have discharged all their obligations to the authorities by their pecuniary contributions." This is contrary to the sources quoted by Fischer and to his own conclusion that the participation of the Jews in defense of the cities resulted from their civic duties and by no means from a specifically Jewish duty. It was Fischer's disregard of the historical development that led to his mistaken conception. He did not search for the origin of the Jews' obligation to take up arms in defense of the cities and did not consider its phases of development. Consequently, he assumed a general influence of the *Kammerknechtschaft* even before this institution was fully developed and effective.

27. Cf. Neubauer and Stern, *op. cit.*, p. 199, *anno* 1171; p. 219, *anno* 1188; cf. also pp. 64, 196, *anno* 1147.

28. So in Hameln, Saxony (Fischer, *op. cit.*, p. 100 and n. 2, *anno* 1320).

29. Aronius, *op. cit.*, No. 168, p. 70; Fischer, *op. cit.*, p. 103 and n. 2.

30. Cf. Adolf Kober, article "Cöln am Rhein," *Germania Judaica*, p. 72: ". . . die Juden besassen wie die Bürger das Waffenrecht"; Koebner, *op. cit.*, p. 447 and n. 3 : "Die spätere Umbildung des 'Bürger'-Rechts der Juden schloss sowohl die Befreiung von Kriegsdiensten wie die von bürgerlichen Steuern ein"; Fischer, *op. cit.*, pp. 100 f. The name of a fortress tower in Cologne, *propugnaculum Judeorum* or *Judenwichhaus*, was a reminder of the Jews' duty of military service (A. Kober, *Cologne* [Philadelphia, 1940], p. 60). As to Hameln see above, n. 28.

31. Cronica S. Petri Erfordensis Moderna, *MG, Scriptores*, XXX, 1, 442, 22 ff.: "Tantum ergo periculum Erphordenses experti, postea muros suos tucius munierunt, tam christianos quam judeos in turribus et propugnaculis collocantes." Cf. Forchhammer, *op. cit.*, p. 178; Erich

Wiemann, "Beiträge zur Erfurter Ratsverwaltung des Mittelalters," *Mitteilungen des Vereins für die Geschichte und Altertumskunde von Erfurt*, LI (Erfurt, 1937), 112; Fischer, *op. cit.*, p. 105, n. 1. Wiemann's argument that, even from the very beginning, full military service was required of the Jews in cases of emergency only, lacks point; for the medieval cities had no body of professional soldiers at their command but generally called their inhabitants to arms only when an emergency arose.

32. Schwsp. L, 260; G 214, 5 (see p. 267). Confirmation is found in an early medieval Hebrew source. Judicial combat between a Jew and a Christian (*milḥama*) is mentioned in a *Responsum* of Rabbenu Gershom (960–1028) (cf. Joel Müller, *Teshubot Ḥaḥme Zarfat ve-Lotair, Réponses faites par de célèbres rabins français et lorrains du XI. et XII. siècle* [Vienna, 1881], pp. 54 ff.; cf. also Sali Levi, "Von der Eigenart der klassischen Handhabung des jüdischen Religionsgesetzes im Rheingebiet," *Minḥat Todah, Max Dienemann zum 60. Geburtstag gewidmet vom Vorstand der israelitischen Religionsgemeinde Offenbach am Main* [Frankfort-on-the-Main, 1935], pp. 69, 72).

33. See below, p. 267; cf. also Otto Stobbe, *Die Juden in Deutschland während des Mittelalters* (Braunschweig, 1866), p. 153; Johannes E. Scherer, *Die Rechtsverhältnisse der Juden in den deutsch-österreichischen Ländern* (Leipzig, 1901), pp. 305–13. The conclusions to be drawn from the instances given gain even greater significance in view of the fact that the Middle Ages knew of an exemption from the obligation of judicial combat as a privilege of the merchants (cf. Robert von Keller, *Freiheitsgarantien für Person und Eigentum im Mittelalter* [Heidelberg, 1933], pp. 220–25; Hans Planitz, "Kaufmannsgilde und städtische Eidgenossenschaft in niederfränkischen Städten im 11. und 12. Jahrhundert," *ZRG*, LX [1940], 112 f.).

34. Cf. Güdemann, Berliner, Abrahams, and Forchhammer as cited above, n. 21.

35. It is therefore an evident misconception when some authors consider the Jews as, in principle, incapable of bearing arms (*waffenunfähige Leute*) (so Fehr, *ZRG*, XXXV [1914], 179; and Elbogen, *Geschichte der Juden in Deutschland* [Berlin, 1935], p. 35). It seems worth mention that a status similar to that in Germany apparently prevailed in England up to the middle of the twelfth century. There was no bar against Jews even becoming knights in the feudal meaning. Only in 1181 was it enacted that "no Jew shall keep with him mail or hauberk, but let him sell or give them away, or in some other way remove them from him" (cf. Joseph Jacobs, *The Jews of Angevin England* [London and New York, 1893], pp. 261, 75; Abrahams, *op. cit.*, pp. 377 f.).

36. Cf. Frensdorff, "Beiträge zur Geschichte und Erklärung der deutschen Rechtsbücher. IV," *Nachrichten der K. Gesellschaft der Wissenschaften zu Göttingen*, 1921 (Berlin, 1921), pp. 157 ff.; Fehr, "Das Waffenrecht der Bauern," p. 150; Gerhard Kallen, "Friedrich Barbarossas Verfassungsreform und das Landrecht des *Sachsenspiegels*," *ZRG*, LVIII (1938), 577.

37. See the literature cited above, n. 8; Kisch, "The Jewry-Law of the *Sachsenspiegel*," pp. 307 ff.; Hugelmann, *Historisches Jahrbuch*, XLVIII (1928), 568, 579.

38. Eichmann, *Historisches Jahrbuch*, XXXVIII (1917), 752. Frensdorff (cited above, n. 7), p. 34, considers "die Ungunst oder Verachtung, in der sie stehen" in general as the reason for the prohibition of the Jews from bearing arms and for their inclusion in the king's peace.

39. This word must be inserted here, for the second part of the sentence cannot refer to Jews; for details on this point see Frensdorff, *op. cit.*, II, 9; Eichmann, *op. cit.*, p. 754.

40. Cf. *Leges Edwardi Confessoris* (*ca.* 1130–35): "non est dignus habere pacem qui non diligit observare pacem"; Felix Liebermann, *Die Gesetze der Angelsachsen*, I (Halle a. S., 1903), 650; *Weichbild-Vulgata* (second half of the thirteenth century), ed. W. von Thüngen (Heidelberg, 1837), art. 175: ". . . wen sy [pfaffen und juden] sullen keyn wophen furen, do mit sy des keysers frid moge brechen."

41. As to the interpretation of this regulation see His, *Das Strafrecht des deutschen Mittelalters*, I, 241 f.; cf. also below, pp. 180, 185.

42. *Die Dresdener Bilderhandschrift des Sachsenspiegels*, Vol. II: *Erläuterungen*, Part I (Leipzig, 1925), p. 458; cf. also pp. 75–77 and 66–75.

43. Cf. the pictures pertaining to Ssp., III, 2, Amira, *op. cit.*, I, Pl. 72, No. 5, and, e.g., to II, 68, Amira, *op. cit.*, I, Dresden MS, fol. 35b, Pl. 70, No. 3 (the horse of the *wegefährtige Mann*, i.e., the traveler) with the war steeds pictured in Dresden MS, fol. 10b, Amira, *op. cit.*, I, Pl. 20, No. 2, and Dresden MS, fol. 45a, Amira, *op. cit.*, I, Pl. 89, No. 5; or the picture of the Bamberg rider of about 1237 in Otto Georg von Simson, "The Bamberg Rider," *Review of Religion*, IV (1940), Pl. I, facing p. 270. Amira, *op. cit.*, II, Part I, 75 ff., in his discussion of the difference between the war steed and the ordinary saddle horse in the *Sachsenspiegel* pictures, failed to include the horse of the Jew in Dresden MS, fol. 36b, Pl. 72, No. 5. As to the clerics mentioned in Ssp., III, 2, it seems also that only those *in itinere* are concerned; as to the origins of Ssp., III, 2, in ecclesiastic law see Eichmann, *op. cit.*, pp. 754 ff.

44. Cf. Amira, "Die Handgebärden in den Bilderhandschriften des Sachsenspiegels," *Abhandlungen der Bayerischen Akademie der Wissenschaf-*

ten, I. Klasse, XXIII (Munich, 1905), 206 f.; Amira, *op. cit.*, II, Part I, 458.

45. For more details see Eichmann, *op. cit.*, pp. 752 ff.

46. See above, pp. 89 f.; cf. the somewhat differing regulation in Schwsp., L 253a; G 207, 4.

47. See above, n. 18, and Fehr, *ZRG*, XXXV (1914), 138, n. 6.

48. Cf. above, n. 19.

49. Cf. G. Kisch, *Sachsenspiegel and Bible* (Notre Dame, Ind., 1941), p. 10; Heinrich Mitteis, *Die deutsche Königswahl, ihre Rechtsgrundlagen bis zur Goldenen Bulle* (Baden bei Wien, 1938), pp. 132 ff., 145; H. Mitteis, "Rechtsgeschichte und Machtgeschichte," in *Wirtschaft und Kultur: Festschrift zum 70. Geburtstag von Alfons Dopsch* (Baden bei Wien, 1938), pp. 557 f.

50. Viewed in this light, the difficult passage, *cum servientibus*, of the Speyer privilege (above, p. 117) receives an unforced and plausible interpretation.

51. For interesting information on this point see *Responsum* by Rabbi Meir of Rothenburg in Zimmels, *Beiträge zur Geschichte der Juden in Deutschland im dreizehnten Jahrhundert*, pp. 36, 97, n. 177, English translation in Agus, *Rabbi Meir of Rothenburg*, II, 534 f., No. 578; cf. also *ibid.*, I, 136; Altmann, *Proceedings*, X (1940), 8, 13–15, 36–37, 47–48.

52. See above, p. 117; cf. also Austrian Jewry privilege of 1244, art. 20: ". . . nos judeis contra suspectum pugilem volumus exhibere"; Scherer, *op. cit.*, pp. 182 and 305–11; Aronius, *op. cit.*, No. 547 (with inaccurate translation).

53. (Ed. Augsburg, 1516), p. 125v: "*Unde joden*] Mercke hir ein grot underscheit: wapen vorbydet men hir den presteren und den schulren tu eren, und vorbydet yt den joden thu schanden." Cf. the legal status of the Jews in National Socialist Germany (prior to 1939), in the light of her military legislation (Heckel, *Wehrverfassung und Wehrrecht des Grossdeutschen Reiches*, I [Hamburg, 1939], 131 f.: ". . . The Jews have not the right of military service. Above all, they have not the right to bear arms and, on the other hand, they are not to be entrusted with the honorable duty of serving in the army. Jews are, therefore, completely excluded from active military service. Even voluntary entrance into the army is denied to them. This prohibition is absolute. There is no exception. . . . In times of war the Jewish members of the state are subject to a special [non-military] duty [defense tax]. It arises from the protection which the Reich gives them").

54. A photographic reproduction, as yet unpublished, is in the possession of the author. On the *Sachsenspiegel* manuscript Varia 1 in the

lebende Jude auf sie berufen konnte, ist selbstverständlich; aber innerhalb dieses Rahmens: jeder, der als Jude geboren ist, oder gar jeder, der
von Juden stammt? Damit sind wir beim Kernproblem der Judenfrage
angelangt. . . .''
    12. Hugelmann, *ibid.*, p. 571: "Es darf . . . übrigens nicht übersehen
werden, dass . . . die Taufe . . . gerade mit Rücksicht darauf, dass
durch dieselbe der Jude aus seinem angeborenen Rechts- und Wirt-
schaftskreis notwendig ausschied, eher als heute als eine auch stammes-
mässige Loslösung vom Judentum zu werten ist.''
    13. Cf. Aronius, *op. cit.*, p. 365, "Sachregister," *s.v.* "Bekehrung zum
Christentum"; Solomon Grayzel, *The Church and the Jews in the XIIIth
Century* (Philadelphia, 1933), p. 367, Index, *s.v.* "Converts to Christianity." On conversion to Christianity and Jewish converts, see below,
p. 315 and chap. xii, nn. 68–71.
    14. Hugelmann's conclusions, moreover, move in a circle: the con-
vert's elimination from his original legal and economic milieu is interpreted as a racial separation from Judaism, and this, in turn, is used to
prove the inapplicability of Jewry-law to converted Jews.
    15. Cf. also chap. iv, Sec. II, pp. 97 f.
    16. So Hugelmann, *Historisches Jahrbuch der Görresgesellschaft*, XLVIII
(1928), 570: "Die Aufstellung von Sonderbestimmungen hat doch of-
fenbar den Sinn, dass die Juden, insoweit nicht eben diese Sonderbestimmungen Platz griffen, im Verhältnis zu Nichtjuden nach denselben
Grundsätzen wie Angehörige der deutschen Stämme gerichtet wurden.
. . . Jeder einzelne Jude wurde vielmehr, insoweit nicht Sonderbestimmungen für ihn als Juden galten, nach dem Recht eines der deutschen
Stämme gerichtet.''
    17. "Jowelk man mût wol vorspreche sîn binnen deme lande zu
Sassen zu lantrechte, sunder paphen, den men an sîme rechte nicht
bescheiden ne mach." Latin version according to Zobel's ed. (Leipzig,
1560): "Quilibet in terra Saxoniae iure civili, dummodo sit bonae
famae, exceptis clericis, ferendarius esse potest.''
    18. Ssp., I, 38, 1: "Kempen unde ir kinder, spellûde, unde alle die
unecht geboren sîn, unde die dûve oder rouf sûnet oder weder gebet,
unde se des vor gerichte verwunnen werden, oder die ir lîph und hût
unde hâr ledeget, die sîn alle rechtelôs.''
    19. For details on this development see below, pp. 248 ff.; cf. also
above, p. 53.
    20. "Swâ men nicht ne dinget under kuninges banne, dâ mût iewelk
man wol ordêl vinden [unde tüch sin] uber den anderen, den men nicht
rechtlôs bescheiden mach, âne die Wend upphe den Sassen unde die

Municipal Archives of Görlitz, Germany, see Richard Jecht, "Über die in Görlitz vorhandenen Handschriften des *Sachsenspiegels*," *Neues Lausitzisches Magazin*, LXXXII (1906), 236–43.

CHAPTER SIX

1. For bibliography see Salo W. Baron, *A Social and Religious History of the Jews* (New York, 1937), II, 22 ff., 47; III, 100 f., n. 9. To this bibliography the following items may be added: Christian Gottlob Haltaus, *Glossarium Germanicum medii aevi* (Lipsiae, 1758), article "Kammerknechte," pp. 1059–63, presenting an interesting theory of his own on the origin of chamber serfdom (p. 1061):

"Nobis sic videtur: Jus illud repetendum est vel ex illo axiomate, quod post instauratum in occidente Imperium Romanum invaluit: Imperatores Germaniae esse successores in omnia jura antiquorum Imperatorum Romanorum (vide tit. *Cod. Justin.*, *de judaeis*); vel ita statuendum: Cum judaei, plebs miserabilis, ingenti numero per provincias Imperii vagarentur, et victum quaererent, omnium ope destituti, omnibus omnium injuriis et vexationibus expositi et exagitati; tutelam eorum pie suscepit summus in terris princeps, Imperator, fisco eos suo addixit, et in conditionem hominum propriorum redegit. Erant itaque judaeorum corpora et bona Imperio addicta et obnoxia, ita ut Imperator de eorum corporibus ac fortunis libere statueret."

Also Ernst Mayer, *Deutsche und französische Verfassungsgeschichte*, II (Leipzig, 1899), 289, n. 32; Simon Deploige, *Saint Thomas et la question juive* (2d ed.; Paris, 1902), pp. 30–34; George Caro, "Zur Geschichte der Reichsjudensteuer im 13. Jahrhundert," *MGWJ*, XLVIII (1904), 73 ff.; Isert Rösel, "Die Reichssteuern der deutschen Judengemeinden von ihren Anfängen bis zur Mitte des 14. Jahrhunderts," *MGWJ*, LIII (1909), 679 f. and n. 1; Ernst Kantorowicz, *Kaiser Friedrich der Zweite* (Berlin, 1927), pp. 244 f.; E. Kantorowicz, *Frederick the Second, 1194–1250* (New York, 1931), pp. 268 f.; Alfred Stern and Raphael Straus, *ZGJD*, II (1930), 68–77; E. Kantorowicz, *Kaiser Friedrich der Zweite, Ergänzungsband* (Berlin, 1931), p. 170; Herbert Fischer, *Die verfassungsrechtliche Stellung der Juden in den deutschen Städten* (Breslau, 1931), pp. 3–7 and 89, n. 1; Fischer, article "Kammerknechtschaft," in *Encyclopaedia Judaica*, IX, 860–62; Richard Schröder and Eberhard Frh. von Künssberg, *Lehrbuch der deutschen Rechtsgeschichte* (7th ed.; Berlin, 1932), pp. 507 f.; Fritz Baer, "Palestine and Exile in the Medieval Conception" (in Hebrew), *Zion*, VI (1934), 153–55; Solomon Grayzel, *The Church and the Jews in the XIIIth Century* (Ph.D. thesis, Dropsie College; Philadelphia, 1933), pp. 51 ff., 348 ff.; Bertold Bretholz, *Geschichte der Juden in Mähren*, I (Brünn, 1934), 71 f.; Ismar Elbogen, article "Deutschland," in *Germania Judaica*, pp. xx ff.; Elbogen, *Geschichte der Juden in Deutschland* (Berlin, 1935), pp. 47 f., 53 f.; G. Kisch, "Otto Stobbe und die Rechtsgeschichte der Juden," *JGJC*, IX (1938), 15 ff.; James Parkes, *The Jew in the Medieval Community* (London, 1938), pp. 106 ff., 155 ff.; Raphael Straus, "Die Speyerer Judenprivilegien von 1084 und 1090," *ZGJD*, VII (1937), 234–39; Hans Lewy, "Josephus the Physician: A Medieval Legend of the Destruction of Jerusalem," *Journal of the Warburg Institute*, I (1938), 232 ff.; Peter Browe, *Die Judenmission im Mittelalter und die Päpste* (Rome, 1942), pp. 185 f.; Irving A. Agus, *Rabbi Meir of Rothenburg*, I (Philadelphia, 1947), 139–49. All investigations hitherto have failed to solve the problem of the history of chamber serfdom, "owing to the fact that they deal exclusively with the German evolution" (cf. Baron, *op. cit.*, III, 100, and *Proceedings*, XII [1942], 38, n. 59). In fact, even the development in Germany has as yet not been fully cleared up. A good survey of the *status causae et controversiae* is found in Jonas Cohn, *Die Judenpolitik der Hohenstaufen* (Hamburg Ph.D. thesis; Hamburg, 1934), Appendix, pp. i–ix.

2. Harry Bresslau, Geiger's *ZGJD*, I (1887), 292: "Unter den einfachen und klaren Rechtsbegriff der Leibeigenschaft lässt sich das komplizierte und seiner rechtlichen Natur nach schwer zu definierende Verhältnis der Kammerknechtschaft, in welchem die deutschen Juden des späteren Mittelalters stehen, nicht subsumieren."

3. *MG, Constitutiones*, III, 368–69, Nos. 388–89; Zeumer, *Quellensammlung zur Geschichte der deutschen Reichsverfassung in Mittelalter und Neuzeit* (Tübingen, 1913), I, 139, No. 107; cf. H. Fischer, *Die verfassungsrechtliche Stellung der Juden*, p. 15, n. 2; Agus, *op. cit.*, I, 139–49.

4. Cf. Eduard Eichmann, "Die Stellung Eikes von Repgau zu Kirche und Kurie," *Historisches Jahrbuch der Görresgesellschaft*, XXXVIII (1917), 752.

5. Zeumer, *op. cit.*, I, 262, No. 166; cf. the similar wording in the electoral land peace of 1438, arts. 3 and 4 (*ibid.*, I, 251, No. 164), where also no mention of the Jews is found.

6. Julius Aronius, *Regesten zur Geschichte der Juden im fränkischen und deutschen Reiche* (Berlin, 1887–1902), Nos. 598, 599, 601, 602, 620; *MG, Constitutiones*, II, 580 ff., No. 428; Zeumer, *op. cit.*, I, Nos. 71, 74; Fischer, *op. cit.*, pp. 85–88. Art. 3 of the document of July 13, 1254, reads: "clerici seculares et omnes religiosi cujuscunque sint ordinis, laici et Judei, hac tuitione perfrui se gaudeant et in tranquillitate sancte pacis valeant permanere." Moreover, Jews are mentioned in the Bavarian land-peace laws of 1244 and 1256, but only with reference to their being allowed to practice moneylending on interest (cf. Schnelbögl, *Die*

innere Entwicklung der bayrischen Landfrieden [Heidelberg, 1932], pp. 185 f.).

7. *MG, Constitutiones*, II, 274 f., No. 204; Geiger's *ZGJD*, I (1887), 137 ff.

8. Cf., e.g., the translation by Parkes, *op. cit.*, p. 162, from the Worms privilege, art. 1, "cum ad cameram nostram attineant": "that they are the *serfs of our treasury.*"

9. See the survey in Cohn, *op. cit.*, pp. ii–iii; and Elbogen, *Germania Judaica*, p. xxiii. It is open to doubt whether the Jewry documents of Regensburg should be used at all for the historical investigation of the problem of chamber serfdom (cf. Straus, *op. cit.*, p. 238). Irrespective of the answer to this question, they, having been introduced into the discussion, cannot remain unnoticed.

10. Täubler, *MGA*, IV (1914), 44–58; Schiffmann, "Die Urkunden für die Juden von Speyer 1090 und Worms 1157," *ZGJD*, II (1930), 37; cf. Cohn, *op. cit.*, p. vii; Straus, *op. cit.*, p. 238.

11. Privilege granted by Frederick I to the church of Arles in 1177: *camere nostre pertinentes*, quoted by Johannes E. Scherer, *Die Rechtsverhältnisse der Juden in den deutsch-österreichischen Ländern* (Leipzig, 1901), p. 76; Täubler, *op. cit.*, p. 54, n. 1. Numerous instances of this kind in Altmann, "Studies in Medieval German Jewish History," *Proceedings*, X (1940), 61–64.

12. *MG, Leges*, V, *Formulae imperiales*, ed. Karolus Zeumer (Hannover, 1886), charter of protection No. 31, p. 310; Aronius, *op. cit.*, No. 82, for the *Hebreos David et Joseph habitantes in Lugduno civitate:* "liceat eis sub mundeburdo et defensione nostra quiete vivere et partibus palatii nostri fideliter deservire"; the same wording (*ibid.*, No. 52, p. 325; Aronius, *op. cit.*, No. 83) for the Hebrew Abraham from Cesaraugusta (Saragossa); cf. *ibid.*, charter of protection No. 37, p. 315, for Christian merchants: "liceat eis, sicut diximus, partibus palatii nostri fideliter deservire."

13. A comprehensive history of medieval law as based on the legal form of privilege is still lacking; cf. G. Kisch, *Das Fischereirecht im Deutschordensgebiete* ("Deutschrechtliche Forschungen," ed. G. Kisch, Vol. V [Stuttgart, 1932]), p. 70, n. 105 (with bibliography of the history of privilege law). Also no attempt has been made to inquire into the legislatorial function of the medieval Jewry privileges. Selma Stern's article, "Judenprivilegien," *Jüdisches Lexikon*, III, 439–42, offers merely an enumeration of medieval charters under the legal aspect of "alien-law"; and the exposition in Parkes, *op. cit.*, pp. 155–238, is confined to a sociological interpretation.

14. Cf. Dominikus Lindner, *Die Lehre vom Privileg nach Gratian und den Glossatoren des Corpus Juris Canonici* (Regensburg, 1917), pp. 1–14. Gratian's pupil, Paucapalea, in his *Summa* to the *Decretum Gratiani* (*ca.* 1144–48) offers the following definition: "[est] privilegium, quod aliquem a jure communi privat seu immunem facit." Cf. also Alexander Gál, *Die Summa legum brevis, levis et utilis des sog. Doctor Raymundus von Wiener-Neustadt* (Weimar, 1926), pp. 141 ff., chap. xv, "De privilegiis."

15. Harry Bresslau, *Handbuch der Urkundenlehre für Deutschland und Italien*, I (2d ed.; Leipzig, 1912), 63, n. 1; Otto Gierke, *Deutsches Privatrecht*, I (Leipzig, 1895), 303; Hinschius-Kahl, article "Privilegium" in Stengel and Fleischmann, *Wörterbuch des deutschen Staats- und Verwaltungsrechts*, III (2d ed.; Tübingen, 1914), 196 ff.

16. MG, *Form. imp.*, Nos. 30, 31, 52; Aronius, *op. cit.*, Nos. 81, 82, 83; all dating from about 825. For a penetrating analysis it is indispensable to study in full the texts of these documents, which are offered only in the *Monumenta Germaniae.*

17. MG, *Form. imp.*, No. 52; Aronius, *op. cit.*, No. 83.

18. MG., *Form. imp.*, Nos 30, 31; Aronius, *op. cit.*, Nos. 81, 82.

19. For a general discussion of the king's special protection see Heinrich Brunner, *Deutsche Rechtsgeschichte*, II (2d ed.; Munich, 1928), 62–73. No new points of view are found in Julius Goebel, *Felony and Misdemeanor: A Study in the History of English Criminal Procedure*, I (New York, 1937), 48 f. Cf. Heinrich Mitteis, *Lehnrecht und Staatsgewalt* (Weimar, 1933), p. 72: "Rechtlich sind diese Kommendationen (vor allem die der Klöster) mit der eines königlichen Schutzjuden oder einer schutzbedürftigen Witwe durchaus auf eine Linie zu stellen."

20. Michael Tangl, "Zum Judenschutzrecht unter den Karolingern," *Neues Archiv für ältere Geschichtskunde*, XXXIII (1907), 197–200. In this important essay, whose results were accepted in Schröder and Künssberg, *op. cit.*, p. 245, but remained unnoticed until now in Jewish historical literature, convincing evidence is brought forward that in *Form. imp.*, Nos. 32 and 37 (Aronius, *op. cit.*, No. 98) Zeumer's readings of the pertinent Tironian notes *sicut ipsi Judei* and *sicut Judeis* are incorrect; they must be replaced by *sicut jam diximus* and *sicut diximus*, respectively. Thus these charters of protection for certain Christian merchants do not refer to Jews or to royal Jewry protection at all, and *Form. imp.*, No. 37, should be eliminated from Aronius. This textual emendation, however, does not prove so negative and worthless for research as Tangl thought when he spoke of an *Ausfall ohne Gegenleistung*. Rather is it fundamental for the legal-historical analysis which is to follow; for, owing to Tangl's researches, the mutual independence of the charters for the Christian and the Jewish merchants has been established.

21. A comprehensive and penetrating discussion of the legal content of the Carolingian Jewry protection formulae is found in Hugo Steinthal, *Die Juden im fränkischen Reiche: Ihre rechtliche und wirtschaftlich-soziale Stellung* (Breslau University Ph.D. thesis; in typescript only; an abstract appeared in print, Breslau, 1922), pp. 25, 30–34, 36–45, 55. It surpasses the interpretation in George Caro, *Sozial- und Wirtschaftsgeschichte der Juden im Mittelalter und der Neuzeit*, I (Frankfort-on-the-Main, 1908), 132–36, and in Parkes, *op. cit.*, pp. 156, 158–60.

22. Cf. Brunner, *op. cit.*, II, 69–71 (English abstract in Goebel, *op. cit.*, pp. 154 f.); Edmund E. Stengel, *Die Immunität in Deutschland bis zum Ende des 11. Jahrhunderts*, I (Innsbruck, 1910), 570–77.

23. *Capitulare missorum generale* of 802, chaps. 2–9; *MG, Leges*, II, 1, 92 f.

24. *MG, Form. imp.*, Nos. 30, 31; cf. Nos. 32, 37, 52. For the relationship of fidelity between subject and king in general see Brunner, *op. cit.*, II, 14, 77 ff.

25. *MG, Form. imp.*, Nos. 31, 37, 52 (see above, n. 12); cf. No. 37 (charter for *non-Jewish* merchants): "ad cameram nostram fideliter unusquisque ex suo negotio ac nostro deservire studeat hasque litteras auctoritatis nostre ostendat." Additional proof in Altmann, *Proceedings*, X (1940), 85 f. Altmann, however, ignored Tangl's textual emendation (see n. 20) and therefore arrived at untenable conclusions. The same is true of Hans Planitz, "Handelsverkehr und Kaufmannsrecht im fränkischen Reich," *Festschrift Ernst Heymann zum 70. Geburtstag überreicht von Freunden, Schülern und Fachgenossen* (Weimar, 1940), p. 189.

26. Cf. Brunner, *op. cit.*, II, 64 and n. 8. Steinthal (*op. cit.*, pp. 41 f., 45 ff., 49 ff., 66, and abstract, p. 4) emphasizes the status of freedom of the Jews in the Frankish empire because of their possession of real property and slaves; cf. also Ernst Mayer, *Deutsche und französische Verfassungsgeschichte*, II, 286 f. Scherer's assertion, based on his "law-of-aliens" theory, that the Jews were considered unfree in the Carolingian era, was disproved by subsequent investigators, chiefly by Eschelbacher, *MGWJ*, XLVI (1902), 390 f.; *Germania Judaica*, pp. xxi, xl, n. 37a; cf. also below, chap. xii, nn. 15 and 18.

27. "Between the general protection enjoyed by all subjects by virtue of the folklaw and the special protection by commendation and charter, an intermediate type of royal protection arose when larger groups were taken under the royal protection such as churches and clerics, widows and orphans, the poor and pilgrims" (Brunner, *op. cit.*, II, 72). It seems unlikely, however, that such a generalizing tendency underlay Louis I's lost capitulary concerning the Jews mentioned in *Form. imp.*, No. 31 (Aronius, *op. cit.*, No. 82), and by Agobard of Lyons, *De insolentia*

Judaeorum, chap. 2 (Migne, *Patr. Lat.*, CIV, 71): "capitularia sanctionum." Apparently, it contained only regulations of criminal procedure (cf. Brunner, *op. cit.*, I, 404 f.; Eschelbacher, *MGWJ*, XLVI [1902], 390). In this connection it should also be pointed out that the charter, *Form. imp.*, No. 31, cannot refer to the entire community of Lyons; otherwise one could not explain how individual Jews were able to enter commendation (cf. Aronius, *op. cit.*, No. 82; Steinthal, *op. cit.*, p. 39).

28. For bibliography on these charters see Parkes, *op. cit.*, pp. 97 f.; in addition: Schiffmann, *ZGJD*, II (1930), 28–39; Straus, *ZGJD*, VII (1937), 234–39; Straus, "The Significance of the Jews in the Medieval German Cities," *Historia Judaica*, III (1941), 107–9.

29. Cf. Bresslau, *Handbuch der Urkundenlehre*, I, 71. In Henry IV's privilege for Worms of January 18, 1074, *judei et coeteri Wormatienses* are mentioned (cf. Aronius, *op. cit.*, No. 162; Täubler, *MGA*, V [1915], 127 ff.).

30. Cf. Täubler, *MGA*, V (1915), 138 ff.; Parkes, *op. cit.*, p. 236; Straus, *ZGJD*, VII (1938), 237–39.

31. A. Hilgard, *Urkunden zur Geschichte der Stadt Speyer*, I (Strassburg, 1885), 11, No. 11; Aronius, *op. cit.*, No. 168, p. 70 (September 13, 1084): ". . . cum ex Spirensi villa urbem facerem, putavi milies amplificare honorem loci nostri, si et judeos colligerem" (cf. Straus, *Historia Judaica*, III [1941], 107–9).

32. Cf. Parkes, *op. cit.*, p. 205; Baron, *op. cit.*, III, 101, n. 10.

33. Cf. Sobieslav II's charter for the Germans in Prague (1176–78), art. 11: *De Romanis et Judeis similiter;* i.e., with regard to the law of evidence, they shall be treated like the Germans (Wilhelm Weizsäcker, "Die älteste Urkunde der Prager Deutschen," *Zeitschrift für sudetendeutsche Geschichte*, I [1937], 181); see also below, chap. x, n. 132.

34. See above, n. 26.

35. Aronius, *op. cit.*, Nos. 129, 133, 140; Siegfried Rietschel, *Markt und Stadt in ihrem rechtlichen Verhältnis* (Leipzig, 1897), pp. 53–55, 58, 61 f.

36. On the reverse legal situation of the peasants during the eleventh century, cf. Fehr, *ZRG*, XXXV (1914), 155, 157, n. 1. The meaning and application of ordeals in general is discussed by Rudolf Hübner in *Reallexikon der germanischen Altertumskunde*, II (Strassburg, 1913–15), 320 ff., *s.v.* "Gottesurteil." It might be interesting to note what the medieval Jews thought of ordeals, which, of course, were not rooted in Jewish law. Ephraim bar Jacob of Bonn (born about 1133), in his account of the Crusade massacres, described a water ordeal performed in his presence and commented: "It is the rule among the Gentiles to apply

the test of the ordeal, 'statutes that were not good and ordinances whereby they should not live' [allusion to Ezek. 20:25]'' (A. Neubauer and M. Stern, *Hebräische Berichte über die Judenverfolgungen während der Kreuzzüge* [Berlin, 1892], pp. 67, 200; cf. also below, chap. x, nn. 101, 102).

37. G. Kisch, *Sachsenspiegel and Bible* (Notre Dame, Ind., 1931), pp. 117 ff.

38. Cf. Hans Hirsch, *Die hohe Gerichtsbarkeit im deutschen Mittelalter* (Prague, 1922), pp. 150–57; Heinrich Glitsch, ''Zum Strafrecht des Zürcher Richtebriefs,'' *ZRG*, XXXVIII (1917), 240–47; Rudolf His, *Das Strafrecht des deutschen Mittelalters*, I (Leipzig, 1920), 6–20.

39. Oswald Holder-Egger and Bernhard von Simson, *Die Chronik des Propstes Burchard von Ursberg* (2d ed.; Hannover, 1916), pp. 54 f., 79; cf. Ferdinand Frensdorff, ''Beiträge zur Geschichte und Erklärung der deutschen Rechtsbücher. IV,'' *Nachrichten der K. Gesellschaft der Wissenschaften zu Göttingen*, 1921, p. 156; V, *ibid.*, 1923, p. 80.

40. Aronius, *op. cit.*, Nos. 178, 203, 205; cf. Täubler, *MGA*, V (1915), 128, n. 1; Parkes, *op. cit.*, pp. 79 ff.

41. Elbogen, *Germania Judaica*, p. xlii, n. 76, in correctly criticizing H. Fischer.

42. Cf. Hirsch, *op. cit.*, pp. 152 f.; Fritz Kern, ''Recht und Verfassung im Mittelalter,'' *Historische Zeitschrift*, CXX (1919), 29 ff.; Kern, *Kingship and Law in the Middle Ages* (Oxford, 1939), pp. 168 ff.

43. See above, p. 109. Interesting confirmation is found in contemporary Hebrew sources. The Jews considered themselves free men possessing the status of free owners of property and endowed with the right to move freely from place to place. In the second half of the twelfth century, Rabbi Isaac ben Samuel, known under the name ''Ri Hazaken,'' wrote in his *Tosaphot* to *Baba Kama*, 58a: ''For we saw throughout the country that the Jews had the legal right, similar to the right of the knights, to live wherever they wanted to; and the law of the kingdom provided that the overlord should not appropriate the Jew's property after he had moved away from his town. This was also the custom throughout Burgundy.'' And elsewhere he stated: ''. . . every Jew had the right, according to the law of the land, to leave his home town at will, and freely to move from place to place.'' Rabbi Meir of Rothenburg (1220–93) in a *Responsum* made the following statement referring to the prevailing customary law: ''The status of the Jew in this land is that of a free landowner who lost his land but did not lose his personal liberty. This definition of the status of the Jews is followed by the government in its customary relations with the Jews.'' For more details see Agus, *Rabbi Meir of Rothenburg*, I, 139–44; II, 553.

428 NOTES TO CHAPTER VI, PAGES 143–147

44. Aronius, *op. cit.*, Nos. 469, 474, 497. According to Kantorowicz, *Kaiser Friedrich der Zweite, Ergänzungsband*, p. 170, "then, for the first time, the Jewish question was considered as of common concern to all European countries"; cf. also Alfred Stern, *ZGJD*, II (1930), 73, and Raphael Straus, *ZGJD*, II (1930), 75.

45. Burchard von Ursberg, *Chronicon* (above, n. 39), p. 65: ". . . quas litteras Alamanni usque in presens 'fridebrief,' id est litteras pacis vocant nec aliis legibus utuntur; sed nec eisdem recte utuntur, tanquam gens agrestis et indomita" (cf. Frensdorff, "Beiträge. II," *Nachrichten der K. Gesellschaft der Wissenschaften zu Göttingen*, 1894, p. 65, n. 4; Hirsch, *op. cit.*, p. 155).

46. Cf. His, *Das Strafrecht des deutschen Mittelalters*, I, 14; Hirsch, *op. cit.*, p. 155.

47. Aronius, *op. cit.*, No. 498: "Judeos autem etsi tam in imperio quam in regno nobis communi jure immediate subjaceant, a nulla tamen ecclesia illos abstulimus, que super eis jus speciale pretenderet, quod communi juri nostro merito preferretur."

48. This is, in my opinion, the only correct designation for the legal concept to be discussed here. It not only clarifies the subject matter involved but is also in accordance with the wording used in the sources (cf., e.g., Bernard of Clairvaux, *De consideratione libri quinque*, chap. 3 [Migne, *Patr. Lat.*, CLXXXII, 732]: ". . . Nulla turpior servitus graviorque, quam *servitus Judeorum* . . ."). The term *servitus Judaica* as used by Täubler (*MGA*, IV [1914], 55), Fischer (*op. cit.*, pp. 3, n. 2, 89, n. 1), and Lewy (*op. cit.*, pp. 234 ff.) (cf., however, Täubler in *Beiträge zur Geschichte der deutschen Juden: Festschrift zum siebzigsten Geburtstag Martin Philippsons* [Leipzig, 1916], pp. 390 ff.) must be avoided because of its ambiguity; the same is true of the English translation "Jewish serfdom" (instead of "servitude of the Jews"). Either may refer to the status of slaves or servants of Jewish masters, as is the case in papal and conciliar decrees. Pope Innocent III's decretal of January 16, 1205 (Migne, *Patr. Lat.*, CCXV, 501–3; Grayzel, *op. cit.*, pp. 104 ff.) clearly states the distinction: "*Judaicam servitutem* illorum libertati preponunt; . . . nec deterior sit Christianorum libertas, quam *servitus Judeorum*."

49. Cf. Willy Cohn, "Kaiser Friedrich II und die deutschen Juden," *MGWJ*, LXIII (1919), 315–32; Jonas Cohn, *Die Judenpolitik der Hohenstaufen*, pp. 28, 39 ff., and bibliography, pp. 7 ff.; Kantorowicz, *Kaiser Friedrich der Zweite*, pp. 245 ff.; and *Frederick the Second*, pp. 269 ff.; Täubler, *MGA*, IV (1914), 53 f.

50. Cf. Justus Hashagen, *Staat und Kirche vor der Reformation* (Essen, 1931), pp. 385–97.

51. Leopold Lucas, *Zur Geschichte der Juden im vierten Jahrhundert* (Berlin, 1910), pp. 97 f., 125, n. 1; Jean Juster, *Les Juifs dans l'empire romain, leur condition juridique, économique et sociale,* I (Paris, 1914), 44 ff., 46, n. 8, 226 ff.; Petrus Browe, "Die Judengesetzgebung Justinians," *Analecta Gregoriana,* VIII (1935), 140 ff.; Yitzhak F. Baer, *Galut* ("Schocken Library," No. 2 [New York, 1947]), pp. 14 ff.; Baron, *op. cit.,* II, 45 f., and *Proceedings,* XII (1942), 38, n. 59; Lewy, *op. cit.,* pp. 234 f.; S. Grayzel, "Christian-Jewish Relations in the First Millennium," in *Essays on Antisemitism,* ed. K. S. Pinson (New York, 1942), pp. 38 ff. On the theologic and canon-law problem of the Jews' responsibility, *culpa,* in Jesus' death and its discussion by the medieval theologians and lawyers, see Stephan Kuttner, *Kanonistische Schuldlehre von Gratian bis auf die Dekretalen Gregors IX* (Città del Vaticano, 1935), pp. 137 f., 143, n. 1, and 267–69.

52. Aurelius Augustinus, *Opera omnia* (Migne, *Patr. Lat.,* XXXIII, 897; XXXVIII, 56; cf. XLI, 543).

53. During this period, however, practice sometimes deviated from theory. This is shown by the report of a Jewish eyewitness of the massacres which opened the Second Crusade in Germany. It reads as follows: "On the second day of the feast of Shabuot [May 8, 1147] the straying rabble from France [i.e., the crusaders] gathered at Rameru and entered the house of our teacher Jacob [i.e., Rabbenu Tam], long may he live, . . . they took and dragged him into the field, spoke roughly to him about his faith and conspired against him, to slay him. They inflicted five wounds on his head saying: "You are the most distinguished man in Israel; therefore, we will avenge on you the Crucified one, and wound you in the same manner as you [Jews] did, inflicting five wounds on our God' " (Neubauer and Stern, *op. cit.,* pp. 64, 195; Lewy, *op. cit.,* p. 240).

54. Cf. Selig Cassel, article "Juden (Geschichte)," in Ersch and Gruber, *Encyclopädie der Wissenschaften und Künste,* II, 27 (Leipzig, 1850), 86, n. 87; Stobbe, *Die Juden in Deutschland während des Mittelalters* (Braunschweig, 1866), p. 17, n. **.

55. Cf. Baer, "Palestine and Exile in the Medieval Conception," *Zion,* VI (1934), 153 f.; A. Lukyn Williams, *Adversus Judaeos: A Bird's-Eye View of Christian Apologiae until the Renaissance* (Cambridge, 1935), p. 394.

56. Thomas Aquinas, *De regimine Judaeorum ad Ducissam Brabantiae,* ed. Joseph Mathis (Turin, 1924), p. 117: ". . . qui licet, ut jura dicunt, judaei merito culpae suae sint vel essent perpetuae servituti addicti, et sic eorum res terrarum domini possint accipere tamquam suas . . ." ;

cf. also *Summa theologiae* ii. 2. 10. 10; *St. Thomae opera omnia*, ed. Fratres Ordinis Praedicatorum, VIII (Rome, 1895), 92: ". . . Nec in hoc injuriam facit ecclesia, quia cum ipsi judaei sint servi ecclesiae, potest disponere de rebus eorum. . . ." Cf. Jacob Guttmann, *Das Verhältnis des Thomas von Aquino zum Judentum und zur jüdischen Literatur* (Göttingen, 1891), pp. 8, 11 f.; Deploige, *Saint Thomas et la question juive*, pp. 35–39.

57. Rupertus Tuitiensis, *De Trinitate et operibus ejus* (Migne, *Patr. Lat.*, CLXVII, 532).

58. See the quotations from Thomas Aquinas in n. 56. In his treatise, *De legibus et consuetudinibus Angliae*, composed before 1256 (ed. Travers Twiss [London, 1883], vi. 51), the famous English thirteenth-century jurist, Henry de Bracton, stated: "But a Jew cannot have anything of his own, because whatever he acquires, he acquires not for himself but for the king, because they do not live for themselves but for others and so they acquire for others and not for themselves" (Baron, *op. cit.*, II, 24). This is the logical application of the Roman-law principles of servitude. As for the history of the latter and the attitude of Christianity toward slavery, cf. Fritz Schulz, *Prinzipien des römischen Rechts* (Munich, 1934), pp. 145–50; Schulz, *Principles of Roman Law* (Oxford, 1936), pp. 215–22; concerning Bracton's borrowings from Roman law see Theodore F. Plucknett, "Bracton," *Encyclopaedia of the Social Sciences*, II, 671.

59. This applies in particular to Baer's remarks on the subject in *Zion*, VI (1934), 153–55. On the basis of a few legal documents from England, Germany, and Spain, in no direct connection with one another, the same as those presented by him in *Encyclopaedia Judaica*, I (1928), 257, he points to the theological doctrines and states: "The political thought of the Middle Ages completed and executed the decrees of the Church Fathers. The legal concept [of the serfdom of the Jews] was created only and exclusively by the theologians." A historical analysis of the ideological connections, however, is missing. Therefore, in the present writer's opinion, Baer's bitter criticism of George Caro and Eugen Täubler (*Zion*, VI, 155, n. 2) is unfounded. Furthermore, it must be emphasized that the development of chamber serfdom and similar institutions must be studied separately and individually for each country, before general conclusions can be reached. For the influence of theological thought upon political theory and practice in the Middle Ages in general, cf. Baer, "Abner aus Burgos," *Korrespondenzblatt der Akademie für die Wissenschaft des Judentums*, X (Berlin, 1929), 20 f.

60. On this problem in general see F. Keutgen, *Der deutsche Staat des*

Mittelalters (Jena, 1918), p. 7; Fritz Kern, "Recht und Verfassung im Mittelalter," *Historische Zeitschrift*, CXX (1919), 27 ff.; Kern, *Kingship and Law in the Middle Ages*, pp. 166 ff.

61. G. Kisch, *Sachsenspiegel and Bible*, pp. 19, 95 ff., and *passim;* G. Kisch, "Biblische Einflüsse in der Reimvorrede des Sachsenspiegels," *Publications of the Modern Language Association of America*, LIV (1939), 20–36.

62. G. Kisch, *Sachsenspiegel and Bible*, pp. 133–46; also G. Kisch, "Biblical Spirit in Mediaeval German Law," *Speculum*, XIV (1939), 48–55.

63. Cf. Philipp Heck, *Eike von Repgow, Verfasser der alten Zusätze zu dem Sachsenspiegel* (Tübingen, 1939), who through his researches rendered it plausible that the author of the "old additions" to the *Sachsenspiegel* was Eike himself; cf., however, Karl August Eckhardt, *ZRG*, LX (1940), 371 f.

64. Aronius, *op. cit.*, No. 509; F. Keutgen, *Urkunden zur städtischen Verfassungsgeschichte* (Berlin, 1899), No. 165, art. 4, p. 211: "Ad hec, catholici principis partes fideliter exequentes, ab officiorum prefectura Judeos excipimus, ne sub pretextu prefecture opprimant Christianos: cum imperialis auctoritas a priscis temporibus ad perpetrati judaici sceleris ultionem eisdem Judeis indixerit *perpetuam servitutem*" (cf. Scherer, *op. cit.*, pp. 85 f., 132; Täubler, *MGA*, IV [1914], 55; Lewy, *op. cit.*, pp. 238 f.).

65. *Cod. Just.* i. 9. 18 [Imp. Theodosius II et Valentinianus; January 31, 439]:
"Hac victura in omne aevum lege sancimus neminem Judaeum, quibus omnes administrationes et dignitates interdictae sunt, nec defensoris civitatis fungi saltem officio nec patris honorem adripere concedimus, ne adquisiti sibi officii auctoritate muniti adversus Christianos et ipsos plerumque sacrae religionis antistites velut insultantes fidei nostrae judicandi vel pronuntiandi quamlibet habeant potestatem."
Cf. also *Cod. Just.* i. 5. 12; *Nov.* 45.

66. Cf. L. Erler, *Archiv für katholisches Kirchenrecht*, XLIII (1880), 366–69 (anti-Semitic); XLVIII (1882), 378; Grayzel, *The Church and the Jews in the XIIIth Century*, pp. 27 f., where many instances are given.

67. Cf. Täubler, *MGA*, IV (1914), 53 f.; Elbogen, *Germania Judaica*, p. xxiv.

68. *Innocentii III Opera omnia* (Migne, *Patr. Lat.*, CCXV, 694 f.; *Corpus juris canonici*, c. 13, X, *de judaeis* 5, 6):
"Etsi Judaeos, quos propria culpa submisit *perpetuae servituti*, quum Dominum crucifixerint . . . ut taliter reprimant Judaeorum excessus, ne

cervicem, *perpetuae servitutis* jugo submissam, praesumant erigere . . .
tanquam servi a Domino reprobati, in cujus mortem nequiter con-
jurarunt, se saltem per effectum operis recognoscant servos illorum, quos
Christi mors liberos, et illos servos effecit . . . Judaei perfidi de cetero
nullatenus insolescant, sed sub timore servili praetendant semper
verecundiam culpae suae, ac revereantur honorem fidei Christianae."
Cf. also Innocent III's letter of January 17, 1208 (Migne, *Patr. Lat.*,
CCXV, 1291; Grayzel, *op. cit.*, No. 24, p. 126).

69. Scherer, *op. cit.*, pp. 85 f., 132; Caro, *op. cit.*, I, 307 f.

70. Täubler (*MGA*, IV [1914], 55, n. 3) declares this assumption as
inadmissible: "das ist natürlich unzulässig"; Baer (*Zion*, VI [1934], 155,
n. 2) takes a stand against Caro and, curiously enough, in spite of
Täubler's n. 4, reproaches Täubler for having followed in Caro's footsteps; he exclaims: "And that is how Jewish history is being written!"

71. Cf. Grayzel, *op. cit.*, pp. 9–12, and bibliography; to be added:
M. Elias, "Die römische Kurie, besonders Innozenz III., und die Juden,"
Jahrbuch der jüdisch-literarischen Gesellschaft zu Frankfurt a.M., XII (1918),
37–82. This entire period and the problem of "Innocent III and the
Jews," in particular, call for re-examination and exhaustive treatment.

72. Emil Friedberg, *Lehrbuch des katholischen und evangelischen Kirchenrechts* (5th ed.; Leipzig, 1903), p. 131.

73. *Corpus juris canonici*, c. 13, X, *de judaeis* 5. 6.

74. Apparently, *Extra, de judaeis* (*Corpus juris canonici* X. 5. 6) soon
became widely known. It was, e.g., cited as early as about 1238–40 by
Alexander of Hales (d. 1245); cf. Willibrord Lampen, "Alexander von
Hales und der Antisemitismus," *Franziskanische Studien*, XVI (1929), 7.

75. Kantorowicz, *Kaiser Friedrich der Zweite*, p. 377 (English ed.,
p. 411).

76. Cf., e.g., the wording in Gregory IX's decretal of May 18, 1233
(Grayzel, *op. cit.*, p. 204): "ne Judaei publicis officiis preponantur,
quoniam sub tali pretextu Christianis plerumque nimium sunt infesti."
According to Scherer's interpretation (*op. cit.*, p. 132), article 4 of the
Vienna privilege excluded Jews only from *presiding* over an office, this
being the milder form of exclusion originally practiced by the church.
If this should be the correct meaning of the passage, another proof for
its origin in canon law would be won. The milder form of the prohibition, however, was definitely abolished as early as the Fourth Council
of Toledo in 633 (c. 65) (J. D. Mansi, *Concilia*, X, 635: "ut Judaei aut hi
qui ex Judaeis, officia publica nullatenus appetant; quia sub hac occasione
Christianis injuriam faciunt"); and the term *praeficere* (*praefectura*) in
later papal and conciliar decrees is hardly used in a restricted sense but

rather refers to exercising authority over Christians by means of public office. The problem requires further investigation.

77. Cf. Kantorowicz, *Kaiser Friedrich der Zweite*, p. 453 (English ed., p. 498); L. Erler, *Archiv für katholisches Kirchenrecht*, XLVIII (1882), 23 ff. On the emperor's relationship to Pope Gregory IX, see *Register* in Kantorowicz, *s.v.* "Gregory IX."

78. Cf. Lewy, "Josephus the Physician: A Medieval Legend of the Destruction of Jerusalem," *Journal of the Warburg Institute*, I (1938), 221–42; Guido Kisch, "A Talmudic Legend as the Source for the Josephus Passage in the *Sachsenspiegel*," *Historia Judaica*, I (1939), 105–18.

79. No other satisfactory explanation has been offered as yet. This applies, in particular, to the suggestions by Alexander Pinthus, *ZGJD*, II (1930), 201 and n. 17; and Jonas Cohn, *Die Judenpolitik der Hohenstaufen*, p. 29, n. 108.

80. G. Kisch, *Sachsenspiegel and Bible*, pp. 144 ff.; G. Kisch, *Speculum*, XIV (1939), 54. The problem is inadequately treated in R. W. Carlyle and A. J. Carlyle, *A History of Mediaeval Political Theory in the West*, III (London, 1915), 89.

81. See above, chap. ii, n. 22.

82. According to Lewy (*op. cit.*, p. 225 and n. 6), one of these sources was the *Vindicta Salvatoris*. This conjecture rests on the assumption that Eike's acquaintance with this work is apparent also from the *Saxon World Chronicle*. This assumption, however, is open to doubt, in view of the fact that the B and C versions of the *Saxon World Chronicle* do not represent its original textual form. The original version (A) refers sometimes to Hegesippus. Cf. below, n. 99, and Ernst von Dobschütz, *Christusbilder: Untersuchungen zur christlichen Legende* (Leipzig, 1899), pp. 240 and n. 4, 279*, No. 8.

83. This hypothesis was first advanced by S. Cassel (see above, n. 54), p. 85, and based on a confusion of the *Schwabenspiegel* with the *Sachsenspiegel*. The southern German lawbook alone, however, relates the assignment of the Jews to the royal chamber by Titus, attributed by Cassel to the *Sachsenspiegel*, whereas chamber serfdom is not mentioned in the latter lawbook at all. Cassel's hypothesis was taken up and elaborated upon by Lewy (*op. cit.*, p. 235), who treats both lawbooks as on the same level; he overlooks the fact that the *Schwabenspiegel*, composed about fifty years after its northern German model, represents a different phase of legal development.

84. Cf. Eichmann, *Historisches Jahrbuch der Görresgesellschaft*, XXXVIII (1917), 720, 745; K. G. Hugelmann, "Der Sachsenspiegel und das vierte

Lateranensische Konzil," *ZRG*, XLIV, kanon. Abt. XIII (1924), 428.

85. Ssp., I, 1: "For the protection of Christendom on earth God confers two swords. The spiritual one is foreordained to the pope, the secular one to the emperor. . . . This means: Any resistance offered to the pope which he cannot overcome with the spiritual court shall be overpowered into obedience to the pope by the emperor with the secular court. Vice versa, the spiritual power shall aid the secular court, if such help is needed" (G. Kisch, *Sachsenspiegel and Bible*, pp. 121 f., with picture from the Dresden manuscript of the *Sachsenspiegel;* also *Speculum,* XIV [1939], 41). Cf. Gerhard Laehr, *Die Konstantinische Schenkung in der abendländischen Literatur des Mittelalters* (Berlin, 1926), p. 83, n. 15; Robert Holtzmann, *Der Kaiser als Marschall des Papstes* (Berlin, 1928), p. 13; R. W. Carlyle and A. J. Carlyle, *A History of Mediaeval Political Theory in the West,* V (Edinburgh and London, 1928), 364–66.

86. As to Frederick II's relationship to the church and to the pope at that time see Karl Hampe, *Deutsche Kaisergeschichte in der Zeit der Salier und Staufer* (5th ed.; Leipzig, 1923), p. 233; K. A Eckhardt," Rechtsbücherstudien, II," *Abhandlungen der Gesellschaft der Wissenschaften zu Göttingen, philol.-hist. Klasse,* Neue Folge, XXIII, No. 2 (Berlin, 1931), 119.

87. Karl Zeumer, "Die Sächsische Weltchronik: Ein Werk Eikes von Repgow," *Festschrift für Heinrich Brunner* (Weimar, 1910), pp. 143 f.: "Eike suchte nach einer historischen Erklärung dieses Königsfriedens." Even Lewy himself (*op. cit.,* p. 233 and n. 3) calls attention to the fact that Eike in his other work, the *Saxon World Chronicle,* introduced stories—sometimes very fanciful—in order to explain the origin of existing customs and habits. But, as Zeumer (*op. cit.*) has already correctly pointed out, it would have been out of place to repeat the Josephus legend in the *World Chronicle;* for, in this work, Eike did not have to strive for a legal-historical explanation of the royal protection enjoyed by the Jews in his day.

88. Lewy's assertion (*op. cit.,* p. 228, n. 3) that in the *Sachsenspiegel* and *Schwabenspiegel* the titles "Emperor" and "King" are often used synonymously is contestable (cf. Heinrich Mitteis, *Die deutsche Königswahl: Ihre Rechtsgrundlagen bis zur Goldenen Bulle* (Baden bei Wien, 1938), p. 138).

89. Cf. Max Fleischmann, "Über den Einfluss des römischen Rechts auf das deutsche Staatsrecht," *Mélanges Fitting,* II (Montpellier, 1908), 670 ff.; Schröder and Künssberg, *op. cit.,* p. 865; Hans von Schubert, *Der Kampf des geistlichen und weltlichen Rechts* (Heidelberg, 1927), pp. 41 ff.; Percy Ernst Schramm, *Kaiser, Rom und Renovatio,* I (Berlin, 1929), 275 ff.

90. Cf. Fehr, *ZRG*, XXXV (1914), 166.

91. Lewy, *op. cit.*, p. 237. It is by no means in accord with this assertion, when Lewy (p. 233, n. 1) considers it as a possibility that "Eike
formed his opinion from a note of Josephus' *Vita* which states that at
his request Titus gave liberty to a few captive Jews." This remark, however, deserves attention, in view of the fact that the contention that the
Vindicta Salvatoris was a source of Eike is doubtful (see above, n. 82).
Cf., on the other hand, the interpretation by Baron (*op. cit.*, II, 23) in
accordance with that offered in the text: ". . . on the insistence of
Josephus, Titus *liberated* them, except for a special tax."

92. For its source history see Lewy, *op. cit.*, pp. 229 ff.; Kisch,
Historia Judaica, I (1939), 114 f.; cf. G. F. Hill, *The Medallic Portraits of
Christ: The False Shekels, the Thirty Pieces of Silver* (Oxford, 1920),
pp. 91–116.

93. Ludwig Weiland, *Sächsische Weltchronik*, in *MG, Deutsche Chroniken*, II, 1 (Hannover, 1876), 101:
"Sin sûn Titus gewan Jerusalem inde zûstorde si; dar wart also vil
Joden geslagen, dat id neyman geagten inkûnde. Ir wart ûyg vil ver-
kocht, 30 umbe eynen penninc, als si verkogten Christum umbe 30
pennige. De hunger was do grois; de mûder as ir kint. *Dit schrift Josephus
inde Egeseppus.* Den selven Josephum hadde gevangen Vespasianus. Do
wickede he eme, dat he keiser sûlde werden, darumbe leis he in vri."

94. Cf. H. Mitteis, *Die deutsche Königswahl*, p. 133.

95. Cf. Lewy, *op. cit.*, pp. 230 f.

96. The law of retaliation is foreign to the *Sachsenspiegel* (cf. G. Kisch,
"Die talionsartige Strafe für Rechtsverweigerung im Sachsenspiegel,"
Tijdschrift voor Rechtsgeschiedenis, XVI [1939], 457–67; G. Kisch, *Sachsen-
spiegel and Bible*, pp. 146–54).

97. G. Kisch, *Sachsenspiegel and Bible*, pp. 131–46; G. Kisch, *Speculum*,
XIV (1939), 47–55. It seems, however, that Eike's doctrine of the origin
of the state is in contradiction to this conception. The state, for Eike, is
the rule of the strong over the conquered weak; the conqueror is in a
position to lay down the law (Ssp., III, 44, 3). In general, these two
doctrines have remained unreconciled in the lawbook. In the case of the
Jews, however, Eike attempted a reconciliation between the two con-
flicting principles of political theory by granting rights to the conquered Jews through introducing the Josephus legend.

98. Weiland, *op. cit.*, p. 49. Zeumer ("Die Sächsische Weltchronik"
[see above, n. 87], pp. 143 f., 154 f.), in accordance with the state of
knowledge at his time, based his discussion on Weiland's assumption
and therefore could not penetrate to the real significance of chap. 44 of
the *Saxon World Chronicle*.

99. Herman Ballschmiede, *Die Sächsische Weltchronik* (Berlin University Ph.D. thesis; Berlin, 1914), appeared also in *Niederdeutsches Jahrbuch*, XL (1914), 81–140; Eckhardt, "Rechtsbücherstudien. II," pp. 72–125; Gustav Korlén, *Die mittelniederdeutschen Texte des 13. Jahrhunderts* (Lund and Kopenhagen, 1945), pp. 72–91.

100. The passage is reproduced above, in n. 93.

101. Aronius, *op. cit.*, No. 518.

102. *MG, Constitutiones*, III, 2–6; cf. Karl Zeumer, "Zur Geschichte der Reichssteuern im früheren Mittelalter," *Historische Zeitschrift*, LXXXI (1898), 24 ff. As to the legal character of this Jewry tax, called *precaria* or *bede*, see George Caro, "Zur Geschichte der Reichsjudensteuer im 13. Jahrhundert," *MGWJ*, XLVIII (1904), 72–75; cf. also *Germania Judaica*, p. xl, n. 34; Altmann, *Proceedings*, X (1940), 43 f.

103. Franz Pfeiffer, *Berthold von Regensburg: Vollständige Ausgabe seiner Predigten*, I (Vienna, 1862), 363: "wan jüden suln sie alsô schirmen alse die kristen an ir lîbe und an ir guote, wan sie sint in den fride genomen. Unde swer einen jüden ze tôde sleht, der muoz in gote büezen unde dem rihter alse einen kristen, wan sie habent eht die keiser in den fride genomen" (cf. also Aronius, *op. cit.*, No. 757; Lewy, *op. cit.*, p. 234).

104. Ballschmiede, *op. cit.*, pp. 7–9. On the disputation see Moritz Güdemann, *Geschichte des Erziehungswesens und der Kultur der abendländischen Juden*, II (Vienna, 1884), 295 ff.

105. In the C version the traditional text reads: "Liker wis alse se Jesum crucegeden an den paschen, also se worden oc vorstoret an den paschen, unde liker wis alse se Jesum koften umbe 30 pennunge, alse worden verkoft ja 30 umbe enen penning. Ir was van hungere dot elleven warve hundert dusent, also vile irslagen, also vile verkoft, jo drittich um enen penning" (Weiland, *Sächsische Weltchronik*, p. 102; cf. the wording in the A version, above, n. 93). A poetic version of the traditional "historical" account similar to that of the C version is found in Heinrich von Hesler's *Evangelium Nicodemi*, written at the end of the thirteenth century or the beginning of the fourteenth (Heinrich von Hesler, *Das Evangelium Nicodemi*, ed. Karl Helm ["Bibliothek des literarischen Vereins in Stuttgart," Vol. CCXXIV (Tübingen, 1902)], vss. 4687–4713):

> "Do vorteilte er mit rehte
> die juden und ir geslehte,
> die kint, wib unde man
> und tet daruber keiseres ban
> nach romischen urteilen.
>
> . . . ."

Cf. also vss. 4991–94:

> "daz ir niht turret sprechen
> und ir nicht turret rechen
> uwers gotes anden
> an sinen vianden."

Cf. Karl Helm, "Untersuchungen über Heinrich Heslers Evangelium Nicodemi," in Paul and Braune, *Beiträge zur Geschichte der deutschen Sprache und Literatur*, XXIV (1899), 142 f. The relationship of this poetic version to the C version of the *Saxon World Chronicle* calls for a new examination, which is not within the scope of the present investigation.

106. On the history of the theological legend see Lewy, *op. cit.*, p. 230. Ballschmiede (*op. cit.*, pp. 9 f.) doubts that Josephus and Hegesippus were really used by the A and B versions; in the case of the C version it seems to him possible, but also subject to doubt.

107. Cf. Ballschmiede, *op. cit.*, pp. 5 f., against Weiland, *op. cit.*, pp. 22 and 102, n. 1 (*Annales Palidenses*, ed. G. H. Pertz, *MG, Scriptores*, XVI, 48–98).

108. See above, p. 132. Fischer (*op. cit.*, p. 88, and similarly on p. 90), in seeking for a reason for the absence of chamber serfdom from these Rhenish land peaces, simply states that "the conception of the relationship between the Jews and their protector based upon the theory of chamber serfdom had no validity in the confederated cities." Here, as he often does, Fischer is anticipating the concept of chamber serfdom in its fullest development. On a similar criticism against Fischer, correctly made by Elbogen, see *Germania Judaica*, p. xlii, n. 76; cf. also Karl Frölich, *ZRG*, LII (1932), 428.

109. *MG, Constitutiones*, II, 612, No. 444; Aronius, *op. cit.*, No. 706; Fischer, *op. cit.*, pp. 88–90, and comments thereupon cited above, n. 108.

110. The pertinent Latin text in *MG* reads *nec parcentes deo;* Aronius has *nec poscendo deo;* Fischer emends it to *nec parentes deo.*

111. G 57, 2: "Wir han daz von der schrift, daz nieman sol eigen sin. Doch ist ez also dar komen mit gewalt und mit twancsal, daz ez nu reht ist, daz eigen liute sin."

L 308: "Nu ist in geseit, daz wir in der heiligen geschrift nuit finden, daz jeman dez andren eigen si oder sullen sin mit rehte. Nu habent ez die herren mit gewonheit darzů braht, daz si ez mit rehte wellent han."

112. According to the lawbook of Ruprecht of Freising (1328), the sale proceeds—not the enslaved Jews—were handed to the imperial chamber (Georg Ludwig von Maurer, *Das Stadt- und Landrechtsbuch*

Ruprechts von Freysing [Stuttgart and Tübingen, 1839], chap. 172, p. 190: "Dise recht erwarb in Josephus von den kaisern Tito und Vespasiano, do sy Jerusalem zerstörten, das sy ye XXX juden umb ain pfenning gabn; dy selben pfennig legtn sy in des reichs kamer; darumb sind dy juden des reichs knecht; darumb sol sy das reich beschirmen"). The passage is missing in Hermann Knapp, *Das Rechtsbuch Ruprechts von Freising* (Leipzig, 1916); chap. 121, p. 70, reads: ". . . Daz recht habent in di roemischen chueng geben"; an identical version is found in Hans-Kurt Claussen, *Freisinger Rechtsbuch* (Weimar, 1941), chap. 122, p. 128.

113. G. Kisch, *Historia Judaica*, I (1939), 110; cf. Lewy, *op. cit.*, pp. 230–32; this omission, however, presents a strong argument against Lewy's contention that the *Schwabenspiegel* "doubtless" borrowed the legend of the sale of the surviving Jews from the *Vindicta Salvatoris*, where the idea of retaliation is clearly emphasized.

114. Though Lewy himself (*op. cit.*, pp. 231 f., n. 4) pointed out the familiar fact that the *Schwabenspiegel* is frequently diffuse, uncritical, and confused, he spent much pains and acumen in clearing up the inconsistencies in that lawbook's narrative and in suggesting a particular reason for each of them (pp. 228 f., 231 f., 235–38). In this way he outlined a seemingly continuous literary history of the Josephus legend as well as of the story of the sale of the Jewish captives after the fall of Jerusalem. Nevertheless, in the present writer's opinion, Lewy's conclusions, in essential points, lack persuasive power. Space does not permit detailed criticism here. In addition to the few remarks in preceding notes, the reader's attention may be called to the following points: (1) The medieval connotation of *eigen* as used in Schwsp., 214, 3, is not "possession" or "ownership" (Lewy, *op. cit.*, pp. 228, 237). *Eigen* means either "landed property," of course not applicable here, or, in contrast to *vri* ("free"), *hörig, leibeigen* ("bondman"), the only meaning that makes sense in this connection (see Matthias Lexer, *Mittelhochdeutsches Handwörterbuch*, I [Leipzig, 1872], 518; Gengler, *Des Schwabenspiegels Landrechtsbuch* [2d ed.; Erlangen, 1875], Wörterbuch, p. 246; cf. also Stobbe, *op. cit.*, pp. 13 f. and above, n. 58). (2) According to Lewy (*op. cit.*, p. 232), the conception of the *Schwabenspiegel* with regard to the story of the Jews' sale is different from that in the *Vindicta Salvatoris*, one more argument, in addition to that advanced above, n. 113, against Lewy's assumption (*op. cit.*, p. 231) that the latter work was a source of the *Schwabenspiegel*. (3) According to Eike, Josephus interceded with *Vespasian*, not with *Titus*, as Lewy (*op. cit.*, p. 233) holds.

115. Cf. above, n. 56.

116. *MG, Constitutiones*, III, 368 f., Nos. 388–89; Zeumer, *Quellen-*

sammlung zur Geschichte der deutschen Reichsverfassung in Mittelalter und Neuzeit, I (2d ed.; Tübingen, 1913), 139, No. 107; reproduced above, pp. 129 f.

117. Friedrich Ortloff, *Das Rechtsbuch nach Distinctionen* (Jena, 1836), III, 17, 31, p. 175; Emil Franz Rössler, *Das altprager Stadtrecht aus dem XIV. Jahrhundert* (Prague, 1845), art. 206, p. 163.

118. Wilhelm von Thüngen, *Das Sächsische Weichbildrecht nach dem Codex Palatinus No. 461* (Heidelberg, 1837), p. 47.

119. J. J. Smits, "De Spiegel van Sassen of zoogenaamde Hollandsche Sachsenspiegel," *Nieuwe Bijdragen voor Regtsgeleerdheit en Wetgeving*, XXII (1872), art. 16, p. 33:

"Want alsoe die papen verde gheboden is vanden paeus, alsoe is den joden vrede geboden vanden keyser, want sy wonen onder des keysers tribuit, alsoe got die ioden gestroeyt heeft in allen eynden der werlt om ghetuichnisse van horen ouden sonden."

The Josephus legend follows on p. 34. Art. 65, p. 192:

"Want Got heeftze ghestroyet in allen eynden der werlt, ons tot enen exempell, daer sellen sy in eygenscap verkeren sonder heerscappie offte ampt. Oick en zellen sy coninck, vorst noch prince hebben, alsoe Amos die propheet zeide."

120. P. Clauswitz, *Das Berlinische Stadtbuch aus dem Ende des XIV. Jahrhunderts* (Berlin, 1883), III, 14, pp. 164 f.: "Here begins the law concerning the Jews, who believe only in the living God, the almighty creator of heaven and earth and all that is therein, and hold by the old law, and are antagonists of the new law, that is, of all Christendom, in that they brought about the innocent death of Christ the true God. Therefore it is puzzling that the Jews are suffered to live in Christendom. Now the sacred teachers of Christendom teach that the Jews are suffered to live among Christians for the sake of four things. First, that we have the law from them wherewith we have testimony to Christ. Second, for the sake of the forefathers from whom Christ took the beginning of his humanity, thus from the line of Jesse. Third, for the sake of the Jews' conversion, as they all shall be converted before the Last Judgment. Fourth, in remembrance of Jesus Christ, for, as stubborn as the Jews are, as stubbornly shall we keep in our hearts the remembrance of His martyrdom." (A similar exposition is found in Purgoldts Rb., VIII, 59). The reference to "the sacred teachers of Christendom" suggests that there must be a model for this introductory article to the Jewry-law section of the *Berliner Stadtbuch* and its reasoning, in the theological or canon-law literature of the Middle Ages. Although much time and effort were spent in searching for such a model, neither the

author nor two of his friends—one a theologian and historian, the other an expert in the history of canon law—were successful in detecting it.

121. M. Wiener, *Regesten zur Geschichte der Juden in Deutschland während des Mittelalters* (Hannover, 1862), No. 137; George Caro, *Sozial- und Wirtschaftsgeschichte der Juden*, II, 136 f., 309.

122. Cf. Isert Rösel, "Die Reichssteuern der deutschen Judengemeinden," *MGWJ*, LIV (1910), 208 ff. It is more than doubtful whether the *guldin pfenning* was, in fact, established in renewal of the ancient yearly poll tax imposed upon the Jews by Vespasian after the destruction of Jerusalem. The proposition was first advanced by S. Cassel, article "Juden (Geschichte)," in Ersch and Gruber, *Encyclopädie der Wissenschaften und Künste*, II, 27, 87 f., and later taken over by H. Graetz, *Geschichte der Juden*, VII (4th ed.; Leipzig, n.d.), 328, as well as by Stobbe, *op. cit.*, p. 31. But there is no documentary evidence for this contention; and the two parallels from Spanish and English sources presented by Lewy, *op. cit.*, pp. 240 f. and nn. 6, 7, offer by no means convincing support.

123. *Rechter Weg*, F 41: ". . . wenne juden nicht under ehn [den fursten] keyn recht habin, wenne was rechtes ehn die fursten gebin und setzin" (cf. below, p. 363).

CHAPTER VII

1. As to the history and jurisdiction of Jewish courts in the Middle Ages, cf. Otto Stobbe, *Die Juden in Deutschland während des Mittelalters* (Braunschweig, 1866), pp. 140–43; J. E. Scherer, *Die Rechtsverhältnisse der Juden in den deutsch-österreichischen Ländern* (Leipzig, 1901), pp. 251, 254–56; Simon Goldmann, *Die jüdische Gerichtsverfassung innerhalb der jüdischen Gemeindeorganisation: Ein Beitrag zur Geschichte des Judenbischofs im Mittelalter in seiner Entwicklung von den ältesten Zeiten bis zum 15. Jahrhundert* (University of Cologne Ph.D. thesis; Cologne, 1924; in typescript only; the copy in the Preussische Staatsbibliothek in Berlin was used by the writer); H. J. Zimmels, *Beiträge zur Geschichte der Juden in Deutschland im 13. Jahrhundert, insbesondere auf Grund der Gutachten des R. Meir Rothenburg* (Vienna, 1926), pp. 40–43; David Menahem Shohet, *The Jewish Court in the Middle Ages* (Columbia University Ph.D. thesis; New York, 1931); Moses Frank, *Kehillot Ashkenaz u-Bate Dinehen* ["The Jewish Communities and Their Courts in Germany from the Twelfth to the End of the Fifteenth Centuries"; in Hebrew] (Tel Aviv, 1938), esp. pp. 117 ff.; James Parkes, *The Jew in the Medieval Community* (London, 1938), pp. 247–50, 255–59; Salo W. Baron, *The Jewish Community: Its History and Structure to the American Revolution* (Philadelphia, 1942), II, 236–43; Abraham A. Neuman, *The Jews in Spain: Their Social, Political,*

and Cultural Life during the Middle Ages, I (Philadelphia, 1942), 112–60; scanty notes also in Herbert Fischer, *Die verfassungsrechtliche Stellung der Juden in den deutschen Städten während des dreizehnten Jahrhunderts* (Breslau, 1931), pp. 123–40.

On the problem of the relationship between Jewish and non-Jewish courts in the Middle Ages see Guido Kisch, "Relations between Jewish and Christian Courts in the Middle Ages," *Louis Ginzberg Jubilee Volume* (New York, 1945), pp. 201–25; cf. Giannino Ferrari delle Spade, "Giurisdizione speciale ebraica nell' Impero Romano-Cristiano," *Scritti in onore di Contardo Ferrini pubblicati in occasione della sua beatificazione,* I (Milan, 1947), 239–61.

2. Heinrich Graetz, *Geschichte der Juden,* VI (4th ed.; Leipzig, n.d.), p. 182; Scherer, *op. cit.,* p. 236; Louis Finkelstein, *Jewish Self-Government in the Middle Ages* (New York, 1924), pp. 155 f. and n. 1; Baron, *op. cit.,* I, 212 f., 312; III, 51 f., n. 3. An interesting parallel is found in medieval canon law, which placed procedure against a cleric before secular courts under punishment and threatened nullification of their sentences (cf. Erwin Jacobi, "Der Prozess im *Decretum Gratiani* und bei den ältesten Dekretisten," *ZRG,* XXXIV, kanon. Abt. III (1913), 236.

3. Finkelstein, *op. cit.,* pp. 42 f., 236 f.; Selig Auerbach, *Die rheinischen Rabbinerversammlungen im 13. Jahrhundert* (University of Würzburg Ph.D. thesis; Würzburg, 1932), pp. 36 f., 53, 68, 80 f. The Christian authorities opposed the prohibition of recourse to secular (Christian) courts by Jewish litigants only sporadically (cf. Stobbe, *op. cit.,* pp. 141, 254 f., n. 132; Augusta Steinberg, *Studien zur Geschichte der Juden in der Schweiz während des Mittelalters* [Zürich, 1903], p. 26 [Zürich]: "If a Jew is wronged by another [Jew], he shall take his cause before the burgomaster and [municipal] council, and as they pass judgment according to their knowledge, so it shall be forever, and in such case no Jew shall seek or receive adjudication by Jewish law against the other"). Cf. also Steinberg, *op. cit.,* p. 27 (Freiburg in Switzerland); Emanuel Forchhammer, "Beiträge zur Geschichte der deutschen Juden mit besonderer Beziehung auf Magdeburg und die benachbarte Gegend," *Geschichtsblätter für Stadt und Land Magdeburg,* XLVI (1911), 386 (Goslar).

Criminal jurisdiction over Jews belonged exclusively to the territorial ruler or town lord and before their respective courts (cf. Stobbe, *op. cit.,* pp. 160 f.; Steinberg, *op. cit.,* pp. 26 f.; Forchhammer, *op. cit.,* pp. 378, 381 ff., 386). For a jury-court decision according to Magdeburg law in a Cracow manuscript from the end of the fourteenth century see Ferdinand Bischoff, "Über eine Sammlung deutscher Schöffensprüche in einer Krakauer Handschrift," *Archiv für Kunde österreichischer Geschichts-*

quellen, XXXVIII (1867), 18, No. 302: "If, then, you have taken the Jew [in a matter of] over six *groschen*, and have to pass judgment on him, you may sentence him as a counterfeiter; but if you have not to judge Jews, then hand him over to him who rightfully has to pass judgment on him, your overlord the *voivode* of Cracow." Cf. also Reg. jur., J 136, 137; MRb., III, 17, 40, and above, p. 102.

4. This is correctly pointed out by Finkelstein (*op cit.*, p. 156, n. 1) with reference to talmudic law (*Gittin*, 84b) and had already been emphasized by Stobbe (*op. cit.*, p. 140; cf. also Parkes, *op. cit.*, p. 255; Baron, *op. cit.*, I, 213 f.; Irving A. Agus, *Rabbi Meir of Rothenburg: His Life and His Works as Sources for the Religious, Legal, and Social History of the Jews of Germany in the Thirteenth Century*, I [Philadelphia, 1947], 57 f., n. 9, 64). Shohet, in contradistinction (*op. cit.*, pp. 103–6, 133), exaggerates the issue by advancing his generalizing thesis that "hardly any provision was made for the Jews in the civil courts, . . . throughout the entire period of the Middle Ages no Jew was allowed anywhere to give testimony, . . . and the Jews were deprived of a judicial standing in the civil courts." The presentation to follow will disprove these assertions. They are contradicted by Shohet's own statement (p. 99, based on Jewish sources) that "Jewish litigants of their own accord" could "give preference to the secular court for the adjudication of their suit," and that such decisions were considered valid according to Rabbi Isaac ben Moses (Or Zarua), an eminent medieval authority on Jewish law.

According to Baron (*op. cit.*, III, 51 f., n. 3), "in considering rabbinic insistence upon a Jewish judiciary, one should not wholly discount the vested interests of lay and rabbinic courts in fees and fines." This hypothesis needs stronger support from the sources in order to become acceptable.

5. The instance of a Jew of Leitmeritz, named Abraham (beginning of the sixteenth century), stands alone, indeed. "Intending to sue the Jew Jacob," Abraham submitted a hypothetically construed law case to the *Schöffen* of Magdeburg and asked for their legal opinion, which was sent to him in writing. The fact that he merely indicated his "intention to sue the Jew Jacob," must be considered as unusual. The regular procedure was to submit an actual law case to the jurors for decision. That this was not done but, instead, a hypothetical form chosen indicates that Abraham did not go so far as to bring actual suit against his fellow-Jew before the Christian court. Abraham's application to the jurors of Magdeburg and their reply are printed in Wilhelm Weizsäcker, *Magdeburger Schöffensprüche und Rechtsmitteilungen für den Oberhof Leitmeritz*

(Stuttgart and Berlin, 1943), No. 102, pp. 358 f., and in Guido Kisch, *Jewry-Law in Medieval Germany: Laws and Court Decisions Concerning Jews* (New York, 1949), p. 236.

6. E.g., Stendal UB., XXVII, 1, p. 112: "Before us came a Jew and a Jewess to the *gehegheden dinge* [the duly inaugurated court session] and laid a complaint against a Christian that he had beaten them black and blue and inflicted bloody wounds"; MFr., I, 4, 7: A Jew lays a complaint against a Christian "vor gehegetem dinge" because of an insult he has suffered from him. Cf. also MSchSpr. Leitmeritz, No. 109, pp. 371 f.

7. Cf. Stobbe, *op. cit.*, p. 143; Hermann Rudorff, *Zur Rechtsstellung der Gäste im mittelalterlichen städtischen Prozess* (Breslau, 1907), p. 37; Hans Planitz, "Studien zur Geschichte des deutschen Arrestprozesses," *ZRG*, XXXIX (1918), 272 ff.; XL (1919), 178; Forchhammer, *op. cit.*, p. 378.

8. Hugo Boehlau, *Die Blume von Magdeburg* (Weimar, 1868), II, 2, 45, pp. 114 f. Cf. charter for the Jews in Basel of 1386: "Were ouch, dass jemande der obgenannten juden deheinen jemer ütschit anzusprechende hette, der sol das recht von inen nemen, in ir judenschul, als es von alter harkomen ist" (*Beiträge zur vaterländischen Geschichte*, VI [Basel, 1857], p. 280, quoted by Herbert Meyer, *Entwerung und Eigentum im deutschen Fahrnisrecht* [Jena, 1902], pp. 173 f.). The court was at times "mixed," i.e., composed of Jewish and non-Jewish jurors, with a Christian or Jew presiding (cf. Forchhammer, *op. cit.*, p. 379).

9. MS Breslau R 568, No. 1, fol. 377; cf. also Guido Kisch, *Leipziger Schöffenspruchsammlung* (Leipzig, 1919), No. 113, p. 137.

10. J. F. Behrend, *Die Magdeburger Fragen* (Berlin, 1865), I, 2, 13; Emil Kalužniacki, "Die polnische Rezension der Magdeburger Urteile," *Sitzungsberichte der kaiserlichen Akademie der Wissenschaften, phil.-hist. Klasse*, CXI (1886), 184, art. O, 101.

11. Cf., e.g., MS Breslau R 568, fol. 406r: "Was mir czugeteilt wirt mit Meydeburgischim rechte, das wil ich vor gut nemen, und was mir geburt czu nemen und czu besitczin, das wil ich stete haldin."

12. For details see G. Kisch, *Leipziger Schöffenspruchsammlung*, "Einleitung"; G. Kisch, "Das Recht am Zeitzer Mühlgraben," in *Sachsen und Anhalt*, V (Magdeburg, 1929), 302, 304 ff.; Walter Becker, *Magdeburger Recht in der Lausitz* (Stuttgart, 1931), pp. 43 ff.; Eugen Wohlhaupter, "Die Spruchtätigkeit der Kieler juristischen Fakultät," *ZRG*, LVIII (1938), 757 f. Cf. also above, chap. ii, n. 93.

13. MS Breslau R 568, fol. 364r: "*Von berichtunge.* Also als ir uns gebetin habit umbe ewir burgere umme dy berichtunge, dorumbe entpite wir euch wedir: Wer czu uns kommit, dem sey wir des phlichtig, das wir

en berichten, wes her uns frogit; off welchim brefe ewir ingesigil cleybit, den wollin wir gern berichtin."

14. MSchSpr. Leitmeritz, No. 109, pp. 371 f.; cf. No. 108, pp. 370 f.

15. Victor Friese and Erich Liesegang, *Magdeburger Schöffensprüche* (Berlin, 1901), III B, 127, p. 591, and III B, 129, pp. 593 f.

16. MSchSpr. Leitmeritz, No. 102, pp. 358 f.

17. Cf. Adolf Stölzel, *Der Brandenburger Schöppenstuhl* (Berlin, 1901), pp. 238 f.; G. Kisch, *Leipziger Schöffenspruchsammlung*, pp. *19–*39.

18. Whoever it actually may have been, this is another clear proof of the fact that the Jews in medieval Germany knew and could employ the German language of their native provinces without admixture of jargon. On this problem, cf. G. Kisch, *Sachsenspiegel and Bible* (Notre Dame, Ind., 1941), pp. 176–78. The Jewry oath had to be taken in German (cf. below, pp. 276 ff.). According to a *Responsum* (No. 101) by Rabbi Jacob ben Judah Weil (first half of the fifteenth century), German was also employed in Jewish courts. A *Takkanah* issued by a rabbinical synod in Nuremberg (date uncertain) made the use of the German language even compulsory on the request of one litigant party, provided that its adversary also had command of written German. Rabbi Weil's *Responsum*, reproduced by Isaac Rivkind in *Pinkos*, I (New York, 1927), 156, was misinterpreted to some extent by A. Berliner, "Die mittelhochdeutsche Sprache bei den Juden," *Jahrbuch für jüdische Geschichte und Literatur*, I (1898), 168 f.

19. Nevertheless, compared with the tremendous mass of general litigations, amounting to thousands, which were decided by the Saxon jury courts, the cases involving Jews were insignificant in number. Accordingly, there is no mention in the available sources of a special day set aside by the court for the trial of suits by Jews against Christians. This was the case in some municipal courts, as in Brünn, Moravia, where the following provision was conditioned by the number of such litigations (Brünn SchB., No. 430, p. 200): "Ultima vero die specialiter est judicium pro judaeis isto videlicet modo, quod judaei tantum agunt in christianos" ("But on the last day justice is administered especially for Jews, that is to say, only Jews bring their suits against Christians").

Although Jews settled in Magdeburg as early as the tenth century (cf. *Germania Judaica*, pp. 163 ff.), no members of that community are represented as parties to litigations decided by the Magdeburg jury court. Magdeburg is mentioned twice in the work *Or Zarua* of Rabbi Isaac ben Moses of Vienna (*ca.* 1180–1250) (ed. Žitomir, 1862), fol. 41a, No. 114, and fol. 230a, No. 775; cf. J. Wellesz, "Über R. Isaak ben Moses 'Or

Zarua,' " *Jahrbuch der jüdisch-literarischen Gesellschaft Frankfurt am Main*, IV (1906), 104; *Germania Judaica*, pp. 166, 169; I. Kahan, "Or Sarua als Geschichtsquelle," *JGJC*, IX (1938), 58. These cases refer to the *Jewish* court in Magdeburg. Louis Rabinowitz ("The Herem Ha-Yishub and the Merchant Guild in Goslar," *Historia Judaica*, II [1940], 14, n. 6) called attention to the fact that parties to litigations concerning the Jewish community of Goslar appealed twice during the thirteenth century to the rabbis of Magdeburg for the decision of law cases. According to Rabinowitz, "such procedure is strongly reminiscent of the Jury Court at Magdeburg and would suggest a similar institution among the Jews of Germany"; cf. also Rabinowitz, *The Ḥerem Hayyishub* (London, 1945), p. 163, n. 9.

20. This opinion was first advanced by Friese and Liesegang, *op. cit.*, pp. 809 f., and was later accepted by K. G. Hugelmann, "Studien zum Recht der Nationalitäten im deutschen Mittelalter. II. Das Judenrecht der Rechtsbücher," *Historisches Jahrbuch der Görresgesellschaft*, XLVIII (1928), 585, n. 40.

21. Hermann Grössler, "Sammlung älterer nach Eisleben ergangener Rechtsbescheide des magdeburgischen Schöppenstuhls," *Zeitschrift des Harzvereins für Geschichte und Altertumskunde*, XXIII (1890), No. 33, 194.

22. Cf. Würzburg *Brückengerichtsordnung* (no date given), manuscript quoted in Christian Gottlob Haltaus, *Glossarium Germanicum medii aevi* (Lipsiae, 1758), p. 1044: "Item von einem yeden urtelbrieff einer person, gibt man fünffundvirtzig pfenning, die juden geben von dem urthel und von den briefen zwyfach; und were ein invocation an den geistlichen richter haben wil, der gibt darvon funffzehen pfenning, aber die juden geben zwyfach; und doch sollen ine die gelter einfach wider bezaln und nit mere."

CHAPTER EIGHT

1. On the history of medieval penal law in general see Rudolf His, *Das Strafrecht des deutschen Mittelalters*, Vols. I (Leipzig, 1920) and II (Weimar, 1935); Victor Friese, *Das Strafrecht des Sachsenspiegels* (Breslau, 1898); Carl Johannes Caspar, *Darstellung des strafrechtlichen Inhaltes des Schwabenspiegels und des Augsburger Stadtrechts* (Berlin University Jur.D. thesis; Berlin, 1892); Johannes Gottfried Ullmann, *Das Strafrecht der Städte der Mark Meissen, der Oberlausitz, des Pleissner-, Oster- und Vogtlandes während des Mittelalters* ("Leipziger Rechtswissenschaftliche Studien," Heft 34 [Leipzig, 1928]); Walter Becker, *Magdeburger Recht in der Lausitz* (Stuttgart, 1931), pp. 79–85.

For full bibliographies see Richard Schröder and Eberhard von Künssberg, *Lehrbuch der deutschen Rechtsgeschichte* (7th ed.; Berlin, 1932); Heinrich Brunner, *Grundzüge der deutschen Rechtsgeschichte* (8th ed. by Claudius von Schwerin; Munich and Leipzig, 1930); also Claudius von Schwerin, *Grundzüge der deutschen Rechtsgeschichte* (Munich, 1934).

On the treatment of Jews in the medieval system of penal law see Otto Stobbe, *Die Juden in Deutschland während des Mittelalters* (Braunschweig, 1866), pp. 42–45, 159–62; J. E. Scherer, *Die Rechtsverhältnisse der Juden in den deutsch-österreichischen Ländern* (Leipzig, 1901), pp. 171 f., 216–30; Forchhammer, "Beiträge zur Geschichte der deutschen Juden . . . ," *Geschichtsblätter für Stadt und Land Magdeburg*, XLVI (1911), 373–91; His, *op. cit.*, I, 239 ff., and *passim*.

2. E.g., RW., Q 60: "Uff ewer rechtes froge thun wir euch zu wissen, das wir nicht des blutis richter sein und uns nicht fuget zu thun, des blutis ortil zu gebin yn sachin, do wir vornemen, das eyner yn hanthaffter that, do es eyme an den hals geht, gefangen were gewest. Yn andern fuglichen sachen thw wir gerne ewern willen." See Hugo Böhlau, "Aus der Praxis des Magdeburger Schöffenstuhls während des 14. und 15. Jahrhunderts," *ZRG*, O.S., IX (1870), 13 and n. 44. Cf., also with regard to the statement following in the text, Becker, *op. cit.*, pp. 79–85; Adolf Stölzel, *Der Brandenburger Schöppenstuhl* (Berlin, 1901), p. 235.

3. See the detailed discussion above, pp. 107–10, 154 ff.; also chap. vii, n. 3.

4. Gustav Adolf Tzschoppe and Gustav Adolf Stenzel, *Urkundensammlung zur Geschichte des Ursprungs der Städte und der Einführung und Verbreitung deutscher Kolonisten und Rechte in Schlesien und der Oberlausitz* (Hamburg, 1832), p. 473; cf. Forchhammer, *op. cit.*, p. 382 and n. 399. On the Magdeburg Law Instruction for Görlitz of 1304 in general see Richard Jecht, Über die in Görlitz vorhandenen Handschriften des *Sachsenspiegels* und verwandter Rechtsquellen," *Neues Lausitzisches Magazin*, LXXXII (Görlitz, 1906), 225 f. and n. 4.

5. See above, pp. 109 f.; furthermore, MRb., VI, 2, 2; Reg. jur., J 132, 139; Bocksd. Rem., 3; Rem. RW., 13.

6. Cf. the quotations in Reg. jur., J 132, of C. *de judeis*, *l. si qui* [*Cod. Just.* i. 9. 8]; in Reg. jur., J 139, of C. *de judeis et celicolis*, *l. nullus* [*Cod. Just.* i. 9. 14], in addition to Ssp., III, 7.

7. See above, pp. 142, 106; cf. also Ferdinand Frensdorff, "Beiträge zur Geschichte und Erklärung der deutschen Rechtsbücher. II," *Nachrichten der K. Gesellschaft der Wissenschaften zu Göttingen*, 1894, p. 33.

8. Karl von Amira, *Die Dresdener Bilderhandschrift des Sachsenspiegels*, Vol. II: *Erläuterungen*, Part I, pp. 465 f.

9. This fact had already struck Karl Friedrich Eichhorn, who remarked in his *Deutsche Staats- und Rechtsgeschichte*, II (5th ed.; Göttingen, 1843), 612, n. a: "Doch kommt der Jude unter den Personen, die ein Wergeld haben, nicht vor, und steht also auch in dieser Hinsicht den Christen nicht ganz gleich." Eichhorn was satisfied with this factual conclusion, without giving the problem involved further consideration. Andreas Heusler (*Institutionen des deutschen Privatrechts*, I [Leipzig, 1885], 152, 155), and, following him, Scherer (*op. cit.*, p. 172), argued: "The Jews had no claim to *Wergeld*, because the *Wergeld* flowed from social standing, while the Jews had no social standing." It was Frensdorff alone (see n. 7, above) who approached the problem with proper understanding.

10. On the *Wergeld* in the *Sachsenspiegel* and under Magdeburg law see His, *op. cit.*, I, 590 ff.; Friese, *op. cit.*, pp. 171–95; Ullmann, *op. cit.*, pp. 43 ff.; Friese and Liesegang, *Magdeburger Schöffensprüche* (Berlin, 1901), pp. 864 f.; G. Kisch, *Leipziger Schöffenspruchsammlung* (Leipzig, 1919), pp. 69–71, 73 f.

11. Cf. His, *op. cit.*, I, 477, 592.

12. On the *Busse* in the *Sachsenspiegel* and under Magdeburg law see His, *op. cit.*, I, 594 ff., 598 ff.; Friese, *op. cit.*, pp. 171–95; Ullmann, *op. cit.*, pp. 44 f.; Friese and Liesegang, *op. cit.*, pp. 752 ff.

13. See above, pp. 87 ff.

14. Stendal UB., XXVII, 1, pp. 112 f.

15. Cf. MFr., I, 1, 19; Forchhammer, *op. cit.*, p. 381.

16. MFr., II, 6, 1; LSchSprS., 444; Helmut Hillmann, *Das Gericht als Ausdruck deutscher Kulturentwicklung im Mittelalter* (Stuttgart, 1930), pp. 105 f.

17. MRb., IV, 45, 21: "Eyns iczlichen mans busse in lantrechte unde wichbilde sin drisig schillinge. . . ."

18. Ssp., III, 45, 2; Friese, *op. cit.*, p. 186; Wasserschleben, RQ., II, 213; IV, 97; His, *op. cit.*, I, 238 and n. 7.

19. Rem. RW., 11: "Whoever abuses a Jew must give him fifteen shillings as *Busse*."

20. MFr., I, 4, 7; MS 170^b, Cracow (Homeyer, No. 645), 182; RW., B 71; cf. Stobbe, *op. cit.*, p. 163; Forchhammer, *op. cit.*, pp. 164, 380 f. A similar case is related in MSchSpr., III B, 96: A Jew called a Christian woman "a hungry harlot [*eyne hongeriche Kotze*]." The *Busse* was also fifteen shillings (cf. Forchhammer, *op. cit.*, p. 387). The abusive name "whoreson," very common in the Middle Ages, was by no means applied to Jews only. It was used to indicate obscure origin (cf. His, *op. cit.*, II, 110, n. 2, 114).

448 NOTES TO CHAPTER VIII, PAGES 183-186

21. MSchSpr., IV, 2, 10; cf. Forchhammer, *op. cit.*, p. 164; Friese and Liesegang, *op. cit.*, p. 810.

22. MSchSpr., III B, 125.

23. MRb., III, 17, 33; cf. Stobbe, *op. cit.*, p. 44.

24. Reg. jur., J 140.

25. Ssp., III, 2; Schwsp., L 255, G 210; cf. above, pp. 119 ff.; Reg. jur., J 149, 153, 154; see also below, n. 109.

26. Documentary evidence in Forchhammer, *op. cit.*, pp. 167 ff.; cf. Stobbe, *op. cit.*, p. 177; H. J. Zimmels, *Beiträge zur Geschichte der Juden in Deutschland* (Vienna, 1926), pp. 13, 23; also the following entry in the "Red Book" of Görlitz from the fourteenth century: "Sara judinne hat uffgegeben er hus, daz Smerlin gewest ist, Isag juden und darnach gemeynlich allen juden czu einer schulen erplichin" (Herbert Zander, *Das rote Buch der Stadt Görlitz [1305-1416]* [Leipzig, 1929], p. 26). On medieval synagogues in general, and from the point of view of architecture in particular, see Richard Krautheimer, *Mittelalterliche Synagogen* (Berlin, 1927). Krautheimer made, however, no inquiry into the property rights in the medieval synagogues.

27. MRb., III, 17, 37; cf. Stobbe, *op. cit.*, pp. 45, 168; Scherer, *op. cit.*, pp. 226 f.; also Georg Phillips, *Kirchenrecht*, II (Regensburg, 1846), 414 f.

28. Reg. jur., J 141; cf. MRb., III, 17, 36. Cf. Scherer, *op. cit.*, pp. 225 f.

29. On the protection of the Sabbath and Jewish holidays under Polish Jewry-law, cf. Isaac Lewin, "The Protection of Jewish Religious Rights by Royal Edicts in Ancient Poland," *Quarterly Bulletin of the Polish Institute of Arts and Sciences in America*, I (1943), 558-62 (pp. 4-8 of the reprint). There the violator is punished "like a robber and thief."

30. Cf. Bocksd. Rem., 8; Rem. RW., 12: "Should a Jew slay a Christian or a Christian a Jew, one shall be judged like the other, as if both were Christians"; Rem. Wolrab, *s.v.* "Juden"; Reg. jur., J 138. See also above, pp. 122 f.

31. Cf. His, *op. cit.*, I, 241 ff.; Forchhammer, *op. cit.*, p. 382; Friese, *op. cit.*, p. 112; Friese and Liesegang, *op. cit.*, pp. 805 f.; Ullmann, *op. cit.*, p. 6.

32. A. von Daniels and Fr. von Gruben, *Das Sächsische Weichbildrecht* (Berlin, 1858), p. 437.

33. For details see Stobbe, *op. cit.*, pp. 160, 265 f., n. 149; His, *op. cit.*, I, 366 and n. 2 (with numerous references), also 493; Augusta Steinberg, *Studien zur Geschichte der Juden in der Schweiz während des Mittelalters* (Zürich, 1902), p. 33; Forchhammer, *op. cit.*, pp. 387 f.

34. On the hanging upside-down see Karl von Amira, *Die germanischen Todesstrafen: Untersuchungen zur Rechts- und Religionsgeschichte* (Munich, 1922), p. 98. On the suspension of dogs on the gallows together with the condemned criminals see *ibid.*, p. 105: "Keine Rede kann davon sein, dass dieser Brauch [suspension of dogs] etwa erst im Mittelalter, insbesondere dass er gar erst als Judenstrafe aufgekommen sei. Er hat sich nur am längsten gerade in dieser Eigenschaft erhalten." On the so-called *Judenspitze* or the "Jews' pinnacle" on the gallows see *ibid.*, p. 251, No. 130 l; p. 325, No. 563 d; p. 326, No. 566. Cf. also Georg Stahm, *Das Strafrecht der Stadt Dortmund bis zur Mitte des XVI. Jahrhunderts* (Heidelberg, 1910), p. 251 and n. 6 with bibliography; in addition, Hans Fehr, *Das Recht im Bilde* (Erlenbach and Zürich, 1923), pp. 84 ff., 183 f., n. 48. Pictorial representations of these kinds of punishment are listed in Amira, *op. cit.*, p. 313, No. 481; p. 328, No. 583; p. 331, No. 598; for reproductions see Fehr, *op. cit.*, Nos. 103 (*a.* 1586), 104 (*a.* 1398); Fehr, "Geschichte der Rechtspflege," in *Wissen ist Macht*, III (1934), 620 f., No. 617 (*a.* 1553); Heinrich Loewe, *Die Juden in der katholischen Legende* (Berlin, 1912), picture facing p. 80 (sixteenth century), not found in the original version of Loewe's essay in *MGWJ*, LVI (1912), 257 ff., 385 ff., 612 ff.; Georg Liebe, *Das Judentum in der deutschen Vergangenheit* (Leipzig, 1903), p. 78, No. 63 (eighteenth century); in the latter picture, strangely enough, the dog is suspended by his neck and not—as usually—by his hind legs. In an essay, "The 'Jewish Execution' in Medieval Germany," *Jewish Social Studies*, V (1943), 3–26, Rudolf Glanz attempted to make an inquiry into the "cultural evolution" of this kind of punishment, called by him "Jewish execution." From secondary sources he collected instances covering the fifteenth to the seventeenth centuries. But Glanz's hypotheses lack adequate documentation, particularly for the medieval period. His reasoning, decisively influenced by the alien-law and racial theories, does not give proper consideration to the general developments in medieval criminal law. The problem has been re-examined by G. Kisch, "The 'Jewish Execution' in Medieval Germany," *Historia Judaica*, V (1943), 103–32.

35. Cf., e.g., *Brünner Schöffenbuch*, composed by the municipal clerk Johannes (middle of the fourteenth century), ed. Emil Franz Rössler, *Die Stadtrechte von Brünn aus dem XIII. und XIV. Jahrhundert* (Prague, 1852), chap. 432, p. 202: ". . . pilleus de scutella ligno quodam elevato superius scutellae more judaico imposito factus cum pice ardente crinibus et capiti judaei impressus cum eodem pilleo, ut a christianis suspensis discerneretur." This form of punishment itself is not designated as "execution 'in the Jewish manner' [*more judaico*]," as interpreted by

Glanz, *op. cit.*, p. 7. The text unequivocally states that a piece of wood was placed on top of the inverted bowl, the improvised Jews' hat, to give it the appearance of the real pointed hat "of the Jewish manner."

36. Amira, *Die germanischen Todesstrafen*, p. 313, No. 481; Amira, *Die Dresdener Bilderhandschrift des Sachsenspiegels*, II, Part I, 466 f.; cf. Hans Fehr, *Das Recht im Bilde*, pp. 84 ff. and No. 102.

37. Forchhammer, *op. cit.*, p. 384 and n. 414; cf. also Dortmund (1411), Stahm, *op. cit.*, p. 244: "Were ok dat jenich jude misdede, de selve jude sal beteren und anders nyman."

38. For details see His, *op. cit.*, I, 405 ff.; Ullmann, *op. cit.*, pp. 55 f.; cf. also Walter Ullmann, "The Right of Asylum in Sixteenth-Century Theory and Practice," *Dublin Review*, CVIII (October, 1944), 103–10.

39. R. Glanz's assertion (*op. cit.*, p. 15) that "even Jews could enjoy such protection [the right of sanctuary], is established by at least one case at Dortmund in 1393" finds no support in the source adduced by him. It is Dietrich Westhoff's "Chronik von Dortmund," in *Die Chroniken der deutschen Städte*, XX (Leipzig, 1887), 287, quoted also by Stahm, *op. cit.*, p. 287. Here is related the case of a Jew who, in 1393, took refuge in the church tower of the monastery of the Preachers, after stabbing a convert to Christianity. The municipal council of Dortmund addressed an inquiry to the "Doctors of the Order," asking under what circumstances the immunity of the asylum could be broken: "warmit einer die vrijheit brecke und watterlei gestalt men einen van derselvigen vrijheit nemen mochte." The "Chronik" continues: "The Doctors replied that the protection of asylum should not be enjoyed by those who betrayed or killed their lord, who robbed the church or its property, or who broke into the asylum with arms or by violence and did not trust themselves to it." The first of the cases enumerated, in its not unintentional ambiguity, unmistakably refers to the crime of betraying and killing the Savior (cast up against the Jews throughout the Middle Ages) in order to exclude them from the right of sanctuary. The stand taken in 1393 is reminiscent of the very similar situation in the late Roman and early canon law, described by Jean Juster, *Les Juifs dans l'empire romain*, II (Paris, 1914), 180. A direct refutation of Glanz's assertion is found in another manuscript, the reference to which in *Die Chroniken der deutschen Städte*, XX, 287, n. 2, escaped his attention. In this manuscript in the Theodor Huning collection the case is related correspondingly, but with the following addition: "The Jew was taken from the asylum and one hand was cut off" ("Der Jude war aus der Freiheit weggeführt und ihm die Hand abgehauen worden").

40. Buch's *Gloss* to Ssp. II, 10 (ed. Zobel; Leipzig, 1560):

"Also thut die Kirch, etc.] Hie soltu wissen, das die Kirch und Kirchhoff beschirmen und freien für dem gefenglichen angrieff alle missthetige leute, *ut 13 q. 2, c. quaesitum [Decretum Gratiani,* c. 30, C. 13, qu. 2] *et c. inter ea., Extra, de immu. eccles.* [c. 6, X, 3, 49] *et C. de his qui ad eccle. confug., l. fideli [Cod. Just.* i. 12. 2]. Doch werden davon ausgenommen fünfferley leute. Die ersten sein die Jüden. . . ."
    Buch's *Gloss* to Ssp. II, 10 (ed. Augsburg, 1516) cites—more correctly —passages treating explicitly of Jews, namely: "*C. de hiis qui ad eccle. confu., l. 1 et l. si servus [Cod. Just.* i. 12. 1 and 4]." On the negative attitude of Roman-canon law in the early Christian centuries see Juster, *op. cit.,* pp. 180 f.
    41. The poem is entitled "Von den Freistätten" and is found in Joseph Freiherr von Lassberg, *Liedersaal, das ist Sammelung altteutscher Gedichte,* I (St. Gallen and Konstanz, 1846), 475 ff. The passage referred to (65, vss. 49–60, p. 476) reads:

"Ich behielt ain yglichen man
Wie er käm geflochen hin dan
Juden haiden morder kätzer
Daz kain boswicht wär so lätzer
Dem min friung wär verspart
Ich behielt jn uff die wart
Daz er käm zu redlichait
Ez wirt oft ain man über sait
Dez er gar unschuldig ist
Da von wolt ich geben frist
Jedem man jn min gemach
Daz ich recht erfür die sach."

    42. MSchSpr., III B, 96; cf. above, pp. 182 f. and n. 20.
    43. Glogau Rb., 476. Cf. the identical provision in the Braunschweig town law of 1350, quoted by His, *op. cit.,* II, 219, where, however, a reference to Glogau Rb., 476, is missing: "men scal it vor duve hebben."
    44. Cf. His, *op. cit.,* II, 218 ff.
    45. Ferdinand Bischoff, "Über eine Sammlung deutscher Schöffensprüche in einer Krakauer Handschrift," *Archiv für Kunde österreichischer Geschichtsquellen,* XXXVIII (1867), 18, No. 302.
    46. Cf. His, *op. cit.,* II, 275 f.; Ullmann, *op. cit.,* pp. 85 ff.; see also below, n. 100.
    47. For details see Stobbe, *op. cit.,* pp. 123 f.; Scherer, *op. cit.,* p. 46, No. 17, pp. 72, 197 ff.; Herbert Meyer, *Entwerung und Eigentum im deutschen Fahrnisrecht: Ein Beitrag zur Geschichte des deutschen Privatrechts*

und des Judenrechts im Mittelalters (Jena, 1902), pp. 210–19; Forchhammer, *op. cit.*, pp. 364 f.; George Caro, *Sozial- und Wirtschaftsgeschichte der Juden*, II (Leipzig, 1920), 162 ff.; Solomon Grayzel, *The Church and the Jews in the XIIIth Century* (Philadelphia, 1933), p. 35, n. 74; Bertold Bretholz, *Geschichte der Juden in Mähren im Mittelalter*, I (Brünn, 1934), 75, 90; G. Kisch, "The 'Jewish Law of Concealment,'" *Historia Judaica*, I (1938), 22–25; James Parkes, *The Jew in the Medieval Community* (London, 1938), pp. 48, 348 f.; Gertrud Schubart-Fikentscher, "Neue Fälle zum Brünner Recht," *Deutsches Archiv für Geschichte des Mittelalters*, III (1939), 441, 492, No. 19*a;* also Friese, *op. cit.*, pp. 36 f. Concerning the treatment of *res sacrae* in canon law, and particularly their alienation, see Paul Hinschius, *System des katholischen Kirchenrechts*, IV (Berlin, 1888), 169; K. G. Hugelmann, "Studien zum Recht der Nationalitäten im deutschen Mittelalter. II. Das Judenrecht der Rechtsbücher," *Historisches Jahrbuch der Görresgesellschaft*, XLVIII (1928), 569 f., n. 9.

48. Buch's *Gloss* to Ssp., III, 7, 4, offers here a restrictive interpretation: "He [Eike von Repgow] speaks here of chalices not yet consecrated or of mass vestments or books that had not yet been in a church."

49. Dsp., F 209; Schwsp., L 261, G 214, 7: ". . . if he conceals it, and it is then found in his possession: he shall be hanged therefor like a thief; otherwise he is bound only to restitution without receiving compensation" (Freising Rb., Maurer, I, 172, Knapp, 122, I). MRb., III, 17, 5, specifies: ". . . books belonging to churches," and adds in III, 17, 6: "All other books, such as schoolbooks and lawbooks, German books, may be publicly accepted as pledges by the Jew in his keeping." He may accept even the other objects, if they remain in the church or are placed in a Christian's custody in the presence of two Christians and one Jew of good reputation. Similarly, Purgoldts Rb., VIII, 92, 93. The latter lawbook (VIII, 94) makes placing in a Christian's custody obligatory also for articles of food accepted as pledges by Jews. Cf. also Ullmann, *op. cit.*, p. 80.

50. BlM., II, 2, 150; Rem. RW., 5; Reg. jur., J 128; Rem. Wolrab, *s.v.* "Juden." Cf. *Glosse* to Wb., 135; Daniels and Gruben, *op. cit.*, p. 437; Forchhammer, *op. cit.*, p. 365.

51. For details see G. Kisch, *Historia Judaica*, I (1938), 22 f.; cf. also M. Elias, "Die römische Kurie, besonders Innozenz III., und die Juden," *Jahrbuch der jüdisch-literarischen Gesellschaft Frankfurt am Main*, XII (1918), 66, n. 1, with references to Jewish literature.

52. Stendal UB., X, 1; cf. Forchhammer, *op. cit.*, pp. 382 f., 390 f.

53. MFr., III, 1, 2; MSchSpr., I, 39, and pp. 866 ff.; LSchSprS., *Wort- und Sachregister, s.v.* "Wunde, kampfbare"; Ullmann, *op. cit.*, pp. 64 ff.

54. Ssp., II, 16, 2; Magdeburg-Breslau Law Instruction of 1261, MRQ., IV, 11.

55. See above, p. 179. Forchhammer (*op. cit.*, pp. 382 f.) arrived at the conclusion that the jurors did not consider this case a criminal matter at all. This opinion was based on a misunderstanding and erroneous interpretation of the Magdeburg court decision (Stendal UB., X, 1). The issue there is not whether the Jews should be tried before the (Christian) municipal court or the Jewish court, nor did the jurors declare the competence of the Jewish court, as supposed by Forchhammer. Instead, the legal problem was restricted to these two questions: (1) Should proof be submitted by the Jewish defendants in the place where municipal justice was administered (*in den ver scaren*) or in a place particularly sacred to the swearer, the synagogue? (2) Should a Jew in taking an oath be supported by Christians or by Jews as oath-helpers? The jurisdiction of a Jewish court was not at all involved in this decision.

56. Such cases are recorded of local municipal courts which, at times, took advantage of transgressions by Jews to free the municipal treasury from burdensome indebtedness to them. Instead of imposing the punishments incurred, the city of Breslau, for instance, was pleased to free itself of a debt of 339 marks groschen and 40 marks interest to the Jew Abraham, and of 800 marks to the Jew Cussiel (cf. Otto Stobbe, "Mitteilungen aus Breslauer Signaturbüchern," *Zeitschrift des Vereins für Geschichte und Altertum Schlesiens*, VIII [1867], 156 f., No. 162, *anno* 1433; 158 f., No. 166, *anno* 1434; 450 f., No. CCVIII, *anno* 1441; cf. also below, n. 89). The benefit of the municipal treasury was, however, not always the concern of the councilmen. Marcus Beckensloer, chairman of the town council of Breslau in 1440, was called to account in the following year because of "gifts" that he had accepted in several cases involving the imprisonment of Jews (see the official protocols in Stobbe, "Mitteilungen aus Breslauer Signaturbüchern," *ibid.*, pp. 451 f., No. CCIX).

57. For bibliography see Hübner, *Grundzüge des deutschen Privatrechts* (5th ed.; Leipzig, 1930), p. 591, n. 1; and His, *op. cit.*, II, 329, n. 7; in addition: G. G. Coulton, *Medieval Panorama: The English Scene from Conquest to Reformation* (Cambridge and New York, 1944), pp. 331–45; Ullmann, *op. cit.*, pp. 75 ff.; Rudolf Ruth, "Das kanonische Zinsverbot, seine ethischen, wirtschaftlichen und rechtlichen Grundlagen," *Festschrift für Ernst Heymann: Beiträge zum Wirtschaftsrecht*, I (Berlin, 1931), 316–48, written prior to Ruth's conversion to nazism (see the following note); T. P. McLaughlin, "The Teaching of the Canonists on Usury

(XII–XIV Centuries)," *Mediaeval Studies*, I (New York, 1939), 81–147; II (1940), 1–22; Carl F. Taeusch, "The Concept of 'Usury,' the History of an Idea," *Journal of the History of Ideas*, III (1942), 291–318, does not delve deeply into the problems, from the point of view of legal history.

58. Parkes, *op. cit.*, pp. 267–382, with bibliography on pp. 270 f., is the fullest analysis from a sociological viewpoint. There "the traditional conception of usury as a Jewish monopoly" is shown to be "a myth." Cf. the review by G. Kisch, *Historia Judaica*, II (1940), 50–54. For the history of usury by the Jews in Germany, the profoundest treatment based on documentary material is still Max Neumann's *Geschichte des Wuchers in Deutschland bis zur Begründung der heutigen Zinsengesetze (1654)* (Halle, 1865), pp. 292–347, although antiquated to some extent; for criticism see Wilhelm Endemann, *Studien in der romanisch-kanonistischen Wirtschafts- und Rechtslehre bis gegen Ende des siebzehnten Jahrhunderts*, II (Berlin, 1883), 381–98. On church law see also the brief survey in Grayzel, *op. cit.*, pp. 43–49. No scientific value attaches to the anti-Semitic essay by Rudolf Ruth, "Wucher und Wucherrecht der Juden im Mittelalter," *Deutsche Rechtswissenschaft*, II (1937), 111–57, based on secondary sources only, and superficially done as Nazi propaganda (cf. the review by G. Kisch, *Historia Judaica*, I [1938], 67–72). On usury, according to Jewish law, for a comparison see Emil Cohn, "Der Wucher im Talmud, seine Theorie und ihre Entwicklung," *Zeitschrift für vergleichende Rechtswissenschaft*, XVIII (1905), 37–72; Salo W. Baron, "The Economic Views of Maimonides," in *Essays on Maimonides: An Octocentennial Volume*, ed. S. W. Baron (New York, 1941), pp. 206–29.

59. Neumann, *op. cit.*, pp. 53 ff.

60. So precisely defined by Theodulfus, bishop of Orleans, at the end of the eighth century: "Quisquis per quodlibet ingenium magis accipit quam praestat, sciat se usuram fecisse" (J. D. Mansi, *Sacrorum conciliorum collectio*, XIII, 1016; quoted by Parkes, *op. cit.*, p. 282).

61. C. 18, X, *de usuris*, 5, 19:
"Quanto amplius Christiana religio ab exactione compescitur usurarum, tanto gravius super his Judaeorum perfidia insolescit, ita, quod brevi tempore Christianorum exhauriunt facultates. Volentes igitur in hac parte prospicere Christianis, ne a Judaeis immaniter aggraventur, synodali decreto statuimus, ut, si de cetero quocunque praetextu Judaei a Christianis graves immoderatasve usuras extorserint, Christianorum eis participium subtrahatur, donec de immoderato gravamine satisfecerint competenter. Unde Christiani, si opus fuerit, per censuram ecclesiasticam appellatione postposita, compellantur ab eorum commerciis abstinere. Principibus autem injungimus, ut propter hoc non

sint Christianis infesti, sed potius a tanto gravamine studeant cohibere Judaeos."

("The more the Christian religion suppresses the collecting of interest, the more does the Jewish unbelief become used to this practice, so that in a short time they [the Jews] exhaust the financial strength of the Christians. Therefore, in our desire to protect the Christians in this matter, that they should not be excessively oppressed by the Jews, we order by a decree of this synod, that when in the future Jews, under any pretext, extort heavy or immoderate interest from Christians, relationship with Christians shall be denied them until they shall have made sufficient amends for the exorbitant exactions. The Christians, moreover, if need be, shall be compelled by ecclesiastical punishment without appeal to abstain from commerce with them [the Jews]. We also impose upon the princes not to be aroused against the Christians because of this, but rather to try to keep the Jews from such grievous practice.")

Cf. Grayzel, *op. cit.*, pp. 306 ff.; Paul Hinschius, *System des katholischen Kirchenrechts*, V (Berlin, 1895), 50 and n. 1.

62. Julius Aronius, *Regesten zur Geschichte der Juden im fränkischen und deutschen Reiche bis zum Jahre 1273* (Berlin, 1887–1902), No. 724; cf. Neumann, *op cit.*, p. 293, n. 1.

63. Cf., e.g., decretal of Pope Gregory IX of October 11, 1229, to the bishop of Palencia, printed in Grayzel, *op. cit.*, pp. 182 ff., No. 60; Council of Albi in 1254, c. 63, Mansi, *op. cit.*, XXIII, 850; Grayzel, *op. cit.*, p. 334, No. XLI.

64. Dsp., F 209, which corresponds to Ssp., III, 7, 4, merely adds: *und nicht den gesuoch*. Only the southern German author of the *Schwabenspiegel*, himself a cleric, took over the canon-law regulations on general usury into art. L 160, G 140 (cf. L 289, G 240) of his lawbook. Thence it was adopted by the Freising Rb. (Maurer, II, 75^{29}; Knapp, 212); cf. also Neumann, *op. cit.*, pp. 69 f. The Freising lawbook treats only of Christian usurers, who, as the author points out at the end of the pertinent article, were commonly called by the name "baptized Jews": "Sie haissent cristen und sein pöser dann juden. Sie haissent wol getaufft juden" (Freising Rb., Maurer, II, 75^{29}; cf. above, p. 51). This designation most probably originated from Bernard of Clairvaux's letter to the clergy and people in eastern France, in 1146, against persecuting Jews during the Second Crusade (*Patr. Lat.*, Vol. CLXXXII, Epistola 363, p. 567 C, No. 7; cf. also Caro, *op. cit.*, I, 224): "Taceo quod sicubi desunt, pejus judaizare dolemus Christianos, feneratores, si tamen Christianos, et non magis *baptizatos Judaeos* convenit appellari."

65. Provisions against usury are also lacking in the medieval town laws of cities such as Goslar, Mühlhausen, Erfurt, Nordhausen, etc. (cf. Forchhammer, *op. cit.*, p. 368, n. 290).

66. *Gloss* on Ssp., I, 54, ed. Augsburg, 1516:

"*We synen tins to rechter tyt nicht en gewet, twifalt schal he en, etc.*]: Wuker is dat ein man mer upnympt wan he uth deit, als oft het bededinget, *ut XIV, qu. 3, c. 1* [*Decretum Gratiani*, c. 1, C. 14, q. 3]. Wo is dat nen wuker oder mut man wuker nemen. Etlike seggen ya. Nach keyserrechte mach men wol wuker nemen [*Cod. Just.* vi. 47. 1; *Nov.* 120, c. 6, § 2 '*Haec etiam*'; *Nov.* 106, *praef.*]. Mer segge, men scole en nenen woker nemen, wen Canones dy vorbydent [*Decretum Gratiani*, c. 2, Dist. XLVII, et X, de usuris, 5, 19 per totum]. Und wat dy Canon vorbydet, dat vorbidet ok dat keyserrecht [*Nov.* 131, *praef.; Nov.* 6, *praef.* . . . ; *Nov.* 133, c. 6]."

Among the five exceptions, in which usury was permitted, usury by Jews is not mentioned in the Augsburg edition of 1516. The edition of the *Gloss* to *Sachsenspiegel* by Cristoff Zobel (Leipzig, 1560), fol. 139b, in contradistinction, enumerates ten exceptions from the prohibition against usury. Usury by Jews is again not mentioned. Among the exceptions permitted, however, there appears as the sixth the permission to Christians to take usury from Jews: "One may well take usury from Jews and heathen. Because they are our and our faith's enemies, we may well take possession of their goods."

"Zum sechsten sagen etliche, man mög wol wucher nemen von Jüden und heiden, *ut 14, qu. 4, c. ab illo* [*Decretum Gratiani*, c. 12, C. 14, q. 4 (*Ubi jus belli, ibi jus usurae*)]. Dann weil sie unsere und unsers glaubens feinde sindt, mögen wir uns ihres guts wol underwinden, *ut Extra, de haere., c. excommunicamus* [c. 15, X, de haereticis, 5, 7]."

For the history and a discussion of this theory, which goes back to Ambrose, see Endemann, *Studien in der romanisch-kanonistischen Wirtschafts- und Rechtslehre*, II, 394 ff.; cf. also Angelo P. Sereni, *The Italian Conception of International Law* (New York, 1943), p. 89, n. 17.

The Stendal *Gloss* to *Sachsenspiegel*, III, 7, 1, referring to the renowned decretalist, Henricus de Segusia Cardin. Hostiensis (d. 1271), and the legist [Jacobus] Goffredus (d. 1245), states: "And Jews are not compelled to restitution by the church through the sanction of the Lateran Council; but there is indirect compulsion in that they are denied commerce with Christians according to Goffredus, who notes this on the said chapter '*quanto*.' "

On Tammo and Theodorich von Bocksdorff's *Glosses* to the *Sachsenspiegel* see Neumann, *op. cit.*, pp. 67, 71, 86.

67. On all the identical passages in this lawbook (IX, 15, 1, 9, 25 and

NOTES TO CHAPTER VIII, PAGES 193–196

26) see above, chap. ii, n. 68; cf. also Neumann, *op. cit.*, p. 298, n. 7, and 299, 305.

68. Friedrich Ortloff, *Das Rechtsbuch des Johannes Purgoldt* (Jena, 1860), p. 239; cf. Neumann, *op. cit.*, pp. 305 f., n. 3.

69. P. Clauswitz, *Das Berlinische Stadtbuch aus dem Ende des XIV. Jahrhunderts* (Berlin, 1883), p. 167; cf. Emil Steffenhagen, "Der Einfluss der Buchschen Glosse auf die späteren Denkmäler. II. Das Berliner Stadtbuch," *Sitzungsberichte der k. Akademie der Wissenschaften zu Wien, philos.-hist. Klasse*, CXXXI, No. 9 (1894), 9–11.

70. Karl Friedrich Eichhorn, *Deutsche Staats- und Rechtsgeschichte*, II (5th ed.; Göttingen, 1843), 614, note g. Hugelmann (*op. cit.*, pp. 577 f.) does not go beyond mere probabilities and unsubstantiated generalities. He did not delve into the problem at all. Even Neumann's comprehensive monograph escaped his attention.

71. Neumann, *op. cit.*, pp. 302 ff.; cf. 63 ff.

72. Neumann, *op. cit.*, pp. 64 and 303.

73. So correctly in Ortloff's edition (p. 168) and in the manuscript of 1387, No. 2680, in the Nationalbibliothek of Vienna (see above, chap. ii, n. 30); *Neun Bücher Magdeburger Rechts*, IX, 15, 2 (Ortloff, *op. cit.*, p. 476) has . . . *gesaczte recht.* . . .

74. MSchSpr., III B, 145, and p. 866. In this case the loan contract between the Jew Shalam and Walman had even been entered in the official court register.

75. MS Breslau J 5, Nos. 30 and 77. Cf. also MS Merseburg 3, No. 4; MSchSpr. Leitmeritz, No. 49, pp. 200, 202 (about 1514): "It does not behoove us, but only the ecclesiastical judge, to pass judgment on usury or whatever touches on usury, since no judge shall pass judgment on usury nor does it belong in his province to pass judgment on it."

76. Several of them are cited in His, *op. cit.*, II, 331, n. 5, and Ullmann, *op. cit.*, pp. 76 f. In general, on the jurisdiction of ecclesiastical courts in law matters of Jews, see Forchhammer, *op. cit.*, pp. 383 f.; Grayzel, *op. cit.*, pp. 58 f. Debtors often tried to bring their disputes with Jewish creditors before ecclesiastical courts, since, owing to the principles of canon law on *usuraria pravitas*, they could there expect more favorable decisions (cf. Otto Stobbe, "Mitteilungen aus Breslauer Signaturbüchern," *ZGS*, VII [1866], 189, n. 2).

77. Wasserschleben, RQ., V, 71, p. 417: "Wyr s[cheppen] czu Meyd[eburg]: Waz wucher sey ader nicht, daz geburt geistlicher gewald czu irkenne unde czu enscheidin unde uns nicht." Cf. MSchSpr., III A, 34, p. 407: "Hetten aber die potticher . . . gelt uff gelt gnomen, das alszo wuckerisch mochte angesehen werden, daruber gebordt uns als

wertlichen richteren nicht zcu erkennen; szundern eyn szotans gebordt billichen dem geystlichen richtere zcu rechtvertigen. Und szo gmelte frauwe . . . die pottichere derwegen anzcuclagen gedechte, das hat sie alszo vor dem geystlichen richtere zcu suchen, . . ." In this connection it seems worth mentioning that the same attitude toward the problem under discussion is found in the *Coutumes de Beauvaisis*, written in 1280–83 by Philippe de Beaumanoir, the greatest French jurist of the feudal period (cf. Beaumanoir, No. 1925, ed. Am. Salmon [Paris, 1899–1900]): "Voirs est que qui veut pledier d'usure, la connoissance en apartient à sainte Église" (quoted by Heinrich Mitteis, "Beaumanoir und die geistliche Gerichtsbarkeit," *ZRG*, XXXV, kanon. Abt. IV [1914], 309 f.).

78. Cf. Neumann, *op. cit.*, pp. 19 f., 142 ff., 152, 308 f.; Parkes, *op. cit.*, pp. 294 f., 329, 280; Coulton, *op. cit.*, pp. 336 f.

79. Cf. MRb., III, 14, 4: "No one may pawn pledges on *wucher(schaden)* with Jews unless upon agreement."

80. It is therefore not surprising that in some of their decisions they referred directly to, or accepted, the canon-law concept of usury. The latter thus found its way also into some lawbooks based on *Schöffensprüche*, such as MFr., II, 1, 1 and 2; MBSchR., III, 2, 12; see an interesting decision of Magdeburg also in [Johannes Ehrenfried Böhme], *Diplomatische Beiträge zur Untersuchung der schlesischen Rechte und Geschichte*, VI (Berlin, 1775), p. 93, §§ 3, 4; cf. Neumann, *op. cit.*, pp. 67 ff.; Ullmann, *op. cit.*, pp. 76, 77, n. 20; and above, n. 76.

81. Cf., e.g., the struggle of the Magdeburg jurors against retrogressive tendencies, apparent from decisions concerning guild statutes, discussed by Becker, *Magdeburger Recht in der Lausitz*, pp. 76 ff.; and concerning liability and exposure to seizure of burghers for debts of their fellow-burghers, discussed below, pp. 258 ff. and chap. x, n. 72. All this offers ample corroboration of, and additional illustration for, Richard Behrend's correct observation concerning the *Schöffen* of Magdeburg (*Göttingische Gelehrte Anzeigen*, Jahrgang CLXV, I [Berlin, 1903], 678): ". . . die sich wandelnden Erwerbs- und Verkehrsverhältnisse brachten zahlreiche Fragen, namentlich obligationenrechtlicher Natur, die aus den Rechtsbüchern nicht ohne weiteres zu beantworten waren. Umso mehr ist anzuerkennen, wie mit gesundem praktischen Verständnisse die Magdeburger Schöffen das Recht handhaben. . . . Die Magdeburger Schöffen legen in einer Zeit, in der die Rezeption des römischen Rechts bereits in vollem Zuge war, Zeugnis dafür ab, dass eine Fortentwicklung des deutschen Rechts aus eigener Kraft an sich nicht unmöglich gewesen wäre."

82. A survey of papal and conciliar legislation of the period from 1198 to 1254 is found in Grayzel, *op. cit.*; see below, chap. xiii, n. 23. Cf. also Louis I. Newman, *Jewish Influence on Christian Reform Movements* (New York, 1925), pp. 360–429.

83. Cf. Willibrord Lampen, "Alexander von Hales und der Antisemitismus," *Franziskanische Studien*, XVI (1929), 8; Peter Browe, "Die religiöse Duldung der Juden im Mittelalter," *Archiv für katholisches Kirchenrecht*, CXVIII (1938), 33 ff.

84. In the original Latin text, with all the quotations from Roman and canon law, no mention is made of *Nov. Just.*, LXXVII, c. 1, §§ 1–2, although the argument employed by the Stendal glossator is clearly set forth in and literally borrowed from this *Novella*.

85. See above, p. 190.

86. See above, pp. 183 f.

87. Reg. jur., J 153, 156.

88. For a survey of the present state of research see Newman, *op. cit.*, pp. 393 ff.; Grayzel, *op. cit.*, pp. 22–26; cf. also Browe, *op. cit.*, pp. 34 f.; and Browe, *Die Judenmission im Mittelalter und die Päpste* (Rome, 1942), pp. 296 ff.

89. Stobbe, "Mitteilungen aus Breslauer Signaturbüchern," ZGS, VIII (1867), 158 f., No. 166, *anno* 1434:

"Excessus et culpe Cussiel Judei.

"Am dinstage an unser frauwen abend nativitatis [September 7, 1434] als die sachen Kussiels des Juden in dis buch geschreben sein, czum ersten, das her eynen Cristen jungen hat lasin heimlichen besneiden und czu eyme Juden wellen machin und den dornoch weg geschicket in andire landt und stete czu smocheit und lesterunge des heiligen cristenlichin glowbens, das ouch Cristen und Juden off in vorbrocht hoben; item so hot derselbe Cussiel Jude sich undirwunden eines Cristen weybes, und die vorantwertet vor eyne Judynne, dy bey im lasen wonen, mit im lasen czu Schule geen, und mit im lasen wuchern; item als uns sulche sachen und broche vormeldet wurden, haben wir in lasen innemen, und in ettliche czeit halden lasen off ein gancz dirfaren sulchir stucke. [He freed himself from prison but was recaptured] . . . das her wider begriffen wardt, wolden wir im umb sulche broche, gewalt, frevel und missetat noch seinem vordinen lasen widerfaren und in richten lasen, und frogten in, ap her umb sulche missetat und broche rechten welde. Do sprach her, her welde nicht rechten und bat, das man im gnade tete, her welde der stat gute tun an sulchin schulden, di im di stat schuldig were, und lis di stat 800 marg ledik und frey von gutem willen unbetwungen und antworte uns die brive dorubir und globte des die stat czu entweren ken allen andern juden, den sulch gelt mete vorschreben was. Darumme im ouch genade getan ist wurden, und sulche missetat vorgeben und vorkoren."

90. *Gregorii I Papae registrum epistolarum,* ed. P. Ewald and Ludov. M. Hartmann (*MG, Epist.,* I [Berlin, 1887]), I, 34, p. 48 (*a.* 591):

"Hos enim, qui a christiana religione discordant, mansuetudine, benignitate, admonendo, suadendo ad unitatem fidei necesse est congregare, ne quos dulcedo praedicationis et praeventus futuri judicis terror ad credendum invitare poterat, minis et terroribus repellatur."

"We never learned of our Lord Jesus Christ that he would have compelled anyone to His service by force. He won people over by humble exhortation alone . . . ," Pope Gregory the Great wrote to Prince Landulf of Benevento in a letter known only through its transmission by Ivo of Chartres (1040–1116):

"Licet ex devotionis studio non dubitamus procedere, quod nobilitas tua iudaeos ad christianum cultum disponit adducere, tamen quia id inordinato videris studio agere, necessarium duximus admonendo tibi litteras nostras dirigere. Dominus enim noster Jesus Christus nullum legitur ad sui servitium violenter coegisse, sed humili exhortatione reservata unicuique proprii arbitrii libertate, quoscunque ad vitam praedestinavit aeternam non vindicando, sed proprium sanguinem fundendo ab errore revocasse" (Peter Browe, *Die Judenmission im Mittelalter und die Päpste,* p. 232, n. 110; cf. p. 13, n. 1).

Cf. canon 57 of the Fourth Council of Toledo (633), which expressly forbade Jews to be brought to Christianity by force or by threat (Mansi, *Concilia,* X, 633; A. Lukyn Williams, *Adversus Judaeos: A Bird's-Eye View of Christian Apologiae until the Renaissance* [Cambridge, Eng., 1935], p. 216). For bibliography on conversion and the legal status of converted Jews in the Middle Ages see below, chap. xii, n. 69.

91. C. 9, X, *de judeis,* 5, 6:

"Statuimus enim, ut nullus Christianus invitos vel nolentes Judaeos ad baptismum [per violentiam] venire compellat. Si quis autem ad Christianos causa fidei confugerit, postquam voluntas eius fuerit patefacta, Christianus absque calumnia efficiatur; quippe Christi fidem habere non creditur, qui ad Christianorum baptismum non spontaneus, sed invitus cogitur pervenire."

Cf. also Newman, *op. cit.,* p. 364; Grayzel, *op. cit.,* pp. 14, 92 ff., No. 5; Browe, *Die Judenmission im Mittelalter und die Päpste,* pp. 235 ff., 285, 49 f.

92. *Summa theologiae,* ed. Ordinis Praedicatorum, Tom. VIII (Rome, 1895), Secunda Secundae, q. 10, art. 8, p. 89. This passage, very sig-

nificant in general, casts light particularly on the previous and following expositions concerning blasphemy by Jews and apostasy by baptized Jews. Therefore, it is worth quoting here in full. The translation is
by the Fathers of the English Dominican Province, in their *The "Summa
Theologica" of St. Thomas Aquinas*, Part II (Second Part), First Number
(QQ. I–XLVI), (London, 1917), pp. 134–36:

"Among unbelievers there are some who have never received the
faith, such as the heathens and the Jews; and these are by no means to be
compelled to the faith, in order that they may believe, because to believe depends on the will: nevertheless they should be compelled by the
faithful, if it be possible to do so, so that they do not hinder the faith,
by their blasphemies, or by their evil persuasions, or even by their open
persecutions. It is for this reason that Christ's faithful often wage war
with unbelievers, not indeed for the purpose of forcing them to believe,
because even if they were to conquer them, and take them prisoners,
they should still leave them free to believe, if they will, but in order to
prevent them from hindering the faith of Christ.

"On the other hand, there are unbelievers who at some time have
accepted the faith, and professed it, such as heretics and all apostates:
such should be submitted even to bodily compulsion, that they may
fulfil what they have promised, and hold what they, at one time,
received.

"Those Jews who have in no way received the faith, ought by no
means to be compelled to the faith: if, however, they have received it,
they ought to be compelled to keep it.

"Just as taking a vow is a matter of will, and keeping a vow, a matter
of obligation, so acceptance of the faith is a matter of the will, whereas
keeping the faith, when once one has received it, is a matter of obligation. Wherefore heretics should be compelled to keep the faith."

93. *Gloss* to Ssp., II, 66, 1; ed. Augsburg, 1516, fol. 121v; ed. Leipzig
(Zobel), 1560, fol. 310v; the clause within brackets is a later addition
found only in Zobel's edition. Johannes Purgoldt, in his *Rechtsbuch*
(VIII, 60), elaborated extensively on Johann von Buch's exposition.
Cases of voluntary conversion seem not to have been frequent in medie-
val Germany. Cf. J. Landsberger, "Mitteilungen aus Breslauer Stadt-,
Schöppen- und Rechnungsbüchern im 14. und 15. Jahrhundert,"
Geiger's *ZGJD*, V (1892), 381; Browe, *Die Judenmission im Mittelalter
und die Päpste*, pp. 207 ff.:

"Ausser diesen wenigen [Victor von Carben, Johann Pfefferkorn, and
Paul Pfeddersheimer], die sich in die Öffentlichkeit drängten, hat sich
in Deutschland kein getaufter Jude und kein Judensprössling in der

Theologie oder auf der Kanzel einen Namen gemacht; auch an der Regierung waren sie nicht beteiligt; zu keiner Zeit des Mittelalters ist einer von ihnen auf einen Bischofssitz gelangt."

94. Cf. Purgoldts Rb., VIII, 96; Stobbe, *op. cit.*, 166 f.; Newman, *op. cit.*, pp. 365 f.

95. For details on this subject see Browe, *Die Judenmission im Mittelalter und die Päpste*, pp. 252 ff.

96. Cf. above, chap. vi, n. 28; Scherer, *op. cit.*, pp. 155 ff.; Browe, *Die Judenmission im Mittelalter und die Päpste*, pp. 178 ff.; Heinrich Rosin, "Beiträge zur Lehre von der Parentelenordnung und Verwandtschaftsberechnung nach deutschem und österreichischem, jüdischem und kanonischem Recht," Grünhut's *Zeitschrift für das Privat- und öffentliche Recht der Gegenwart*, XXVIII (1901), 359, n. 49. On the Jewish legal maxim that "the court may declare anyone's property as belonging to no one" and its application by Maimonides particularly to the purpose of salvaging the property of an apostate for his Jewish heirs see Baron, "The Economic Views of Maimonides," *Essays on Maimonides*, pp. 164 f.

97. C. 5, X, *de judeis*, 5, 6:
"Si qui praeterea Deo inspirante ad fidem se converterint Christianam, a possessionibus suis nullatenus excludantur, cum melioris conditionis ad fidem conversos esse oporteat, quam antequam fidem susceperint, habeantur. Si autem secus fuerit factum, principibus seu potestatibus eorundem locorum iniungimus sub poena excommunicationis, ut portionem hereditatis suae et bonorum suorum ex integro eis faciant exhiberi" [cf. Browe, *Die Judenmission im Mittelalter und die Päpste*, pp. 180 ff.].

The interconnection of the customary right of the Jews to dispossess and disinherit apostates, with the financial interests of their protective secular lords can here be left untouched; on this problem see Scherer, *op. cit.*, pp. 156 ff.; Newman, *op. cit.*, p. 367; Grayzel, *op. cit.*, p. 19; Baron, *A Social and Religious History of the Jews*, II (New York, 1937), 51 f.; Browe, *op. cit.*, pp. 180 ff., 192 f.

98. Cf. His, *op. cit.*, II, 18 ff., especially 21 and nn. 6, 7; see also below, n. 99.

99. Cf. Paul Hinschius, *System des katholischen Kirchenrechts*, V (Berlin, 1895), 51; 387, n. 7; 378 ff., esp. 384, n. 9; 385, n. 1; 487, 562 f.; Emil Friedberg, *Lehrbuch des katholischen und evangelischen Kirchenrechts* (5th ed.; Leipzig, 1903), pp. 302 ff.; Richard Schmidt, "Die Herkunft des Inquisitionsprozesses," *Festschrift der Universität Freiburg zum fünfzigjährigen Regierungsjubiläum Grossherzogs Friedrich* (Freiburg i.B. and Leip-

zig, 1902), p. 88, n. 1; Eduard Eichmann, *Acht und Bann im Reichsrecht des Mittelalters* (Paderborn, 1909), pp. 32–34; Hugelmann, *ZRG*, XLIV, kanon. Abt. XIII (1924), 487, n. 1; G. G. Coulton, *The Death Penalty for Heresy from 1184–1921* (London, 1924), pp. 1–19; Newman, *op. cit.*, pp. 373 ff.; Justus Hashagen, *Staat und Kirche vor der Reformation* (Essen, 1931), pp. 52–66; [Sebastian Castellio], *De haereticis—Concerning Heretics*, trans. Roland H. Bainton ("Records of Civilization," Vol. XXII [New York, 1935]), Introd., p. 29; G. Kisch, "The Yellow Badge in History," *Historia Judaica*, IV (1942), 111 ff., 143.

100. This punishment was actually carried out in several cases: in Constance, in 1390 (cf. His, *op. cit.*, II, 23, n. 4); in Görlitz, in 1476, according to the *Ratsrechnungen*, in *Codex diplomaticus Lusatiae Superioris*, III, 733: "Item umbe holz 5 gr., als man den cristen, der sich getaufter jude nante, richtete" (cf. Ullmann, *op. cit.*, p. 76, n. 6); for more instances see Browe, *Die Judenmission im Mittelalter und die Päpste*, pp. 261, 297. The execution at the stake of thirteen Jews in Troyes, France, in 1288, cited as the earliest example of this kind by Newman (*op. cit.*, p. 378), was due to different reasons and therefore does not come under this heading (cf. Arsène Darmesteter, "L'Autodafé de Troyes," *Revue des études juives*, II [1881], 242 ff.). Nor does another fact, namely, the punishment of Jewish counterfeiters with death by fire, as recorded in the *Vehmbuch der Stadt Zerbst*, ed. Friedrich Heine (Zerbst, 1912), p. 30 (*anno* 1482) (for the text, see below, chap. x, n. 63). At the end of the Middle Ages, fraudulent imitation of money, originally threatened with the loss of one hand (see above, p. 189), was generally punished by death by fire (cf. His, *op. cit.*, II, 277 f.).

101. *Bullarium diplomatum et privilegiorum sanctorum Romanorum pontificum*, III (Turin, 1857/60), 786:

"*Turbato corde* audivimus et narramus, quod quamplurimi reprobi christiani, veritatem catholicae fidei abnegantes, se ad ritum iudaeorum damnabiliter transtulerunt. Quod tanto magis reprobum fore dignoscitur, quanto ex hoc Christi nomen sanctissimum quadam familiari hostilitate securius blasphematur. Cum autem huic pesti damnabili, quae, ut accepimus, non sine subversione praedictae fidei nimis excrescit, congruis et festinis deceat remediis obviari, universitati vestrae per apostolica scripta mandamus, quatenus terminos vobis ad inquirendum contra haereticos auctoritate sedis apostolicae designatos, super praemissis, *tam per christianos quam etiam per iudaeos*, inquisita diligenter et fideliter veritate, *contra Christianos, quos talia inveneritis commisisse, tamquam contra haereticos procedatis*."

Cf. Browe, *Die Judenmission im Mittelalter und die Päpste*, pp. 257 f.,

238, n. 148. Grayzel (*op. cit.*, p. 15, n. 15) cites merely a decree of 1277 by Pope Nicholas III, who, "in answer to a question of a Dominican Inquisitor, replied that Jews baptized while in fear of death, and later reverting to Judaism and refusing to live as Christians even after prolonged imprisonment, must be treated as ordinary heretics, i.e., burned at the stake. This was later repeated by Nicholas IV [May 7, 1288]." Scherer (*op. cit.*, p. 46, No. 20) refers to a Mainz council as late as 1310. Israel Levi (*Les Juifs et l'inquisition dans la France méridionale* [Paris, 1891], p. 7) mentions a bull issued by Pope Gregory X (March 1, 1274) (cf. Newman, *op. cit.*, pp. 374, 376). Joshua Starr ("The Mass Conversion of Jews in Southern Italy [1290–1293]," *Speculum*, XXI [1946], 205, n. 15) made the following statement: "Although it is frequently stated that the bull *Turbato corde* of Clement IV (26 July 1267) specifically authorized the Inquisition to condemn crypto-Jews to death, it was not until the renewal of that bull by Nicholas IV (5 September 1288) that the explicit authorization was given: 'Quidam de iudaicae caecitatis errore ad lumen fidei christianae conversi, ad priorem reversi esse perfidiam dignoscuntur' (*Bullarium diplomatum et privilegiorum sanctorum pontificum* [Turin, 1859], IV, 88)." From the point of view of canon law, however, there can be no doubt that the equation of reversion to Judaism with ordinary heresy was first expressly stated in Clement IV's bull, *Turbato corde*. For the early Christian centuries, cf. Juster, *Les Juifs dans l'empire romain*, I (Paris, 1914), 272–74; Scherer, *op. cit.*, pp. 15 f. In Visigothic law, relapse of baptized Jews to Judaism was threatened with death by fire (*Lex Visigothorum*, ed. Karl Zeumer [Hannover, 1894], XII, 2, 11; cf. Hinschius, *op. cit.*, IV, 848; Browe, *Die Judenmission im Mittelalter und die Päpste*, pp. 252–54).

102. Ssp., II, 13, 7: "Swelk cristen man ungeloubich ist oder mit zoubere umme geit oder mit vorgiftnisse, unde des virwunnen wirt, den sol men ûph der hurt burnen" ("Whatever Christian man is an unbeliever or applies sorcery or poison, if convicted thereof shall be burned at the stake"). A number of manuscripts have the variant reading *unde mit zoubere*, which is considered to be the original version; in another group the clause *ungeloubich ist unde* is missing. Cf. Ernst Theodor Gaupp, *Germanistische Abhandlungen* (Mannheim, 1853), p. 109; Herman Ballschmiede, *Die sächsische Weltchronik*, University of Berlin Ph.D. thesis (Berlin, 1914), pp. 36, 59. On Ssp., II, 13, 7, taken over by Zwickau Rb., II, 38, see Otto Stobbe, *Geschichte der deutschen Rechtsquellen*, I (Braunschweig, 1860), 311, n. 56; Frensdorff, "Beiträge zur Geschichte und Erklärung der deutschen Rechtsbücher. II," *Nachrichten der Gesellschaft der Wissenschaften zu Göttingen*, 1894, pp. 25 f.; Eichmann,

op. cit., p. 34, n. 6; Fehr, "Die Staatsauffassung Eikes von Repgau," *ZRG*, XXXVII (1916), 162, 218, 244; Eichmann, "Die Stellung Eikes von Repgau zu Kirche und Kurie," *Historisches Jahrbuch der Görresgesellschaft*, XXXVIII (1917), 751, n. 6; Hugelmann, *op. cit.* (above, n. 99); Hans von Voltelini, "Forschungen zu den deutschen Rechtsbüchern. III. Der Sachsenspiegel und die Zeitgeschichte," *Sitzungsberichte der Akademie der Wissenschaften in Wien, phil.-hist. Kl.*, CCI, Abh. 4–5 (Vienna, 1924), 66; Schröder and Künssberg, *op. cit.*, p. 721; Eckhardt, "Rechtsbücherstudien. II," *Abhandlungen der k. Gesellschaft der Wissenschaften zu Göttingen, philol.-hist. Kl.*, N.F., XXIII, 2 (1931), 67 f.; His, *op. cit.*, II, 21 and n. 7.

103. Cf. Stobbe, *Die Juden in Deutschland während des Mittelalters*, p. 162; Scherer, *op. cit.*, pp. 39 f.; Friedberg, *op. cit.*, pp. 424 f.; Israel Abrahams, *Jewish Life in the Middle Ages* (London, 1896), p. 94; Baron, *A Social and Religious History of the Jews*, II, 53 f. Cf. also Louis I. Newman, "Intermarriage between Jews and Christians during the Middle Ages," *Jewish Institute Quarterly*, II (1926), No. 2, 2–8; No. 3, 22–28, based on secondary sources only; L. Günther, *Die Idee der Wiedervergeltung in der Geschichte und Philosophie des Strafrechts*, I (Altenburg, 1889), 261 f.

104. On the different kinds of punishment for sexual offenses in general, as applied all over Europe prior to the middle of the twelfth century, see J. R. Reinhard, "Burning at the Stake in Mediaeval Law and Literature," *Speculum*, XVI (1941), 186–209.

105. See above, n. 99. In Spain sexual relations between Christians and Jews or Moors were placed under the sanction of death by fire as early as the last quarter of the twelfth century; in the municipal laws of Teruel, Aragon, in 1176; and Cuenca, Castile, in 1190–91 (Fritz Baer, *Die Juden im christlichen Spanien*, I [Berlin, 1929], 1037; II [1936], 41 n.; cf. also *ibid.*, I, 717, No. 456 [1393]). As late as the second half of the thirteenth century, on the other hand, regional church councils threatened sexual relations between Jews and Christians with varying punishments of a milder character. In 1267, the Council of Breslau, for instance, imposed upon the Jew imprisonment pending his payment of a fine of at least ten marks, and upon the Christian woman public flogging and permanent banishment from the city (Aronius, *op. cit.*, No. 724). The obvious cause of such an alleviation of the punishments may easily be found in the ecclesiastical limitations of the church's criminal jurisdiction (cf. Hinschius, *System des katholischen Kirchenrechts*, V, 50).

Secular law experienced theoretical difficulties in finding a solid juridical basis for an appropriate penalty of such transgressions. This is

evident from the pertinent discussions in the glossators and commentators of the Roman law and the theorists of canon law. They prove at
the same time that the cases under consideration were not as infrequent
as Friedberg (*Lehrbuch des katholischen und evangelischen Kirchenrechts*,
p. 424) believed. This is also confirmed by Marquardus de Susannis,
Tractatus de iudaeis et aliis infidelibus (Venice, 1558), fol. 53r–v: ". . .
qualiter puniatur judaeus se carnaliter jungens cum Christiana, et
Christianus rem habens veneream cum judaea, *quod saepe solet contingere.*
. . ."

It is well known that intermarriage between Christians and Jews was
threatened with capital punishment by Constantius in 339, and such
alliances were equated in 388 to adultery (*Cod. Just.* i. 9. 6; cf. Juster,
op. cit., II, 46–49). On this basis Alexander Tartagnus of Imola (*fl.* 1445–
77) urged the death penalty for the Jew (cf. Anna T. Sheedy, *Bartolus on
Social Conditions in the Fourteenth Century* [New York, 1942], p. 238).
But Oldradus de Ponte (de Laude) (*fl.* 1302–35), in the last period of his
life (d. 1335) advocatus consistorialis at the papal curia in Avignon,
had argued differently. True, in his *Consilia* (ed. Romae, 1478), No. 333,
he considered sexual relations between Jews and Christians an offense
against Christianity (see below, n. 108). Yet his conclusion, based on
Roman law sources, reads: "Ideo non est talis ut adulter puniendus
capitaliter, *C. de adul., que adulterium* [*Cod. Just.* ix. 9. 28] ubi nota. Non
dico tamen quod hec feda commixtio civiliter ad arbitrium iudicantis
non sit aliqualiter punienda." In a *postscriptum* to his *consilium* Oldradus
tells of the punishment actually inflicted as follows: "Ego Oldradus
predicta scripsi et sigillum apposui. Sed dominus R. de Apulea et
dominus Antho. de Cruce qui tunc preerant in officio iudicatus Avinio-
nensis, dictum iudeum in amissione virilium condemnaverunt, cuius
nomen erat Pandonus et ego vidi virilia incisa ante palacium." Cf.
also Marquardus de Susannis, *op. cit.*, fol. 54v. As late as the middle of
the eighteenth century, reference to this case is found in Johannes
Jodocus Beck, *Tractatus de juribus Judaeorum: Von Recht der Juden* (Nürnberg, 1741), p. 364; and even in K. A. Schaab, *Diplomatische Geschichte
der Juden zu Mainz und dessen Umgebung mit Berücksichtigung ihres
Rechtszustandes* (Mainz, 1855), p. 104.

106. The municipal and mining law of Iglau, Moravia (1249), applied a unique sanction to such cases: burying alive of the transgressors:
"Et si aliquis Judeorum cum christiana muliere adulteratus fuerit,
raptus et duobus viris convictus, ambo vivi sepeliantur." Cf. J. A.
Tomaschek, *Deutsches Recht in Österreich im 13. Jahrhundert auf Grundlage
des Stadtrechtes von Iglau* (Vienna, 1859), pp. 296 f.; Aronius, *op. cit.*,

No. 573, p. 244; G. Kisch, "The Jews in Medieval Law," in *Essays on Antisemitism*, ed. K. S. Pinson (New York, 1942), pp. 63 f.

107. This fact must have been Baron's reason (*A Social and Religious History of the Jews*, II, 54) for omitting this clause from his translation of the *Schwabenspiegel* passage under consideration, although its complete text is reproduced in Aronius, *op. cit.*, No. 771, pp. 330 f. The explanatory clause is indispensable for an understanding of the regulation as a whole. It was not given proper consideration by Carl J. Caspar, *Darstellung des strafrechtlichen Inhaltes des Schwabenspiegels* (Berlin, 1892), p. 23, nor by Hermann Knapp, "Das Rechtsbuch Ruprechts von Freising (1328) in seiner Bedeutung als strafrechtliche Quelle des Mittelalters," Goltdammer's *Archiv für Strafrecht und Strafprozess*, LXI (1914), 233, 241, 251.

108. Cf. His, *op. cit.*, II, 149, 171; Eberhard Schmidt, *ZRG*, LVI (1936), 626: "Der schwere Fall der Unzucht zwischen Christen und Juden (His, S. 149) erhält für mittelalterliches Rechtsdenken seine besondere Bedeutung 'als Verleugnung des christlichen Glaubens.' . . . Das sexuelle Moment als solches tritt bei der Wertung durchaus zurück, um andersartigen Gesichtspunkten Platz zu machen" (see also Schmidt, *loc. cit.*, p. 635). For instances of actual execution of the punishment (death by fire) see Steinberg, *Studien zur Geschichte der Juden in der Schweiz*, pp. 37 f.; Abrahams, *Jewish Life in the Middle Ages*, p. 94, n. 5.

The interesting argumentation on the problem in Oldradus de Ponte, *Consilia* (ed. Romae, 1478), No. 333, reads:

"Qualiter puniatur iudeus cognoscens carnaliter christianam. Fateri quidem oportet, prohibitum esse iudeum christiane coniungi, quia cum matrimonium sit comunicatio divini iuris . . . hoc autem cum non sit, constat matrimonium non esse . . . et talis contrahens tanquam adulter puniretur . . . sed de alia commixtione iudei cum christiana licet sit prohibita extra non occurrit ius expressum dicens eum tanquam adulterum puniri. Et si forte diceretur arguendo quod, si puniretur talis commixtio sub velamine matrimonii commissa, ut supra dictum est, fortius sine velamine tali, ut *ff. de adul., si adulterium cum incestu* [Dig., 48, 5, 39 (38)]. Sed hec multum non cogit. Primo quia commixtionem illicitam committit et *matrimonii sacramento iniuriam facit, C. ne sacrum bapt. rei., l. 1* [*Cod. Just.* 1. 6. 1]. . . ."

109. It is appropriate here to recall the provision in Schwsp., L 255, G 210: Jews—treated there on an equal footing with clerics—forfeit the king's peace and pass under the peace of the common laity "if they are found in [public inns or] whore-houses, and someone should there do something to them" (cf., above, pp. 122 f. and 183 f.).

110. This stand had already been taken in Roman law. In the *Code* of Justinian, Jews and heretics are treated under separate rubrics as separate groups: *Cod. Just.* i. 5: *de haereticis et manichaeis;* i. 9: *de judaeis et caelicolis.* On the interesting discussion of this difference by the glossators and commentators of Roman law see Sheedy, *Bartolus on Social Conditions in the Fourteenth Century,* pp. 230 ff.

111. For details on policy and decrees of the Fourth Lateran Council on the subject see G. Kisch, "The Yellow Badge in History," *Historia Judaica,* IV (1942), 103–13, and below, pp. 295 ff. Additional evidence testifying to the correctness of the argument as presented in the above context can be gleaned from c. 14, X, *de judaeis,* 5, 6, immediately followed, in the *Corpus juris canonici,* by canon 68 of the Fourth Lateran Council (= c. 15, X, 5, 6) concerning the garb distinguishing Jews and Saracens from Christians.

112. It is found in Freising Rb., Maurer, I, 173, but missing in Knapp, 122, II, and in Claussen, 123 (cf. below, p. 297).

CHAPTER NINE

1. On the history of medieval civil law in general see Rudolf Hübner, *Grundzüge des deutschen Privatrechts* (5th ed.; Leipzig, 1930), with extensive bibliography on pp. 45 ff. [pp. liii ff.]. (The second edition of this work was translated into English and appeared as Vol. IV of "The Continental Legal History Series" under the title *A History of Germanic Private Law* [Boston, 1918]. The page numbers of this English version are added in brackets to the references to Hübner's work.) The following basic standard works on medieval German private law should be mentioned here: Otto Stobbe, *Handbuch des deutschen Privatrechts* (5 vols.; Berlin, 1871–85; 3d ed., 1893–1900); Andreas Heusler, *Institutionen des deutschen Privatrechts,* Vols. I, II (Leipzig, 1885–86); Otto von Gierke, *Deutsches Privatrecht,* Vols. I (Leipzig, 1895), II (1905), III (1917); Theodor Kraut, *Grundriss zu Vorlesungen über das deutsche Privatrecht* (6th ed. by Ferdinand Frensdorff; Berlin, 1886). Cf. also Walter Becker, *Magdeburger Recht in der Lausitz* (Stuttgart, 1931), pp. 91–100.

On the treatment of Jews in the medieval system of private law see Otto Stobbe, *Die Juden in Deutschland während des Mittelalters* (Braunschweig, 1866), pp. 103–31; J. E. Scherer, *Die Rechtsverhältnisse der Juden in den deutsch-österreichischen Ländern* (Leipzig, 1901), pp. 147–62, 185–216; Herbert Meyer, *Entwerung und Eigentum im deutschen Fahrnisrecht* (Jena, 1902), pp. 166–278; Moses Hoffmann, *Der Geldhandel der deutschen Juden während des Mittelalters bis zum Jahre 1350* (Leipzig, 1910), pp. 64–76, 94–118; Emanuel Forchhammer, "Beiträge zur Geschichte der deutschen Juden . . . ,'' *Geschichtsblätter für Stadt und Land Magdeburg*, XLVI (1911), 358–73, 400–407; H[irsch] J[acob] Zimmels, *Beiträge zur Geschichte der Juden in Deutschland im 13. Jahrhundert, insbesondere auf Grund der Gutachten des R. Meir Rothenburg* (Vienna, 1926), pp. 46–61.

2. For details on the problem see Guido Kisch, "Studien zur Kulmer Handfeste," *ZRG*, L (1930), 205–12.

3. See above, pp. 100 ff.

4. See above, pp. 86 ff.

5. See above, p. 184; cf. also Forchhammer, *op. cit.*, pp. 166 ff.

6. Stobbe, *op. cit.*, 176 ff.; cf. Otto H. Stowasser, "Zur Frage der Besitzfähigkeit der Juden in Österreich während des Mittelalters," *Mitteilungen des Vereines für Geschichte der Stadt Wien*, IV (1923), 23–27.

7. LSchSprS., 500.

8. MSchSpr., III, B, 90 and 104; cf. Forchhammer, *op. cit.*, pp. 403 f.

9. See above, p. 193; cf. also Purgoldts Rb., VIII, 31, 85, 99.

10. Stobbe, *op. cit.*, p. 276, n. 171.

11. H. Meyer, *op. cit.*, pp. 192 ff.; cf. G. Kisch, "The 'Jewish Law of Concealment,' " *Historia Judaica*, I (1938), 4 f., n. 7. Even Hugelmann ("Studien zum Recht der Nationalitäten im deutschen Mittelalter. II. Das Judenrecht der Rechtsbücher," *Historisches Jahrbuch der Görresgesellschaft*, XLVIII [1928], 569) avoids the use of the term *Jüdisches Hehlerrecht* and employs it only with reference to Meyer (p. 571). From the above text as well as from the very first sentence in this writer's essay in *Historia Judaica*, I, 4, the characteristics of the so-called *Jüdisches Hehlerrecht* emerge clearly: (1) it was an old trade privilege accorded to merchants; (2) it was not restricted to Jewish merchants but was bestowed on non-Jewish merchants as well. No misunderstanding on the part of the reader needs to be feared, therefore, if for the sake of brevity the designation "Jewish trade privilege" or "trade privilege of the Jews" is used in the discussion to follow.

12. See above, pp. 78 f. and chap. ii, nn. 149–51.

13. G. Kisch, "The 'Jewish Law of Concealment,' " pp. 3–30; cf. also Boaz Cohen, "The So-called 'Jüdisches Hehlerrecht' in the Light of Jewish Law," *Historia Judaica*, IV (1942), 145–53. The hypothesis of the possible origin of that trade privilege in talmudic law—to be sure, without any derogatory implication—was first set forth by Stobbe, *op. cit.*, pp. 120 and 242, n. 111, upon the suggestion of the Jewish historian, Heinrich Graetz, who was no talmudic scholar. Stobbe's theory was, however, strongly opposed by two eminent authorities on medieval legal history: Konrad Maurer, *Kritische Vierteljahrsschrift für Gesetzgebung und Rechtswissenschaft*, IX (1867), 570; and

Heinrich Brunner, *Deutsche Rechtsgeschichte*, II (Leipzig, 1892), 507, n. 82. Brunner's original stand remained unchanged in the second edition of his work (Munich and Leipzig, 1928), p. 663, n. 86. Its editor, Claudius von Schwerin, even supported it by further documentary proof from English municipal law of the twelfth century. Cf. also Alfred Schultze, "Gerüfte und Marktkauf in Beziehung zur Fahrnisverfolgung," offprint from *Festgabe für Felix Dahn*, I (Breslau, 1905), 50 ff.; for more details see G. Kisch, "The 'Jewish Law of Concealment,' " pp. 10 f. Stobbe himself was not free of doubts concerning Graetz's suggestion, as is shown in Stobbe, *op. cit.*, p. 241, n. 109. Of different opinion, Salo W. Baron, "The Economic Views of Maimonides," in *Essays on Maimonides*, ed. S. W. Baron (New York, 1941), pp. 159 f.: "This law of the Talmud indirectly seems to have influenced various privileges granted to Jews in medieval Europe and, through them, the development of a significant legal institution in Western lands. . . ."

14. See above, chap. vi, n. 28. In the Speyer charter the original text of art. 6 reads: "Si autem res furtiva apud eos inventa fuerit, si dixerit Judeus se emisse, juramento probet secundum legem suam quanti emerit, et tantundem accipiat et sic rem ei cujus erat restituat." The Worms charter reads *recipiat* instead of *accipiat;* the word *sic* is missing.

An interesting passage from an anti-Jewish letter of Peter the Venerable of Cluny (1094–1156) to his king, Louis VII, written probably in 1146, must be quoted here. It was not referred to in any of the previous writings concerned with the trade privilege of the Jews under consideration. Although nonjuridical in character, this document is remarkable from the point of view of legal history, for two reasons. First, in the history of that trade privilege it offers a connecting link between the era of the Rhenish charters for the Jews (*ca.* 1090) and the era of the *Sachsenspiegel* (*ca.* 1221–24). Second, it represents contemporary evidence from an authority above suspicion that this trade privilege was conferred upon the Jews for commercial reasons. The passage (Migne, *Patr. Lat.*, CLXXXIX, 368C) reads:

"Insuper, ut tam nefarium furtum, *Judaeorumque commercium tutius esset*, lex jam vetusta, sed vere diabolica, ab ipsis Christianis principibus processit, ut si res ecclesiastica, vel (quod deterius) aliquod sacrum vas, apud Judaeorum repertum fuerit, nec rem sacrilego furto possessam reddere, nec nequam furem Judaeus prodere compellatur."

("Moreover, that such nefarious theft and Jewish commerce be even safer, a law, very old but truly diabolic, issued from Christian princes: in case a church object or [even worse] a sacred vessel were found among Jewish belongings, no Jew should be compelled to restore the object obtained by sacrilegious theft or to betray the thief.")

The English rendering in A. Lukyn Williams, *Adversus Judaeos: A Bird's-Eye View of Christian Apologiae until the Renaissance* (Cambridge, England, 1935), p. 394, is inaccurate and omitted the relevant clause of the sentence. On an identical conception in Maimonides see Baron, *op. cit.*, p. 160.

15. Cf. above, p. 190. Karl G. Hugelmann (*op. cit.*, p. 569) correctly interprets this clause (Ssp., III, 7, 4 [1]) to constitute only an exception from the privilege accorded the Jews in the clause following it (Ssp., III, 7, 4 [2]); the Jews are thus subject to the general rule with regard to the sacred objects mentioned. Compared with Ssp., II, 36, 1, the exemption in Ssp., III, 7, 4 (1) is even a disadvantage for the Jews, a *privilegium odiosum*, according to Hugelmann: exculpation by proof of purchase in open daylight was here prohibited.

16. Similar regulations on the publicity of purchase or acceptance in pledge by the Jew are found in Dsp., F 209; Schwsp., L 261, G 214, 7; Freising Rb., Maurer, I, 172, Knapp, 121; MRb., III, 17, 3, 4, 25, 27 (particularly detailed); Breslau-Glogau Law Instruction of 1302, art. 5, in G. A. Tzschoppe and G. A. Stenzel, *Urkundensammlung zur Geschichte des Ursprungs der Städte . . . in Schlesien und der Oberlausitz* (Hamburg, 1832), p. 445 and n. 2; Glogau Rb., 476, 477; BlM., II, 2, 151; Wasserschleben, RQ., V, 44, p. 400; Reg. jur., J 127; Rem. R.W., 3, 4, 10; Purgoldts Rb., VIII, 62, 86–88, and below, chap. x, n. 142. Cf. Meyer, *op. cit.*, pp. 220 ff. Cf. also the general rule in Ssp., II, 36.

17. The scheme of the *Sachsenspiegel*, in III, 7, 1, was adopted without change in Dsp., FE 207 (cf. Eckhardt, "Rechtsbücherstudien. I," 81); Magdeburg-Görlitz Law Instruction of 1304, art. 118 (Tzschoppe and Stenzel, *op. cit.*, p. 473); *Gloss* Wb., 135 (A. von Daniels and F. von Gruben, *Das Saechsische Weichbildrecht* [Berlin, 1858], p. 436); cf. Latin translation of Wb., 138, 1 (Daniels and Gruben, *op. cit*, p. 174: ". . . Judaeus illum varendare non potest, nisi in quantum jus immutet suum, hoc est, nisi ut Christianus respondere velit"); Pölmann, IX, 16, 3; *Neun Bücher Magdeburger Rechts*, by Walter Eckhardi, IX, 16, 1, quoted by Meyer, *op. cit.*, pp. 233 f.; Reg. jur., C 35, 36, J 124; Bocksd. Rem., 1; Purgoldts Rb., VIII, 95. Cf. also MRb., IV, 42, 22.

Another group of medieval lawbooks eliminated the condition "unless he is willing to respond [assume the defense] by taking the Christian's place," and thereby excluded Jews unconditionally from warranty: MBSchR., II, 2, 69: ". . . no Jew be warrantor [*gewer*] in court" (cf. Th. Goerlitz, *ZRG*, LIX [1939], 161); *Richtsteig Landrechts*, 13, 7, ed. Homeyer (Berlin, 1857), p. 132: "Tüt ok jene up enen joden, so vrag oft en jode moge enes kersten gewere sin. Dat vint me he en moge"; Kalužniacki, "Die polnische Rezension der Magdeburger Urteile . . . ,"

Sitzungsberichte der kaiserlichen Akademie der Wissenschaften zu Wien, phil.-hist. Klasse, CXI (1885), 184, art. O 80; C. K. Leman, *Das alte Kulmische Recht* (Berlin, 1838), II, 81, p. 46; Rem. RW., 6. Wb. 135, 1 (Daniels and Gruben, *op. cit.*, p. 173), and Wb. 116, 3 (Daniels, *Dat buk wichbelde recht*, p. 53) offer a peculiar argument in restricting warranty to the house of the Jew: "... wenn kein jude vordir geweren mag kouffis, wenn alzo verre, alz sien huz went"; similarly, Glogau Rb., 482; Reg. jur., J 125. On the last-mentioned point, cf. Meyer, *op. cit.*, pp. 234, 230 f.; Forchhammer, *op. cit.*, p. 402.

18. The clause "unless . . . law," missing in L, appears only in the later manuscripts of type G.

19. H. Meyer ("Das Hehlerrecht der Juden und Lombarden," in *Forschungen zur Judenfrage*, I [Hamburg, 1937], 100) connects this clause with the Josephus passage occurring in an entirely different context in Ssp., III, 7, 3. From Meyer (*ibid.*, p. 106, n. 4) the unmistakable conclusion must be drawn, however, that the context was well known to him. On the Josephus passage, Ssp., III, 7, 3, see above, pp. 154 ff. and 164 ff.

20. Cf. Purgoldts Rb., VIII, 95. Fanatical Jew hatred reveals itself in the pertinent art. 145 of the *Wiener Stadtrechtsbuch*, ed. Schuster, p. 131; cf. above, p. 56; cf. also MRb., IV, 42, 22.

21. Johann von Buch was the first to propound this reasoning for the continuance of the Jewish trade privilege. The passage is found in the Augsburg edition (1516), as well as in Zobel's edition of the *Gloss* (Leipzig, 1560); cf. also K. Schilling, *Das objektive Recht in der Sachsenspiegel-Glosse* (Berlin, 1931), p. 61. From Buch's *Gloss* to Ssp., III, 7, 1, his argument was taken over and elaborated on by the glossator of the *Weichbild-Vulgata*, art. 135 (Daniels and Gruben, *op. cit.*, pp. 436 f.). Cf. Stobbe's interpretation (*op. cit.*, pp. 125 f.), which seems preferable to that by Meyer, *Entwerung und Eigentum*, p. 235. Meyer misunderstood the passage in the *Weichbild Gloss;* and its model in Buch's *Gloss* to *Sachsenspiegel* remained unknown to him. The passage recurs also in Bocksd. Rem., 3: "A Jew may buy stolen goods; this for the reason that one may the better find his lost goods, and they be the sooner restored to him."

22. Tzschoppe and Stenzel, *op. cit.*, p. 473.

23. Wasserschleben, RQ., V, 44, p. 400.

24. MSchSpr., III B, 90.

25. MSchSpr., III B, 104.

26. SchwSp., L 261; G 214, 7; Freising Rb., Maurer, I, 172, Knapp, 121. Cf. Levin Goldschmidt, "Über den Erwerb dinglicher Rechte von

dem Nichteigentümer," *Zeitschrift für das gesamte Handelsrecht*, VIII (1865), 274 f.; Meyer, *Entwerung und Eigentum*, pp. 236 ff.

27. So does, furthermore, a decision handed down by the jury court of Brünn, Moravia, probably in the middle of the fourteenth century (cf. Gertrud Schubart-Fikentscher," Neue Fälle zum Brünner Recht," *Deutsches Archiv für Geschichte des Mittelalters*, III [1939], 440 f., 492, No. 19b).

28. This fact has been admitted even by Meyer (*Entwerung und Eigentum*, p. 238) and by Rudolf Ruth ("Wucher und Wucherrecht der Juden im Mittelalter," *Deutsche Rechtswissenschaft*, II [1937], 133). For more instances see Hoffmann, *Der Geldhandel der deutschen Juden*, p. 99.

29. MRb., III, 17, 25; Stobbe, *op. cit.*, p. 118.

30. Magdeburg-Breslau Law Instruction for Olmütz, of the fourteenth century, reproduced in Wilhelm Weizsäcker, "Die Rechtsmitteilung Breslaus an Olmütz," *Festschrift für Otto Peterka* (Brünn, 1936), p. 96; cf. Wasserschleben, RQ., V, 44, p. 400.

31. Cf. Forchhammer, *op. cit.*, p. 364, and n. 261; see also above, p. 115.

32. Cf. above, chap. viii, n. 47; Stobbe, *op. cit.*, pp. 118, 125, 246, n. 120; Meyer, *Entwerung und Eigentum*, pp. 214 f , with more references; Forchhammer, *op. cit.*, p. 404. Ruth's purely anti-Semitic argument (*op. cit.*, p. 137) needs no refutation.

33. Cf. MRb., III, 17, 5, 25, 27; also Brünn jury-court decision (middle of the fourteenth century) (Schubart-Fikentscher, *op. cit.*, pp. 492 f., No. 19a and c: "nulla de hiis requisitione facta").

34. Cf. Hübner, *op. cit.*, pp. 433 ff. [pp. 407 ff.].

35. MS Dresden M 20a, fol. 110r, *s.v.* "furman."

36. Cf. Purgoldts Rb., VIII, 86–88; Meyer, *Entwerung und Eigentum*, p. 225.

37. MRb., III, 17, 4; cf. III, 17, 3; Purgoldts Rb., VIII, 88, 84, 90 (see above, p. 99); Glogau Rb., 476; Meyer, *Entwerung und Eigentum*, p. 229; Ullmann, *Das Strafrecht der Städte der Mark Meissen* (Leipzig, 1928), p. 80.

38. Dsp , FE 73, 3; Schwsp., L 81, G 66; MRb., III, 14, 4; Purgoldts Rb., VII, 102. Stobbe (*op. cit.*, p. 239, n. 103, and *Zur Geschichte des deutschen Vertragsrechts* [Leipzig, 1855], pp. 93 f.) interprets this regulation in MRb. in a restricted sense as referring only to the legal transaction of *Schadennehmen* (see below, pp. 239 ff.). But the context in Schwsp. does not support such a restrictive interpretation.

39. Cf. Hübner, *op. cit.*, pp. 473 ff. [pp. 443 ff.].

40. Cf. Stobbe, *Die Juden in Deutschland*, pp. 126 f.; 247, n. 121. What

Rudolf Ruth ("Wucher und Wucherrecht der Juden im Mittelalter," pp. 132–38) has to say on the subject, particularly his objections against Stobbe and the alleged, yet unproved, influence of the Talmud on medieval German law, show clearly the anti-Semitic bias of his National Socialist outlook.

41. On the details of the procedure, cf. MRb., III, 17, 15, 16; Purgoldts Rb., VIII, 76, 77; see also Forchhammer, *op. cit.*, pp. 406 f.

42. Cf. also Wasserschleben, RQ.², I, 264, p. 83. Schwsp., L 192 b, G 165, 7, contains a provision disadvantageous to the Jewish creditor: "If one forbids the pennies [i.e., if new coins are issued to replace the money in circulation], one shall be allowed a fortnight to pay and redeem pledges with the old ones; except in the case of the Jews, redemption of pledges from whom is permitted [with old coins] for four weeks."

43. On this problem, cf. Stobbe, *op. cit.*, pp. 126 f.; Max Neumann, *Geschichte des Wuchers in Deutschland bis zur Begründung der heutigen Zinsengesetze (1654)* (Halle, 1865), pp. 309–12; cf. also Ssp., III, 5, 5.

44. The same regulation in Purgoldts Rb., VIII, 78. Characteristically enough, these regulations were suppressed by Ruth in his essay (*op. cit.*, p. 134).

45. [Johannes Ehrenfried Böhme], *Diplomatische Beiträge zur Untersuchung der schlesischen Rechte und Geschichte*, VI (Berlin, 1775), 113, 3; the same solution is found in Glogau Rb., 475.

46. The same regulation in Purgoldts Rb., VIII, 83; cf. VIII, 89; also in King Venceslas II's confirmation of Přemysl Otakar II's Jewry privilege of 1268, in E. F. Rössler, *Die Stadtrechte von Brünn aus dem XIII. und XIV. Jahrhundert* (Prague, 1852), pp. 368 f., No. 119; cf. Schubart-Fikentscher, "Neue Fälle zum Brünner Recht," p. 475 and n. 4; also Scherer, *op. cit.*, p. 207. Accordingly, a decision in Brünn SchB., No. 439, p. 206, whereby public announcement was made an obligatory requirement: "And this decision rests on the privileges of the Jews where it is written: 'If a Jew sustains the loss of his property together with objects pledged with him through fire, theft or violence, and if this is established [*hoc constiterit*], and the Christian, who has pledged those objects, nevertheless sues him, the Jew shall clear himself by his personal oath.' From the fact that it reads *constiterit*, it is patent that the loss of the pledge must be made public and not be kept in secret. Hence note what great weight attaches to this publication, which is called *urkund* in the vernacular, because it removes suspicion."

Cf. Julius Weiske, "Bemerkungen über das Brünner Schöffenbuch,"

Zeitschrift für deutsches Recht und deutsche Rechtswissenschaft, XIV (1853), 115. Correspondingly, another interesting decision in Brünn SchB., pp. 143 f., No. 313. In this case pledges of Christian debtors were stolen from the house of a Jew. He made no public announcement but later advanced the theory that those pledges included his own money lent on them. Consequently, the holder's own belongings were lost, together with the stolen pledges: "The Jew replied: since he had had his own money in the lost pledges, whether, the pledges having been stolen, that which belonged to him had not likewise been stolen." In its final decision the court did not accede to this argument, but stated: "The Jew is required to make compensation for the pledges; reference to the loss of money that he suffered does not avail the Jew in this case, for [only] property of his own which is separated and distinct from the pledges can here be taken into consideration." (The text in Rössler's edition is corrupt; the emendation above was made by Bertold Bretholz, *Quellen zur Geschichte der Juden in Mähren vom XI. bis zum XV. Jahrhundert* [Prague, 1935], p. 20, n. 1, on the basis of the manuscript.)

47. Cf. James Parkes, *The Jew in the Medieval Community* (London, 1938), pp. 267–382, with bibliography on pp. 270 f.; George Caro, *Sozial- und Wirtschaftsgeschichte der Juden im Mittelalter und der Neuzeit*, I (Leipzig, 1908), 225 ff., 436 ff.; II (Leipzig, 1920), 143–71; Forchhammer, *op. cit.*, pp. 364 ff. Bibliographical notes also in Baron, *A Social and Religious History of the Jews*, III (New York, 1937), 132, n. 6. Werner Sombart (*Die Juden und das Wirtschaftsleben* [1st ed.; Leipzig, 1911; fourteenth and fifteenth thousand, Munich and Leipzig, 1927; English translation under the title, *The Jews and Modern Capitalism*, London, 1913]), excluded from his presentation the period prior to 1492. The voluminous work by Eugen Nübling, *Die Judengemeinden des Mittelalters, insbesondere die Judengemeinde der Reichsstadt Ulm* (Ulm, 1896), [pp. xliv–lx, 89–152, 173–241, 362–435] is based on secondary sources only and written with an anti-Semitic tendency, influenced by the teachings of Eugen Dühring.

48. Moses Hoffmann, *Der Geldhandel der deutschen Juden während des Mittelalters;* H. J. Zimmels, *Beiträge zur Geschichte der Juden in Deutschland im 13. Jahrhundert*, pp. 53–61; Irving A. Agus, *Rabbi Meir of Rothenburg: His Life and His Works as Sources for the Religious, Legal, and Social History of the Jews of Germany in the Thirteenth Century* (Philadelphia, 1947). All these books, however meritorious, give no consideration at all to problems of legal history; they merely narrate the historical facts from the sources.

49. The eminent Belgian historian, Henri Pirenne, in his *Economic*

and Social History of Medieval Europe (New York, 1937), p. 133, judges the economic role of the Jews in the Middle Ages as follows: "Compared with the efflorescence and ubiquity of Italian credit, that of the Jews appears a very small affair and the part which they played in the Middle Ages has certainly been much exaggerated." L. Rabinowitz (*The Herem Hayyishub: A Contribution to the Medieval Economic History of the Jews* [London, 1945], pp. 170 f., n. 7) offers a different view on the part played by the Jews in medieval commerce in general. This has, however, no bearing on the question at issue. But even Forchhammer, who cannot be suspected of a philo-Semitic tendency, admits (*op. cit.*, p. 367) various facts leading to a conclusion similar to that of Pirenne; and Herbert Meyer ("Das Hehlerrecht der Juden und Lombarden," *Forschungen zur Judenfrage*, I [Hamburg, 1937], 95) writes: "As Christian moneylenders the Lombards [or Caorsins] were the greatest competitors of the Jews." Cf. also Kisch, "The 'Jewish Law of Concealment,' " *Historia Judaica*, I (1938), 7. G. G. Coulton (*Medieval Panorama: The English Scene from Conquest to Reformation* [Cambridge and New York, 1944], p. 357) states: ". . . the worst sinners of all were the Caursins," quoting (pp. 337 ff.) a description by Matthew Paris (*ca.* 1200–1259) of the role these "manifest usurers" played in economic life in the middle of the thirteenth century. As late as the fifteenth century, Johann Rothe in his *Ritterspiegel*, a book of rules for knights, pointed out that it would blemish the noble name to cheat the poor people out of their earnings. This should be left to Jews and "Caorsins, the wicked Christians":

> "Sugit her der armen lute blud,
> so werdit sin adil gar kleine.
> den judin sal her ez befelin
> und kawerzinern, den besin Cristin."

("If he sucks the poor people's blood, his nobility is disgraced. He should leave it to the Jews and Caorsins, the wicked Christians.") See Gudde, *Social Conflicts in Medieval German Poetry* (Berkeley, Calif., 1934), p. 96; cf. also pp. 93 f. On the Caorsins see below, n. 120. On moneylending by monasteries, cf. Coulton, *op. cit.*, pp. 342 ff.

50. MSchSpr., III B, 121.

51. RW., F 42. MS Breslau 568, No. 2: 8 *schock;* MS Breslau J 5, No. 19: 100 marks; No. 30: 20 marks *houptgutis* plus 8 marks *wuchir;* No 69: 145 marks; No. 180: 60 florins; RW., F 42: $24\frac{1}{4}$ marks; MS Görlitz, Varia 4, fols. 207 ff., No. 4: 30 marks; MSchSpr., II, 19: $18\frac{1}{2}$ *schock groschen;* III B, 92: 26 Rhenish florins; III B, 99: 18 new *schock*.

52. MSchSpr., III B, 92: principal of 30 old *schock groschen* plus 2 *gute*

nuwe phennige zcu wucher for each *schock* and week; III B, 120: 7 old *schock groschen* plus 2 pennies for each *schock* and week; III B, 121: 8 Hungarian florins and 4 old *schock groschen* plus 3 new pennies for each florin and *schock* per week; III B, 122: 3 old *schock groschen* and 15 old *groschen* plus 2 pennies for each *schock* and week; LSchSprS., 495: 51 florins and *gesuch*.

53. On medieval rates of interest for Jews and in general see Stobbe, *Die Juden in Deutschland*, pp. 110 ff.; Hoffmann, *op. cit.*, pp. 70 ff.; Forchhammer, *op. cit.*, p. 362; Zimmels, *op. cit.*, pp. 55 ff.; Artur Rosenberg, *Beiträge zur Geschichte der Juden in Steiermark* (Vienna, 1914), pp. 58 ff., 133 ff.; Aloys Schulte, *Geschichte des mittelalterlichen Handels und Verkehrs*, I (Leipzig, 1900), 319: "Der Zins von 43, 3%, den Juden und Astigianen in Deutschland erhielten, war gegenüber dem, der auf den Champagnermessen als Verzugszinsen erhoben wurde—60%—noch niedrig zu nennen." Cf. also Coulton, *op. cit.*, pp. 337, 340.

54. MSchSpr., III B, 92, 121.

55. MS Breslau 568, No. 3; MS Breslau J 5, No. 69, 180; MSchSpr., II, 19; III B, 92, 99, 120, 121; LSchSprS., 495, 500, 505, 519, 520, 525, 609, 651.

56. MS Breslau 568, No. 2.

57. MS Breslau J 5, No. 19; on similar cases see Forchhammer, *op. cit.*, pp. 361 f. For numerous instances of large amounts borrowed from Jews by the city of Breslau see Otto Stobbe, "Mitteilungen aus Breslauer Signaturbüchern," *ZGS*, VI (1865), Heft 2, 354–56; in 1434 the city council of Breslau extended the city's peace and safe-conduct to several foreign Jews and their families "for as long as the city is indebted to them and has to deal with them because of debt," thereby putting them on an equal footing with the resident Jews of Breslau (Stobbe, *ZGS*, VIII [1867], 158, No. CLXV); on a debt of 1,000 Hungarian florins owed by the city of Neisse, Silesia, to the Jewess Hester and the Jew Smoyl see *ibid.*, pp. 445 f., No. CCIII, *anno* 1440. For more cases see I. Landsberger, "Mitteilungen aus Breslauer Stadt-, Schöppen- und Rechnungsbüchern im 14. und 15. Jahrhundert," in Geiger's *ZGJD*, V (1892), 376–79: "Fürsten und Städte als Schuldner jüdischer Gläubiger."

58. Hermann Grössler, "Sammlung älterer nach Eisleben ergangener Rechtsbescheide des Magdeburger Schöppenstuhls," *Zeitschrift des Harzvereins für Geschichte und Altertumskunde*, XXIII (1890), 193 f., No. 33.

59. RW., F 42; MS Görlitz, Varia 4, fols. 207 ff., No. 4; MSchSpr., III B, 99; LSchSprS., 113, 495, 727. Cf. also Landsberger, *loc. cit.*

60. LSchSprS., 727.

61. MS Breslau J 5, No. 30.

62. LSchSprS., 727.

63. The same observation, though made in medieval German sources of a different type, had already struck Caro (*Sozial- und Wirtschaftsgeschichte der Juden*, I, 226, 437). He explained the causes of this phenomenon also from the point of view of economic history. Whether the situation was materially different in southwestern Germany in the period of the Peasant Wars, early in the sixteenth century, still awaits clarification (cf. Alfred Stern, "Die Juden im grossen deutschen Bauernkriege 1525," *Jüdische Zeitschrift für Wissenschaft und Leben*, VIII [1870], 62 f., 70 f.). Günther Franz, who studied the history of the Peasant Wars prior to his conversion to National Socialist doctrines, contented himself with hypothetical assertions but did not adduce full or convincing evidence that the peasants' indebtedness to Jews may have been one of the principal causes for their uprising. In his book, *Der deutsche Bauernkrieg* (Munich and Berlin, 1933), pp. 74, 78, he writes:

"Die Judenverfolgungen nahmen von den Städten ihren Ausgang. Ursprünglich hatten religiöse Gründe, Kreuzzugsbegeisterung, den Vorrang gehabt, sie hatten sich rasch mit wirtschaftlichen Interessen verschmolzen. Die grosse Verfolgung im Pestjahr 1348 hatte wesentlich sozialen Charakter. Sie war ein Aufstand der arbeitenden Schichten gegen die Rentenbezieher und Kapitalisten. . . . Ihre [der Bauern] Fahne war das Kreuz. Sie beriefen sich auf eine göttliche Weissagung, die ihnen befohlen habe, die Juden als Feinde Christi zu vernichten. Trotzdem hat wohl nicht Glaubenseifer, sondern die wirtschaftliche Verschuldung den Anstoss gegeben. . . . Juden- und Pfaffenhass wurzeln nahe beieinander. Beide sind in den mittelalterlichen Städten entstanden und haben erst später das flache Land ergriffen. In beiden suchen religiöse, nationale und wirtschaftliche Gegensätze nach einem Ausgleich."

Ruth ("Wucher und Wucherrecht der Juden im Mittelalter," pp. 117 ff.), on the other hand, advanced the assertion that, from the fourteenth century on, peasants were the principal debtors of Jewish moneylenders. But he was unable to support this thesis with even one single example such as the sources should have supplied.

64. Cf., e.g., RW., F 42; MS Breslau J 5, No. 69; MS Görlitz, Varia 4, fols. 207 ff., No. 4; LSchSprS., 495, 519, 520, 609; MSchSpr., III B, 127, 129; cf. also Wasserschleben, RQ., IV, 173, 174; also the instances quoted in the note following.

65. E.g., MSchSpr., III B, 92, I and II, 120, 121, 122; cf. also, below, n. 99.

66. Here follows a characteristic example in faithful translation from the medieval German (MSchSpr., III B, 120):

"I, Hans Glogaw, citizen at Naumburg, personal debtor and all my heirs, and I, Wenceslaus von Glogaw, citizen at Naumburg, surety, publicly acknowledge in this letter before all good people that we are indebted and shall pay with joint responsibility [*mid gesampter hand*] the rightful debt to Junger and Kanold, Jews, resident in Naumburg, their wives and all their heirs and to anyone who holds this letter with the aforementioned Jews' free will and knowledge, seven old *schock* of *groschen* of Freiberg coinage, three of which are worth one new *schildichter groschen*. This aforementioned sum of *groschen* we promise to pay, without demur, to the aforementioned Jews on the next Saint Jacob the Apostle's day. Failing to do this, we promise to give to the aforementioned Jews each week two good *pfennige* as interest on each *schock groschen*, the while the aforementioned sum of *groschen* is not paid, three of which are worth one. And we, the aforementioned personal debtors and sureties, shall be obligated and are willing to cover and pay the aforementioned money, principal and interest [*wúcher*], messengers' fees, letter-money, expenses of travel and board, such as might arise, in ready money or good pledges, as will satisfy the Jews, without recourse to an ecclesiastical or secular court, [payment to be made] in the city of Naumburg or within a circuit of seven miles, in whatever town they claim payment from us. No lord's service, request, or order shall impede us therefrom, and nothing shall be found therein that may be injurious to the aforementioned Jews regarding their aforementioned money, be it of ecclesiastic or secular jurisdiction. As long as the Jews hold this letter, no one shall swear away nor void it, nor claim payment of the debt. If it also be that words or seals in this letter should be displaced, missing, or broken, or if there were any omission or defect in this letter or seal, this shall work no injury to the Jews mentioned as to their aforementioned money, on our good faith. In attestation thereof and for greater security that all that has been written above, words, clauses, and articles of this letter, shall be kept by us steadfastly and wholly and inviolably, I, aforementioned Hans Glagaw, personal debtor, and I, aforementioned surety, Wenceslaus von Glagaw, have with our free will and knowledge attached our seals to this open letter, which is given in the fourteen hundred and seventeenth year after the birth of Christ, on the Friday next before the day of Saint Donatus the bishop [August 6, 1417]."

67. Caro, *op. cit.*, I, 437, 440 f., 514: "der Schuldbrief spielte jedenfalls eine sehr geringe Rolle" (p. 437). Assenting, Forchhammer, *op.*

cit., p. 361; cf. also Stobbe, *Die Juden in Deutschland*, p. 128.

68. Caro himself, in his second volume (*op. cit.*, pp. 148 ff.), adduced documentary material contradicting the thesis set forth in his first volume (*ibid.*, pp. 437, 440 f., 514) and suggested a French model for the German bonds in favor of Jewish creditors (*ibid.*, II, 145). If the custom of promissory notes had, in fact, penetrated into western and southern Germany from France only later in the Middle Ages, the wide dissemination and common use of this legal instrument in central Europe in the thirteenth and fourteenth centuries could hardly find a reasonable explanation. Even Caro (*ibid.*, II, 145) had to admit with reference to the years 1259–62: "Ungewöhnlich kann freilich das Leihen gegen Schuldbrief schon damals in diesen Gegenden [Switzerland] nicht gewesen sein." Rosenberg, *Beiträge zur Geschichte der Juden in Steiermark*, Appendix (*Beilagen*, pp. 150–76), published promissory notes for Jewish creditors, of the fourteenth and fifteenth centuries, also one of 1281, from the Styrian Provincial Archives in Graz, Austria. Viewed in the light of the above text, the provision of art. 25 in the Austrian Jewry privilege of 1244 (Scherer, *op. cit.*, p. 183) will receive its proper meaning, different from Caro's (*op. cit.*, I, 440 f., 514) interpretation.

69. Except when differently specified, this and all other statements under the present heading are based on the group of Magdeburg jury-court decisions, MSchSpr., III B, 92, 120, 121, 122 (about 1413–17), in which promissory notes to Jewish creditors are included. As to their legal-historical and paleographic analysis, cf. Victor Friese and Erich Liesegang, *Magdeburger Schöffensprüche* (Berlin, 1901), pp. 745 ff., 842 f.; Forchhammer, *op. cit.*, pp. 397–400.

70. MSchSpr., III B, 120; RW., F 42; LSchSprS., 495.

71. LSchSprS., 519. Cf. Hübner, *Grundzüge des deutschen Privatrechts*, pp. 746 f. [705 f.], 513 [482].

72. LSchSprS., 609; cf. 651. In another case—MSchSpr., III B, 127—the *Oberhof* of Magdeburg declared the heirs of a creditor unconditionally "liable, in accordance with the wording of the letter, to pay the money which you [the Jew Margkard] had lent to the deceased." It does not appear from the *Schöffenspruch* whether the heirs had been included as co-debtors in the promissory note. There is reference only to the copy of it sent to Magdeburg and not reproduced in the *Schöffenspruch*. It may be safe to assume that the heirs had been named in the document as debtors *mit gesampter hand*.

73. Cf. Hübner, *op. cit.*, pp. 574 [543]; Friese and Liesegang, *op. cit.*, pp. 801 ff.

74. RW., F 42; MSchSpr., III B, 120.

75. MSchSpr., III B, 92 (I). Jewish women also figure as principal creditors in the sources, e.g., LSchSprS., 525; cf. Hoffmann, *op. cit.*, pp. 99 f.; Caro, *op. cit.*, II, 148 ff.

76. MSchSpr., III B, 120; the clause following the words "all their heirs" is omitted from the promissory notes in MSchSpr., III B, 121, 122; in MS Breslau J 5, No. 69, the clause reads: "Also we promise on our faith and honor to everyone who holds this letter and therewith demands payment of us with the consent of the aforementioned Jews, to him we pledge ourselves in the same manner as to the aforementioned Jews themselves."

77. Cf. Hübner, *op. cit.*, pp. 564 ff. [533 ff.]. As late as the end of the fourteenth century it was still necessary to enter in the municipal register a special contract between creditor and debtor, to enable the creditor legally to transfer his claim to a third party without the debtor's specific consent; cf., e.g., Otto Stobbe, "Mitteilungen aus Breslauer Signaturbüchern," *ZGS*, VI (1865), Heft 2, 338, *anno* 1390: "Auch haben sy sich an beiden teilen vorlobt, were sache, das Albertus [the creditor] des geldes selber nicht gefordern mochte, weme her denne des befule und mechtig machte, czu vorderen, der sal des fordern, alz her selber"; cf. a similar case, *ibid.*, p. 342, *anno* 1399, No. 19; cf. also Stobbe, *Handbuch des deutschen Privatrechts*, III (3d ed. by H. O. Lehmann; Berlin, 1898), 249, n. 6.

78. MS Breslau J 5, No. 69.

79. Cf. Hübner, *op. cit.*, pp. 602 f. [570 f.].

80. Cf. also MSchSpr., III B, 127, 129.

81. MSchSpr., III B, 92 (II). The application of this clause to the heirs of a debtor was, however, flatly denied to a Jewish creditor by the *Oberhof* of Magdeburg (MSchSpr., III B, 129), and this in spite of the fact that the heir's obligation to pay the debt of the deceased had been recognized previously by the same superior court (MSchSpr., III B, 127).

82. Cf. a quite similar decision by the *Schöffenstuhl* of Dohna (MS Dresden M 20a, pp. 23v, 203v): ". . . if the prince and his sureties do not acknowledge the letter, they must disengage their seals, according to law. If they would then proceed against the Jew as forger of the letter, they must convict him, else he could find protection in his right."

83. MSchSpr., III B, 120 (cf. III B, 121): "If it also be that words or seals in this letter should be displaced, missing or broken, or if there were any omission or defect in this letter or seal, this shall work no injury to the Jews mentioned as to their aforementioned money, on our good faith."

84. MSchSpr., III B, 122.

85. MSchSpr., III B, 121.

86. Actual payment of expenditures of the kind described here is attested in a Leipzig *Schöffenstuhl* decision (LSchSprS., 495, p. 348).

87. MSchSpr., III B, 120, 121, 122.

88. MSchSpr., III B, 92 (I).

89. MSchSpr., III B, 92 (I); the same principle appears very strictly applied also to the debtor's heirs in MSchSpr., III B, 127; cf. also III B, 92 (II); LSchSprS., 519. On the authenticity and legal significance of seals on promissory notes in general see Harry Bresslau, *Handbuch der Urkundenlehre für Deutschland und Italien*, I (2d ed., Leipzig, 1912), 718–30.

90. See above, pp. 230 f.

91. MSchSpr., III B, 92 (II); III B, 121; cf. III B, 65. From the beginning of the fifteenth century onward a peculiar legal procedure was practiced in medieval Austria in order to invalidate promissory notes in the hands of Jewish creditors. The debtor (or his heirs) declared publicly readiness to redeem all promissory notes standing to his debit if presented in court within a definite time. After this had elapsed, unclaimed bonds held by Jewish creditors would be declared void by decision of the court. For details on this procedure see Arnold Luschin, "Das Berufen von Brief und Siegel," *ZRG*, O.S., XII (1876), 46–80.

92. RW., F 42. Cf. LSchSprS., 495, p. 347: the promissory note must be returned; MS Breslau, J 5, No. 180: no *quitancia* was ever issued that the debt was paid. For more details on the entire history of this interesting lawsuit between Moshe and Bartusch Koslig, decided by the *Schöffen* of Magdeburg probably in 1432, see Otto Stobbe, "Mitteilungen aus Breslauer Signaturbüchern," *ZGS*, VII (1866), 188, No. LXXXIX, and n. 3; pp. 351 ff., No. CXVII; p. 352, n. 1; more data about Ichel (Michel) of Reichenbach, *ibid.*, pp. 182 f. and note, 188, 351 ff., 358 f. In another Magdeburg jury-court decision (about 1377–82), the promissory note still in the hand of the creditor, Jacob the Jew, was declared old and long invalidated by tacit preclusion (*Verschweigung*): "zo sint [the defendants] . . . neher zu bliben, wenne die juden mit den aldin briuen, die se lange cziet fursuegen sint, en abgewinnen mogen" (Theodor Goerlitz and Paul Gantzer, *Die Magdeburger Schöffensprüche und Rechtsmitteilungen für Schweidnitz* [Stuttgart and Berlin, 1940], II, No. 8, p. 90).

93. MSchSpr., III B, 121. A similar case (not decided by the *Oberhof* of Magdeburg) is reported in Stobbe, *ZGS*, VIII (1867), 445, No. CCII, *anno* 1440.

94. MSchSpr., III B, 121, 122.

95. MSchSpr., III B, 92 (I), 120; RW., F 42; MS Görlitz, Varia 4, fols. 207 ff., No. 4 (Dohna); MS Dresden M 20a, fols. 23v, 203v (Dohna); cf. MSchSpr., III B, 127, 129. Cf. Bresslau, *Handbuch der Urkundenlehre*, I, 728 f.

96. Even an author like Forchhammer admits in general (*op. cit.*, p. 361, n. 237): "Betrügereien waren dabei [namely, in connection with promissory notes] bei Christen und Juden an der Tagesordnung"; cf. also Stobbe, *Die Juden in Deutschland*, p. 129; Stobbe, "Mitteilungen aus Breslauer Signaturbüchern," *ZGS*, VII (1866), 352, n. 1; Otto H. Stowasser, *Vierteljahrschrift für Sozial- und Wirtschaftsgeschichte*, XVI (1922), 110.

97. In a case decided by the *Oberhof* of Magdeburg, MS Merseburg 3, No. 4, the plaintiff refers to the following facts as conclusive evidence for the genuineness of the seal which allegedly had been attached to the deed in a fraudulent manner: "Since Diterich Buckelwicz used the seal before contracting the debt, and also thereafter, and can adduce no proof that he ever lost or missed his seal, etc."

98. Another decision of the *Schöffen* of Magdeburg, in a very similar case, reads (MS Merseburg 3, No. 4):

"Hereon we, *Scheppen* of Magdeburg, state the law: If the letter shows no erasure or [other] tampering, and if Diterich acknowledges his seal on it, then Diterich, the question standing thus, if he would redeem his seal, must state on oath (to be supported by two honorable persons in full possession of their rights, against whose giving testimony no objection can be raised) by what deception or fraud the seal may have become attached to the letter, else he must observe it according to its tenor; premium or usury being excluded; thereon we pass no judgment."

On analogous cases between Christian parties see MBSchR., III, 2, 37; Wasserschleben, RQ., V, No. 32, p. 384; Wasserschleben, RQ.², 197, p. 65. If the heirs of the debtor have to go through this procedure, the oath is prescribed to be taken with the support of six (instead of only two) witnesses (MSchSpr., III B, 129).

99. MSchSpr., III B, 145; Wasserschleben, RQ., IV, 173–74; both *Schöffensprüche* contain the full text of obligations by non-Jewish debtors to their Jewish creditors; cf. LSchSprS., 495, p. 348; MS Breslau 568, Nos. 2, 3; Stobbe, "Mitteilungen aus Breslauer Signaturbüchern," *ZGS*, VII (1866), 182–89; Forchhammer, *op. cit.*, p. 396; also Richard Jecht, *Quellen zur Geschichte der Stadt Görlitz bis 1600* (Görlitz, 1909), p. 62. Cf. an interesting case in which a deed could not be executed

484 NOTES TO CHAPTER IX, PAGES 234–238

because the Jews lacked a seal of their own (*propriis carentes sigillis*). Thus, in substitution, recourse was taken to an entry in "authoritative records," namely, the *Stadtbuch* of Brünn (cf. Bertold Bretholz, *Geschichte der Juden in Mähren im Mittelalter*, I [Brünn and Vienna, 1934], 126 ff., with further reference on p. 127, n. 1). These decisions are also of importance for the history of the law of evidence.

100. Caro, *op. cit.*, I, 228; cf. Hoffmann, *op. cit.*, pp. 100 ff.; Zimmels, *op. cit.*, p. 61.

101. For details and bibliography on the problem see Otto von Gierke, *Deutsches Privatrecht*, III, 358 ff., § 187; the excellent work on the subject by Otto Stobbe, *Zur Geschichte des deutschen Vertragsrechts* is still not outdated.

102. On Christian moneylenders see below, p. 240.

103. See above, pp. 217 ff.

104. Guido Kisch, "Die Pfändungsklausel: Ein Beitrag zur Geschichte des deutschen Vollstreckungsrechts," *ZRG*, XXXV (1914), 41–68.

105. For details and instances see Kisch, *ibid.*, p. 66, n. 1.

106. G. Kisch, "Ehrenschelte und Schandgemälde," *ZRG*, LI (1931), 514–20, including bibliography, to which should be added: RW., Q 77, Böhlau, *ZRG*, O.S., IX (1870), 13 f., n. 44; Gerhard Brauer, *Das Ehrenwort im Vermögensrecht* (University of Greifswald Jur.D. thesis; Greifswald, 1930), pp. 28 ff.; Wilhelm Weizsäcker, "Zur Geschichte des Zittauer Landgerichts," *Neues Lausitzisches Magazin*, CX (1934), 18; Hans Fehr, *Die Dichtung im Recht* (Bern, 1936), pp. 207–11; G. Kisch, "The 'Jewish Execution' in Medieval Germany," *Historia Judaica*, V (1943), 128 f.

107. A. Heusler, *Institutionen des deutschen Privatrechts*, II (Leipzig, 1886), 248: "Des Schuldners Ehre ist durch seine Zahlungsunfähigkeit dem Gläubiger verfallen und kann öffentlich ausgeboten und weggeworfen werden." See also Hübner, *Grundzüge des deutschen Privatrechts*, p. 527 [495].

108. Reproductions of the picture (second half of the fifteenth century) are found in Otto Hupp, *Scheltbriefe und Schandbilder: Ein Rechtsbehelf aus dem 15. und 16. Jahrhundert* (Schleissheim near Munich, 1930), p. 23; and Kisch, "The 'Jewish Execution,' " pl. 3. The inscription reads:

"Saydro Straubinger und Isaac, Juden von Regensburg contra Hansen Judmann zu Afekhing der mit sambt hern Johansen von Degenberg sel. ihr rechter borge für Heinrich Schenkh von Geyern, dene Judman sie nit haben ermahnen mögen umb aussrichtung, als die er geleistet hett laut brieff und Sigl, warnen derhalben Fürsten, Grafen, Freye Ritter und Knecht und meniglich, das sie sich hueten vor dem ehr- und treulosen sigelbrüchigen mann."

In contradistinction to the usual way of picturing the debtor, namely, hanged on the gallows by the neck, Hans von Judmann appears suspended by the feet. The Jewish creditors, then, made use on their *Schandgemälde* of the kind of execution applied at that time particularly to Jewish thieves. This was intended as an especially cutting humiliation for a member of the Christian nobility. Dogs do not appear in the picture. Beside the nobleman's figure his coat-of-arms is also suspended upside-down from the gallows. In its middle field it shows three silver Jews' hats, and it is surmounted by a fourth of very large size. The Jews' hats as well as the name "Judmann" indicate the Jewish origin of the incriminated nobleman, possibly another reason for the figurative application of the "Jewish execution."

109. G. Kisch, "Ehrenschelte und Schandgemälde," p. 519, n. 1; Otto Stobbe ("Mitteilungen aus Breslauer Signaturbüchern," *ZGS*, VII [1866], 352, n. 1) mentions a *Schmähbrief* of 1389, issued by the Jew Ichel of Reichenbach (see above, p. 233 and n. 92) entered in the *Stadtbuch* of the Silesian town of Schweidnitz: Ichel complains against "the wicked rogue [*bösen Schalk*] Jacob Zanne who summoned him before the ecclesiastical court for usury, although he never gave him a loan"; cf. also the following entry in the Breslau *Signaturbücher*, No. CXXXIII, p. 4, of 1428 (Stobbe, *ibid.*, p. 360):

"Lazarus the Jew has pledged himself for Abraham the Jew that, between now and Pentecost and eight days thereafter, he would not defame nor post letters against Gregor von Gregersdorf on account of the matter and debt, as he has pledged himself to the same Abraham for Andris Cannengisser, our fellow-citizen; but that, as to what they have to do thereafter with one another regarding such debt, they shall leave it to the course of justice."

In the Bavarian State Archives (Bayrisches Reicharchiv), under "Reichsstadt Regensburg, Literalien, fol. 117," a document of January 19, 1458, refers to a *Schandgemälde* issued by a Jew who "den von Aw [a patrician family of Regensburg] toten auf der par gemalten angeslagen" (information in a letter of May 12, 1931, by Professor Otto Hupp of Schleissheim, Germany, to this writer).

110. In Poland, in contradistinction, the Jews had not the right of *Schelmenschelten* (cf. S. Rundstein, "Ächtungs- und Schmähungsklausel im polnischen Obligationenrecht des Mittelalters," *Zeitschrift für vergleichende Rechtswissenschaft*, XVII [1905], 27).

111. Cf. Hübner, *op. cit.*, pp. 514 ff. [482 f.]; G. Kisch, "Das Einlager im älteren Schuldrechte Mährens," *Zeitschrift des deutschen Vereins für die Geschichte Mährens und Schlesiens*, Vol. XV (Brünn, 1912), Heft 4; separate edition, Prague, 1912.

112. Cf. Stobbe, *Die Juden in Deutschland*, pp. 130, 248 f., n. 123; Stobbe, *Zur Geschichte des deutschen Vertragsrechts*, p. 198, n. 28; Adolf Lechner, *Das Obstagium oder die Giselschaft nach schweizerischen Quellen* (Bern, 1906), pp. 66–73; Caro, *op. cit.*, I, 357, and II, 148–50, 154, 155, 158–61; Forchhammer, *op. cit.*, pp. 362 f.; Siegmar Bromberger, *Die Juden in Regensburg bis zur Mitte des 14. Jahrhunderts* (University of Berlin, Ph.D. thesis; Berlin, 1934), p. 53. On rabbinic sources see Hoffmann, *op. cit.*, p. 70 (comment by George Caro in *Deutsche Literaturzeitung*, XXXII [1911], 753 ff.); Zimmels, *op. cit.*, pp. 60 and 115, n. 408.

113. Stobbe, *Die Juden in Deutschland*, p. 130; Konrad Maurer, *Kritische Vierteljahrsschrift für Gesetzgebung und Rechtswissenschaft*, IX (1867), 567; Hoffmann, *op. cit.*, p. 70; Forchhammer, *op. cit.*, pp. 362, n. 250, and 363, n. 252. Cf. Andreas Würfel, *Historische Nachrichten von der Judengemeinde, welche ehehin in der Reichsstadt Nürnberg angericht gewesen, aber anno 1499 ausgeschaffet worden* (Nürnberg, 1755), pp. 30 f. Restrictions in the application and execution of the *Einlager* clause to the disadvantage of Jewish creditors were also practiced in Bohemia and Moravia at the end of the fifteenth and during the sixteenth century (for details see František Čáda, *Ležení podle Českého práva zemského* ["*Einlager* According to the Czech Territorial Law"] ["Práce ze Semináře Českého Práva na Karlově Universitě v Praze," No. 6 (Prague, 1922)], p. 40).

114. MS Breslau J 5, No. 69.

115. G. Kisch, "Das Schadennehmen: Ein Beitrag zur Geschichte des deutschen mittelalterlichen Vollstreckungsrechts," *Rheinische Zeitschrift für Zivil- und Prozessrecht*, V (Mannheim, 1913), 477–506; also separate edition (Mannheim, 1913). Cf. Stobbe, *Zur Geschichte des deutschen Vertragsrechts*, pp. 40–49; and Stobbe, *Die Juden in Deutschland*, pp. 114–16, 239 f., n. 104; Hoffmann, *op. cit.*, pp. 98 f.; Forchhammer, *op. cit.*, p. 363. Some of Stobbe's statements have been previously rectified by this writer. The legal-historical nature of *Schadennehmen* was not recognized by Bertold Bretholz, *Geschichte der Juden in Mähren im Mittelalter*, I, 124; nor by Parkes, *op. cit.*, p. 332; nor by Bromberger, *op. cit.*, p. 49.

116. G. Kisch, "Die Pfändungsklausel," *ZRG*, XXXV (1914), 66, n. 1. In medieval English documents a legal device is not infrequent that bears no specific name but is unmistakably identical with the central European *Schadennehmen*. Jacob J. Rabinowitz ("Some Remarks on the

Evasion of the Usury Laws in the Middle Ages," *Harvard Theological Review*, XXXVII [1944], 49–59) quotes the following clause from *Select Pleas, Starrs and Other Records from the Rolls of the Exechequer of the Jews* ("Selden Society Publications," Vol. XV), pp. 65 f., *anno* 1272: "Diei, le Evesk', Judeus, recognovit per starrum suum, quod tenetur Abrahe, filio Joscei, de Eboraco, in XII L sterlingorum . . . et si dictum terminum transierit, dicto Abrahe [the lender] licebit mutuo accipere dictos denarios per mannum alicujus Christiani ad usuram." Thus in England the stipulation was customary between the Jewish parties to a loan contract, the eventual new creditor being a Christian. The aim of evading the usury laws may have been in play. The selection of a Christian as new creditor by the Jewish parties seems to indicate this. But it was certainly not the main point in that stipulation, as Rabinowitz assumes on the basis of some alleged legal fictions for which there is no support in the sources. The medieval English form of *Schadennehmen* calls for monographic treatment by a competent legal historian.

117. Cf., e.g., Purgoldts Rb., VIII, 10, 11; *Gerichtsleuft zu Eisenach*, ed. Ortloff, art. 59, p. 368; *Wiener Stadtrechtsbuch*, ed. Schuster, art. 10, p. 51; art. 135, pp. 124 f.; for full references see Kisch, "Das Schadennehmen," pp. 481 f. [separate ed., pp. 9 f.]. Meissen Rb., III, 14, 4, claimed by Stobbe, *Die Juden in Deutschland*, p. 239, n. 104, to refer to *Schadennehmen*, and similarly Wasserschleben, RQ.², I, chap. 264, p. 83, most probably refer merely to pawning with Jewish creditors (cf. Kisch, "Das Schadennehmen," p. 498, n. 8 [p. 26, n. 8]; and above, n. 38 and chap. viii, n. 79.

118. RW., L 84; cf. Böhlau, ZRG, O.S., IX (1870), 29, n. 91; MS Breslau 568, Nos. 2, 3; MS Görlitz, Varia 4, fols. 271v–272r; MSchSpr., III B, 65, 99; LSchSprS., 495, 519, 727; Wasserschleben, RQ., IV, 1, pp. 130 ff.; V, 95, pp. 442 f.; for full references and numerous instances of documents with the *Schadennehmen* clause see Kisch, "Das Schadennehmen," pp. 481 ff. [9 ff.]; cf. also Rudolf His, "Eine eigentümliche Klausel in westfälischen Schuldurkunden," ZRG, XLII (1921), 481 ff. As late as the fifteenth century, a formulary of legal documents contains a form of promissory note with *Schadennehmen* clause (Leopold Hallein, *Mainzer Gerichtsformeln aus dem fünfzehnten Jahrhundert* [Würzburg, 1891], p. 44, No. X e). Cf. also Adolf Stölzel, *Urkundliches Material aus den Brandenburger Schöppenstuhlsakten*, I (Berlin, 1901), 22, No. 17, *anno* 1474; 68, No. 43, *anno* 1510.

119. Kisch, "Das Schadennehmen," pp. 483 f. [pp. 11 f.], 484, n. 4 [p. 12, n. 4].

120. See *ibid*. The Caorsins (*Caorsini*) took their name from the French

city of Cahors, about a hundred miles inland from Bordeaux on the river Lot (cf. Aloys Schulte, *Geschichte des mittelalterlichen Handels und Verkehrs*, I, 308–27; N. Denholm-Young, "The Merchants of Cahors," *Medievalia et Humanistica*, IV [1946], 37–44). By kings and town lords they were granted trade privileges which, to some extent, resemble the medieval Jewry privileges. On the role of the Caorsins in medieval economic life, cf. above, n. 49.

121. Rotenburg, January 7, 1364; Meir Wiener, *Regesten zur Geschichte der Juden in Deutschland während des Mittelalters* (Hannover, 1862), p. 135, No. 240.

122. RW., L 84, Böhlau, *ZRG*, O.S., IX (1870), 29, n. 91.

123. MSchSpr., III B, 65.

124. This fact as established here is reminiscent of Pope Innocent III's statement in his letter of April 19, 1208, to Bishop Radolfus of Arras that "in the city and diocese of Arras, [Christian] usurers are said to be in such number that it would become necessary to close the churches altogether because of their multitude, if the penalty decreed by the [Third] Lateran Council for such [c. 3, X, *de usuris*, 5, 19] were to be inflicted on all of them:

". . . in usurarios, qui tantum in civitate ac dioecesi tua excrevisse dicuntur quod si censura in Lateranensi concilio prodita contra tales proferretur in omnes, omnino claudi ecclesias prae multitudine oporteret [Innocentii III, *Opera omnia*, II (*Patr. Lat.*, CCXV, 1380 D)].

Cf. also L. Erler, "Die Juden des Mittelalters," *Archiv für katholisches Kirchenrecht*, XLVIII (1882), 399. On the rates of interest of Christian moneylenders and their relation to those demanded by Jews, cf. Coulton, *Medieval Panorama*, pp. 337, 340.

125. Similarly, *Gerichtsleuft zu Eisenach*, ed. Ortloff, art. 59, p. 368.

126. Wasserschleben, RQ., V, 95, p. 442 f.

127. MS Breslau 568, No. 2. In this case the stipulation of *Schadennehmen* was even entered in the official municipal records, *in der stad toffel*.

CHAPTER TEN

1. On the history of criminal and civil procedure in the Middle Ages in general see Carl Gustav Homeyer, "Das Gerichtswesen nach dem Richtsteige," in his book, *Der Richtsteig Landrechts nebst Cautela und Premis* (Berlin, 1857), pp. 411–520; Julius Wilhelm Planck, *Das deutsche Gerichtsverfahren im Mittelalter*, Vols. I and II (Braunschweig, 1879); Paul Laband, *Die vermögensrechtlichen Klagen nach den sächsischen Rechtsquellen des Mittelalters* (Berlin, 1869). A good abstract and a select bibliography are found in H. Brunner, *Grundzüge der deutschen Rechtsge-*

schichte (8th ed. by C. von Schwerin; Munich and Berlin, 1930), pp. 176–86. Monographs on individual topics of procedural law to be treated here will be cited at the head of the subsections to follow. On the history of procedure according to canon law see Nicolaus München, *Das kanonische Gerichtsverfahren und Strafrecht*, Vol. I (Cologne and Neus, 1865; 2d ed., 1874); Paul Hinschius, *System des katholischen Kirchenrechts mit besonderer Rücksicht auf Deutschland*, Vol. V (Berlin, 1895); Erwin Jacobi, "Der Prozess im Decretum Gratiani und bei den ältesten Dekretisten," *ZRG*, XXXIV, kanon. Abt. III (1913), 223–343.

On the treatment of Jews in the medieval system of criminal and civil procedure see Otto Stobbe, *Die Juden in Deutschland während des Mittelalters* (Braunschweig, 1866), pp. 143–45, 148–59; Johannes E. Scherer, *Die Rechtsverhältnisse der Juden in den deutsch-österreichischen Ländern* [Leipzig, 1901), pp. 162 ff., 230–313; Emanuel Forchhammer, "Beiträge zur Geschichte der deutschen Juden . . . ," *Geschichtsblätter für Stadt und Land Magdeburg*, XLVI (1911), 389–400.

2. Cf. G. Kisch, *Sachsenspiegel and Bible* (Notre Dame, Ind., 1941), pp. 155, 131, n. 27; Helmut Hillmann, *Das Gericht als Ausdruck deutscher Kulturentwicklung im Mittelalter* (Stuttgart, 1930), pp. 27 ff., 31 ff., 87 ff. Buch's *Gloss* to Ssp., III, 69, 1, ed. Zobel (Leipzig, 1560):
". . . sie [richter und schöppfen] sollen mit blossen heuptern sein, und keine kappen oder kogelen noch hauben daruff haben. Solches geschiehet zu einer beweisung, das sie Gottes bildt sindt, das ist, dass sie ihrer seelen durch unrechtes urteln nie sein missgestalt und unehnlich worden."

3. See above, pp. 173 ff.

4. See above, pp. 88 f.

5. The principle of equality of birth and rank, as pointed out in Ssp., II, 12, 2, also played a considerable role in the appointment of judges and courts (cf. Scherer, *op. cit.*, pp. 235 f., n. 4).

6. Cf. Stobbe, *op. cit.*, pp. 144 f., 256, n. 134; Scherer, *op. cit.*, pp. 239, 257; Forchhammer, *op. cit.*, p. 379; also above, chap. vii, n. 8. It is unlikely that the court mentioned in Brünn SchB., No. 432, p. 202, before which the accused Jew deposed his confession ("judaeus ipse promissis et tormentis de veritate dicenda monitus et inductus confessus est") was a "mixed" court, as assumed by Stobbe (*op. cit.*, p. 256, n. 134). The absence of the Jewish jurors remains unaccounted for. But the actual institution of a mixed court, as provided in Brünn SchB., No. 441, p. 207, was not mentioned by Stobbe (*ibid.*):
"In quaestione, quam judaeus movet judaeo, soli jurati judaeorum sententias dicere possunt, nisi fortassis nolint, vel partibus habeantur

suspecti; tunc enim christiani jurati cum judaeis ad pronuntiandum sententias assumantur. Sic sententiatum est in Radisch.''

("In an action by a Jew against a Jew the jurors of the Jews alone can pronounce judgment, unless they should perhaps be unwilling or be suspected by the parties; then Christian jurors shall be appointed to pronounce judgment together with the Jewish jurors. Such was the decision [of the court] in Radisch.")

For details see G. Kisch, "Relations between Jewish and Christian Courts in the Middle Ages," *Louis Ginzberg Jubilee Volume* (New York, 1945), pp. 214–17.

7. See above, pp. 173 f.

8. For more details on this subject see below, p. 256.

9. The passage in parentheses is added in the *Schwabenspiegel*. Cf. also Rudolf Limmer, *Bildungszustände und Bildungsideen des 13. Jahrhunderts* (Munich and Berlin, 1928), p. 38 and n. 19. It is worth while noting that Brünn SchB., No. 403, p. 185, has an identical passage: "Homo in judicem eligendus non debet esse perjurus, nec etiam debet esse proscriptus nec excommunicatus, nec sit etiam judaeus nec haereticus vel paganus, sitque legitimi matrimonii filius. . . ." This evidently goes back to Schwsp., W 71; L 86; G 71, 2. It is known that a codex of the *Schwabenspiegel*, still in existence, had been used in Brünn as early as the beginning of the fourteenth century, namely, the manuscript Homeyer, Rbb., No. 213; cf. Rössler, *Die Stadtrechte von Brünn aus dem XIII. und XIV. Jahrhundert* (Prague, 1852), pp. cxxviii ff. Unfortunately, the problem of the German-law sources of the Brünn SchB. has hardly been touched by research as yet. The first author who sensed some connections with older German lawbooks was Julius Weiske, "Bemerkungen über das Brünner Schöffenbuch," *Zeitschrift für deutsches Recht und deutsche Rechtswissenschaft*, XIV (1853), 115. Gertrud Schubart-Fikentscher (*Deutsches Archiv für Geschichte des Mittelalters*, I [1937], 467, and III [1939], 480) did not see the aforementioned connection with the Schwsp., which had also escaped the attention of all previous writers. From the entire tenor of chapter 403 in the *Brünner Schöffenbuch* it is clear beyond doubt that it was an insertion of the redactor, and not an original *Schöffenspruch*. Herewith the hypothesis that a Jew may have been considered for the office of municipal judge in a Moravian town as late as the middle of the fourteenth century does not gain much probability. This hypothesis was advanced by Bertold Bretholz, *Geschichte der Juden in Mähren im Mittelalter*, I (Brünn, 1934), 137.

10. Zobel's edition (Leipzig, 1560), p. 141, whereas the passage is not in the Augsburg edition of 1516. Similarly, *Holländ. Sachsenspiegel* (ed. Smits), 65, 1, with reference to the *Authentica, De judicibus* (Auth.

LXXXIII, Coll. VI, tit. 10): "Clerics, Jews, and women, and also persons of illegitimate birth shall not be judges nor pass judgment on anyone, as is stated in the *Authentica, de judicibus*, in the first paragraph of the sixth collation." On the exclusion of the Jews from the bar in Roman law, cf. *Cod. Just.* i. 4. 15; ii. 6. 8; Jean Juster, *Les Juifs dans l'empire romain*, II (Paris, 1914), 263 f.

11. Ssp., II, 12, 4; III, 26, 1: "Der kuning is gemeyne richtêre uber al"; cf. Ssp., III, 33, 1; I, 58, 2.

12. The clause, "oder der ein heide oder ein jude oder ein kezzer ist," is missing in Schwsp., L 122.

13. See Ssp., III, 54, 3; cf. Ferdinand Frensdorff, "Beiträge zur Geschichte und Erklärung der deutschen Rechtsbücher. V. 2, Die Rechtsbücher und die Königswahl," *Nachrichten der k. Gesellschaft der Wissenschaften zu Göttingen, phil.-hist. Klasse,* 1924, pp. 209 f.; Heinrich Mitteis, *Die deutsche Königswahl, ihre Rechtsgrundlagen bis zur Goldenen Bulle* (Baden bei Wien, 1938), p. 142.

14. Hans Voltelini, "Forschungen zu den deutschen Rechtsbüchern, III," *Sitzungsberichte der Akademie der Wissenschaften in Wien, phil.-hist. Klasse,* CCI, Abh. 4–5 (Vienna, 1924), 122.

15. See pp. 173–78.

16. *Decretum Gratiani*, c. 18, 23–25, C. II, qu. 7; cf. Jacobi, *op. cit.*, p. 251 and n. 4. According to the Brünn SchB., No. 431, p. 201, in a lawsuit the question was once raised as to "whether a Jew, being an infidel, is capable of acting in the capacity of a respectable man either as plaintiff or as defendant." The influence of canon law is patent. The decision of the secular court was in favor of the Jew: "Thereupon it was decided: As a Jew is a man and is capable of being a man with regard to age, sex, intellect, i.e., discretion, honesty, and manly action, and if in all these respects he gives no cause for doubting that he is respectable: he is capable of acting in the capacity of a respectable man, though not of a respectable Christian [man], both as plaintiff and as defendant, so long as he is not in ill repute. Therefore, his not being a believer is patent only from the fact that he cannot be a man with regard to marriage; for there is no matrimony or other sacrament outside the church."

17. See pp. 92 f.; cf. *ibid.*, also the comments on Johann von Buch's methodology in harmonizing the German with Roman and canon law.

18. *Gloss* to Ssp., III, 7, 1.

19. Also *Cod. Just.* i. 9. 15. Cf. Scherer, *op. cit.*, p. 16; Juster, *op. cit.*, II, 101–6; G. Kisch, "Relations between Jewish and Christian Courts in the Middle Ages," pp. 201 f.

20. See above, pp. 173 ff. In addition, some other examples of Jews or

Jewesses as plaintiffs before Christian courts: MS Breslau, J 5, No. 19; MFr., I, 2, 13, I, 4, 7; LSchSprS., No. 495, p. 348, Nos. 500, 506a, 525, 609, 651; Wasserschleben, RQ.², chap. 204, p. 67; cf. also Richard Jecht, *Quellen zur Geschichte der Stadt Görlitz bis 1600* (Görlitz, 1909), p. 45; Planck, *op. cit.*, I, 183.

21. See above, p. 174 and n. 10.

22. RW., F 41: "If the Jew is indebted or obligated to give something to someone, he [the latter] may well claim this from the Jew in court. Thereby neither the prince's letter nor peace is broken with respect to the Jew"; RW., B 97: "And the fact that he [the Jew David] is the emperor's *kemmerer* [chamber serf] and belongs to his chamber, cannot be of any help to him."

23. Cf. Brunner, *Grundzüge der deutschen Rechtsgeschichte* (8th ed. by C. von Schwerin; Munich and Leipzig, 1930), p. 177; Planck, *op. cit.*, I, 194–217.

24. MFr., I, 5, 1:
"*Wer vorspreche mag gesyn unde nicht gesyn.*

"Euwir vroge stet umme recht, wer vorspreche mag gesyn unde nicht gesyn mag, unde umme was sachen man ym vorspreche mag geweygern.

"Hiruff sprechen wir scheppin zcu Magdeburg recht: Eyn iczlich man, der kein gewiet pfaffe ist noch geistlich man nicht en ist, der mag in eyme iczlichen wertlichen gerichte, do her nicht ynne vorfestent ist, vorspreche wesen, unde den man nicht beschelden mag an syme rechte, den sal der richter von rechte zcu vorspreche gebin, wer umme yn bittet, vor yn czu reden, her en were is sich denne mit rechte. Der borggreve noch der richter noch dy wedirsachen mogen keynem manne geweigern, vorspreche zcu syn dorumme, ab her usz eyme andern lande ist adir in eyner andern herschafft gesessen ist adir das her keyn erbe do hat in deme gerichte. Von rechtis wegen. Zcu orkunde have wir unser insigel an dessen briff gehangen."

25. Homeyer, *Sachsenspiegel*, on *Landrecht*, I, 61, 4; see also above, p. 53.

26. *Gloss* to Ssp., I, 60 (Zobel's ed., Leipzig, 1560; ed. Augsburg, 1516): "Kettere und joden und ungelovige lüde muten nicht vorspreken yegen christen lüde; *C. de. postul., l. nemo* [*Cod. Just.* ii. 6. 8], et *Extra, de hereti., c. excommunicamus,* § *credentes* [c. 13, § 5, X, *de haereticis,* 5, 7]." Cf. Homeyer, *Der Richtsteig Landrechts* (Berlin, 1857), pp. 96 f.: "Wete ok dat papen, joden, wif, rechtlose lude nene vorspreken sin muten." On the exclusion of the Jews from the bar in Roman law see above, n. 10.

27. MS Breslau, J 5, No. 69; cf. above, pp. 224 f.

28. MS Breslau, J 5, No. 180: "Mosshe, Jew of Sagan, mandatory of Isaac Jew, onetime Abraham Meysner's brother proving his mandate before us, . . ."; cf. Magdeburg jury-court decision for the court of Schweidnitz (1377–82): "Since he [the Jew Jacob] brought suit into court as a guardian on behalf of his mother and his brothers . . ." (Theodor Goerlitz and Paul Gantzer, *Die Magdeburger Schöffensprüche und Rechtsmitteilungen für Schweidnitz* [Stuttgart and Berlin, 1940], II, 89, No. 7).

29. MS Breslau, J 5, No. 69. The advantages of employing a Christian *prolocutor* for a Jewish litigant come to light from a case related in Brünn SchB., No. 241, p. 114. A certain statement made by the *prolocutor* was considered an offense against the court. Since it had not been explicitly corroborated by his Jewish client, the fine for a minor offense only was imposed.

30. RW., F 41; Rem. RW., 14.

31. Ssp., III, 70, 1; cf. above, pp. 88 f., and below, pp. 269 ff.; also Stobbe, *op. cit.*, p. 150; Forchhammer, *op. cit.*, pp. 391 f.

32. MS Breslau, R 568, No. 3. For *Schadennehmen* see above, pp. 239 ff.

33. This translation renders the text in the Zobel edition (Leipzig, 1560), which is more elaborate on the point than is the original text in the Augsburg edition of 1516. Cf. also Reg. jur., J 151; Rem. RW., 1; MRb., IV, 46, 12; moreover, Brünn SchB., No. 664, pp. 307 ff., where the canon-law standpoint is clearly exposed.

34. Cf., e.g., Planck, *op. cit.*, I, 183, with reference to the Saxon prerogative of the oath of purgation, also denied to Jews according to *Gloss*, Ssp., III, 7, 1 (see also below, pp. 269 ff.).

35. MS Breslau, R 568, No. 3. Similar conditions prevailed within the jurisdiction of the *Oberhof* of Brünn in Moravia (see above, n. 33; cf. also Bretholz, *Geschichte der Juden in Mähren im Mittelalter*, I, 138). For details on Jews as witnesses see the section, "Law of Evidence" (below, pp. 260 ff.).

36. Cf. Brunner-Schwerin, *op. cit.*, pp. 180 ff.; Paul Laband, *Die vermögensrechtlichen Klagen nach den sächsischen Rechtsquellen des Mittelalters* (Berlin, 1869).

37. See, e.g., LSchSprS., 505: ". . . so schuldigte er [Isaac juda] in einer schlechten schulde. . . ."

38. MS Breslau, J 5, No. 19; cf. also LSchSprS., 520.

39. Cf., e.g., MS Breslau, J 5, No. 30; here the Jew Kussil takes recourse to his *gewere*, his legitimate possession of the pledges in dispute.

40. MS Breslau, R 568, No. 1.

41. LSchSprS., 520.

42. Cf. Brunner-Schwerin, *op. cit.*, p. 181; Julius Goebel, *Felony and Misdemeanor: A Study in the History of English Criminal Procedure*, I (New York, 1937), 66.

43. Wasserschleben, RQ.², No. 204, p. 67.

44. Ssp., II, 13, 1; MFr., I, 1, 25, 26. Cf. Rudolf His, *Das Strafrecht des deutschen Mittelalters*, II (Weimar, 1935), 183 ff.

45. Cf. Rudolf Hübner, *Grundzüge des deutschen Privatrechts* (5th ed.; Leipzig, 1930), pp. 438 ff. [Eng. ed., pp. 411 ff.].

46. Wasserschleben, RQ., V, 4, p. 400; cf. above, p. 213. Cf. a civil-law case of the Jew Abraham of Leipzig (MS Merseburg 3, No. 24). He was put under obligation to make restitution for goods unlawfully received, prior to the possible initiation of a lawsuit between the participants in the unlawful act.

47. O. Stobbe, "Mitteilungen aus Breslauer Signaturbüchern," *ZGS*, VII (1866), 178, No. LXIII of 1417: "Heylias Jew has pledged himself for the Jew Michil of Reychembach, residing in Canthe, to produce him again before the next Pentecost under the penalty of giving three oven bricks to the city for failing to produce him, for that he [Michil] had offensively threatened another Jew before the Council."

48. Cf. Brunner-Schwerin, *op. cit.*, pp. 179 f.; Planck, *op. cit.*, I, 379 ff.; Victor Friese and Erich Liesegang, *Die Magdeburger Schöffensprüche* (Berlin, 1901), pp. 858 ff.; Herbert Menzel, *Die Klagengewere* (University of Königsberg i.P., Jur. D. thesis, 1922; in typescript only), p. 90, n. 119.

49. MS Breslau, J 5, No. 180. According to another decision of the *Schöffen* of Magdeburg (1377–82), "the Jew Jacob was not considered to be bound by law to insure the performance of the act of *Klagengewere* by sureties" (Goerlitz and Gantzer, *Die Magdeburger Schöffensprüche und Rechtsmitteilungen für Schweidnitz*, II, No. 7, p. 87). In still another case at the beginning of the sixteenth century, the sureties of a Jewish plaintiff were held responsible for the latter's disregard of his duties arising from his pledge of *Klagengewere* (MSchSpr., Leitmeritz, No. 106, pp. 366 f.).

50. Cf. LSchSprS., 169, 706; Menzel, *op. cit.*, pp. 41, 44.

51. LSchSprS., 525. In LSchSprS., 651, the Jew Josse loses his claim on account of his ignorance that a relevant legal act was not valid.

52. On contumacy of Jews, cf. Scherer, *op. cit.*, pp. 288 f.

53. Cf., e.g., LSchSprS., 500: "By court decision the Jew Jordan has obtained the real estate of Hans Lasitz of Eilenburg with all rights, so that execution was awarded to him; thereupon the *schöpfen* decided

that the Jew might sell it, give it away or pledge it as security, which judge and jurors acknowledge." In LSchSprS., 525, it is taken for granted that execution (*hulfe*) would be carried out in favor of a Jewess "just as for other people" (*als ander leute*), provided that all formal requirements were met by her (cf. also MSchSpr., III B, 90, 145).

54. See above, chap. vii, n. 12.

55. MSchSpr., III B, 129, in connection with III B, 127; cf. also LSchSprS., 506, 606a. On *Läuterung* in general see Friese and Liesegang, *op. cit.*, pp. 810 ff.; Hildegard Berthold, Karl Hahn, and Alfred Schultze, *Die Zwickauer Stadtrechtsreformation 1539/69* (Leipzig, 1935), p. 133, n. 1.

56. On arbitration in medieval law in general see Hugo Böhlau, "Die 'Summa der rechte Weg gnant,' " ZRG, O.S., VIII (1869), 193–97; Böhlau, "Aus der Praxis des Magdeburger Schöffenstuhls während des 14. und 15. Jahrhunderts," ZRG, O.S., IX (1870), 40–50; Hermann Krause, *Die geschichtliche Entwicklung des Schiedsgerichtswesens in Deutschland* (Berlin, 1930), pp. 29–39, chiefly based on the *Schöffenspruch* material published in G. Kisch, *Leipziger Schöffenspruchsammlung;* cf. also Anna T. Sheedy, *Bartolus on Social Conditions in the Fourteenth Century* (New York, 1942), pp. 236 f.

57. MS Breslau, J 5, No. 180; cf. MS Breslau, J 7, No. F 42; LSchSprS., 505; Breslau *Signaturbuch* of 1396, p. 49, quoted by Stobbe, *Die Juden in Deutschland*, p. 256, n. 134; more instances in Stobbe, "Mitteilungen aus Breslauer Signaturbüchern," ZGS, VII (1866), *passim;* VIII (1867), 445 f., No. CCIII, *anno* 1440.

58. Cf. above, p. 243.

59. The case mentioned by Stobbe, *Die Juden in Deutschland*, p. 256, n. 134, is related by him *in extenso* in "Mitteilungen aus Breslauer Signaturbüchern," ZGS, VI (1865), Heft 2, 341 f., No. 17. The interesting text found in this obscure place may be quoted here in full:

"An des heilgin Crucz abunde Invencionis sint vor uns komen Hannes Domnic und Lazar der Jude und haben becant, das sy alle sachen zwisschen Czenke Domninge und Joseph Juden von der Swidnicz und nemlich von der sebinhundert und dry und czwenczig tucatyn, dy Czenco Joseph schuldig ist, und itzunt czu Venedegin legin, gutlich und vruntlich vorricht haben, das in an beyden teylen wol genuget: Also das Czenco Domnig schicken und bestellen sal, das Josephe dy 723 tucatyn uff sante Jocobs tag nestkommende czu Venedigin ane hinderniss werden beczalet. Ab her des nicht tete, so sal her Josephe drysig Schock gr. geben czu wandilgelde. Gebreche abir dy betzalunge an Josephe, also das her dy 723 tucaten von Czenken uff den tag nicht uffneme, so sal im Czenco in den 30 schocken wendilgeldis nicht seyn vorfallin. Beczalt im abir Czenco dy 723 tuc[atyn] alz abenges[chreben] stet, so sal im Joseph syne quytbrive geben, also das Czenco und syne nachkomen von Joseph und synen nachkomen von weyne der 723 tuc[atyn] vorbasme ewiglich ane ansprache seyn sulle, und Joseff sal auch Czenken synen briff wedir geben den her hat obir dy uorges[chreben] tucatyn."

60. MS Breslau, J 7, No. F 42 (above, chap. ix, nn. 70 and 92). In a case related in the municipal records of Görlitz, the local town *Schöffen* arbitrated a dispute "between Peter Crobeinis and the Jewess Zepphor over a well," ownership of which was adjudged to the Jewess; for the full text of the decision see Herbert Zander, *Das Rote Buch der Stadt Görlitz (1305–1416)* (Leipzig, 1929), p. 75.

61. Cf. Böhlau, *op. cit.* (above, n. 56); Krause, *op. cit.*, pp. 35 f. Cf., e.g., the general decision of the *Schöffen* of Leipzig, hitherto unpublished, MS University Library Leipzig 945, No. 292, fol. 127v (no date given; probably first half of the fifteenth century): ". . . habin beide part dem amptmann, dem voite macht gegebin und gebetin sie zu entscheiden in fruntschaft ader in rechte und hat Erhard Arnold das den andern tag darnoch wedirsprochen, das hat Erhard Arnold nicht mogin thun, sunder is blibet noch billich do bie. Von rechtis wegin."

62. Cf. Carl Georg von Wächter, *Beiträge zur deutschen Geschichte insbesondere zur Geschichte des deutschen Strafrechts* (Tübingen, 1845), pp. 194–96; Theodor Lindner, *Die Veme* (Münster, 1888; new ed., Paderborn, 1896), pp. xx, 557 f.; Scherer, *op. cit.*, p. 258, n. 3.

63. Stobbe, *Die Juden in Deutschland während des Mittelalters*, p. 258, n. 137; Lindner, *op. cit.*, p. 558; Friedrich Heine, "Das Vehmgericht und die Beziehungen der Stadt Zerbst zu westfälischen Freistühlen," *Mitteilungen des Vereins für anhaltische Geschichte und Altertumskunde*, XI (1912), 486, March 30, 1482: "Eyn jode Mossze genant, umb valschunge der munte . . . is hy vam rade van Brandeborch ut der Nyenstat gefordert worden und gebrant met füre [namely, in Zerbst]"; for two more instances see Forchhammer, *op. cit.*, p. 380.

64. Cf. Hermann Rudorff, *Zur Rechtsstellung der Gäste im mittelalterlichen städtischen Prozess* (Breslau, 1907); Alfred Schultze, "Über Gästerecht und Gastgerichte in den deutschen Städten des Mittelalters," *Historische Zeitschrift*, CI (1908), 473 ff.; Hans Planitz, "Studien zur Geschichte des deutschen Arrestprozesses," *ZRG*, XXXIX (1918), 223–308; XL (1919), 87 ff.; also the essay by Wilhelm Weizsäcker, "Das Recht der Fremden in Böhmen," *Mitteilungen des Vereins für Geschichte der Deutschen in Böhmen*, LIX (1921), 52.

65. *Gastrecht* is here used for *gastgericht* as was frequently done (cf.

Christian Gottlob Haltaus, *Glossarium Germanicum medii aevi* [Lipsiae, 1758], p. 587).

66. MS Breslau, J 5, No. 69.

67. See above, p. 229.

68. On the procedure of seizure or *Arrest* in medieval Germany in general see Guido Kisch, *Der deutsche Arrestprozess in seiner geschichtlichen Entwicklung* (Vienna and Leipzig, 1914); Hans Planitz, "Studien zur Geschichte des deutschen Arrestprozesses," *ZRG*, XXXIV (1913), 49–140; XXXIX (1918), 223–308; XL (1919), 87–198; Planitz, *Grundlagen des deutschen Arrestprozesses* (Leipzig, 1922); Wilhelm Brunner, *Der Arrestprozess im mittelalterlichen Rechte der deutschen Schweiz* (University of Halle, Jur.D. thesis; Leipzig, 1933).

69. LSchSprS., 506, 506a; 525.

70. MSchSpr. Leitmeritz, No. 106, pp. 365–67 (*ca.* 1500).

71. On reprisal arrest see Kisch, *Der deutsche Arrestprozess*, pp. 32 ff.; Planitz, *ZRG*, XL (1919), 167 ff.

72. Kisch, *Der deutsche Arrestprozess*, pp. 33 ff.; Planitz, *op. cit.*, pp. 171 ff. Cf. the letter of the city of Deventer to the city of Cologne of May 15, 1271: *absurdum est, quod malitia unius pluribus innocentibus sit in damnum* (quoted after Theodor Goerlitz, "Die Haftung des Bürgers und Einwohners für Schulden der Stadt und ihrer Bewohner nach Magdeburger Recht," *ZRG*, LVI [1936], 173). Reprisals of the kind here under consideration were also contrary to the principles of law as set forth by the *Oberhof* of Magdeburg (cf. Goerlitz, *op. cit.*, pp. 174–77). In medieval France, Jews and Lombards were generally exempt from the execution of reprisals, because of regard for the necessary services which they rendered to public economy through their banking business (cf. M. René de Mas Latrie, *Du droit de marque ou droit de représailles au moyen-âge* [2d ed.; Paris, 1875], p. 20; Erich Schumann, *Die Repressalie*, "Rostocker Abhandlungen, Rechtswissenschaftliche Reihe," Heft III [Rostock, 1927], pp. 7 ff.).

73. This kind of liability and the various phases of its legal development received thorough treatment, with particular reference to Magdeburg law, in a stimulating essay by Goerlitz, *op. cit.*, pp. 150–77.

74. Cf. MS Breslau, G 5, 36, p. 137, *anno* 1447; Goerlitz, *op. cit.*, p. 158: "Civitas Franckenstein cum incolis habet treugas vor der stat schulde *exceptis Judeis.*"

75. MS Breslau, G 5, 29, p. 78; Goerlitz, *op. cit.*, p. 159: "Canald und Ysaac jude Yco genant von Calis haben geleite dis gancze jar, also das sie nymand von der stat schulde wegin zu Kalis anlangen noch beteydingen mag, sunder vor eigene schuld haben si keyn geleyte." Cf. also MS

Breslau, G 5, 28, pp. 91 and 64 (Goerlitz, *op. cit.*, p. 159; see above, chap. iv, n. 35: "Mosshe [of Brega] shall not have safe-conduct until he is absolved of the Jewish ban, under which he is said to stand."

76. For details see Goerlitz, *op. cit.*, pp. 161–67.

77. The prevalent opinion, founded by Otto Stobbe, received its definite shape by Otto von Gierke. It considers the collective liability of the city as a corporate body, *genossenschaftliche Gesamthaftung*, the juridical basis of all personal liability for municipal debt on the part of the inhabitants (cf. Otto Stobbe, *Zur Geschichte des deutschen Vertragsrechts* [Leipzig, 1855], pp. 150–53; Otto Gierke, *Das deutsche Genossenschaftsrecht*, II [Berlin, 1873], 383 f., 387 ff., 770 ff.). This theory was also accepted by Alfred Schultze, *Historische Zeitschrift*, CI (1908), 511 f.; and G. Kisch, *Der deutsche Arrestprozess*, p. 32. Another interpretation was advanced by H. Planitz, *ZRG*, XL (1919), 186 f.: the burgher's liability for municipal debt originates from "der eine gewisse Gegenseitigkeit verbürgenden städtischen Einung." Accordingly, the city protects the citizens, to a certain extent, particularly against foreigners; and the citizen, vice versa, has to take upon himself liability for municipal debt, with respect to foreigners. The diversity of these historical constructions has no bearing on the present writer's explanation as to why Jews had to share in that responsibility (see above, pp. 259 f.). None of the authors concerned with the problem here under discussion gave heed to the fact that Jews, too, were subjected to liability for municipal debt. To class this liability with that of bondmen for debts of their lord, as Goerlitz does (*op. cit.*, pp. 161 f.), is neither admissible nor acceptable, however; for the Jews were not bondmen, either of the town lord or of the municipal magistracy. Their liability, as to juridical qualification, was, moreover, in no way different from that of the Christian burghers. And, finally, in the very promissory note quoted by Goerlitz (*op. cit.*, pp. 160 f.) the community as debtor is designated as *burgermeyster, rathmanne, und die gancze gemeine, arm und reich*, indicating that all inhabitants should be included in the liability for municipal debt.

78. On the history of the medieval law of evidence in general see J. W. Planck, *Das deutsche Gerichtsverfahren im Mittelalter*, II (Braunschweig, 1879), 1–234; Richard Loening, *Der Reinigungseid bei Ungerichtsklagen* (Heidelberg, 1880); Victor Hasenöhrl, "Die Beweiszuteilung im österreichischen Rechte des Mittelalters," *Sitzungsberichte der kaiserlichen Akademie der Wissenschaften zu Wien, phil.-hist. Klasse*, Vol. CXXXIX, Abh. 7 (Vienna, 1898); Edwin Mayer-Homberg, *Beweis und Wahrscheinlichkeit nach älterem deutschem Recht* (Marburg, 1921), includes a complete bibliography of all older writings on the subject. Especially on Magdeburg law, see Friese and Liesegang, *Magdeburger Schöffensprüche*, pp. 720–

44; Erich Holdefleiss, *Der Augenscheinsbeweis im mittelalterlichen deutschen Strafverfahren* ("Deutschrechtliche Forschungen," ed. G. Kisch, Vol. VI [Stuttgart, 1933]); Rudolf Ruth, *Zeugen und Eideshelfer in den deutschen Rechtsquellen des Mittelalters* (Breslau, 1922), *passim*.

On the treatment of Jews in the medieval law of evidence see Stobbe, *Die Juden in Deutschland*, pp. 148–53; J. F. Behrend, *Ein Stendaler Urteilsbuch aus dem vierzehnten Jahrhundert* (Berlin, 1868), pp. 50 f., note a; Scherer, *op. cit.*, pp. 162–67, 290–93, 299–303, 305–12; Friese and Liesegang, *op. cit.*, p. 809; Forchhammer, *op. cit.*, pp. 378 f., 389–408; Mayer-Homberg, *op. cit.*, pp. 165 f.

79. Mayer-Homberg, *op. cit.;* Claudius von Schwerin, *ZRG*, XLII (1921), 579–83.

80. Ulrich Stutz, "Die Beweisrolle im altdeutschen Rechtsgang," *ZRG*, XLIX (1929), 1–25; Rudolf Bechert, "Recht oder Pflicht zur Beweisführung," *ZRG*, XLIX (1929), 26 ff.

81. Mayer-Homberg, *op. cit.*, pp. 165 f.

82. "Lex Visigothorum Reccessvindiana," XII, 2, 9 in *Leges Visigothorum antiquiores*, ed. Karolus Zeumer (Hannover, 1894), p. 304; see also Mayer-Homberg, *op. cit.*, p. 165, n. 835.

83. Von Schwerin, *ZRG*, XLII (1921), 582: "Vollends sollten die Fälle, in denen Juden und Christen, Staatsangehörige und Staatsfremde sich gegenüberstehen, hier ausscheiden; die Regel für die Beweiszuteilung kann nur im Prozess zwischen Volksgenossen klar werden."

84. Cf. Rem. RW., 7; MS Breslau, J 5, No. 19. Glogau Rb., 482: "If, however, the Christian maintains that he has paid him, he may prove this with two Christian men rather than that the Jew may produce witness." An identical decision by the *Oberhof* of Magdeburg is found in MS Breslau, J 5, No. 180.

85. Cf. Otto Gierke, *Deutsches Privatrecht*, I (Leipzig, 1895), 424; Georg von Below, "Unehrliche Leute," in Johannes Hoops, *Reallexikon der germanischen Altertumskunde*, IV (Strasbourg, 1918–19), 373; Hübner, *Grundzüge des deutschen Privatrechts*, p. 118 [Eng. ed., p. 104].

86. Cf. Eduard Graf and Mathias Dietherr, *Deutsche Rechtssprichwörter* (Nördlingen, 1864), p. 369.

87. Cf. Stutz, *op. cit.*, p. 14.

88. See above, p. 181.

89. MBrSchR., III, 2, 39:
"*Von clage und wibis ansproche.* Spricht ouch eyn weip eynyn man an umme gelt, des ist der man nehir czu untgende, wenne ze en obirczugin moge; wenne keyn weip mag umme gelt eynyn man obirczugin. Aber umme ungerichte, als umme campirwunden und lemde unde totslag,

mag ze eryn vredebrecher in frischir tot obirwindin, glich als eyn man tun mochte, mit sechs mannyn geczugin."

According to *Sachsenspiegel*, III, 70, 2 (cf. III, 70, 1), the same principle applies to the Wends in their relation to Saxons with reference to their ability to pass judgment and bear witness (cf. Karl G. Hugelmann, "Die Rechtsstellung der Wenden im deutschen Mittelalter," *ZRG*, LVIII [1938], 249–51).

90. See above, chap. viii, n. 18.

91. Such argument remained foreign to Mayer-Homberg, *op. cit.*, pp. 165 f. and n. 840; cf., on the other hand, a similar train of thought in Stutz, *ZRG*, XLIX (1929), 18 and 11, n. 4. A very similar stand as in the quotation from the *Schwabenspiegel* (L 260; G 214, 4) is taken also in Brünn SchB., No. 437, p. 204, in favor of the Jew. The latter was accused of having libeled an advocate in the presence of the (Christian) jurors. His opponent desired to convict him by the jurors' testimony. The decision reads:

"The answer is: If some other Jews, as is quite likely, were present in the court before which the Jew is said to have called the Christian advocate a thief, then the Jew shall be convicted by [the testimony of] Christians and Jews."

If Jews were absent, the Christian jurors alone should be qualified as witnesses, their judicial office notwithstanding.

92. For details see above, p. 185.

93. Magdeburg-Breslau Law Instruction of 1261, art. 11, in MRQ., IV, 11 (Laband, p. 15): "Ist iz also, daz ein man gewûnt wirdit, geschriet her daz ruocht unde begrifet her den man unde bringet her in vor gerichte und havet er des sine schreiman selbe siebende, her ist naher in zu vorziugende, danne her ime untgan muge"; Wasserschleben, RQ.[2], p. 108, chap. 384: ". . . szo muste sze sick des myt hulpe unde tugen alzo starck entleddigen, alsze sze anspraken were; sunder bauen VII manne tuchnisse scal men nicht tolaten . . ."; cf. MS Breslau, J 5, No. 140: ". . . so einer mit gezeugen angesprochen wirt, der mus mit also vil gezeugen entgeen, doch uber sieben menner gezeuge khan nimand gedrungen werden." Cf. also Forchhammer, *op. cit.*, p. 390; Friese and Liesegang, *op. cit.*, p. 722.

94. MBSchR., III, 2, 38; Wasserschleben, RQ.[2], p. 67, chap. 204:

"Hereupon [we state the law]: The Jew shall convict the Christian with the support of VII [actually VI] Christian men, who shall swear by the Saints that the object was tied on the back of the Christian, that they have knowledge thereof; this is the evidence to be produced by the Jew against the Christian in this matter; so says the law."

Erroneously, or by a mistake in transcribing, seven witnesses are required here instead of—correctly—six. The expression in the sources, *selbsiebent,* which means that "himself" (the swearer) is the seventh, might easily cause such a mistake.

95. RW., B 97; cf. Rem. RW., 9.

96. In the case submitted from Stendal to Magdeburg and referred to earlier in this work, however, each of the Jews indicted was ordered to free himself by taking an oath with six Jewish oath-helpers (Stendal UB., X, 1; see above, p. 191).

97. MSchSpr., III B, 125, and p. 757; cf. Forchhammer, *op. cit.,* p. 389.

98. Cf. LSchSprS., 737; Wasserschleben, RQ.², p. 115, chap. 407; cf. Planck, *op. cit.,* I, 784 ff.

99. With reference to the last alternative as found in Ssp., I, 39, Forchhammer (*op. cit.,* p. 389) remarks sarcastically: "Auf den letzten Fall [namely, judicial combat] verzichtet also der vorsichtige Jude." This is not to the point at all. More reasons can be found, different from that adduced in the text (above), such as the Jews' exclusion from bearing arms or the abolition of ordeals in general. They will be discussed hereafter. Forchhammer overlooked, in particular, the well-known fact that substitution of a professional and paid *kemphe* was explicitly permitted by law to a Jew (cf. MRb., III, 17, 44; above, p. 127; Austrian Jewry privilege of 1244, art. 20, in Scherer, *op. cit.,* pp. 182, 305 f.; Nübling, *Die Judengemeinden des Mittelalters insbesondere die Judengemeinde der Reichsstadt Ulm* [Ulm, 1896], pp. 32 f.).

100. Cf. LSchSprS., 111: "[The *Schöffen* of] Leipzig state: Self-exculpation by means of carrying a hot iron or plunging one's hand into boiling water is prohibited by Holy Church." Cf. also Victor Friese, *Das Strafrecht des Sachsenspiegels* (Breslau, 1898), pp. 212 f., n. 14; Scherer, *op. cit.,* pp. 307 f., n. 3; Hans Planitz, "Gottesurteile," in *Handwörterbuch der Rechtswissenschaft,* III (Berlin and Leipzig, 1928), pp. 13 f.; Heinrich Glitsch, *Gottesurteile* ("Voigtländers Quellenbücher," Vol. XLIV [Leipzig, n.d.]); Mayer-Homberg, *op. cit.,* pp. 42 ff.; Robert von Keller, *Freiheitsgarantien für Person und Eigentum im Mittelalter* (Heidelberg, 1933), pp. 220 ff.

101. *MG., Form. imp.,* No. 30 (about 825); Julius Aronius, *Regesten zur Geschichte der Juden im fränkischen und deutschen Reiche bis zum Jahre 1273* (Berlin, 1887–1902), No. 81: "et nullatenus volumus, ut predictos judeos ad nullum judicium examinandum, id est nec ad ignem nec ad aquam calidam seu etiam ad flagellum, nisi liceat eis secundum illorum legem vivere vel ducere." Cf. Steinthal, *Die Juden im fränkischen Reiche, ihre rechtliche und wirtschaftlich-soziale Stellung* (University of Breslau

Ph.D. thesis, in typescript, 1922), pp. 32 f.; also Stobbe, *Die Juden in Deutschland*, p. 153; Scherer, *op. cit.*, p. 310; above, p. 139.

102. Art. 12, Geiger's *ZGJD*, I (1887), 140: "Et nemo judeum ad ignitum ferrum vel ad calidam aquam vel frigidam cogat, nec flagellis cedat, nec in carcerem mittat, sed juret secundum legem suam post quadraginta dies."

103. See above, p. 117. On judicial combat between a Christian and a Jew in the Christian legend literature of the Middle Ages see Heinrich Löwe, *Die Juden in der katholischen Legende* (Berlin, 1912), pp. 68–71; also in *MGWJ*, LVI (1912), 408–11.

104. In the better manuscripts of the *Schwabenspiegel* the word *eit* in the passage, *deheines juden eit gêt gegen einen christen*, is emended into *kampf*, as required by the meaning, in view of the succeeding sentence (cf. Hans von Voltelini, "Der Wiener und Kremser Judeneid," *Mitteilungen des Vereines für Geschichte der Stadt Wien*, XII [Vienna, 1932], 64, n. 5; *Schwabenspiegel* manuscript of about 1500 in the library of Guido Kisch [Homeyer, Rbb., No. 578], fol. 21v). Thus the passage reads: "No Jew's [challenge to] combat can be issued against a Christian. But if a Christian challenges him, the Jew is bound to do combat with him."

105. MRb., III, 17, 44: "When a Jew is clandestinely put in confinement [by anyone] or seized and held for ransom, and escapes, the Jew shall be entitled to sue; and if he would make a claim against him, the Jew may do so through a *kemphe* whom he may procure with his money" (cf. Planck, *op. cit.*, I, 791 f.; Scherer, *op. cit.*, pp. 311 f.; see also above, n. 99).

106. Cf. Planck, *op. cit.*, I, 797 ff.; Hans Fehr, *Der Zweikampf* (Berlin, 1908), pp. 14 ff.; Gertrud Schubart-Fikentscher, "Neue Fälle zum Brünner Recht," *Deutsches Archiv für Geschichte des Mittelalters*, III (1939), 454; for medieval France see Axel Vorberg, *Der Zweikampf in Frankreich* (Leipzig, 1899), pp. 5 ff.

107. See above, pp. 119 ff.

108. Cf. Fritz Baer, *Die Juden im christlichen Spanien*, I (Berlin, 1929), 1027.

109. Homeyer, *Sachsenspiegel*, II, 1, pp. 33 f., No. 79; H. G. Ph. Gengler, *Deutsche Stadtrechte des Mittelalters* (Nuremberg, 1866), pp. 394–407; Mayer-Homberg, *op. cit.*, p. 166.

110. Gengler, *op. cit.*, p. 406:

Salzwedel Lawbook, § 83, 2

"Sleit eyn jode einen kerstenman edder dodet he ene, de jode ne mach to nener antworde komen, he mot dogen dar umme, wat en recht is,

wente he ne het nenen namen an der krystenheit, unde is goddes
vorvolgere unde eyn morder der kristenheit."

Sachsenspiegel Landrecht, III, 7, 2

"Sleit die jode eynen kerstenen man, oder dûth her yme ungerichte,
dâ her mede begriffen wirt, men richtet uber ine alse uber eynen kerstenen man."

111. Cf. Böhlau, *ZRG*, O.S., IX (1870), 32, 38 ff.; cf. Forchhammer,
op. cit., p. 395.

112. LSchSprS., 113; cf. Forchhammer, *op. cit.*, p. 394, n. 480.

113. For more details on the reasoning in Buch's *Glosse* see above,
pp. 91 f. Buch's standpoint is shared in Reg. jur., J 166.

114. The last sentence in Schwsp., G 214, 2, "it was the Roman kings
who gave the Jews this right" (*Daz reht hânt in die romischen künige
gegeben*), has no connection with this rule. It belongs to the following
paragraph, Schwsp., G 214, 3, as has already been recognized by Hans
Lewy, *Journal of the Warburg Institute*, I (1938), 228. Herewith the traditional interpretation in Stobbe, *Die Juden in Deutschland*, p. 151, and
Scherer, *op. cit.*, p. 166, previously supported by the present writer
(*Proceedings*, X [1940], 181, n. 159) has to be discarded.

115. Ed. Daniels and Gruben, p. 173 (ed. Daniels, 116, 4, 5); cf.
Forchhammer, *op. cit.*, p. 397. According to an addition in Zobel's edition of Ssp. *Gloss*, III, 2 (fol. 321v), not found in the Augsburg edition
of 1516, a Jew needs two Christians and one Jew to convict a Christian;
and, vice versa, a Christian against a Jew, one Christian and one Jew.

116. Cf. also MRb., III, 11, 4; III, 17, 18; Purgoldts Rb., VII, 97;
VIII, 71. For more references concerning municipal law and Jewry
privileges see Stobbe, *op. cit.*, pp. 259 ff.

117. MS Breslau, J 5, No. 27.

118. Wasserschleben, RQ., V, 44, p. 400; cf. above, pp. 216 f.

119. Forchhammer, *op. cit.*, p. 394.

120. MSchSpr., II, 19; Friese and Liesegang, *op. cit.*, p. 743; Forchhammer, *op. cit.*, p. 400. A different procedural situation is found in
LSchSprS., 505, where the Jew Isaac is denied evidence *mit gezeugnus
nach toder hand.*

121. Cf. MFr., II, 3; Friese and Liesegang, MSchSpr., pp. 742 ff.;
Forchhammer, *op. cit.*, p. 400.

122. MSchSpr., III B, 129; cf. III B, 127; Forchhammer, *op. cit.*,
p. 399 f. Cf., in contradistinction, the decision in Brünn SchB., No. 19,
p. 12.

123. Wasserschleben, RQ., IV, 173, 174.

124. MSchSpr., III B, 96; Friese and Liesegang, *op. cit.*, p. 809; Forchhammer, *op. cit.*, pp. 394 f.

125. Hermann Grössler, "Sammlung älterer nach Eisleben ergangener Rechtsbescheide des Magdeburgischen Schöppenstuhls," *Zeitschrift des Harz-Vereins für Geschichte und Altertumskunde*, XXIII (1890), 194, No. 33; cf. Forchhammer, *op. cit.*, p. 397.

126. *Arg.: zcu besseren des unsaligen joden recht, ist gefraget.*

127. Cf. Kisch, *Leipziger Schöffenspruchsammlung*, pp. *20 ff.

128. So Friese and Liesegang, *op. cit.*, p. 809.

129. See above, p. 269.

130. MSchSpr., II, 19.

131. MS Breslau, J 5, No. 27; Wasserschleben, RQ., V, 44, p. 400.

132. The specific reference to Jews in Duke Sobieslav II's charter for the Germans in Prague (1176–78) does not seem a basis sufficiently broad and pertinent to derive the general principle governing mixed evidence in medieval German procedure. Such a generalization was made by Stobbe, *Die Juden in Deutschland*, pp. 152 f., whose path was followed by later authors, e.g., by Nübling, *Die Judengemeinden des Mittelalters*, pp. 30 f.

The *Sobieslaum* states (Wilhelm Weizsäcker, "Die älteste Urkunde der Prager Deutschen," *Zeitschrift für sudetendeutsche Geschichte*, I [1937], 181):

Art. 9.—"When a Bohemian [Czech] has a legal cause against a German, which is to be proved through witnesses, the Bohemian shall have against the German two Germans and one Bohemian, all faithful."

Art. 10.—"In like manner when a German has a legal cause against a Bohemian, then the German shall have against the Bohemian two Bohemians and one German, but faithful."

Art. 11.—"The like holds of Latins and Jews."

Hence, a German against a Jew needed two Jewish witnesses and one Christian; and vice versa. One must bear in mind that in all civil lawsuits covered by the aforementioned articles of the *Sobieslaum* the German court was competent exclusively. This fact in itself meant a far-reaching privilege decisively favoring the Germans. The peculiarity of the political and legal situation in the Slavic regions opened to German colonization does not permit generalization as to the legal status in the German empire proper. On the Jews in the *Sobieslaum*, cf. Adolf Zycha, *Prag: Ein Beitrag zur Rechtsgeschichte Böhmens im Beginn der Kolonisationszeit* (Prague, 1912), pp. 143 ff., 197.

133. Cf. G. Kisch, "Nationalism and Race in Medieval Law," *Seminar*, I (1943), 65 ff.; G. Kisch, "The 'Jewish Execution' in Medieval

Germany," *Historia Judaica*, V (1943), 110 and *passim;* see also below, pp. 305 ff.

134. See above, p. 262, on MBSchR., III, 2, 38; cf. also the pertinent Magdeburg jury-court decision in Heinrich Mühler, *Deutsche Rechtshandschriften des Stadtarchivs zu Naumburg an der Saale* (Berlin, 1838), p. 81, No. 25.

135. See above, pp. 225, 232, and 234.

136. Cf. Otto Stobbe, *Zur Geschichte des deutschen Vertragsrechts*, pp. 88 ff.; 92 f.; Stobbe, *Die Juden in Deutschland*, pp. 114, 118; Forchhammer, *op. cit.*, pp. 395 f. Cf. also Reg. jur., J 126. The same principle was upheld by the superior court of Brünn in a decision of 1390, published in German translation in Bertold Bretholz, *Quellen zur Geschichte der Juden in Mähren vom XI. bis zum XV. Jahrhundert (1067–1411)* (Prague, 1935), No. 387, pp. 224 f.

137. This rule is analogous to that applied to Christian creditors in MRb., III, 14, 8:

"If someone says he would like to redeem his pledge and offers his money; if then the other who holds the pledge says there is more due on it: the latter shall have the preference of proof by the pledge and [swearing] by the Saints, which is not open to the other one."

Unfortunately, no specific evidence is available to support the (most probable) assumption that this principle had universal validity also under Magdeburg law.

138. Cf. above, p. 219; also Stobbe, *Zur Geschichte des deutschen Vertragsrechts*, pp. 102 f.; Victor Hasenöhrl, "Die Beweiszuteilung im österreichischen Rechte des Mittelalters (above, n. 78), pp. 109 f.

139. See above, pp. 239 ff.

140. MSchSpr., III B, 65; RW., L 84; Böhlau, *ZRG*, O.S., IX (1870), 29, n. 91; cf. G. Kisch, "Das Schadennehmen," pp. 505 f. [33 f.].

141. Heinrich M. Schuster, *Das Wiener Stadtrechts- oder Weichbildbuch* (Vienna, 1873), art. 10, p. 51: ". . . Als er das pringt, so muez der jud sagen pei seinen treuen, und pei seiner ee, daz er dieselben phenning auf des mannes schaden des tages gelichen hat, und nenn auch den man und den tag."

142. See above, chap. ix, n. 16 and pp. 218 f.; Ssp., III, 7, 4 (2); Glogau Rb., 477; Wasserschleben, RQ., V, No. 44, p. 400; Magdeburg-Breslau Law Instruction sent to Olmütz, in W. Weizsäcker, "Die Rechtsmitteilung Breslaus an Olmütz," *Festschrift für Otto Peterka* (Brünn and Prague, 1936), p. 96, n. 2; MS Dresden, M 20a, fol. 110r, *s.v.* "furman"; cf. also BlM., II, 2, 151; Reg. jur., J 126.

143. As to evidence in favor of Jewish creditors by the production in

court of promissory notes or entry of loan contracts in official records of public authenticity see above, pp. 225 ff., 234 f. and chap. ix, n. 127.

144. For bibliographies on the Jewry oath in general see G. Kisch, "Studien zur Geschichte des Judeneides im Mittelalter," *Hebrew Union College Annual*, XIV (1939), 432 f. and n. 5; S. W. Baron, *The Jewish Community: Its History and Structure to the American Revolution*, III (Philadelphia, 1942), 180 f., n. 31.

As to the history of the Jewry oath in Germany see Christian Gottlob Haltaus, *Glossarium Germanicum medii aevi*, pp. 1051–53, *s.v.* "Judeneid"; Stobbe, *Die Juden in Deutschland*, pp. 153–59; Heinrich Gottfried Gengler, *Deutsche Stadtrechtsaltertümer*, pp. 115–17; Nübling, *op. cit.*, pp. 199 f.; Scherer, *op. cit.*, pp. 293–99; Emil Goldmann, "Zur Geschichte des fränkischen Eidganges," *Fetschrift für Karl von Amira zu seinem sechzigsten Geburtstage* (Berlin, 1908), pp. 87, 91–93; Forchhammer, *op. cit.*, pp. 392–94; Mayer-Homberg, *Beweis und Wahrscheinlichkeit nach älterem deutschen Recht*, p. 65, n. 313; Hans von Voltelini, "Der Wiener und Kremser Judeneid," pp. 64–70; Hans Fehr, *Die Dichtung im Recht* (Bern, 1936), pp. 69–72; G. Kisch, "A Fourteenth-Century Jewry Oath of South Germany," *Speculum*, XV (1940), 331–37; G. Kisch, "Nuremberg Jewry Oaths," *Historia Judaica*, II (1940), 23–38.

On the Jewry oaths in the medieval German lawbooks in particular see Thea Bernstein, *Die Geschichte der deutschen Judeneide im Mittelalter* (University of Hamburg Ph.D. thesis, in typescript only; 1922), pp. 46–62; Hans-Kurt Claussen, "Der Judeneid: Ein Beitrag zur Geschichte des Rechtsschutzes," *Deutsche Rechtswissenschaft*, II (Berlin, 1937), 179–84; G. Kisch, "Studien zur Geschichte des Judeneides im Mittelalter," *Hebrew Union College Annual*, XIV (1939), 437 f., 440–42, 445 ff.

At present there is no complete collection of all the Jewry-oath formulas handed down from the Middle Ages, some of which are printed in the above-mentioned works. A selection of such oath material is found in K. Müllenhoff and W. Scherer, *Denkmäler deutscher Poesie und Prosa aus dem VIII. bis XII. Jahrhundert*, II (3d ed.; Berlin, 1892), 465–74. The formulas of numerous Jewry oaths published in various scholarly periodicals are not listed bibliographically as yet. The formulas found in the medieval German lawbooks are reproduced in Guido Kisch, *Jewry-Law in Medieval Germany: Laws and Court Decisions Concerning Jews* ("Texts and Studies," pub. by the American Academy for Jewish Research, Vol. III [New York, 1949]). A systematic compilation of all the source material available is decidedly a desideratum.

Concerning the oaths taken by Jews in Jewish courts during the geonic period, i.e., from the seventh to the middle of the eleventh century, cf. H. Tykocinski, *Die gaonäischen Verordnungen* (Berlin, 1929), pp. 67–98; on oaths according to Jewish law in general, Zacharias Frankel, *Die Eidesleistung der Juden in theologischer und historischer Beziehung* (2d ed.; Dresden and Leipzig, 1847), is still useful.

145. Müllenhoff and Scherer, *op. cit.*, pp. 465, 467; facsimile reproduction in Georg Liebe, *Das Judentum in der deutschen Vergangenheit* ("Monographien zur deutschen Kulturgeschichte," Vol. XI [Leipzig, 1903]), p. 15; cf. Herbert Meyer, *Das Mühlhäuser Reichsrechtsbuch* (2d ed.; Weimar, 1934), pp. 69 ff. (with text); Claussen, *op. cit.*, pp. 173 ff. (with text).

146. Müllenhoff and Scherer, *op. cit.*, p. 467; facsimile reproduction in Conrad Borchling, "Das Alter des Görlitzer Judeneides," *Neues Lausitzisches Magazin*, LXXXVI (1910), between 244 and 245; Richard Jecht, "Über die in Görlitz vorhandenen Handschriften des Sachsenspiegels und verwandter Rechtsquellen," *Neues Lausitzisches Magazin*, LXXXII (1906), 231 f. [pp. 9 f.] (with text); Meyer, *op. cit.*, pp. 70 f. (with text); Claussen, *op. cit.*, pp. 175 ff. (with text).

147. Cf. Heinrich Brunner, *Deutsche Rechtsgeschichte*, I (2d ed.; Leipzig, 1906), 257 ff.; Johannes Hoops, *Reallexikon der germanischen Altertumskunde*, I, 522–24; Hans Fehr, "Die gerechte Vergeltung im Diesseits und Jenseits," in *Wirtschaft und Kultur*, Festschrift zum 70. Geburtstag von *Alfons Dopsch* (Baden bei Wien, 1938), pp. 593–96; in general, Hanns Bächtold-Stäubli, *Handwörterbuch des deutschen Aberglaubens*, II (Berlin and Leipzig, 1929–30), 659 ff.

148. Talmud, *Shebuot*, 38*b;* cf. *Encyclopaedia Judaica*, VI, 331; Leopold Zunz, *Gesammelte Schriften*, II (Berlin, 1876), 256 f.

149. On the history of the institution of *den Eid staben* see Karl von Amira, "Der Stab in der germanischen Rechtssymbolik," *Abhandlungen der kgl. Bayerischen Akademie der Wissenschaften, philos.-philol. und hist. Klasse*, Vol. XXV, No. 1 (Munich, 1909), pp. 92–94. Two interesting law cases decided by the superior court of Brünn, Moravia, for the Moravian town of Ungarisch-Hradisch, may be mentioned here. In one, this question was disputed and submitted for decision: Has the swearer to repeat the entire oath formula recited to him, or is confirmation by his merely saying "Amen" to be considered satisfactory? According to the Brünn SchB., No. 435, p. 204, it was left to the swearer to choose between these alternatives: "judaeus jurans manum ponat, et sive repetat verba post illum, qui sibi formam proponit, sive proponens totam formam pro se loquatur, judeus subjungat solum Amin, forma valet." In the case under consideration, the Jew Hasco explicitly referred to

this older decision. The court, however, decided that the Jew was to repeat a brief prescribed formula ending with "Amen" (Bertold Bretholz, *Quellen zur Geschichte der Juden in Mähren*, No. 329, p. 188 [*anno* 1384]). In the other case (Bretholz, *op. cit.*, No. 338, p. 193 [*anno* 1385]), the question came up as to whether the swearer's son should be permitted to function as *Eidstaber* to his father in the oath ceremony. The decision read that the reciting of the oath formula by the swearer's son is more efficient than that by another person; for it is to be supposed that a son will defend his father's honor much more than anyone else, and *fraus duplex duplam dampnaret animam*.

150. See above, p. 100.

151. On this so-called *Langform* (*Handschriftenklasse* II) see Homeyer, Rbb., pp. *20 ff.

152. Claussen, *op. cit.*, pp. 182 f.

153. Homeyer, Nos. 286 (Donaueschingen, Fürstlich Fürstenbergische Hofbibliothek, Cod. Lützelnheimeri, No. 738 [a] of 1287, on which Lassberg's edition of the *Schwabenspiegel* was based); 1240 (Zürich, Zentralbibliothek, MS Z XI, 302, of the end of the thirteenth century, also used for his edition by Lassberg); 866 (Munich, Stadtarchiv, Cod. No. 14, probably late thirteenth century, intended by Ludwig Rockinger to be used as basis for his *Schwabenspiegel* edition, which was never published). In the second edition of his *Rechtsbücher* (No. 491), Homeyer attributed the last-mentioned manuscript (Homeyer, No. 866) to the fourteenth century, changing thereby the previous attribution to the thirteenth century, no reasons being given. From a later analysis by Rockinger it is clear that the manuscript belongs probably to the end of the thirteenth century but to no later date than to the first decade of the fourteenth (cf. Ludwig Rockinger, "Berichte über die Untersuchung von Handschriften des sogenannten *Schwabenspiegels*," XII, *Sitzungsberichte der kaiserlichen Akademie der Wissenschaften in Wien, phil.-hist. Klasse*, CXX [1890], 64, No. 284).

154. Cf. Voltelini, "Der Wiener und Kremser Judeneid," p. 67, n. 39.

155. Maurer, I, 174; Knapp, 218; Claussen, 219.

156. Hermann Ernst Endemann, *Das Keyserrecht nach der Handschrift von 1372* (Cassel, 1846), IV, chap. 24, pp. 248–50.

157. The descriptive analysis of the *Sachsenspiegel* codices in Homeyer, *Die deutschen Rechtsbücher des Mittelalters und ihre Handschriften*, and in Emil Steffenhagen, "Die Entwicklung der Landrechtsglosse des Sachsenspiegels," VIII and IX, *Sitzungsberichte der kaiserlichen Akademie der Wissenschaften in Wien, phil.-hist. Klasse*, CXIV (1887), 309 ff. and 691 ff., is not full and accurate enough to make the compilation of a

complete list of all *Sachsenspiegel* manuscripts containing the Jewry-oath formula possible. The provisional list to follow hereafter will have to be supplemented when the complete manuscript material becomes available. The first number refers to the third edition of Homeyer's *Rechtsbücher*, while the number in Homeyer's second edition appears in parentheses.

1. 188 (89). Breslau University Library, II, Q 2, fourteenth century.
2. 466 (275). Göttweih, Benedictine Abbey, No. 364, fifteenth century.
3. 496 (301). Halberstadt, Gymnasium Library, No. 65, *ca.* 1463.
4. 548 (347). Jena, University Library, MS Bud. f.376, 1457.
5. 634 (369). Copenhagen, Royal Library, Thott Collection, 336, 1412.
6. 195 (413). Breslau, University Library, Depositum Löwenberg, first half of fourteenth century.
7. 1043 (608). Schweidnitz, Municipal Archives, Cod. A, second half of fourteenth century.
8. 1132 = 1075 (664 = 606). Strasbourg, Bibliothèque Nationale, L.germ.193,2°, 1382.
9. 1140 (726). Wernigerode Prince Stolberg Library, MS Zb. 37, fifteenth century.

158. Fols. 221v–222r; the oath formulas are missing in Zobel's *Sachsenspiegel* edition (Leipzig, 1560); and in Carl Wilhelm Gärtner, *Eykens von Repgow Sachsenspiegel* (Leipzig, 1732), which is the only critical work on the *Sachsenspiegel* published in the eighteenth century.

159. Homeyer, No. 41; cf. above, pp. 46–48. One must be careful not to confuse this third group, the *Weichbild* Jewry-oath formulas, with the others; for *Sachsenspiegel* and *Weichbild-Vulgata* sometimes occur in the same codex, such as, e.g., in Homeyer, No. 41. Thus confusing the different groups of oath formulas, Thea Bernstein (*Die Geschichte der deutschen Judeneide*, pp. 46 ff.) barred herself from a proper understanding of their relationship.

160. III, 17, 46; cf. Ortloff's ed., pp. 177 f., 484; Stobbe, p. 264, n. 148.

161. E.g., *Sechsisch Weichbild, Lehenrecht und Remissorium* (Budissin: Nicolaus Wolrab, 1557), fol. 107v. On the various versions of the *Weichbild* oath formula see Stobbe, p. 264, n. 148. A hitherto unpublished oath formula in the manuscript MS jur. 2584a of the Hamburg University Library (Homeyer, No. 509) is reproduced and discussed in Bernstein, *op. cit.*, pp. 47 ff. (cf. *ibid.*, pp. 55 ff., 60 f. [Homeyer, No. 63]; cf. above, p. 47). Related to the *Weichbild* formula is the Braun-

schweig Jewry oath, reproduced by A. Lewinsky, "Nachtrag zum 'Judeneid,' " *Zeitschrift für hebräische Bibliographie*, IX (1905), 148–50. The historical evolution and topographical dissemination of the *Weichbild* Jewry oath and its derivatives would deserve special treatment.

162. Voltelini, "Der Wiener und Kremser Judeneid," pp. 66–69.

163. Schwsp., L 260; G 214, 1; Ssp., III, 7, 1.

164. Thus Claussen's assertion ("Der Judeneid," pp. 179 f.), "die [sächsischen] Eidesformeln haben ihren Ursprung im Magdeburger Recht und verbreiten sich von Magdeburg in derselben Weise wie das Magdeburger Recht selbst," is not accurate.

165. See G. Kisch, *Speculum*, XV (1940), 337. The same conclusion applies to the brief version of the *Weichbild* oath (ed. 1557) and to the oath in Glogau Rb., 485, where the final curse reads: ". . . that God disgrace me forever and send me to the devil, body and soul."

166. Cf. Kisch, *Speculum*, XV (1940), 336 f. The oath formula in MS Boruss. fol. 240, in the Preussische Staatsbibliothek in Berlin (Homeyer, No. 134), published in Wasserschleben, RQ., III b, 99, p. 127, has a related and unique clause: "that you never enter Abraham's bosom for the resurrection when Christians, Jews and heathen rise up before our Creator."

167. See Kisch, *Hebrew Union College Annual*, XIV (1939), 437 ff. Cf. also some interesting decisions handed down on the subject by the superior court of Brünn to the jurors of Hradisch, both in Moravia, in Bertold Bretholz, *Quellen zur Geschichte der Juden in Mähren*, No. 329, p. 188 (*anno* 1384); No. 338, p. 193 (*anno* 1385); No. 400, p. 227 (*anno* 1391).

168. Similarly, *Berliner Stadtbuch* (ed. Clauswitz), III, 19; Forchhammer, *op. cit.*, p. 162; Claussen, *op. cit.*, p. 181; cf. Scherer, *op. cit.*, p. 296; Bernstein, *op. cit.*, pp. 50 f. According to the shorter *Sachsenspiegel* oath formula, "the Jew shall present his *Eidstaber* with one pound of pepper and a pair of fine breeches" (as an obligatory payment) (cf. Müllenhoff and Scherer, *op. cit.*, p. 471; Bernstein, *op. cit.*, p. 50; Lewinsky, *Zeitschrift für hebräische Bibliographie*, IX [1905], p. 148).

169. Cf. above, pp. 100 f.; also Voltelini, "Der Wiener und Kremser Judeneid," p. 65, n. 15. It is considered a *resereye* ("aberration") according to a gloss on art. 133, in the *Weichbild* manuscript of Görlitz of *ca.* 1387, probably Varia 5 (Homeyer, No. 419) (cf. W. Wackernagel, *Die altdeutschen Handschriften der Basler Universitätsbibliothek* [Basel, 1836], pp. 38 f.; Bernstein, *op. cit.*, p. 63). A Christian author, Christian Gottlob Haltaus, in his *Glossarium Germanicum medii aevi* (pp. 1052 f.), wrote in 1758 with reference to the pigskin ceremony:

"An vero Judaei ceremonia hac ipsis abominabili, ad majorem jura-
menti observantiam adigantur? Aliis judicandum relinquo: ego autem
vehementer dubito."

170. Cf. F. Ortloff, *Das Rechtsbuch nach Distinctionen* [MRb.], p. 485.
Middle High German: *hût* = *Haut* ("skin"), *hût* = *Hut* ("hat"). Cf.
also Forchhammer, *op. cit.*, p. 393, n. 470; Voltelini, *op. cit.*, p. 66; also
MS 946 in the University Library at Leipzig (Homeyer, No. 681); cf.
Haltaus, *op. cit.*, p. 1053, *s.v.* "Judeneid."

171. Homeyer, No. 931; Müllenhoff and Scherer, *op. cit.*, p. 468;
Stobbe, *op. cit.*, p. 155; Scherer, *op. cit.*, p. 297; Claussen, *op. cit.*, p. 181, n.
4. An identical formula is found in MS Boruss. fol. 240, in the Preussische
Staatsbibliothek in Berlin (Homeyer, No. 134), published in Wasserschleben, RQ., III b, 98, pp. 126 f.; cf. below, n. 187; also Bernstein,
op. cit., pp. 56 ff., 64 f. (Löwenberg Jewry oath, see below, n. 180).
Voltelini (*op. cit.*, p. 66) considers the procedure of standing on a stool
with the consequence of losing the suit in case of falling off, an ordeal.

172. Cf., e.g., *Jewish Encyclopaedia*, XI (New York, 1905), 677, picture at bottom; cf. also Bernstein, *op. cit.*, p. 57, referring to the Breslau
Jewry-oath picture of the seventeenth century, often reproduced and
also reprinted in *Encyclopaedia Judaica*, IX (Berlin, 1922), 535. For comparative material on this subject from the legal history of various
peoples see Jan Kapras, "Der altböhmische Grenzeid im Grabe unter
dem Rasen: Ein Beitrag zur Geschichte des Ordalwesens," *Zeitschrift für
vergleichende Rechtswissenschaft*, XXXIV (1916), 313–22. The requirement that the swearer "shall stand barefoot, wearing nothing but
nether garment and a hair-cloth about his body" (above, p. 282), is
not peculiar to the Jewry oath but represents a general ancient custom
found also in the ritual for Christians taking a solemn legal oath (cf.
Kapras, *op. cit.*, pp. 292 ff., 298, 300). But there is no parallel to account
for the fact that sometimes the Jew was ordered to stand on a pig's skin
or a stool. This cannot possibly be interpreted as meaning that the Jew
was excluded from a share in the earth; for this would be contradictory
to the invocation of the earth, that should swallow him if perjurious,
like Dathan and Abiram.

173. Glogau Rb., 485, Wasserschleben, RQ., I, 59; Claussen, *op. cit.*,
p. 182, n. 1. For the text following see also above, n. 172.

174. For more details see Gengler, *Deutsche Stadtrechtsaltertümer*, pp.
115–17; G. Kisch, *Hebrew Union College Annual*, XIV (1939), 446 ff. According to a decision of the superior court of Brünn, *ubi judicium
judeorum exercetur* (Bretholz, *Quellen zur Geschichte der Juden in Mähren*,
No. 338, p. 193 [*anno* 1385]).

175. Ed. Daniels and Gruben, 137, 2, p. 174; cf. also 134, 2, p. 173; also ed. Daniels, 116, 2, p. 53; Glogau Rb., 479, Wasserschleben, RQ., I, p. 58; here the obligation is restricted to cases "if a Jew promises a Christian to act rightly by him, under penalty of excommunication."

176. *Weichbild-Vulgata, versio Latina*, ed. Daniels and Gruben, 139, 2, p. 174; cf. Claussen, *op. cit.*, p. 180; Voltelini, "Der Wiener und Kremser Judeneid," p. 65, n. 14; and p. 69 with n. 54; Emil Goldmann, "Zur Geschichte des fränkischen Eidganges," *Festschrift für Karl von Amira*, p. 87. Owing to the war, this writer was unable to secure a photostat of the picture in the *Weichbild* manuscript No. 2 of the Petro-Paulinian Library in Liegnitz, Germany, mentioned by Goldmann, which shows a swearing Jew grasping the ring at the synagogue door.

177. The term *Rodale*, also used in the Austrian Jewry privilege of 1244 (Scherer, *op. cit.*, p. 182, art. 19), derives from the Latin *rotulus* and refers to the scroll form of the Torah (MRb., III, 17, 46, note on p. 484 in Ortloff's edition; cf. also Scherer, *op. cit.*, pp. 298 f.; Forchhammer, *op. cit.*, pp. 393 f.; Voltelini, *op. cit.*, p. 65, n. 13; Kisch, *Hebrew Union College Annual*, XIV, 441). Interesting examples of how the term *Rodale* was misunderstood and misinterpreted in the practice of law are found in sixteenth-century Poland. In one case the opponent of a Jew asserted that *Rodale* is a tripod on which the Jew had to stand with one leg(!) in taking the oath. In another case, *Rodale* was interpreted to be a pig's skin! (cf. Philipp Bloch, *Die Generalprivilegien der polnischen Judenschaft* [Posen, 1892], pp. 95 ff.).

178. See below, chap. xi, n. 28. Cf. also Reg. jur., J 130; Bocksd. Rem., 12; Rem. Wolrab, last item.

179. G. Kisch, *Hebrew Union College Annual*, XIV, 439 f., 447 ff. Claussen's assertion (*op. cit.*, p. 183) that "ebenso wie im Gebiete des sächsischen Rechts hat auch nach dem *Schwabenspiegel* der Jude seine Eide nicht in der Synagoge zu leisten, sondern an der ordentlichen Gerichtsstätte" is therefore not accurate.

180. Wb. 117, 1, ed. Daniels, p. 53:
"And let the oath be recited to him thus: Thou sayest on thy Law and upon thy Judaism that this book upon which thou hast thy hand, is the five-books in which thou shalt exculpate thyself according to the law of all of which thou art accused."

Similarly, Oxford MS Cod. Laud. misc. 741, fol. 35b, of the fourteenth century (Müllenhoff and Scherer, *op. cit.*, p. 468; Bernstein, *op. cit.*, pp. 58 f.; G. Kisch, *Hebrew Union College Annual*, XIV, 455); cf. also Löwenberg Jewry oath from the beginning of the fourteenth century, Stobbe, *op. cit.*, p. 158; Bernstein, *op. cit.*, pp. 63 ff.

181. Purgoldts Rb., VIII, 66, 67, pp. 247 f.; cf. Stobbe, p. 264, n. 148; Bernstein, *op. cit.*, pp. 23 f.; Claussen, *op. cit.*, p. 182.

182. Cf. Berlin StB., III, 19, p. 168: "This oath was changed into a short oath by those in authority; the Jews shall take it in their synagogue upon Moses' books or Yosaphantis book" (on similar instances see Stobbe, *op. cit.*, p. 159; Claussen, *op. cit.*, p. 184).

183. Cf. Wb., 137, ed. 1557, fol. 107v; cf. Voltelini, *op. cit.*, pp. 67 f.

184. For instance, the pigskin ritual was there persistently adhered to. Its practical application is found as late as 1562 in the "Procedure According to the Law of Olomouc" (*Proces Práva Olomuckého*); cf. V. Prasek, *Organisace práv Magdeburských na severní Moravě a v rakouském Slezsku* ("The Organization of Magdeburg Law in Northern Moravia and Austrian Silesia"; in Czech) (Olomouc, 1900), p. 227; in general also W. Weizsäcker, "Die Altstadt Prag und das Nürnberger Recht," *ZRG*, LX (1940), 117 ff.

185. Cf. Heinrich Mühler, *Deutsche Rechtshandschriften des Stadtarchivs zu Naumburg au der Saale* (Berlin, 1838), p. 81. The oath formula is introduced with the clause: *Also get der juden eyt nach wychhelde rechte.*

186. Cf. V. Prasek, *Tovačovská kniha ortelů Olomuckých* ("Tovačov Book of Olomouc Court Decisions"; a collection of decisions according to Magdeburg law handed down from Olomouc to Tovačov, 1430–1689; in Czech) (Olomouc, 1896), pp. 60 f. It is noteworthy that in the Jewry-oath formula the German language was retained, whereas the decisions are in Czech.

187. MS Breslau, J 7, fol. 241v, O 47; cf. also MS Cracow, No. 169 (Homeyer, No. 643), Ferdinand Bischoff, "Über einen deutschen Rechtskodex der Krakauer Universitätsbibliothek," *Sitzungsberichte der kaiserlichen Akademie der Wissenschaften zu Wien*, XLVIII (1864), 19, 28; cf., moreover, above, n. 171.

188. Cf., e.g., MS Breslau, J 5, No. 140: "Die von Magdeburg sprechen nichts uf der stad genad oder willkhor"; No. 180 (in a lawsuit of a Jew); Wasserschleben, RQ, IV, 2, p. 136; 26, p. 162: ". . . had die stad eyne willekor, do spreche wir keyn recht obir, von rechtis wegen"; LSchSprS., Nos. 797, 810; Hugo Böhlau, "Aus der Praxis des Magdeburger Schöffenstuhls während des 14. und 15. Jahrhunderts," *ZRG*, O.S., IX (1870), 14–24; Paul Rehme, "Schöffen als 'Boten' bei gerichtlichen Vorgängen im Magdeburgischen Rechtskreise," in *Festschrift Heinrich Brunner zum 70. Geburtstag dargebracht von Schülern und Verehrern* (Weimar, 1910), p. 30 of the reprint.

189. Grössler, *Zeitschrift des Harz-Vereins für Geschichte und Altertums-*

kunde, XXIII (1890), 175, No. 7; Kisch, *Hebrew Union College Annual*, XIV, 446, n. 40.

190. MS Breslau, R 568, fol. 377r–v, No. 1; LSchSprS., No. 113; Stendal UB., X, 1, pp. 49 f.

191. Cf. Forchhammer, *op. cit.*, p. 392, n. 467. In this connection it is noteworthy that, as late as 1580, the Polish King Stephan Bathory, in an edict concerning the Jews of Poznan, forbade insulting forms of the Jewry oath as contradictory to the statutes and to Magdeburg law: "Cavemus sexto loco, juramenta a judeis ulterius contemptis formulis exigi non debent, qua [*sic*] denique ex statutorum libris et jure Maidemburgensi peti possunt, hoc est vel supra rodale, si est summa aliqua pecuniaria insignis, vel ad valvas sinagogae, si minor est summa" (Philipp Bloch, *Die Generalprivilegien der polnischen Judenschaft* [Posen, 1892], p. 99).

On the influence of medieval German law on the Polish Jewry-law regarding the oath, cf. also Isaac Lewin, "The Protection of Jewish Religious Rights by Royal Edicts in Ancient Poland," *Quarterly Bulletin of the Polish Institute of Arts and Sciences in America*, I (1943), 565–69 [pp. 11–15 of the reprint].

192. Stendal UB., X, 1, p. 49 (cf. above, chap. viii, n. 55). Thus it is also prescribed in the decisions mentioned above, nn. 189 and 190. Hence Claussen's assertion (*op. cit.*, p. 180) that, according to Magdeburg law, "the oath ceremony did not take place in the synagogue but in the regular meeting place of the court" is not accurate if so generalized (cf. Kisch, *Hebrew Union College Annual*, XIV, 446, and above, n. 179).

193. Stendal UB., X, 1, p. 50; cf. above, pp. 100 f.

194. So MS Breslau, R 568, No. 1; Grössler, *op. cit.*, No. 7, p. 175. In MS Breslau, R 568, No. 1, the passage reads clearly: "*das der clegir* den eyd *sehe und hore*"; this is fully in accord with the medieval German law. A clause in the privilege for the Jews of Stendal of December 7, 1297, should be noted here: "cum judeus aliquis causabitur, et justicia persecutus usque ad juramentum publice faciendum, et hoc quidem ante scolas judeorum faciet lingua teutonica, ita quod christiani universi intelligant suum juramentum" (H. G. Ph. Gengler, *Deutsche Stadtrechte des Mittelalters*, p. 461; Stendal UB., X, 1, p. 50; Gengler, *Deutsche Stadtrechtsaltertümer*, p. 116, n. 160). Attention may also be directed to the identical practice at the jury court of Brünn. The Jewry-oath formula was to be recited by the *Eidstaber*, as well as the swearer, *in vulgari*, that is, in German, and, accordingly, its text appears in German inserted in the Latin text of the court decisions (cf. Brünn SchB., No.

435, p. 204; Bretholz, *Quellen zur Geschichte der Juden in Mähren*, No. 329, p. 188 [*anno* 1384]).

195. Stendal UB., X, 1, pp. 50 f.

196. See Planck, *op. cit.*, II, 88, 95 f.; as to the sequence of the oaths, under Magdeburg law it was customary for the litigant to take the oath prior to the oath-helpers or witnesses (cf. *ibid.*, II, 84).

CHAPTER ELEVEN

1. Cf. Ernst Freund, "Administrative Law," *Encyclopaedia of the Social Sciences*, I (New York, 1937), 452 ff.

2. The history of *Polizeirecht* in medieval Germany has hitherto received but little attention from scholars. For a brief survey of the literature see Claudius von Schwerin, *Grundzüge der deutschen Rechtsgeschichte* (Munich, 1934), pp. 193 f.; cf. also Fritz Fleiner, *Institutionen des deutschen Verwaltungsrechts* (8th ed.; Tübingen, 1928), pp. 385 f.; Walter Becker, "Die Anfänge von Polizei und Polizeirecht im mittelalterlichen Goslarer Rechtskreise," *Thüringisch-Sächsische Zeitschrift für Geschichte und Kunst*, XIX (1930), 163–67.

3. Cf. Walter Becker, *Magdeburger Recht in der Lausitz* (Stuttgart, 1931), pp. 76–78 and 70–75.

4. *Sachsenspiegel* (ed. Augsburg, 1516), fol. 130v; ed. Zobel (Leipzig, 1560), fols. 331v–332r; Rem. RW. 1; Bocksd. Rem., 6.

5. Jean Juster, *Les Juifs dans l'empire romain, leur condition juridique, économique et sociale*, Vols. I, II (Paris, 1914), *passim;* Peter Browe, "Die Judengesetzgebung Justinians," *Analecta Gregoriana*, VIII (1935), 109–46, esp. 130 ff.

6. Otto Stobbe, *Die Juden in Deutschland während des Mittelalters* (Braunschweig, 1866), pp. 176 f.; Heinrich Gottfried Gengler, *Deutsche Stadtrechtsaltertümer* (Erlangen, 1882), pp. 97–120, containing an important and well-documented chapter, "Die Judenwohnplätze" (including the older bibliography), almost completely overlooked in Jewish historical literature; Eugen Nübling, *Die Judengemeinden des Mittelalters, insbesondere die Judengemeinde der Reichsstadt Ulm* (Ulm, 1896), pp. 475 ff.; Johannes E. Scherer, *Die Rechtsverhältnisse der Juden in den deutsch-österreichischen Ländern* (Leipzig, 1901), pp. 44 f.; Emanuel Forchhammer, "Beiträge zur Geschichte der deutschen Juden . . . ," *Geschichtsblätter für Stadt und Land Magdeburg*, XLVI (1911), 172–77, 166–70, 334 f.; James Parkes, *The Jew in the Medieval Community* (London, 1938), pp. 85, 108, 189, 215; also Louis Wirth, *The Ghetto* (Chicago, 1928).

7. For the first theory, Samuel Krauss, personally consulted and quoted by K. G. Hugelmann, "Studien zum Recht der Nationalitäten

im deutschen Mittelalter. II. Das Judenrecht der Rechtsbücher," *Historisches Jahrbuch der Görresgesellschaft*, XLVIII (1928), 577, n. 25; for the second theory, Hugelmann, *ibid.*, p. 577.

8. Alexander Pinthus, *Die Judensiedlungen der deutschen Städte: Eine stadtbiologische Studie* (Technische Hochschule of Hannover Dr. Ing. thesis, 1931), first published in *ZGJD*, II (1930), 101–30, 197–217, 284–300.

9. Cf. Stobbe, *op. cit.*, p. 176; Ellen Littmann, *Studien zur Wiederaufnahme der Juden durch die deutschen Städte nach dem Schwarzen Tode* (University of Cologne Ph.D. thesis [Breslau, 1928]), pp. 24 f.; also published in *MGWJ*, LXXII (1928), 594.

10. Cf. G. Kisch, "The Yellow Badge in History," *Historia Judaica*, IV (1942), 103 f.

11. Cf. Julius Aronius, *Regesten zur Geschichte der Juden im fränkischen und deutschen Reiche bis zum Jahre 1273* (Berlin, 1887–1902), No. 463, p. 204; F. J. Mone, "Kirchenverordnungen der Bistümer Mainz und Strassburg," *Zeitschrift für die Geschichte des Oberrheins*, III (1852), 136, No. 4 (provincial statute of the archdiocese of Mayence of 1233): "Christianos quoque, qui cum Judeis habitant, eis serviendo, excommunicamus. . . ." This is probably the regulation that Pinthus (*op. cit.*, p. 8, n. 3; *ZGJD*, II [1930], 102, n. 3) alluded to in his wrong citation and erroneous interpretation. It was merely the old prohibition of employing Christian servants and their living in Jewish homes that was here enforced through excommunication.

12. Aronius, *op. cit.*, No. 724, p. 302; cf. S. W. Baron, *The Jewish Community: Its History and Structure to the American Revolution*, I (Philadelphia, 1942), 225.

13. MS Breslau, J 5, No. 27.

14. See above, p. 184; cf. also Hugelmann, *op. cit.*, p. 575.

15. *Cod. Theod.* xvi. 8. 25: "Synagogae de cetero nullae protinus extruantur, veteres in sua forma permaneant."

C. 7, X, *de judaeis, 5, 6:*

"Judaei veteres synagogas in priorem statum reformare possunt; de novo exigere non possunt.

"Consuluit Judaeos *etiam* de novo construere synagogas, ubi *eas* non habuerunt, pati non debes. Verum, si antiquae corruerint, vel ruinam minantur, ut eas reaedificent, potest aequanimiter tolerari, non autem, ut eas exaltent, aut ampliores aut pretiosiores faciant, quam antea fuisse noscuntur; qui utique hoc pro magno debent habere, quod in veteribus synagogis et suis observantiis tolerantur."

Cf. Juster, *op. cit.*, I, 464–72; Scherer, *op. cit.*, p. 45 (16).

16. *Sachsenspiegel* (ed. Augsburg, 1516), fol. 130v; ed. Zobel (Leipzig,

1560), fol. 331v, cf. also Buch's *Gloss* on III, 2, where in the latter edition the following addition to the original text is inserted: *auch keine nawe schulen bawen.*

17. Reg. jur., J 131; Bocksd. Rem., 6.

18. Homeyer, No. 1024 (formerly 590); Homeyer, *Sachsenspiegel*, I, 307, n. 5; Aronius, *op. cit.*, No. 458, p. 201, second paragraph.

19. Cf. Stobbe, *op. cit.*, pp. 173–76; Nübling, *op. cit.*, pp. 52–54, 161 f.; Scherer, *op. cit.*, pp. 41–44; Forchhammer, *op. cit.*, pp. 152–55; Kisch, "The Yellow Badge in History," pp. 95–144, with bibliography; the following additions should be made: p. 142, under III, between Jacobs and Forchhammer: Henry C. Lea, *A History of the Inquisition of Spain*, I (New York, 1906), 68 f., n. 2; p. 143, under IV, as first title: Paul Hinschius, *System des katholischen Kirchenrechts*, V (Berlin, 1895), 390, n. 4; cf. also p. 487. The following presentation is largely based on the present writer's essay, "The Yellow Badge in History." The latter goes into much more detail on the subject than the space available here permits.

20. It was later incorporated in the *Corpus Juris canonici as* c. 15, X, *de judeis, Sarracenis, et eorum servis*, 5, 6. Latin text in J. D. Mansi, *Sacrorum conciliorum amplissima collectio*, XXII, 1055, often reprinted; see S. Grayzel, *The Church and the Jews in the XIIIth Century* (Philadelphia, 1933), p. 308.

"In nonnullis provinciis a christianis Judaeos seu Sarracenos habitus distinguit diversitas; sed in quibusdam sic quaedam inolevit confusio, ut nulla differentia discernantur. Unde contingit interdum, quod per errorem Christiani Judaeorum seu Sarracenorum, et Judaei seu Sarraceni Christianorum provincia et omni tempore qualitate habitus publice ab mixtionis excessus per velamen erroris huiusmodi ulterioris excusationis possint habere diffugium: statuimus, ut tales utriusque sexus in omni Christianorum provincia et omni tempore qualitate habitus publice ab aliis populis distinguantur [cum etiam per Moysen hoc ipsum legatur eis injunctum]."

21. For an extensive discussion of all details involved see Kisch, "The Yellow Badge in History," pp. 103 ff., 109 ff.

22. *Von rehte, nâch rehte, wol*, or *als er sol; junkherren und knehte, gekleidet nâch ir rehte* (Hartmann von Aue, *Iwein*, 307 f.); cf. Moriz Heyne, *Körperpflege und Kleidung bei den Deutschen von den ältesten geschichtlichen Zeiten bis zum 16. Jahrhundert* (Leipzig, 1903), pp. 303 f. and n. 223b.

23. See the illustrations reproduced in Guido Kisch, *Jewry-Law in Medieval Germany: Laws and Court Decisions Concerning Jews* (New York, 1949), pp. 38, 50.

24. See below, chap. xii, n. 158. Recently an attempt has been made

to question that Süsskind von Trimberg was Jewish (cf. Raphael Straus, "Was Süsskint von Trimperg a Jew?" *Jewish Social Studies*, X [1948], 19–30). Because of the unquestionable pictorial representation in the Manesse manuscript, the conclusions drawn above are obviously not dependent on what the final reply to Straus's question will be.

25. The same conclusion flows from the fact that the Jewish hat was, among other symbols, employed as a sort of coat-of-arms on Jewish official and private seals in the thirteenth and fourteenth centuries. Jews would never voluntarily have used symbols of degradation as their personal emblems. The argument of Chayim Lauer, who takes the Jewish hats as chalices, is not based on unobjectionable premises, nor is it at all convincing (C. Lauer, "Zur Geschichte des 'Zürcher Semak,' " *Jahrbuch der jüdisch-literarischen Gesellschaft zu Frankfurt a.M.*, XII [1918], 16, 326). And the occurrence of a variety of emblems on medieval Jewish seals, such as the crescent, the signs of the zodiac, fishes, the *Magen David* ("Shield of David"), etc., is proof that their choice was left to the Jews. On medieval seals of German Jews using the Jewish hat as emblem see Alexander Kisch, "Trois sceaux juifs du moyen âge," *Revue des études juives*, IV (1882), 279; cf. Émile Ouverleaux, "Notes et documents sur les juifs de Belgique," *Revue des études juives*, VII (1883), 125; Forchhammer, *op. cit.*, pp. 155, 388, n. 434; Richard Grünfeld, *Ein Gang durch die Geschichte der Juden in Augsburg* (Augsburg, 1917), pp. 1, 18, and picture, reproduced also in *Encyclopaedia Judaica*, III (1929), 687–88.

26. A provincial council held in Breslau in 1267 (Aronius, *op. cit.*, No. 724, p. 302) stated:

"Item statuimus atque ordinavimus ut judei cornutum pileum, quem quondam in istis partibus consueverunt deferre et sua temeritate deponere praesumpserunt, resumerent, ut a Christianis discerni valeant evidenter, sicut olim in generali concilio fuit definitum. Quicumque autem judaeus sine tali signo deprehensus fuerit incedere, ad morem terrae poena pecuniaria puniatur."

Similar decrees were issued by the church councils of Vienna in 1267, Olmütz in 1342, Prague in 1355 (*pilea lata*), Salzburg, 1418 (cf. Stobbe, *op. cit.*, pp. 273 f., n. 166; Gerson Wolf, "Zur Geschichte der Juden in Österreich," Geiger's *ZGJD*, I [1887], 249).

27. Cf. above, p. 207 and chap. viii, n. 112.

28. Ed. Daniels and Gruben, art. 139, p. 176 (cf. *Gloss*, Daniels and Gruben, p. 438): "Judaeus etiam synagogam exire non debet sine mitra judaica." Cf. A. von Daniels, *Dat buk wichbelde recht: Das sächsische Weichbildrecht* (Berlin, 1853), art. 117, p. 54: "Die jode sal ok nümmer üt siner scule oder ut siner sinagogen komen ane joden hud." Cf. also Forchhammer, *op. cit.*, pp. 154 f.

29. Cf. above, p. 283. Similarly, according to the Jewry-oath formula found in a fourteenth-century manuscript of the Leipzig University Library (Homeyer, *Rechtsbücher*, No. 681); C. G. Haltaus, *Glossarium Germanicum medii aevi*, p. 1053; cf. also Stobbe, *op. cit.*, p. 274, n. 167. The same headgear also accompanied the Jewish offender sentenced to death on his last journey and on the gallows (cf. G. Kisch, "The 'Jewish Execution' in Medieval Germany," *Historia Judaica*, V [1943], 109 f.). The Jews' hat was also employed for publicly pillorying Christian usurers and women convicted of sexual relations with Jews (cf. Stobbe, *op. cit.*, pp. 274, n. 167; 266 f., n. 151).

30. The Jews' prohibition from wearing particular kinds of boots and compulsion to wear certain others is similarly found in Islamic countries in the beginning of the fourteenth century (cf. Ilse Lichtenstadter, "The Distinctive Dress of Non-Muslims in Islamic Countries," *Historia Judaica*, V [1943], 50).

31. Cf. Stobbe, *op. cit.*, pp. 170–73, 179–81; Nübling, *op. cit.*, pp. 54–89; Scherer, *op. cit.*, pp. 39–50; Forchhammer, *op. cit.*, pp. 151 f., 156–64; Hugelmann, *op. cit.*, pp. 574–76, 578, 582 f.; Grayzel, *op. cit.*, pp. 9–12, 25–35; see also below, chap. xiii, n. 40.

32. E. F. Jacob, "Innocent III," *Encyclopaedia of the Social Sciences*, VIII (1937), 57 f., with bibliography.

33. *Innocentii III Opera omnia* (Migne, *Patr. Lat.*, CCXV, 502 f.); Grayzel, *op. cit.*, pp. 104 ff.

34. See above, p. 150.

35. C. 18, X, *de usuris*, 5, 19 and c. 13, 15–17, X, *de judeis*, 5, 6; cf. *Decretum Gratiani*, C. XXVIII, qu. 1, c. 13, 14; see Scherer, *op. cit.*, pp. 39–50, citing all church councils, before and after the Fourth Lateran Council, which issued similar or identical decrees; cf. also M. Elias, "Die römische Kurie, besonders Innozenz III, und die Juden," *Jahrbuch der jüdisch-literarischen Gesellschaft zu Frankfurt a.M.*, XII (1918), 52–58.

36. The translation follows the text in the Augsburg edition of 1516, inclosing in brackets additions or variants as found in Zobel's edition (Leipzig, 1560).

37. Prohibitions from taking meals together with Jews, Bocksd. Rem., 2, Rem. RW. 15, Purgoldts Rb., VIII, 97, 98 ("It is also prohibited by law that Christians eat their *Osterkuchen* [unleavened bread as used for Passover] or accept it from them"), 100, 103 (cf. also 94) (an exception is made only for Christian missionaries, Purgoldts Rb., VIII, 98); selling meat from animals slaughtered by Jews, in the stalls for the sale of meat, MRb., V, 5, 3, Zwickau Rb. (ed. Ullrich and Planitz), I, 6, 1 (such meat should be offered for sale only before the slaughter-

house; cf. Stobbe, *op. cit.*, pp. 171, 271 f., n. 162; Hugelmann, *op. cit.*, pp. 575 f. and n. 17); bathing with Jews, Purgoldts Rb., VIII, 106; using Jewish physicians or their medicines, Bocksd. Rem. 2, Purgoldts Rb., VIII, 106; employing Jewish servants or nurses, under penalty of excommunication, Reg. jur., J 160, 161, Rem. RW., 1 (cf. Purgoldts Rb., VIII, 103); Jews' attaining public office, Buch's *Gloss* to Ssp., III, 2 (Hugelmann's assertion [*op. cit.*, p. 578] that this prohibition is unknown to the lawbooks, is erroneous; cf. also K. Schilling, *Das objektive Recht in der Sachsenspiegelglosse* [Berlin, 1931], p. 65); the public appearance of Jews during Holy Week, particularly on Good Friday, Reg. jur., J 149, Bocksd. Rem., 4; Jews' remaining in the street when meeting a procession bearing the Host, MRb., III, 17, 34; gifts or bequests of Christians in favor of Jews and vice versa, Buch's *Gloss* to Ssp., III, 7, 1 (9); Reg. jur., J 146, 147; Rem. RW., 1 (bequests by Jews exempted; cf. also below, chap. xiii, n. 66); private religious discussions between Jews and Christians, Purgoldts Rb., VIII, 105; playing with Jews in the streets, *ibid.*, 106; intercourse between Jews and Christians, Reg. jur., J 144, Purgoldts Rb., VIII, 106.

38. Cf. Stobbe, *op. cit.*, pp. 27–45; Nübling, *op. cit.*, pp. 261–81; Scherer, *op. cit.*, pp. 81 f., 529–42; Forchhammer, *op. cit.*, pp. 170, 178, 329–31, 340–43, 348 f., 352 f., 354 ff.

39. Cf. Stobbe, *op. cit.*, p. 41.

40. *Sachsenspiegel* (ed. Augsburg, 1516), fol. 130r.

41. C. 18, X, *de usuris*, 5, 19; cf. Grayzel, *op. cit.*, pp. 36, 38, 308; Scherer, *op. cit.*, p. 535. On the general literature relating to the tithe see Catherine E. Boyd, "The Beginnings of the Ecclesiastical Tithe in Italy," *Speculum*, XXI (1946), 158 ff.

42. Aronius, *op. cit.*, No. 724, p. 303.

CHAPTER TWELVE

1. The *Jewish* aspects and their effect on internal Jewish life, as a complementary counterpart to this picture, are described in Salo W. Baron, *The Jewish Community: Its History and Structure to the American Revolution* (Philadelphia, 1942); see, in particular, Vol. I, chap. vii, "European Corporation"; Vol. II, chaps. xiv, "Law Enforcement," and xv, "Public Finance." Cf. also Fritz Baer, *Galut* ("Schocken Bücherei," No. 61 [Berlin, 1936]), pp. 16–49; English translation (New York, 1947), pp. 22–59; Gershom G. Scholem, *Major Trends in Jewish Mysticism* (Jerusalem, 1941), esp. pp. 79–118.

2. On the doctrine of God as the creator of law see G. Kisch, *Sachsenspiegel and Bible* (Notre Dame, Ind., 1941), pp. 117–19, 120–46.

3. Cf. Solomon Grayzel, "Christian-Jewish Relations in the First Millennium," *Essays on Antisemitism*, ed. K. S. Pinson (New York, 1942), pp. 25–44; also above, pp. 147 ff.

4. See above, pp. 136 f.

5. See above, pp. 100 ff.

6. See above, pp. 275 ff.

7. See above, pp. 102 ff.

8. See above, pp. 184 f.

9. Cf., e.g., J. E. Scherer, *Die Rechtsverhältnisse der Juden in den deutsch-österreichischen Ländern* (Leipzig, 1901), p. 3; R. Schröder and E. von Künssberg, *Lehrbuch der deutschen Rechtsgeschichte* (7th ed.; Berlin and Leipzig, 1932), pp. 506, 508; Rudolf Hübner, *A History of Germanic Private Law* (Boston, 1918), p. 83: Hugo Steinthal, *Die Juden im fränkischen Reiche, ihre rechtliche, und wirtschaftlich-soziale Stellung* (Breslau University Ph.D. thesis, 1922; of which only a summary was published [Breslau, 1922]), pp. 20, 23, and *passim;* see also the following note.

10. This doctrine is already found in Karl von Amira's article "Recht," in Hermann Paul's *Grundriss der germanischen Philologie*, II (1st ed.; Strasbourg, 1893), 124, later published separately under the title, *Grundriss des germanischen Rechts* (3d ed.; Strasbourg, 1913), p. 148, and in Otto Gierke, *Deutsches Privatrecht*, I (Leipzig, 1895), 437, which also lists the older writings on the subject. The theory that the legal treatment of the Jews during the medieval period was motivated mainly by the "law of aliens" was developed most fully and propounded most profoundly by Johannes E. Scherer (*op. cit.*, pp. 4–8, 62–105). Cf., e.g., the following passages in Scherer, showing the wide compass of this doctrine; "Die Gesetze . . . gehen von der Anschauung aus, dass die Juden Angehörige einer fremden Nation, Ausländer und daher nach dem Fremdenrechte zu behandeln sind" (p. 4). "Nach diesem Fremdenrechte wurden im karolingischen Reiche, in Deutschland, in den meisten Ländern Österreichs und bis in das 13. und 14. Jahrhundert in Aragonien, England, Frankreich, in Kastilien, Portugal und Süditalien auch die Juden behandelt" (p. 6). Scherer's conception was adopted in almost the entire literature of legal history and thus also found acceptance in the leading textbooks and encyclopedic works; cf., e.g., Rudolf Hübner, *Grundzüge des deutschen Privatrechts* (5th ed., Leipzig, 1930), pp. 94 ff.; Hübner, *A History of Germanic Private Law*, pp. 83 ff.; Claudius von Schwerin, *Deutsche Rechtsgeschichte* ("Grundriss der Geschichtswissenschaft," ed. Aloys Meister, Vol. II, No. 5 [2d ed.; Leipzig, 1915]), pp. 41 f.; Hans Schreuer, *Deutsches Privatrecht* (Stuttgart, 1921), p. 78; Hans Planitz, *Grundzüge des deutschen Privatrechts* (2d ed.;

Berlin, 1931), p. 23; Karl Haff, *Institutionen des deutschen Privatrechts auf rechtsvergleichender und soziologischer Grundlage*, I (Stuttgart, 1927), 51; Paul Rehme, *Geschichte des Handelsrechts* (separate ed. from *Handbuch des gesamten Handelsrechts*, ed. by Victor Ehrenberg), I (Leipzig, 1914), 113, 131.

Of the monograph literature, cf., e.g., the following: Alfred Schultze, "Über Gästerecht und Gastgerichte in den deutschen Städten des Mittelalters," *Historische Zeitschrift*, CI (1908), 526: "Das städtische Gästerecht des Mittelalters war nicht eine Anwendung oder Nachwirkung des alten germanischen Fremdenrechtes, wie es etwa das mittelalterliche Judenrecht war"; Hans von Frisch, *Das Fremdenrecht, die staatsrechtliche Stellung der Fremden* (Berlin, 1910), pp. 42–68; Karl G. Hugelmann, "Studien zum Recht der Nationalitäten im deutschen Mittelalter," *Historisches Jahrbuch der Görresgesellschaft*, XLVIII (1928), 565–85.

Jewry-law is treated in the same section with alien law, though separately, by Heinrich Brunner, in his *Deutsche Rechtsgeschichte*, I (2d ed.; Leipzig, 1906), 399–405, and esp. 403, n. 22. Andreas Heusler, *Institutionen des deutschen Privatrechts*, I (Leipzig, 1885), 144–53, treating of the Jews under the heading "Einfluss der Ausländerqualität auf die Rechtsfähigkeit: A. Bei Angehörigen auswärtiger Staaten, B. Bei den Juden," excluded Jewry-law from his presentation as a law of a group of people considered foreigners nationally and ethnically, though not regarded as aliens politically.

To the law of aliens as the origin and basis of medieval Jewry-law no reference was made by Otto Stobbe, *Die Juden in Deutschland während des Mittelalters* (Braunschweig, 1886); Schröder and Künssberg, *op. cit.*, pp. 245, 505 ff.; Georg von Below, "Juden," in Johannes Hoops's *Reallexikon der Altertumskunde*, II (Strasbourg, 1913–15), 617 f.; Ernst Freiherr von Schwind, *Deutsches Privatrecht* (Vienna and Leipzig, 1921), p. 93.

11. Recent special investigation devoted to the historical development of alien law in Germany paid no attention to the problem of medieval Jewry-law (cf. the literature cited in Hübner, *Grundzüge des deutschen Privatrechts*, pp. 83 f., n. 2). The only exception is H. von Frisch's book mentioned above, n. 10, which, however, in its pertinent pp. 42–90, is based on secondary literature only, without independent research in the sources.

12. Cf. below, p. 314 and nn. 57, 58.

13. See above, n. 10 and for criticism, G. Kisch, *ZRG*, LVII (1937), 723 ff. The distinguished historian of economics, Lujo Brentano, pro-

pounded a modification of the alien-law theory, interesting, "whether tenable or not," to use his own words. "The Jews always felt and remained aliens with regard to the peoples among whom they settled in the Diaspora" ("Die Juden fühlten sich und blieben stets gegenüber den Völkern, unter denen sie sich in der Diaspora niedergelassen hatten, fremd") (L. Brentano, *Die Anfänge des modernen Kapitalismus* [Munich, 1916], pp. 192–95).

14. Cf., e.g., Eugen Täubler, "Urkundliche Beiträge zur Geschichte der Juden in Deutschland im Mittelalter," *Mitteilungen des Gesamtarchivs der deutschen Juden*, IV (1913), 58: "Die Grundlage der Entwicklung ist das Fremdenrecht"; Jean Juster, *Les Juifs dans l'empire romain*, II (Paris, 1914), 26 f.; Selma Stern, "Judenprivilegien," *Jüdisches Lexikon*, III (Berlin, 1929), 440.

15. Objections to Scherer's conception and theory were first expressed in a review of his book by Max Eschelbacher, *MGWJ*, XLVI (1902), 388–94, meritorious, though itself not free from misconceptions. Thereafter a stand of resolute opposition against Scherer was taken by George Caro, renowned authority on the medieval economic history of the Jews, in his *Sozial- und Wirtschaftsgeschichte der Juden*, I (Leipzig, 1908), 459: "Where the Jews were regarded as aliens, when this process began and in what respects the Jews were so regarded, would first have to be investigated. In no case is it permissible to have them treated as aliens by the Franks after Clovis' conquest of Gaul, as they previously were considered Romans." Later, with reference to Alfons Dopsch's studies on the economic and social foundations of European civilization up to the Carolingian era, stout resistance was offered to Scherer's views by Steinthal, *op. cit.*, p. 3 of the summary: "The Jews' *status civitatis* remained untouched in the Frankish era; they were *Volksgenossen* of a different faith. They were not treated, as is frequently held, as 'aliens' according to so-called alien-law"; this was explained *in extenso* on pp. 25 ff. of the unpublished dissertation.

16. National Socialist doctrine as expressed in the party platform of February 25, 1920, arts. 4 and 5, demanded that the Jews should be treated according to laws regulating the behavior of "aliens" (*Fremdengesetzgebung*), this being represented as the return to the "ancient basis of Germanic alien law." For a detailed discussion of the question of the historical basis and validity of this theory see G. Kisch, "Jewry-Law in Central Europe—Past and Present," *Journal of Central European Affairs*, II (1943), 412.

17. For references see above, nn. 10 and 14.

18. This is a recent formulation by S. W. Baron, "The Jewish Factor

in Medieval Civilization," *Proceedings*, XII (1942), 36. Baron believes (*ibid.*, p. 36 and n. 55) that, in abandoning Scherer's original theory, the pendulum has swung too far to the other extreme: "There is no denying that in the mental picture of most medieval men the Jew appeared as a permanent stranger"; cf. also Baron, *The Jewish Community*, I, 243: ". . . the 'alien' character of the Jews was doubtless more pronounced in the north than in the more heterogeneous south"; Baron, *A Social and Religious History of the Jews*, II (New York, 1937), 22, 26 f., 31 f., and *passim;* III, 102 f., n. 11, 107 f., n. 18 (for criticism see G. Kisch, *Speculum*, XIV [1939], 367 f.).

Another formulation, different from Baron's yet moving in a similar direction, by a Christian author, reads: "Von den Juden, die stets eine besondere Stellung einnahmen, indem sie zwar als volksfremd, aber nur zutreffendenfalls als Fremde galten, sei hier abgesehen" (Wilhelm Weizsäcker, "Das Recht der Fremden in Böhmen," *Mitteilungen des Vereins für Geschichte der Deutschen in Böhmen*, LIX [1921], 52). Weizsäcker follows the older pattern of Andreas Heusler, who speaks of the *Vaterlandslosigkeit* of the Jews, regarding them as of foreign nationality and ethnically foreign, though not as aliens politically (Heusler, *Institutionen des deutschen Privatrechts*, I, 147 ff.).

The conception of the Jew as "an alien without a motherland" was dogmatically developed from the point of view of legal theory in a monograph chiefly concerned with the status of aliens under modern public law, by H. von Frisch, *Das Fremdenrecht, die staatsrechtliche Stellung der Fremden*, p. 43: "Erstere [the Jews] waren tatsächlich heimatlos; sie hatten kein Territorium, in das sie zurückkehren konnten, und keine Staatsgewalt, die sie unter Umständen in der Fremde schützte." The actual "homelessness" of the Jews may have been conspicuous indeed in the initial period of their emergence in Europe, preceding the era of their permanent settlement. Thus it may well explain some peculiarities in their legal situation compared with that of other traveling merchants in that period. After their permanent settlement, however, this aspect hardly impressed itself on the medieval mind, least of all in the refined implications of modern juridical thinking. Such present-day forms of legal construction have no foundation in concept or phrasing of the medieval sources. For this reason James Parkes (*The Jew in the Medieval Community* [London, 1938], p. 206) correctly refused to apply the modern conception of "statelessness" to the medieval conditions under consideration.

19. A summary survey of the present state of knowledge has been offered by G. Kisch, "Nationalism and Race in Medieval Law,"

Seminar: An Annual Extraordinary Number of the Jurist, I (1943), 48–64. Cf., below, n. 23.

20. James Westfall Thompson, *Feudal Germany* (Chicago, 1928), pp. 366 ff.

21. Cf. Walther Merk, "Die deutschen Stämme in der Rechtsgeschichte," *ZRG*, LVIII (1938), 38–41.

22. Claudius von Schwerin, *Grundzüge der deutschen Rechtsgeschichte* (Munich and Leipzig, 1934), pp. 123 ff.

23. For details on the awakening of "nationalism" in medieval Germany see G. Kisch, "Nationalism and Race in Medieval Law," pp. 56 ff., and the literature cited there, particularly Erich Maschke, *Das Erwachen des Nationalbewusstseins im deutsch-slavischen Grenzraum* (Leipzig, 1933).

Only after publication of my aforementioned essay and completion of the present chapter in manuscript form were two books on the history of nationalism published: Hans Kohn, *The Idea of Nationalism: A Study in Its Origins and Background* (New York, 1944), and Frederick Hertz, *Nationality in History and Politics: A Study of the Psychology and Sociology of National Sentiment and Character* (New York, 1944). The results of Kohn's research on medieval Germany (esp. pp. 78 f., 85) are basically in agreement with this writer's conclusions, presented above and derived from more restricted but more specific source material. True, "people looked upon everything not from the point of view of their 'nationality' or 'race,' but from the point of view of religion" (Kohn, *op. cit.*, p. 79). "Religion was definitely regarded as superior to national sentiment, at least in principle, though in the later Middle Ages there was a widespread national movement against the abuses of Papacy" (Hertz, *op. cit.*, p. 286). In my opinion, however, both authors partly underestimated, partly left unheeded, certain phenomena and developments in medieval law important for a study of the roots of nationalism, as set forth in my "Nationalism and Race," pp. 56 ff.; cf. also *Historia Judaica*, VI (1944), 195 ff. No revision of the original text of the present chapter was necessitated by the reading of these valuable additions to the literature on the history of nationalism.

24. Cf. G. Kisch, "Nationalism and Race," p. 59 and n. 23. Additional proof of the importance of the language issue in the process of national evolution can be derived from the illuminating study by Josef Kliment, "Státní občanství a národnost v českém právu do Bílé Hory" ("Citizenship and Nationality in Czech Law up to the Battle of the White Mountain"), *Sborník prací z dějin práva československého*, Vol. I

("Práce ze semináře českého práva na Karlově Universitě," No. 15 [Prague, 1930]), pp. 50–59.

25. Cf. G. Kisch, *Sachsenspiegel and Bible*, pp. 176 ff.

26. Ernst Hoyer, "Das Sprachenrecht des *Sachsenspiegels*," *Jahrbuch des Vereins für Geschichte der Deutschen in Böhmen*, II (Prague, 1929), 21 ff.; Karl Gottfried Hugelmann, "Die Rechtsstellung der Wenden im deutschen Mittelalter," *ZRG*, LVIII (1938), 224 ff.

27. See also, with reference to the following presentation, G. Kisch, "Nationalism and Race," pp. 62 f.

28. See above, pp. 100 ff.

29. See above, p. 89 and G. Kisch, *Jewry-Law in Medieval Germany: Laws and Court Decisions Concerning Jews* (New York, 1949), picture to Ssp., III, 70, 1, facing p. 50.

30. In his essay on the legal status of the Wends in Germany in the Middle Ages (*ZRG*, LVIII [1938], 249–56) Hugelmann also refers to Ssp., III, 69 and 70, and, in his interpretation, shares the views presented above. But the illustrations to Ssp., III, 70, 1, in the illuminated manuscripts escaped his attention. Moreover, he was guided by his basic conception of the Jews as a racially different national group (*rassenfremde Volksgruppe*). These two facts prevented him from drawing the proper conclusions regarding the Jews as they are borne out, with no ambiguity, by the sources.

31. Cf. Hugelmann, *ZRG*, LVIII (1938), 223, 237 f.

32. An interesting example of such a complete assimilation of Jews by baptism is found in R. Hoeniger's essay, "Zur Geschichte der Juden Deutschlands im frühern Mittelalter," Geiger's *ZGJD*, I (1887), 90–94, which was criticized by Adolf Kober, *Studien zur mittelalterlichen Geschichte der Juden in Köln am Rhein, insbesondere ihres Grundbesitzes* (University of Breslau Ph.D. thesis; Breslau, 1903), pp. 13 f., n. 1. The point at issue here, however, is not invalidated by this critique.

33. *Vita Sturmii*, chap. 7, *MG, Scriptores*, II (Hannover, 1829), 369: ". . . ubi platea illa super flumen Fuldam vadit, ibi magnam Sclavorum multitudinem reperit eiusdem fluminis alveo natantes, lavandis corporibus se immersisse, . . . et ipse vir Dei eorum foetorum exhorruit" (G. Kisch, "Jewry-Law in Central Europe," pp. 402 f.).

34. For instances see Maschke, *Das Erwachen des Nationalbewusstseins*, pp. 9 f.

35. For instances see Joshua Trachtenberg, *The Devil and the Jews: The Medieval Conception of the Jew and Its Relation to Modern Antisemitism* (New Haven, 1943), pp. 47–50, 227 f., nn. 13 ff.; pp. 116, 250, n. 22.

36. Cf. Siegfried Stein, *Die Ungläubigen in der mittelhochdeutschen Litera-*

tur von 1050 bis 1250 (University of Heidelberg Ph.D. thesis; Berlin, 1933), p. 93; see below, nn. 113, 134; Erwin Gustav Gudde (*Social Conflicts in Medieval German Poetry* ["University of California Publications in Modern Philology," Vol. XVIII, No. 1 (Berkeley, Calif., 1934)], p. 33) says: "It is interesting and noteworthy, however, that the Jews, who so often are the targets of poetic criticism in later centuries, are hardly ever mentioned by these early Meistersinger [namely, of the first half of the thirteenth century]. Occasional attacks upon them are caused by religious animosity . . ." ; "During the period of classical knightly poetry, the attitude of the poets had been one of tolerance toward Christians, heathens, and Jews alike, an attitude which we still find in *Der welsche Gast* [by Thomasin von Zirclaria]. As a matter of fact we read repeatedly that writers believe that the Jews, as well as the Christians, are obviously under God's protection" (p. 40).

37. The epithets used for the Jews are: *verteilt* [*verurteilt*], *ubel*, *unsaelig, ungelaeubig, boes, vil ungetriwe*. They are, of course, not original creations of the medieval German literature but have their history in the writings of the Church Fathers, where such adjectives are used of the Jews as: *infideles, increduli, rebelles, miseri*, and, particularly, *perfidi;* furthermore, they have their precursors in the ancient Roman literature. Erik Peterson, "Perfidia Iudaica," *Ephemerides liturgicae,* L, N.S., X (1936), 296–308: "Dass *perfidia* die Bedeutung *Unglaube* und *perfidus* den Sinn von *ungläubig* in der christlichen Literatur erhalten hat, ist mit zahlreichen Beispielen aus der patristischen Literatur zu belegen" (p. 299); "der aktive Sinn in dem Adjektiv *perfidus* muss lebendig gewesen sein, sodass wohl mehr die Bedeutung von *nicht glaubend* als von *nicht gläubig* empfunden worden ist" (p. 302); "irgend eine moralische Kränkung der Juden ist also nicht ausgesprochen, wenn in der Liturgie der hl. Kirche von der *perfidia iudaica* die Rede ist" (p. 308). Cf. Stein, *op. cit.*, p. 24; N. W. Goldstein, "Cultivated Pagans and Ancient Anti-Semitism," *Journal of Religion*, XIX (1939), 353 f., 361; Peter Browe, *Die Judenmission im Mittelalter und die Päpste* (Rome, 1942), p. 136, n. 24: "*Perfidi iudaei* bedeutet *ungläubige, nicht an Christus glaubende Juden*. . . . Den Nebensinn *treulos*, *perfid* hat das Volk erst in viel späterer Zeit hineingelegt"; cf. also Herman Hailperin, "The Hebrew Heritage of Mediaeval Christian Biblical Scholarship," *Historia Judaica*, V (1943), 148. It is conspicuous that the expression "Jew" as a term of abuse is not found in medieval German law sources (cf. R. His, *Das Strafrecht des deutschen Mittelalters*, II [Weimar, 1935], 107 ff.).

38. Cf. Stein, *op. cit.*, pp. 13, 17, 22, 24, 34; cf. Browe, *op. cit.*, pp. 306 ff.

39. Other factors which, at times, came to play a more or less important role, will be given proper consideration in the sections to follow.

40. A similar view, well conceived though somewhat vague, was propounded hypothetically by Hoeniger (Geiger's, *ZGJD*, I [1887], 94 f.); cf. also Forchhammer ("Beiträge zur Geschichte der deutschen Juden . . . ," *Geschichtsblätter für Stadt und Land Magdeburg*, XLVI [1911], 124), an early proponent of the racial theory: "Von einem wirklich bewusst nationalen Gegensatz hören wir im Mittelalter fast gar nichts." As to the Carolingian era, cf. Hugo Steinthal, *op. cit.* (above, n. 9), pp. 24 f.

41. The presentations now to follow are largely based on this writer's studies on "Race and Law in Medieval Germany," published in his essay, "Nationalism and Race in Medieval Law," pp. 65–73. There the reader will also find cited the scanty literature on the general problem under consideration.

42. Cf. Friedrich Hertz, *Race and Civilization* (London and New York, 1928), pp. 67, 73, n. 54.

43. The "historical lands" of the Bohemian crown are here excluded from consideration because of their peculiar political and ethnographical status, the connection with the Roman-German Reich being always loose and the majority of the population remaining Slav.

44. See above, p. 310.

45. Buch's *Gloss* on *Sachsenspiegel*, III, 70, 1 (Zobel's ed. [Leipzig, 1560], fol. 446a), offers this historical explanation for the difference before the law between Saxons and Wends:

"Diss ist darumb, das sie von alters her unter einander sind feinde gewesen. . . . Und solchs ist di ursach, das ir keiner uber den andern urtel finden mag: Dann niemand mag uber seinen feind oder schwertgenossen urtel finden" ("This is because they have been, of old, mutual enemies. . . . And this is the reason why neither may pass judgment on the other: for no one may pass judgment on his enemy or companion in arms").

Cf. Hugelmann, *ZRG*, LVIII (1938), 251, 255; Maschke, *op. cit.* (above, n. 23), p. 18.

46. Hugelmann, *ZRG*, LVIII (1938), 223.

47. See above, pp. 89 and 310.

48. The meaning of the Middle Low German term *art* was originally "plowing" (*das Pflügen*) and later, derived from this, the plowed land, then land in general. A subsequent derivation attached to *art* the sense of descent (*Abstammung, Abkunft*) and quality or kind (*natürliche Beschaffenheit*). Cf. Karl Schiller and August Lübben, *Mittelnieder-*

deutsches Wörterbuch, I (Bremen, 1875), 130 f.; also Hugelmann, *Historisches Jahrbuch der Görresgesellschaft*, XLVII (1927), 278 ff.; Herman Ballschmiede, *Die sächsische Weltchronik* (Berlin University Ph.D. thesis; Berlin, 1914), p. 36. The term received a specifically racial connotation only under the impact of the modern racial doctrines.

49. MBSchR., III, 1, 4: "Ab sich czwene undir en andir wundin bynnyn weichbilde unde beyde von windischer art sint her komyn, unde doch nicht wendin sint, . . ." (cf. Hugelmann, *ZRG*, LVIII [1938], 237).

50. True, as late as the fifteenth and sixteenth centuries, some guilds required for admission to membership evidence that the candidates were "of genuine German and not of Wendish *Art*." But even protagonists of the race theory concede in this case that this restriction on the part of the craftsmen guilds was due only to considerations of the competitive struggle, not of racial enmity (cf. Hugelmann, *ZRG*, LVIII [1938], 223). This interpretation is applicable also to the similar restrictions on admission to guilds in late medieval Spain, as emerges clearly from the presentation by Julius Klein, "Medieval Spanish Guilds," in *Facts and Factors in Economic History: Articles by Former Students of Francis Gray* (Cambridge, Mass., 1932), pp. 179 (n. 3) and 183 f. Such discrimination was extended even to non-Jews. In the course of the sixteenth century the indigenous German burgher class of Cracow was pushed into the background by the Polish population, steadily increasing in number. Therefore, a *Gesellenordnung* of the "Kordiwans" of 1583 stated that a member of the German nation able to produce evidence of legitimate birth and of good conduct should be admitted as apprentice for learning a handicraft, whereas it should be illicit "einen Behmen, Polackhen, Ungern und anderer derenern zugethanern nationen an- und aufzunehmen" (W. Weizsäcker, "Das deutsche Recht des Ostens im Spiegel der Rechtsaufzeichnungen," *Deutsches Archiv für Landes- und Volksforschung*, III [1939], 67).

51. Hugelmann, *ZRG*, LVIII (1938), 237. A similar process of gradual assimilation of non-Hungarian "minorities" is found in medieval Hungary (cf. Elemir Mályusz, "Le Problème de l'assimilation au moyen âge," *Nouvelle Revue de Hongrie*, LXIV [April, 1941], 291–301).

52. G. Kisch, *Sachsenspiegel and Bible*, pp. 176 ff.

53. Ssp., III, 70, 1 (see above, pp. 89 and 310).

54. See Hugelmann, *ZRG*, LVIII (1938), *passim*.

55. See above, pp. 100 ff.

56. See above, p. 310.

57. Cf. Friedrich Wiegand, "Agobard von Lyon und die Judenfrage,"

separate edition from *Festschrift der Universität Erlangen zur Feier des achtzigsten Geburtstages des Prinzregenten Luitpold von Bayern* (Erlangen, 1901): "... werden bereits Anschauungen laut und gewinnen Gesetzeskraft, welche, über das Mass des Erforderlichen weit hinausgehend, den klerikalen Übermut und Rassenhass auf der Höhe zeigen" (p. 9); "Aber die Tendenz, die Juden unter Berufung auf Schrift und Kirchenrecht als eine inferiore Rasse gesellschaftlich zu ächten, war einmal ausgesprochen und verstummte nicht wieder" (p. 31). Forchhammer, *op. cit.*, p. 122: "... als man gelernt hatte, im Juden nicht allein den oft glücklicheren Nebenbuhler, sondern auch den fremden, anderer Rasse angehörenden Menschen zu sehen und zu hassen." Cf. also Hugelmann, *Historisches Jahrbuch der Görresgesellschaft*, XLVIII (1928), 565 ff., *passim;* Karl Frölich, *ZRG*, LII (1932), 428.

58. Cf. R. Foss, "Leben und Schriften Agobards, Erzbischofs von Lyon," *Beiträge zur Förderung christlicher Theologie*, I (1897), Heft 3, 116: "Von einem Rassenkampfe ist aber nirgend die Rede"; Karl von Amira, *Grundriss des germanischen Rechts* (3d ed.; Strasbourg, 1913), p. 140: "Den Juden wies nach südgermanischen Rechten weniger die Rasse als die Religion eine Sonderstellung an"; Johannes Nohl, *Der schwarze Tod, eine Chronik der Pest 1348–1720* (Potsdam, 1924), pp. 252 f.; Gertrud Schaaf, *Über die Besonderheiten des jüdischen Geistes und ihre Ursachen* (Heidelberg University Ph.D. thesis; 1931), p. 74. Even an author such as Max Hildebert Boehm wrote, prior to 1933 (*Encyclopaedia of the Social Sciences*, XI, 236): "Whereas the antisemitism of the Middle Ages was grounded on a religious basis and was appeased by the conversion of the Jews, the racial or nationalistic antisemitism of today passionately opposes change of faith as mimicry." Similarly, Georg Dahm (*Das Strafrecht Italiens im ausgehenden Mittelalter* [Berlin and Leipzig, 1931], p. 28, n. 74) says: "Bei diesen Zurücksetzungen spielt der Rassenhass wohl gar keine, eine umso grössere Rolle aber religiöser Eifer und wirtschaftlicher Konkurrenzneid." Cf. also F. M. Powicke, *The Christian Life in the Middle Ages* (Oxford, 1935), p. 44: "Anti-Semitism and also the hatred of the infidel was grounded in Biblical exegesis, not on race prejudice."

59. Wilhelm Grau, *Antisemitismus im späten Mittelalter: Das Ende der Regensburger Judengemeinde 1450–1519* (University of Munich Ph.D. thesis; Munich, 1934), pp. 134–37; Herbert Meyer, "Das Hehlerrecht der Juden und Lombarden," *Forschungen zur Judenfrage*, I (Hamburg, 1937), 92–109; H. Meyer, "Das jüdische Hehlerrecht," in *Deutsche Rechtswissenschaft*, II (1937), 97–111 (for criticism see G. Kisch, *Historia Judaica*, I [1938], 3–30; Boaz Cohen, *Historia Judaica*, IV [1942], 145–53); Rudolf

Ruth, "Wucher und Wucherrecht der Juden im Mittelalter," *Deutsche Rechtswissenschaft*, II (1937), 111–57 (criticism by G. Kisch, *Historia Judaica*, I [1938], 66–72); Günther Franz, "Der Jude im katholischen Kirchenrecht," *Deutsche Rechtswissenschaft*, II (1937), 157–66 (criticism, G. Kisch, *Historia Judaica*, I [1938], 67); George A. Löning, "Juden im mittelalterlichen Bremen und Oldenburg," *ZRG*, LVIII (1938), 270 f.; Hugelmann, *ZRG*, LVIII (1938), 216, 254.

60. Cecil Roth, "The Mediaeval Conception of the Jew: A New Interpretation," *Essays and Studies in Memory of Linda R. Miller*, ed. Israel Davidson (New York, 1938), p. 176; Cecil Roth, "Marranos and Racial Antisemitism," *Jewish Social Studies*, II (1940), 243 (for criticism see G. Kisch, *Seminar*, I [1943], 71 f., and *Historia Judaica*, VI [1944], 196); Joseph Reider, "Jews in Medieval Art," *Essays on Antisemitism*, ed. K. S. Pinson (New York, 1942), pp. 45–56 (for criticism see G. Kisch, *Historia Judaica*, IV [1942], 102 f.; Paul Frankl, *Historia Judaica*, V [1943], 162 ff.). In contradistinction, S. W. Baron takes a cautious stand but still admits "latent racial feelings," in his essay "The Jewish Factor in Medieval Civilization," *Proceedings*, XII (1942), 2: "The racial concept of the Jew may have played but a minor role in the consciousness of medieval man. Yet there undoubtedly existed certain ethnic and social characteristics which, aside from his religion, set the Jew apart from his neighbors and caused him to 'influence' them in a variety of often intangible ways"; and p. 16: "To be sure, 'race' was still an unknown concept, and whatever racial feeling there existed was latent rather than overt" (for criticism see G. Kisch, *Speculum*, XIV [1939], 367 f.). George Caro (*Sozial- und Wirtschaftsgeschichte der Juden*, Vol. I) expressed himself decidedly against the race conception; but a detailed argument is missing in his presentation, p. 93: "Ein Gefühl der Rassenverschiedenheit dem Absonderungsbestreben unterschieben könnte nur doktrinäres Vorurteil"; p. 213: "Was man als notwendige Folge angeborener Rasseneigenschaft hinzustellen beliebt, war nichts als das Ergebnis religiöser Erziehung und Bildung."

61. G. Kisch, "Die Rechtsstellung der Wormser Juden im Mittelalter," *ZGJD*, V (1934), 126 ff. This fact was recognized by Rudolf Ruth, even after his conversion to national socialism, in his essay "Wucher und Wucherrecht der Juden im Mittelalter," p. 142, n. 1. Cf. also below, chap. xiii, n. 8.

62. See Hoeniger, Geiger's *ZGJD*, I (1887), 72 f., 90 f., 93. On the Christian name *Judeus*, indicating Jewish origin with no racial discrimination implied, cf. Stobbe, *op. cit.*, pp. 268 f., n. 156; A. Lewinsky, *MGWJ*, XLIX (1905), 748, n. 5; Bruno Jacob, "Die Rittergeschlechter

Jude und Judemann in Hessen," *Jüdische Familienforschung: Mitteilungen der Gesellschaft für jüdische Familienforschung*, VI (1930), Heft 22, 248–51; Peter Browe, *Die Judenmission im Mittelalter und die Päpste*, pp. 207 f.

63. Cf. Peter Browe, "Die kirchenrechtliche Stellung der getauften Juden und ihrer Nachkommen," *Archiv für katholisches Kirchenrecht*, CXXI (1941), 188: "Das Altertum und Hochmittelalter hat weder eine tatsächliche noch eine rechtliche Zurücksetzung der getauften Juden gekannt, höchstens hat man, der Mahnung des Apostels (I Tim., 3, 6) entsprechend, eine Bewährungsfrist abgewartet, bis man sie als Kleriker annahm. Nie aber hat man es ihre Nachkommen büssen lassen, dass sie von Juden abstammten, sondern man hat die wenigen, die sich meldeten, unter denselben Voraussetzungen zu den kirchlichen Weihen und Ämtern zugelassen wie die Altchristen."

64. See above, pp. 186 f.; G. Kisch, "The 'Jewish Execution' in Mediaeval Germany," *Historia Judaica*, V (1943), 132.

65. Schwsp., L 322, G 272.

66. For a detailed discussion of this case and its juridical evaluation see above, pp. 205 f.

67. Ambrose, *De Abraham*, i. 9 (Migne, *Patr. Lat.*, XIV, 473C, D: "Et ideo cave, Christiane, gentili aut Judaeo filiam tuam tradere. Cave, inquam, gentilem aut judaeam atque alienigenam, hoc est, haereticam et omnem alienam a fide tua uxorem arcessas tibi. . . . Primum ergo in conjugio religio quaeritur." On the social significance of the *impedimentum disparitatis cultus*, cf. Hans Liermann, "Rasse und Recht," *Zeitschrift für die gesamte Staatswissenschaft*, LXXXV (1928), 292 f.

68. Cf., e.g., Julius Aronius, *Regesten zur Geschichte der Juden im fränkischen und deutschen Reiche bis zum Jahre 1273* (Berlin, 1887–1902), No. 226 (1137): ". . . qua Judeos christianos factos frequenter viderat . . ."; No. 250 (1147): A document issued by Archbishop Arnold of Cologne mentions as witnesses the "burgenses . . . Everhardus ex Judeo christianus et frater ejus Walterus"; No. 274 (1153): "Coloniae quidam ⟨Judaeus⟩ ex patre Judeo set converso"; No. 297 (1147–65): "[Josephus] qui nunc factus cristianus Petrus vocatur"; No. 445 (1229): "quidam videlicet de Judaicae coecitatis errore ad Christum lumen verum adductus"; Hoeniger, Geiger's *ZGJD*, I (1887), 73 (prior to 1159): ". . . eo tempore, quo Egebreth (qui Judeus fuit) et Harduwic filius Giroldi erant magistri vicinorum parrochie St. Laurentii"; cf. also Stobbe, pp. 268 f.; from papal decretals, Grayzel, *The Church and the Jews in the XIIIth Century* (Philadelphia, 1933), No. 8 (1199): "ab renuntiato errore Judaico a tenebris se convertunt ad lucem et fidem recipiunt

Christianam"; No. 48 (1221): "uxori et filiis magistri B. quondam Judei
ad fidem Christianam de infidelitate conversi"; No. 75 (1234): ". . .
dilectus filius Wilhelmus canonicus . . . , natus quondam magistri B.
Judei . . ." ; No. 76 (1234): "B., quondam Judei ad fidem Christianam
de Judaismo conversi"; No. 124 (1250): "Philippum patrem vestrum de
Judaice cecitatis tenebris conversum ad fidem Catholicam"; similarly
also in *Corpus juris canonici*. Numerous convincing examples from later
centuries are found in Peter Browe, "Die kirchenrechtliche Stellung der
getauften Juden und ihrer Nachkommen," pp. 3–22, 165–91. Browe, *Die
Judenmission im Mittelalter und die Päpste*, pp. 219 f.:

"Diese immer wiederholten Rückfälle liessen den mittelalterlichen
Christen fast alle Bekehrungen von Juden, auch derjenigen, die sich
freiwillig zum Übertritt gemeldet hatten, verdächtig erscheinen, und es
bildete sich allmählich die allgemeine Volksmeinung heraus, dass der
Jude auf alle Fälle Jude bleibe. Nicht wenige Sprichwörter gingen um,
die dieses Misstrauen zum Ausdruck brachten."

69. The legal and social status of converted Jews in the Middle Ages
demands thoroughgoing monographic treatment. The most recent essay
on this subject by Peter Browe, "Die kirchenrechtliche Stellung der
getauften Juden und ihrer Nachkommen," *Archiv für katholisches Kirchenrecht*, CXXI (1941), 3–22, 165–91, is devoted exclusively to the question
of "whether baptized Jews and their descendants became actually full-
fledged members of the Church, were received in religious orders, and
admitted to priesthood and bishophood." The older literature is scanty;
cf. Georg Phillips, *Kirchenrecht*, II (Regensburg, 1846), 400 ff.; Stobbe,
pp. 164–67, 268 f.; Julius Aronius, "Hermann der Prämonstratenser,"
Geiger's *ZGJD*, II (1888), 217–31; Reinhold Seeberg, *Hermann von
Scheda, ein jüdischer Proselyt des 12. Jahrhunderts* (Leipzig, 1891); Leopold
Lukas, "Judentaufen und Judaismus zur Zeit des Papstes Innocenz III.,"
*Beiträge zur Geschichte der deutschen Juden, Festschrift zum siebzigsten
Geburtstage Martin Philippsons* (Leipzig, 1916), pp. 25–38; Grayzel, *The
Church and the Jews in the XIIIth Century*, pp. 13–21. Much documentary
material and information are to be found in Fritz Baer, *Die Juden im
christlichen Spanien*, I, 1, 2 (Berlin, 1929, 1936), Index, *s.v.* "Conversos";
and in Browe, *Die Judenmission im Mittelalter und die Päpste, passim*.

70. Cf. G. Kisch, "Nationalism and Race," pp. 71 f. Their conversion, it was held, was ineffective. For these converts remained at heart
deeply attached to the ideals of their former brethren in faith; baptism
had not affected these *marranos* spiritually (cf. Cecil Roth, "Marranos
and Racial Antisemitism," *Jewish Social Studies*, II [1940], 241–43).
To draw from this the conclusion that "the prejudice which had pre-

viously been ostensibly religious became 'racial' " (Roth) means, indeed, reading modern racist conceptions into medieval sources where no justification can be found for such interpretation. That did Roth (*ibid.*, p. 243), faithfully leaning on Henry Charles Lea, *A History of the Inquisition of Spain*, I (New York, 1906), p. 126, who wrote: "Thus the hatred which of old had been merely a matter of religion had become a matter of race." Contradictory, however, are Roth's remarks on the "deliberate misbelief, considered typical of the New Christians," in his, "The Mediaeval Conception of the Jew" (above, n. 60), p. 176. The fact also deserves attention that the term "race" in Henry Charles Lea's days carried a meaning quite different from its present-day implications. The overwhelming evidence recently brought to light by Browe, "Die kirchenrechtliche Stellung der getauften Juden und ihrer Nachkommen," *passim*, and esp. pp. 188–91, leaves no doubt that it was really suspicion of infidelity in matters of faith alone which constantly endangered the New Christians in Spain. Racial sentiments must therefore be definitely denied because they were actually absent, not because "the original sources fail to call them by their modern names," as was recently implied by S. W. Baron, *Modern Nationalism and Religion* (New York and London, 1947), p. 276, n. 26. Baron, who, in principle, shares Roth's opinion, nevertheless attenuates it considerably in stating that only "indirectly" the church "contributed to some of the early manifestations of racialism in the treatment of the Iberian *conversos*" (*ibid.*, p. 15). Against Lea (*op. cit.*) and Hans Kohn (*The Idea of Nationalism*, p. 623, n. 31), both emphasizing certain disabilities imposed on *conversos* by Spanish guilds, see above, n. 50.

71. C. 7, X, *de rescriptis*, 1, 3:

". . . mandatum dedimus et praeceptum, ut dilectum filium nostrum P. praesentium latorem, qui de gente Judaeorum originem duxit, et divina gratia fidem Christi humiliter et devote suscepit . . . quod ecclesiastico beneficio dignus non immerito reputatur, receptis literis nostris in canonicum reciperent et praebendam, si qua vacaret, vel quam primo vacare contingeret, liberaliter sibi conferre deberent. . . . Pro eo vero, quod Judaeus extiterit, ipsum dedignari non debes."

72. The unusual choice of words in the papal decree was caused, in all probability, by the contents or text of the complaint of the converted prebend-seeker, who felt that he had been slighted only because of his Jewish origin. On a similar case under Pope Innocent IV and on papal letters in favor of Jewish converts to Christianity see Caro, *op. cit.*, I, 295, 497.

73. Ssp., I, 18, 3: "Dar zû behîlden se al ir alde recht, wâr iz weder der

kristlicher ê unde weder deme gelouben nicht ne was" (G. Kisch, *Sachsenspiegel and Bible*, pp. 122, 124).

74. G. Kisch, *Sachsenspiegel and Bible*, pp. 144 f.

75. Caro, *Sozial- und Wirtschaftsgeschichte der Juden*, I, 213: "Die Religion hat die soziale Klassenbildung verursacht, indem sie Lebensweise und Denkart bestimmend eine Scheidewand aufrichtete zwischen sonst Gleichstehenden."

76. Parkes, *The Jew in the Medieval Community*, p. 40; cf. also pp. 66, 221, 205 f.; also the comment by G. Kisch, *Historia Judaica*, II (1940), 52 f.

77. Caro's *Sozial- und Wirtschaftsgeschichte der Juden* is still outstanding and unsurpassed, although it is not complete and is in some respects antiquated. On Werner Sombart's *Die Juden und das Wirtschaftsleben* (1st ed.; Leipzig, 1911; English translation by M. Epstein, under the title, *The Jews and Modern Capitalism* [London and New York, 1913]), "one of the most deplorable publications of German scholarship," as L. Brentano called it ("eine der betrüblichsten Erscheinungen auf dem Gebiete der deutschen Wissenschaft"), cf. Brentano, *Die Anfänge des modernen Kapitalismus*, pp. 158–99. The polemical literature concerning that book is listed in Alfred Philipp, *Die Juden und das Wirtschaftsleben, eine antikritisch-bibliographische Studie* (Berlin University Ph.D. thesis; Strasbourg, 1919), which was published upon Sombart's suggestion and under his guidance and thus is not impartial. Cf. also Ignaz Schipper, "Anfänge des Kapitalismus bei den abendländischen Juden im früheren Mittelalter bis zum Ausgang des XII. Jahrhunderts," reprinted from *Zeitschrift für Volkswirtschaft, Sozialpolitik und Verwaltung*, Vol. XV (1906) [Vienna, 1907]. Bibliographical notes in Parkes, *op. cit.*, pp. 270 f.; Baron, *Proceedings*, XII (1942), 18 ff., nn. 29, 30, 34. For comparative aspects see Baron, "The Economic Views of Maimonides," in *Essays on Maimonides*, ed. S. W. Baron (New York, 1941), pp. 127–264. Cf. also the brief survey in Cecil Roth, "The Jews in the Middle Ages," *Cambridge Medieval History*, VII (Cambridge, 1932), 643 ff.; and a meritorious essay by Raphael Straus, "The Jews in the Economic Evolution of Central Europe," *Jewish Social Studies*, III (1941), 15–40.

78. Cf., also with reference to the two sentences which follow hereafter, August Oncken, *Geschichte der Nationalökonomie*, I (1st ed., Leipzig, 1902; 2d ed., Leipzig, 1920), 131, referring to Thomas Aquinas, *De regimine principum*, ii. 3; Horst Jecht, "Studien zur gesellschaftlichen Struktur der mittelalterlichen Städte," *Vierteljahrschrift für Sozial- und Wirtschaftsgeschichte*, XIX (1926), 57 ff., 82 f.; John A. Ryan, "The

Economic Philosophy of St. Thomas," in *Essays in Thomism*, ed. Robert E. Brennan (New York, 1942), pp. 252 ff.

79. In *Summa theologiae*, ii. 2. 77. 4, Thomas Aquinas pointed out that there is such a thing as trading for the public good, "to provide a house or a city with the necessities of life," which may be distinguished from trading "not for the necessities of life but for the sake of gain" (cf. G. G. Coulton, *Medieval Panorama* [Cambridge and New York, 1944], p. 333).

80. See above, p. 126.

81. See above, pp. 211 ff. and 217 f.

82. See above, pp. 228 f.

83. See above, p. 229.

84. See above, pp. 196 f. and 240 f.

85. See above, pp. 237 f.

86. See above, pp. 240 f.

87. See above, p. 126 and the immediately preceding notes.

88. See above, pp. 259 f.

89. See above, p. 240.

90. Wilhelm Roscher, "Die Stellung der Juden im Mittelalter, betrachtet vom Standpunkte der allgemeinen Handelspolitik," *Zeitschrift für die gesamte Staatswissenschaft*, XXXI (1875), 503–26; reprinted in Roscher's *Ansichten der Volkswirtschaft aus dem geschichtlichen Standpunkte*, II (3d ed.; Leipzig, 1878), 321–54; English translation by Solomon Grayzel, in *Historia Judaica*, VI (1944), 13–26. On Roscher, cf. Guido Kisch, "The Jews' Function in the Medieval Evolution of Economic Life," *Historia Judaica*, VI (1944), 1–12. Roscher (*op. cit.*, p. 511, n. 1) designates as his predecessor the German historian, Karl Dietrich Hüllmann: "Ein Keim der von uns hier entwickelten Ansicht findet sich bereits in Hüllmann, *Geschichte des Ursprungs der Regalien* [*in Deutschland*], [Frankfurt a.O., 1806], S. 54." The passage reads: "Von mehreren der berüchtigten Judenverfolgungen waren keineswegs blinder Religionseifer oder gewisse Verbrechen, die man den Juden andichtete, z.B. Vergiftung der Brunnen, die Ursache, sondern Verdruss über die Schuldenlast, von der sich der Haufe durch Vertreibung oder Ermordung der Gläubiger auf ein Mal befreien konnte. *Chronicon S. Petri Erfurtense*, *a.* 1349, *apud* Menken, *Scriptores Rerum Germanicarum*, T. III, col. 341: 'Credo, fuisse exordium eorum magnam et infinitam pecuniam, quam barones cum militibus, cives cum rusticis, ipsis solvere tenebantur.' "

91. Raphael Straus, "The Jews in the Economic Evolution of Central Europe," pp. 15–40.

92. Roscher, *Zeitschrift für die gesamte Staatswissenschaft*, XXXI (1875), 504, 506, 516, 511.

93. Heusler, *Institutionen des deutschen Privatrechts*, I, 149 f.; cf. Otto Gierke, *Deutsches Privatrecht*, I, 438, n. 2.

94. Forchhammer, *op. cit.*, pp. 122 ff., 132; Georg Liebe, "Die rechtlichen und wirtschaftlichen Zustände der Juden im Erzstift Trier," *Westdeutsche Zeitschrift für Geschichte und Kunst*, XII (1893), 316, 334; Liebe, "Die wirtschaftliche Bedeutung der Juden in der deutschen Vergangenheit," separate edition from *Jahrbücher der königlichen Akademie gemeinnütziger Wissenschaften zu Erfurt*, N.S., Heft XXVI (Erfurt, 1900), pp. 116 ff., (4 ff.); Karl G. Hugelmann, "Studien zum Recht der Nationalitäten im Mittelalter," p. 580, n. 32. Cf. also L. Erler, "Historisch-kritische Übersicht der nationalökonomischen und sozialpolitischen Literatur," *Archiv für katholisches Kirchenrecht*, XLII (1879), 35 ff., 73 ff.

95. Forchhammer (*op. cit.*, pp. 122 ff., 132) lays particular emphasis on commercial competition and jealousy. He considers the religious motives as of only secondary weight.

96. E.g., Ruth, "Wucher und Wucherrecht der Juden im Mittelalter," pp. 111–57; cf. G. Kisch, *Historia Judaica*, I (1938), 69.

97. George Caro, "Die Juden des Mittelalters in ihrer wirtschaftlichen Betätigung," *MGWJ*, XLVIII (1904), 587 f., 592 f., especially stressing the organization of handicraft in guilds "in which Jews participated as little as the patricians"; cf. also Caro, *Sozial- und Wirtschaftsgeschichte*, I, 198, 429 ff.; cf., however, Caro, *MGWJ*, XLVIII (1904), 597, 603, where some aspects of Roscher's theory are nevertheless accepted. Ignaz Schipper (*op. cit.* [above, n. 77], p. 3) finds fault with Roscher's methodology, particularly the adducing of evidence *per analogiam* but, nonetheless, accepts some of his views (pp. 26, 38). Julius Guttmann, "Die wirtschaftliche und soziale Bedeutung der Juden im Mittelalter," *MGWJ*, LI (1907), 280–84, propounds a whole series of interesting counterarguments of diverse nature. Eugen Täubler, "Zur Handelsbedeutung der Juden in Deutschland vor Beginn des Städtewesens," in *Beiträge zur Geschichte der deutschen Juden, Festschrift zum siebzigsten Geburtstage Martin Philippsons* (Leipzig, 1916), pp. 370–81, assembles all negative criteria against Roscher from the field of general economic history, maintaining that Roscher's theory was invalidated through the studies of Alfons Dopsch, *Die Wirtschaftsentwicklung der Karolingerzeit* (Weimar, 1913; 2d ed., 1921). According to Täubler, new detailed investigations are required to prepare an appropriate basis for reconsideration of the entire problem. Täubler's own contribution was confined to

early Jewish slave trade; the further studies in this field which he promised, unfortunately remained unpublished. Täubler's criticism of Roscher and Stobbe could not prevail, however (cf. Straus, p. 34). Salo W. Baron, "Nationalism and Intolerance," *Menorah Journal*, XVI (1929), 504 (reprint, p. 2), rejected Roscher's theory for its failure to explain the relation between the national structure of the state and the treatment accorded Jews throughout Diaspora history.

98. Karl Bücher, *Die Bevölkerung von Frankfurt am Main im XIV. und XV. Jahrhundert*, I (Tübingen, 1886), 572 f., 589 ff.; cf. Täubler, "Zur Handelsbedeutung der Juden in Deutschland," pp. 371, 377. Cf. *contra* also Georg Below, "Juden," in Hoops's *Reallexikon der Altertumskunde*, II (Strasbourg, 1913–15), 618.

99. Cf. Hoeniger, Geiger's *ZGJD*, I (1887), 78 f., 86 ff., 90 f., 93 f. (for criticism see Täubler, "Zur Handelsbedeutung der Juden . . . ," pp. 373 f., 377); Grayzel, "Christian-Jewish Relations in the First Millennium," p. 43; Baron, "The Jewish Factor in Medieval Civilization," *Proceedings*, XII (1942), 19 ff.; Straus, "The Jews in the Economic Evolution of Central Europe," pp. 21 ff., 30, 32 ff., and *passim*.

100. See above, n. 78. Cf. also Georg Brodnitz, *Englische Wirtschaftsgeschichte* (Jena, 1918), p. 327.

101. In his book, *The Jew in the Medieval Community*, Parkes did not enter into a critical discussion of Roscher's theory, unless the brief remarks on pp. 326 f. be regarded as such. Cf., however, Parkes, "Christian Influence on the Status of the Jews in Europe," *Historia Judaica*, I (1938), 34 ff., where Roscher's theory is tacitly assumed.

102. See above, p. 317.

103. Parkes, *The Jew in the Medieval Community*, p. 237.

104. Parkes, *ibid.*, p. 266. The italics are those of Parkes.

105. Investigation of the psychic behavior of the masses as a general postulate for modern research in legal history was rightfully emphasized by Hans Fehr, "Mehr Geistesgeschichte in der Rechtsgeschichte," *Deutsche Vierteljahrsschrift für Literaturwissenschaft und Geistesgeschichte*, V (1927), 7 f. Karl W. Deutsch ("Anti-Semitic Ideas in the Middle Ages: International Civilizations in Expansion and Conflict," *Journal of the History of Ideas*, VI [1945], 239–51) aims at a historical-sociological comparison between medieval and modern anti-Semitism, as to motives, techniques, and effects. Well-known historical events and social trends are reinterpreted in terms of "expansion and conflict" of "international civilizations." But Deutsch's "provisional and tentative conclusions" are based on secondary sources only and often even on thirdhand information alone. They suffer, moreover, from a complete lack of

understanding of the moving forces in medieval civilization and of the Jewish status in the Christian world in particular. In addition, the necessary differentiation of periods of history is missing. This article, merely playing with sociological conceptions and terms, does not add to our knowledge or make a contribution to the discussion of the problems involved.

106. Cf. Andreas Heusler, *Institutionen des deutschen Privatrechts*, I, 148.

107. Cecil Roth, "The Mediaeval Conception of the Jew: A New Interpretation," pp. 171–90, esp. pp. 174–76, 180 ff., 188 f., from which the quotations in the text are taken; cf. also Peter Browe, *Die Judenmission im Mittelalter und die Päpste*, pp. 111 f., 125, 293, 306 f.

108. James Parkes, *The Conflict of the Church and the Synagogue* (London, 1934), p. 158; Trachtenberg, *The Devil and the Jews: The Medieval Conception of the Jew and Its Relation to Modern Antisemitism*, p. 163. Cf. G. Kisch, "The 'Jewish Execution' in Mediaeval Germany," *Historia Judaica*, V (1943), 122 ff., with reference to the monkey symbolism applied in 1398 to a Jew, indicating that, as the monkey is like man in figure only, the Jew, too, has nothing in common with a human being except the human figure.

109. A. Lukyn Williams, *Adversus Judaeos: A Bird's-Eye View of Christian Apologiae until the Renaissance* (Cambridge, 1935); cf. also Baron, "The Jewish Factor in Medieval Civilization," p. 31 and n. 50.

110. Trachtenberg, *op. cit.*, *passim*. According to him (pp. 174–78), the Jew was looked upon in popular thinking as a heretic—indeed, *the* heretic.

111. So Roth, "The Mediaeval Conception of the Jew: A New Interpretation," p. 176 and n. 3.

112. See below, p. 347 and chap. xiii, n. 11.

113. On Heinrich der Teichner see above, p. 188 and n. 41; cf. also Theodor Georg von Karajan, "Über Heinrich den Teichner," *Denkschriften der kaiserlichen Akademie der Wissenschaften in Wien, phil.-hist. Klasse*, VI (Vienna, 1855), 131 f. According to Heinrich, many Christians are worse than the poor Jews:

> "Den armen judam
> ist manger unbillich gram,
> der vil böser ist denn er."

["Many a man, who is himself much worse, bears an unjust grudge against the poor Jew"]; Joseph Freiherr von Lassberg, *Liedersaal, das ist Sammelung altteutscher Gedichte*, III (St. Gallen and Konstanz, 1846), 223, 27 ff., 383; E. G. Gudde, *Social Conflicts in Medieval German Poetry*, pp. 74 ff. The quotation from Jan van Boendale reads in the original as follows:

> "Want mi dunct emmer dat si
> also wel menschen syn als wi
> ende oec comen van Adame."

Léon Vanderkindere, *Le Siècle des Artevelde: Études sur la civilisation morale et politique de la Flandre et du Brabant* (Brussels, 1879), p. 347, n. 1; cf. Gudde, *op. cit.*, pp. 61 f., 67. It is interesting to note that Jan van Boendale was a lawyer, namely, a clerk at the jury court (*Schöppenstuhl*) at Antwerp (cf. W. J. A. Jonckbloet, *Geschichte der niederländischen Literatur*, I [Leipzig, 1870], 259 ff.).

114. See above, pp. 275 ff.

115. See above, pp. 191 ff.

116. See above, pp. 40 f. and 55 f.

117. See above, pp. 299 ff.; cf. also Aronius, Geiger's *ZGJD*, II (1888), 230 f.

118. Stobbe, "Mitteilungen aus Breslauer Signaturbüchern," *Zeitschrift des Vereins für Geschichte und Altertum Schlesiens*, VIII (1867), 158 (*anno* 1434): ". . . Ipo jude . . . und hot geredt wider denselbin Franczken, her hette eczliche herren in dem rate, die im des wol beistendig wurden sein."

119. MS Breslau, R 568, No. 3.

120. Cf. Herbert Fischer, *Die verfassungsrechtliche Stellung der Juden in den deutschen Städten während des dreizehnten Jahrhunderts* (Breslau, 1931), pp. 45–53; however, there were also some elements unfriendly to the Jews, particularly in the lower strata of the city populations (cf. *ibid.*, p. 49, n. 4).

121. Cf. above, pp. 115 and chap. v, n. 16; 116 and chap. v, n. 22; chap. xii, n. 36.

122. See above, p. 311.

123. See above, pp. 323 f.

124. So Israel Abrahams, *Jewish Life in the Middle Ages* (London, 1896), pp. 400, 404 ff. Cf. Trachtenberg, *op. cit.*, pp. 161 ff., 207; Gudde, *op. cit.*, p. 107: "Attacks upon the Jews are less numerous in the folk songs than one would expect in view of the increased animosity against them after the great plague in the middle of the fourteenth century."

125. Cf. above, p. 191, and the literature cited in the notes, especially Parkes, *The Jew in the Medieval Community*, pp. 334 ff.

126. See above, chap. viii, n. 64.

127. Cf. Hoeniger, Geiger's *ZGJD*, I (1887), 97; Caro, *MGWJ*, XLVIII (1904), 592.

128. Cf. Stein, *Die Ungläubigen in der mittelhochdeutschen Literatur von 1050–1250*, pp. 74 f. It was left to the Teutonic knight-poet, Heinrich von Hesler, at the end of the thirteenth or in the beginning of the fourteenth century, "to voice for the first time that unreasonable hatred with which the Jews were pursued in the following centuries: he calls usury worse than robbery . . ." (Gudde, *op. cit.*, pp. 40 f.; cf. also below, chap. xiii, n. 47). Heinrich von Hesler, *Das Evangelium Nicodemi*, ed. Karl Helm ("Bibliothek des literarischen Vereins in Stuttgart," Vol. CCXXIV [Tübingen, 1902]), verses 4930 f., writes:

> "mit wucher ob irs geloubet,
> daz is arger dan geroubet";

verses 5279 ff.:

> "Welt ir juden vor u wesen
> und mit der judeschaft genesen,
> so lazet wucher und besuch,—
> wen daz vorbutet uwer buch,
> (daz ist allen den wol kundic,
> die der buche sint vorstundic,)
> und ist sunde und ouch schande."

Cf. also Karl Helm, "Untersuchungen über Heinrich Heslers Evangelium Nicodemi," in Paul and Braune, *Beiträge zur Geschichte der deutschen Sprache und Literatur*, XXIV (1899), 139 ff. The attitude of the poet toward the Jews in his other biblical paraphrase, the *Apokalypse*, is more moderate: he expresses the hope that the Jews will be converted. Like his contemporary, Heinrich von Hesler, a satirist known in literary history as "Seifried Helbling" also attacked the Jews with unrestrained violence (cf. Gudde, *op. cit.*, pp. 41, 45).

129. See above, p. 195.

130. See above, p. 127.

131. See above, chap. viii, n. 64.

132. See above, chap. viii, n. 64.

133. Cf., e.g., Max Neumann, *Geschichte des Wuchers in Deutschland*, *passim;* Georg Liebe, *Das Judentum in der deutschen Vergangenheit* (Leipzig, 1903; anti-Semitic), pp. 10, 22 ff.; Hans Fehr, *Das Recht in der Dichtung* (Bern, 1931), pp. 272, 541 f.; Trachtenberg, *op. cit.*, pp. 188–94.

134. For details concerning the attitude of medieval German poetry toward *wuocher* in this period see Erwin G. Gudde, *Social Conflicts in*

Medieval German Poetry, pp. 81 ff., 84, 87 f., 98, n. 298. One of Muskat-
blüt's attacks on the Jews reads:

> "Juodischer glaub vil [wil?] machen daube
> die cristenheit, ir gewalt ist breit
> und duot die werelt krenken.
> ir gebt friheit juodischer diet
> vur priesteren und vur leyen"

["The Jewish faith will ruin Christendom; its power is great and does
harm to the world. You give the Jewish people more liberty than priests
and laymen"]. E. von Groote, *Lieder Muskatblüts* (Cologne, 1852), 75,
19 ff.; Gudde, *op. cit.*, p. 82, n. 249 (wrong citation).

On the attitude of the minnesingers in the beginning of the fourteenth century see above, n. 128. Hugo von Trimberg (*ca.* 1260—after
1313) was comparatively tolerant toward the Jews. In his work, *Der
Renner*, he assails the power of *wuocher* by paraphrasing a passage from
Freidank's *Bescheidenheit* (cf. edition by H. E. Bezzenberger [Halle,
1872]), No. 27, ll. 1–6:

> "Got hât drîerleie kint,
> daz juden, kristen, heiden sint,
> daz vierde geschuof des tiufels list,
> daz dirre drîer meister ist:
> daz ist wuocher genant
> und roubet liute und ouch daz lant"

["God has three kinds of children: Jews, Christians, and heathen. The
fourth was created by the devil's cunning, and it is the master of these
three: it is called *wuocher* and it robs alike people and land"]. Gustav
Ehrismann, *Der Renner von Hugo von Trimberg*, I ("Bibliothek des
literarischen Vereins in Stuttgart," Vol. CCXLVII [Tübingen, 1908]),
vss. 5177–82; cf. Gudde, *op. cit.*, pp. 53 ff. In various places, Hugo puts
the Jews on a par with the Christians. His criticism of Christian merchants is much more biting than that of Jewish moneylenders (e.g.,
op. cit., vss. 4865–72):

"Lord God, I lament to Thee that spices, grain, silk, and wine, and
cloth, whose threads have not yet been spun and whose color has not
yet been exposed to the sun and air, are now sold by wicked Christians
who with cursed cunning make money in worse ways than the Jews,
who are called the devil's hounds."

Cf. also Schwsp., L 160, G 140; Freising Rb., Maurer II, 75, n. 29;
Knapp 212; above, chap. viii, n. 64. Even in the early part of the
fifteenth century a similar attitude was taken in the didactic poem, *Des*

Tüfels Segi ("The Devil's Net") (cf. Gudde, *op. cit.*, pp. 93 f.).

135. See above, p. 262.

136. See above, pp. 107–28.

137. See above, pp. 129–53, 166–68.

138. Cf. Horst Jecht, "Studien zur gesellschaftlichen Struktur der mittelalterlichen Städte," *Vierteljahrschrift für Sozial- und Wirtschaftsgeschichte*, XIX (1926), 83 ff.

139. See Caro, *op. cit.* (above, n. 97).

140. See above, pp. 308 ff. The concluding clause in Bishop Rüdiger's charter for the Jews of Speyer, of September 13, 1084 (Aronius, *op. cit.*, No. 168, p. 70) reads:

"Ad summam pro cumulo benignitatis concessi illis legem, quamcumque meliorem habet *populus judeorum* in qualibet urbe theutonici regni."

This is the only reference to the *populus judeorum* occurring in medieval German law sources that has come to the author's attention. That phrase, however, does not refer to the "Jewish people," the *jüdisches Volk*, as translated, with wrong interpretation of the entire passage, by Herbert Meyer, *Entwerung und Eigentum im deutschen Fahrnisrecht* (Jena, 1902), p. 194 (for criticism see G. Kisch, *Historia Judaica*, I [1938], 17 f.). The same error in translating the phrase *populus judeorum* was incurred independently by I. Elbogen, *Germania Judaica*, p. xxi, and by Solomon Zeitlin, "Judaism as a Religion," *Jewish Quarterly Review*, XXXIV (1943), 238. In contemporary sources of medieval town law, the term *populus* designates "community," *communitas, civitas, gemeinde*, as is evidenced by the instances listed in F. Keutgen, *Urkunden zur städtischen Verfassungsgeschichte* (Berlin, 1899), p. 632, *s.v.* "populus," "populares"; cf. also Du Cange, *Glossarium mediae et infimae latinitatis*, VI, 413, *s.v.* "2 populus"; Eugen Haberkern and Joseph F. Wallach, *Hilfswörterbuch für Historiker—Mittelalter und Neuzeit* (Berlin, 1935), pp. 432, *s.v.* "populus," 192 f., *s.v.* "Gemeinde, politische." Aronius (*op. cit.*, No. 168, p. 70) correctly translated "die Judenschaft."

141. See above, p. 308.

142. For details see G. Kisch, "Nationalism and Race in Medieval Law," pp. 61 ff.

143. See G. Kisch, *ibid.*, pp. 62 f.; see also above, p. 309.

144. See above, pp. 100 ff. and 172 f.

145. Cf. Roscher, *Zeitschrift für die gesamte Staatswissenschaft*, XXXI (1875), 504; English translation in *Historia Judaica*, VI (1944), p. 14. On the mutual Jewish-Christian relations up to the middle of the thir-

teenth century see Elbogen, *Germania Judaica*, pp. xxxiii–xxxvii; Parkes, *The Jew in the Medieval Community, passim;* Browe, *Die Judenmission im Mittelalter und die Päpste,* p. 64.

146. See G. Kisch, "Nationalism and Race in Medieval Law," p. 64. The dynamic factor in the process of this transformation seems to have been considerably underestimated by Otto Peterka, in *Wirtschaft und Kultur, Festschrift zum 70. Geburtstag von Alfons Dopsch* (Baden bei Wien, 1938), p. 655; and by Kohn, *The Idea of Nationalism,* pp. 107 ff.

147. Such a relationship of causality, as a historical law with no exceptions, was suggested by Salo W. Baron in his "Nationalism and Intolerance," *Menorah Journal,* XVI (1929), 503–15; XVII (1929), 148–58; *A Social and Religious History of the Jews,* II, 38 ff.; III, 107 f.; "The Jewish Factor in Medieval Civilization," *Proceedings,* XII (1942), 40 f. and nn. 64, 65; *Modern Nationalism and Religion,* p. 20. Baron concedes (*Proceedings,* XII, p. 41, n. 65) that "in Germany and Italy, particularly, the operation of these factors [*sc.* nationalism and religious intolerance] was greatly complicated by the conflict between Papacy and Empire, the struggle between the imperial and the territorial powers, etc." Nonetheless, he pleads for full validity of his theory with regard to those countries also. As far as Germany in the medieval period is concerned, the evidence adduced in the above text is opposed to that assumption. Apart from this fact, to consider Germany as consisting of "numerous *Nationalteilstaaten,*" of which "each small subdivision was a State embracing only part of a nationality" (*Menorah Journal,* XVI, 512; p. 10 of the reprint) will hardly correspond to the actual political state of medieval Germany and its conception in contemporary law and public opinion (cf. G. Kisch, "Nationalism and Race in Medieval Law," pp. 57–64).

148. See above, pp. 145–53.

149. G. Kisch, "Otto Stobbe und die Rechtsgeschichte der Juden," *JGJC,* IX (1938), 1–11.

150. Cf. the recent evaluations by Parkes, *The Jew in the Medieval Community,* pp. 79–89, and Trachtenberg, *op. cit.,* pp. 167 ff., and *passim.* Cf. also Heinrich Mitteis, "Beaumanoir und die geistliche Gerichtsbarkeit," *ZRG,* XXXV, kanon. Abt. IV (1914), 296, n. 2: "Schon Heinrich Brunner hat in der *Entstehung der Schwurgerichte* (Berlin, 1872), S. 324, wenn auch in anderem Zusammenhange, auf einen rechtlichen Niederschlag der wirtschaftlichen Bewegung, die durch die Kreuzzüge hervorgerufen wurde, hingewiesen."

151. Trachtenberg, *op. cit.,* pp. 166 f. The following quotation is from

Trachtenberg (*ibid.*, p. 161). Within the realm of Middle High German poetry, Heinrich von Hesler seems to have been the first German poet who attacked the Jews as a group within the social system (cf. above, n. 128). In the fourteenth century, Barthel Regenbogen, blacksmith and wandering minstrel, also directed against the Jews invectives which were primarily dictated by religious animosity. His unrestrained desire to exterminate the Jewish element gives them a highly social-political significance. "I hate you Jews beyond measure" ("ich hazze iuch juden sunder maze") is the refrain of his abusive poems. For details and specimens of this type of poetry see Gudde, *Social Conflicts in Medieval German Poetry*, pp. 71 f.

152. Cf. the lists of regional expulsions of the Jews from German cities in the fifteenth century in Forchhammer, *op. cit.*, p. 141, n. 152, and p. 146; and *Encyclopaedia Judaica*, II (Berlin, 1928), 986.

153. Cf. also Forchhammer, *op. cit.*, pp. 128 ff.; Joseph Hansen, *Quellen und Untersuchungen zur Geschichte des Hexenwahns und der Hexenverfolgung im Mittelalter* (Bonn, 1901); Hans Fehr, *Massenkunst im 16. Jahrhundert* (Berlin, 1924), pp. 22 ff.; Hanns Bächtold-Stäubli, *Handwörterbuch des deutschen Aberglaubens*, III, 1827 ff.

154. On this subject see the several items in Trachtenberg, *op. cit.*, Bibliography, pp. 256-67; cf. also M. Blakemore Evans, *The Passion Play of Lucerne: An Historical and Critical Introduction* ("Modern Language Association of America, Monograph Series," Vol. XIV [New York, 1943]), with bibliography on pp. 242-45; on the Jews in Catholic legends in particular see Heinrich Loewe, *Die Juden in der katholischen Legende* (Berlin, 1912), p. 62.

155. Cf. Fehr, *op. cit.*, pp. 3 ff.; G. Kisch, "The Yellow Badge in History," *Historia Judaica*, IV (1942), 102 f. (12 f. of the separate edition).

156. Cf. the reproduction in Liebe, *Das Judentum in der deutschen Vergangenheit*, p. 20, picture No. 15. Only in the middle or second half of the fifteenth century, it seems, did the so-called "Jewish nose" become an attribute characteristic of Jews (cf. G. Kisch, "The Yellow Badge in History," p. 103). The sole reference to this distinctive mark in a non-pictorial document from the Middle Ages known to this author is from the year 1451. Jacobus Grunow, "a priest and scribe of Magdeburg," demanded legal aid from the municipal council of Zerbst, Anhalt, against a fraudulent citizen of Zerbst who previously had sold bad beer to him. Since Grunow was unable to ascertain his identity, he gave a detailed personal description, which contained the following passage: ". . . dat gij en deste bat kennen, he heft en lang antlat mit eyner langen nesen und is also en jode geschapen unde spricket ok also"

(". . . that you may recognize him the better: he has a long face with a long nose and is formed like a Jew and also speaks like one"); Gustav Hertel, *Urkundenbuch der Stadt Magdeburg*, II ("Geschichtsquellen der Provinz Sachsen," Vol. XXVII [Halle, 1894]), No. 608, p. 633. This document was also quoted by Forchhammer, *op. cit.*, p. 122, n. 27, and by Liebe, *Die wirtschaftliche Bedeutung der Juden in der deutschen Vergangenheit* (see above, n. 94), p. 121 (9). Both (anti-Semitic) authors omitted, however, to relate the aforementioned details characteristic of this case and important for its historical evaluation.

157. See the reproduction in *Encyclopaedia Judaica*, IX (Berlin, 1932), 403–4.

158. The best reproduction in multicolor is found in *Philo-Lexikon, Handbuch des jüdischen Wissens* (Berlin, 1936), pl. 7, facing pp. 151–52.

159. See the reproductions in Guido Kisch, *Jewry-Law in Medieval Germany: Laws and Court Decisions Concerning Jews* (New York, 1949), facing pp. 38, 50. The fact that no caricatural connotation attaches to the pictorial representations of Jews in the illuminated *Sachsenspiegel* manuscripts can be best demonstrated by their comparison with actual caricatural features occurring in the same manuscripts. In the illumination on *Sachsenspiegel*, *Lehnrecht*, 78, 3, for instance, the enemies of the law are symbolized in two figures, one of which, with head thrown back, makes a rejecting gesture, while the other, ugly of profile and with an expression of hatred, spits and kicks at the author of the *Sachsenspiegel*. The latter, manifestly no Jew, is portrayed with a nose of exaggerated dimension. This picture is reproduced in G. Kisch, *Speculum*, XIV (1939), plate facing p. 43, and in G. Kisch, *Sachsenspiegel and Bible*, pl. 8, facing p. 122; cf. also *ibid.*, p. 125; Karl von Amira, *Die Dresdener Bilderhandschrift des Sachsenspiegels*, Vol. II: *Erläuterungen*, Part II, p. 332.

160. So Trachtenberg, *op. cit.*, p. 163; similarly, Cecil Roth, "The Mediaeval Conception of the Jew," p. 190: "On the assumption advanced in the foregoing pages, it is possible to acquit the ordinary man of the Middle Ages of unreasoning cruelty in his relations with a people whom he was encouraged to consider in so distorted a light, but not our own contemporaries, who have revived an equally preposterous conception in this enlightened age." The very fact that Roth would not acquit our own contemporaries does not lend much support to his first judgment, for the absence of modern enlightenment holds equally true of medieval theology. And "the medieval mind was as keen, as logical, and as eminently reasonable as is ours," as Roth (*ibid.*, p. 173) correctly recognized.

CHAPTER THIRTEEN

1. A detailed exposition is found in G. Kisch, *Sachsenspiegel and Bible* (Notre Dame, Ind., 1941), pp. 118 ff. Cf. also Maria Mackensen, "Soziale Forderungen und Anschauungen der früh-mittelhochdeutschen Dichter," *Neue Heidelberger Jahrbücher*, N.F., Jahrbuch 1925 (Heidelberg, 1925), pp. 146–48.

2. For a detailed exposition see Fritz Kern, "Recht und Verfassung im Mittelalter," *Historische Zeitschrift*, CXX (1919), 1–79; Kern, *Kingship and Law in the Middle Ages* (Oxford, 1939). Cf. Otto von Gierke, *Der germanische Staatsgedanke* (Berlin, 1919), p. 27: "Den grossen germanischen Gedanken, dass sich alle staatliche Willensmacht vor der sittlichen Macht des Rechtes zu beugen hat, . . ."

3. For details see Helmut Hillmann, *Das Gericht als Ausdruck deutscher Kulturentwicklung im Mittelalter* (Stuttgart, 1930), pp. 87 ff.

4. Gustav Homeyer, *Die deutschen Rechtsbücher des Mittelalters und ihre Handschriften* (Weimar, 1931–34), No. 642; Ferdinand Bischoff, "Beiträge zur Geschichte des Magdeburgerrechtes," *Sitzungsberichte der philosophisch-historischen Klasse der kaiserlichen Akademie der Wissenschaften zu Wien*, L (1865), p. 339:

"Ich swere gote und meynem herre dem konige und dem gerichte, do ich czu gekorn bin, das ich dem richter noch dem rechte gehorsam wil seyn, und den leuten arm und reych in dem lande rechte orteil fünden wil und den scheppen stuel noch dem deutcze rechte vorsten wil, so ich rechte konne und wisse und des folge haben wurde und den durch keyne sache noch durch liebe adir gobe lossen wil als mir got helfe und dy heyligen."

5. MS Breslau, R 568, fol. 375r: ". . . wenn der richter sal eym iczlichin helffin, das ym gerecht geschee, wenne her das geheisen wirt." *Sachsenspiegel*, Prologue, ll. 11–14: "Dâr umme sên sie sich vore alle die, den gerichte van gottis halven bevolen ist, daz sie alsô richten, daz gottis zorn unde sîn gerichte gnêdelîchin obir sie irgân mûze." *Magdeburger Fragen*, I, 3, 2: "Alle schrifft syn den luten geschreben unde gegeben zcu wissentschafft unde zcu lere. Hirumb wer eyn scheppe ist unde gesworen hat zcu dem rechte, der mag noch syner redelicheit synes besten synnes unde noch wissenheit der schriffte unde des rechten orteil vinden uff synen eid." Cf. also Hillmann, *op. cit.*, p. 127.

6. This seems not to have been the attitude of German courts toward Jews in the sixteenth and seventeenth centuries; in the words of a Christian observer, Christian Gottlob Haltaus, "jus haud raro male redditum postulantibus [judaeis], ita ut non tam judicati quam elusi viderentur"

(Haltaus, *Glossarium Germanicum medii aevi* [Leipzig, 1758,] p. 1044).

7. See also, with reference to the expositions following in the text, G. Kisch, "The Jews in Medieval Law," *Essays on Antisemitism*, ed. K. S. Pinson (New York, 1942), pp. 61–63; (2d ed., New York, 1946), pp. 106–8.

8. For a detailed discussion see G. Kisch, "Die Rechtsstellung der Wormser Juden im Mittelalter," *ZGJD*, V (1934), 126–31 (pp. 7–12 of the reprint). The political and legal status of the Jews in the medieval cities, despite numerous monographs on various Jewish communities, still calls for comprehensive treatment by a legal historian (cf. Kisch, "Research in Medieval Legal History of the Jews," *Proceedings*, VI [1934–35], pp. 273 ff.; also Baron, "The Jewish Factor in Medieval Civilization," *Proceedings*, XII [1942], 39, n. 60). "Citizenship of Jews in Medieval Cities," a study on a restricted problem, namely, the legal position of the Jews in the light of the medieval concepts of citizen, *Bürger*, and denizen, *Einwohner*, is being prepared by the author. The precise meaning of the term *Bürger*, at times explicitly applied to Jews in thirteenth- and fourteenth-century documents, needs elucidation. According to Otto Stobbe, *Die Juden in Deutschland während des Mittelalters* (Braunschweig, 1866), pp. 38 f., "ist dies nur im uneigentlichen Sinne zu nehmen," the term being used either "merely to differentiate Jews permanently residing in a city from transient visitors" or to point out their inclusion in the city's peace. This opinion was accepted by later students without independent re-examination of the sources. For the present, far-reaching generalizations can naturally not be drawn from the legal situation in Worms. On Jewish craftsmen in medieval German cities see I. Elbogen, *Germania Judaica*, p. xxxii and n. 152.

9. Cf., as a counterpart, the keystone in the anti-Jewish "legislation" of National Socialist Germany, a law promulgated as late as 1943, by which the competence to pass judgment over Jews was transferred from the courts to the police. Thereby Jews were denied any recourse to judicial investigation and trial (Thirteenth Decree under the Reich Citizens' Law of April 1, 1933; English translation in *Jewish Comment*, I, No. 13 [October 8, 1943], 1; cf. Robert Kempner, "Hitlers neuester Schlag: Gerichte nicht mehr für Juden zuständig," *Aufbau-Reconstruction*, IX [August 6, 1943], 1).

10. G. Kisch, "Jewry-Law in Central Europe—Past and Present," *Journal of Central European Affairs*, II (1943), 401 f.; G. Kisch, "Research," pp. 259 f. Cf. Otto Gierke, *Das deutsche Genossenschaftsrecht*, III (Berlin, 1881), 517 ff.; Gierke, *Political Theories of the Middle Age [sic]*, trans. Frederic W. Maitland (Cambridge, 1900), pp. 9 ff.; Eduard Eich-

mann, *Acht und Bann im Reichsrecht des Mittelalters* (Paderborn, 1909), pp. 5 f.; Selma Stern, "Das Judenproblem im Wandel der Staatsformen," *ZGJD*, II (1930), 2 ff.; Willy Andreas, *Deutschland vor der Reformation* (2d ed.; Stuttgart, 1934), pp. 375–79; Fritz Baer, "Palestine and Galut in the Medieval Conception" (Hebrew), *Zion*, VI (1934), 153–55; also Hans Kohn, *The Idea of Nationalism: A Study in Its Origins and Background* (New York, 1944), pp. 79, 82; Ernst H. Kantorowicz, "The Problem of Medieval World Unity," in *The Quest for Political Unity in World History*, ed. for the American Historical Association by Stanley Pargellis (Vol. III of the *Annual Report of the American Historical Association for the Year 1942* [Washington, D.C., 1944]), pp. 31–37; Gerhard B. Ladner, "Aspects of Mediaeval Thought on Church and State," *Review of Politics*, IX (1947), 403–22.

11. It was a confirmation of King Přemysl Otakar II's Jewry privilege of 1268 (cf. Bertold Bretholz, *Quellen zur Geschichte der Juden in Mähren vom XI. bis zum XV. Jahrhundert (1067–1411)* [Prague, 1935], No. 16, p. 11). The *arenga* in its contemporaneous German translation was published by Emil Franz Rössler, *Die Stadtrechte von Brünn aus dem XIII. und XIV. Jahrhundert* (Prague, 1852), p. 367:

"Merchent und vornement alle di nu in disem alter lebent, di leut, und di hernach chunftig werdent, di rede diser hantveste, daz etwen der juden vater ier poshait wegangen und erczaiget habent an unserem herren Jesu Christo, gotes sun, dez lemtigen, der hantvest des angeporn rechtes weraubet sint und in di sunde der vordampnusse iemerleich vurvuert sint; und wie si uns doch gleich sein an der gestalt der menschlichen natur und wir mit unserm heilichen christenleichen gelauben von in gesundert sein, so lert uns christenleich guet daz, daz wier ab schullen werfen unsir hertichait und schullen unser guet warten czu in; und schullen die menshait an in lieb haben und nicht irn unglauben."

On the spiritual and moral dignity of man and the divinely ordained rights of man, according to Christian teaching, cf. Anton-Hermann Chroust, "The Corporate Idea and the Body Politic in the Middle Ages," *Review of Politics*, IX (1947), 450.

12. Baron, *Proceedings*, XII (1942), pp. 34 ff.; S. W. Baron, *A Social and Religious History of the Jews*, II (New York, 1937), 46 f.; S. W. Baron, "Ghetto and Emancipation," *Menorah Journal*, XIV (1928), 516–20 (pp. 2–6 of the reprint). Cf. Cecil Roth, "The Jews in the Middle Ages," *Cambridge Medieval History*, VII (Cambridge, 1932), 647: "Their [the Jews'] relations with the government were essentially as a collective body. . . . Of the manifold corporations of the Middle Ages, that of the Jews was perhaps the closest and the most rigidly controlled, for

there was no way out of it except through apostasy." See also Joshua Trachtenberg, *The Devil and the Jews: The Medieval Conception of the Jew and Its Relation to Modern Antisemitism* (New Haven, 1943), pp. 167, 176 f.

In this connection an interesting theory may be recalled, which was propounded eighty years ago. In his review of Stobbe's work on the legal history of German Jewry, Konrad Maurer emphasized the corporate structure of the political and legal organization in medieval Germany and its significance for the status of the Jews. This sociological aspect accounts, according to Maurer—and in contrast to Baron—for the oppression and the persecutions of the Jews in medieval Germany. This is, incidentally, a reflection of the "lachrymose conception of Jewish history" transmitted to Maurer by Stobbe from one of its protagonists, the Jewish historian, Heinrich Graetz. The pertinent passage from Maurer's review may be reproduced here in the original German wording:

"Der eigentümliche Standpunkt, von welchem aus die rechtliche Behandlung der Juden im Mittelalter normiert wurde, und welcher insbesondere auch zu deren Unterwerfung unter den besonderen Schutz des Königs oder seiner Vertreter führte, ist an und für sich ganz und gar nicht aus einer besonderen Gehässigkeit gegen das Judentum hervorgegangen, sondern lediglich eine Konsequenz der genossenschaftlichen Struktur der älteren germanischen Rechtsordnung in Verbindung mit der Tatsache, dass der Jude seiner Nationalität und Sitte wie seinem Glauben und Recht nach von der Gemeinschaft der Christen und Deutschen sich schied. Aber allerdings ist richtig, dass jener Standpunkt die Möglichkeit verschaffte, in aller Form Rechtens die Juden in unbilligster Weise zu drücken, und dass von dieser Möglichkeit in mehr als reichlichem Masse Gebrauch gemacht wurde" (Konrad Maurer, *Kritische Vierteljahrsschrift für Gesetzgebung und Rechtswissenschaft*, IX [1867], 574, cf. also 578 f.; cf. also G. Kisch, "Otto Stobbe und die Rechtsgeschichte der Juden," *JGJC*, IX [1938], 9 f.).

This theory, closely linked to the "alien" doctrine, was discussed and, for interesting reasons, rejected by Andreas Heusler, *Institutionen des deutschen Privatrechts*, I (Leipzig, 1885), 150 f., although he himself regarded the Jews as foreigners nationally and ethnically (see above, chap. xii, n. 10); cf. also Jean Juster, *Les Juifs dans l'empire romain*, II (Paris, 1914), 27, n. 1.

13. Cf. Otto Gierke, *Das deutsche Genossenschaftsrecht*, I (Berlin, 1868), 337 f.: "Als besondere Gemeinden in der Stadt sind ferner die Judengemeinden hervorzuheben, welche eine zugleich lokal und per-

sönlich von der Bürgerschaft abgesonderte Genossenschaft bildeten. . . .
Ganz wie die Bürgerschaft in der Stadt und vielfach in direkter Nachah-
mung derselben hatte aber diese Genossenschaft eine besondere Organisation. . . ."

14. Cf. above, p. 138 and chap. vi, n. 31; and chap. xii, n. 140.

15. Cf. Richard Krautheimer, "Die Synagoge zu Worms," *ZGJD*, V
(1934), 90 ff.; G. Kisch, "Die Rechtsstellung der Wormser Juden im
Mittelalter," *ZGJD*, V (1934), 122 f.

16. Cf. A. Epstein, "Der Wormser Judenrat," *MGWJ*, XLVI (1902),
157 ff.; Kisch, "Die Rechtsstellung der Wormser Juden im Mittelalter,"
pp. 122 f., 132 f.; similarly in Schweidnitz, Silesia, cf. Heinrich Gottfried Gengler, *Deutsche Stadtrechtsaltertümer* (Erlangen, 1882), p. 104.
In Worms the Jewish community council consisted of twelve members
elected for life; in Schweidnitz it numbered four, and elections took
place annually.

17. As to *Judenmeister*, cf. Adolf Kober, article "Judenmeister,"
Jüdisches Lexikon, III, 433 f.; as to *Judenbischof*, see Gengler, *op. cit.*,
pp. 103 f.; H. J. Zimmels, *Beiträge zur Geschichte der Juden in Deutschland
im 13. Jahrhundert* (Vienna, 1926), pp. 41, 123; Adolf Kober, article
"Judenbischof," *Jüdisches Lexikon*, III, 416 f.; Kisch, "Die Rechtsstellung der Wormser Juden im Mittelalter," pp. 132 f.; Simon Goldmann,
"Die jüdische Gerichtsverfassung innerhalb der jüdischen Gemeindeorganisation, ein Beitrag zur Geschichte des Judenbischofs im Mittelalter in seiner Entwicklung von den ältesten Zeiten bis zum 15. Jahrhundert" (University of Cologne unpublished Ph.D. thesis, 1924),
pp. 24-40; esp. p. 30:

". . . Als genossenschaftliche Korporationen wurden auch die Judengemeinden des Mittelalters (*universitas judeorum*), die sich allerdings
schon lange vor dieser um die Mitte des 12. Jahrhunderts begonnenen
Entwicklung auf der Grundlage ihres althergebrachten ausgebildeten
Rechts aus sich selbst heraus organisiert hatten, betrachtet, und in
Analogie dazu wurden auch für ihre Vorsteher ähnliche Bezeichnungen
gewählt. Wir haben es somit nicht mit einer den Gilden und Zünften
parallel sich bildenden Entwicklung zu tun, sondern mit einer von
aussen herantretenden analogen Begriffsübertragung. Die Namen 'Judenbischof' und 'Judenpapst' sind aber unzweifelhaft in Analogie zu den
höchsten Würdenträgern der katholischen Kirche, den Inhabern der
geistlichen Gerichtsbarkeit, gewählt und wollen damit einen geistlichen Würdenträger bezeichnet wissen, ebenso wie der Titel 'Hoch-
meister' der christlichen Ordensverfassung entlehnt ist."

Cf. also Baron, "Rashi and the Community of Troyes," *Rashi An-*

niversary Volume ("Texts and Studies," Vol. I, pub. by the American Academy for Jewish Research [New York, 1941]), p. 57: "It has long been suspected that the extensive synodal activity of Franco-German Jewry, which so obviously marked a complete departure from the long established practice of the Mediterranean communities, owed its origin to the example set by the provincial councils of the Church."

18. Arthur Zuckerman, *Speculum*, XXII (1947), 658, for example, suggests that "the term *Ḥerem Hayyishub* ('ban of settlement') is the Hebrew equivalent, if not translation, of a medieval legal concept. In all likelihood, the *bannus civitatis* or *Burgbann* connoting exclusive jurisdiction, and the *Bannmeile*, defining a trade monopoly, were included in the original meaning of *Ḥerem Hayyishub*. Similarly, the related *Ḥerem Bet Din* ('judicial ban') is a Hebrew equivalent of a medieval legal concept and signifies the immunity enjoyed by a local Jewry from the jurisdiction of another community, the *jus de non evocando*."

19. Cf., e.g., S. W. Baron, *The Jewish Community: Its History and Structure to the American Revolution*, II (Philadelphia, 1942), 55 f.

20. Heusler, *op. cit.*, p. 151: "Das Judenrecht des Mittelalters ist ein aus zufälligen und verschiedenartigen Begünstigungen und Beschränkungen zusammengesetztes Privilegienrecht."

21. On this subject, cf. Baron, *Proceedings*, XII (1942), 44. The state of permanent instability, however, was by no means something peculiar to the Jewish status alone. It applied in general to the law of privilege and to any legal status based on it. This was well observed and aptly pointed out by Peter Krebil (d. 1484), member of the municipal council of Breslau, who stated:

"Previlegium heen, previlegium her. Wenne der herre genadig ist, so sinth dy previlegia nütze und gut. Wil der landisherre abir ungenadig sein, so sintd sy wenig nütze. Dorumbe müs man ofte dem landishern gebin unde sich demüttiglich dinstlich irczeygen, uff das man recht und previlegia behalden mag in genade."

["Privilege or no privilege. If the prince is gracious, the privileges are useful and good; but if the prince should become ungracious, they are of little use. Therefore one must frequently give offerings to the prince and must serve him in humility in order to keep rights and privileges through his grace."]

This statement, which "Peter Krebil dixit et experiencia docet," was reproduced on the front page of a manuscript collection of privileges of the city of Breslau (cf. Theodor Goerlitz, "Der Verfasser der Breslauer Rechtsbücher *Rechter Weg* und *Remissorium*," *Zeitschrift des Vereins für Geschichte Schlesiens*, LXX [1936], 199).

22. Attention has rightly been directed to the fact that the church employed the term "Jew" as all-inclusive, embracing the totality of Jews, past, present, and future. The principle of corporate responsibility prevailing during the Middle Ages lent added force to the traditional generalization (cf. Trachtenberg, *op. cit.*, p. 167; Peter Browe, "Die Judenbekämpfung im Mittelalter," *Zeitschrift für katholische Theologie*, LXII [1938], 383 f.).

23. An exhaustive investigation and presentation of medieval church legislation concerning the Jews in comparison with secular Jewry-law and the mutual influences of both is a most important and pressing desideratum of the legal history of the Jews. As for medieval Germany, the two valuable publications of pertinent sources available (besides Aronius) are both limited in scope: Moritz Stern, *Urkundliche Beiträge über die Stellung der Päpste zu den Juden*, Vol. I (Kiel, 1893), Vol. II, Part I (Kiel, 1895); Solomon Grayzel, *The Church and the Jews in the XIIIth Century* (Dropsie College Ph.D. thesis; Philadelphia, 1933); still valuable is the survey by Selig Cassel in his article "Juden (Geschichte)," in Ersch and Gruber, *Encyklopädie der Wissenschaften und Künste*, II, Part 27 (Leipzig, 1850), 70–84; cf. also Konrad Eubel, "Zu dem Verhalten der Päpste gegen die Juden," *Römische Quartalschrift für christliche Altertumskunde und für Kirchengeschichte*, XIII (1899), 29–42 and XVII (1903), 183–87; Max Simonsohn, *Die kirchliche Judengesetzgebung im Zeitalter der Reform-Konzilien von Konstanz und Basel* (University of Freiburg i.B. Ph.D. thesis; Breslau, 1912). These are comparatively small but important segments. The treatises by L. Erler, "Die Juden des Mittelalters: Die Päpste und die Juden," *Archiv für katholisches Kirchenrecht*, XLVIII (1882), 369–416; L (1883), 3–64; LIII (1885), 3–70, though written from a most extreme anti-Semitic viewpoint, are still useful as guides to the sources and for their bibliographical notes. Cf. also L. Erler, "Historisch-kritische Übersicht der nationalökonomischen und sozialpolitischen Literatur," *Archiv für katholisches Kirchenrecht*, XLI (1879), 75–96; XLII (1879), 3–80; XLIII (1880), 361–408; XLIV (1880), 353–416. For bibliography see G. Kisch, "Research," p. 275, n. 106; Grayzel, *op. cit.*, pp. 359–64; Baron, *A Social and Religious History of the Jews*, III, p. 109, n. 20; Baron, *Proceedings*, XII (1942), pp. 41 f., n. 66; also above, chap. xii, n. 69. In addition to the works enumerated there, Parkes's *The Jew in the Medieval Community* (London, 1938) and the studies of Peter Browe (see below, n. 26) deserve scholars' attention; cf. also Willibrord Lampen, "Alexander von Hales und der Antisemitismus," *Franziskanische Studien*, XVI (1929), 1–14; Cecil Roth, "The Popes and the Jews," *Church Quarterly Review*, CXXIII (London,

1936), 75–92; Grayzel, article "Popes," *Universal Jewish Encyclopedia*, VIII (1942), 587–99; Grayzel, "The Avignon Popes and the Jews," *Historia Judaica*, II (1940), 1–12; George La Piana, "Catholic Church," in the encyclopedia, "The Jews" (New York, to appear in 1950); Parkes, "Christian Influence on the Status of the Jews in Europe," *Historia Judaica*, I (1938), 31–38.

24. Grayzel, *The Church and the Jews, passim;* Grayzel, "Christian-Jewish Relations in the First Millennium," *Essays on Antisemitism*, ed. K. S. Pinson, esp. pp. 41–44. Grayzel's opinion is fully shared and elaborated on in great detail by Parkes, *The Jew in the Medieval Community, passim*, esp. pp. 84 ff., 383 ff.; also Parkes, *Historia Judaica*, I (1938), 33. Opposed to this "scholastically long outworn conception" is Baron, *Proceedings*, XII (1942), p. 42, n. 66.

25. Baron, *Proceedings*, XII (1942), pp. 37 f., 41, 45, 47; cf. also Baron, *A Social and Religious History of the Jews*, II, 44–48. Baron's interpretation of the church's attitude toward the Jews is strongly influenced by his doctrine of "nationalism and intolerance."

26. Peter Browe, S.J., "Die Judenbekämpfung im Mittelalter," *Zeitschrift für katholische Theologie*, LXII (1938), 197–231, 349–84, and *passim*, esp. pp. 382–84; Browe, "Die religiöse Duldung der Juden im Mittelalter," *Archiv für katholisches Kirchenrecht*, CXVIII (1938), 3–76, *passim*, esp. p. 76; and, particularly, Browe, *Die Judenmission im Mittelalter und die Päpste* (Rome, 1942), *passim;* cf. also Browe, "Die Judengesetzgebung Justinians," *Analecta Gregoriana*, VIII (1935), 109–46.

27. Cf. Parkes, *The Jew in the Medieval Community*, pp. 215 f.; Parkes, *Historia Judaica*, I (1938), p. 34.

28. Cf. Grayzel, *The Church and the Jews*, pp. 76 ff.

29. "Quae eis concessa sunt," in Innocent III's *Constitutio pro Judaeis* of 1199, in Grayzel, *The Church and the Jews*, p. 92.

30. See above, p. 245.

31. See above, p. 203.

32. See above, pp. 203 f.

33. See above, p. 205.

34. See pp. 295 ff. and 291 ff.

35. See pp. 195 f.

36. See pp. 164 ff., where also can be found references to the influence of the theological doctrine and canon Jewry-law on other lawbooks.

37. See pp. 323 ff.

38. See pp. 327 ff.

39. See pp. 143–53.

40. That aim and effect of the canon-law regulations were first em-

phasized, though not fully expounded and evaluated, by George Caro (*MGWJ*, XLVIII [1904], 588–91, 601 f.), who did not even include it, still less elaborate it, in his *Sozial- und Wirtschaftsgeschichte der Juden* (Leipzig, 1908) (cf. the remark in I, 457). According to Konrad von Ammenhausen, a Swiss cleric, who completed his *Schachzabelbuch* in 1337, Christians should be separated socially from the Jews because of the pertinent rules of the canon law:

> "Und wissent niht, das man alsô list
> an dem rehtbuoch, das dâ heist decrêt,
> dâ alsô geschriben stêt,
> das man sol merken gar wol,
> das weder pfaffe noch leije sol
> der juden brôt niht essen.
> ouch sol man niht vergessen,
> das dâbî geschriben stât,
> dâ das selb rehtbuoch geboten hât,
> das kein kristan mit in sol wonung hân
> in ir hûse; ouch vint man stân,
> das kein kristaner siech ir rât sol nemen
> noch ir arzenîe im lân gezemen
> noch in einem bade mit in baden
> noch juden zuo der kristanen wirtschaft laden
> noch kein kristan zuo der juden wirtschaft gân.
> dis vint man an dem rehtbuoch stân."

["They do not know that one can read this in the lawbook called *Decret*. There it is written thus, to be remembered well: Neither cleric nor layman should eat the Jews' bread. It should also not be forgotten that the same lawbook prescribes that no Christian shall lodge in their houses; one finds it also written that no Christian in sickness shall accept the Jews' counsel, nor take their medicine, nor bathe in the same bathhouse, nor invite Jews to a Christian's inn, nor shall a Christian go to a Jew's inn. This is written in the lawbook."]

See Ferdinand Vetter, *Das Schachzabelbuch Kunrats von Ammenhausen* ("Bibliothek älterer Schriftwerke der deutschen Schweiz" [Frauenfeld, 1892], vss. 15466–82; Erwin G. Gudde, *Social Conflicts in Medieval German Poetry* ("University of California Publications in Modern Philology," Vol. XVIII, No. 1 [Berkeley, Calif., 1934]), p. 60; cf. Browe, *Die Judenmission im Mittelalter und die Päpste* (Rome, 1942), p. 34. Cf. Schwsp., L 262, G 214, 9, 11; and above, pp. 299 ff. The reference to the "lawbook called *Decret*" refers, of course, to the *Decretum Gratiani*, C. XXVIII, qu. 1, c. 13, 14:

"13. Nullus eorum, qui in sacro sunt ordine, aut laicus azima eorum manducet, aut cum eis habitet aut aliquem eorum in infirmitatibus suis vocet, aut medicinam ab eis percipiat, aut cum eis in balneo lavet. Si vero quisquam hoc fecerit, si clericus est, deponatur, laicus vero, excommunicetur.

"14. Omnes deinceps clerici sive laici judeorum convivia vitent, nec eos quisquam ad convivium excipiat, quia, cum apud Christianos communibus cibis non utantur, indignum atque sacrilegum est eorum cibos a Christianis sumi, cum ea, que Apostolo permittente [I Tim. 4: 3–5] nos sumimus, ab illis judicentur inmunda, ac si inferiores Christiani incipient esse, quam judei, si nos que ab illis apponuntur utamur, illi vero a nobis oblata contempnant."

41. So Innocent III, in his letter to the Count of Nevers, of January 17, 1208, reproduced in Grayzel, *The Church and the Jews*, pp. 126 ff., n. 24.

42. P. Browe offers impressive evidence for this fact in his book, *Die Judenmission im Mittelalter und die Päpste*, which came to the writer's attention only after the completion of the present work. This unimpeachable witness summarizes his historical observations thus (pp. 286 f.):

"Die Christen, die Laien und die Kleriker, haben der Bekehrung der Juden, ohne es zu beabsichtigen, nicht wenige Hindernisse in den Weg gelegt. Zunächst durch ihre Interesselosigkeit und ihre Nichtunterstützung. . . . Die Bemühungen, die Juden für die Kirche zu gewinnen, haben kein Echo geweckt und keine lebendige Unterstützung gefunden. Im Gegenteil haben ihnen Laien und Kleriker nur zu oft sogar entgegengewirkt und geschadet. . . . Noch mehr erregten und verbitterten sie die gesetzlichen und ungesetzlichen Verfolgungen, die seit dem Ende des 11. Jahrhunderts über sie hereinbrachen, die zahlreichen kirchlichen und weltlichen Gesetze, die darauf ausgingen, sie von den Christen zu trennen und in eine mindere gesellschaftliche und rechtliche Stellung herabzudrücken. Sie erzeugten auf die Dauer eine Abneigung und einen Hass, die eine freundliche Einwirkung ungemein erschwerten. Wenn die Missionäre überhaupt an sie herankommen wollten, mussten sie die Behörden zu Zwangsmassregeln veranlassen, die neue Erbitterung hervorriefen. Aufs äusserste wurde aber die Erbitterung dadurch gesteigert, dass man sie direkt oder indirekt zum Übertritt nötigte oder ihre Kinder ihnen gewaltsam wegnahm und taufte, so dass sie es gelegentlich vorzogen, sie zu töten und so diesem Schicksal zu entziehen. Dazu kam noch die Behandlung der Getauften, denen man fast immer misstraute, auch wenn sie freiwillig und ehrlich in die Kirche gekommen waren."

43. See p. 197. It is worth noting here that a similar attitude prevailed in the legal life of fourteenth-century Italy. According to Lucas of Penna (born *ca.* 1320), noted Italian jurist and philosopher of law, civil law, even if contrary to canon law, was to be observed in its proper domain, that is, before the civil courts: "Leges etiam si sint directe contrariae canonibus, tamen servandae sunt in foro civili, ubi possunt sine periculo animae observari . . . nam servantur canones in foro ecclesiastico" (Walter Ullmann, "A Mediaeval Philosophy of Law," *Catholic Historical Review*, XXXI [1945], 28, n. 148).

44. There is no comprehensive monograph on the reception of the Roman law in general. For bibliography see R. Schröder and E. von Künssberg, *Lehrbuch der deutschen Rechtsgeschichte* (7th ed.; Berlin and Leipzig, 1932), pp. 864 ff.; Eberhard Freiherr von Künssberg, article "Rezeption," in *Handwörterbuch der Rechtswissenschaft*, V (Berlin, 1928), 128 f.; Heinrich Brunner, *Grundzüge der deutschen Rechtsgeschichte* (8th ed. by Cl. von Schwerin; Munich and Leipzig, 1930), pp. 258–66; Rudolf Hübner, *Grundzüge des deutschen Privatrechts* (5th ed.; Leipzig, 1930), p. 18, n. 1; Claudius von Schwerin, *Grundzüge der deutschen Rechtsgeschichte* (Munich and Leipzig, 1934), pp. 233–40. Cf., in particular, Georg von Below, *Die Ursachen der Rezeption des römischen Rechts in Deutschland* (Munich and Berlin, 1905); Paul Vinogradoff, *Roman Law in Medieval Europe* (2d ed. by F. de Zulueta; Oxford, 1929); Woldemar Engelmann, *Die Wiedergeburt der Rechtskultur in Italien durch die wissenschaftliche Lehre* (Leipzig, 1938); Erich Genzmer, "Kritische Studien zur Mediaevistik. I," *ZRG*, Roman. Abt. LXI (1941), pp. 276–354; Paul Koschaker, *Europa und das römische Recht* (Munich, 1947); Harold D. Hazeltine, "Roman and Canon Law in the Middle Ages," *Cambridge Medieval History*, V (Cambridge, 1926), 697–764. Cf. also Hermann Kantorowicz, "Note on the Development of the Gloss to the Justinian and the Canon Law," in Beryl Smalley, *The Study of the Bible in the Middle Ages* (Oxford, Eng., 1941), pp. 36–39; Walter Ullmann, *The Medieval Idea of Law as Represented by Lucas de Penna: A Study in Fourteenth-Century Legal Scholarship* (London, 1946).

45. Cf. Roderich Stintzing, *Geschichte der populären Literatur des römisch-kanonischen Rechts in Deutschland am Ende des fünfzehnten und im Anfang des sechzehnten Jahrhunderts* (Leipzig, 1867); Emil Seckel, *Beiträge zur Geschichte beider Rechte im Mittelalter*, Vol. I: *Zur Geschichte der populären Literatur des römisch-kanonischen Rechts* (Tübingen, 1898); Guido Kisch, "Juridical Lexicography and the Reception of Roman Law," *Seminar*, II (1944), 51–81.

46. Cf. *Schwabenspiegel*, L 262, 322; G 214, 8–13, 272; see also above, pp. 159 ff. The method of the author of the *Schwabenspiegel* in incorporating foreign-law matter has rightly been designated as "naïve" (cf. Hermann U. Kantorowicz, "Zu den Quellen des Schwabenspiegels," *Neues Archiv der Gesellschaft für ältere deutsche Geschichtskunde*, XXXVIII [1913], 688).

47. See above, p. 291. It is worth noting that, as early as the end of the thirteenth century or the beginning of the fourteenth, the Teutonic knight-poet, Heinrich von Hesler, in his *Evangelium Nicodemi* tried to convince his readers that "the Jews had fewer rights under the Roman than they have under the German law" (Gudde, *op. cit.*, p. 41). Heinrich von Hesler, *Das Evangelium Nicodemi*, ed. Karl Helm (Tübingen, 1902), vss. 4721 ff.:

> "daz die juden und ir kindt
> vorteilde couflunge sint
> under romischer echte."

Cf., above, p. 161.

48. Cf. von Schwerin, *Grundzüge der deutschen Rechtsgeschichte*, p. 129; Emil Steffenhagen, "Die Entwicklung der Landrechtsglosse des Sachsenspiegels. XII. Johann von Buch und die kanonische Glosse," *Sitzungsberichte der philosophisch-historischen Klasse der kaiserlichen Akademie der Wissenschaften zu Wien*, CXCV, Abh. 1 (1923), 4 f., n. 3. Strangely enough, Wolfgang Stammler, *Die deutsche Literatur des Mittelalters, Verfasserlexikon* (Berlin and Leipzig, 1931–43), has no article on Johann von Buch.

49. See above, pp. 91 ff., and below, p. 359.

50. See above, p. 206. Both are treated in the *Corpus juris canonici* under separate *tituli* as separate groups: X, *de Judaeis, Sarracenis et eorum servis*, 5, 6; X, *de haereticis*, 5, 7; cf. also Thomas Aquinas, *Summa theologiae* ii. 2. 10. 8 (*St. Thomae Opera omnia*, ed. Fratres Ordinis Praedicatorum, Tom. VIII [Rome, 1895], p. 89): ". . . quod infidelium quidam sunt, qui nunquam susceperunt fidem, sicut gentiles et Judaei. . . . Alii vero sunt infideles, qui quandoque fidem susceperunt et eam profitentur, sicut haeretici vel quicumque apostatae." On Alexander of Hales's *Summa theologica* see W. Lampen, "Alexander von Hales und der Antisemitismus," *Franziskanische Studien*, XVI (1929), 9.

51. See above, pp. 91 f.

52. This becomes particularly clear with regard to the problem as to whether Jews can be considered as heretics, referred to in the text (above, p. 359). Both are treated under separate rubrics and as separate groups in Justinian's *Code* (cf. above, p. 206 and chap. xiii, n. 50).

Although heretics and Jews are occasionally mentioned together in the commentaries of the Italian jurists, it was recognized by Bartolus and Baldus that the Jews practicing their own rites could not properly be considered and treated as heretics (cf. Anna T. Sheedy, *Bartolus on Social Conditions in the Fourteenth Century* [New York, 1942], pp. 230 f.). Another example is found in Oldradus de Ponte (de Laude) (d. 1335), *Consilia*, No. 87: Even opposing the general opinion, he demanded a just cause for the confiscation of Jewish property (Walter Ullmann, *The Medieval Idea of Law*, p. 188, n. 1). Cf. also the fair discussion among Italian lawyers concerning the *status civitatis* of the Jews, in Vittore Colorni, *Legge ebraica e leggi locali: Ricerche sull'ambito d'applicazione del diritto ebraico in Italia dall'epoca romana al secolo XIX* (Milan, 1945), pp. 75 ff.

53. Among the more than 1,260 legal manuscripts listed in Homeyer, *Die deutschen Rechtsbücher und ihre Handschriften* (3d ed.; Weimar, 1931–34), this writer came across one isolated instance of a legal treatise by an Italian jurist (Bartolus) included in a German law manuscript, as early as the fifteenth century. It is Homeyer, *op. cit.*, No. 466. Another instance from the first, and a few more from the second, half of the fifteenth century (again Bartolus) are mentioned in J. L. J. van de Kamp, *Bartolus de Saxoferrato, 1313–1357, Leven, Werken, Invloed, Beteekenis* (Amsterdam, 1936), p. 211. Cf. also R. Stintzing, *Geschichte der deutschen Rechtswissenschaft*, I (Munich and Leipzig, 1880), p. 79: "Im Vergleich zu dieser populären Literatur erscheint die typographische Verbreitung der grossen Kommentarien der italienischen Legisten und der Quellen des römischen Rechts in Deutschland sehr gering"; cf. also van de Kamp, *op. cit.*, pp. 209 ff.

54. An exception is the so-called Stendal *Gloss* (*ca.* 1374–1410) by whose Italian-trained author a great number of Italian jurists were cited (cf. Emil Steffenhagen, "Die Entwicklung der Landrechtsglosse des Sachsenspiegels, II. Die Stendaler Glosse," *Sitzungsberichte der philosophisch-historischen Klasse der kaiserlichen Akademie der Wissenchaften zu Wien*, C [1882], 896 f.).

55. As to Johann von Buch, cf. Steffenhagen, "XI. Johann von Buch und die Accursische Glosse," *ibid.*, CXCIV, Abh. 3 (Vienna, 1922); "XII. Johann von Buch und die kanonische Glosse," *ibid.*, CXCV, Abh. 1 (Vienna, 1923). On the *Glossa ordinaria*, cf. the brief survey by Hermann Kantorowicz, "Note on the Development of the Gloss to the Justinian and the Canon Law," in Beryl Smalley, *The Study of the Bible in the Middle Ages*, pp. 36–39.

56. In this connection the attitude of Italian jurisprudence toward the literal interpretation of laws and statutes is noteworthy. As is well

known, in the Middle Ages literal or historical interpretation of the law was considered typically Jewish (cf. Herman Hailperin, "The Hebrew Heritage of Mediaeval Christian Biblical Scholarship," *Historia Judaica*, V [1943], 147, with further references; Hailperin, "Nicolas de Lyra and Rashi," in *Rashi Anniversary Volume* ["Texts and Studies," Vol. I, pub. by the American Academy for Jewish Research (New York, 1941)], pp. 126 f.). Literal interpretation of laws and statutes was, however, unsympathetic to, and rejected by, the leading Italian lawyers, who compared this juridical method with that customary among Jews in the interpretation of Scripture and designated it as *inhaerere tamquam Judaei*. See gloss *amplexus* ad *Cod. Just.* i. 14. 5: "Id est circumplectens adeo, ut a verbis tamquam Judaeus recedere nolit." Baldus de Ubaldis (1327–1400) repeatedly turned against such misunderstanding of law and pleaded for its interpretation by the most minute searching-out of the true meaning, *mens*, the legislator had in mind: "Lex et statutum non sunt intelligenda judaice"; "non enim sunt verba statuti sic judaice intelligenda, quia pravus intellectus non recipitur in statutis." For numerous quotations see W. Engelmann, *Die Wiedergeburt der Rechtskultur in Italien durch die wissenschaftliche Lehre*, pp. 148, 151 f. Logically, such a method of interpretation operated, at times, also in favor of the Jews (cf. G. Kisch, "Medieval Italian Jurisprudence and the Jews," *Historia Judaica*, VI [1944], 78–82; and below, n. 66).

57. Cf. van de Kamp, *op. cit.*, pp. 212–18.

58. For the text see G. Kisch, *Jewry-Law in Medieval Germany: Laws and Court Decisions Concerning Jews* (New York, 1949), pp. 127 f.

59. Cf. Trachtenberg, *op. cit.*, pp. 67, 232, n. 25, 254, n. 1.

60. Gl. Wb., 137 (ed. Wolrab [Budissin, 1557]), fol. CVIIr; the passage is missing from Gl. Wb., 135 (ed. Daniels and Gruben), p. 437. Rem. Wolrab, *s.v.* "Juden."

61. Matthias Lexer, *Mittelhochdeutsches Taschenwörterbuch* (13th ed.; Leipzig, 1915), p. 231: "slahtunge=*das Töten, Schlachten, Gemetzel, Mord.*"

62. C. 5, X, *de judaeis*, 5, 6.

63. *Cod. Just.* x. 1. 5 and 10; x. 2. 4; x. 6. 2. The citation in Reg. jur., J 148, "ut C. de jure fisci, l. inter tantulas," is not identifiable. The only *lex* with a similarly sounding *initium* is *Cod. Just.* x. 2. 5 (*inter chartulas*) but has no connection with the subject matter involved here. Careless citations were not infrequent among the writers of the reception era. They were less concerned with the substance of their citations than with their multiplicity.

64. For details see Stobbe, *Die Juden in Deutschland*, pp. 54 f., 99 ff.

Cf. also Charles IV's document for the Counts of Pappenheim (*anno* 1349): ". . . wan die juden in unser und des richs kamer gehören und mit in tun mugen waz wir wellen" (Wilhelm Kraft, "Zur Geschichte der Juden in Pappenheim," *MGWJ*, LXX [1926], 280). Charles IV favored for his chancellery jurists who were trained in Roman law (cf. Schubart-Fikentscher, *ZRG*, LXV (1947), 89.

65. A parallel from recent history seems worth noting. In 1943, the National Socialist government of Germany issued a law, according to which "upon the death of a Jew his property goes to the Reich" (for full text see *Jewish Comment*, I, No. 13 [October 8, 1943], 1). The Reich lawyers of 1943, in contradistinction to those of 1349, were not supposed to search for or refer to any legalistic support. The Italian fourteenth-century lawyers, on the contrary, argued quite differently. According to their doctrine (e.g., Lucas de Penna, who died in 1390), the ruler is overlord of person and property; his overlordship is, however, trusteeship. The ruler is overlord, but he is not the owner of the property of his subjects. He has the duty to protect their life and property intrusted to him by God: "Quemlibet in sua possessione tueri." He is permitted to expropriate possessions for the common good but is obliged to compensate their owner. His permission is derived from the consideration of the public interest—hence the requirement of a *legitima causa*, on whose behalf he encroaches upon the rights of his subjects. In the case of the Jews, this means the requirement of a just cause for the confiscation of Jewish property (W. Ullmann, *The Medieval Idea of Law*, pp. xxxv, 187 f.; cf. also above, n. 52).

66. See above, chap. xi, n. 37. It was no less a jurist than Bartolus who propounded a broad interpretation of the pertinent passage, *Cod. Just.* i. 9. 1, favoring the Jews concerned. While he agreed that no bequest could be made to an association of Jews, on account of the wording, *universitati Judaeorum*, forbidding such associations, in his opinion a bequest could lawfully be made to any individual Jew (cf. Sheedy, *Bartolus on Social Conditions in the Fourteenth Century*, p. 238).

67. Cf. G. Kisch, "The 'Jewish Execution' in Medieval Germany," *Historia Judaica*, V (1943), 115–18, 122 ff.

68. See above, p. 148, and chap. xiii, n. 64.

69. This specific result suggests an inquiry into its significance for the history of the reception of Roman law in general. The historical function of the latter's impact on the several autochthonous legal systems has not been subjected to a comprehensive analysis since the publication of Georg von Below's *Die Ursachen der Rezeption des römischen Rechts in Deutschland*, in 1905; and special studies of the manifold problems in-

volved have also been few. Below (*op. cit.*, p. 66) had arrived at this conclusion: "Weitere Forschungen werden wohl zu dem Resultat führen, dass das römische Recht verschiedenen Zwecken dienstbar geworden und als eine an sich im wesentlichen neutrale Macht anzusehen ist." One of his disciples probed into the problem of "The Influence of the Reception of Roman Law on the Status of the German Peasantry" (cf. Gustav Aubin, "Der Einfluss der Rezeption des römischen Rechtes auf den deutschen Bauernstand," *Jahrbücher für Nationalökonomie und Statistik* [3d ser.] XLIV [1912], 721–42). Through his research, Below's thesis was confirmed, yet somewhat modified: "Das römische Recht war an sich eine neutrale Macht, die verschiedenen Zwecken dienstbar gemacht worden ist" (p. 742). The reception of Roman law, though not solely responsible for the deterioration in the peasant's status, nonetheless turned out to be an important factor in this process. With respect to the Jews' legal status and its considerable deterioration, the role played by the adoption of Roman law in Germany was much more pronounced. This detailed study thus adds to the clarification of the general picture, on which still more research will have to be expended.

70. To illustrate the text, only a few examples from the vast legal literature of that period can be quoted. Theodorus Reinkingk, *Tractatus de regimine seculari et ecclesiastico . . . circa hodiernum S. Imperii Romani statum ac gubernationem* (Giessen, 1619), lib. II, cl. I, c. 2, p. 240, nn. 23–27: "Denique ita tractandi Judei ut Christianis subjiciantur et ab iis pro sola humanitate foveantur. . . ." Henricus Kornmann, *Responsum Juris über die Frag, ob und wie die Juden von und unter Christlicher Obrigkeit zu dulden* (Marburg, 1622), pp. 2 f.:

"Nach solcher Zerstreuung sind sie [the Jews] hin und wider von heidnischer und christlicher Herrschaft angenommen und geduldet worden: doch mit solcher condition und verstand, dass, nachdem sie einmal per passionem Christi, servi und dienstbare leibeigne leut worden, sie in solcher servitut und ewiger last bleiben und beharren sollen, bis dass sie sich solcher durch bekehrung und annehmung der Heil. Christlichen Tauff etwas entschüttet und frey gemacht, also zu Christlichen Würden befordert werden könen. Wie dann hierüber sacratiss. Imp. Justinianus heilsame gesetz statuirt, *C. de Judaeis*, Pontifex in *tit. Extr., de Judaeis*."

Ibid., pp. 32–34:

"Jure Romano in potestate Dominorum erant servi. . . . Bey den Römern und andern Völckern hatten die Herrn macht und gewalt, mit ihrem leibeignen knecht nach ihrem gefallen zu handlen, ja sie gantz und gar ums leben zu bringen; doch ist solche asperitet und schärpffe etwas von dem Kayser Antonino moderirt worden. Solche servitut und dienstbarkeit ist zwar bey den Christen uffgehaben, aber nicht gäntzlich, sondern es ist noch ein schein von der alten servitut und leibeigschafft noch im brauch und gewonheit, also dass, so ein leibeigner stürbt, sein haussfrau oder kinder das beste haupt geben und verstehen müssen, das ist entweder das beste pferd oder viehe, oder solches mit einer gewissen summ gelts nach des verstorbenen leibeigenen vermögen redimiren und losmachen . . . Wird nun solches noch bey und unter den Christen gehalten, wie viel mehr solte es also mit den Juden . . . gehalten werden."

Ibid., p. 39:

"Der Jud aber, weil er leibeigen, ein Schlav und knecht, also keiner ehr noch würden fähig, kan und soll keinen Christen, wes stands der auch sey, tutzen, dann durch das tutzen wird ein Superioritet im hohen grad, oder im mittlern ein gleichheit verstanden, welches beydes dem Juden gegen den Christen benommen."

Georg Theodor Dietrich, *De jure et statu judeorum in republica Christianorum discursus* (Marburg, 1648), p. 80:

". . . de civibus loquens, de veris civibus accipi debere, non de his qui in oppido tantum commorantur, quales sunt die Pfalbürger et Judei."

Johannes Carolus Lochner, *Dodecas legalis de Judaeorum receptione ac tolerantia: Von Juden-Schutz* (Jena, 1729), p. 17:

"Ast respondeat εἰ τύχοι adversarius: Judeos ex consuetudine et stylo Camerae pro civibus Romanis haberi: Verum sine ἀκρίβια."

Ibid., p. 21:

". . . Judaei itaque non secus jure communi Romano vivunt ac carnifices, meretrices aut alii infames et turpitudine aspersi. Quippe inter quos referuntur, in Ord. Polit. verbis: Dass sich die unehrlichen Weiber, Nachrichter und Juden solcher Kleidung gebrauchen, dadurch die Ehrbarkeit verdruckt und eines jeden Wesen und Stand nicht erkennet werden mag. Infamia autem non juris sed facti. . . . Eapropter, ut eo melius ab honestis et spectatis discernantur viris, prudenter alibi provisum: Dass die Juden einen gelben Ring an dem Rock oder Kappen allenthalben ohnverborgen zu ihrer Erkäntnüs offentlich tragen."

On the voluminous source material of the *Judenrechtswissenschaft*, consisting of a large number of doctoral theses, professorial dissertations, and lawyers' responsa see above, p. 72. As yet, it has almost completely escaped scholarly investigation. For a brief discussion of the *status civitatis* of the Jews according to this literature see Vittore Colorni, *Legge ebraica e leggi locali* (Milan, 1945), pp. 82 ff.

71. RW., F 41, fols. 106v–107r. Cf. Parkes, *Historia Judaica*, I (1938), 36: "In the Middle Ages the Jews enjoyed no right except such as the princes directly conferred on them." The similarity in wording is worth noting. Parkes had no knowledge of the manuscript quoted here.

72. Cf. Otto Stobbe, *Geschichte der deutschen Rechtsquellen*, I (Braunschweig, 1860), 281 f.

73. G. Kisch, *Zur sächsischen Rechtsliteratur der Rezeptionszeit* ("Beiträge zur Geschichte der Rezeption," ed. G. Kisch, Vol. I; Leipzig, 1923), p. 21 and n. 1; G. Kisch, "Juridical Lexicography and the Reception of Roman Law," *Seminar*, II (1944), 57 f.

74. This very fact disproves and exposes as nonsensical a transparent misstatement of National Socialist anti-Semitic propaganda, namely, that the reception of Roman law, a "Jew-made law" (*Judenrecht*), served Jewish purposes. Such distortions were contradicted by Otakar Sommer, "Třetí Říše a římské právo" ("The Third Reich and Roman Law" [in Czech]), reprinted from the anniversary volume, *Pocta k šedesátým narozeninám Dra. Alberta Miloty* (Prague, 1937), pp. 6 ff., including full bibliographical references. The National Socialist statements were based, no doubt, on Oswald Spengler's untenable assertion (*Der Untergang des Abendlandes*, II [Munich, 1924], 78) that all the "classics" among the Roman jurists were Aramaeans (". . . den 'klassischen' Juristen, die sämtlich Aramäer waren"). For contrary arguments see Sommer, *op. cit.*, p. 6 and n. 27; cf. also Fritz Schulz, *Prinzipien des römischen Rechts* (Munich and Leipzig, 1934), pp. 90 f.; Schulz, *Principles of Roman Law* (Oxford, 1936), pp. 132 f.; Paul Koschaker, *Die Krise des römischen Rechts und die romanistische Rechtswissenschaft* (Munich and Berlin, 1938), p. 73 and n. 1; and recently, Koschaker, *Europa und das römische Recht* (Munich, 1947), pp. 158, 134.

BIBLIOGRAPHY

BIBLIOGRAPHY

The following works, arranged under appropriate headings, represent a selected working bibliography. No attempt has been made to be exhaustive. Only those works providing material on, or an introduction to, the various subjects indicated or those actually employed have been listed. Through them the reader will find guidance in the entire field of research covered in the present volume. Further bibliographical references on each individual topic are given in the notes.

As a rule, the quotations from the sources have been faithfully translated into English. They are accompanied by precise citations of the originals referred to by their titles or sigla. The texts in the medieval languages are reproduced in full in a separate volume, Guido Kisch, *Jewry-Law in Medieval Germany: Laws and Court Decisions Concerning Jews* ("Texts and Studies," published by the American Academy for Jewish Research, Vol. III [New York: American Academy for Jewish Research, and 's Gravenhage: Martinus Nijhoff, 1947]).

ABBREVIATIONS

Auth.	Authentica	MFr.	*Magdeburger Fragen*
BlM.	*Blume von Magdeburg*	MG	*Monumenta Germaniae*
BlSsp.	*Blume des Sachsenspiegels*	MRb.	*Meissener Rechtsbuch (Rechts-*
Bocksd. Rem.	*Bocksdorfs Remissorium*		*buch nach Distinctionen)*
Cod. Just.	*Codex Justinianus*	MRQ.	*Magdeburger Rechtsquellen*
Cod. Theod.	*Codex Theodosianus*	MS	manuscript
Coll.	Collatio	MSchSpr.	*Magdeburger Schöffensprüche*
Decr. Grat.	*Decretum Gratiani*	*Nov.*	Novella, Novellae
Dig.	Digesta	O.S.	Old Series
Dsp.	*Deutschenspiegel*	Rb., Rbb.	Rechtsbuch, Rechtsbücher
E	Eckhardt	Reg. jur.	*Regulae juris*
ed.	edidit, editor	Rem.	*Remissorium*
F	Ficker	RQ.	*Rechtsquellen*
Form. imp.	*Formulae imperiales*	RW.	*Rechter Weg*
G	Gengler	SchB.	*Schöffenbuch*
Gl.	Gloss, Glosse	Schwsp.	*Schwabenspiegel*
Glogau Rb.	*Glogauer Rechtsbuch* (ed. Was-	Ssp.	*Sachsenspiegel*
	serschleben)	StB.	*Stadtbuch*
L	Lassberg	UB.	*Urkundenbuch, Urteilsbuch*
Ldr.	*Landrecht*	W	Wackernagel
LSchSprS.	*Leipziger Schöffenspruchsamm-*	Wb.	*Weichbild, Weichbild-Vulgata*
	lung	X	*Liber Extra (Decretales Gre-*
MBSchR.	*Magdeburg-Breslauer syste-*		*gorii IX)*
	matisches Schöffenrecht		

A. PRIMARY SOURCES

I. MANUSCRIPTS

1. LAWBOOKS

Blume des Sachsenspiegels [BlSsp.].

Compiled by NICHOLAS WURM at the end of the fourteenth century, written in the fifteenth century.

Breslau, Stadtarchiv, MS J 15. GUSTAV HOMEYER, *Die deutschen Rechtsbücher des Mittelalters und ihre Handschriften* (3d ed.; Weimar, 1931–34), No. 210.

BOCKSDORF, THEODOR VON. *Remissorium.*

Compiled in the middle of the fifteenth century (1449); copied in 1468.

Breslau, Stadtarchiv, MS J 16. Homeyer, No. 211; cf. *ibid.*, p. *57; Homeyer (2d ed.; Berlin, 1856), pp. 59–60, No. 7.

Meissener Rechtsbuch [MRb.].

Compiled between 1357 and 1387.

Vienna, Nationalbibliothek, MS 2680. Homeyer, No. 1144.

Regulae juris "Ad decus" [Reg. jur.].

Compiled at the end of the fourteenth century, possibly by NICHOLAS WURM; written in the fifteenth century.

a) Breslau, Stadtarchiv, MS J 15. Homeyer, No. 210.

b) Breslau, Stadtarchiv, MS J 3. Homeyer, No. 204.

Remissorium "Rechter Weg" [Rem. RW.].

Compiled between 1484 and 1493, by CASPAR POPPLAW, author of the collection, *Der Rechte Weg.*

Breslau, Stadtarchiv, MS J 8. Homeyer, No. 207.

Schwabenspiegel Landrecht [Schwsp. Ldr.].

Compiled about 1275; written about 1500.

New York City, Library of Guido Kisch. Homeyer, No. 578.

Weichbild-Vulgata.

Compiled in the second half of the thirteenth century; written in 1382.

Berlin, Preussische Staatsbibliothek, MS Germ. fol. 391. Homeyer, No. 50.

Weichbild-Vulgata and *Sachsenspiegel Landrecht.* Berlin-Steinbeck Manuscript.

Written in the fourteenth century.

Berlin, Preussische Staatsbibliothek, MS Germ. fol. 631. Homeyer, No. 63.

2. COURT DECISIONS

BOCKSDORF, DIETRICH VON. *Informationes.*

A collection of court decisions from Magdeburg and excerpts from various Saxon lawbooks; compiled in 1433, but the decisions are older.

Görlitz, Ratsarchiv, MS Varia 4. Homeyer, No. 418.

Collection of Magdeburg Court Decisions.

Compiled in 1464, the decisions being older.

Breslau, Stadtbibliothek, MS R 568. Photostat in New York City, Library of Guido Kisch. Not in Homeyer.

Collection of 234 Magdeburg Court Decisions.
Of the first half of the fifteenth century, with additions from the sixteenth century.
Breslau, Stadtarchiv, MS J 5. Homeyer, No. 205.

Liegnitz-Görlitz Collection of Court Decisions.
Decisions of the jury court of Dohna, Saxony, sent to Görlitz during the first half of the fifteenth century.
Görlitz, Ratsarchiv, MS Varia 4. Homeyer, No. 418.

Merseburg Collection of 165 Magdeburg Jury Court Decisions.
From the period of 1424–52; compiled in the fifteenth century.
Merseburg, Stadtbibliothek, MS No. 3. Partial apograph in New York City, library of Guido Kisch. Homeyer, No. 788.

Revised Collection of Magdeburg Court Decisions.
Compiled and written in the beginning of the fifteenth century; related to the *Magdeburger Fragen.*
Cracow, Poland, University Library, MS 170ᵇ.
Apograph in New York City, Library of Guido Kisch. Homeyer, No. 645.

Summa "Der Rechte Weg" [RW.].
By CASPAR POPPLAW; end of the fifteenth century.
Breslau, Stadtarchiv, MS J 7. Homeyer, No. 206.

Summaries of Court Decisions of Magdeburg, Leipzig, and Dohna.
Completed in 1504, the decisions originating in the fifteenth century.
Dresden, Sächsische Landesbibliothek, MS M 20a. Homeyer, No. 304.

3. CENSUS OF MANUSCRIPTS OF MEDIEVAL GERMAN LAWBOOKS

HOMEYER, GUSTAV. *Die deutschen Rechtsbücher des Mittelalters und ihre Handschriften.* Erste Abteilung: *Verzeichnis der Rechtsbücher*, bearbeitet von KARL AUGUST ECKHARDT. Zweite Abteilung: *Verzeichnis der Handschriften*, bearbeitet von CONRAD BORCHLING und JULIUS VON GIERKE, Weimar: Hermann Böhlaus Nachfolger, 1931–34.
Cited as "Homeyer."
The book contains a full bibliography on pp. 314–23. An analogous census of the extant manuscripts of medieval German court decisions is a desideratum.

4. LITERARY HISTORY OF THE MEDIEVAL GERMAN LAW SOURCES

GAUPP, ERNST THEODOR. *Das alte Magdeburgische und Hallische Recht: Ein Beitrag zur Deutschen Rechtsgeschichte.* Breslau: Josef Max & Co., 1826.

———. *Das Schlesische Landrecht oder eigentlich Landrecht des Fürstentums Breslau.* Leipzig: C. H. F. Hartmann, 1828.

KISCH, GUIDO. *Sachsenspiegel and Bible. Researches in the Source History of the Sachsenspiegel and the Influence of the Bible on Medieval German Law* ("Publications in Mediaeval Studies," Vol. V.) Notre Dame, Ind.: University of Notre Dame, 1941.
Comprehensive bibliography on pp. 180–85.

Kisch, Guido. "Schöffensprüche als historische Quellen," *Niederdeutsche Mitteilungen*, IV (Lund, Sweden, 1948), 50–58.

————. "Schöffenspruchsammlungen," *Zeitschrift der Savigny-Stiftung für Rechtsgeschichte, Germanistische Abteilung*, XXXIX (1918), 346–65.

Martitz, Ferdinand von. *Das eheliche Güterrecht des Sachsenspiegels und der verwandten Rechtsquellen*. Mit einer Einleitung über die Quellen des sächsischen Rechts. Leipzig: H. Haessel, 1867.

Stobbe, Otto. *Geschichte der deutschen Rechtsquellen*. 2 vols. Brunswick: C. A. Schwetschke & Sohn, 1860, 1864.

II. Printed Editions

1. lawbooks

Amira, Karl von. *Die Dresdener Bilderhandschrift des Sachsenspiegels*, Vol. I: *Ausgabe*. 2 parts. Leipzig: Karl W. Hiersemann, 1902. Vol. II: *Erläuterungen*. 2 parts. Leipzig: Karl W. Hiersemann, 1925–26.

Boehlau, Hugo. *Die Blume von Magdeburg*. Weimar: Hermann Boehlau, 1868.

Claussen, Hans-Kurt. *Freisinger Rechtsbuch*. ("Germanenrechte," Neue Folge, "Stadtrechtsbücher.") Weimar: Hermann Böhlaus Nachfolger, 1941.

Clauswitz, P. *Das Berlinische Stadtbuch aus dem Ende des XIV. Jahrhunderts*. Berlin, 1883.

Daniels, A. von. *Dat buk wichbelde recht: Das sächsische Weichbildrecht nach einer Handschrift der königlichen Bibliothek zu Berlin von 1369*. Berlin: Th. Chr. Fr. Enslin, 1853.

Daniels A. von, and Gruben, Fr. von. *Das Saechsische Weichbildrecht: Jus municipale Saxonicum*. Vol. I: *Weltchronik und Weichbildrecht in [C]XXXVI Artikeln mit der Glosse*. Berlin: Mylius, 1858.

Eckhardt, Karl August. *Sachsenspiegel: Land- und Lehnrecht*. ("Monumenta Germaniae historica: Fontes iuris Germanici antiqui," N.S., Vol. I.) Hannover: Hahnsche Buchhandlung, 1933.

Eckhardt, Karl August, and Hübner, Alfred. *Deutschenspiegel und Augsburger Sachsenspiegel*. ("Monumenta Germaniae historica: Fontes iuris Germanici antiqui," N.S., Vol. III.) 2d rev. ed. Hannover: Hahnsche Buchhandlung, 1933.

Endemann, Hermann Ernst. *Das Kayserrecht nach der Handschrift von 1372*. Cassel: J. C. Krieger, 1846.

FICKER, JULIUS. *Der Spiegel deutscher Leute: Textabdruck der Innsbrucker Handschrift.* Innsbruck: Wagnersche Buchhandlung, 1859.

FIDICIN, EDUARD. *Historisch-diplomatische Beiträge zur Geschichte der Stadt Berlin,* Part I: *Berlinisches Stadtbuch.* Berlin: A. W. Hayn, 1837.

GEER VAN JUTPHAAS, B. J. L. BARON DE. *De Saksenspiegel in Nederland.* 's Gravenhage: Martinus Nijhoff, 1888.

GENGLER, HEINRICH GOTTFRIED. *Des Schwabenspiegels Landrechtsbuch.* 2d rev. ed. Erlangen: Andreas Deichert, 1875.

HIRSCH, HANS CHRISTOPH. *Eike von Repgow: Der Sachsenspiegel (Landrecht), in unsere heutige Muttersprache übertragen und dem deutschen Volke erklärt.* Berlin and Leipzig: Walter de Gruyter & Co., 1936.

HOMEYER, CARL GUSTAV. *Der Richtsteig Landrechts nebst Cautela und Premis.* Berlin: Georg Reimer, 1857.

———. *Des Sachsenspiegels Erster Teil, oder das Sächsische Landrecht, nach der Berliner Handschrift vom Jahre 1369 herausgegeben.* 3d rev. ed. Berlin: Ferdinand Dümmler, 1861.

Quotations citing book, article, and paragraph without any further addition, e.g., III, 7, 3, always refer to *Sachsenspiegel Landrecht.*

KNAPP, HERMANN. *Das Rechtsbuch Ruprechts von Freising (1328).* Leipzig: R. Voigtländer, 1916.

LASSBERG, F. L. A. FREIHERR VON. *Der Schwabenspiegel oder Schwäbisches Land- und Lehenrechtbuch nach einer Rezension vom Jahr 1287 mit späteren Zusätzen.* Tübingen: Ludwig Friedrich Fues, 1840.

LUDOVICI, JACOB FRIEDERICH. *Das Sächsische Weichbild in der lateinischen und jetzo gebräuchlichen hoch-teutschen Sprache aus alten bewährten Codicibus, nebst nöthigen Auszügen aus der Glosse.* Halle: Waysenhaus, 1721.

MAURER, G. LUDWIG VON. *Das Stadt- und das Landrechtbuch Ruprechts von Freysing: Ein Beitrag zur Geschichte des Schwabenspiegels.* Stuttgart and Tübingen: J. G. Cotta, 1839.

MEINARDUS, OTTO. *Das Neumarkter Rechtsbuch und andere Neumarkter Rechtsquellen.* ("Darstellungen und Quellen zur schlesischen Geschichte," Vol. II.) Breslau: E. Wohlfarth, 1906.

MEYER, HERBERT. *Das Mühlhäuser Reichsrechtsbuch aus dem Anfang des 13. Jahrhunderts: Deutschlands ältestes Rechtsbuch nach den altmitteldeutschen Handschriften herausgegeben, eingeleitet und übersetzt.* 2d rev. ed. Weimar: Hermann Böhlaus Nachfolger, 1934.

ORTLOFF, FRIEDRICH. *Das Rechtsbuch nach Distinctionen [Meissener Rechtsbuch] nebst einem Eisenachischen Rechtsbuch.* Jena: Crökersche Buchhandlung, 1836.

ORTLOFF, FRIEDRICH. *Das Rechtsbuch Johannes Purgoldts nebst statutarischen Rechten von Gotha und Eisenach.* Jena: Friedrich Frommann, 1860.

PLANITZ, HANS. "Das Zwickauer Stadtrechtsbuch," *Zeitschrift der Savigny-Stiftung für Rechtsgeschichte, Germanistische Abteilung,* XXXVIII (Weimar: Hermann Böhlaus Nachfolger, 1917), 321–66.

RÖSSLER, EMIL FRANZ. *Das altprager Stadtrecht aus dem XIV. Jahrhunderte.* ("Deutsche Rechtsdenkmäler aus Böhmen und Mähren," Vol. I.) Prague: J. G. Calve, 1845.

Sassenspegel mit velen nyen Addicien san dem Leenrechte vnde Richtstige [Latin and Low German text of the *Sachsenspiegel* with Johann von Buch's and the Stendal *Gloss*]. Augsburg: Sylvanus Othmer, 1516. Described in Homeyer, *Sachsenspiegel*, p. 70, No. 15; Homeyer, *Des Sachsenspiegels Zweiter Theil nebst den verwandten Rechtsbüchern,* I (Berlin: Ferdinand Dümmler, 1842), 42 f., No. 7.

SCHUSTER, HEINRICH MARIA. *Das Wiener Stadtrechts- oder Weichbildbuch.* Vienna: G. J. Manz, 1873.

Sechsisch Weichbild, Lehenrecht, vnd Remissorium, auffs new an vielen orten in Texten, Glossen, vnd derselben allegaten, aus den warhafftigen glossen Keiserlicher vnd Bepstlicher Recht, vnd also den hauptquellen, mit fleis anderwerts corrigiert vnd restituiret, darzu etliche Vrteil, in teglichen fürfallenden sachen sehr richtig vnd dienstlich, zum teil vor nicht gedruckt. Budissin: Nicolaus Wolrab, 1557.

SMITS, J. J. "De Spiegel van Sassen of zoogenaamde Hollandsche Sachsenspiegel," *Nieuwe Bijdragen voor Regtsgeleerdheid en Wetgeving,* XXII (1872), 5–72, 169–237.

THÜNGEN, W. VON. *Das Sächsische Weichbildrecht nach dem Codex Palatinus Nro. 461* [of 1504]. Heidelberg: August Osswald, 1837.

ULLRICH, GÜNTHER, and PLANITZ, HANS. *Zwickauer Rechtsbuch.* ("Germanenrechte," Neue Folge, "Abteilung Stadtrechtsbücher.") Weimar: Hermann Böhlaus Nachfolger, 1941.

WACKERNAGEL, WILHELM. *Der Schwabenspiegel in der ältesten Gestalt mit den Abweichungen der gemeinen Texte und den Zusätzen derselben,* Part I: *Das Landrecht des Schwabenspiegels.* Zürich and Frauenfeld: Christian Beyel, 1840.

ZOBEL, CHRISTOFF. *Sachsenspiegel, auffs newe vbersehen, mit Summarijs vnd newen Additionen, so aus den gemeinen Keyserrechten vnd vieler vornemer dieser Lande Doctorn bericht vnd Radtschlegen, auch der Hoffgericht vnd Schöppenstuel vblichen Rechtsprüchen zusammenbracht, vnd an den Glossen vnnd Allegaten vielfeltig gebessert.* Edited by GEORGIUS MENIUS. Leipzig: Ernestus Vögelin, 1560[-61].

2. COURT DECISIONS

BEHREND, J[AKOB] FR[IEDRICH]. *Die Magdeburger Fragen.* Berlin: I. Guttentag, 1865.
Cited as "MFr."

————. *Ein Stendaler Urteilsbuch aus dem vierzehnten Jahrhundert als Beitrag zur Kenntnis des Magdeburger Rechts.* Berlin: I. Guttentag, 1868.
Cited as "Stendal UB."

BISCHOFF, FERDINAND. "Über eine Sammlung deutscher Schöffensprüche in einer Krakauer Handschrift," *Archiv für Kunde österreichischer Geschichtsquellen,* XXXVIII (Vienna, 1867), 1–24.

[BÖHME, JOHANNES EHRENFRIED]. *Diplomatische Beyträge zur Untersuchung der schlesischen Rechte und Geschichte,* Part VI [zweyten Bandes, zweyter Theil]. Berlin: Haude & Spener, 1775.

FRIESE, VICTOR, and LIESEGANG, ERICH. *Die Magdeburger Schöffensprüche für Gross-Salze, Zerbst und Anhalt, Naumburg und aus dem Codex Harzgerodanus.* ("Magdeburger Schöffensprüche," Vol. I.) Berlin: Georg Reimer, 1901.
Cited as "MSchSpr."

GOERLITZ, THEODOR. *Magdeburger Schöffensprüche für die Hansestadt Posen und andere Städte des Warthelandes.* ("Die Magdeburger Schöffensprüche und Rechtsmitteilungen," herausgegeben VON FRITZ MARKMANN, Ser. VIII, "Wartheland," Vol. I.) Stuttgart and Berlin: W. Kohlhammer, 1944.

GOERLITZ, THEODOR, and GANTZER, PAUL. *Die Magdeburger Schöffensprüche und Rechtsmitteilungen für Schweidnitz.* ("Die Magdeburger Schöffensprüche und Rechtsmitteilungen," herausgegeben von FRITZ MARKMANN, Ser. VII. "Schlesien," Vol. I.) Stuttgart and Berlin: W. Kohlhammer, 1940.

GRÖSSLER, HERMANN. "Sammlung älterer nach Eisleben ergangener Rechtsbescheide des magdeburgischen Schöppenstuhls," *Zeitschrift des Harzvereins für Geschichte und Altertumskunde,* XXIII (1890), 171–201.

KALUŽNIACKI, EMIL. "Die polnische Rezension der Magdeburger Urteile und die einschlägigen deutschen, lateinischen und czechischen Sammlungen," *Sitzungsberichte der Kaiserlichen Akademie der Wissenschaften in Wien, phil.-hist. Klasse,* CXI (Vienna: Carl Gerolds Sohn, 1885), 113–330.

KISCH, GUIDO. *Leipziger Schöffenspruch-Sammlung.* ("Quellen zur Geschichte der Rezeption," Vol. I.) Leipzig: S. Hirzel, 1919.
Cited as "LSchSprS."

LABAND, PAUL. *Das Magdeburg-Breslauer systematische Schöffenrecht aus der Mitte des XIV. Jahrhunderts.* Berlin: Ferdinand Dümmler, 1863.
Cited as "MBSchR."

————. *Magdeburger Rechtsquellen.* Königsberg: Hübner & Matz, 1869.

LEMAN, C. K. *Das Alte Kulmische Recht, mit einem Wörterbuche.* Berlin: Ferdinand Dümmler, 1838.

MÜHLER, HEINRICH. *Deutsche Rechtshandschriften des Stadtarchivs zu Naumburg an der Saale.* Berlin: Ferdinand Dümmler, 1838.

PRASEK, V. *Tovačovská Kniha ortelů Olomuckých* ["Tovačov Book of Court Decisions from Olomouc: A Collection of Decisions according to Magdeburg Law from Olomouc to Tovačov, 1430–1689."] Olomouc: Museum, 1896.

RÖSSLER, EMIL FRANZ. *Die Stadtrechte von Brünn aus dem XIII. und XIV. Jahrhundert.* ("Deutsche Rechtsdenkmäler aus Böhmen und Mähren," Vol. II.) Prague: J. G. Calve, 1852.
Cited as "Brünn SchB."

SCHUBART-FIKENTSCHER, GERTRUD. "Neue Fälle zum Brünner Recht," *Deutsches Archiv für Geschichte des Mittelalters,* III (Weimar, 1939), 430–96.

STOBBE, OTTO. "Mitteilungen aus Breslauer Signaturbüchern," *Zeitschrift des Vereins für Geschichte und Altertum Schlesiens,* VI (Breslau, 1864), 335–56; VII (1866), 176–91, 344–62; VIII (1867), 151–66, 438–53; IX (1868), 165–81; X (1870), 192–96.

TZSCHOPPE, GUSTAV ADOLF, and STENZEL, GUSTAV ADOLF. *Urkundensammlung zur Geschichte des Ursprungs der Städte und der Einführung und Verbreitung deutscher Kolonisten und Rechte in Schlesien und der Oberlausitz.* Hamburg: Friedrich Perthes, 1832.

WASSERSCHLEBEN, HERRMANN. *Deutsche Rechtsquellen des Mittelalters.* Leipzig: Veit & Co., 1892.
Cited as "RQ²."

————. "Das Glogauer Rechtsbuch," in H. WASSERSCHLEBEN, *Sammlung deutscher Rechtsquellen,* pp. 1–79. Giessen: E. Heinemann, 1860.
Cited as "Glogau Rb."

————. *Sammlung deutscher Rechtsquellen,* Vol. I. Giessen: Ernst Heinemann, 1860.
Cited as "RQ."

WEIZSÄCKER, WILHELM. *Magdeburger Schöffensprüche und Rechtsmitteilungen für den Oberhof Leitmeritz.* ("Die Magdeburger Schöffensprüche und Rechtsmitteilungen," herausgegeben von FRITZ MARKMANN,

Ser. IX, "Sudetenland," Vol. I.) Stuttgart and Berlin: W. Kohlhammer, 1943.
Cited as "MSchSpr. Leitmeritz."

———. "Die Rechtsmitteilung Breslaus an Olmütz," *Festschrift für Otto Peterka,* pp. 85–103. Brünn and Prague: R. Rohrer, 1936.

3. HISTORICAL AND LEGAL DOCUMENTS
a) GERMANY AND CENTRAL EUROPE

ARONIUS, JULIUS. *Regesten zur Geschichte der Juden im fränkischen und deutschen Reiche bis zum Jahre 1273.* Bearbeitet unter Mitwirkung von ALBERT DRESDNER UND LUDWIG LEWINSKI. Berlin: Nathansen & Lamm, 1887–1902.
Cited as "Aronius."

BONDY, GOTTLIEB, and DWORSKÝ, FRANZ. *Zur Geschichte der Juden in Böhmen, Mähren und Schlesien von 906 bis 1620.* 2 vols. Prague: Gottlieb Bondy, 1906.

BRETHOLZ, BERTOLD. *Quellen zur Geschichte der Juden in Mähren vom XI. bis zum XV. Jahrhundert (1067–1411).* ("Schriften der Gesellschaft für Geschichte der Juden in der Čechoslovakischen Republik," Vol. I.) Prague: Taussig & Taussig, 1935.

GEYER, RUDOLF, and SAILER, LEOPOLD. *Urkunden aus Wiener Grundbüchern zur Geschichte der Wiener Juden im Mittelalter.* ("Quellen und Forschungen zur Geschichte der Juden in Deutsch-Österreich," Vol. X.) Vienna: Deutscher Verlag für Jugend und Volk, 1931.

GOLDMANN, ARTUR. *Das Judenbuch der Scheffstrasse zu Wien (1389–1420).* ("Quellen und Forschungen zur Geschichte der Juden in Deutsch-Österreich," Vol. I.) Vienna and Leipzig: Wilhelm Braumüller, 1908.

———. "Das verschollene Wiener Judenbuch," in A. GOLDMANN, B. WACHSTEIN, and J. TAGLICHT, *Nachträge zu den zehn bisher erschienenen Bänden der Quellen und Forschungen zur Geschichte der Juden in Österreich,* pp. 1–14. Vienna: Selbstverlag der Historischen Kommission, 1936.

GRAYZEL, SOLOMON. *The Church and the Jews in the XIIIth Century: A Study of Their Relations during the Years 1198–1254, Based on the Papal Letters and the Conciliar Decrees of the Period.* Philadelphia: Dropsie College, 1933.

HERZOG, DAVID. *Das "Juden-Puech" des Stiftes Rein.* Sonderabdruck aus dem 28. Jahrgang der *Zeitschrift des Historischen Vereines für Steiermark.* Graz: Leuschner & Lubensky, 1934.

———. *Urkunden und Regesten zur Geschichte der Juden in der Steiermark*

(1475–1585). ("Quellen und Forschungen zur Geschichte der Juden in der Steiermark," Vol. I.) Graz: Israelitische Kultusgemeinde, 1934.

HOENIGER, ROBERT, [and STERN, MORITZ]. *Das Judenschreinsbuch der Laurenzpfarre zu Köln.* ("Quellen zur Geschichte der Juden in Deutschland," Vol. I.) Berlin: Leonhard Simion, 1888.

KEUTGEN, FRIEDRICH. *Urkunden zur städtischen Verfassungsgeschichte.* ("Ausgewählte Urkunden zur deutschen Verfassungsgeschichte," von G. VON BELOW und F. KEUTGEN, Vol. I.) Berlin: Emil Felber, 1899.

KISCH, GUIDO. *Jewry-Law in Medieval Germany: Laws and Court Decisions Concerning Jews.* ("Texts and Studies," published by the American Academy for Jewish Research, Vol. III.) New York: American Academy for Jewish Research, 1949.

KOBER, ADOLF. *Grundbuch des Kölner Judenviertels 1135–1425: Ein Beitrag zur mittelalterlichen Topographie, Rechtsgeschichte und Statistik der Stadt Köln.* ("Publikationen der Gesellschaft für Rheinische Geschichtskunde," Vol. XXXIV.) Bonn: Hansteins Verlag, 1920.

KRACAUER, ISIDOR. *Urkundenbuch zur Geschichte der Juden in Frankfurt am Main von 1150–1400,* Vol. I: *Urkunden, Rechenbücher, Bedebücher.* Frankfort-on-the-Main: J. Kauffmann, 1914.

MARCUS, JACOB R. *The Jew in the Medieval World: A Source Book 315–1791.* Cincinnati: Union of American Hebrew Congregations, 1938.
Selected medieval sources with introductory explanations and bibliographical notes intended for the use of the college student.

NEUBAUER, ADOLF, and STERN, MORITZ. *Hebräische Berichte über die Judenverfolgungen während der Kreuzzüge.* Ins Deutsche übersetzt von S. BAER. ("Quellen zur Geschichte der Juden in Deutschland," Vol. II.) Berlin: Leonhard Simion, 1892.

OELSNER, LUDWIG. *Schlesische Urkunden zur Geschichte der Juden im Mittelalter.* Reprinted from *Archiv für Kunde österreichischer Geschichtsquellen,* Vol. XXXI. Vienna: Karl Gerolds Sohn, 1864.

ROSENBERG, ARTUR. *Beiträge zur Geschichte der Juden in Steiermark.* ("Quellen und Forschungen zur Geschichte der Juden in Deutsch-Österreich," Vol. VI.) Vienna and Leipzig: Wilhelm Braumüller, 1914.

SALFELD, SIEGMUND. *Das Martyrologium des Nürnberger Memorbuches.* ("Quellen zur Geschichte der Juden in Deutschland," Vol. III.) Berlin: Leonhard Simion, 1898.

STERN, MORITZ. *König Ruprecht von der Pfalz in seinen Beziehungen zu den Juden: Ungedruckte Königsurkunden nebst ergänzenden Aktenstücken.* Kiel: H. Fiencke, 1898.

———. *Die päpstlichen Bullen über die Blutbeschuldigung.* Berlin: 1893. 2d ed. Munich: August Schupp, 1900.

———. "Papsturkunden: Ein Beitrag zur Geschichte der Juden, aus Archiven mitgeteilt," *Beilage zum Berichte der israelitischen Religionsschule zu Kiel über das Schuljahr 1892–1893.* Kiel: Israel. Religionsschule, 1893.

———. *Urkundliche Beiträge über die Stellung der Päpste zu den Juden.* Vol. I. Kiel: H. Fiencke, 1893. Vol. II, Heft I. Kiel: H. Fiencke, 1895.

STRAUS, RAPHAEL. *Urkunden und Aktenstücke zur Geschichte der Juden in Regensburg im ausgehenden Mittelalter. Im Auftrage des Verbandes bayerischer israelitischer Gemeinden herausgegeben.* 1938.
This volume was never officially published. It was ready for publication when almost all copies were burned by the Munich Gestapo. Only four or five sets of page proofs survived.

SÜSSMANN, ARTHUR. "Das Erfurter Judenbuch (1357–1407)," *Mitteilungen des Gesamtarchivs der deutschen Juden,* V (Leipzig, 1914), 1–126.

TÄUBLER, EUGEN. "Urkundliche Beiträge zur Geschichte der Juden in Deutschland im Mittelalter," *Mitteilungen des Gesamtarchivs der deutschen Juden,* IV (Leipzig, 1914), 31–62; V (1915), 127–48.

ULRICH, JOHANN CASPAR. *Sammlung jüdischer Geschichten, welche sich mit diesem Volk in dem XIII. und folgenden Jahrhunderten bis auf MDCCLX in der Schweitz von Zeit zu Zeit zugetragen.* Basel, 1768.

WIENER, MEIR. *Regesten zur Geschichte der Juden in Deutschland während des Mittelalters,* Part I. Hannover: Hahnsche Hofbuchhandlung, 1862.

WILLIAMS, A. LUKYN. *Adversus Judaeos: A Bird's-Eye View of Christian Apologiae until the Renaissance.* Cambridge: At the University Press, 1935.
A collection and survey of medieval Christian treatises on Jews and Judaism, from various countries.

ZEUMER, KARL. *Quellensammlung zur Geschichte der deutschen Reichsverfassung in Mittelalter und Neuzeit.* (HEINRICH TRIEPEL's "Quellensammlungen zum Staats-, Verwaltungs- und Völkerrecht," Vol. II.) 2 vols. Tübingen: J. C. B. Mohr, 1913.

b) BYZANTINE EMPIRE

MANN, JACOB. *Texts and Studies in Jewish History and Literature.* Vol. I. Cincinnati, Ohio: Hebrew Union College Press, 1931.

STARR, JOSHUA. *The Jews in the Byzantine Empire 641–1204.* ("Texte und Forschungen zur byzantinisch-neugriechischen Philologie," No. 30.) Athens: Byzantinisch-Neugriechische Jahrbücher, 1939.

c) ENGLAND

ABRAHAMS, ISRAEL; STOKES, H. P.; and LOEWE, HERBERT. *Starrs and Jewish Charters Preserved in the British Museum.* 3 vols. London: Jewish Historical Society of England, 1930, 1932.

DAVIS, M. D. *Shetaroth: Hebrew Deeds of English Jews before 1290.* ("Publications of the Anglo-Jewish Historical Exhibition.") London: Jewish Chronicle, 1888.

JACOBS, JOSEPH. *The Jews of Angevin England: Documents and Records from Latin and Hebrew Sources.* ("English History by Contemporary Writers.") New York and London: G. P. Putnam's Sons, 1893.

RIGG, JAMES MACMULLEN. *Select Pleas, Starrs and Other Records from the Rolls of the Exchequer of the Jews, A.D. 1220–1284.* London: Jewish Historical Society of England, 1902.

RIGG, JAMES MACMULLEN, and JENKINSON, HILARY. *Calendar of the Plea Rolls of the Exchequer of the Jews Preserved in the Public Record Office.* 3 vols. London: Jewish Historical Society of England, 1905, 1910, 1929.

TOVEY, D'BLOSSIERS. *Anglia Judaica or the History and Antiquities of the Jews in England.* Oxford: James Fletcher, 1738.

d) FRANCE

ARONIUS, JULIUS. *Regesten zur Geschichte der Juden im fränkischen und deutschen Reiche bis zum Jahre 1273.* Berlin: Nathansen & Lamm, 1887–1902.
Cited as "Aronius."

e) HUNGARY

Magyar-Zsido Oklevéltár—Monumenta Hungariae Judaica, publicari fecit Societas Litteraria Hungarico-Judaica. Vol. I: *1092–1539,* ed. ARMIN FRISS [and MAURICE WEISZ]. Budapest: F. Wodnianer, 1903. Vol. IV: *1371–1564,* ed. FERENC KOVÁTS. Budapest, 1938.

f) ITALY

LAGUMINA, BARTOLOMEO and GIUSEPPE. *Codice diplomatico dei Giudei di Sicilia.* 3 vols. ("Documenti per servire alla storia di Sicilia pub-

blicati a cura della Società Siciliana per la Storia Patria," Prima
Serie, "Diplomatica," Vols. VI, XII, and XVII.) Vol. I, Part I,
Palermo, 1884. Vol. II of Part I, Palermo, 1890. Vol. III of Part I,
Palermo, 1895.

SALZMAN, MARCUS. *The Chronicle of Ahimaaz*. ("Columbia University
Oriental Studies," Vol. XVIII.) New York: Columbia University
Press, 1924.

g) POLAND

BERSOHN, MATHIAS. *Dyplomataryusz dotyczący Żydów w dawnej Polsce na
żródłach archiwalnych osnuty (1388–1782)* ["Collection of Documents
concerning Jews in Ancient Poland from Archival Sources"]. Warsaw: Edward Nicz, 1910.

BLOCH, PHILIPP. *Die Generalprivilegien der polnischen Judenschaft*. Revised
and enlarged separate edition from *Zeitschrift der Historischen Gesellschaft für die Provinz Posen*, Vol. VI. Posen: Joseph Jolowicz, 1892.

h) RUSSIA

[ANONYMOUS]. *Regesti i Nadpisi: Svod materialov dla istoriyi yevreyev v
Rossiyi* ["Documents and Inscriptions: Collection of Materials for the
History of the Jews in Russia"]. Vol. I (*80–1670*). [Published by the
Society for the Diffusion of Culture among the Jews of Russia.] St.
Petersburg: Z. Kreiz & Co., 1899.

BERSCHADSKI, SERGEI A. *Rusko-Yevreiski Archiv: Dokumenty i materialy dlia
istorii Yevreyev v Rossii* ["Russian-Jewish Archives: Documents and
Materials on the History of the Jews in Russia"]. 3 vols. St. Petersburg, 1882–83, 1903.
In Russian.

i) SPAIN

BAER, FRITZ. *Die Juden im christlichen Spanien*. Part I: *Urkunden und Regesten*. Vol. I: *Aragonien und Navarra*. Vol. II: *Kastilien, Inquisitionsakten*.
Berlin: Vol. I, Akademie-Verlag, 1929; Vol. II, Schockenverlag,
1936.

B. LITERATURE

I. POLITICAL AND CULTURAL HISTORY OF MEDIEVAL JEWRY

1. BIBLIOGRAPHY
(See also under the following heading)

[FREIDUS, ABRAHAM SOLOMON]. *The New York Public Library: List of
Works Relating to the History and Condition of the Jews in Various Countries*. New York: New York Public Library, 1914.

FREIMANN, ARON. *Stadtbibliothek Frankfurt am Main: Katalog der Judaica und Hebraica.* Vol. I: *Judaica.* Frankfort-on-the-Main: Stadtbibliothek, 1932.

KISCH, GUIDO. "Dissertationenliteratur zur Geschichte der Juden aus den Jahren 1922–1928," *Zeitschrift für die Geschichte der Juden in Deutschland*, III (1931), 117–23.

KLAUS, BRUNO. "Die Juden im deutschen Mittelalter," *Deutsche Geschichtsblätter, Monatsschrift zur Förderung der landesgeschichtlichen Forschung*, II (1901), 241–48, 273–92.
This survey article is accompanied by a bibliography, arranged according to individual countries (Landschaften) and localities.

KOBER, ADOLF. "Die Geschichte der deutschen Juden in der historischen Forschung der letzten 35 Jahre," *Zeitschrift für die Geschichte der Juden in Deutschland*, I (1929), 13–32.

ROTH, CECIL. "The Jews in the Middle Ages," *Cambridge Medieval History*, VII, 937–47. Cambridge: At the University Press, 1932.

SCHWAB, MOÏSE. *Répertoire des articles relatifs à l'histoire et à la littérature juives, parus dans les Periodiques, de 1665 à 1900.* Paris: P. Geuthner, 1914–23.
This bibliography is based mainly on Jewish historical journals. A similar work compiled from non-Jewish historical periodicals is a desideratum.

STEINSCHNEIDER, MORITZ. *Die Geschichtsliteratur der Juden in Druckwerken und Handschriften*, Part I: *Bibliographie der hebräischen Schriften.* Frankfort-on-the-Main: J. Kauffmann, 1905.
Only this volume was published.

———. *Die hebraeischen Uebersetzungen des Mittelalters und die Juden als Dolmetscher: Ein Beitrag zur Literaturgeschichte des Mittelalters, meist nach handschriftlichen Quellen.* 2 vols. Berlin: Bibliographisches Bureau, 1893.
Only this volume was published.

STERN, MORITZ. *Quellenkunde zur Geschichte der deutschen Juden.* Vol. I: *Die Zeitschriftenliteratur.* Kiel: H. Fiencke, 1892.
Only this volume was published.

ZUNZ, LEOPOLD. *Zur Geschichte und Literatur.* Vol. I. Berlin: Veit & Co., 1845.

2. GENERAL WORKS

ABRAHAMS, ISRAEL. *Jewish Life in the Middle Ages.* London: Macmillan & Co., 1896; 2d ed., by CECIL ROTH. London: Edward Goldston, 1932.

BARON, SALO W. *The Jewish Community: Its History and Structure to the American Revolution.* 3 vols. Philadelphia: Jewish Publication Society of America, 1942.

————. *A Social and Religious History of the Jews.* 3 vols. New York: Columbia University Press, 1937.

CASSEL, SELIG. "Juden (Geschichte)," in J. S. ERSCH and J. G. GRUBER, *Allgemeine Encyklopädie der Wissenschaften und Künste*, Zweite Section, 27. Teil, pp. 1–238. Leipzig: F. A. Brockhaus, 1850.

DEPPING, GEORGES BERNARD. *Les Juifs dans le moyen âge: Essai historique sur leur état civil, commercial, et littéraire.* Paris: Imprimerie Royale, 1834. A German translation appeared under the title, *Die Juden im Mittelalter* (Stuttgart: E. Schweizerbart, 1834).

DUBNOW, SIMON. *Weltgeschichte des jüdischen Volkes von seinen Uranfängen bis zur Gegenwart.* 10 vols. Berlin: Jüdischer Verlag, 1928–30.

GRAETZ, HEINRICH. *Geschichte der Juden von den ältesten Zeiten bis auf die Gegenwart.* 11 in 13 vols. 4th unrev. ed. Leipzig: Oskar Leiner, n.d. Originally published 1853–75.

————. *History of the Jews.* 6 vols. Philadelphia: Jewish Publication Society, 1891–98.

NEWMAN, LOUIS I. *Jewish Influence on Christian Reform Movements.* ("Columbia University Oriental Studies," Vol. XXIII.) New York: Columbia University Press, 1925.

PARKES, JAMES. *The Conflict of the Church and the Synagogue.* London: Soncino Press, 1934.

————. *The Jew in the Medieval Community: A Study of His Political and Economic Situation.* London: Soncino Press, 1938.

SCHOLEM, GERSHOM G. *Major Trends in Jewish Mysticism.* Jerusalem: Schocken Publishing House, 1941.

SMALLEY, BERYL. *The Study of the Bible in the Middle Ages.* Oxford: Clarendon Press, 1941.

STEINSCHNEIDER, MORITZ. "Allgemeine Einleitung in die jüdische Literatur des Mittelalters," *Jewish Quarterly Review*, O.S., XV (London, 1903), 302–29; XVI (1904), 373–95, 734–64; XVII (1904–5), 148–62, 354–69, 545–82.

ZIMMELS, HIRSCH JACOB. *Die Marranen in der rabbinischen Literatur: Forschungen und Quellen zur Geschichte und Kulturgeschichte der Anussim.* Berlin: Rubin Mass, 1932.

3. GERMANY AND CENTRAL EUROPE

Beiträge zur Geschichte der deutschen Juden: Festschrift zum siebzigsten Geburtstage Martin Philippsons. Herausgegeben vom Vorstande der Gesellschaft zur Förderung der Wissenschaft des Judentums. Leipzig: Gustav Fock, 1916. A collection of essays by several authors on various topics, including articles on the history of the Jews in medieval Germany.

BERLINER, ABRAHAM. *Aus dem Leben der deutschen Juden im Mittelalter zugleich als Beitrag für deutsche Culturgeschichte.* Berlin: M. Poppelauer, 1900.

BRANN, MARCUS. "Geschichte der Juden in Schlesien," *Jahresbericht des jüdisch-theologischen Seminars Fraenckelscher Stiftung* [Breslau]. Breslau: 1896, 1897, 1901, 1907, 1910.

BRETHOLZ, BERTOLD. *Geschichte der Juden in Mähren im Mittelalter.* Part I: *Bis zum Jahre 1350.* Brünn and Leipzig: Rudolf M. Rohrer, 1934.

COHN, JONAS. *Die Judenpolitik der Hohenstaufen.* Ph.D. thesis, University of Hamburg. Hamburg, 1934.

DICKER, HERMANN. *Die Geschichte der Juden in Ulm: Ein Beitrag zur Wirtschaftsgeschichte des Mittelalters.* Rottweil a.N.: M. Rothschild, 1937.

ELBOGEN, ISMAR. *Geschichte der Juden in Deutschland.* Berlin: Erich Lichtenstein, 1935.

ELBOGEN, I.; FREIMANN, A.; TYKOCINSKI, H.; [and BRANN, M.]. *Germania Judaica: Von den ältesten Zeiten bis 1238.* Breslau: M. & H. Marcus, 1934.
A history of medieval German Jewry up to 1238, alphabetically arranged according to the names of individual countries and towns.

FORCHHAMMER, EMANUEL. "Beiträge zur Geschichte der deutschen Juden mit besonderer Beziehung auf Magdeburg und die benachbarte Gegend," *Geschichtsblätter für Stadt und Land Magdeburg,* XLVI. Jahrgang (Magdeburg, 1911), 119–78, 328–408.
Anti-Semitic. Cited as "Forchhammer."

GÜDEMANN, MORITZ. *Geschichte des Erziehungswesens und der Cultur der Juden in Deutschland während des XIV. und XV. Jahrhunderts.* Vienna: Alfred Hölder, 1888.

———. *Geschichte des Erziehungswesens und der Cultur der Juden in Frankreich und Deutschland (X.–XIV. Jahrhundert.)* Vienna: Alfred Hölder, 1880.

HEISE, WERNER. *Die Juden in der Mark Brandenburg bis zum Jahre 1571.* (EMIL EBERING's "Historische Studien," Heft 220.) Berlin: Emil Ebering, 1932.

HOENIGER, ROBERT. "Zur Geschichte der Juden im frühen Mittelalter," Geiger's *Zeitschrift für die Geschichte der Juden in Deutschland,* I (1887), 65–97, 136–51.

————. *Der Schwarze Tod in Deutschland: Ein Beitrag zur Geschichte des vierzehnten Jahrhunderts*. Berlin: Eugen Grosser, 1882.

KEYSER, ERICH. *Bevölkerungsgeschichte Deutschlands*. Leipzig: S. Hirzel, 1938.
Anti-Semitic; yet valuable because of the compilation of statistical data for the medieval period.

KOBER, ADOLF. "Aus der Geschichte der Juden im Rheinland," in *Rheinischer Verein für Denkmalpflege und Heimatschutz, 1931*, Heft 1, pp. 11–39. Düsseldorf: L. Schwann, 1931.

KRACAUER, ISIDOR. *Geschichte der Juden in Frankfurt am Main (1150–1824)*. 2 vols. Frankfort-on-the-Main: J. Kauffmann, 1925.

KRAUSS, SAMUEL. *Die Wiener Geserah vom Jahre 1421*. Vienna and Leipzig: Wilhelm Braumüller, 1920.
This book has only a limited historical value; see the critical review by Otto H. Stowasser in *Vierteljahrschrift für Sozial- und Wirtschaftsgeschichte*, XVI (1922), 104–18.

KRAUSS, SAMUEL, and FISCHER, ISIDOR. *Geschichte der jüdischen Ärzte vom frühesten Mittelalter bis zur Gleichberechtigung*. Vienna: Moritz Perles, 1930.

KRAUTHEIMER, RICHARD. *Mittelalterliche Synagogen*. Berlin: Frankfurter Verlagsanstalt, 1927.

LANDSBERGER, FRANZ. *A History of Jewish Art*. Cincinnati: Union of American Hebrew Congregations, 1946.

LIEBE, GEORG. *Das Judentum in der deutschen Vergangenheit*. ("Monographien zur deutschen Kulturgeschichte," Vol. XI.) Leipzig: Eugen Diederichs, 1903; 2d ed., 1924.
Anti-Semitic.

LITTMANN, ELLEN. *Studien zur Wiederaufnahme der Juden durch die deutschen Städte nach dem Schwarzen Tode: Ein Beitrag zur Geschichte der Judenpolitik der deutschen Städte im späten Mittelalter*. Ph.D. thesis, University of Cologne. Breslau: Th. Schatzky, 1928.
Appeared in part also in *Monatsschrift für Geschichte und Wissenschaft des Judentums*, LXXII (1928), 576–600.

MENCZEL, J. S. *Beiträge zur Geschichte der Juden von Mainz im XV. Jahrhundert: Eine quellenkritische Untersuchung mit Quellenabdruck*. Berlin: Rubin Mass, 1933.

NEUFELD, SIEGBERT. *Die halleschen Juden im Mittelalter*. Ph.D. thesis, University of Strasbourg. Berlin, 1915.

————. *Die Juden im thüringisch-sächsischen Gebiet während des Mittelalters*. Vol. I: *Von den ältesten Zeiten bis zum "schwarzen Tod" (1348)*. Berlin: M. Poppelauer, 1917. Vol. II: *Vom "schwarzen Tod" (1348) bis zum Ausgang des Mittelalters.* Halle a.d. Saale: Gebauer-Schwetsch-ke, 1927.

Volume II originally appeared in *Thüringisch-sächsische Zeitschrift für Geschichte und Kunst*, IX (1919), 6–16; XII (1924), 66–87; XV (1927), 158–78.

NOHL, JOHANNES. *Der schwarze Tod, eine Chronik der Pest, 1348–1720.* Potsdam: Gustav Kiepenheuer, 1924.

NÜBLING, EUGEN. *Die Judengemeinden des Mittelalters, insbesondere die Judengemeinde der Reichsstadt Ulm: Ein Beitrag zur deutschen Städte- und Wirtschaftsgeschichte.* Ulm: Gebrüder Nübling, 1896.

Anti-Semitic. Cited as "Nübling."

PINTHUS, ALEXANDER. *Die Judensiedlungen der deutschen Städte: Eine stadtbiologische Studie.* Doctor of Engineering thesis, Technische Hochschule of Hannover, 1931.

Appeared also in *Zeitschrift für die Geschichte der Juden in Deutschland*, II (1930), 101–30, 197–217, 284–300.

RIEMER, ALFRED. *Die Juden in niedersächsischen Städten des Mittelalters.* Ph.D. thesis, University of Göttingen. Göttingen, 1907.

The complete version appeared in *Zeitschrift des historischen Vereins für Niedersachsen*, 1907, pp. 303–64; 1908, pp. 1–57.

SCHIFFMANN, SARA. *Heinrich IV. und die Bischöfe in ihrem Verhalten zu den deutschen Juden zur Zeit des ersten Kreuzzuges.* Ph.D. thesis, University of Berlin. Berlin, 1931.

Appeared also in *Zeitschrift für die Geschichte der Juden in Deutschland*, III (1931), 39–58, 233–50.

SCHWARZ, IGNAZ. *Geschichte der Juden in Wien bis zum Jahre 1625.* Separatabdruck aus Band V der *Geschichte der Stadt Wien*, herausgegeben vom Altertumsvereine zu Wien. Vienna: Gilhofer & Ranschburg, 1913.

STEINBERG, AUGUSTA. *Studien zur Geschichte der Juden in der Schweiz während des Mittelalters.* Zürich: Schulthess & Co., 1902.

STERN, MORITZ. *Die israelitische Bevölkerung der deutschen Städte: Ein Beitrag zur deutschen Städtegeschichte.* 7 vols. Frankfort, Kiel, Berlin, Breslau, 1890–1937.

STRAUS, RAPHAEL. *Die Judengemeinde Regensburg im ausgehenden Mittelalter.* ("Heidelberger Abhandlungen zur mittleren und neueren Geschichte," Heft 61.) Heidelberg: Carl Winter, 1932.

SÜSSMANN, ARTHUR. *Die Judenschuldentilgungen unter König Wenzel.* Berlin: Louis Lamm, 1907.

ZIMMELS, HIRSCH J. *Beiträge zur Geschichte der Juden in Deutschland im 13. Jahrhundert insbesondere auf Grund der Gutachten des R. Meir Rothenburg.* Vienna: Israelitisch-theologische Lehranstalt, 1926.

ZUNZ, LEOPOLD. *The Sufferings of the Jews during the Middle Ages.* Translated from the German [*Die synagogale Poesie des Mittelalters*, Berlin, 1855] by REV. DR. A. LÖWY. Revised and edited with notes by GEORGE A. KOHUT. New York: Bloch Publishing Co., 1907.

4. OTHER COUNTRIES
a) BELGIUM
ULLMANN, SALOMON. *Studien zur Geschichte der Juden in Belgien bis zum XVIII. Jahrhundert.* Antwerp: S. Kahan, 1909.

b) BYZANTINE EMPIRE
STARR, JOSHUA. *The Jews in the Byzantine Empire 641–1204.* ("Texte und Forschungen zur byzantinisch-neugriechischen Philologie," No. 30.) Athens: Byzantinisch-Neugriechische Jahrbücher, 1939.

c) ENGLAND
ADLER, MICHAEL. *Jews of Medieval England.* London: Edward Goldston, 1939.
A collection of essays on individual topics.

COULTON, GEORGE GORDON. *Medieval Panorama: The English Scene from Conquest to Reformation*, pp. 346–65. Cambridge: At the University Press; New York: Macmillan Co., 1944.

HYAMSON, ALBERT M. *A History of the Jews in England.* London and New York: Macmillan & Co., 1907.

ROTH, CECIL. *A History of the Jews in England.* Oxford: Clarendon Press, 1941.

———. *Magna Bibliotheca Anglo-Judaica: A Bibliographical Guide to Anglo-Jewish History.* New, rev., and enl. ed. London: Jewish Historical Society of England, 1937.

STOKES, H. P. *Studies in Anglo-Jewish History.* London: Jewish Historical Society of England, 1913.

JEWISH HISTORICAL SOCIETY OF ENGLAND. *Transactions.* 15 vols. London: Edward Goldston, 1895–1946.

———. *Miscellanies.* 5 vols. London: Jewish Historical Society of England, 1925–48.

Jewish Quarterly Review, O.S., Vols. I–XX. London, 1889–1908.

d) FRANCE
ANCHEL, ROBERT. *Les Juifs de France.* [Paris]: J. B. Janin, 1946.
Contains critical, bibliographical notes on pp. 279–85.

BERMAN, LÉON. *Histoire des juifs de France des origines à nos jours.* Paris: Librairie Lipschutz, 1937.
This book offers a popular, often inaccurate, presentation of the history of the Jews in

France, including the medieval period, with no documentation. It is listed despite this fact, since no comprehensive scholarly work on the subject exists, except the preceding item, which was inserted in the course of proofreading.

EPHRAÏM, MAX. *Histoire des juifs d'Alsace et particulièrement de Strasbourg depuis le milieu du XIIIᵉ jusqu'à la fin du XIVᵉ siècle.* Paris: Durlacher, 1925.
Appeared originally in *Revue des études juives*, LXXVII (1923), 127–65; LXXVIII (1924), 35–84.

GROSS, HEINRICH. *Gallia Judaica: Dictionnaire géographique de la France d'après les sources rabbiniques.* Paris: Léopold Cerf, 1897.
A history of French Jewry, alphabetically arranged according to geographical names.

MOSSÉ, ARMAND. *Histoire des juifs d'Avignon et du comtat Venaissin.* Paris: Lipschutz, 1934.

RABINOWITZ, LOUIS. *The Social Life of the Jews of Northern France in the XII–XIV Centuries as Reflected in the Rabbinical Literature of the Period.* London: Edward Goldston, 1938.

Revue des études juives, Vols. I ff. Paris, 1880 ff.

e) HOLLAND

BRUGMANS, HENDRIK, and FRANK, A. *Geschiedenis der Joden in Nederland.* Eerste Deel tot circa 1795. Amsterdam: Van Holkema & Warendorf, 1940.

f) HUNGARY

BERGL, JOSEPH. *Geschichte der ungarischen Juden.* Kaposvar: Hermann Jeiteles, 1879.

g) ISLAMIC COUNTRIES

EPSTEIN, ISIDORE. *The Responsa of Rabbi Simon b. Ẓemaḥ Duran as a Source of the History of the Jews in North Africa.* London: Humphrey Milford, 1930.

FISCHEL, WALTER J. *Jews in the Economic and Political Life of Mediaeval Islam.* ("Royal Asiatic Society Monographs," Vol. XXII.) London: Royal Asiatic Society, 1937.

GINSBERG, DAVID. "Prilozi k Historiji Jevreja na Balkanu" ["Contributions to the History of the Jews in the Balkan Peninsula"], *Omanut*, V, Nos. 1–2 (Zagreb, 1941), 7–28.
In the Croatian language.

ROSANES, SOLOMON A. *Dibre Yeme Israel be-Togarmah* ["A History of the Jews in Turkey"]. 5 vols. 2d ed. Tel Aviv: Dvir, 1930–38.
In Hebrew.

STRAUSS, ELI. *Toledot ha-Yehudim be-Mitzraim ve-Syria Tahath Sulton ha-*

Mamelukim ["A History of the Jews in Egypt and Syria under the Mameluke Dynasty"]. Jerusalem: Rav Kook Foundation, 1944.
In Hebrew.

b) ITALY

BERLINER, ABRAHAM. *Geschichte der Juden in Rom, von der ältesten Zeit bis zur Gegenwart (2050 Jahre).* 2 vols. Frankfort-on-the-Main: J. Kauffmann, 1893.

CASSUTO, UMBERTO. *Gli Ebrei a Firenze nell'età del Rinascimento.* Florence: Galletti & Cocci, 1918.

CISCATO, ANTONIO. *Gli Ebrei in Padova (1300–1800): Monografia storica documentata.* Padua: Società Cooperativa Tipographica, 1901.

FERORELLI, NICOLA. *Gli Ebrei nell'Italia meridionale dall'eta romana al secolo XVIII.* Turin: Il Vessillo Israelitico, 1915.

GABRIELI, GIUSEPPE. *Italia Judaica.* ("Guide Bibliografiche.") Rome: Fondazione Leonardo, 1924.
A bibliography.

GÜDEMANN, MORITZ. *Geschichte des Erziehungswesens und der Cultur der Juden in Italien während des Mittelalters.* Vienna: Alfred Hölder, 1884.

LUCAS, LEOPOLD. *Zur Geschichte der Juden im vierten Jahrhundert.* Berlin: Mayer & Müller, 1910.

MILANO, ATTILIO. *Gli Ebrei in Italia nei secoli XI° e XII°.* Città di Castello: Unione Arti Graphiche, 1938.

MUNKÁCSI, ERNST. *Der Jude von Neapel: Die historischen und kunstgeschichtlichen Denkmäler des süditalienischen Judentums.* Zürich: "Die Liga" Verlag, [1937].

RODOCANACHI, EMMANUEL. *Le Saint-Siège et les juifs: Le Ghetto à Rome.* Paris: Firmin-Didot et Cie., 1891.

ROTH, CECIL. *The History of the Jews of Italy.* Philadelphia: Jewish Publication Society of America, 1946.

STRAUS, RAPHAEL. *Die Juden im Königreich Sizilien unter Normannen und Staufern.* ("Heidelberger Abhandlungen zur mittleren und neueren Geschichte," Heft 30.) Heidelberg: Carl Winter, 1910.

VOGELSTEIN, HERMANN, and RIEGER, PAUL. *Geschichte der Juden in Rom.* 2 vols. Berlin: Mayer & Müller, 1895–96.
An abbreviated translation into English appeared in the "Jewish Communities Series" under the title, *Rome* (Philadelphia: Jewish Publication Society of America, 1940). It supplements the German original and brings it up to date.

La Rassegna mensile di Israel, Vols. I–XII (Rome, 1925–37).

Rivista israelitica, Vols. I–X (1904–13).

i) POLAND AND RUSSIA

CZACKI, TADEUSZ. *Rozprawa o żydach i Karaitach.* Vilna, 1807. 2d ed., by K. J. TUROWSKI. Cracow: Biblioteka Polska, 1860. 3d ed., Lwów: A. D. Bartoszewicz, 1885.

DUBNOW, SIMON M. *History of the Jews in Russia and Poland from the Earliest Times until the Present Day.* 3 vols. Philadelphia: Jewish Publication Society of America, 1916.

EISENSTEIN, ARON. *Die Stellung der Juden in Polen im XIII. und XIV. Jahrhundert.* Cieszyn, 1934.

MEISL, JOSEF. *Geschichte der Juden in Polen und Russland.* 3 vols. Berlin: C. A. Schwetschke, 1921–25.

STERNBERG, HERMANN. *Geschichte der Juden in Polen unter den Piasten und den Jagiellonen, nach polnischen und russischen Quellen bearbeitet.* Leipzig: Duncker & Humblot, 1878.

Evreiskaia Starina, Vols. I–XIII. St. Petersburg and Leningrad, 1909–30. In Russian. This journal includes only a few items on medieval Jewish history. It is indexed in Abraham G. Duker, " 'Evreiskaia Starina': A Bibliography of the Russian-Jewish Historical Periodical," *Hebrew Union College Annual,* VIII–IX (1931–32), 525–603.

Kwartalnik poświęcony badaniu przeszłości Żydów w Polsce [A Quarterly Devoted to the Study of the History of the Jews in Poland], I, 1–3 (Warsaw, 1912–13). In Polish.

j) SPAIN AND PORTUGAL

AMADOR DE LOS RIOS, DON JOSÉ. *Historia social, política y religiosa de los Judíos de España y Portugal.* 3 vols. Madrid: T. Fortanet, 1875–76.

BAER, FRITZ. *Studien zur Geschichte der Juden im Königreich Aragonien während des 13. und 14. Jahrhunderts.* ("Historische Studien," Heft 106.) Berlin: Emil Ebering, 1913.

BAER, ISAAC (FRITZ). *Toledoth ha-Yehudim be-Sepharad ha-Notzrith* ["History of the Jews in Christian Spain"]. 2 vols. Tel Aviv: Am Oved, 1945. In Hebrew.

GÜDEMANN, MORITZ. *Das jüdische Unterrichtswesen während der spanisch-arabischen Periode.* Vienna: Carl Gerold's Sohn, 1873.

HERSHMAN, ABRAHAM M. *Rabbi Isaac ben Sheshet Perfet and His Times.* New York: Jewish Theological Seminary of America, 1943.

KAYSERLING, MEYER. *Bibliotheca española-portugueza-judaica: Dictionnaire bibliographique des auteurs juifs, de leur ouvrages espagnols et portugais et des œuvres sur et contre les juifs et le judaisme.* Strasbourg: Charles J. Trubner, 1890.

———. *Geschichte der Juden in Portugal*. Leipzig: Oscar Leiner, 1867.

———. *Die Juden in Navarra, den Baskenländern und auf den Balearen.* Berlin: Julius Springer, 1861.

LEA, HENRY CHARLES. *A History of the Inquisition of Spain.* 4 vols. New York: Macmillan Co., 1906.

NEUMAN, ABRAHAM A. *The Jews in Spain: Their Social, Political and Cultural Life during the Middle Ages.* 2 vols. Philadelphia: Jewish Publication Society of America, 1942.

ROTH, CECIL. *A History of the Marranos.* Philadelphia: Jewish Publication Society of America, 1932.

II. HISTORY OF LAW IN MEDIEVAL GERMANY

1. GENERAL WORKS AND BIBLIOGRAPHY

AMIRA, KARL VON. *Grundriss des germanischen Rechts.* ("Grundriss der germanischen Philologie," Vol. V.) 3d rev. and enl. ed. Strasbourg: Karl J. Trübner, 1913.

BELOW, GEORG VON. *Der deutsche Staat des Mittelalters: Ein Grundriss der deutschen Verfassungsgeschichte.* Leipzig: Quelle & Meyer, 1914.

BRUNNER, HEINRICH. *Deutsche Rechtsgeschichte.* (KARL BINDING's "Systematisches Handbuch der deutschen Rechtswissenschaft," II. Abteilung, erster Teil.) 2 vols. 2d ed. Leipzig: Duncker & Humblot, 1906, 1928.

———. *Grundzüge der deutschen Rechtsgeschichte.* 8th ed. by CLAUDIUS VON SCHWERIN. Munich and Leipzig: Duncker & Humblot, 1930.

EICHHORN, KARL FRIEDRICH. *Deutsche Staats- und Rechtsgeschichte.* 4 vols. 5th rev. ed. Göttingen: Vandenhoeck & Ruprecht, 1843–44.

FEHR, HANS. *Deutsche Rechtsgeschichte.* ("Grundrisse der Rechtswissenschaft," Vol. X.) 2d ed. Berlin and Leipzig: W. de Gruyter & Co., 1925.

GENGLER, HEINRICH GOTTFRIED. *Deutsche Stadtrechtsaltertümer.* Erlangen: A. Deichert, 1882.

GIERKE, OTTO. *Das deutsche Genossenschaftsrecht.* 4 vols. Berlin: Weidmann, 1868, 1873, 1881, 1913.
Only excerpts from this work are available in English translation: Otto Gierke, *Political Theories of the Middle Age*, translated with an Introduction by Frederic W. Maitland (Cambridge, 1913); Otto Gierke, *Natural Law and the Theory of Society 1500–1800*, translated by Ernest Barker (2 vols.; Cambridge, 1934).

HEUSLER, ANDREAS. *Deutsche Verfassungsgeschichte.* Leipzig: Duncker & Humblot, 1905.

Kern, Fritz. *Kingship and Law in the Middle Ages.* ("Studies in Mediaeval History," ed. by Geoffrey Barraclough, Vol. IV.) Oxford: Basil Blackwell, 1939.

Keutgen, Friedrich. *Der deutsche Staat des Mittelalters.* Jena: Gustav Fischer, 1918.

Mitteis, Heinrich. *Der Staat des hohen Mittelalters: Grundlinien einer vergleichenden Verfassungsgeschichte des Lehnszeitalters.* Weimar: Hermann Böhlaus Nachfolger, 1940; 2d ed., 1944.

Planitz, Hans. "Forschungen zur Stadtverfassungsgeschichte," Parts 1–3, *Zeitschrift der Savigny-Stiftung für Rechtsgeschichte, Germanistische Abteilung,* LX (1940), 1–116; LXIII (1943), 1–91; LXIV (1944), 1–85.

Schröder, Richard, and Künssberg, Eberhard Freiherr von. *Lehrbuch der deutschen Rechtsgeschichte.* 7th ed. Berlin and Leipzig: Walter de Gruyter, 1932.
The only bibliographical reference work concerning all fields of the history of medieval German law. Cited as "Schröder and Künssberg."

Schubart-Fikentscher, Gertrud. *Die Verbreitung der deutschen Stadtrechte in Osteuropa.* ("Forschungen zum deutschen Recht," Vol. IV, Heft 3.) Weimar: Hermann Böhlaus Nachfolger, 1942.

Schwerin, Claudius Freiherr von. *Einführung in das Studium der germanischen Rechtsgeschichte und ihrer Teilgebiete.* Freiburg i.B.: Julius Boltze, 1922.

——. *Grundzüge der deutschen Rechtsgeschichte.* Munich and Leipzig: Duncker & Humblot, 1934.

Waitz, Georg. *Deutsche Verfassungsgeschichte.* 8 vols. I and II, 3d ed., Berlin: Weidmann, 1880, 1882; III–VI, 2d ed., Berlin: Weidmann, 1883–96; VII, Kiel: E. Homann, 1876; VIII, Kiel: E. Homann, 1878.

Zeitschrift für Rechtsgeschichte, Vols. I–XIII. Weimar: Hermann Böhlau, 1861–78.

Zeitschrift der Savigny-Stiftung für Rechtsgeschichte, Germanistische Abteilung, Vols. I–LXV. Weimar: Hermann Böhlaus Nachfolger, 1880–1947.

2. CIVIL LAW

Gierke, Otto. *Deutsches Privatrecht.* (Karl Binding's "Systematisches Handbuch der Deutschen Rechtswissenschaft," II. Abteilung, dritter Teil.) 3 vols. Leipzig: Duncker & Humblot, 1895, 1905, 1917.

Heusler, Andreas. *Institutionen des deutschen Privatrechts.* (Karl Bin-

DING's "Systematisches Handbuch der Deutschen Rechtswissen-schaft," II. Abteilung, zweiter Teil.) 2 vols. Leipzig: Duncker & Humblot, 1885, 1886.

HÜBNER, RUDOLF. *Grundzüge des deutschen Privatrechts.* 5th rev. ed. Leipzig: A. Deichert, 1930.

————. *A History of Germanic Private Law.* ("Continental Legal History Series," Vol. IV.) Boston: Little, Brown, & Co., 1918.

An English translation of the second (1913) edition of Hübner's *Grundzüge des deutschen Privatrechts.*

KRAUT, WILHELM THEODOR. *Grundriss zu Vorlesungen über das deutsche Privatrecht.* 6th rev. ed. by FERDINAND FRENSDORFF. Berlin: J. Guttentag, 1886.

STOBBE, OTTO. *Handbuch des deutschen Privatrechts.* 5 vols. Berlin: Wilhelm Hertz, 1871–85. 3d ed., 1893–1900.

3. CRIMINAL LAW

AMIRA, KARL VON. *Die germanischen Todesstrafen: Untersuchungen zur Rechts- und Religionsgeschichte.* ("Abhandlungen der Bayerischen Akademie der Wissenschaften, philosophisch-philologische und historische Klasse," Vol. XXXI, 3. Abhandlung.) Munich, 1922.

CASPAR, CARL JOHANNES. *Darstellung des strafrechtlichen Inhaltes des Schwabenspiegels und des Augsburger Stadt-Rechts.* Jur.D. thesis, University of Berlin. Berlin: Gustav Schade, 1892.

FRIESE, VICTOR. *Das Strafrecht des Sachsenspiegels.* (OTTO GIERKE's "Untersuchungen zur deutschen Staats- und Rechtsgeschichte," Heft 55.) Breslau: M. & H. Marcus, 1898.

HIS, RUDOLF. *Das Strafrecht des deutschen Mittelalters.* 2 vols. I, Leipzig: Theodor Weicher, 1920. II, Weimar: Hermann Böhlaus Nachfolger, 1935.

ULLMANN, JOHANNES GOTTFRIED. *Das Strafrecht der Städte der Mark Meissen, der Oberlausitz, des Pleissner-, Oster- und Vogtlandes während des Mittelalters.* ("Leipziger Rechtswissenschaftliche Studien," Heft 34.) Leipzig: Theodor Weicher, 1928.

WÄCHTER, CARL GEORG VON. *Beiträge zur deutschen Geschichte, insbesondere zur Geschichte des deutschen Strafrechts.* Tübingen: L. F. Fues, 1845.

4. COURT JURISDICTION AND PROCEDURE

HILLMANN, HELMUT. *Das Gericht als Ausdruck deutscher Kulturentwicklung im Mittelalter.* (GUIDO KISCH's "Deutschrechtliche Forschungen," Heft 2.) Stuttgart: W. Kohlhammer, 1930.

HINSCHIUS, PAUL. *Das Kirchenrecht der Katholiken und Protestanten in Deutschland: System des katholischen Kirchenrechts mit besonderer Rücksicht auf Deutschland.* 6 vols. Berlin: I. Guttentag, 1869–97.

HOMEYER, CARL GUSTAV. "Das Gerichtswesen nach dem Richtsteige," in his *Der Richtsteig Landrechts nebst Cautela und Premis*, pp. 411–520. Berlin: Georg Reimer, 1858.

JACOBI, ERWIN. "Der Prozess im Decretum Gratiani und bei den ältesten Dekretisten," *Zeitschrift der Savigny-Stiftung für Rechtsgeschichte*, XXXIV, Kanonistische Abteilung, III (1913), 223–343.

KISCH, GUIDO. *Der deutsche Arrestprozess in seiner geschichtlichen Entwicklung.* Vienna and Leipzig: F. Tempsky, 1914.

KRAUSE, HERMANN. *Die geschichtliche Entwicklung des Schiedsgerichtswesens in Deutschland.* Berlin: Carl Heymann, 1930.

LABAND, PAUL. *Die vermögensrechtlichen Klagen nach den sächsischen Rechtsquellen des Mittelalters.* Berlin: Weidmann, 1869.

MAYER-HOMBERG, EDWIN. *Beweis und Wahrscheinlichkeit nach älterem deutschen Recht.* Marburg: N. G. Elwert, 1921.

MÜNCHEN, NICOLAUS. *Das kanonische Gerichtsverfahren und Strafrecht.* 2 vols. Cologne-Neuss, 1865. 2d ed., Cologne: L. Schwann, 1874.

PLANCK, JULIUS WILHELM. *Das deutsche Gerichtsverfahren im Mittelalter.* 2 vols. Brunswick: C. A. Schwetschke, 1879.

PLANITZ, HANS. *Grundlagen des deutschen Arrestprozesses.* Leipzig: Felix Meiner, 1922.

RUDORFF, HERMANN. *Zur Rechtsstellung der Gäste im mittelalterlichen städtischen Prozess.* (OTTO GIERKE's "Untersuchungen zur deutschen Staats- und Rechtsgeschichte," Heft 88.) Breslau: M. & H. Marcus, 1907.

5. LAW OF EVIDENCE

HASENÖHRL, VICTOR. "Die Beweiszuteilung im österreichischen Rechte des Mittelalters," *Sitzungsberichte der kaiserlichen Akademie der Wissenschaften zu Wien, philosophisch-historische Klasse*, Vol. CXXXIX. Abhandlung 7 (Vienna, 1898).

HOLDEFLEISS, ERICH. *Der Augenscheinsbeweis im mittelalterlichen deutschen Strafverfahren.* (GUIDO KISCH's "Deutschrechtliche Forschungen," Heft 6.) Stuttgart: W. Kohlhammer, 1933.

LÖNING, RICHARD. *Der Reinigungseid bei Ungerichtsklagen im deutschen Mittelalter.* Heidelberg: Carl Winter, 1880.

MAYER-HOMBERG, EDWIN. *Beweis und Wahrscheinlichkeit nach älterem deutschen Recht.* Marburg: N. G. Elwert, 1921.

PLANCK, JULIUS WILHELM. *Das deutsche Gerichtsverfahren im Mittelalter.* 2 vols. Brunswick: C. A. Schwetschke, 1879.

RUTH, RUDOLF. *Zeugen und Eideshelfer in den deutschen Rechtsquellen des Mittelalters.* (OTTO GIERKE's "Untersuchungen zur deutschen Staats- und Rechtsgeschichte," Heft 133.) Breslau: M. & H. Marcus, 1922.

III. LEGAL AND SOCIAL HISTORY OF THE JEWS

1. JEWRY-LAW IN GENERAL

KISCH, GUIDO. "Jewry-Law in Central Europe—Past and Present," *Journal of Central European Affairs*, II, No. 4 (January, 1943), 396–422.

———. "The Jewry-Law of the Medieval German Law-Books," Parts I and II, *Proceedings of the American Academy for Jewish Research*, VII (1935–36), 61–145; X (1940), 99–184.

———. "The Jewry-Law of the Sachsenspiegel," *Occident and Orient: Gaster Anniversary Volume*, pp. 306–11. London: Taylor, 1936.

———. "Jüdisches Recht und Judenrecht: Ein Beitrag zur wissenschaftlichen Grundlegung für eine Rechtsgeschichte der Juden," *Festschrift Dr. Jakob Freimann zum 70. Geburtstag*, pp. 94–105. Berlin, 1937.

———. "Magdeburg Jury Court Decisions as Sources of Jewry-Law," *Historia Judaica*, V (1943), 27–34.

———. "Otto Stobbe und die Rechtsgeschichte der Juden," *Jahrbuch der Gesellschaft für die Geschichte der Juden in der Czechoslovakischen Republik*, IX, 1–41. Prague: Taussig & Taussig, 1938.

———. "Research in Medieval Legal History of the Jews," *Proceedings of the American Academy for Jewish Research*, VI (1934–35), 229–76.

LANDAUER, GEORG. "Zur Geschichte der Judenrechtswissenschaft: Hinweis auf ein Kapitel aus der Rechtsgeschichte der Juden," *Zeitschrift für die Geschichte der Juden in Deutschland*, II (1931), 255–61.

2. GERMANY AND CENTRAL EUROPE

EICHMANN, EDUARD. "Die Stellung Eikes von Repgau zu Kirche und Kurie," *Historisches Jahrbuch der Görresgesellschaft*, XXXVIII (1917), 746–57.
This article deals with the passage in *Sachsenspiegel*, III, 2, concerning "clerics and Jews who bear arms and who are not shaven in accordance with their law."

FISCHER, HERBERT. "Die Judenprivilegien des Goslarer Rates im 14. Jahrhundert," *Zeitschrift der Savigny-Stiftung für Rechtsgeschichte, Germanistische Abteilung*, LVI (1936), 89–149.

———. *Die verfassungsrechtliche Stellung der Juden in den deutschen Städten während des dreizehnten Jahrhunderts.* (OTTO GIERKE's "Untersuchungen

zur deutschen Staats- und Rechtsgeschichte," Heft 140.) Breslau: M. & H. Marcus, 1931.
Cited as "Fischer."

GROTEFEND, ULRICH. *Geschichte und rechtliche Stellung der Juden in Pommern von den Anfängen bis zum Tode Friedrich des Grossen*. Ph.D. thesis, University of Marburg, Marburg, 1931.
Appeared also in *Baltische Studien*, Neue Folge, XXXII (Stettin, 1930), 83–198.

HUGELMANN, KARL GOTTFRIED. "Studien zum Recht der Nationalitäten im deutschen Mittelalter. II. Das Judenrecht der Rechtsbücher," *Historisches Jahrbuch der Görresgesellschaft*, XLVIII (1928), 565–85.

KISCH, GUIDO. "The Jewish Execution in Medieval Germany," *Historia Judaica*, V (1943), 103–32.

———. "The 'Jewish Law of Concealment,' " *Historia Judaica*, I (1938), 3–30.

———. "The Jews in Medieval Law," *Essays on Antisemitism*, ed. KOPPEL S. PINSON. New York: Conference on Jewish Relations, 1942, pp. 57–66, 2d rev. ed. (1946), pp. 103–11.

———. "Die Rechtsstellung der Wormser Juden im Mittelalter," *Zeitschrift für die Geschichte der Juden in Deutschland*, V (1934), 122–33.
Appeared also in a separate edition (Halle-on-the-Saale, 1934).

———. "Das Schadennehmen: Ein Beitrag zur Geschichte des deutschen mittelalterlichen Vollstreckungsrechtes," *Rheinische Zeitschrift für Zivil- und Prozessrecht*, V (1913), 477–506.

KOBER, ADOLF. *Das Salmannenrecht und die Juden*. (KONRAD BEYERLE'S "Deutschrechtliche Beiträge," Vol. I, Heft 3.) Heidelberg: Carl Winter, 1907.

LÖNING, GEORGE A. "Juden im mittelalterlichen Bremen und Oldenburg," *Zeitschrift der Savigny-Stiftung für Rechtsgeschichte, Germanistische Abteilung*, LVIII (1938), 257–74.
Anti-Semitic.

NEUMANN, MAX. *Geschichte des Wuchers in Deutschland bis zur Begründung der heutigen Zinsengesetze (1654). Aus handschriftlichen und gedruckten Quellen*. Halle: Waisenhaus Buchhandlung, 1865.

RÖSEL, ISERT. *Die Reichssteuern der deutschen Judengemeinden von ihren Anfängen bis zur Mitte des 14. Jahrhunderts*. Berlin: Louis Lamm, 1910.
Originally published in *Monatsschrift für die Geschichte und Wissenschaft des Judentums*, LIII (1909), 679–708; LIV (1910), 55–69, 206–23, 333–47, 462–73.

ROSENTHAL, EDUARD. *Beiträge zur deutschen Stadtrechtsgeschichte*. Heft 1 und 2: *Zur Rechtsgeschichte der Städte Landshut und Straubing nebst Mitteilungen aus ungedruckten Stadtbüchern*. Würzburg: A. Stuber, 1883.

SAITSCHIK, R. *Beiträge zur Geschichte der rechtlichen Stellung der Juden namentlich im Gebiet des heutigen Österreich-Ungarn vom zehnten bis sechszehnten Jahrhundert.* Frankfort-on-the-Main: J. Kauffmann, 1890.

SCHERER, JOHANNES E. *Die Rechtsverhältnisse der Juden in den deutsch-österreichischen Ländern.* Mit einer Einleitung über die Prinzipien der Judengesetzgebung in Europa während des Mittelalters. ("Beiträge zur Geschichte des Judenrechtes im Mittelalter mit besonderer Bedachtnahme auf die Länder der österreichisch-ungarischen Monarchie.") Leipzig: Duncker & Humblot, 1901.
The only volume published in the series.
Cited as "Scherer."

STEINTHAL, HUGO. *Die Juden im fränkischen Reiche, ihre rechtliche und wirtschaftlich-soziale Stellung.* Ph.D. thesis, University of Breslau, 1922.
In typescript only, of which an abstract was published under the same title (Breslau: Hochschulverlag, 1922).

STOBBE, OTTO. *Die Juden in Deutschland während des Mittelalters in politischer, socialer und rechtlicher Beziehung.* Brunswick: C. A. Schwetschke, 1866. 2d ed. Leipzig: Duncker & Humblot, 1902. Photostatic 3d ed., Berlin: Louis Lamm, 1923.
Cited as "Stobbe."

WEIZSÄCKER, WILHELM. "Aus der Geschichte des Judenrechts in Böhmen und Mähren," *Zeitschrift für osteuropäisches Recht,* VI (1939–40), 457–67.
Not available to the author.

WYLER, FRITZ. *Die staatsrechtliche Stellung der israelitischen Religionsgenossenschaften in der Schweiz.* Jur.D. thesis, University of Zürich. ("Glarner Beiträge zur Geschichte, Rechtswissenschaft, Sozialpolitik und Wirtschaftskunde," Heft 10.) Glarus: Rudolf Tschudy, 1929.

Historia Judaica: A Journal of Studies in Jewish History, Especially in the Legal and Economic (Social) History of the Jews. Edited by GUIDO KISCH. Vols. I–X. New York: Historia Judaica, 1938–48.

3. OTHER COUNTRIES

a) ENGLAND

LINCOLN, F. ASHE. "The Legal Background to the Starrs," in HERBERT LOEWE, *Starrs and Jewish Charters Preserved in the British Museum,* II, lvii–lxxiv. London: Jewish Historical Society of England, 1932.
Appeared also separately under the same title (London: Edward Goldston, 1932).

———. *The Starra: Their Effect on Early English Law and Administration.* London: Oxford University Press, 1939.

Picciotto, Cyril M. "The Legal Position of the Jews in pre-Expulsion England, as Shown by the Plea Rolls of the Jewish Exchequer," *Transactions of the Jewish Historical Society of England*, IX (1922), 67–84.

Schechter, Frank I. "The Rightlessness of Mediaeval English Jewry," *Jewish Quarterly Review*, N.S., IV (1913–14), 121–51.

b) FRANCE

Gasnos, X. *Étude historique sur la condition des juifs dans l'ancien droit français.* Jur.D. thesis, Faculté de droit de Rennes. Angers: A. Burdin, 1897.

c) ITALY

(See under "Roman Empire and Medieval Italy")

d) POLAND AND RUSSIA

Berschadski, Sergei A. *Litovskie Yevrei* ["History of the Legal and Social Conditions of the Jews in Lithuania, 1388–1569"]. St. Petersburg: M. M. Stasupevitsch, 1883.
In Russian.

Gumplowicz, Ludwik. *Prawodawstwo Polskie względem Żydów* ["Polish Legislation concerning the Jews"]. Cracow: J. M. Himmelblau, 1867.

Kutrzeba, Stanislaw. "Stanowisko prawne Żydów w Polsce w XV st. ['The Legal Status of the Jews in Poland in the Fifteenth Century']," *Przewodnik naukowy i literacki* (1901).
Not available to the author.

Lewin, Isaac. "The Protection of Jewish Religious Rights by Royal Edicts in Ancient Poland," *Quarterly Bulletin of the Polish Institute of Arts and Sciences in America*, I (1943), 556–77.

Maciejowski, Wacław Aleksander. *Żydzi w Polsce, na Rusi i Litwie* ["The Jews in Poland, Ruthenia, and Lithuania"]. Warsaw: K. Kowalewski, 1878.

Schorr, Moses. *Rechtsstellung und innere Verfassung der Juden in Polen, ein geschichtlicher Rundblick.* Berlin and Vienna: R. Löwit, 1917.

e) ROMAN EMPIRE AND MEDIEVAL ITALY

Browe, Petrus. "Die Judengesetzgebung Justinians," *Analecta Gregoriana*, VIII (1935), 109–46.

Colorni, Vittore. *Legge ebraica e leggi locali: Ricerche sull'ambito d'applicazione del diritto ebraico in Italia dall'epoca romana al secolo XIX.* ("R. Università di Roma: Pubblicazioni dell'Istituto di Diritto Romano dei Diritti dell'Oriente Mediterraneo e di Storia del Diritto," Vol. XXIII.) Milan: A. Giuffrè, 1945.

FERRARI DELLE SPADE, GIANNINO. "Giurisdizione speciale ebraica nell'impero romano-cristiano," *Scritti in onore di Contardo Ferrini pubblicati in occasione della sua beatificazione*, I, 239–61. Milan: "Vita e Pensiero," 1947.

JUSTER, JEAN. *Les Juifs dans l'empire romain, leur condition juridique, économique et sociale.* 2 vols. Paris: Paul Geuthner, 1914.

SENIGAGLIA, QUINTO. "La Condizione giuridica degli ebrei in Sicilia," *Rivista Italiana per le scienze giuridiche*, XLI (Turin, 1906), 75–102.

f) SPAIN

JUSTER, JEAN. "La Condition légale des juifs sous les rois Visigoths," pp. 275–335. Separate edition from *Études d'histoire juridique offertes à Paul Frédéric Girard.* Paris: Paul Geuthner, 1912.

MELICHER, THEOPHIL. *Der Kampf zwischen Gesetzes- und Gewohnheitsrecht im Westgotenreiche.* Weimar: Hermann Böhlaus Nachfolger, 1930.

4. IN THE REALM OF THE CHURCH

BROWE, PETER. "Die Judenbekämpfung im Mittelalter, *Zeitschrift für katholische Theologie*, LXII (1938), 197–231, 349–84.

———. *Die Judenmission im Mittelalter und die Päpste.* ("Miscellanea historiae pontificiae edita a Facultate Historiae Ecclesiasticae in Pontificia Universitate Gregoriana," Vol. VI, Collectionis totius, No. 8.) Rome: Herder, 1942.

———. "Die kirchenrechtliche Stellung der getauften Juden und ihrer Nachkommen," *Archiv für katholisches Kirchenrecht*, CXXI (1941), 3–22, 165–91.

———. "Die religiöse Duldung der Juden im Mittelalter," *Archiv für katholisches Kirchenrecht*, CXVIII (1938), 3–76.

ELIAS, M. "Die römische Kurie, besonders Innozenz III., und die Juden," *Jahrbuch der Jüdisch-literarischen Gesellschaft zu Frankfurt am Main*, XII (1918), 37–82.

ENDEMANN, WILHELM. *Studien in der romanisch-kanonistischen Wirtschafts- und Rechtslehre bis gegen Ende des siebzehnten Jahrhunderts.* 2 vols. Berlin: J. Guttentag, 1883.

ERLER, L. "Die Juden des Mittelalters: Die Päpste und die Juden," *Archiv für katholisches Kirchenrecht*, XLVIII (1882), 369–416; L (1883), 3–64; LIII (1885), 3–70; cf. also XLI (1879), 75–96; XLII (1879), 3–80; XLIII (1880), 361–408; XLIV (1880), 353–416. Although written from an anti-Semitic viewpoint, these studies are still useful as guides to the sources and because of their bibliographical notes.

GRAYZEL, SOLOMON. *The Church and the Jews in the XIIIth Century.* Philadelphia: Dropsie College, 1933.

LA PIANA, GEORGE. "Catholic Church," in the encyclopedia, "The Jews." New York, to be published in 1950.

SIMONSOHN, MAX. *Die kirchliche Judengesetzgebung im Zeitalter der Reformkonzilien von Konstanz und Basel.* Ph.D. thesis, University of Freiburg i.B. Breslau: S. Lilienfeld, 1912.

IV. SPECIFIC JEWRY-LAW

1. CHAMBER SERFDOM

COHN, JONAS. "Die Entwicklung der Kammerknechtschaft unter den Hohenstaufen," pp. i–ix ("Anhang"). Appended to his *Die Judenpolitik der Hohenstaufen.* Ph.D. thesis, University of Hamburg. Hamburg, 1934.

FISCHER, HERBERT. *Die verfassungsrechtliche Stellung der Juden in den deutschen Städten während des dreizehnten Jahrhunderts.* Breslau: M. & H. Marcus, 1931.

KISCH, GUIDO. "The Jewry-Law of the Medieval German Law-Books," Part II. *Proceedings of the American Academy for Jewish Research,* X (1940), 130–84.

2. JEWISH TRADE PRIVILEGE

KISCH, GUIDO. "The 'Jewish Law of Concealment,'" *Historia Judaica,* I (1938), 3–30.

MEYER, HERBERT. *Entwerung und Eigentum im deutschen Fahrnisrecht: Ein Beitrag zur Geschichte des deutschen Privatrechts und des Judenrechts im Mittelalter.* Jena: Gustav Fischer, 1902.

3. COURT JURISDICTION

KISCH, GUIDO. "Relations between Jewish and Christian Courts in the Middle Ages," *Louis Ginzberg Jubilee Volume,* ed. by the American Academy for Jewish Research, pp. 201–25 of the English section. New York: American Academy for Jewish Research, 1945.

4. JEWRY OATH

BERNSTEIN, THEA. "Die Geschichte der deutschen Judeneide im Mittelalter," Ph.D. thesis, University of Hamburg, 1922.
In typescript only, of which an abstract was published under the same title (Königsberg i.Pr.: E. Steinbacher, 1922).

CLAUSSEN, HANS-KURT. "Der Judeneid: Ein Beitrag zur Geschichte des Rechtsschutzes," *Deutsche Rechtswissenschaft,* II (1937), 166–89.

KISCH, GUIDO. "A Fourteenth-Century Jewry Oath of South Germany," *Speculum*, XV (1940), 331–37.

———. "Nuremberg Jewry Oaths," *Historia Judaica*, II (1940), 23–38.

———. "Studien zur Geschichte des Judeneides im Mittelalter," *Hebrew Union College Annual*, XIV (Cincinnati, 1939), 431–56.

MÜLLENHOFF, K., and SCHERER, W. *Denkmäler deutscher Poesie und Prosa aus dem VIII.–XII. Jahrhundert*, II, 465–74. 3d ed. Berlin, 1892.

VOLTELINI, HANS VON. "Der Wiener und Kremser Judeneid," *Mitteilungen des Vereines für Geschichte der Stadt Wien*, XII (Vienna, 1932), 64–70.

5. GHETTO AND DRESS REGULATIONS

GENGLER, HEINRICH GOTTFRIED. *Deutsche Stadtrechtsaltertümer*, pp. 97–120. Erlangen: A. Deichert, 1882.

KISCH, GUIDO. "The Yellow Badge in History," *Historia Judaica*, IV (1942), 95–144.
Appeared also in a separate edition.

PINTHUS, ALEXANDER. *Die Judensiedlungen der deutschen Städte: Eine stadtbiologische Studie*. Doctor of Engineering thesis, Technische Hochschule of Hannover, 1931.

WIRTH, LOUIS. *The Ghetto*. Chicago, Ill.: University of Chicago Press, 1928.

V. JEWISH LAW IN MEDIEVAL GERMANY

AGUS, IRVING A. "The Development of the Money Clause in the Ashkenazic Ketubah," *Jewish Quarterly Review*, N.S., XXX (1940), 221–56.

———. *Rabbi Meir of Rothenburg, His Life and His Works as Sources for the Religious, Legal, and Social History of the Jews of Germany in the Thirteenth Century*. Ph.D. thesis, Dropsie College for Hebrew and Cognate Learning. 2 vols. Philadelphia: Dropsie College, 1947.

AUERBACH, SELIG. *Die rheinischen Rabbinerversammlungen im 13. Jahrhundert*. Ph.D. thesis, University of Würzburg. Würzburg: P. Halbig, 1932.

FINKELSTEIN, LOUIS. *Jewish Self-government in the Middle Ages*. New York: Jewish Theological Seminary of America, 1924.

FRANK, MOSES. *Kehillot Ashkenaz u-Bate Dinehen* ["The Jewish Communities and Their Courts in Germany from the Twelfth to the End of the Fifteenth Centuries"]. Ph.D. thesis, University of Jerusalem. Tel Aviv: Dvir, 1938.
In Hebrew.

GOLDMANN, SIMON. "Die jüdische Gerichtsverfassung innerhalb der jüdischen Gemeindeorganisation, ein Beitrag zur Geschichte des Judenbischofs im Mittelalter in seiner Entwicklung von den ältesten Zeiten bis zum 15. Jahrhundert." Ph.D. thesis, University of Cologne, 1924.
In typescript only.

KISCH, GUIDO. "Die talionsartige Strafe für Rechtsverweigerung im *Sachsenspiegel*," *Tijdschrift voor Rechtsgeschiedenis*, XVI (1939), 457–67.

LEVI, SALI. "Von der Eigenart der klassischen Handhabung des jüdischen Religionsgesetzes im Rheingebiet," in *Minhat Todah, Max Dienemann zum 60. Geburtstag gewidmet vom Vorstand der israelitischen Religionsgemeinde Offenbach am Main*, pp. 66–75. Frankfort-on-the-Main: J. Kauffmann, 1935.

RABINOWITZ, LOUIS. *The Ḥerem Hayyishub: A Contribution to the Medieval Economic History of the Jews*. London: Edward Goldston, 1945.

ROSIN, HEINRICH. "Beiträge zur Lehre von der Parentelenordnung und Verwandtschaftsberechnung nach deutschem und österreichischem, jüdischem und canonischem Rechte," *Zeitschrift für das Privat- und öffentliche Recht der Gegenwart*, XXVIII (Vienna, 1901), 341–404.

SHOHET, DAVID MENAHEM. *The Jewish Court in the Middle Ages: Studies in Jewish Jurisprudence according to the Talmud, Geonic, and Medieval German Responsa*. Ph.D. thesis, Columbia University. New York, 1931.

VI. THE JEWS' FUNCTION IN THE MEDIEVAL EVOLUTION OF ECONOMIC LIFE

BELOW, GEORG VON. *Probleme der Wirtschaftsgeschichte: Eine Einführung in das Studium der Wirtschaftsgeschichte*. Tübingen: J. C. B. Mohr, 1920.

CARO, GEORG. "Die Juden des Mittelalters in ihrer wirtschaftlichen Betätigung," *Monatsschrift für Geschichte und Wissenschaft des Judentums*, XLVIII (1904), 423–39, 576–603.

———. *Sozial- und Wirtschaftsgeschichte der Juden im Mittelalter und der Neuzeit*. ("Grundriss der Gesamtwissenschaft des Judentums.") 2 vols. Leipzig: Gustav Fock, 1908, 1920. 2d [unchanged] edition of the first volume, Frankfort-on-the-Main: J. Kauffmann, 1924.
Cited as "Caro."

GRAU, WILHELM. *Antisemitismus im späten Mittelalter: Das Ende der Regensburger Judengemeinde 1450–1519*. Ph.D. thesis, University of Munich. Munich and Leipzig: Duncker & Humblot, 1934.
Anti-Semitic.

GUTTMANN, JULIUS. "Die wirtschaftliche und soziale Bedeutung der Juden im Mittelalter," *Monatsschrift für Geschichte und Wissenschaft des Judentums*, LI (1907), 257–90.

HAHN, BRUNO. *Die wirtschaftliche Tätigkeit der Juden im fränkischen und deutschen Reich bis zum 2. Kreuzzug.* Ph.D. thesis, University of Freiburg i.B. Freiburg i.B.: Hammerschlag & Kahle, 1911.

HOFFMANN, MOSES. *Der Geldhandel der deutschen Juden bis zum Jahre 1350: Ein Beitrag zur deutschen Wirtschaftsgeschichte im Mittelalter.* (GUSTAV SCHMOLLER's "Staats- und sozialwissenschaftliche Forschungen," Heft 152.) Leipzig: Duncker & Humblot, 1910.

KELTER, ERNST. "Die Juden in der deutschen Wirtschaftsgeschichte," in *Festschrift Adolf Zycha zum 70. Geburtstag überreicht von Freunden, Schülern und Fachgenossen*, pp. 551–588. Weimar: Hermann Böhlaus Nachfolger, 1941.
Anti-Semitic; based exclusively on secondary sources and chiefly on pseudo-scholarly writings of National Socialist propagandists.

KISCH, GUIDO. "The Jews' Function in the Mediaeval Evolution of Economic Life," *Historia Judaica*, VI (1944), 1–12.

KÖTZSCHKE, RUDOLF. *Allgemeine Wirtschaftsgeschichte des Mittelalters.* (GEORG BRODNITZ's "Handbuch der Wirtschaftsgeschichte.") Jena: Gustav Fischer, 1924.

LIEBE, GEORG. "Die rechtlichen und wirtschaftlichen Zustände der Juden im Erzstift Trier," *Westdeutsche Zeitschrift für Geschichte und Kunst*, XII (Trier, 1893), 311–74.

———. "Die wirtschaftliche Bedeutung der Juden in der deutschen Vergangenheit," *Jahrbücher der königlichen Akademie gemeinnütziger Wissenschaften zu Erfurt*, N. S., Heft XXVI (Erfurt, 1900), 113–127.
Anti-Semitic.

NEUMANN, MAX. *Geschichte des Wuchers in Deutschland bis zur Begründung der heutigen Zinsengesetze (1654). Aus handschriftlichen und gedruckten Quellen.* Halle: Waisenhaus Buchhandlung, 1865.

PARKES, JAMES. *The Jew in the Medieval Community: A Study of His Political and Economic Situation.* London: Soncino Press, 1938.

———. "The Jewish Money-Lender and the Charters of English Jewry in Their Historical Setting," *Miscellanies of the Jewish Historical Society of England*, III (1937), 34–41.

PHILIPP, ALFRED. *Die Juden und das Wirtschaftsleben: Eine antikritisch-bibliographische Studie zu Werner Sombart, "Die Juden und das Wirtschaftsleben."* Ph.D. thesis, University of Berlin. Strasbourg: Heitz & Co., 1929.

PIRENNE, HENRI. *Economic and Social History of Medieval Europe.* New York: Harcourt, Brace & Co., 1937.

ROESEL, ISERT. *Die Reichssteuern der deutschen Judengemeinden von ihren Anfängen bis zur Mitte des 14. Jahrhunderts.* Berlin: Louis Lamm, 1910.

ROSCHER, WILHELM. "Die Stellung der Juden im Mittelalter, betrachtet vom Standpunkte der allgemeinen Handelspolitik," *Zeitschrift für die gesamte Staatswissenschaft*, XXXI (1875), 503–26.

Roscher's famous essay was reprinted in his *Ansichten der Volkswirtschaft aus dem geschichtlichen Standpunkte*, II (Leipzig, 1878), 321–54. An English translation by Solomon Grayzel was published in *Historia Judaica*, VI (1944), 13–26.

RUTH, RUDOLF. "Wucher und Wucherrecht der Juden im Mittelalter," *Deutsche Rechtswissenschaft*, II (1937), 111–57.

Anti-Semitic.

SCHIPPER, IGNAZ. *Anfänge des Kapitalismus bei den abendländischen Juden im früheren Mittelalter (bis zum Ausgang des XII. Jahrhunderts).* Reprinted from *Zeitschrift für Volkswirtschaft, Sozialpolitik und Verwaltung*, Vol. XV (1906). Vienna: Wilhelm Braumüller, 1907.

SCHIPPER, IGNACY. *Studya nad stosunkami gospodarczymi żydów w Polsce podczas średniowiecza* ["Studies in the Economic Conditions of the Jews in Poland during the Middle Ages"]. Lwów: B. Poloniecki, 1911.

SCHIPPER, ISAAC. *Yidishe Geshichte (Wirtshaftsgeshichte).* 4 vols. Warsaw: Ahisefer-Central, 1930.

In Yiddish.

SCHULTE, ALOYS. *Geschichte des mittelalterlichen Handels und Verkehrs zwischen Westdeutschland und Italien mit Ausschluss von Venedig.* 2 vols. Leipzig: Duncker & Humblot, 1900.

SOMBART, WERNER. *Die Juden und das Wirtschaftsleben.* Leipzig: Duncker & Humblot, 1911.

Numerous later impressions; the fourteenth and fifteenth thousands were published in 1927.

An English translation by M. Epstein appeared under the title, *The Jews and Modern Capitalism* (London and New York, 1913).

STOWASSER, OTTO H. "Zur Geschichte der Wiener Geserah," *Vierteljahrschrift für Sozial- und Wirtschaftsgeschichte*, XVI (1922), 104–18.

STRAUS, RAPHAEL. "The Jews in the Economic Evolution of Central Europe," *Jewish Social Studies*, III (1941), 15–40.

TÄUBLER, EUGEN. "Zur Handelsbedeutung der Juden in Deutschland vor Beginn des Städtewesens," in *Beiträge zur Geschichte der deutschen Juden: Festschrift zum siebzigsten Geburtstage Martin Philippsons*, pp. 370–81. Leipzig: Gustav Fock, 1916.

THOMPSON, JAMES WESTFALL. *Economic and Social History of Europe in the Later Middle Ages (1300–1530)*. New York: Century Co., 1931.

VII. MEDIEVAL POETRY ON THE JEWISH STATUS

AMIRA, KARL VON. *Das Endinger Judenspiel*. ("Neudrucke deutscher Litteraturwerke des XVI. und XVII. Jahrhunderts," No. 41.) Halle: Max Niemeyer, 1883.

EVANS, M. BLAKEMORE. *The Passion Play of Lucerne: An Historical and Critical Introduction*. ("Modern Language Association of America, Monograph Series," Vol. XIV.) New York: Modern Language Association of America, 1943.

GUDDE, ERWIN GUSTAV. *Social Conflicts in Medieval German Poetry*. Ph.D. thesis, University of California. ("University of California Publications in Modern Philology," Vol. XVIII, No. 1.) Berkeley, California: University of California Press, 1934.

LIFSCHITZ-GOLDEN, MANYA. *Les Juifs dans la littérature française du moyen âge (mystères, miracles, chroniques)*. New York: Columbia University Press, 1935.

LOEWE, HEINRICH. *Die Juden in der katholischen Legende*. Berlin: Jüdischer Verlag, 1912.
Enlarged reprint from *Monatsschrift für Geschichte und Wissenschaft des Judentums*, LVI (1912), 257–84, 385–416, 612–21.

PFLAUM, HEINZ. *Die religiöse Disputation in der europäischen Dichtung des Mittelalters. Erste Studie: Der allegorische Streit zwischen Synagoge und Kirche*. Genève and Firenze: Leo S. Olschki, 1935.

STEIN, SIEGFRIED. *Die Ungläubigen in der mittelhochdeutschen Literatur von 1050 bis 1250*. Ph.D. thesis, University of Heidelberg. Heidelberg, 1933.

STRUMPF, DAVID. *Die Juden in der mittelalterlichen Mysterien-, Mirakel- und Moralitätendichtung Frankreichs*. Ph.D. thesis, University of Heidelberg. Ladenburg a.N., 1920.

VIII. THE MEDIEVAL CONCEPTION OF THE JEW

BAER, YITZHAK FRITZ. *Galut*. ("Schocken Library," Vol. II.) New York: Schocken Books, 1947.

BARON, SALO W. "The Jewish Factor in Medieval Civilization," *Proceedings of the American Academy for Jewish Research*, XII (1942), 1–48.

KISCH, GUIDO. "Nationalism and Race in Medieval Law," *Seminar: An Annual Extraordinary Number of "The Jurist,"* I (Washington, D.C., 1943), 48–73.

REIDER, JOSEPH, "Jews in Medieval Art," *Essays on Antisemitism*, edited by Koppel S. Pinson. New York: Conference on Jewish Relations, 1942, pp. 45–56; 2d ed., 1946, pp. 93–102.

Roth, Cecil. "The Medieval Conception of the Jew: A New Interpretation," *Essays and Studies in Memory of Linda R. Miller*, ed. Israel Davidson, pp. 171–90. New York: Jewish Theological Seminary of America, 1938.

Stern-Täubler, Selma. "Das Judenproblem im Wandel der Staatsformen," *Zeitschrift für die Geschichte der Juden in Deutschland*, II (1930), 1–13.

Trachtenberg, Joshua. *The Devil and the Jews: The Medieval Conception of the Jew and Its Relation to Modern Antisemitism.* New Haven: Yale University Press, 1943.

C. ENCYCLOPEDIC WORKS

Encyclopaedia Judaica: Das Judentum in Geschichte und Gegenwart. 10 vols. Berlin: Verlag Eschkol, 1928–34.
Not completed.

Encyclopaedia of the Social Sciences. 15 vols. New York: Macmillan Co., 1930, 1935, 1937.

Germania Judaica: Von den ältesten Zeiten bis 1238. Breslau: M. & H. Marcus, 1934.

Glossarium Germanicum medii aevi maximam partem e diplomatibus multis praeterea aliis monimentis tam editis quam ineditis. Ed. Christianus Gottlob Haltaus. Tom. I, II. Lipsiae: Joh. Frid. Gleditsch, 1758.

The Jewish Encyclopedia. 12 vols. New York: Funk & Wagnalls Co., 1901–6.

Jüdisches Lexikon: Ein enzyklopädisches Handbuch des jüdischen Wissens. 4 vols. Berlin: Jüdischer Verlag, 1927–30.

Stammler, Wolfgang. *Die deutsche Literatur des Mittelalters: Verfasserlexikon.* 3 vols. Berlin and Leipzig, 1931–43.
Not completed.

D. PERIODICALS

Geiger's ZGJD   *Zeitschrift für die Geschichte der Juden in Deutschland*, Vols. I–V. Herausgegeben von Ludwig Geiger. Braunschweig, 1887–92.

JGJC   *Jahrbuch der Gesellschaft für Geschichte der Juden in der Čechoslovakischen Republik*, Vols. I–IX. Herausgegeben von Samuel Steinherz. Prague, 1929–38.

MGA   *Mitteilungen des Gesamtarchivs der deutschen Juden*, Vols. I–VI. Leipzig and Berlin, 1909–26.

MGWJ   *Monatsschrift für Geschichte und Wissenschaft des Judentums*, Vols. I–LXXXIII. Breslau, 1851–1939.

Proceedings   *Proceedings of the American Academy for Jewish Research*, Vols. I–XVI. New York, 1930–47.

VSWG   *Vierteljahrschrift für Sozial- und Wirtschaftsgeschichte*, Vols. I–XXIX. Leipzig and Stuttgart, 1903–36.

ZGJD   *Zeitschrift für die Geschichte der Juden in Deutschland*, Vols. I–VII. Herausgegeben von ISMAR ELBOGEN, ARON FREIMANN, und MAX FREUDENTHAL. Berlin, 1929–37.

ZGS   *Zeitschrift des Vereins für Geschichte und Altertum Schlesiens*, Vols. I ff. Breslau, 1859 ff.

ZRG, O.S.   *Zeitschrift für Rechtsgeschichte*, Vols. I–XIII. Weimar, 1861–78.

ZRG   *Zeitschrift der Savigny-Stiftung für Rechtsgeschichte, Germanistische Abteilung* [unless otherwise stated], Vols. I–LXV. Weimar, 1880–1947.

INDEXES

GENERAL INDEX

God—*Continued*
Jews as children of, 325
name of, in Jewry-oath formulas, 276, 282
omnipotence of, 280
protects Jews and Christians, 527, n. 36
as source of all law, 316, 342; 520, n. 2
Godfrey of Bouillon, Duke, leader in First Crusade, 141
Görlitzer Rechtsbuch, 50
Gold penny; see *Guldin pfenning*
Good Friday, public appearance of Jews forbidden on, 183–84, 199, 300–301, 351; 520, n. 37
Gregory the Great, Pope
against forced baptism of Jews, 200–201; 460, n. 90
on Jews, 325
restrictions of, on building of synagogues, 294
Gregory IX, Pope, 144
accusations against Talmud, 151
anti-Jewish attitude of, 151
approval of death penalty for heresy by, 203–4
codification of church law by, 151–52, 361
and Emperor Frederick II, 153; 433, n. 77
on exclusion of Jews from public office, 432, n. 76
Liber Extra, 354
Gregory X, Pope, bull of 1274 on apostasy of Jewish converts, 464, n. 101
Guard duty
money payment by Jews instead of, 126, 130
of Jews, 114, 116, 126; 416, n. 24; 417, n. 26
see also Military service
Guardians, by law, for women, 254
Guest courts; see *Gastgericht*
Guilds
admission to, 290; 529, n. 50
Christian character of, 318
Jews barred from membership in, 59, 194, 318, 347; 537, n. 97
municipal control of, 288
see also Craftsmen
Guldin pfenning [gold penny, a tax imposed on Jews], 167–68; 440, n. 122

"*Hand wahre Hand*" ["hand must warrant hand"], 219
Handhaftige Tat (Handhafte Tat); see Handhaving crimes; Handhavingness
Handhaving crimes
committed against Jews, 253, 262; 500, n. 94
committed by Jews, 407, n. 27

conviction of the accused, 254, 265; 500, n. 93
see also Crimes; Handhavingness
Handhavingness
concept of, 185
as condition for special procedure, 266
procedure in, 253–54, 257
Handicrafts, Jews barred from, 59, 194
Hanging; see Gallows
Hatred: see Jew hatred
Head-covering
not practiced by French Jews, 296
in synagogue, 284
Heathen, 5, 59
excluded from imperial privileges, 91
incapable for judgeship, 244
not to be compelled to the Christian faith, 461, n. 92
usury taken from, 194
Heeresrecht; see Military service
Heirs; see Liability; Obligations; Promissory notes
Henry of Avranches, 152
Henry IV, King, 140
charter for Worms of 1074, 138
Jewry privileges by, 95–96, 101, 108–9, 134, 138
protection of Jews by, 141
see also Charters for Jews
Henry VII, King, 109
Herem; see Jewish ban
Herem Bet Din [judicial ban], 552, n. 18
Herem Hayyishub [ban of settlement], 552, n. 18
Heresy (*Ketzerei*)
of Christians, 85, 202–6, 353, 360; 464, n. 102
of converts to Christianity, 203, 353; 463, n. 100; 464, n. 101
death at the stake for, 85, 202–5, 206, 353; 464, n. 102
a *delictum mere ecclesiasticum*, 203
relapse into Judaism equated with, 204, 353; 463 f., n. 101
Sachsenspiegel on, 204
suppression of, 323
usury as, 192
see also Heretics
Heretics (*Ketzer*)
conviction of, in legal procedure, 91, 269
exclusion of
from being plaintiffs, 245–46
from imperial privileges, 90
from marriage with Christians, 315
extermination of, 203
incapacity of
for judgeship, 244
for spokesmanship, 249; 492, n. 26

Interregnum, 132

Intolerance; *see* Anti-Jewish agitation, etc.; Discrimination; Hostility against Jews; Jew hatred; Jewish persecutions; National socialism; Nationalism

Irregularity of clerics, 127, 130

Jacob ben Meir Tam, Rabbi, 172; 429, n. 53

Jerusalem
  conquest of, 156–58, 165
  destruction of, 154, 160–62; 440, n. 122
  sale of Jews after conquest of, 157–62; 165; 435, n. 93; 436, n. 105; 437 f., n. 112; 438, n. 113

Jesus Christ
  Jews accused
    of killing, 337; 450, n. 39
    of torturing, 278
  Jews' crime against, 347; 450, n. 39; 549, n. 11
  martyrdom of, 439, n. 120
  no compulsion to Christian faith by, 460, n. 90
  see also Crucifixion

"Jew," as term of abuse, 327; 527, n. 37

Jew hatred
  causes of, 321 ff., 336, 339; 478, n. 63
  medieval, 339
  of modern authors, 80
  no nationalistic, 336
  in *Salzwedeler Stadtrechtsbuch*, 54–55
  in *Wiener Stadtrechtsbuch*, 56

Jewish ban, 103; 172; 512, n. 175
  recognized by Christian court, 103; 306; 412, n. 35; 498, n. 75
  see also Ḥerem Bet Din; Ḥerem Hayyishub

Jewish bishop, 348

Jewish-Christian relations
  amicable, 300, 326, 351
  Crusade period turning point in, 337–38
  deterioration of, 339, 352, 355
  rules on, in *Sachsenspiegel*, 86–90, 94
  see also Segregation of Jews; Social relation between Jews and Christians

Jewish community
  ancient law of, 349
  basis of origin of, 348
  charters for, 138
  concept of medieval, 307–9
  development of, 349
  head of, 348
  integration of, into medieval community, 347–48
  organizational form of, 348; 550 f., nn. 13, 17
  protection of, 184–85
  religious and social history of, 19
  responsibility for transgressions of individual members of, 187–88; 450, n. 37

spirit of, 352
  see also Charters for Jews; Self-government

Jewish courts; *see* Courts of law, Jewish

"Jewish execution," 186–87; 449, n. 34; 485, n. 108

Jewish garb; *see* Dress, Jewish

"Jewish hat"; *see* Jews' hat

Jewish history
  "lachrymose conception" of, 21; 550, n. 12
  terminology of, 369, n. 14

Jewish law, 6, 7, 9, 20, 64, 67, 99–103, 124–25, 172–73, 208, 269, 274, 296; 373, n. 44; 404, n. 7; 410, n. 15
  forfeiting of, 102
  of inheritance, 228
  medieval, 172
  no reference to in *Sachsenspiegel*, 100, 277
  oath in accordance with, 100–101, 191, 254, 275–76, 287, 306, 325
  oath formulas of, 276–77
  punishment according to, 186
  rule of, 101, 173, 208, 289
  supported by Christian jurists and courts, 103
  terminology, 369, n. 14
  validity of
    denied, 441, n. 3
    recognized in German law and lawbooks, 100–102, 172, 186, 208, 306, 309, 313, 336
  see also Jewry oath

"Jewish nose," 545, n. 156

Jewish people, eternal servitude of, 147

Jewish persecutions
  during "Black-Death" period, 4, 311, 317, 321; 478, n. 63
  causes of, 321 ff., 352; 478, n. 63; 550, n. 12
  at Lauda and Fulda, 143
  successive waves of, 351
  see also Crusades

Jewish quarters, 264, 289
  compulsory segregation of Jews in, 291–93, 298, 351, 353
  construction of, 290–93
  literature on, 515, n. 6
  originally voluntary, 292, 298
  separated by fence or wall, 293
  theories on origin of, 291–92

"Jewish question" in the Middle Ages, 86, 131, 151, 305, 310, 336, 338, 352–53; 428, n. 44

Jewish religion
  cause for different treatment of Jews in law, 251
  neither church nor state interferes with, 198

Poelmannsche Distinctionen; see *Neun Bücher Magdeburger Rechts*

Poetry, medieval German
on Jews and Jewry-law, 80–81, 311, 325–26, 328, 340, 355; 527, n. 36
on law and Christianity, 305

Pogrom
in Germany on November 10, 1938, 414, n. 15
"*slahtunge,*" 360–61; 560, n. 61

Poisoning of wells, 4; 536, n. 90

Police service, judicial, 111, 330

Polizei, 288

Polizeirecht [laws concerning public welfare]
Jewish, 289
Jews not subjected to general, 289
medieval German, 515, n. 2
municipal, 288–89

Poll tax for Jews, 167, 333

Polygamy, forbidden, 172

Popular beliefs concerning Jews
favorable, 326
unfavorable, 324–25

Populus Judeorum, 543, n. 140

Prager Rechtsbuch, 54

Prayers, 283, 292

Precaria; see *Bede*

Priests
armed on horseback, 124
equal legal treatment of, with Jews, 123–24
as "journeying" people, 124
under king's peace, 107–8, 119
as "masters of Christendom," 157

Princeps legibus solutus, 363

Privilege (*privilegium*)
abrogation of, 9
common imperial, enjoyed by Jews, 92
definition of, 135
forfeiture of, 141
as form of bestowal of Jewry protection, 131, 133
as form of recorded law, 8, 95, 135, 140; 408, n. 36; 423, n. 13
for Jews and non-Jews, 137
privilegia favorabilia, 98
privilegia odiosa, 98; 402, n. 146; 471, n. 15
recognition of
in *Meissener Rechtsbuch,* 99
in *Sachsenspiegel,* 96
revokable, 141
special imperial, not for Jews, heathen, and heretics, 91, 407 f., n. 33
value of, 552, n. 21
see also Charters for Jews

Procedure; *see* Civil procedure; Criminal procedure; Judicial procedure

Procession, Jews not to stay in street during, 520, n. 37

Prolocutor; see Spokesmanship

Promissory notes, 225–35, 319, 479–83
clause of attorney in, 228–29, 249, 258, 319, 481
clauses in, 226, 229–32; 479, n. 66; 481, n. 83
copies of, 175, 178, 225
date in, 230, 232, 233
evidence by, 225, 253, 273
formulas for, 226, 231; 479, n. 66
importance of, in lawsuits, 225
inclusion in, of heirs of debtors, 226–27; 480, n. 72
invalidation of, 235; 482, nn. 91, 92
loans without, 224
loss of, 235
as pledges in the hands of Jewish creditors, 229–30, 232
redemption of, 230, 232–33
seals on, 230–35, 274; 479, n. 66; 481, n. 82; 483, n. 97
validity of, 230, 232–35; 483, n. 98

Propaganda; *see* Anti-Jewish propaganda

Property
acquisition of movable, 210–18, 269
confiscation of, 361
confiscation of Jewish, 129–30, 166
just cause required for, 561, n. 65
prohibited, 427, n. 43
embezzlement of intrusted, 189
illegal acquisition of, 190
immovable, 217, 302, 361; 496, n. 60
Jews excluded from, 59, 99, 193–94, 210
Jews not excluded from, 116
lawful acquisition of, from nonowner; *see* Trade privilege of Jewish merchants
of massacred Jews, 141, 360–61
protection of, 143
see also Real property

Propugnaculum Judeorum [Cologne], 417, n. 30

Prosecution under criminal law, 185, 203

Proselytes; *see* Conversion; Converts

Protection, royal
of ecclesiastical institutions, 84, 136
in general, 424, n. 19
of Jewish religious institutions, 184–85, 290, 306
of Jews, 108, 136–37, 141, 143–45, 153–59, 162–63, 167, 199, 330–31, 338, 347
of merchants, 108, 136, 330
of non-Jews, 136–37, 330
see also Charters of protection; Jewry protection

INDEX OF AUTHORS

[Only those authors are listed whose works or theories are discussed in this volume.]

INDEX OF GEOGRAPHICAL NAMES

INDEX OF JEWISH NAMES

INDEX OF LAW SOURCES

[Italic page numbers indicate English translations of quotations from the sources. The original texts are reproduced in full in the author's *Jewry-Law in Medieval Germany: Laws and Court Decisions concerning Jews* (New York, 1949).]